THE

STOICS, EPICUREANS

AND

SCEPTICS

THE

STOICS, EPICUREANS

AND

SCEPTICS

TRANSLATED FROM THE GERMAN OF

DR E. ZELLER

Professor of the University of Heidelberg

BY

OSWALD J. REICHEL, B.C.L. & M.A.

A NEW AND REVISED EDITION

NEW YORK

RUSSELL & RUSSELL · INC

1962

REISSUED, 1962, BY RUSSELL & RUSSELL, INC.
L. C. CATALOG CARD NO: 62-10701

PRINTED IN THE UNITED STATES OF AMERICA

PREFACE.

THE present translation aims at supplying an introductory volume to a later period of the history of
mind in Greece, which may be collectively described
as the *post-Aristotelian*. To the moralist and theo-
logian no less than to the student of philosophy this
period is one of peculiar interest; for it supplied
the scientific mould into which Christianity in the
early years of its growth was cast, and bearing the
shape of which it has come down to us.

SPARSHOLT VICARAGE:
October, 1879.

CONTENTS.

—◆◇◆—

PART I.

STATE OF CULTURE IN GREECE.

———

CHAPTER I.

THE INTELLECTUAL AND POLITICAL STATE OF GREECE AT THE CLOSE OF THE FOURTH CENTURY, B.C.

CHAPTER II.

CHARACTER AND CHIEF FEATURES OF THE POST-ARISTOTELIAN PHILOSOPHY.

PART II.

THE STOICS.

CHAPTER III.

HISTORY OF THE STOICS UNTIL THE END OF THE SECOND CENTURY, B.C.

CHAPTER IV.

AUTHORITIES FOR THE STOIC PHILOSOPHY; ITS PROBLEM AND DIVISIONS.

CONTENTS.

CHAPTER V.

LOGIC OF THE STOICS.

CHAPTER VI.

THE STUDY OF NATURE: 1. FUNDAMENTAL POSITIONS.

CHAPTER VII.

THE STUDY OF NATURE: 2. COURSE, CHARACTER, AND GOVERNMENT OF THE UNIVERSE.

CHAPTER VIII.

THE STUDY OF NATURE: 3. IRRATIONAL NATURE. THE ELEMENTS.—THE UNIVERSE.

CHAPTER IX.

THE STUDY OF NATURE: 4. MAN.

CHAPTER X.

ETHICS: 1. THE GENERAL PRINCIPLES OF THE STOIC ETHICS. ABSTRACT THEORY OF MORALITY.

CHAPTER XI.

ETHICS: 2. THE STOIC THEORY OF MORALS AS MODIFIED IN PRACTICE.

CHAPTER XII.

ETHICS : 3. APPLIED MORAL SCIENCE.

CHAPTER XIII.

THE RELATION OF THE STOICS TO RELIGION.

CHAPTER XVII.

THE EPICUREAN VIEWS ON NATURE.

CHAPTER XVIII.

VIEWS OF EPICURUS ON RELIGION.

CHAPTER XIX.

THE MORAL SCIENCE OF THE EPICUREANS:
1. GENERAL VIEWS.

CHAPTER XX.

THE EPICUREAN ETHICS CONTINUED: 2. SPECIAL POINTS.

CHAPTER XXI.

THE EPICUREAN SYSTEM AS A WHOLE.
ITS POSITION IN HISTORY.

PART IV.

THE SCEPTICS: PYRRHO AND THE OLDER ACADEMY.

CHAPTER XXII.

PYRRHO.

CHAPTER XXIII.

THE NEW ACADEMY.

PART I.

STATE OF CULTURE IN GREECE.

CHAPTER I.

In Plato and Aristotle Greek Philosophy reached its greatest perfection. In their hands the Socratic philosophy of conceptions had been developed into elaborate systems, embracing the whole range of contemporary knowledge, and grouping it from definite points of view so as to afford a connected view of the universe. The study of nature had been supplemented by careful enquiries into morals, and had been itself transformed, enlarged, and enriched by Aristotle. In metaphysics, the foundations of a philosophical building had been by him laid deeply, everything that is having been thoroughly referred to first principles, so as no previous philosopher had attempted. A multitude of phenomena which earlier thinkers had carelessly passed by, in particular the phenomena of mental life, had been pressed into the service of research; new questions had been raised;

CHAP.
I.

A. *Merits and defects of the systems of Plato and Aristotle.*

B

new answers given. Into every branch of knowledge new ideas had reached and penetrated. Idealism, that beautiful and telling expression of the Greek mind, had been set forth by Plato in pure brilliancy, and had been united by Aristotle with the most careful observation. Practice and theory had brought the dialectic method to the position of an art, and a valuable instrument of thought had been gained in the scientific use of terms of which Aristotle was the real originator. Within a few generations the intellectual treasures of Greece had been increased manifold both in extent and value. The heritage received by Socrates from his predecessors could hardly be recognised as the same left by Aristotle to his successors.

Great as was the progress made by Greek philosophy in the fourth century before Christ, equally great, however, were the difficulties with which it had perpetually to contend; not less difficult the problems for the solution of which it had to labour. Already Aristotle had pointed out the weak points in the system of Plato, rendering it impossible for him to rest therewith content. From the platform of present knowledge still further objections would be naturally urged. And again as regards Aristotle, even in his system inconsistencies on some of the most important points may be found concealed under a certain indefiniteness of expression, fatal if once brought to light to the soundness of the whole. With all his ingenuity, Aristotle had not succeeded in blending into one harmonious whole all the elements out of which his system was composed. Hence the divergencies of his immediate followers from the original Aristotelian teaching may be explained.

Nor were these defects of a kind that could be easily got over. On the contrary, the more the matter is gone into, the clearer it becomes that these defects were embedded in the foundations of the systems both of Plato and Aristotle, underlying in short the whole previous career of philosophic thought. Leaving details and minor points out of consideration, they all ultimately may be traced to two main sources, either to an imperfect knowledge and experience of the world, or to the hasty conclusions of an idealistic philosophy of conceptions. To the former cause may be attributed the mistakes in natural science into which Plato and Aristotle fell, and the limited character of their view of history; to the latter, the Platonic theory of ideas with all that it involves—the antithesis of ideas and appearances, of reason and the senses, of knowledge and ignorance, of the present world and the world to come—and likewise the corresponding points in the system of Aristotle ; such, for instance (to mention some of the principal ones only), as the relation of what is particular and what is general, of form and matter, of God and the world, of the theory of final causes and of natural explanations, of the rational and the irrational parts of the soul, of speculative theory and practice.

Both causes are, however, closely connected. The Greek philosophers were content with an uncertain and defective knowledge of facts, because they trusted conceptions too implicitly, being ignorant of their origin and worth; and they had this unconditional trust in the truth of conceptions because the study of nature was yet in its infancy. Their knowledge of history was as yet too limited for them to note the difference between the results of a careful observation and those of ordinary unmethodical experience, the uncertainty of most of the traditional principles and the necessity for a more stringent method of induction. The fault common to both Plato and Aristotle lay in attaching undue prominence to the dialectical method inherited from Socrates to the neglect of observation, and in supposing that conceptions expressing the very essence of things can be deduced in a purely logical way from current beliefs and the uses of language. In Plato this dialectical exclusiveness appears more strongly, finding expression in a telling manner in the theory of recollection. For certainly, if all our conceptions are inherent from the moment of birth, needing only the agency of sensible things to make us conscious of their existence, it may be legitimately inferred that, to know the essence of things, we must look within and not without, obtaining our ideas by development from the mind rather than by abstraction from experience. It may be inferred with equal reason, that the ideas drawn from the mind are the true standard by which experience must be judged. Whenever ideas and experience disagree, instead of regarding ideas as at fault, we ought to look upon the data of experience as imperfect, and as inadequately expressing the

ideas which constitute the thing as it really exists.
The whole theory of ideas, in short, and all that it
implies, is a natural corollary from the Socratic
theory of conceptions. Even those parts of this
theory which seem most incongruous are best explained by being referred to the principles of the
Socratic process.

From the onesidedness of these suppositions
Aristotle is only partly free. Undoubtedly he attempted to supply the defects in the Socratic and
Platonic theory of conceptions by observation, with
which Plato's experimental knowledge cannot be
compared, either in point of accuracy or extent.
Neither can it be ignored that therewith is connected that complete transformation of the Platonic metaphysics, whereby the same right is
secured for particulars over against the universal, as
the philosopher had already secured for observation
over against conceptional knowledge. But Aristotle
did not go far enough. In his theory of knowledge
he cannot wholly discard the supposition that the
soul has its knowledge by a process of development
from within, being not only endowed with the capacity of thinking, but possessing from its birth the
substance of ideas. In his scientific method the
critical investigation of common notions and of idiom,
that in fact which he himself calls proof by probabilities, is constantly taking the place of strict
induction. His endeavours to harmonise the two
antagonistic currents in Plato's teaching may have
been undertaken in all sincerity, but the antagonism

was too deep-seated to yield to his efforts. It not only reappears in the fundamental ideas, but colours the most general results of his system. Beginning with the antithesis between *form* and *matter*, it ends in the contrast between the *world* and a *soul* outside the world, in the conception of reason regarded even in man as something coming from without, and never combining with the lower parts of his nature to form one complete living unity.

B. *Connection between the theories of Aristotle and Greek character.*

Granting that the above features may be proximately deduced from the Socratic theory of conceptions, still that philosophy, it must be owned, expresses the character of the nation to which it belonged. In an earlier work it has been shown [1] that the commonest peculiarity of life in Greece consists in the undisturbed unity of the outer and the inner world, in an artless belief that mind and matter were originally connected, and are still in perfect harmony with one another. When the whole mental life of a people bears this impress, it is not likely to be wanting in its philosophy also. Besides the advantages, therefore, which accrue from the close connection of those two elements, philosophy will also share the defects unavoidably connected with any view of their intimacy which ignores a real distinction between them. Only gradually and imperfectly will the mind become aware of the distinctive peculiarity of mental life, of the notion of personality, of the independence of moral rights and duties of all external circum-

[1] Zeller's Philosophie der Griechen. Part I. 96.

stances, of the share of our own will in creating our ideas. On the other hand, it will have less hesitation in transferring the phases of consciousness immediately to things themselves, in regarding the world from ideal points of view borrowed from the domain of our own minds, in accepting our own notions of things as something real, without testing their actual truth, nay, even treating them as higher compared with the reality of the senses, and in confounding the critical analysis of a notion with the experimental investigation of a thing. If in the time of its highest perfection the philosophy of Greece was not free from these mistakes; if, further, these were the cause of all the important faults in the systems of Plato and Aristotle, not the framers of these systems only and their immediate successors ought to bear the blame, but rather the whole mental peculiarity of that people, of which within the province of science these men were the greatest representatives.

In proportion as the close connection of the faults of the Platonic and Aristotelian systems with the whole character of Greek thought becomes apparent, the more difficult, it will be felt, was it for Greek thought to emancipate itself from these faults. To compass this a sweeping change of the customary lines of thought would be requisite. The origin of our ideas, the primary meaning of our conceptions, must needs be examined much more closely; a sharper distinction made between what is supplied from without and what is supplied from within; the truth of several axioms received in metaphysics more carefully investigated, than had been done as yet. Science must accustom itself to an accuracy of observation, and to a strictness of inductive process, never as yet reached in Greece. Sciences resting on observation must have attained a pitch of completeness which it was vain to hope to reach by the methods and means then in vogue. The anthropomorphic way of looking at nature, allowing questions as to facts to be answered by speculations on final causes and the desire of nature to realise beauty, must be dropped. Enquiries into man's moral nature and functions would have to be severed from a regard for purely natural relations, the disturbing influences of which may be seen in the national exclusiveness of the Greeks, in the onesided political character of their morality, in the institution of slavery.

How much would have to be changed in the conditions and views of Greece before this pass would be reached! Could it be expected that a stricter and more scientific method would obtain rule so long as the tendency to look upon the life of nature as analogous to the life of man was kept alive by a religion such as that of Hellas? Or that moral science would shake off the trammels of the Greek propriety of conduct, whilst in all practical matters those trammels were in full force? Or that a sharper distinction between what comes from without and what from within in our ideas—a distinction which we vainly look for in Aristotle—would prevail, until a depth and an intensity had been given to the inner life, and the rights and value of the individual as such had obtained a recognition which it required the combined influence of Christianity and the peculiar Germanic character to bring about? The more vividly we realise the national stamp and the surrounding national conditions of the Greek philosophy, with all the characteristics of the national life, the more ready to hand is the conviction, that to heal its defects—defects which are apparent even in its greatest and most brilliant achievements—nothing short of an actual revolution in the mental tone of Greece would avail—such as history has at length seen accomplished after many shifts and many centuries.

On the platform of the ancient life of Greece such a change could not possibly have come about. Thereby certainly the possibility is not excluded, that under more favourable circumstances a further development of Greek philosophy might have taken place in the same course of purely intellectual enquiry which it had followed hitherto in the hands of its earlier representatives, and more particularly of Aristotle, with the most important results. The results which might in this way have been possibly attained, we cannot exactly determine. Speculation is, however, useless. In point of fact, the historical circumstances under which philosophy had to grow cannot be ignored. It had only become what it had under the influences of these circumstances. The Socratic theory of conceptions, and the Ideal theory of Plato, presuppose on the one hand the high culture of the age of Pericles, and the brilliant career of Athens and Greece following on the Persian war.

CHAP. I.

Not less do they presuppose the political degradation and the moral exhaustion of Greece during and after the Peloponnesian war. In his purely intellectual attitude, despairing of every direct practical activity, in his broad view of things, his knowledge of every kind, in his system matured and elaborate, and embracing all the results of previous enquiry—Aristotle appears as the child of an age which was bearing to its grave a great historical development, in which intellectual labour had begun to take the place of hearty political action.

The bloom of Greek philosophy was short-lived, but not more so than the bloom of national life. A closer examination shows that the one depended on the other, and that both of these phenomena were due to the operation of the same causes. With a high appreciation of freedom, with a ready aptitude for politics, with a genius for artistic creations, the Greeks produced, within the sphere of politics, one result of its kind unrivalled and unique. They neglected, however, to lay the foundations wide and deep. Their political duration could not keep pace with their versatility and excitability. Communities limited in extent and simple in arrangement sufficed for them, which, however, could not include all branches of the Greek family, nor satisfy at once all legitimate interests. Within the range of science we likewise see them forming rash conclusions, advancing from individual experiences at once and without any mediating links to the most general conceptions, and constructing theories upon a foundation of limited and imperfect experience, which it was wholly inadequate to bear. Whether, and in how far, the intellect of Greece, if left to itself, might have remedied these defects in a longer protracted, undisturbed development, is a question which it is impossible to answer. That intellect was far too intimately bound up with the political, the moral, and the religious life—in short, with the whole mental tone and culture of the people—not to be seriously affected by any of their changes. It lay, too, in the character and historical progress of this people to have only a brief period of splendour, and one soon over. At the time that the philosophy of Greece reached its highest point in Plato and Aristotle, in all other respects Greece was then in a hopeless state of decline. Notwithstanding individual attempts to resuscitate it, the old morality and propriety of conduct had disappeared since the beginning of the Peloponnesian war. Together with them, too, the old belief in the gods was gone. To the bulk of the people the rising philosophy with its ethics afforded no substitute. Art, however carefully cultivated, could no longer come up to the excellence of the strictly classic period. Political relations became daily more unsatisfactory. If in the fifth century before Christ the rivalry of Athens and Sparta had ranged the states of Greece into two groups, in the succeeding century disunion spread further. Even the attempt of Thebes under Epaminondas to found a new leadership only multiplied parties. Destitute of a political centre of gravity, the Greeks, of their own choice, drifted into a disgraceful dependence on the conquered and now declining Persian empire. Persian gold wielded an influence which Persian arms had never been able to exercise. The petty jealousies of little states and tribes wasted in endless local feuds resources which needed only unity and leadership to do wonders. With the decline of civil order the well-being and martial prowess of the nation declined also; and the increasing technical cultivation of the art of war contributed to take the decision of battle more and more out of the hands of free citizens, and to place it in those of the numerous mercenaries which are one of the most injurious phenomena of this age, a sure sign of the decline of freedom, and of the approach of a military despotism. As this danger with the threatening rise of the Macedonian power came nearer, patriots in Greece might still deceive themselves with the hope that their self-devotion would avert the danger. An unbiassed glance at history can, however, only see in the failure of this attempt the natural and inevitable consequence of causes so deeply rooted in the Greek character and the course of Greek history, that not even the most heroic exertions of individuals, nor the resistance of the divided states, which came too late, could for one moment render the final issue doubtful.

*C. Greece
after the
battle of
Chæronea.*

By the battle of Chæronea the doom of Greece was sealed. Never since then has Greece attained to real political freedom. All attempts to shake off the Macedonian supremacy ended in exhausting disasters. In the subsequent struggles Hellas, and Athens in particular, was the play-ball of changing rulers, the continual arena of their warfare. Not until the second half of the third century was a purely Grecian power formed—the Achæan League—round which the hopes of the nation rallied. How inadequate, however, was this attempt compared with what the real wants of the country required! How soon it became apparent that no remedies were here to be found to heal the ills from which it was suffering! That old hereditary failing of the Greeks, internal discord, still rendered it impossible for them to be independent in foreign relations, and to be united and settled at home. In perpetual struggles between Achæans, Ætolians, and Spartans, their best resources were squandered. The very individual who had led the Achæans against the Macedonians, in the cause of independence, now summoned the Macedonians back to the Peloponnesus, to gain their support against Sparta. When the supremacy of Macedonia was broken by the arms of Rome, a more avowed dependence on Italian allies succeeded. And when, in the year 146 B.C., the province of Achaia was incorporated in the Roman empire, even the shadow of freedom which up to this time had been assured, departed for ever.

Sad as the affairs of Greece at this period became, and marked as was the decline of its internal resources, not less important was the extension of its mental horizon, and the more general diffusion of its culture. The Macedonian ascendancy, dealing as it did a death-blow at the independence of Greece, also

broke down the boundaries which had hitherto separated Greeks from foreigners. A new world was
opened out before the gaze of Greece, and a vast
territory offered for her energies to explore. She
was brought into manifold contact with the Eastern
nations belonging to the Macedonian monarchy,
securing for her culture the place of honour among
the nations of the East, but producing at the same
time a tardy, but, in the long run, important back-
current of Oriental thought, traces of which appeared
in the philosophy of Greece a few centuries later.
By the side of the old famed centres of learning in
the mother country of Hellas, new centres arose,
suited by position, inhabitants, and peculiar circumstances, to unite the culture of East and West, and
to fuse into one homogeneous mass the intellectual
forces of different races. Whilst Hellas, by the
number of emigrants who left her shores to settle in
Asia and Egypt, was losing her population; whilst
the Greeks in their ancestral homes were succumbing
to foreigners; the most extensive intellectual con-
quests were being gained by her over nations by
whom and with whom she had been oppressed.

CHAPTER II.

CHARACTER AND CHIEF FEATURES OF THE POST-ARISTOTELIAN PHILOSOPHY.

THE circumstances which have been hastily sketched in the preceding chapter, are of the greatest importance as affecting the character of the post-Aristotelian philosophy. Greek philosophy, like Greek art, is the offspring of Greek political freedom. In the play of political life, throwing every one on himself and his own resources, in the rivalry of unlimited competition for all the good things of life, the Greeks had learned to make free use of all their mental powers. From his consciousness of dignity—connected by a Greek far more closely than by us with the privilege of citizenship—from his superiority to the needs of daily life, a freedom of thought had sprung up in his mind which could boldly attack the problem of knowledge, without any ulterior aim.[1] With the decline of political independence, however, the mental powers of the nation received a fatal blow. No longer borne up by a powerful *esprit de corps*, weaned from the habit of working for the common weal, the majority gave

CHAP. II.

A. *Causes producing the post-Aristotelian philosophy.*

(1) *Political causes.*

---

[1] Conf. *Arist.* Metaph. I. 2, 282 b, 19.

themselves up to the petty interests of private life and their personal affairs. Even the better disposed were too much occupied in contending with the low tone and corruption of the times, to be able to devote themselves in their moments of relaxation to a free and speculative consideration of things. What could be expected in such an age as that which preceded the rise of the Stoic and Epicurean systems, but that philosophy would take a decidedly practical turn, if indeed it were studied at all?

An age like this did not require theoretical knowledge. It required to be morally braced and strengthened. If these desiderata were no longer to be met with in the popular religion in its then state; if amongst all the cultivated circles philosophy had taken the place of religion, it was only natural that philosophy should meet the existing need. Is it more particularly asked what course, under the circumstances, was it possible and more especially necessary for moral energy to take? the answer is not far to seek. There was less scope for creative ingenuity than for resolute self-devotion; less for outward actions than for inward feeling; less opportunity for public achievements, more for private reforms. So utterly hopeless had the public state of Greece become, that even the few who made it their business to provide a remedy could only gain for themselves the honour of martyrdom. As matters then stood, no other course seemed open for the best-intentioned, save to withdraw entirely within themselves, to entrench themselves within the safe barriers of their own inner life against outward misfortunes, and to make happiness dependent entirely on their own inward state.

Stoic apathy, Epicurean self-contentment, and Sceptic imperturbability, were the doctrines which suited the political helplessness of the age. They were therefore the doctrines which met with the most general acceptance. Suited, too, was that sinking of national distinctions in the feeling of a common humanity, that severance of morals from politics which characterise the philosophy of the Alexandrian and Roman period. Together with national independence, the barriers between nations had been swept away. East and West, Greeks and barbarians, were united in large empires, placed in communication, and compared in most important respects. In declaring that all men are of one blood and equally privileged citizens of one empire, that morality rests on the relation of man to man independently of his nationality and his position in the state, philosophy was only explicitly stating a truth which had been already partly realised in actual fact, and which was certainly implied therein.

By the course, too, which it had taken during the last century and a half, philosophy itself had prepared the way for the turn which now set in. Socrates and the Sophists, in different ways no doubt, had each devoted themselves to the practical side of philosophy; and more definitely still the Cynic School had paved the way for Stoicism, the Cyrenaic for Epicureanism. These two Schools, it is true, play

CHAP. II.

(2) *Intellectual causes.*

a subordinate part in the general conditions of the philosophy of the fourth century, and sophistry by the close of the same century was already a thing of the past. Nor can Socrates, although turning his back on physical enquiries, be at all compared with the post-Aristotelian philosophers, the desire for knowledge being still keen in him. He wished, however, to busy himself only with subjects which were of practical use in life; and yet his theory of knowledge involved a reform quite as much of speculative as of practical philosophy, and that reform was accomplished on a grand scale by Plato and Aristotle. Little as the course of development taken by Greek philosophy during the fourth century agrees with the course of its subsequent development, still the speculations of Plato and Aristotle helped to prepare the way for the coming change. The chasm between the ideal and phenomenal worlds which Plato set up, and Aristotle vainly attempted to bridge over, leads ultimately to a contrast between what is within and what is without, between thought and the object of thought. The generic conceptions or forms, which Plato and Aristotle regard as most truly real, are, after all, fabrications of the human mind. The conception of reason, even in its expanded form as the divine Reason, or reason of the world, is an idea formed by abstraction from our inner life. And what is really meant by identifying form in itself with what *is*, and matter only with what is *possible*, or even (as Plato does) with what *is not*, or by placing God over against and in contrast to the world, except that man finds in his own mind a higher and more real existence than any which he finds outside of it in the world, and that what is truly divine and unlimited must be *in* the mind in its ideal nature, apart from and independent of all impressions from without? Plato and Aristotle in fact declared that reason constitutes the real essence of man—reason coming from above and uniting itself with the body, but being in itself superior to the world of sense and life in time—and that man's highest activity is thought, turned away from all external things, and meditating only on the inner world of ideas. It was only one step further in the same direction for the post-Aristotelian philosophy to refer man back to himself, in complete severance from the outer world, that he may find that peace within which he can find nowhere in the world besides.

This step was taken by the Schools of the Stoics, Epicureans, and Sceptics. Appearing in the first half of the third century before Christ, superseding the influence of the older Schools, and asserting this supremacy without great variation in their teaching until the beginning of the first century, these three Schools, however else they may differ, at least agree in two fundamental points—in subordinating theory to practice, and in the peculiar character of their practical philosophy.

B. Common characteristics of the post-Aristotelian philosophy.

The former point appears most clearly, as will be seen, in the School of Epicurus. It is nearly as clear in the case of the Sceptics, who, denying all possi-

(1) Theory subordinated to practice.

bility of knowledge, left as the only ground of action
conviction based on probabilities; and both these
Schools agree in considering philosophy as only a
means for securing happiness. By the Stoics, on the
other hand, the need of philosophic speculation was
felt more pressingly; but even in their case it may be
readily seen- that this need was not felt simply and
for its own sake, but was subordinated to practical
considerations and determined by these. For, first
of all, the Stoics, like the Epicureans, restricted themselves in the speculative part of their system to more
ancient views—a fact of itself proving that speculation
was not the cause of their philosophical peculiarities,
but that other investigations were of greater value in
their eyes, in which, too, they considered themselves
more proficient. Moreover, they expressly stated that
the study of nature was only necessary as a help to the
study of virtue. It is also beyond question, that their
chief peculiarities, and those which give them an
importance in history, are ethical—the other parts of
their system, and those in which their distinctive
tenets appear, being only regulated by practical considerations. Hereafter, these statements will be substantiated in detail. It may therefore suffice to
observe here, that the most important question in
the logic of the Stoics—the question of a standard of
truth—was decided by a practical postulate; that the
fundamental principles of the Stoic metaphysics are
only intelligible from the ground of their ethics; that
for natural science the Stoics did very little; that in
their theory of final causes on which they lay so much

stress nature is explained by moral considerations; even their natural as well as their positive theology bearing ample testimony to the practical tone of their system. Standing in advance of the Epicureans by their higher intellectual bearing and their learned energy, and decidedly opposing the Sceptics by their dogmatism, the Stoics nevertheless agree with both these Schools in the essentially practical character of their teaching.

CHAP. II.

This relationship is more strikingly seen in the way in which they dealt with practical problems. The Epicurean imperturbability is akin to that of the Sceptics; both resemble the Stoic apathy. All three Schools are agreed that the only way to happiness consists in peace of mind, and in avoiding all those disturbances which sometimes arise from external influences, at other times from internal emotions; they are only divided as to the means by which peace of mind may be secured. They are also agreed in making moral activity independent of external circumstances, and in separating morals from politics, although only the Stoics set up the doctrine of the original unity of the whole human family, and insisted on being citizens of the world. Through all the Schools runs the common trait of referring everything to the subject, of withdrawing everything within the sphere of mind and of the inner life, one consequence of which is to press into notice practice rather than speculation, another being that the satisfaction of this want can only be had in internal self-consciousness, and in a mental equilibrium attained

(2) Peculiar mode of dealing with the practical problem.

CHAP.
II.

(3) *Their
peculiari-
ties illus-
trated by
subsequent
philo-
sophy.*

by the exercise of the will and the cultivation of the intellect.

The same character attaches to philosophy in the centuries succeeding the rise of these three Schools; nor were the circumstances out of which it grew materially altered. In addition to the followers of the old Schools, Eclectics were now to be met with, gathering from every system what was true and probable. In this process of selection, however, the determining element was a regard for the practical wants of man, and the ultimate standard of truth was placed in our own immediate consciousness, everything being referred to the subject as its centre. In ethics, too, and natural theology the Eclectics were also mainly indebted to the Stoics. A new School of Sceptics also arose, not differing, however, in its tendencies from the older one. Neopythagoreans and Platonists appeared, not satisfied with human knowledge, but aspiring to higher revelations. Professing to appeal to the metaphysics of Plato and Aristotle, these philosophers nevertheless betray their connection with the later post-Aristotelian Schools, not only because they borrowed extensively from the Stoics the material for their theology and ethics, but far more by their general tone, knowledge being for them even far less than for the Stoics an end in itself, and they are further from natural science. Their philosophy is subservient to the interests of religion, its aim being to bring men into proper relation with God; and the religious needs of mankind are the highest authority for science.

The same observations apply also to Plotinus and his successors. These philosophers are not lacking in a developed science of metaphysics. The care, too, with which they elaborated this science leaves no doubt as to their lively interest in scientific completeness and systematic correctness. Still these scientific efforts bear with them the same relation to the practical aim of philosophy as with the Stoics, who in point of learning and logical elaboration of a system are quite their match. Undoubtedly a real interest in knowledge was one of the elements which brought Neoplatonism into being; but it was not strong enough to counterbalance another element, the practical and religious one. The mind was not sufficiently independent to be able to get on without appealing to intellectual and theological authorities; the scientific procedure was too complex to lead to a simple study of things as they are. As in the case of the Neopythagoreans, the ultimate ground of the system is a religious want. The divine world is only a portion of human thought projected out of the mind, and incapable of being fully grasped by the understanding. The highest business of philosophy is to reunite man with the divine world external to himself. To attain this end, all the means which science supplies are employed. Philosophy endeavours to explain the steps by which the finite gradually came to be separated from the original infinite being; it seeks to bring about a return by a regular and systematic course; and in this attempt the philosophic spirit of Greece, by no

means extinct, proved its capabilities by a result of
its kind unrivalled. If, in the first instance, the
problem was so raised as to impress philosophy into
the service of religion; still, in the long run, it
could not fail to be seen that, with the premises
assumed, a scientific solution of the religious question was impossible. With its idea of an original
being, the system had started from a conception
which in this form was a reflex of the religious sentiment, and not the result of scientific research. In
its doctrine of a mystical union with a transcendental
being, it had concluded with a religious postulate,
the gratuitous assumption of which betrays an origin
in the mind of the thinker. Neoplatonism, therefore, in its whole bearing, stands on the same ground
as the other post-Aristotelian systems; and it is
hardly necessary in further proof of this relationship
to point to its agreement in other respects with
Stoicism, and especially in ethics. Far as these two
systems lie asunder, the one standing at the beginning the other at the end of the post-Aristotelian
philosophy, nevertheless both display one and the
same attitude of thought; and we pass from one to
the other by a continuous series of intermediate
links.

The character of the post-Aristotelian philosophy
assumed, as might be expected, various modifications
in course of time in passing from School to School;
nevertheless, it reproduced certain common elements. Such was the neglect of intellectual originality, which drove some thinkers to a sceptical

denial of all knowledge, and induced others to take their knowledge at second hand from older authorities. Such was the prominence given to practical over speculative questions. Such was the disregard for natural science, and, in comparison with former times, the greater importance attached to theology, appearing not only in the controversy between the Epicureans and Stoics, but also in the apologetical writings of the Stoics and Platonists. Such, too, was the negative morality which aimed at independence of the outer world, at mental composure, and philosophic contentment; the separating of morals from politics ; the moral universalism and citizenship of the world; the going within self into the depths of the soul, the will, and the thinking powers ; the deepening of the consciousness accompanied at the same time by a narrowing and isolation of it, and the loss of a lively interest in the world without, and in the simple scientific study thereof.

This mental habit, first of all, found a dogmatic expression in philosophy. Not only moral science, but logic and natural science were treated in a way corresponding therewith, though partially built on to the older teaching. In the treatment of moral science in particular, two Schools come to view, markedly different and decided in their peculiarities. The Stoics regard almost exclusively the universal element in the man who seeks contentment within, the Epicureans catch at the individual side of his being. The Stoics regarded man exclusively as a thinking being, the Epicureans as a creature of feel-

C. *Development of post-Aristotelian philosophy.*
(1) *Dogmatic Schools.*
(a) *Stoics and Epicureans.*

ing. The Stoics made happiness consist in his subordination to the law of the whole, in the suppression of all personal feelings and inclinations, in virtue; the Epicureans in the independence of the individual from everything external, in the unruffled serenity of the inner life, in painlessness. The theoretical assumptions on which their teaching was based corresponded with these fundamental ethical positions.

(b) Dogmatic scepticism.

Violent as was the rivalry between these two Schools, both, nevertheless, stand on the same platform. Absolute composure of mind, freedom of the inner life from every external disturbance, is the goal at which both Schools aim, although following different courses. Therewith arises the demand to elevate this common element, making it the essential aim and subject matter of philosophy. If the philosophic axioms of these systems contradict one another, what may be thence concluded save that the aim may be attained independently of any definite dogmatic view; in short, that we may despair of knowledge in order to pass from the knowledge of our ignorance to a general indifference to everything and to an unconditional repose of mind. Thus Scepticism joins on to Stoicism and Epicureanism, as the third chief form of the philosophy of that age, finding detached representatives in Pyrrho's School, and most influentially represented in the New Academy.

(2) Sceptical Schools.

The rise, the growth, and the conflict of these three Schools, by the side of which the older Schools have only a subordinate value, occupies the first portion of the period of post-Aristotelian philosophy, extending from the end of the fourth to the beginning of the first century before Christ. The distinctive features of this epoch consist partly in the predominance of the above tendencies, and partly in their separate existence, without being modified by intermixture. After the middle of the second century a gradual change may be observed. Greece was now a Roman province, and the intellectual intercourse between Greece and Rome was continually on the increase. Many learned Greeks resided at Rome, frequently as the companions of families of high birth ; others living in their own country, were visited by Roman pupils. How, in the face of the clearly defined and sharply expressed Roman character, could the power and independence of the Greek intellect, already unquestionably on the decline, assert its ancient superiority ? How could Greeks become the teachers of Romans without accommodating themselves to their requirements, and experiencing in turn a reflex influence ? Nor could the philosophy of Greece be exempt from such an influence, its originality long since in abeyance, its Scepticism now openly avowing that it could place no trust in itself. To the practical sense of a Roman no philosophical system could commend itself which did not make for practical results by the shortest possible route. To him practical needs were the ultimate standard of truth. Little did he care for rigid logic and conclusive accuracy in the scientific procedure. Differences of schools, so long as they

CHAP. II.

(a) *Influences producing Scepticism.*

(a) *Political influence of Rome.*

*(β) Intel-
lectual in-
fluence of
Alexan-
dria.*

had no practical bearing, were for him of no importance. No wonder that Greek philosophy, touched
by the breath of Rome, lent herself to Eclecticism !

Whilst on the one side of the world the Greeks
were experiencing the influence of the nation that
had subdued them, on the other they were assimila-
ting the views of the Oriental nations whom they had
subdued alike by martial as by mental superiority.
For two centuries, in philosophy at least, Greece had
held her own against Oriental modes of thought.
Now, as her internal incapacity continually increased,
those modes of thought gained for themselves a
foothold in her philosophy. Alexandria was the
place where first and most completely the connection
of Greece with the East was brought about. In that
centre of commerce for all parts of the globe, East
and West entered into a connection more intimate
and more lasting than in any other centre; nor was
this connection a mere accident of circumstances;
it was also a work of political forecast. From its
founder, Ptolemy Soter, the Ptolemæan dynasty inherited as its principle of government the maxim of
always combining what is native with what is foreign,
and of clothing things new in the old and venerable
forms of Egyptian custom and religious ceremony.
At Alexandria, accordingly, there arose, towards the
beginning of the first century before Christ, a School
calling itself at first Platonic, afterwards Pythagorean,
which later still, in the shape of Neoplatonism,
gained the ascendency over the whole domain of
philosophy. The very fact, however, that such a

change in philosophic views did not appear before, may suffice to show that it was called for and produced by external circumstances, but that notwithstanding these circumstances it would never have come into being had not the intellect of Greece in the course of its own development been ripe for the change.

The same remark holds good of the rise of that practical Eclecticism which we have before traced to the influence of Rome. Even in the period of its intellectual exhaustion, Greek philosophy became what it did not simply from the force of circumstances, but, under the influence of those very surroundings, it developed in a direction to which its previous course already pointed. If we except the lingering remains of a few small Schools, which soon expired, there existed, after the beginning of the third century before Christ, only four great philosophic Schools—the Peripatetic, the Stoic, the Epicurean, and the School of Platonists, converted to Scepticism by Arcesilaus. These four Schools were all permanently established at Athens, and thus a lively interchange of thought, and a thorough comparison of their several teachings were rendered comparatively easy. That they would not long exist side by side without making some overtures towards union and agreement was a perfectly natural prospect, one, too, hastened on by Scepticism, which, after denying the possibility of knowledge, only allowed a choice between probabilities, that choice being decided by the standard of practical needs. Hence, towards the close of the second century before Christ, these

CHAP. II.

(*b*) *Scepticism and Electicism.*

philosophic Schools may be observed to emerge more
or less from their exclusiveness. An eclectic tendency steals over philosophy, aiming not so much at
scientific knowledge as at attaining certain results
of a practical kind. The distinctive doctrines of
each School drop into the background ; and in the
belief that infallibility resides solely in the mind
itself, such portions were selected from each system
as seemed most in harmony with the selecting mind.
Yet just as this eclectic mode of thought lay in
germ in Scepticism, so, on the other hand, Eclecticism involves doubt, which appears again, soon after
the Christian era, in a new school of doubt, continuing
until the third century. There is thus, on the one
hand, an urgent demand for knowledge, which is
first sought for in the practical interest of religion
and morals ; and, on the other hand, a disbelief in
the truths of existing knowledge, and, indeed, of
knowledge generally, which some openly avow as
Sceptics, others clearly enough betray in the unset-
tledness of their Eclecticism. These two currents
coalescing, we arrive at the thought that truth,
which could not be attained in the form of intellectual knowledge, exists outside of it, and is partly to
be sought in the religious traditions of the early
days of Greece and the East, partly by immediate
divine revelation. This effort gives rise to such a
notion of God, and of His relations to the world, as
is suited to this belief in revelation. Man knowing
that truth lies outside himself, and doubting his own
capacities to attain thereto, has removed deity, as

the absolute source of truth, into another world. The need of a revelation of truth still existing, the interval between God and the world is peopled with intermediate beings, who were sometimes conceived of as purely metaphysical entities, and at others appeared, according to the popular belief, as demons. This mental habit, which, among the older systems, belongs particularly to the Platonic and Pythagorean, forms the transition to Neoplatonism, the appearance of which introduces the last stage in the development of Greek philosophy.

Yet even this last phase of Greek philosophy was not uninfluenced by the circumstances of history. Since the end of the second century after Christ, the decline of the Roman Empire, the terrible dangers which threatened it on all sides, the pressure and the necessity of the time, had made startling progress. All means of defence hitherto employed proved unavailing to stem destruction. With ruin everywhere staring in the face, the desire and longing for some higher assistance increased. Such assistance could no longer be obtained from the old Gods of Rome or the religious faith of the day. Despite these circumstances were daily becoming more hopeless. Stronger and stronger became the inclination which had been gradually spreading over the Roman world since the last days of the Republic, and which the circumstances of the empire had greatly favoured, to have recourse to foreign forms of worship. The highest power in the state had, moreover, favoured this inclination under the Oriental and half Oriental emperors who for nearly half a century after Septimius Severus occupied the imperial throne. The state and the Gods of the state were continually losing their hold on the respect of men. Meanwhile, on the one hand, Oriental worships, mysteries new and old, and foreign heathen religions of the most varying kinds, were ever gaining fresh adherents. On the other, Christianity was rapidly gaining a power which enabled it openly to enter the lists for supremacy among the recognised religions of the state. The attempts of a series of powerful monarchs about the middle of the third century to build up the Empire afresh, could not have for their object a restoration of a specifically Roman form of government. Their only aim was to bring the various elements which composed the Empire under one sovereign will by fixed forms of administration; a result which was actually reached under Diocletian and Constantine. The Roman character asserted itself, indeed, as a ruling and regulating power, but it was at the same time subordinate to another of an originally foreign character. The Empire was a congeries of nations artificially held together, and arranged on a carefully designed plan; their centre of gravity lay not within the nation, but in the simple will of a prince, standing above all rules and laws of state, and deciding everything without appeal and without responsibility.

In a similar manner Neoplatonism united all the elements of previous philosophical Schools into one comprehensive and well-arranged system, in which

each class of existences had its definite place assigned to it. The initial point in this system,
however, the all-embracing unity, was a being lying
beyond it, soaring above every notion that experience
and conception can supply, unmixed with the pro
cess of life going on in the world, and from his un-
attainable height causing all things, but himself
subject to no conditions of causality. Neoplatonism
is the intellectual reproduction of Byzantine Imperialism. As Byzantine Imperialism combines Oriental despotism with the Roman idea of the state,
so Neoplatonism fills out with Oriental mysticism
the scientific forms of Greek philosophy.

In Neoplatonism the post-Aristotelian philosophy
had manifestly veered round into its opposite. Self-
dependence, and the self-sufficingness of thought,
have made way for a resignation to higher powers,
for a longing for some revelation, for an ecstatic
departure from the domain of conscious mental activity. Man has resigned the idea of truth within
for truth to be found only in God. Removed into
another world, God stands over against man and the
world of appearances, in abstract spirituality. All
the attempts of thought have but one aim—to explain the procession of the finite from the infinite,
and the conditions of its return into the absolute.
But neither the one nor the other of these problems
could meet with a satisfactory intellectual solution.
That even this form of thought betrays undeniably the
personal character of the post-Aristotelian philosophy
has been already seen, and will be seen still more in

CHAP.
II.

the sequel. Therewith undoubtedly the creative
powers of the Greek mind were exhausted. Losing
the platform of her national existence for centuries
step by step, Greece saw the last remaining fragments
torn from her grasp by the victory of Christianity.
Before surrendering them, Neoplatonism made one
more futile attempt to rescue the forms of Greek
culture from her mighty rival. With the failure of
that attempt Greek religion and Greek philosophy
set together.

PART II.

THE STOICS.

CHAPTER III.

HISTORY OF THE STOICS UNTIL THE END OF THE
SECOND CENTURY B.C.

A STRIKING feature in the history of the post-Aristotelian philosophy, and one which at the same time
brings forcibly home to us the thorough change
of all circumstances, is the fact that so many of its
representatives come from eastern countries in which
Greek and Oriental modes of thought met and mingled.
For centuries still Athens continued to have the reputation of being the chief seat of Greek philosophy;
nor did she cease to be one of the most important
seminaries of philosophy, even when she had to share
that reputation with other cities, such as Alexandria,
Rome, Rhodes, and Tarsus. Yet even at Athens there
were teachers not a few whose foreign extraction indicates the age of Hellenism. Next to the later Neoplatonic School, this remark is of none more true
than the Stoic. With this fact we may always connect the world-citizenship of this School, whilst we

CHAP.
III.

CHAP.
III.

A. Zeno.

are careful not to attribute a general characteristic of the then state of the world to purely external circumstances. Nearly all the most important Stoics before the Christian era belong by birth to Asia Minor, to Syria, and to the islands of the Eastern Archipelago. Then follow a series of Roman Stoics, by the side of whom the Phrygian Epictetus occupies a prominent place; but Greece proper is exclusively represented by men of third or fourth rate capacity.

The founder of the Stoic School, Zeno[1] by name, was the son of Mnaseas,[2] and a native of Citium[3] in Cyprus. Leaving his home, he repaired to Athens,[4]

[1] For the life of Zeno, Diogenes is the chief authority, who appears to be chiefly indebted for his information to Antigonus of Carystus, who lived about 250 B.C. In proof of this, compare the account of Diogenes with the extracts given by Athenæus (viii. 345, d; xiii. 563, e; 565, d; 603, e; 607, e; and, in particular, ii. 55, f) from Antigonus' life of Zeno. Of modern authorities, consult *Wagenmann*, in *Pauly's* Realencyclop.

[2] *Diog.* vii. 1. *Suid.* Ζήνων. *Plut.* Plac. i. 3, 29. *Pausan.* ii. 8, 4. He is called by others Demeas.

[3] Citium, which the ancients unanimously call the native city of Zeno, was, according to *Diog.* vii. 1, a πόλισμα Ἑλληνικὸν Φοίνικας ἐποίκους ἐσχηκὸς, i.e. Phœnician immigrants had settled there by the side of the old Greek population, whence its inhabitants are sometimes called ' e Phœnicia profecti ' (*Cic.* Fin. iv. 20, 56), and Zeno

is himself called a Phœnician (*Diog.* vii. 3; 15; 25; 30; ii. 114. *Suid.* Ζήν. *Athen.* xiii. 563, e. *Cic.* l. c.). A continuous connection between Citium and Phœnicia is implied in *Diog.* vii. 6; οἱ ἐν Σιδῶνι Κιτιεῖς.

[4] The details are differently given by *Diog.* 2–5; 31; *Plut.* Inimic. Util. 2, p. 87; and *Sen.* Tranq. An. 14, 3. Most accounts relate that he came to Athens for trading purposes, and accidentally became acquainted with Crates and philosophy after being shipwrecked. According to other accounts, he remained at Athens, after disposing of his merchandise, and devoted himself to philosophy. Demetrius of Magnesia (*Themist.* Or. xxiii. 295, D) further relates that he had already occupied himself with philosophy at home, and repaired to Athens to study it more fully —a view which seems most likely, because the least sensational.

about the year 320 B.C.,[1] where he at first joined the
Cynic Crates.[2] He appears, however, to have been
previously disgusted with the extravagances of the
Cynic mode of life.[3] Besides, his keen desire for
knowledge could find no satisfaction in a teaching so
meagre as that of the Cynics.[4] To supply its defects
he had recourse to Stilpo, who united to the moral
teaching of the Cynics the logical accuracy of the

[1] The dates in Zeno's life are
very uncertain. He is said to
have been thirty when he first
came to Athens (*Diog.* 2). Persæus, however (*Ibid.* 28), his
pupil and countryman, says
twenty-two. These statements
are of little use, since the date
of his coming to Athens is unknown. If it is true that after
reading with Crates he was for
ten years a pupil of Xenocrates,
who died 314 B.C. (*Timocrates*
in *Diog.* 2), he must have come
to Athens not later than 328
B.C. But this fact may be
doubted. For his whole line of
thought resembles that of Crates
and Stilpo. How then can he
have been for ten years a pupil
in the Academy, and in addition have enjoyed Polemo's
teaching? Altogether he is
said to have frequented the
schools of different philosophers
for twenty years before opening
his own (*Diog.* 4). According
to Apollon. in *Diog.* 28, he presided over his own school for
fifty-eight years, which is
hardly reconcileable with the
above data, even if he attained
the age of ninety-eight (*Diog.*
28; *Lucian.* Macrob. 19). According to Persæus (*Diog.* 28),

he only attained the age of
seventy-two (*Clinton* Fast.
Hell. II. 368 capriciously suggests 92), and was altogether
only fifty years in Athens. On
the other hand, in his own
letter to Antigonus (*Diog.* 9),
he distinctly calls himself an
octogenarian, but the genuine-
ness of this letter, borrowed by
Diogenes from Apollonius, the
Tyrian about 50 B.C., may perhaps be doubted. The year of
Zeno's death is likewise unknown. His relations to Antigonus Gonatas prove at least
that he was not dead before the
beginning of his reign in 278
B.C., and probably not till long
afterwards. It would appear
from the calculation of his age,
that his death did not take
place till 260 B.C. He may,
then, have lived circa 350 to
260 B.C.; but these dates are
quite uncertain.

[2] *Diog.* vii. 2 ; vi. 105.

[3] *Diog.* 3 · ἐντεῦθεν ἤκουσ ἐτοῦ
Κράτητος, ἄλλως μὲν εὔτονος πρὸς
φιλοσοφίαν, αἰδήμων δὲ ὡς πρὸς
τὴν κυνικὴν ἀναισχυντίαν.

[4] Conf., besides what immediately follows, *Diog.* 25 and
15: ἦν δὲ ζητητικὸς καὶ περὶ
πάντων ἀκριβολογούμενος.

Megarians. He also studied under Polemo; it is said likewise under Xenocrates and Diodorus the logician, with whose pupil Philo[1] he was on terms of intimacy. After a long course of intellectual preparation, he at last appeared as a teacher, soon after the beginning of the third, or perhaps during the last years of the fourth century B.C. From the Stoa ποικίλη, the place which he selected for delivering his lectures, his followers derived their name of Stoics, having first been called after their master Zenonians.[2] Such was the universal respect inspired by his earnestness, moral strictness,[3] and simplicity of life,[4] and the dignity, modesty, and affability of his conduct,[5]

[1] *Diog.* vii. 2; 4; 16; 20; 24; ii. 114; 120. Numen. in *Eus.* Pr. Ev. xiv. 5, 9; 6, 6. Polemo is called his teacher by *Cic.* Fin. iv. 16, 45; Acad. i. 9, 35. *Strabo,* xiii. 1, 67, p. 614. On Xenocrates compare p. 37, 1. How ready he was to learn from others is proved by the saying in *Diog.* 25; *Plut.* Fragm. in Hesiod. ix. T. V. 511. W.

[2] *Diog.* 5, according to whom, he gave instruction walking to and fro, like Aristotle, but never to more than two or three at a time (*Diog.* 14). It is not probable that he gave any formal lectures.

[3] Which, however, must be judged by the standard of that time and of Greek customs. Conf. *Diog.* 13; and the quotations in *Athen.* xiii. 607, e; 563, e, from Antigonus of Carystus.

[4] See Musonius in *Stob.* Serm. 17, 43. His outward circumstances also appear to have been

very simple. According to one account (*Diog.* 13), he brought to Athens the fabulous sum of 1000 talents, and put it out to interest. *Themist.* Or. xxi., p. 252, says that he forgave a debtor his debt. He is said to have paid a logician 200 drachmas, instead of the 100 which he asked for (*Diog.* 25). Nor is there any mention of a Cynical life or of poverty. But, according to *Diog.* 5, *Plut.* and *Sen.*, however, he had lost his property almost entirely. According to *Sen.* Consol. ad Helv. 12, 5 (contradicted by *Diog.* 23), he owned no slave. Had he been well to do, he would hardly have accepted the presents of Antigonus. That Zeno was unmarried appears from *Diog.* 13.

[5] Conf. *Diog.* 13; 16; 24; 26; *Athen.* in the passage quoted p. 36, 1; *Suid.*; *Clem.* Strom. 413, A. It is mentioned as a peculiarity of Zeno, that he avoided

that Antigonus Gonatas vied with the city of Athens   CHAP.
in showing his appreciation of so estimable a philo-   III.
sopher.[1] Although lacking smoothness of style and
using a language far from pure,[2] Zeno had neverthe-

all noise and popular display
(*Diog.* 14); that, though generally grave, he relaxed over
his wine, and that too much;
that he could not tolerate many
words, and was very fond of
epigrams. See *Diog.* 16 ; 20 ;
24 ; *Athen.* l.c. *Stob.* Serm. 34 ;
10 ; 36 ; 19 ; 23. He is said to
have carried his parsimonious-
ness too far—in this respect a
thorough Phœnician (*Diog.* 16).
The presents of Antigonus he
never sought, and broke with
an acquaintance who asked for
his interest with the King.
Still he did not despise them,
without abating from his dignity. The loss of his property
he bore with the greatest composure (*Diog.* 3; *Plut.* and *Sen.*).
   [1] Antigonus (conf. *Athen.*
xiii. 603, e; *Arrian*, Diss. Epict.
ii. 13, 14; *Simpl.* in Epict. Enchir. 283, c ; *Æl.* V. H. ix. 26)
was fond of his society, attended
his lectures, and wished to have
him at court—an offer which
Zeno declined, sending two of
his pupils instead. The Athenians, to whom, according to
Ælian's untrustworthy account
V. H. vii. 14 he had rendered
political services, honoured him
with a public panegyric, a golden crown, a statue, and burial
in the Ceramicus. That the
keys of the city were left in
his keeping is not probable.
The offer of Athenian citizenship he declined (*Plut.* Sto.
Rep. 4, 1, p. 1034). Nor did

his countrymen in Citium fail
to show their appreciation
(*Diog.* 6; *Plin.* H. N. xxxiv. 19,
32) of him, and Zeno always
insisted on being a Citian
(*Diog.* 12 ; *Plut.* l.c.).
   [2] He himself (*Diog.* vii. 18)
compares the λόγοι ἀπηρτισμένοι
of the ἀσόλοικοι to the elegant
Alexandrian coins, which, instead of being better, were often
lighter than those of Athens.
He is charged in particular
with using words in a wrong
sense, and with inventing new
ones, whence *Cic.* Tusc. v. 11,
34, calls him 'ignobilis verborum
opifex,' and Chrysippus, in a
treatise περὶ τοῦ κυρίως κεχρῆσθαι
Ζήνωνα τοῖς ὀνόμασιν, dispar-
ages this καινοτομεῖν ἐν τοῖς
ὀνόμασι (*Galen.* Diff. Puls. III.
1., vol. viii. 642, K.). He is also
charged with maintaining that
nothing should be concealed,
but that even the most indeli-
cate things should be called by
their proper names. He is further charged with having propounded no new system, but
with having appropriated the
thoughts of his predecessors,
concealing his plagiarism by
the use of new terms. In *Diog.*
vii. 25, Polemo says: κλέπτων τὰ
δόγματα Φοινικῶς μεταμφιεννύς ;
and Cicero frequently repeats
the charge (Fin. v. 25, 74 ; iii.
2, 5 ; iv. 2, 3 ; 3, 7 ; 26 ; 72 ; v.
8, 22 ; 29, 88. Acad. ii. 5, 15.
Legg. i. 13, 38 ; 20 ; 53. Tusc.
ii. 12, 29).

CHAP.
III.

less an extensive following. Leading a life of singular moderation, he reached an advanced age untouched
by disease, although he naturally enjoyed neither
robust health nor an attractive person.[1] A slight
injury having at length befallen him, which he regarded as a hint of destiny, he put an end to his own
life.[2] His not very numerous writings[3] have been
lost, with the exception of a few fragments, some no
doubt dating from the time when, as a pupil of Crates,
he adhered more strictly to Cynic ideas than was
afterwards the case;[4] nor ought this point to be forgotten in sketching his teaching.

B. Pupils
of Zeno.
(1) Cle-
anthes.

The successor to the chair of Zeno was Cleanthes,[5]
a native of Assos in the Troad,[6] a man of a strong and
firm character, of unusual endurance, energy, and con-

[1] Diog. 28, 1. The statement that he was ἄνοσος must be taken with some limitation, according to Diog. vii. 162; Stob. Floril. 17, 43.

[2] Diog. 28; 31. Lucian, Macrob. 19. Lactant. Inst. iii. 18. Stob. Floril. 7, 45. Suid.

[3] The list of them in Diog. 4, to which additions are made Diog. 34; 39; 134. The Διατριβαὶ (Diog. 34; Sext. Pyrrh. iii. 205; 245; Math. xi. 90) may perhaps be identical with the Ἀπομνημονεύματα Κράτητος (Diog. 4), the Τέχνη ἐρωτική (Diog. 34), with Τέχνη (Diog. 4). An ex-position of Hesiod, which had been inferred to exist, from Cic. N. D. i. 14, 36, Krische, Forsch. 367, rightly identifies with the treatise περὶ τοῦ ὅλου, and this with the treatise περὶ τῆς φύσεως (Stob. Ecl. i. 178). Other au-

thorities are given by Fabric. Bibl. Gr. iii. 580.

[4] This appears at least prob-able from Diog. 4: ἕως μὲν οὖν τινὸς ἤκουσε τοῦ Κράτητος · ὅτε καὶ τὴν πολίτειαν αὐτοῦ γράψαντος, τινὲς ἔλεγον παίζοντες ἐπὶ τῆς τοῦ κυνὸς οὐρᾶς αὐτὴν γεγραφέναι.

[5] Mohnike, Cleanthes d. Sto.: Greifsw. 1814. Cleanthis Hymn. in Jovem, ed Sturz, ed. nov. cur. Merzdorf.: Lips. 1835.

[6] Strabo, xiii. 1, 57, p. 610. Diog. vii. 168. Ælian, Hist. Anim. vi. 50. How Clemens, Protrept. 47, A, comes to call him Πισαδεὺς, it is hard to say, nor is it of any moment. Moh-nike, p. 67, offers conjectures. Mohnike also rightly maintains, p. 77, that Cleanthes ὁ Ποντικὸς in Diog. ix. 15 must be the same as this Cleanthes, and Cobet strikes out the words ὁ Ποντικὸς after Κλεάνθης.

ARISTO AND HERILLUS.

---

tentment, but also slow of apprehension, and somewhat heavy in intellect. Resembling Xenocrates in mind, Cleanthes was in every way adapted to uphold his master's teaching, and to recommend it by the moral weight of his own character, but he was incapable of expanding it more completely, or of establishing it on a wider basis.[1]

Besides Cleanthes, the best known among the pupils of Zeno are Aristo of Chios,[2] and Herillus of

CHAP. III.

(2) *Aristo and Herillus.*

[1] According to Antisthenes (the Rhodian), in *Diog.* l. c., Cleanthes was a pugilist, who came to Athens with four drachmae, and entered the school of Zeno (according to *Hesych.* v. *Suid.*, that of Crates, which is impossible for chronological reasons. Conversely, *Valer. Max.* viii. 7, ext. 11, makes him a pupil of Chrysippus, confounding the relations of pupil and teacher, as we have met with elsewhere), in which he studied for nineteen years (*Diog.* 176), gaining a maintenance by working as a labourer (*Diog.* 168; 174; *Plut.* Vit. Ær. Al. 7, 5, p. 830; *Sen.* Ep. 44, 3; *Krische* Forsch.). A public maintenance, which was offered him, Zeno induced him to refuse, who, in other ways, tried his power of will by the severest tests. It is, therefore, all the more improbable that Antigonus gave him 3000 minæ (*Diog.* 169). On the simplicity of his life, his constant application, his adherence to Zeno, &c., see *Diog.* 168; 170; 37; *Plut.* De Audi. 18, p. 47; *Cic.* Tusc. ii. 25, 60. He also refused to become an Athenian citizen (*Plut.*

Sto. Rep. 4, p. 1034). He died of self-imposed starvation (*Diog.* 176; *Lucian*, Macrob. 19; *Stob.* Floril. 7, 54). His age is stated by *Diog.* 176, at eighty; by *Lucian* and *Valer. Max.* viii. 7, ext. 11, at ninety-nine. *Diog.* 174, gives a list of his somewhat numerous writings, mostly on moral subjects, which is supplemented by *Fabric.* Bibl. iii. 551, Harl. and *Mohnike*, p. 90. Cleanthes was held in great esteem in the Stoic School, even in the time of Chrysippus (*Diog.* vii. 179; 182; *Cic.* Acad. ii. 41, 126). At a later time, the Roman Senate erected a statue to him at Assos (*Simpl.* in *Epict.* Enchir. c. 53, 329, b).

[2] Aristo, son of Miltiades, a Chian, discussed most fully by *Krische*, Forsch. 405, known as the Siren, because of his persuasive powers, and also as the Baldhead, was a pupil of Zeno (*Diog.* 37; 160; *Cic.* N. D. i. 14, 37; Acad. ii. 42, 130; *Sen.* Ep. 94, 2), but is said, during Zeno's illness, to have joined Polemo (Diocl. in *Diog.* 162). Although it may be objected that his teaching does not diverge in the direction of Pla-

41

Carthage,[1] who diverged from his teaching in the most opposite directions, Aristo confining himself

tonism, but rather in the opposite direction, still Polemo's contempt (*Diog.* iv. 18) for dialectic may at one time have had its attractions for him. It is a better established fact that his attitude towards pleasure was less indifferent than it ought to have been, according to his principles (Eratos and Apollophanes in *Athen.* vii. 281, c); but the charge of flattery towards his fellow-pupil Persæus appears not to be substantiated (*Athen.*vi.251,c). His letters show that he was on intimate terms with Cleanthes (*Themist.* Or. xxi. p. 255, b). His loquacity is said to have been displeasing to Zeno (*Diog.* vii. 18). He appeared as a teacher in the Cynosarges, Antisthenes' old locality (*Diog.* 161), thus claiming descent from Cynicism. Of his numerous pupils (*Diog.* 182; *Plut.* C. Princ. Philos. i. 4, p. 776), two are mentioned by Diogenes, 161; Miltiades and Diphilus. Athenæus names two more: Apollophanes, and the celebrated Alexandrian sage, Eratosthenes, both of whom wrote an 'Aristo.' The latter is also named by *Strabo*, i. 2, 2, p. 15, *Suid.* 'Ερατοσθ. Apollophanes, whilst adopting Aristo's views of virtue in *Diog.* vii. 92, did not otherwise adopt his ethics. His natural science is mentioned by *Diog.* vii. 140, his psychology by *Tertul.* De An. 14. Since Erastosthenes was born 276 B.C., Aristo must have been alive in 250 B.C., which agrees

with his being called a cotemporary and opponent of Arcesilaus (*Strabo*, 1. c.; *Diog.* vii. 162; iv. 40, and 33). According to *Diog.* vii. 164, he died of sunstroke. Not only had his School disappeared in the time of Strabo and Cicero (*Cic.* Legg. i. 13, 38; Fin. ii. 11, 35; v. 8, 23; Tusc. v. 30, 85; Off. i. 2, 6; *Strabo*, l. c.), but no traces of it are found beyond the first generation. The writings enumerated by *Diog.* vii. 163, with the single exceptiou of the letter to Cleanthes, are said to have been attributed by Panætius and Sosicrates to the Peripatetic; but Krische's remarks, p. 408, particularly after *Sauppe's* demurrer (Philodemi de Vit. Lib. X. Weimar, 1853, p. 7), raise a partial doubt as to the accuracy of this statement. The fragments, at least, of Ὁμοιώματα preserved by Stobæus seem to belong to a Stoic. Perhaps from the Ὅμοια come the statements in *Sen.* Ep. 36, 3; 115, 8; *Plut.* De Aud. 8, p. 42; De Sanit. 20, p. 133; De Exil. 5, p. 600; Præc. Ger. Reip. 9, 4, p. 804; Aqua an Ign. Util. 12, 2, p. 958.

[1] Herillus's native place was Carthage (*Diog.* vii. 37; 165). If Χαλχηδόνιος is read by *Cobet* in the last passage, we have again the same confusion between Καλχηδών and Καρκηδῶν, which made Xenocrates a Καρχηδόνιος. He came as a boy under Zeno (*Diog.* 166; *Cic.* Acad. ii. 42, 129). *Diog.* l. c. enumerates the writings of Herillus, calling

rigidly to Cynicism, Herillus approximating to the
leading positions held by the Peripatetic School.

Other pupils of Zeno were Persæus, a countryman
and companion of Zeno;[1] Aratus, the well-known
poet of Soli;[2] Dionysius of Heraclea in Pontus,

CHAP.
III.

(3) *Other
pupils.*

them, however, ὀλιγόστιχα μὲν
δυνάμεως δὲ μεστά. *Cic.* De
Orat. iii. 17, 62, speaks of a
School bearing his name, but no
pupil belonging to it is known.
   [1] Citium was his birthplace.
His father's name was Demetrius (*Diog.* 6 ; 36), and his own
nickname Dorotheus (*Suid.*
Περσ.). According to *Diog.*
36 ; Sotion and Nicias in *Athen.*
iv. 162, d ; *Gell.* ii. 18, 8; *Orig.*
C. Cels. iii. 483, d ; he was first
a slave of Zeno's, which agrees
with his being a pupil and in-
mate of his house (*Diog.* 36;
13; *Cic.* N. D. i. 15, 38 ; *Athen.*
xiii. 607, e ; *Pausan.* ii. 8, 4).
It is less probable that he was
presented by Antigonus to Zeno
as a copyist (*Diog.* 36). He
subsequently lived at the court
of Antigonus (*Athen.* vi. 251, c ;
xiii. 607,a ; *Themist.* Or. xxxii.,
p. 358), whose son Halcyoneus
(*Ælian*, V. H. iii. 17, says
falsely himself) he is said to
have instructed (*Diog.* 36), and
with whom he stood in high
favour (*Plut.* Arat. 18 ; *Athen.*
vi. 251, c). He allowed, however, the Macedonian garrison
in Corinth to be surprised by
Aratus, in 243 B.C., and, according to *Pausan.* ii. 8, 4 ; vii. 8,
1, perished on that occasion.
The contrary is asserted by
Plut. Arat. 23, and *Athen.* iv.
162, c. In his teaching and
manner of life, he appears to

have taken a very easy view of
the Stoic principles (*Diog.* 13 ;
36 ; *Athen.* iv. 162, b ; xiii. 607,
a). It is therefore probable
that he did not agree with
Aristo's Cynicism (*Diog.* vii.
162), and his pupil Hermagoras
wrote against the Cynics (*Suid.*
Ἑρμαγ.). Political reasons were
at the bottom of Menedemus'
hatred for him (*Diog.* ii. 143).
Otherwise, he appears as a
genuine Stoic (*Diog.* vii. 120 ;
Cic. N. D. i. 15, 38; *Minuc. Felix*
Octav. 21, 3 ; *Philodem.* De
Mus., Vol. Herc. i. col. 14).
Compare p. 39, 2. The treatises
mentioned by *Diog.* 36 are
chiefly ethical and political. In
addition to these, there was a
treatise on Ethics (*Diog.* 28) ;
the συμποτικὰ ὑπομνήματα, or
συμποτικοὶ διάλογοι, from which
Athen. (iv. 162, b ; xiii. 607, a)
gives some extracts ; and the
Ἱστορία (in *Suid.*). Whether
Cicero's statement is taken
from a treatise omitted by Diogenes, or from that περὶ ἀσεβείας,
it is hard to say.
   [2] According to the sketch of
his life in *Buhle* (Arat. Opp. i.
3), Aratus was a pupil of Persæus at Athens, in company
with whom he repaired to Antigonus in Macedonia, which
can only mean that he was, together with Persæus, a pupil of
Zeno. Another writer in *Buhle*
(ii. 445) calls him so, mention-

who afterwards joined the Cyrenaic or Epicurean
School ;[1] and Sphærus from the Bosporus, who studied
first in the School of Zeno, and afterwards in that
of Cleanthes, and was the friend and adviser of
Cleomenes, the unfortunate Spartan reformer.[2] Of
a few other pupils of Zeno the names are also known ;[3]
but nothing is known beyond their names. No ap-

ing one of his letters addressed
to Zeno. Other accounts (*Ibid.*
ii. 431; 442 ; 446) describe him
as a pupil of Dionysius of Heraclea, or of Timon and Menedemus. A memorial of his Stoicism is the introduction to his
'Phænomena,' a poem resembling the hymn of Cleanthes.
Asclepiades (Vita in *Buhle* ii.
429), in calling him a native of
Tarsus, is only preferring a
better-known Cilician town to
one less known.

[1] Hence his name ὁ Μεταθέμενος. On his writings, consult
Diog. vii. 166; 37; 23; v. 92 ;
Athen. vii. 281, d; x. 437, e;
Cic. Acad. ii. 22, 71 ; Tusc. ii.
25, 60; Fin. v. 31, 94. Previously to Zeno, he is said to
have studied under Heraclides
ὁ Ποντικὸς, Alexinus, and Menedemus.

[2] *Diog.* 177; *Plut.* Cleomen.
2; 11; *Athen.* viii. 354, e.
Sphærus' presence in Egypt
seems to belong to the time before he became connected with
Cleomenes. He was a pupil of
Cleanthes (*Diog.* vii. 185 ;
Athen. l. c.) when he went to
Egypt, and resided there, at
the court of Ptolemy, for several
years. He had left him by 221

B.C., but was then himself no
longer a member of the Stoic
School at Athens. It is possible that Sphærus may first
have come to Cleomenes on a
commission from the Egyptian
king. In that case, the Ptolemy
referred to must have been
either Ptolemy Euergetes or
Ptolemy Philadelphus — certainly not Philopator, as *Diog.*
177 says. If, however, the
view is taken that it was Ptolemy Philopator, it may be supposed that Sphærus repaired to
Egypt with Cleomenes in 221
B.C. Sphærus' numerous writings (*Diog.* 178: Λακωνικὴ πολιτεία
also in *Athen.* iv. 141, 6) refer
to all parts of philosophy, and
to some of the older philosophers. According to *Cic.* Tusc.
iv. 24, 53, his definitions were
in great esteem in the Stoic
School.

[3] Athenodorus, a native of
Soli (*Diog.* vii. 38 ; 100); Cal-
lippus of Corinth (*Diog.* 38) ;
Philonides of Thebes, who went
with Persæus to Antigonus
(*Diog.* 9; 38); Posidonius of
Alexandria (*Diog.* 38) ; Zeno of
Sidon, a pupil of Diodorus
Cronus, who joined Zeno (*Diog.*
38 ; 16 ; *Suid.*).

preciable addition was made to the Stoic doctrine by any one of them.

It was therefore fortunate for Stoicism that Cleanthes was followed in the presidency of the School by a man of learning and argumentative power like Chrysippus.[1] In the opinion of the ancients, Chrysippus was the second founder of Stoicism.[2] Born[3] in the year 280 B.C.,[4] at Soli in Cilicia,[5] after being a pupil of Cleanthes[6] and it is said even of Zeno[7] himself, he succeeded, on the death of Cleanthes, to the conduct of his School.[8] He is also

CHAP. III.

C. Chrysippus and the later Stoics.

(1) Chrysippus.

[1] Baguet, De Chrysippo. Annal. Lovan. vol. iv. Lovan. 1822.
[2] Εἰ μὴ γὰρ ἦν Χρύσιππας οὐκ ἂν ἦν στοά (Diog. 183). Cic. Acad. ii. 24, 75: Chrysippum, qui fulcire putatur porticum Stoicorum. Athen. viii. 335, b: Χρύσιππον τὸν τῆς στοᾶς ἡγεμόνα. See Baguet, p. 16.
[3] It is recorded (Diog. 179) that he was brought up in early life as a racer, which is an exceedingly suspicious statement (confer D, 168); and that his paternal property was confiscated (Hecato in Diog. 181). Subsequently, his domestic establishment was scanty, consisting of one old servant (Diog. 185; 181; 183); but whether this was the result of Stoicism or of poverty is not known. The Floril. Monac. (in Stob. Floril. ed. Mcin. iv. 289) 262 calls him λιτὸς, ἔχων χρήματα πολλά.
[4] According to Apollodorus in Diog. 184, he died c. 205 B.C., in his 73rd year, which would give 281 to 276 as the year of

his birth. According to Lucian, Macrob. 20, he attained the age of 81, and, according to Valer. Max. viii. 7 ext. 10, completed the 39th book of his logic in his eightieth year.
[5] This is the view of Diog. 179; Plut. De Exil. 14, p. 605; Strabo, xiii. 1, 57, p. 610; xiv. 4, 8, p. 671, and most writers. Alexander Polyhistor, however, in Diog. and Suid. Ζήν. call him a native of Tarsus; and since his father Apollonius migrated from Tarsus to Soli (Strabo, p. 671), it is possible that Chrysippus may have been born in Tarsus.
[6] On this point all authorities are agreed. When and how he came to Athens is not recorded. He subsequently obtained the rights of a citizen (Plut. Sto. Rep. 4, 2, p. 1034).
[7] Diog. 179. This statement cannot be tested by chronology. Authorities, however, do not look promising.
[8] Diog. Pro. 15. Strabo, xiii. 1, 57, 610.

said to have attended the lectures of Arcesilaus and
Lacydes, philosophers of the Middle Academy;[1] and
so thoroughly had he appropriated their critical
methods, that later Stoics accused him of furnishing
Carneades with the necessary weapons for attacking
them,[2] by the masterly manner in which he raised
philosophical doubts, without being able to answer
them satisfactorily. This critical acuteness and
skill, more than anything else, entitle him to be regarded as the second founder of Stoicism.[3] In
learning, too, he was far in advance of his predecessors, and passed for the most industrious and learned
man of antiquity.[4] Independent in tone, as his other
conduct and the intellectual self-reliance which ani-

[1] *Diog.* vii. 183. It is possible, as *Ritter*, iii. 524, supposes, that he was for some
time in doubt about Stoicism,
under the influence of the
Academic Scepticism, and that
during this time he wrote the
treatise against συνήθεια. This
is possible, but not probable.
But that he should have separated from Cleanthes, setting
up a school in the Lyceum in
opposition to him, is not contained in the words of *Diog.*
179 ; 185.

[2] *Diog.* 184 ; iv. 62. *Cic.*
Acad. ii. 27, 87. *Plut.* Sto.
Rep. p. 10, 3, 1036. These passages refer particularly to
Chrysippus' six books κατὰ τῆς
συνηθείας. On the other hand,
his pupil Aristocreon, in *Plut.*
l. c. 2, 5, commends him as
being τῶν Ἀκαδημιακῶν στραγ-
γαλίδων κοπίδα. (Conf. *Plut.*

Comm. Not. i. 4, p. 1059).

[3] When a learner, he is said
to have used these words to
Cleanthes : 'Give me the principles ; the proofs I can find
myself.' Subsequently it is
said of him : 'If the Gods have
any logic, it is that of Chrysippus' (*Diog.* 179). See *Cic.*
N. D. i. 15, 30, where the
Epicurean calls him Stoicorum
somniorum vaferrimus inter-
pres : ii. 6, 16 ; iii. 10, 25 ;
Divin. i. 3, 6 : Chrysippus
acerrimo vir ingenio. *Senec.*
Benefic. i. 3, 8 ; 4, 1, who complains of his captiousness.
Dionys. Hal. Comp. Verb. 68,
calls him the most practised
logician, but the most careless
writer. *Krische*, Forsch. i.
445.

[4] *Diog.* 180. *Athen.* xiii. 565,
a. *Damasc.* V. Isid. 36. *Cic.*
Tusc. i. 45, 108.

mated him[1] often proved,[2] he deviated from the CHAP.
teaching of Zeno and Cleanthes, as might be expected, III.
in many respects.[3] Still, the fundamental principles
of the system were not altered by him; only their
intellectual treatment was perfected and deepened.
In fact, the Stoic doctrine was expanded by him with
such completeness in details, that hardly a gleaning
was left for his successors to gather up.[4] In multitude of writings[5] he exceeded Epicurus;[6] their titles,
and a comparatively small number of fragments,
being all that have come down to us.[7] With such
an extraordinary literary fertility, it will be easily
understood that their artistic value does not keep
pace. The ancients are unanimous in complaining
of their careless and impure language, of their dry
and often obscure style, of their prolixity, their endless repetitions, their frequent and lengthy citations,

---

[1] *Diog.* 179; 183.
[2] *Diog.* 185, mentions it as
deserving of especial notice,
that he refused the invitation
of Ptolemy to court, and dedicated none of his numerous
writings to a prince.
[3] *Cic.* Acad. ii. 47, 143. *Diog.*
179. *Plut.* Sto. Rep. 4, 1, p.
1034. According to the latter
passage, Antipater had written
a special treatise περὶ τῆς Κλεάν-
θους καὶ Χρυσίππου διαφορᾶς.
[4] Quid enim est a Chrysippo
prætermissum in Stoicis? *Cic.*
Fin. i. 2, 6.
[5] According to *Diog.* 180,
there were not fewer than 750.
Conf. *Valer. Max.* viii. 7, ext.
10; *Lucian*, Hermotim. 48.
[6] This appeared to the Epi-

cureans disparaging to the
honour of their master. Hence
the charge that Chrysippus had
written against Epicurus in
rivalry (*Diog.* x. 26, and the
criticism of Apollodorus in
Diog. vii. 181).
[7] *Baguet*, pp. 114-357, discusses the subject very fully,
but omitting several fragments.
On logical treatises, of which
alone there were 311 (*Diog.*
198), see *Nicolai*, De logicis
Chrysippi libris: Quedlinb.
1859. *Prantl*, Gesch. d. Log.
i. 404. *Petersen* (Philosoph.
Chrysip. Fundamenta: Ham-
burg, 1827, 321) attempts a
systematic arrangement of all
the known books.

and their too frequent appeals to etymologies, authorities, and other irrelevant proofs.[1] But by Chrysippus the Stoic teaching was brought to completeness; and when he died, in the year 206 B.C.,[2] the form was in every respect fixed in which Stoicism would be handed down for the next following centuries.

(2) *Later Stoics.*

A cótemporary of Chrysippus, but probably somewhat his senior, was Teles, a few extracts[3] from whose writings have been preserved by Stobæus,[4] in the shape of popular moral considerations written from a Cynic or Stoical point of view. The same age also produced the Cyrenaic Eratosthenes,[5] a man distinguished in every branch of knowledge, but particularly celebrated for his mathematical attainments,

[1] See *Cic.* De Orat. i. 11, 50; *Dionys.* Hal. See above 46, 3; *Diog.* vii. 180; x. 27. *Galen,* Differ. Puls. ii. 10; vol. viii. 631 K; Hippocr. et Plat. Plac. ii. 2; iii. 2; vol. v. 213, 295, 308, 312, 314, and *Baguet,* 26. See also *Plut.* Sto. Rep. 28, 2; and *Bergk,* Commentat. de Chrys. lib. περὶ ἀποφατικῶν: Cassel, 1841.

[2] The circumstances of his death are related differently in *Diog.* 184; but both stories are untrustworthy. The story of the ass is also told in *Lucian,* Macrob. 25 of Philemon; the other version in *Diog.* iv. 44; 61 of Arcesilaus and Lacydes. On the statue of Chrysippus in the Ceramicus see *Diog.* vii. 182; *Cic.* Fin. i. 11, 39; *Pausan.* i. 17, 2; *Plut.* Sto. Rep. 2, ó.

[3] In 40, 8, mention is made of the honourable position enjoyed by the Athenian Chremonides, who had been banished from his country. The banishment of Chremonides being in the year 263 B.C., Teles' treatise περὶ φυγῆς must have been written between 260 and 250 B.C. This is further proved by the fact that there is no reference in the fragments preserved to persons or circumstances later than this date. The philosophers to whom reference is made are the Cynics Diogenes, Crates, Metrocles, Stilpo, Bio the Borysthenite, Zeno, and Cleanthes (95, 21), the latter being called ó Ἄσσιος.

[4] Floril. 5, 67; 40, 8; 91, 33; 93, 31 98, 72; 108, 82 and 83.

[5] According to *Suid.,* born c. 275 B.C., and he died in his 80th year.

who was gained for Stoicism by Aristo.[1] Another
cotemporary of Chrysippus, and perhaps his fellow-
student,[2] who in many respects approximated to the
teaching of the Peripatetics,[3] was the Stoic Boëthus.
The proper scholars of Chrysippus were without doubt
numerous;[4] but few of their names are known to us.[5]
The most important among them appear to have
been Zeno of Tarsus,[6] and Diogenes of Seleucia,[7] who

[1] See p. 41, 2.

[2] Conf. *Diog.* 54 : ὁ δὲ Χρύσιππος διαφερόμενος πρὸς αὐτόν. . .
κριτήριά φησιν εἶναι αἴσθησιν καὶ
πρόληψιν. That he was junior
to Aratus appears by his
commentary on Aratus' poem.
See Appendix to *Geminus,*
Elem. Astron. (Petavii Doctr.
Temp. III. 147). The Vita
Arati (Von Buhle's Aratus,
vol. ii. 443), probably confounding him with the Peripatetic Boëthus, calls him a
native of Sidon.

[3] We shall have occasion to
prove this in speaking of his
views of a criterion, and of his
denial of a conflagration and
destruction of the world. Nevertheless, he is frequently appealed to as an authority among
the Stoics. *Philo,* Incorruptib.
M. 947, c, classes him among
ἄνδρες ἐν τοῖς Στωϊκοῖς δόγμασιν
ἰσχυκότες.

[4] This follows from the
great importance of Chrysippus, and the esteem in which
he was held from the very first,
and is confirmed by the number of persons to whom he
wrote treatises. See the list
from *Diog.* 189 in *Fabric.* Bibl.
iii. 549. It is, however, am-

biguous whether πρὸς means *to*
or *against.*

[5] Aristocreon, the nephew
of Chrysippus, is the only pupil
who can be definitely mentioned by name. See *Diog.* vii.
185; *Plut.* Sto. Rep. 2, 5, p. 1033.

[6] What is known of this
philosopher is limited to the
statements in *Diog.* 35; *Suid.*
Ζήν. Διοσκ.; *Eus.* Pr. Ev. xv.
13, 7; Arius Didymus, *Ibid.* xv.
17, 2; that he was a native of
Tarsus (in *Suid.* τινὲς say of
Sidon, evidently confounding
him with the Zeno mentioned
p. 44, 3) ; that he was the son of
Dioscorides, the pupil and follower of Chrysippus; that he
left many pupils, but few
writings; and that he doubted
a conflagration of the world.

[7] According to *Diog.* vi. 81 ;
Lucian, Macrob. 20, he was
a native of Seleucia on the
Tigris; but he is sometimes
called a native of Babylon
(*Diog.* vii. 39; 55 ; *Cic.* N. D.
i. 15, 41 ; Divin, i. 3, 6 ; *Plut.*
Dc Exll. 14, p. 605). *Cic.* Divin.
i. 3, 6, calls him a pupil of
Chrysippus; and Acad. ii. 30,
98, the instructor of Carneades
in dialectic. *Plut.* Alex. Virt.
5, p. 328, calls him a pupil of

succeeded Chrysippus in the presidency of the School.[1]
The pupil and successor of Diogenes, in his turn, was
Antipater of Tarsus,[2] in connection with whom his
countryman Archedemus is frequently mentioned.[3]

Zeno (of Tarsus). Zeno, he
says, Διογένη τὸν Βαβυλώνιον
ἔπεισε φιλοσοφεῖν. Diog. vii.
71, mentions a διαλεκτικὴ τέχνη
of his ; and, vii. 55 and 57, a
τέχνη περὶ φωνῆς. Cic. Divin.
i. 3, 6, speaks of a treatise on
divination. Athen. iv. 168, e,
of a treatise περὶ εὐγενείας, xii.
526, d, of a work περὶ νόμων—
the same work probably which,
according to Cic. Legg. iii. 5,
14, was written 'a Dione Stoico.'
Cic. Off. iii. 12, 51, calls him
'magnus et gravis Stoicus ; '
Seneca, De Ira, iii. 38, 1, mentions a trait showing great
presence of mind. Diogenes
was, without doubt, aged in
156 B.C. (Cic. De Senec. 7, 23).
According to Lucian, he attained the age of 88, and may
therefore have died 150 B.C.

[1] It was often supposed,
on the strength of Cic. N. D.
i. 15, 41, Divin. i. 3, 6, that
Diogenes was the immediate
successor of Chrysippus. The
words, however, consequens
or subsequens, by no means
necessarily imply it. On the
authority of Arius, Eusebius,
and Suidas, it would seem that
Zeno was the successor of
Chrysippus, and that Diogenes
followed Zeno.

[2] Cic. Off. iii. 12, 51, only
calls him his pupil ; but it is
clear that he taught in Athens
from Plut. Ti. Gracch. c. 8, as
Zumpt, Ueber die philos.
Schulen in Athen. Abh. d. Berl.

Acad. 1842, Hist. phil. kl. p. 103,
already remarks ; and Plut.
Tranq. An. 9, p. 469, seems to
imply that he continued to live
at Athens after leaving Cilicia.
The same fact is implied by
the mention of Diogenists and
Panætiasts at Athens (Athen.
v. c. 2, p. 186, a) ; by the charge
brought against Antipater
(Plut. Garrul. c, 23, p. 514 ;
Numen. in Eus. Pr. Ev. xiv.
8, 6 ; Cic. Acad. ii. 6, 17, and
the fragment from Acad. Post.
I. in Non. p. 65), that he never
ventured to dispute with Carneades ; and by Diog. iv. 65 ;
Stob. Floril. 119, 19. According
to these two authorities, he
voluntarily put an end to his
own life. In Acad. ii. 47, 143,
Cicero calls him and Archedemus 'duo vel principes
dialecticorum, opiniosissimi homines.' It appears from Off.
iii. 12, 51, where he is also
called 'homo acutissimus,' that
he pronounced a severer judgment on several moral questions
than Diogenes. Sen. Ep. 92, 5,
reckons him among the magnos
Stoicæ sectæ auctores. Epictet.
Diss. iii. 21, 7, speaks of the
φορὰ 'Αντιπάτρου καὶ 'Αρχεδήμου.
See Van Lynden, De Panætio,
33 ; and Fabric. Biblioth. iii.
538 for his numerous lost
treatises.

[3] Cic. l. c. ; Strabo xiv. 4, 14,
p. 674, Epictet. l. c. ; Diog. vii.
55. It does not follow that they
were cotemporaries, but only

Under Panætius, Antipater's scholar, Stoicism entered the Roman world, and there underwent internal changes, to which attention will be drawn in the sequel.[1]

CHAP.
III.

that their writings and philosophy were the same. We have otherwise no accurate information as to the date of Archedemus. Passages where he is mentioned may be found in *Fabric.* Bibl. III. 540. He also appears to be meant in *Simpl.* De Coelo Schol. in Arist. 505, a, 45. In *Diog.* 134, he appears to be placed between Chrysippus and Posidonius. In *Plut.* De Exil. 14, 605, he follows Antipater. According to this authority he established a school in Babylon, and because he came there from Athens, Plutarch appears to have considered him an Athenian.

[1] Apollodorus of Athens, the compiler of the Βιβλιοθήκη, a well-known grammarian, is also mentioned as a pupil of Diogenes (*Scymnus*, Chius Perieges. v. 20). His chronicle, dedicated to Attalus II., Philadelphus of Pergamum (158–138 B.C.), and probably drawn up 144 B.C., would seem to corroborate this assertion. Panætius, whose pupil he is elsewhere called (*Suid.* Ἀπολλόδ.), was himself a pupil of Diogenes' successor, Antipater (*Cic.* Divin. i. 3, 6), and can hardly have been older than Apollodorus.

Another grammarian belonging to the School of Diogenes is Zenodotus (*Diog.* vii. 30), supposing him to be identical with the Alexandrian

Zenodotus (*Suid.* Ζηνόδ.). A third is perhaps the celebrated Aristarchus, whom Scymnus calls a fellow-disciple of Apollodorus. A fourth, Crates of Mallos, called by *Strabo*, xiv. 5, 16, p. 676, the instructor of Panætius, by *Suid.* a Stoic philosopher, who in *Varro*, Lat. ix. 1, appeals to Chrysippus against Aristarchus.

Antipater's pupils are Heraclides of Tarsus (*Diog.* vii. 121); Sosigenes (*Alex. Aphr.* De Mixt. 142); C. Blossius of Cumæ (*Plut.* Ti. Gracch. 8, 17 and 20 ; *Val. Max.* iv. 7, 1 ; *Cic.* Læl. 11, 37). Eudromus, mentioned by *Diog.* vii. 39, appears to belong to the time between Chrysippus and Panætius. Between Zeno of Tarsus and Diogenes, *Diog.* vii. 84, names a certain Apollodorus, the author, probably, of the fragments in *Stob.* Ecl. i. 408 and 520. Possibly, however, he may be identical with the Apollodorus mentioned by *Cic.* N. D. i. 34, 93, and consequently a cotemporary of Zeno. In *Diog.* vii. 39, he is called Ἀπολλόδωρος ὁ Ἐφίλλος, instead of which Cobet reads Ἀπολλόδωρος καὶ Σύλλος. Apollodorus the Athenian, mentioned by *Diog.* vii. 181, is without doubt the Epicurean, known to us also from *Diog.* x. 2 and 25. *Krische*, Forsch. 26, thinks even that the passages in Cicero refer to him.

CHAP.
III.

The age of Diogenes of Ptolemais (*Diog.* vii. 41), of Œnopides mentioned by *Stob.* Ecl. i. 58; *Macrob.* Sat. i. 17, together with Diogenes and Cleanthes, and of Nicostratus, mentioned by Philodemus περὶ θεῶν διαγωγῆς Tab. I. 2 and perhaps by Artemidorus Oneirocrit. I. 2 Sch. is quite unknown. Nicostratus, however, must have written before the middle of the first century before Christ. He is probably distinct from the Nicostratus who wrote on the Aristotelian categories in an adverse spirit, and is re-

ferred to by *Simpl.* in Categ. Schol. in Arist. 40, a; 24, b, 16; 41, b, 27; 47, b, 23; 49, b, 43; 72, b, 6; 74, b, 4; 81, b, 12; 83, a, 37; 84, a, 28; 86, b, 20; 87, b, 30; 88, b, 3 and 11; 89, a, 1; 91, a, 25; b, 21. For this Nicostratus used the treatise of a certain Roman Lucius, whereas Roman treatises on the Categories can hardly have existed before the time of Philodemus, a cotemporary of Cicero. However, both Lucius and Nicostratus appear to have been Stoics.

CHAPTER IV.

AUTHORITIES FOR THE STOIC PHILOSOPHY: ITS
PROBLEM AND DIVISIONS.

To give a faithful exposition of the Stoic philosophy is a work of more than ordinary difficulty, owing to the circumstance that all the writings of the earlier Stoics, with the exception of a few fragments, have been lost.[1] Those Stoics whose complete works are still extant—Seneca, Epictetus, Marcus Aurelius, Heraclitus, Cornutus—lived under the Roman Empire, and therefore belong to a time in which all Schools alike exposed to foreign influences had surrendered or lost sight of many of their original peculiarities, substituting new elements in their place. The same remark applies to writers like Cicero, Plutarch, Diogenes, Sextus Empiricus, and the commentators on Aristotle, who may be considered as authorities at second hand for the teaching of the Stoics; but it is more than doubtful whether everything which they mention as Stoic teaching really belongs to the older members of that School.

CHAP.
IV.

A. *Authorities for the Stoic philosophy.*
(1) *Review of authorities.*

[1] Already *Simpl.* in Cat. Schol. in Arist. 49, a, 16, says: παρὰ τοῖς Στωϊκοῖς, ὧν ἐφ' ἡμῶν καὶ ἡ διδασκαλία καὶ τὰ πλεῖστα τῶν συγγραμμάτων ἐπιλέλοιπεν.

That teaching can, however, be ascertained with sufficient certainty on most of the more important points, partly by comparing accounts when they vary, partly by looking to definite statements on which authorities agree for the teaching and points of difference between individual philosophers, such as Zeno, Cleanthes, Chrysippus; partly too by consulting such fragments of their writings as are still extant. Yet, when the chief points have been settled in this way, many difficulties still remain. In the first place, it will be found that only isolated points of their teaching, with at most a few arguments on which to base them, are recorded; but the real connection of those tenets, and the motives which gave rise to them, can only be known by conjecture. Had the writings of Zeno and Chrysippus come down to us in their entirety, we should have had a much surer foundation on which to build, and far less would have been left to conjecture. An opportunity, too, would then have been afforded us of tracing the inward growth of the Stoic teaching, and of deciding how much of that teaching was due to Zeno, and how much to Chrysippus. That now this work of arrangement can only be done very imperfectly, is the second difficulty which arises from the nature of our authorities. It may be ascertained without difficulty what the teaching of the Stoics was since the time of Chrysippus, but only on a few points are the differences between Chrysippus and his predecessors known. For the most part, the authorities do not hesitate to attribute to the founder of the School all that was known to them as belonging to its later members, just as everything Pythagorean was directly attributed to Pythagoras, and everything Platonic to Plato. Still, there can be no doubt that the Stoic teaching was very considerably expanded by Chrysippus, and that it was altered in more than one respect. But how considerable the alterations were, and in what they consisted, are questions upon which there is little direct evidence.

The path is thus marked out, which must be followed in giving an exposition of the Stoic philosophy. Could only full information be obtained respecting the rise of the Stoic system and the form it assumed under each one of its representatives, it would be most natural to begin by reviewing the motives which led Zeno to his peculiar teaching, and to describe the system as it grew thereout. Next it would be right to trace step by step the changes and expansions which it received in the hands of each succeeding teacher. But, in default of the necessary information for such a treatment of the subject, it will be better to pursue another course. The Stoic teaching will have to be treated as a whole, in which the contributions of individuals can no longer be distinguished. It will have to be set forth in the form which it assumed after the time of Chrysippus. Nor can the share of individuals in constructing the system, nor their deviations from the general type, be considered, except in cases where they are placed beyond doubt by the statements of the ancients, or by well-founded historical surmises. Stoicism will have to be de-

(2) *Use to be made of authorities.*

scribed in the first place as it is traditionally known,
without having its principles explained or resolved
into their component factors; without even considering how they grew out of previous systems. Not till
this has been done will it be possible to analyse the
purport and structure of the system, so as to fathom
its leading motives, to understand the connection of
its various parts, and thus to ascertain its true position in history.

*B. Problem
proposed
to the Stoic
philoso-
phy.*

Proceeding next to ask in what form the problem
of philosophy presented itself to the Stoics, three
points deserve to be specially noticed. In the first
place, philosophy was determined practically by an
end in view. The character of this end was decided by
the idea of conformity with reason; and this view
was substantiated by an intellectual proof.

*(1) Its
practical
character.*

The real business of all philosophy, according to
the Stoics, is the moral conduct of man. Philosophy
is the exercise of an art, and more particularly of the
highest art—virtue:[1] it is therefore the learning of
virtue. Now virtue can only be learnt by exercise,
and therefore philosophy is at the same time virtue,[2]

---

[1] *Plut.* Plac. Pro. 2 : οἱ μὲν
οὖν Στωϊκοὶ ἔφασαν, τὴν μὲν
σοφίαν εἶναι θείων τε καὶ ἀνθρωπίνων ἐπιστήμην· τὴν δὲ φιλοσοφίαν ἄσκησιν τέχνης ἐπιτηδείου·
ἐπιτήδειον δ᾽ εἶναι μίαν καὶ ἀνωτάτω
τὴν ἀρετήν· ἀρετὰς δὲ τὰς γενι-
κωτάτας τρεῖς, φυσικὴν, ἠθικὴν,
λογικὴν, κ.τ.λ. See also *Diog.*
vii. 92.

[2] In *Seneca*, Ep. 89, 4, wisdom is the highest good for the
human mind, and philosophy

is a striving after wisdom :
wisdom is defined to be the
knowledge of things human
and divine; philosophy to be
studium virtutis, or *studium
corrigendæ mentis.* This striving
after virtue cannot be distinguished from virtue itself :
Philosophia studium virtutis
est, sed per ipsam virtutem.
Seneca further observes (Fr. 17,
in *Lactant.* Inst. iii. 15) : Philosophia nihil aliud est quam

and the several parts of philosophy are so many distinct virtues.[1] Morality is the central point towards which all other inquiries converge: even natural science, although lauded as the inmost shrine of philosophy, is, according to Chrysippus, only necessary for the philosopher to enable him to distinguish between things good and evil, between what should be done and what should be left undone.[2] Pure speculation, on the contrary, which Plato and Aristotle had commended as the height of human happiness, Chrysippus so far from approving, plainly asserted that to live for speculation is equivalent to living only for pleasure.[3] With this view of Chrysippus most of the statements of the Stoics as to the relation of various branches of philosophy to each other agree, although there is a certain amount of vagueness about them, owing to reasons which will shortly be mentioned; and on no other hypothesis can the internal structure and foundation of their system be

recta vivendi ratio, vel honeste vivendi scientia, vel ars rectæ vitæ agendæ. Non errabimus, si dixerimus philosophiam esse legem bene honesteque vivendi, et qui dixerit illam regulam vitæ, suum illi [nomen] reddidit. *Plut.* see previous note.

[1] See *Diog.* vii. 46 : αὐτὴν δὲ τὴν διαλεκτικὴν ἀναγκαίαν εἶναι καὶ ἀρετὴν ἐν εἴδει περιέχουσαν ἀρετὰς, κ.τ.λ.

[2] *Chrys.* in *Plut.* Sto. Rep. 9, 6 : δεῖ γὰρ τούτοις [sc. τοῖς φυσικοῖς] συνάψαι τὸν περὶ ἀγαθῶν καὶ κακῶν λόγον, οὐκ οὔσης ἄλλης ἀρχῆς αὐτῶν ἀμείνονος οὐδ' ἀναφορᾶς, οὐδ' ἄλλου τινὸς ἕνεκεν τῆς φυσικῆς

θεωρίας παραληπτῆς οὔσης ἢ πρὸς τὴν περὶ ἀγαθῶν ἢ κακῶν διάστασιν.

[3] *Chrys.* in *Plut.* Sto. Rep. 3, 2 : ὅσοι δὲ ὑπολαμβάνουσι φιλοσόφοις ἐπιβάλλειν μάλιστα τὸν σχολαστικὸν βίον ἀπ' ἀρχῆς, οὗτοί μοι δοκοῦσι διαμαρτάνειν ὑπονοοῦντες διαγωγῆς τινος ἕνεκεν δεῖν τοῦτο ποιεῖν ἢ ἄλλου τινὸς τούτῳ παραπλησίου, καὶ τὸν ὅλον βίον οὕτω πως διελκύσαι τοῦτο δ' ἔστιν, ἂν σαφῶς θεωρηθῇ, ἡδέως. Διαγωγὴ had, it is true, been treated by Aristotle, whose school is here referred to, as an end in itself ; but Aristotle had carefully distinguished διαγωγὴ from ἡδονή.

CHAP.
IV.

satisfactorily explained. It is enough to remark here, as has been done before,[1] that the most important and most distinctive points established by the Stoic School belong to the domain of ethics. In logic and natural science that School displays far less independence, for the most part following older teachers; and it is expressly noted, as a deviation from the ordinary teaching of the School, that Herillus, the pupil of Zeno, declared knowledge to be the highest good, thus making it the chief end in philosophy.[2]

(2) *Neces-sity for intellectual knowledge.*

This view of the problem of philosophy is more precisely defined by the Stoic doctrine of virtue. Philosophy should lead to right action and to virtue. But right action is, according to the Stoics, only rational action, and rational action is action which is in harmony with human and inanimate nature. Virtue consists therefore in bringing man's actions into harmony with the laws of the universe, and with the general order of the world. This is only possible when man knows that order and those laws;

---

[1] P. 19.

[2] *Cic.* Acad. ii. 42, 129: Herillum, qui in cognitione et scientia summum bonum ponit: qui cum Zenonis auditor esset, vides quantum ab eo dissenserit, et quam non multum a Platone. Fin. ii. 13, 43 : Herillus autem ad scientiam omnia revocans unum quoddam bonum vidit. iv. 14, 36 : In determining the highest good, the Stoics act as one-sidedly, as if ipsius animi, ut fecit Herillus, cognitionem amplexarentur, ac-

tionem relinquerent. v. 25, 73 : Sæpe ab Aristotele, a Theophrasto mirabiliter est laudata per se ipsa rerum scientia. Hoc uno captus Herillus scientiam summum bonum esse defendit, nec rem ullam aliam per se expetendam. *Diog.* vii. 165 : Ἡρίλλος. . . τέλος εἶπε τὴν ἐπιστήμην. Ibid. vii. 37. With less accuracy, it is asserted by *Iambl.* in *Stob.* Ecl. i. 918, that we are raised to the society of the gods, κατὰ Ἡρίλλον, ἐπιστήμῃ.

and thus the Stoics are brought back to the principles of Socrates, that virtue may be learnt; that
knowledge is indispensable for virtue, or rather that
virtue is identical with right knowledge. They
define virtue in so many words as knowledge, vice
as ignorance. If sometimes they seem to identify
virtue with strength of will, it is only because they
consider strength of will to be inseparable from
knowledge, so that the one cannot be conceived
of without the other. Hence the practical problem
of philosophy conducts with them to the intellectual;
philosophy is not only virtue, but without philosophy
no virtue is possible.[1] Granting that the attainment of virtue, and the happiness of a moral life are
the chief ends which the Stoics propose to themselves, still the possession of a comprehensive
scientific knowledge is indispensable, as the only
means thereto.

These remarks prove the need for the Stoics of
that kind of scientific knowledge which has to do
with life, the morals and the actions of mankind, in
short, of Ethics. Whether in addition thereto further scientific knowledge is necessary, was a question
on which the earliest adherents of the Stoic teaching
expressed different opinions. Zeno's pupil, Aristo of
Chios, held that the sole business of man is to pursue
virtue,[2] and that the sole use of language is to purify

(3) *Posi-
tion to-
wards logic
and
natural
science.*

(a) *Aris-
to's views.*

---

[1] *Sen.* Ep. 89, 8 : Nam nec
philosophia sine virtute est nec
sine philosophia virtus. Ibid.
53, 8: We all lie in the slumber
of error: sola autem nos philosophia excitabit . . . illi te
totum dedica.

[2] *Lact.* Inst. vii. 7: Ad
virtutem capessendam nasci
homines, Ariston disseruit. See
Stob. Ecl. 4, 111.

the soul.[1] This purifying process, however, is
neither to be found in logical subtleties nor in
natural science. Logic, as doing more harm than
good, he compared to a spider's web, which is as
useless as it is curious;[2] or else to the mud on a
road.[3] Those who studied it he likened to people
eating lobsters, who take a great deal of trouble for
the sake of a little bit of meat enveloped in much
shell.[4] Convinced, too, that the wise man is free
from every deceptive infatuation,[5] and that doubt,
for the purpose of refuting which logic had been
invented, can be more easily overcome by a healthy
tone of mind[6] than by argument, he felt no particular necessity for logic. Nay, more, he considered
that excessive subtlety transforms the healthy action
of philosophy into an unhealthy one.[7] Just as little
was Aristo disposed to favour the so-called *encyclical*
knowledge : those who devote themselves to this·
knowledge instead of to philosophy he compared to
the suitors of Penelope, who won the maids but not
the mistress.[8] Natural science would probably have
received a more favourable treatment at the hands of
Aristo, had he not shared the opinion of Socrates,
that it is a branch of knowledge which transcends

---

[1] *Plut.* De Audiendo, c. 8,
p. 42 : οὔτε γὰρ βαλανείου, φησὶν
ὁ Ἀρίστων, οὔτε λόγου μὴ καθαί-
ροντος ὄφελός ἐστιν.
[2] *Stob.* Floril. 82, 15. *Diog.*
vii. 161.
[3] *Stob.* Floril. 82, 11.
[4] *Ibid.* 7.
[5] *Diog.* vii. 162 : μάλιστα δὲ
προσεῖχε Στωϊκῷ δόγματι τῷ τὸν

σόφον ἀδόξαστον εἶναι.
[6] See *Diog.* vii. 163.
[7] Aristo (in the Ὁμοιώματα)
in *Stob.* Floril. 82, 16 : ὁ ἐλλέ-
βορος ὁλοσχερέστερος μὲν ληφθεὶς
καθαίρει, εἰς δὲ πάνυ σμικρὰ τριφ-
θεὶς πνίγει· οὕτω καὶ ἡ κατὰ
φιλοσοφίαν λεπτολογία.
[8] *Stob.* l. c. 4, 110.

the capacity of the human mind ;[1] and having once
embraced this notion, he was inclined to pronounce
all physical enquiries useless. His attitude towards
other sciences has therefore been generally expressed
by saying that he excluded from philosophy both
logic and natural science, on the ground that both
are useless; the former being irrelevant, and the
latter transcending our powers.[2] Even ethics was
limited by Aristo to most fundamental notions—to
inquiries into good and evil, virtue and vice, wisdom
and folly. The special application of these notions
to the moral problems suggested by particular relations in life, he declared to be useless and futile ;
proper for nursemaids and trainers of young children,
but not becoming for philosophers;[3] wherever there

---

[1] See following note and *Cic.*
Acad. ii. 39, 123 : Aristo Chius,
qui nihil istorum (*sc.* phy-
sicorum) sciri putat posse.

[2] *Diog.* vii. 160 : τόν σε φυσικὸν τόπον καὶ τὸν λογικὸν ἀνῄρει,
λέγων τὸν μὲν εἶναι ὑπὲρ ἡμᾶς,
τὸν δ' οὐδὲν πρὸς ἡμᾶς, μόνον δὲ
τὸν ἠθικὸν εἶναι πρὸς ἡμᾶς. *Stob.*
Floril. 80, 7 : Ἀρίστων ἔφη τῶν
ζητουμένων παρὰ τοῖς φιλοσόφοις
τὰ μὲν εἶναι πρὸς ἡμᾶς, τὰ δὲ μηδὲν
πρὸς ἡμᾶς, τὰ δ' ὑπὲρ ἡμᾶς. πρὸς
ἡμᾶς μὲν τὰ ἠθικά, μὴ πρὸς ἡμᾶς
δὲ τὰ διαλεκτικά· μὴ γὰρ συμβάλλεσθαι πρὸς ἐπανόρθωσιν βίου·
ὑπὲρ ἡμᾶς δὲ τὰ φυσικά· ἀδύνατα
γὰρ ἐγνῶσθαι καὶ οὐδὲ παρέχειν
χρείαν. *Minuc. Fel.* Octav. 13,
and *Lactant.* Inst. iii. 20, attribute this utterance to Socrates. According to *Cic.* De
Nat. De. I. 14, 37, Aristo expressed doubts about the existence of a God.

[3] *Sext.* Math. vii. 13 : καὶ
Ἀρίστων δὲ ὁ Χῖος οὐ μόνον, ὥς
φασι, παρῃτεῖτο τήν τε φυσικὴν
καὶ λογικὴν θεωρίαν διὰ τὸ ἀνωφε-
λὲς καὶ πρὸς κακοῦ τοῖς φιλοσο-
φοῦσιν ὑπάρχειν, ἀλλὰ καὶ τοῦ
ἠθικοῦ τόπου τινὰς συμπεριέγραψε
καθάπερ τόν τε παραινετικὸν καὶ
τὸν ὑποθετικὸν τόπον· τούτους γὰρ
εἰς τίτθας ἂν καὶ παιδαγωγοὺς
πίπτειν· — (almost a literal
translation is given of these
words by *Seneca*, Ep. 89, 13)—
ἀρκεῖσθαι δὲ πρὸς τὸ μακαρίως
βιῶναι τὸν οἰκειοῦντα μὲν πρὸς
ἀρετὴν λόγον, ἀπαλλοτριοῦντα δὲ
κακίας, κατατρέχοντα δὲ τῶν
μεταξὺ τούτων, περὶ ἃ οἱ πολλοὶ
πτοηθέντες κακοδαιμονοῦσιν. *Seneca,* Ep. 94, 1 : Eam partem
philosophiæ, quæ dat propria
cuique personæ præcepta . . . .
quidam solam receperunt . . . .
sed Ariston Stoicus e contrario
hanc partem levem existimat

is a proper knowledge and a right disposition, such particular applications will come of themselves without teaching ; but when these are wanting, all exhortations are useless.[1]

(b) Views of Zeno and Cleanthes.

These views are mentioned as peculiar to Aristo, and as points in which he differed from the rest of his School ; and, to judge from his controversial tone, the opposite views were those almost universally entertained by Stoics. That controversial tone, in fact, appears to have been directed not only against assailants from without—such as the Peripatetics and Platonists—but far more against those members of the Stoic School, who attached greater importance than he did to special ethical investigations, and to logical and physical inquiries. Among their number must have been Zeno and Cleanthes ; for had not Zeno set the example to his School of dividing philosophy into logic, ethics, and natural science ?[2] Do not the titles of his logical and physical treatises[3]

---

et quæ non descendat in pectus usque ; ad illam habentem præcepta [? ad vitam beatam] plurimum ait proficere ipsa decreta philosophiæ constitutionemque summi boni, quam qui bene intellexit ac didicit, quid in quaque re faciendum sit, sibi ipse præcepit. This is then further expanded following Aristo.

[1] *Seneca*, § 12, asks for whom should such exhortations be necessary—for him who has right views of good and evil, or for him who has them not ? Qui non habet, nihil a te adjuvabitur ; aures ejus contraria monitionibus tuis fama possedit ; qui habet exactum judicium de fugiendis petendisque, scit, quid sibi faciendum sit, etiam te tacente ; tota ergo pars ista philosophiæ submoveri potest. In § 17, he continues : A madman must be cured, and not exhorted ; nor is there any difference between general madness and the madness which is treated medically.

[2] *Diog.* vii. 39.

[3] Logical treatises, those περὶ λέξεων, λύσεις καὶ ἔλεγχοι, περὶ λόγου—and if there were a rhetoric (see p. 40, 3) the τέχνη

prove this fact; as also statements in reference to
theoretical knowledge and natural science which are
expressly attributed to him? Moreover, Zeno himself recommended to others, and himself pursued,
logical inquiries.[1] Indeed, his whole mental habit,[2]
with its keen appreciation of even the subtleties of
the Megarians, bears testimony to an intellectual
line of thought which is far removed from that of
Aristo.[3] It was, moreover, Zeno who chose that curt
and unadorned logical style, which is found in its
greatest perfection in Chrysippus.[4] Logical and
scientific treatises are also known to have been
written by Cleanthes,[5] who, in his division of phi-

—physical treatises, those περὶ
ὅλου and περὶ οὐσίας. *Diog.* 4,
39.

[1] *Plut.* Sto. Rep. 8, 2 : ἔλυε
δὲ σοφίσματα καὶ τὴν διαλεκτικὴν,
ὡς τοῦτο ποιεῖν δυναμένην, ἐκέλευε
παραλαμβάνειν τοὺς μαθητάς.
That he occasionally not only
solved but propounded sophisms
is proved by the fallacy quoted
Ibid. i. Conf. *Diog.* vii. 25.
[2] See above p. 36.
[3] According to *Diog.* 32, he
declared at the beginning of
his polity the ἐγκύκλιος παιδεία
to be useless — a testimony
worth very little; for it is a
moot point, in what sense Zeno
made this statement. Perhaps
he was only anxious to exclude
those studies from the narrower
sphere of philosophy (as *Sen.*
Ep. 88). Perhaps his polity
was nearer Cynicism than any
other of his writings.
[4] Proofs will be given later.
[5] The Catalogue in *Diog.*
174, περὶ λόγου 3, B (*Mohnike*

Cleanth. 102, believes this work
was a treatise on life according
to reason. The title is against
this view, and it is also improbable, inasmuch as treatises
by Sphærus and Chrysippus
bearing the same title, are exclusively logical), mentions
logical treatises περὶ λόγου,
περὶ ἐπιστήμης, περὶ ἰδίων, περὶ τῶν
ἀπόρων, περὶ διαλεκτικῆς, περὶ
κατηγορημάτων. To these may
be added, from *Athen.* 467, d ;
471, b, the rhetorical treatises
περὶ τρόπων and περὶ μεταλήψεως.
Of greater importance were
the physical and theological
treatises : περὶ τῆς τοῦ Ζήνωνος
φυσιολογίας (2, B); τῶν Ἡρακλείτου ἐξηγήσεις (4, B); πρὸς
Δημόκριτον, περὶ θεῶν, περὶ μαντικῆς (*Cic.* Divin. i. 3, 6); περὶ
γιγάντων (in *Plut.* De Flum.
5, 3); and the μυθικὰ (*Athen.*
xiii. 572, e), which is probably
identical with the ἀρχαιολογία
of Diogenes.

losophy, allotted separate parts to logic, to rhetoric,
and to natural science,[1] and the name of Cleanthes is
one of frequent occurrence, not only in the natural
science, but more particularly in the theology of
the Stoics. Still more exhaustive inquiries into
logic and natural science appear to have been set on
foot by Sphærus ;[2] all proving that the energies of
the Stoic School must have been directed to these
subjects before the time of Chrysippus, although
these branches of science were no doubt subservient
to ethics, ethics holding the most important and
highest place in their philosophy. At a later time,
when Chrysippus had expanded the system of the
Stoics in every direction, and especial attention had
been devoted to logic, the necessity for these sciences
came to be generally recognised. More especially
was this the case with regard to natural science, including 'theology.' All ethical inquiries must start,
according to Chrysippus, with considering the universal order and arrangement of the world. Only by
a study of nature, and a knowledge of what God is,
can anything really satisfactory be stated touching
good and evil, and all that is therewith connected.[3]

---

[1] *Diog.* 41.

[2] *Diog.* vii. 178, mentions (1) logical and rhetorical writings : περὶ τῶν Ἐρετρικῶν φιλοσόφων, περὶ ὁμοίων, περὶ ὅρων, περὶ ἕξεως, περὶ τῶν ἀντιλεγομένων (3, B), περὶ λόγου, τέχνη διαλεκτικὴ (2, B), περὶ κατηγορημάτων, περὶ ἀμφιβολιῶν ; (2) treatises on science : περὶ κόσμου (2, B), περὶ στοιχείων, περὶ σπέρματος, περὶ τύχης, περὶ ἐλαχίστων, πρὸς τὰς

ἀτόμους καὶ τὰ εἴδωλα, περὶ αἰσθητηρίαν, περὶ Ἡρακλείτου (5, B), περὶ μαντικῆς. That Sphærus' definitions were particularly valued, has been already seen, 44, 2.

[3] *Chrys.* in the 3rd B, περὶ θεῶν (in *Plut.* Sto. Rep. 9, 4) : οὐ γάρ ἐστιν εὑρεῖν τῆς δικαιοσύνης ἄλλην ἀρχὴν οὐδ' ἄλλην γένεσιν ἢ τὴν ἐκ τοῦ Διὸς καὶ τὴν ἐκ τῆς κοινῆς φύσεως · ἐντεῦθεν γὰρ δεῖ

Less obvious is the connection between logic and the ultimate aim of all philosophical inquiries. Logic is compared by the Stoics to the shell of an egg, or to the wall of a city or garden;[1] and is considered to be of importance, because it contributes towards the discovery of truth and the avoiding of error.[2] The value of logic in their eyes is, therefore, essentially due to its scientific method; its proper aim is the art of technical reasoning; and thus, following Aristotle, an unusually full treatment is allowed to the doctrine of the syllogism.[3] That the value, however, attached to it must have been considerable is proved by the extraordinary care which Chrysippus

πᾶν τὸ τοιοῦτον τὴν ἀρχὴν ἔχειν, εἰ μέλλομέν τι ἐρεῖν περὶ ἀγαθῶν καὶ κακῶν. The same writer, in φυσικαὶ θέσεις (Ibid. 5): οὐ γάρ ἐστιν ἄλλως οὐδ' οἰκειότερον ἐπελθεῖν ἐπὶ τὸν τῶν ἀγαθῶν καὶ κακῶν λόγον οὐδ ἐπὶ τὰς ἀρετὰς οὐδ' ἐπὶ εὐδαιμονίαν, ἀλλ' ἢ ἀπὸ τῆς κοινῆς φύσεως καὶ ἀπὸ τῆς τοῦ κόσμου διοικήσεως. Further details above p. 47, 2.

[1] *Sext.* Math. vii. 17 ; *Diog.* 40.

[2] The chief divisions of the logic of the Stoics (*Diog.* 42, 46) are considered important for special purposes. The doctrine περὶ κανόνων καὶ κριτηρίων is of use, helping us to truth, by making us examine our notions; ὁρικὸν, because it led to the knowledge of things by means of conceptions; διαλεκτικὴ (which includes the whole of formal logic), because it produced ἀπροπτωσία (= ἐπιστήμη τοῦ πότε δεῖ συγκατατίθεσθαι καὶ μή), ἀνεικαιότης (= ἰσχυρὸς

λόγος πρὸς τὸ εἰκὸς, ὥστε μὴ ἐνδιδόναι αὐτῷ), ἀνελεγξία (= ἰσχὺς ἐν λόγῳ, ὥστε μὴ ἀπάγεσθαι ὑπ' αὐτοῦ εἰς τὸ ἀντικείμενον), ἀματαιότης (= ἕξις ἀναφέρουσα τὰς φαντασίας ἐπὶ τὸν ὀρθὸν λόγον). Its value was therefore chiefly negative, preserving from error. See *Seneca,* Ep. 89, 9 : Proprietates verborum exigit et structuram et argumentationes, ne pro vero falsa subrepant. *Sext.* Math. vii. 23 : ὀχυρωτικὸν δὲ εἶναι τῆς διανοίας τὸν διαλεκτικὸν τόπον ; Pyrrh. ii. 247 : ἐπὶ τὴν τέχνην τὴν διαλεκτικὴν φασὶν ὡρμηκέναι οἱ διαλεκτικοὶ (the Stoics), οὐχ ἁπλῶς ὑπὲρ τοῦ γνῶναί τι ἐκ τίνος συνάγεται, ἀλλὰ προηγουμένως ὑπὲρ τοῦ δι' ἀποδεικτικῶν λόγων τὰ ἀληθῆ καὶ τὰ ψευδῆ κρίνειν ἐπίστασθαι.

[3] This may be seen in *Sext.* Pyrrh. ii. 134-203, 229 ; Math. viii. 300 ; as well as from the catalogue of the writings of Chrysippus in *Diogenes.*

devoted to the subject;[1] hence, the Stoics would
never allow, in dispute with the Peripatetics, that
logic was only an instrument, and not a part of philosophy. To later writers that stiff logical mode of
description, regardless of all beauty of language,
appeared to be a peculiarity of the Stoic school,[2] and
hence that school was characteristically known as
the School of the Reasoners.[3] Frequent instances
will be found hereafter of the Stoic preference for
dry argument and formal logic;[4] in Chrysippus this
fondness degenerated to a dry formalism devoid of
taste.[5]

*C. Divi-
sions of
philoso-
phy.*

The foregoing remarks have already established
the three main divisions of philosophy[6] which were
universally acknowledged by the Stoics[7]—Logic,

[1] The only part which incurs
the blame of Chrysippus (in
Plut. Sto. Rep. 10, 1) is the
sceptical logic, which leaves
contradictions unsolved: τοῖς
μὲν γὰρ ἐποχὴν ἄγουσι περὶ πάντων
ἐπιβάλλει, φησί, τοῦτο ποιεῖν, καὶ
συνεργόν ἐστι πρὸς ὃ βούλονται·
τοῖς δ' ἐπιστήμην ἐνεργαζομένοις,
καθ' ἣν ὁμολογουμένως βιωσόμεθα
τὰ ἐναντία στοιχειοῦν.

[2] *Cic.* Parad. Procem.: Cato
autem perfectus mea sententia
Stoicus . . . in ea est hæresi,
quæ nullum sequitur florem
orationis neque dilatat argumentum: minutis interroga-
tiunculis, quasi punctis, quod
proposuit efficit. *Cic.* Fin. iv. 3,
7 : Pungunt quasi aculeis inter-
rogatiunculis angustis, quibus
etiam qui assentiuntur nihil
commutantur animo. See also
Diog. vii. 18, 20.

[3] In Sextus Empiricus,

Διαλεκτικοὶ is their ordinary
name. It is also found in
Plut. Qu. Plat. x. 1, 2, p. 1008.
Cic. Top. 2, 6 ; Fin. iv. 3, 6.
[4] After the example of the
Megarians, the Stoics were in
the habit of couching their
arguments in the form of a
question. Hence the terms
λόγον ἐρωτᾶν (*Diog.* vii. 186),
interrogatio (*Sen.* Ep. 82, 9 ;
85, 1 ; 87, 11), *interrogatiuncula*
(*Cic.*), which are employed
even when their arguments
were not in this form.
[5] See p. 48, 1.
[6] Called μέρη, according to
Diog. 39 also τόποι, εἴδη, γένη.
[7] *Diog.* 39: τριμερῆ φασιν
εἶναι τὸν κατὰ φιλοσοφίαν λόγον·
εἶναι γὰρ αὐτοῦ τὸ μέν τι φυσικὸν,
τὸ δὲ ἠθικὸν, τὸ δὲ λογικόν. οὕτω
δὲ πρῶτος διεῖλε Ζήνων ὁ Κιτιεὺς
ἐν τῷ περὶ λόγου καὶ Χρύσιππος ἐν
τῷ α' περὶ λόγου καὶ ἐν τῇ α'

Natural Science, and Ethics. As regards the relative worth and sequence of these divisions, very opposite views may be deduced from the principles of the Stoic teaching. There can be no doubt, and, indeed, all are agreed in allowing, that logic was subservient to the other two branches of science, being only an outpost of the system. If therefore in arranging the parts the advance is from the less important to the more important, logic will hold the first place. It will occupy the last place if the opposite mode of procedure is followed. But the relation existing between ethics and natural science is an open question. On the one hand, ethics appears to be the higher science, the crowning point of the system, the subject towards which the whole philosophical activity of the school was directed; for was not philosophy practical knowledge? and was not its object to lead to virtue and happiness? On the other hand, virtue and the destiny of man consist in subordination to the laws of nature, which it is the province of science to investigate. Has not, therefore, natural science the higher object? Does it not lay down the universal laws which in ethics are applied to man? Does not, therefore, to it, in the graduated scale of sciences, belong the higher rank?

In attempting to harmonise these opposite considerations, the Stoics did not always succeed. At one

τῶν ψυσικῶν, καὶ ᾿Απολλόδωρος ὁ ῎Εφιλλος ἐν τῷ πρώτῳ τῶν εἰς τὰ δόγματα εἰσαγωγῶν, καὶ Εὔδρομος ἐν τῇ ἠθικῇ στοιχειώσει, καὶ Διο-γένης ὁ Βαβυλώνιος, καὶ Ποσειδώ-νιος. *Sext.* Math. vii. 16. *Sen.*

Ep. 89, 9; 14. The six divisions enumerated by Cleanthes (*Diog.* 41)—Dialectic, Rhetoric, Ethics, Politics, Physics, Theology (*Diog.* 41)—are easily reducible to three.

CHAP.
IV.
___
(2) Rela-
tive im-
portance
of each
part.

time natural science is preferred to ethics, at another
time ethics to natural science,[1] in the enumeration
of the several branches of philosophy. In the comparisons by means of which their relations to each
other were explained,[2] ethics appears at one time,
at another time natural science, to be the aim and
soul of the whole system. Different views were even
entertained in reference to the order to be followed

[1] According to *Diog.* 40, the
first place was assigned to
Logic, the second to Science,
the third to Ethics, by Zeno,
Chrysippus, Archedemus, Eudemus, and others. The same
order, but inverted, is found in
Diogenes of Ptolemais, and in
Seneca, Ep. 89, 9. The latter,
however, observes (Nat. Qu.
Prol. 1) that the difference between that part of philosophy
which treats about God, and
that which treats about man,
is as great as the difference
between philosophy and other
departments, or even as between
God and man. On the other
hand, Apollodorus places Ethics
in the middle, as also Cleanthes
does, and likewise Panætius and
Posidonius, if it is certain that
they began with science. This
appears, however, only to have
reference to their order in discussion (see *Sext.* Math. vii. 22,
probably on the authority of
Posidonius.) A few (*Diog.* 40)
asserted that the parts could
be so little separated, that they
must be always treated at the
same time. The statement of
Chrysippus (in *Plut.* Sto. Rep.
9, 1), that Logic must come
first, and be followed by Ethics
and Science, so that the theo-

logical part may form the conclusion, only refers to the order
in which they ought to be
taught.

[2] In *Diog.* 39; *Sext.* Math.
vii. 17; *Philo*, Mut. Nom. p.1055,
E. Hösch. (589 M); De Agricul.
189, D (302), philosophy is
compared to an orchard, Logic
answering to the fence, Science
to the trees, Ethics to the fruit;
so that Ethics is the end and
object of the whole. Philosophy is also compared to a
fortified town, in which the
walls are represented by Logic,
but in which the position of the
other two is not clear; to an
egg, Logic being the shell, and,
according to Sextus, Science
being the white and Ethics the
yolk, but the reverse according
to Diogenes. Dissatisfied with
this comparison, Posidonius preferred to compare philosophy
to a living creature, in which
Logic constituted the bones
and muscles, Science the flesh
and blood, and Ethics the soul.
But Diogenes has another version of this simile, according
to which Science represents the
soul; and Ritter, iii. 432, considers the version of Diogenes
to be the older of the two.

in teaching these sciences.[1] In describing the Stoic system, preference will be here given to that arrangement which begins with logic and goes on to natural science, ending with ethics; not only because that arrangement has among its supporters the oldest and most distinguished adherents of the Stoic School, but far more because in this way the internal relation of the three parts to each other can be most clearly brought out. For, granting that, in many essential respects, natural science is modified by ethical considerations; still, in the development of the system, the chief results of science are used as principles on which ethical doctrines are founded; and logic, although introduced later than the other two branches of study, is the instrument by means of which they are put into scientific shape. If the opportunity were afforded of tracing the rise of the Stoic teaching in the mind of its founder, it would probably be possible to show how the physical and logical parts of the system gradually gathered about the original kernel of ethics. But knowing Stoicism only as we do from the intellectual development which it attained after the time of Chrysippus, it will be enough, in analysing the form which it then assumed, to proceed from without to within, and to advance from logic through natural science to ethics. When this has been done it will be time to attempt to re-trace our steps backwards, and to explain how, from the ethical tone of Stoicism, its peculiar speculative tenets may be deduced.

[1] See *Sext.* Pyrrh. ii. 13.

CHAPTER V.

LOGIC OF THE STOICS.

CHAP.
V.

A. *General remarks.*

(1) *Field of logic.*

UNDER the head of Logic, in the Stoic use of the term after the time of Chrysippus, a number of intellectual inquiries were included which would not now be considered to belong to philosophy at all. One common element, however, characterised them all—they all referred to the formal conditions of thought and expression.

Logic was primarily divided into two parts, sharply marked off from each other, roughly described as the art of speaking continuously and the art of conversing—the former being known as Rhetoric, the latter as Dialectic.[1] To these two parts was added, as a third part, the

---

[1] *Diog.* 41: τὸ δὲ λογικὸν μέρος φασὶν ἔνιοι εἰς δύο διαιρεῖσθαι ἐπιστήμας, εἰς ῥητορικὴν καὶ διαλεκτικήν . . τήν τε ῥητορικὴν ἐπιστήμην οὖσαν τοῦ εὖ λέγειν περὶ τῶν ἐν διεξόδῳ λόγων καὶ τὴν διαλεκτικὴν τοῦ ὀρθῶς διαλέγεσθαι περὶ τῶν ἐν ἐρωτήσει καὶ ἀποκρίσει λόγων. *Sen.* Ep. 89, 17 : Superest ut rationalem partem philosophiæ dividam : omnis oratio aut continua est aut inter respondentem et interrogantem discissa ; hanc διαλεκτικήν, illam ῥητορικὴν pla-

cuit vocari. *Cic.* Fin. ii. 6, 17 ; Orat. 32, 113. *Quintil.* Inst. ii. 20, 7. According to these passages, Rhetoric was by Zeno compared to the palm of the hand, and Dialectic to the fist : quod latius loquerentur rhetores, dialectici autem compressius. The Stoics agree with Aristotle in calling rhetoric ἀντίστροφος τῇ διαλεκτικῇ (*Sop.* in Hermog. v. 15, Walz.). See *Prantl*, Gesch. der Log. i. 413.

doctrine of a standard of truth, or the theory of knowledge ; and, according to some authorities,[1] a fourth part, consisting of inquiries into the formation of conceptions. By others, these inquiries were regarded as the third main division, the theory of knowledge being included under dialectic.[2] By rhe-

[1] *Diog.* 41 :. Some divide logic into rhetoric and dialectic: τίνες δὲ καὶ εἰς τὸ ὁρικὸν εἶδος, τὸ περὶ κανόνων καὶ κριτηρίων· ἔνιοι δὲ τὸ ὁρικὸν περιαιροῦσι. (We have no reason to read as Menage does περιδιαιροῦσι, or to conjecture, as Meibom and Nicolai, De Log. Chrys., Lib. 23, do, παραδιαιροῦσι.) According to this passage, ὁρικὸν must be identical with the doctrine of a criterium. In a subsequent passage, however, the two are distinguished ; the doctrine of a criterium is said to be useful for the discovery of truth : καὶ τὸ ὁρικὸν δὲ ὁμοίως πρὸς ἐπίγνωσιν τῆς ἀληθείας· διὰ γὰρ τῶν ἐννοιῶν τὰ πράγματα λαμβάνεται. We may therefore suppose that in the passage first quoted the words should be τὸ ὁρικὸν εἶδος καὶ τὸ περὶ κανόνων, κ.τ.λ. In this case, we may understand by ὁρικὸν not only the theory of definition—a theory to which Aristotle devoted a separate section at the end of his Analytics (Anal. Post. ii.)—but besides a theoretical disquisition on the formation of definitions, a collection of definitions of various objects. Such collections are found in the treatises of Chrysippus (*Diog.* 199, 189): περὶ τῶν ὅρων ζ'. ὅρων διαλεκτικῶν στ'. ὅρων τῶν κατὰ γένος ζ'. ὅρων τῶν κατὰ τὰς ἄλλας τέχνας αβ'.

ὅρων τῶν τοῦ ἀστείου β'. ὅρων τῶν τοῦ φαύλου β'. ὅρων τῶν ἀναμέσων β'; besides the further treatises περὶ τῶν οὐκ ὀρθῶς τοῖς ὅροις ἀντιλεγομένων ζ'. Πιθανὰ εἰς τοὺς ὅρους β'. The treatise περὶ εἰδῶν καὶ γενῶν may also be included here ; perhaps also that περὶ τῶν κατηγορημάτων πρὸς Μητρόδωρον ι'. πρὸς Πάσυλον περὶ κατηγορημάτων δ', *Diog.* 191.

[2] No description of their system can dispense with this fundamental inquiry, which had been already instituted by Zeno. It appears, however, to have been treated by several writers as a branch of dialectic. *Diog.* 43 says that the branch of dialectic which treats of σημαινόμενα may be divided εἴς τε τὸν περὶ τῶν φαντασιῶν τόπον καὶ τῶν ἐκ τούτων ὑφισταμένων λεκτῶν. (See *Nicolai* p. 23.) Compare with this the words of *Diocles*, in Diog. 49 : ἀρέσκει τοῖς Στωϊκοῖς περὶ φαντασίας καὶ αἰσθήσεως προτάττειν λόγον, καθότι τὸ κριτήριον ᾧ ἡ ἀλήθεια τῶν πραγμάτων γινώσκεται, κατὰ γένος φαντασία ἐστὶ καὶ καθότι ὁ περὶ συγκαταθέσεως καὶ ὁ περὶ καταλήψεως καὶ νοήσεως λόγος προάγων τῶν ἄλλων οὐκ ἄνευ φαντασίας συνίσταται. According to this passage, the branch of dialectic which treated of φαντασία included the theory of knowledge. *Diog.* 43, *Peter-sen's* conjecture is singular

toric, however, little else was meant but a collection of artificial rules, without philosophical worth;[1] and dialectic was in great measure occupied with inquiries referring only to precision of expression. Dialectic was defined to be the science or art of speaking well;[2] and since speaking well consists in saying what is becoming and true,[3] dialectic is used

(Phil. Chrys. Fund. p. 25) that the theory of knowledge may have been understood by Chrysippus under the name rhetoric.
[1] Our information on this head is very small. In the words : ῥητορικὴ verba curat et sensus et ordinem, a division of rhetoric is implied by Seneca, little differing, except in the position of the chief parts, from that of Aristotle. A fourth part is added to the three others by *Diog.* 43—on Delivery— εἶναι δ' αὐτῆς τὴν διαίρεσιν εἴς τε τὴν εὕρεσιν καὶ εἰς τὴν φράσιν, καὶ εἰς τάξιν καὶ εἰς τὴν ὑπόκρισιν. Diogenes also claims for the Stoics the Aristotelian distinction between three ways of speaking—συμβουλευτικὸς, δικανικὸς, ἐγκωμιαστικός—and four parts in a speech : προοίμιον, διήγησις, τὰ πρὸς τοὺς ἀντιδίκους, ἐπίλογος. Definitions of διήγησις and παράδειγμα are given from Zeno by the anonymous author in *Spengel,* Rhet. Gr. i. 434, 23; 447, 11. The same author (*Ibid.* 454, 4) says that, according to Chrysippus, the ἐπίλογος must be μονομερής. The Stoic definition of rhetoric has been already given, p. 70, 1. Another— τέχνη περὶ κόσμου καὶ εἰρημένου λόγου τάξιν — is attributed to Chrysippus by *Plut.* Sto. Rep.

28, 1. *Cic.* Fin. iv. 3, 7, observes, in reference to the Stoic rhetoric, and in particular to that of Chrysippus, that such was its nature that si quis obmutescere concupierit, nihil aliud legere debeat — that it dealt in nothing but words, being withal scanty in expressions, and confined to subtleties. This neglect of the truly rhetorical element appears already in the quotations from *Plut.* Sto. Rep. 28, 2. We have not the slightest reason to complain, as *Prantl* does, p. 413, of the purely rhetorical value of dialectic with the Stoics.
[2] See p. 70, 1, *Alex.* Aphr. Top. 3 : οἱ μὲν ἀπὸ τῆς Στοᾶς ὁριζόμενοι τὴν διαλεκτικὴν ἐπιστήμην τοῦ εὖ λέγειν ὁρίζονται, τὸ δὲ εὖ λέγειν ἐν τῷ ἀληθῆ καὶ προσήκοντα λέγειν εἶναι τιθέμενοι, τοῦτο δὲ ἴδιον ἡγούμενοι τοῦ φιλοσόφου, κατὰ τῆς τελεωτάτης φιλοσοφίας φέρουσιν αὐτὸ καὶ διὰ τοῦτο μόνος ὁ φιλόσοφος κατ' αὐτοὺς διαλεκτικός. Aristotle had used the term dialectic in another sense, but with Plato it expressed the mode of procedure peculiar to a philosopher.
[3] See Anon. Prolegg. ad Hermog. Rhet. Gr. vii. 8, W. : οἱ Στωϊκοὶ δὲ τὸ εὖ λέγειν ἔλεγον τὸ ἀληθῆ λέγειν.

to express the knowledge of what is true or false, or
what is neither one nor the other,[1] correctness of
expression being considered inseparable from correctness of thought. Words and thoughts are, according
to this view, the very same things regarded under
different aspects. The same idea (λόγος), which is
a thought as long as it resides within the breast, is
a word as soon as it comes forth.[2] Accordingly, dialectic consists of two main divisions, treating respectively of utterance and the thing uttered, thoughts
and words.[3] Both divisions, again, have several sub-

[1] *Diog.* 42: ὅθεν καὶ οὕτως
αὐτὴν [τὴν διαλεκτικὴν] ὁρίζονται,
ἐπιστήμην ἀληθῶν καὶ ψευδῶν καὶ
οὐδετέρων. (The same, p. 62,
quoted from Posidonius, and in
Sext. Math. xi. 187, and *Suid.*
Διαλεκτικῆ.) οὐδετέρων being probably used, because dialectic
deals not only with judgments,
but with conceptions and inter-
rogations. Conf. *Diog.* 68.

[2] This is the meaning of the
Stoic distinction between λόγος
ἐνδιάθετος and προφορικός, a distinction subsequently employed
by Philo and the Fathers, and
really identical with that of
Aristotle (Anal. Post. i. 10, 76 b,
24): οὐ πρὸς τὸν ἔξω λόγον, ἀλλὰ
πρὸς τὸν ἐν τῇ ψυχῇ. On this distinction see *Heraclit.* Alleg.
Hom. c. 72, p. 142 : διπλοῦς ὁ
λόγος· τούτων δ' οἱ φιλόσοφοι (the
Stoics are meant) τὸν μὲν ἐνδιάθετον καλοῦσι, τὸν δὲ προφορικόν.
ὁ μὲν οὖν τῶν ἔνδον λογισμῶν ἐστιν
ἐξάγγελος, ὁ δ' ὑπὸ τοῖς στέρνοις
καθείρκται. φασὶ δὲ τούτῳ χρῆσθαι καὶ τὸ θεῖον. *Sext.* Math.
viii. 275 (conf. Pyrrh. i. 76) :
οἱ δὲ Δογματικοὶ . . . φασὶν ὅτι

ἄνθρωπος οὐχὶ τῷ προφορικῷ λόγῳ
διαφέρει τῶν ἀλόγων ζώων . . .
ἀλλὰ τῷ ἐνδιαθέτῳ. The Stoics
alone can be meant by the νεώτεροι in *Theo. Smyrn.* Mus. c.
18, who are contrasted with the
Peripatetics for using the terms
λόγος ἐνδιάθετος and προφορικός.
They are also referred to by
Plut. C. Prin. Phil. 2, 1, p.777 :
τὸ δὲ λέγειν, ὅτι δύο λόγοι εἰσὶν,
ὁ μὲν ἐνδιαθετὸς, ἡγεμόνος Ἑρμοῦ
δῶρον, ὁ δ' ἐν προφορᾷ, διάκτορος
καὶ ὀργανικὸς ἔωλόν ἐστι. The
double form of Hermes is explained by *Heraclitus* as referring to the twofold λόγος—
Ἑρμῆς Χθόνιος representing λόγον
ἐνδιάθετον, and the heavenly
Hermes (διάκτορος) representing
the προφορικόν. The distinction
passed from the Stoics to others,
like *Plut.* Solert. An. 19, 1, p.
973 ; *Galen,* Protrept. i. 1.

[3] *Diog.* 43: τὴν διαλεκτικὴν
διαιρεῖσθαι εἴς τε τὸν περὶ τῶν ση-
μαινομένων καὶ τῆς φωνῆς τόπον.
Ibid. 62 : τυγχάνει δ' αὕτη, ὡς ὁ
Χρύσιππός φησι, περὶ σημαίνοντα
καὶ σημαινόμενα. *Seneca* l. c.: διαλεκτικὴ in duas partes dividitur,

divisions,[1] which are only imperfectly known to us.[2]
Under the science of utterance, which was generally
placed before the science of things uttered,[3] they included, not only instruction as to sounds and speech,
but also the theories of poetry and music, these arts
being ranked under the head of the voice and of
sound on purely external considerations.[4] What
is known to us of the teaching of the Stoics on these
subjects, consisting, as it does, of a mass of definitions,
differences, and divisions, has so little philosophical
value, that it need not detain our attention longer.[5]

in verba et significationes, i.e.
in res, quæ dicuntur, et voca-
bula, quibus dicuntur. The
distinction between τὸ σημαῖνον
and τὸ σημαινόμενον, to which
τὸ τυγχάνον (the real object)
must be added as a third, will
be hereafter discussed in another place. A much narrower
conception of dialectic, and
more nearly approaching to
that of the Peripatetics, is to be
found in the definition given
by *Sext.* Pyrrh. ii. 213. The
division there given is also
found in the Platonist *Alcinous*,
Isag. c. 3, as Fabricius pointed
out. It appears, therefore, not
to belong to the Stoic School,
but, at most, to a few of its
later members.

[1] *Seneca* continues: Ingens
deinde sequitur utriusque divisio, without, however, giving
it.

[2] There is much which is
open to doubt in *Petersen's*
attempt (Phil. Chrys. Fund.
221) to settle these divisions.
At the very beginning, his referring the words of *Sext.* Math.

viii. 11, to the parts of logic is
unhappy. *Nicolai* (De Logic.
Chrys. Lib. 21) has acted with
greater caution, but even much
of what he says is doubtful.

[3] *Diog.* 55.

[4] *Diog.* 44: εἶναι δὲ τῆς διαλεκτικῆς ἴδιον τόπον καὶ τὸν προει-
ρημένον περὶ αὐτῆς τῆς φωνῆς, ἐν
ᾧ δείκνυται ἡ ἐγγράμματος φωνὴ
καὶ τίνα τὰ τοῦ λόγου μέρη, καὶ
περὶ σολοικισμοῦ καὶ βαρβαρισμοῦ
καὶ ποιημάτων καὶ ἀμφιβολιῶν καὶ
περὶ ἐμμελοῦς φωνῆς καὶ περὶ μουσικῆς καὶ περὶ ὅρων κατά τινας
καὶ διαιρέσεων καὶ λέξεων. The
theory of the determination
and division of conceptions
occupies such an important
place in the section περὶ φωνῆς,
that we might feel disposed to
suppose some mistake in the
authority. Still, from the later
authorities, pp. 60-62, it is seen
that by many it is usually so
represented.

[5] Further particulars may be
obtained in *Schmidt's* Stoicorum
Grammatica (Halle, 1839) ;
Lersch, Sprachphilosophie der
Alten ; *Steinthal,* Gesch. der

Two parts only of the Stoic logic possess for us any real interest—the theory of knowledge, and that part of dialectic which treats of ideas, and which in the main agrees with our formal logic.

The Stoic theory of knowledge turns about the inquiry for a criterion or standard by which what is true in our notions may be distinguished from what is false. Since every kind of knowledge, no matter what be its object, must be tested by this standard, it follows that the standard cannot be sought in the

CHAP.
V.

B. *Theory of knowledge.*
(1) *General character of this theory.*

Sprachwissenschaft, i. 265–363; *Nicolai*, De Log. Chrys. Lib. 31. This part of dialectic began with inquiries into the voice and speech. Voice is defined to be sound and speech, to be air in motion, or something hearable—ἀὴρ πεπληγμένος ἢ τὸ ἴδιον αἰσθητὸν ἀκοῆς; the human voice as ἔναρθρος καὶ ἀπὸ διάνοιας ἐκπεμπομένη, is distinguished from the sounds of other animals, which are ἀὴρ ὑπὸ ὁρμῆς πεπληγμένος (*Diog.* 55; *Simpl.* Phys. 97; *Sext.* Math. vi. 39; `Gell.` N. A. vi. 15, 6). That the voice is something material is proved in various ways (*Diog.* 55; *Plut.* Plac. iv. 20, 2; *Galen,* Hist. Phil. 27). The voice, in as far as it is ἔναρθρος, or composed of letters, is called λέξις; in as far as it expresses certain notions, it is λόγος (*Diog.* 56; *Sext.* Math. i. 155). A peculiar national mode of expression (λέξις κεχαραγμένη ἐθνικῶς τε καὶ Ἑλληνικῶς ἢ λέξις ποταπὴ) was called διάλεκτος (*Diog.* 56). The elements of λέξις are the 24 letters, divided into 7 φωνήεντα, 6 ἄφωνα, and 11 semivowels

(*Diog.* 57); the λόγος has 5 parts, called στοιχεῖα by Chrysippus— ὄνομα, προσηγορία, ῥῆμα, σύνδεσμος, ἄρθρον—to which Antipater added the μεσότης, or adverb (*Diog.* 57; *Galen,* De Hippocrat. et Plat. viii. 3; *Lersch,* ii. 28; *Steinthal,* 291). Words were not formed by caprice, but certain peculiarities of things were imitated in the chief sounds of which they are composed. These peculiarities can therefore be discovered by etymological analysis (*Orig.* c. Cels. i. 24; *Augustin.* Dialect. c. 6; Opp. T. I. Ap. 17, c.). Chrysippus, however, observes (in *Varro,* L. Lat. ix. 1) that the same things bear different names, and vice versâ, and (in *Gell.* N. A. xi. 12, 1) that every word has several meanings. See *Simpl.* Cat. 8, ζ. Five advantages and two disadvantages of speech are enumerated *Diog.* 59; *Sext.* Mat: i. 210; and poetry (*Diog.* 60), various kinds of amphibolia (*Diog.* 62; *Galen,* De Soph. P. Dict. c. 4), the formation of conceptions, and division, are treated of.

subject-matter of our notions, but, on the contrary, in their form. The inquiry after a standard becomes therefore identical with another—the inquiry as to what *kind* of notions supply a knowledge that may be depended upon, or what activity of the power of forming conceptions carries in itself a pledge of its own truth. It is impossible to answer these questions without investigating the origin, the various kinds, and the value and importance of our notions. Hence the problem proposed to the Stoics is reduced to seeking by an analysis of our notions to obtain a universally valid standard by which their truth may be tested.

Whether this inquiry was pursued by the older Stoics in all its comprehensiveness is a point on which we have no information. Boëthus, whose views on this subject were attacked by Chrysippus, had assumed the existence of several standards, such as Reason, Perception, Desire, Knowledge. Others, in the vaguest manner, had spoken of Right Reason (ὀρθὸς λόγος) as being the standard of truth.[1] Hence it may be inferred that before the time of Chrysippus the Stoics had no distinctly developed theory of knowledge. Nevertheless there are expressions of Zeno and Cleanthes still extant which prove that the essential parts of the later theory were already held by these philosophers,[2] although it is no doubt true

[1] *Diog.* vii. 54.
[2] The statements of Zeno and Cleanthes, for instance, in reference to φαντασία, prove that these Stoics deduced their theory of knowledge from general principles respecting notions. They therefore started from the data supplied by the senses. A passage in Zeno, ex-

that it first received that scientific form in which
alone it is known to us at the hands of Chrysippus.

The character of this theory of knowledge appears
mainly in three particulars :—(1) In the importance
attached by the Stoics to the impressions of the
senses. This feature they inherited from the Cynics
and shared with the Epicureans. (2) In the exaltation of expression into a conception—a trait distinguishing this from either of the two other
contemporary schools. (3) In the practical turn
given to the question of a criterion or standard of
truth. We proceed to the expansion of this theory
in detail.

*(2) Promi-
nent points
in the
theory of
knowledge.*

The origin of all perceptions (φαντασίαι) may be
referred to the action of some object (φανταστὸν) on
the soul,[1] the soul at birth resembling a blank page,
and only receiving definite features by experience
from without.[2] By the elder Stoics, this action of

*(a) Per-
ceptions
the result
of impres-
sions from
without.*

plaining the relations of various forms of knowledge, shows
that even Zeno required progress to be from perception to
conception and knowledge, and
that he distinguished these
states only by the varying
strength of conviction which
they produced.

[1] *Plut.* Plac. iv. 12. *Diog.*
vii. 50. *Nemes.* Nat. Hom. 76.
Φαντασία is πάθος ἐν τῇ ψυχῇ γινόμενον, ἐνδεικνύμενον ἑαυτό τε καὶ
τὸ πεποιηκός, in the same way,
it is added, that light shows
other things as well as itself;
φανταστὸν is τὸ ποιοῦν τὴν φαντασίαν, and therefore πᾶν ὅ τι
ἂν δύνηται κινεῖν τὴν ψυχήν.
Φαντασία is distinguished from

φανταστικόν, because no φανταστὸν corresponds to φανταστικόν·
it is διάκενος ἑλκυσμὸς, πάθος ἐν
τῇ ψυχῇ ἀπ' οὐδενὸς φανταστοῦ
γινόμενον· and the object of such
an empty perception is a φάντασμα. Compare also *Sext.*
Math. vii. 241 : διάκενος ἑλκυσμὸς
is called φαντασία τῶν ἐν ἡμῖν
παθῶν. Impressions wholly unfounded, which give the impression of being actual perceptions, are called by *Diog.*
51, ἐμφάσεις αἱ ὡσανεὶ ἀπὸ ὑπαρχόν-
των γινόμεναι. In a wider sense,
φαντασία means any kind of
notion.

[2] *Plut.* Plac. iv. 11 : οἱ Στωϊκοί
φασιν· ὅταν γεννηθῇ ὁ ἄνθρωπος
ἔχει τὸ ἡγεμονικὸν μέρος τῆς ψυχῆς

objects on the soul was regarded as grossly material,
Zeno defining a perception to be an *impression*
(τύπωσις) made on the soul,[1] and Cleanthes taking
this definition so literally as to compare the impression on the soul to the impression made by a seal on
wax.[2] Being himself a very exact pupil of Zeno's,
Cleanthes probably rendered the views of Zeno correctly in this comparison. The difficulties of this
view were recognised by Chrysippus, who accordingly
defined a perception to be the *change* (ἑτεροίωσις)
produced on the soul by an object, or, more accurately, the change produced thereby in the ruling part
of the soul;[3] and whereas his predecessors had only

ὥσπερ χάρτης (χάρτην as *Galen*,
H. Phil. 24, vol. xix. reads),
ἐνεργῶν εἰς ἀπογραφήν. εἰς τοῦτο
μίαν ἑκάστην τῶν ἐννοιῶν ἐναπο-
γράφεται· πρῶτος δὲ ὁ τῆς ἀπογρα-
φῆς τρόπος ὁ διὰ τῶν αἰσθήσεων.
See p. 79, 2, *Orig.* c. Cels. vii. 37,
720, b, says that they taught
αἰσθήσει καταλαμβάνεσθαι τὰ κα-
ταλαμβανόμενα καὶ πᾶσαν κατάληψιν ἠρτῆσθαι τῶν αἰσθήσεων.

[1] *Plut.* Comm. Not. 47: φαντασία τύπωσις ἐν ψυχῇ. The
same in *Diog.* vii. 45 and 50.
That this was also the view of
Diogenes appears from what
follows.

[2] *Sext.* Math. vii. 228:
Κλεάνθης μὲν γὰρ ἤκουσε τὴν
τύπωσιν κατὰ εἰσοχὴν τε καὶ
ἐξοχὴν ὥσπερ καὶ διὰ τῶν δακτυ-
λίων γινομένην τοῦ κηροῦ τύπωσιν.
Conf. *Ibid.* vii. 372; viii. 400.

[3] *Sext.* vii. 229, continues:
Χρύσιππος δὲ ἄτοπον ἡγεῖτο τὸ
τοιοῦτον· — according to this
view, it would be necessary for
the soul to receive at once

many different forms, if it had
to retain different notions at
the same time—αὐτὸς οὖν τὴν
τύπωσιν εἰρῆσθαι ὑπὸ τοῦ Ζήνωνος
ὑπενόει ἀντὶ τῆς ἑτεροιώσεως,
ὥστε εἶναι τοιοῦτον τὸν λόγον·
φαντασία ἐστὶν ἑτεροίωσις ψυχῆς.
Objection had, however, been
raised to this definition, on the
ground that not every change
of the soul gives rise to a perception, and therefore the
Stoics had defined a perception
more accurately: φαντασία ἐστὶ
τύπωσις ἐν ψυχῇ ὡς ἂν ἐν ψυχῇ,
which was equivalent to saying
φαντασία ἐστὶν ἑτεροίωσις ἐν ἡγε-
μονικῷ· or else in Zeno's definition of φαντασία as τύπωσις
ἐν ψυχῇ they had taken ψυχῇ in
a restricted sense for τὸ ἡγεμονικὸν, which really comes to the
same thing. Even this definition had, however, been found
too wide, and hence ἑτεροίωσις
was limited to mean change in
feeling (ἑτεροίωσις κατὰ πεῖσιν).
But the definition is still too

considered sensible things to be objects, he included
among objects conditions and activities of the
mind.[1] The mode, however, in which the change
was produced in the soul did not further engage his
attention.

It follows, as a necessary corollary from this view,
that the Stoics regarded sensation as the only source
of all our perceptions : the soul is a blank leaf, sensation is the hand which fills it with writing. But
this is not all. Perceptions give rise to memory,
repeated acts of memory to experience,[2] and conclusions based on experience suggest conceptions
which go beyond the sphere of direct sensation.
These conclusions rest either upon the comparison, or
upon actual combination of perceptions, or else upon

*(b) Con-
ceptions
formed
from per-
ceptions.*

---

wide, as Sextus already remarked; for a perception is
not the only feeling of change
in the soul. A more accurate
definition has already been
quoted, 77, 1. The statements
in *Sext.* Math. vii. 372 ; viii.
400 ; *Diog.* vii. 45 and 50;
Alex. Aphro. De Anim. 135, b;
Boëth. De Interpret. ii. 292
(Schol. in Arist. 100), are in
agreement with the above remarks.
　[1] Chrys. in *Plut.* Sto. Rep.
19, 2 : ὅτι μὲν γὰρ αἰσθητά ἐστι
τἀγαθὰ καὶ τὰ κακὰ, καὶ τούτοις
ἐκποιεῖ λέγειν· οὐ γὰρ μόνον τὰ
πάθη ἐστὶν αἰσθητὰ σὺν τοῖς
εἴδεσιν, οἷον λύπη καὶ φόβος καὶ
τὸ παραπλήσια, ἀλλὰ καὶ κλοπῆς
καὶ μοιχείας καὶ τῶν ὁμοίων ἔστιν
αἰσθέσθαι · καὶ καθόλου ἀφροσύνης
καὶ δειλίας καὶ ἄλλων οὐκ ὀλίγων

κακιῶν· οὐδὲ μόνον χαρᾶς καὶ εὐερ-
γεσιῶν καὶ ἄλλων πολλῶν κατορ-
θώσεων, ἀλλὰ καὶ φρονήσεως καὶ
ἀνδρείας καὶ τῶν λοιπῶν ἀρετῶν.
This passage must not be understood to mean that the *conceptions* of good and evil, as such,
are objects of sensation (*Ritter*,
iii. 558). The only objects of
that kind are *individual* moral
states and activities. The
general conceptions derived
from them are, according to
the Stoic theory of knowledge,
only obtained by a process of
abstraction.
　[2] *Plut.* Plac. iv. 11, 2 : αἰσθα-
νόμενοι γάρ τινος οἷον λευκοῦ
ἀπελθόντος αὐτοῦ μνήμην ἔχουσιν,
ὅταν δὲ ὁμοειδεῖς πολλαὶ μνῆμαι
γένωνται τότε φασὶν ἔχειν ἐμπει-
ρίαν.

analogy;[1] some add, upon transposition and contrast.[2] The formation of conceptions by means of these agencies sometimes takes place methodically and artificially, at other times naturally and spontaneously.[3] In the latter way are formed the primary conceptions, προλήψεις or κοιναὶ ἔννοιαι, which were regarded by the Stoics as the natural types of truth and virtue, and as the distinctive possession of rational beings.[4] To judge by many expressions, it

---

[1] *Diog.* vii. 52 : ἡ δὲ κατάληψις γίνεται κατ᾽ αὐτοὺς αἰσθήσει μὲν, ὡς λευκῶν καὶ μελάνων καὶ τραχέων καὶ λείων · λόγῳ δὲ τῶν δι᾽ ἀποδείξεως συναγομένων, ὥσπερ τὸ θεοὺς εἶναι καὶ προνοεῖν τούτους · τῶν γὰρ νοουμένων τὰ μὲν κατὰ περίπτωσιν (immediate contact) ἐνοήθη, τὰ δὲ καθ᾽ ὁμοιότητα, τὰ δὲ κατ᾽ ἀναλογίαν, τὰ δὲ κατὰ μετάθεσιν, τὰ δὲ κατὰ σύνθεσιν, τὰ δὲ κατ᾽ ἐναντίωσιν . . . νοεῖται δὲ καὶ κατὰ μετάβασιν (transition from the sensuous to the supersensuous) τινὰ, ὡς τὰ λεκτὰ καὶ ὁ τόπος. *Cic.* Acad. i. 11, 42 : Comprehensio [= κατάληψις] facta sensibus et vera illi [Zenoni] et fidelis videbatur : non quod omnia, quæ essent in re, comprehenderet, sed quia nihil quod cadere in eam posset relinqueret, quodque natura quasi normam scientiæ et principium sui dedisset, unde postea notiones rerum in animis imprimerentur. *Ibid.* Fin. iii. 10, 33 : Cumque rerum notiones in animis fiant, si aut usu (experience) aliquid cognitum sit, aut conjunctione, aut similitudine, aut collatione rationis : hoc quarto, quod extremum posui, boni notitia facta est.

Sext. (Math. iii. 40 ; ix. 393) also agrees with the Stoic doctrine of the origin of conceptions, in saying that all our ideas arise either κατ᾽ ἐμπέλασιν τῶν ἐναργῶν or κατὰ τὴν ἀπὸ τῶν ἐναργῶν μετάβασιν (cf. *Diog.* vii. 53), and in the latter case either by comparison, or actual combination, or analogy.

[2] *Diog.* l. c. Compare the passage quoted from Seneca, 81, 2.

[3] *Plut.* Plac. iv. 11 : τῶν δ᾽ ἐννοιῶν αἱ μὲν φυσικαὶ γίνονται κατὰ τοὺς εἰρημένους τρόπους (according to the context, this must mean by memory and experience), but perhaps the author of the placita has been careless in his extracts here, καὶ ἀνεπιτεχνήτως · αἱ δ᾽ ἤδη δι᾽ ἡμετέρας διδασκαλίας καὶ ἐπιμελείας · αὗται μὲν οὖν ἔννοιαι καλοῦνται μόναι, ἐκεῖναι δὲ καὶ προλήψεις. *Diog.* vii. 51 : [τῶν φαντασιῶν] αἱ μέν εἰσι τεχνικαὶ, αἱ δὲ ἄτεχνοι.

[4] *Plut.* Plac. iv. 11 : ὁ δὲ λόγος καθ᾽ ὃν προσαγορευόμεθα λογικοὶ ἐκ τῶν προλήψεων συμπληροῦσθαι λέγεται κατὰ τὴν πρώτην ἑβδομάδα (the first seven years of life). Comm. Not. 3,

might seem that by primary conceptions, or κοιναὶ
ἔννοιαι,[1] *innate ideas* were meant; but this view
would be opposed to the whole character and connection of the system. In reality, these primary conceptions, or κοιναὶ ἔννοιαι, are only those conceptions
which, by reason of the nature of thought, can be
equally deduced by all men from experience; even
the highest ideas, those of good and evil, having no
other origin.[2] The artificial formation of conceptions

1, says that to the Stoics belonged τὸ παρὰ τὰς ἐννοίας καὶ
τὰς προλήψεις τὰς κοινὰς φιλοσοφεῖν, ἀφ᾽ ὧν μάλιστα τὴν αἵρεσιν
. . . καὶ μόνην ὁμολογεῖν τῇ φύσει
λέγουσιν. *Sen.* Epist. 117, 6 :
multum dare solemus præsum-
tioni (πρόληψις) omnium hominum ; apud nos argumentum
veritatis est, aliquid omnibus
videri. Frequent instances will
occur of appeals to communes
notitiæ and consensus gentium.

[1] *Diog.* vii. 53 : φυσικῶς δὲ
νοεῖται δίκαιόν τι καὶ ἀγαθόν. 54 :
ἔστι δ᾽ ἡ πρόληψις ἔννοια φυσικὴ
τῶν καθόλου. In the same strain
Chrysippus (in *Plut.* Sto. Rep.
17) speaks of ἔμφυτοι προλήψεις
of good and evil. In *Plut.*
Frag. De Anim. vii. 6 T. V.
487 Wytt., the question is
asked, How is it possible to
learn what is not already
known? The Stoics reply, By
means of φυσικαὶ ἔννοιαι.

[2] Compare *Cic.* Fin. iii. 10 :
hoc quarto [collatione rationis]
boni notitia facta est; cum enim
ab iis rebus, quæ sunt secundum
naturam, adscendit animus collatione rationis, tum ad noti-

tiam boni pervenit. Similarly
Sen. Ep. 120, 4, replying to the
question, Quomodo ad nos prima
boni honestique notitia per-
venerit? observes, Hoc nos
natura docere non potuit: semina nobis scientiæ dedit,
scientiam non dedit . . . nobis
videtur observatio collegisse
[speciem virtutis], et rerum
sæpe factarum inter se collatio :
per analogiam nostri intellectum et honestum et bonum
judicant. The notion of mental
health and strength has grown
out of the corresponding bodily
notions; the contemplation of
virtuous actions and persons
has given rise to the conception
of moral perfection, the good
points being improved upon,
and defects being passed over,
the experience of certain faults
which resemble virtues serving
to make the distinction plainer.
Even belief in a God was produced, according to *Diog.* vii.
52, by ἀπόδειξις. See p. 80, 1.
Conf. *Stob.* Ecl. i. 792 : οἱ μὲν
Στωϊκοὶ λέγουσι μὲν εὐθὺς ἐμφύε-
σθαι τὸν λόγον, ὕστερον δὲ συνα-
θροίζεσθαι ἀπὸ τῶν αἰσθήσεων καὶ
φαντασιῶν περὶ δεκατέσσαρα ἔτη.

gives rise to knowledge, which is defined by the
Stoics to be a fixed and immoveable conception, or
system of such conceptions.[1] Persistently maintaining,
on the one hand, that knowledge is a system of
artificial conceptions, impossible without a logical
process ; on the other hand, occupying the ground
they did, they must have felt it imperative that
knowledge should agree in its results with primary
conceptions,[2] agreement with nature being in every
department their watchword. For their system,
moreover, it was as natural to derive support from a
supposed agreement with nature, as it was easy for
their opponents to show that their agreement with
nature was imaginary ; many of their assertions, on
the contrary, being wholly opposed to general
opinions.[3]

Perceptions, and the conclusions based upon
them,[4] being thus, according to the Stoics, the two

---

[1] *Stob.* Ecl. ii. 128 : εἶναι δὲ
τὴν ἐπιστήμην κατάληψιν ἀσφαλῆ
καὶ ἀμετάπτωτον ὑπὸ λόγου· ἑτέραν
δὲ ἐπιστήμην σύστημα ἐξ ἐπιστημῶν τοιούτων, οἷον ἡ τῶν κατὰ
μέρος λογικὴ ἐν τῷ σπουδαίῳ ὑπάρ-
χουσα· ἄλλην δὲ σύστημα ἐξ
ἐπιστημῶν τεχνικῶν ἐξ αὑτοῦ ἔχον
τὸ βέβαιον ὡς ἔχουσιν αἱ ἀρεταί·
ἄλλην δε (knowledge in a relative
sense) ἕξιν φαντασιῶν δεκτικὴν
ἀμετάπτωτον ὑπὸ λόγου, ἥντινά
φασιν ἐν τόνῳ καὶ δυνάμει (sc. τῆς
ψυχῆς) κεῖσθαι. *Diog.* vii. 47 :
αὐτήν τε τὴν ἐπιστήμην φασὶν ἢ
κατάληψιν ἀσφαλῆ ἢ ἕξιν ἐν φαντασιῶν προσδέξει ἀμετάπτωτον ὑπὸ
λόγου. (This explanation, which
Herillus used according to
Diog. vii. 165, certainly belongs

to Zeno.) οὐκ ἄνευ δὲ τῆς διαλεκτικῆς θεωρίας τὸν σοφὸν ἄπτωτον
ἔσεσθαι ἐν λόγῳ.

[2] See p. 80, 4.

[3] This was the object of
Plutarch's treatise περὶ τῶν
κοινῶν ἐννοιῶν. In the same
way, the Peripatetic Diogenianus
(in *Euseb.* Pr. Ev. vi. 8,
10) casts it in the teeth of
Chrysippus that, whilst appealing
to generally-received
opinions, he was always going
contrary to them, and that he
considered all men, with one
or two exceptions, to be fools
and madmen.

[4] *Diog.* 52 : ἡ δὲ κατάληψις
γίνεται κατ' αὐτοὺς αἰσθήσει μὲν
λευκῶν, κ.τ.λ. λόγῳ δὲ τῶν δι'

sources of all notions, the further question arises, How are these two sources related to each other? It might have been expected that only perceptions would be stated to be originally and absolutely true, since all general conceptions are based on them. Nevertheless, the Stoics are far from saying so. Absolute certainty of conviction they allow only to knowledge, and therefore declared that the truth of the perceptions of the senses depends on their relation to thought.[1] Truth and error not belonging to disconnected notions, but to notions combined in the form of a judgment, and a judgment being produced by an effort of thought, it follows that sensations, taken alone, are the source of no knowledge, knowledge first arising when the activity of the understanding is allied to sensation.[2] Or, starting from

ἀποδείξεως συναγομένων, ὥσπερ τὸ θεοὺς εἶναι, κ.τ.λ.

[1] *Sext.* Math. viii. 10 : οἱ δὲ ἀπὸ τῆς στοᾶς λέγουσι μὲν τῶν τε αἰσθητῶν τινα καὶ τῶν νοητῶν ἀληθῆ, οὐκ ἐξ εὐθείας δὲ τὰ αἰσθητὰ, ἀλλὰ κατὰ ἀναφορὰν τὴν ὡς ἐπὶ τὰ παρακείμενα τούτοις νοητά.

[2] *Sext.* l. c. continues : ἀληθὲς γάρ ἐστι κατ' αὐτοὺς τὸ ὑπάρχον καὶ ἀντικείμενόν τινι, καὶ ψεῦδος τὸ μὴ ὑπάρχον καὶ μὴ (this μὴ is obviously redundant as appears from Math. viii. 85, 88 ; xi. 220, where the same definition is given without the μὴ) ἀντικείμενόν τινι, ὅπερ ἀσώματον ἀξίωμα καθεστὼς νοητὸν εἶναι · every sentence containing an assertion or negative, and therefore being opposed to every other. *Ibid.* viii. 70 : ἠξίουν οἱ

Στωϊκοὶ κοινῶς ἐν λεκτῷ τὸ ἀληθὲς εἶναι καὶ τὸ ψεῦδος · λεκτὸν δὲ ὑπάρχειν φασὶ τὸ κατὰ λογικὴν φαντασίαν ὑφιστάμενον · λογικὴν δὲ εἶναι φαντασίαν καθ' ἣν τὸ φαντασθὲν ἔστι λόγῳ παραστῆσαι. τῶν δὲ λεκτῶν τὰ μὲν ἐλλιπῆ καλοῦσι τὰ δὲ αὐτοτελῆ (conceptions and propositions ; conf. *Diog.* vii. 63) . . . προσαγορεύουσι δέ τινα τῶν αὐτοτελῶν καὶ ἀξιώματα, ἅπερ λέγοντες ἤτοι ἀληθεύομεν ἢ ψευδόμεθα. *Ibid.* 74 ; *Diog.* vii. 65 : ἀξίωμα δέ ἐστιν, ὃ ἐστιν ἀληθὲς ἢ ψεῦδος (see *Cic.* Tusc. I. 7, 14) ἢ πρᾶγμα (better λεκτὸν as *Gell.* N. A. xvi. 8, 4 reads) αὐτοτελὲς ἀποφαντὸν ὅσον ἐφ' ἑαυτῷ · ὡς ὁ Χρύσιππός φησιν ἐν τοῖς διαλεκτικοῖς ὅροις. Aristotle had already observed that the distinction between false and

the relation of thought to its object, since like can
only be known by like according to the well-known
adage, the rational element in the universe can only
be known by the rational element in man.[1] But
again, the understanding has no other material to
work upon but that supplied by sensation, and general conceptions are only obtained therefrom by conclusions. The mind, therefore, has the capacity of
formally working up the material supplied by the
senses, but to this material it is limited. Still, it can
progress from perceptions to notions not immediately
given in sensation, such as the conceptions of what is
good and of God. And since, according to the Stoic
teaching, material objects only possess reality, the
same vague inconsistency may be observed in their
teaching as has been noticed in Aristotle[2]—reality
attaching to individuals, truth to general notions.
This inconsistency, however, is more marked in their
case than in that of Aristotle, the Stoics so far adhering to the Cynic nominalism[3] as to assert that no
reality attaches to thought.[4]   Such an assertion

true first appears in judgment.
See *Zeller,* Philosophie der
Griechen, vol. ii. b, 156, 2; 157, 1.
  [1] *Sext.* Math. vii. 93 ; ὡς τὸ
μὲν φῶς, φησὶν ὁ Ποσειδώνιος τὸν
Πλάτωνος Τίμαιον ἐξηγούμενος,
ὑπὸ τῆς φωτοειδοῦς ὄψεως κατα-
λαμβάνεται, ἡ δὲ φωνὴ ὑπὸ τῆς
ἀεροειδοῦς ἀκοῆς, οὕτω καὶ ἡ τῶν
ὅλων φύσις ὑπὸ συγγενοῦς ὀφείλει
καταλαμβάνεσθαι τοῦ λόγου. Conf.
Plato, Rep. vi. 508, B.
  [2] See *Zeller's* Philosophie
der Griechen, vol. ii. b, 231.
  [3] *Ibid.* ii. a, 211.

  [4] *Diog.* 61 : ἐννόημα (object
of thought) δέ ἐστι φάντασμα
διανοίας, οὔτε τί ὂν οὔτε ποιόν,
ὡσανεὶ δὲ τί ὂν καὶ ὡσανεὶ ποιόν.
Stob. Ecl. i. 332 : τὰ ἐννοήματα
φησὶ μήτι τινὰ εἶναι μήτι ποιά,
ὡσανεὶ δὲ τινὰ καὶ ὡσανεὶ ποιὰ
φαντάσματα ψυχῆς · ταῦτα δὲ ὑπὸ
τῶν ἀρχαίων ἰδέας προσαγορεύε-
σθαι . . . ταῦτα [ταύτας] δὲ οἱ
Στωϊκοὶ φιλόσοφοι φασὶν ἀνυπάρ-
κτους εἶναι, καὶ τῶν μὲν ἐννοημάτων
μετέχειν ἡμᾶς, τῶν δὲ πτώσεων,
ἃς δὴ προσηγορίας καλοῦσι, τυγχάνειν. Although defended by

makes it all the harder to understand how greater truth can be attributed to thought, unreal as it is said to be, than to sensations of real and material objects. Do we then ask in what the peculiar character of thought consists, the Stoics, following Aristotle, reply that in thought the idea of universality is added to that which presents itself in sensation as a particular.[1] More importance was attached by them to another feature—the greater certainty which belongs to thought than to sensation. All the definitions given above point to the immovable strength of conviction

Prantl, Gesch. d. Log. I. 420, 63, the last words as they stand do not appear capable of any tolerable meaning. They are more probably corrupt. *Plut.* Plac. i. 10, 4: οἱ ἀπὸ Ζήνωνος Στωϊκοὶ ἐννοήματα ἡμέτερα τὰς ἰδέας ἔφασαν. *Simpl.* Categ. 26, e : Χρύσιππος ἀπορεῖ περὶ τῆς ἰδέας, εἰ τόδε τι ῥηθήσεται. συμπαραληπτέον δὲ καὶ τὴν συνήθειαν τῶν Στωϊκῶν περὶ τῶν γενικῶν ποιῶν πῶς αἱ πτώσεις κατ' αὐτοὺς προφέρονται καὶ πῶς οὕτινα τὰ κοινὰ παρ' αὐτοῖς λέγεται. *Syrian* on Met. p. 59. (In *Petersen's* Philos. Chrys. Fund. 80): ὡς ἄρα τὰ εἴδη . . . οὔτε πρὸς τὴν ῥῆσιν τῆς τῶν ὀνομάτων συνηθείας παρήγετο, ὡς Χρύσιππος καὶ 'Αρχέδημος καὶ οἱ πλείους τῶν Στωϊκῶν ὕστερον ᾠήθησαν . . . οὐ μὴν οὐδὲ νοήματά εἰσι παρ' αὐτοῖς αἱ ἰδέαι, ὡς Κλεάνθης ὕστερον εἴρηκε. *Prantl*, l. c. takes objection to what Stobæus and Plutarch here say; yet this view is not that the Stoics regarded their conception of the ἐννόημα as identical with Plato's concep-

tion of ideas, but that they asserted that these ideas were only ἐννοήματα—an assertion which had also been made by Antisthenes. Compare what is said on p. 92 respecting the unreality of the λεκτόν, likewise what *Sext.* Math. vii. 246, quotes, as belonging to the Stoics : οὔτε δὲ ἀληθεῖς οὔτε ψευδεῖς εἰσιν αἱ γενικαὶ [φαντασίαι] · ὧν γὰρ τὰ εἴδη τοῖα ἢ τοῖα τούτων τὰ γένη οὔτε τοῖα οὔτε τοῖα · if mankind be divided into Greeks and barbarians, the γενικὸς ἄνθρωπος will be neither one nor the other. The further therefore a conception is removed from individual limitations, the further it is removed from truth.
  [1] *Diog.* vii. 54 : ἔστι δ' ἡ πρόληψις ἔννοια φυσικὴ τῶν καθόλου. Exc. e *Joan. Damasc.* (*Stob.* Floril. ed. Mein. iv. 236), Nr. 34: Χρύσιππος τὸ μὲν γενικὸν ἡδὺ νοητόν, τὸ δὲ εἰδικὸν καὶ προσπίπτον ἤδη (*Petersen*, 83 without cause suggests ἡδὺ) αἰσθητόν.

as the distinctive feature of knowledge;[1] and of like
import is the language attributed to Zeno,[2] comparing simple sensation with an extended finger, assent,
as being the first activity of the power of judgment,
with a closed hand, conception with the fist, and
knowledge with one fist firmly grasped by the other.
According to this view, the whole difference between
the four processes is one of degree, depending on the
greater or less strength of conviction, on the mental
exertion and tension.[3] It is not an absolute difference
of kind, but a relative difference, a gradual shading
off of one into the other.

*(d) The
standard
of truth.*

*(a) Prac-
tical need
of such a
standard.*

From these considerations it follows that in the
last resort only a relative distinction is left whereby
the truth of notions may be tested. Even the general argument for the possibility of knowledge proceeds
with the Stoics by practically taking something for
granted. Without failing to urge intellectual objections against Scepticism, as was indeed natural, particularly since the time of Chrysippus[4]—and often
most pertinent ones[5]—the Stoics nevertheless speci-

[1] See p. 82, 1.

[2] *Cic.* Acad. ii. 47, 145.

[3] *Stob.* Ecl. ii. 128 : Knowledge is defined to be ἕξις φαντασιῶν δεκτικὴ ἀμετάπτωτος ὑπὸ
λόγου, ἥντινά φασιν ἐν τόνῳ καὶ
δυνάμει κεῖσθαι.

[4] Chrysippus opposed Arcesilas, with such success, according to the view of the
Stoic School, that Carneades
was refuted by anticipation;
and it was considered a special
favour of Providence that the
labours of Chrysippus had occu-

pied an intermediate place
between two of the most important Sceptics. *Plut.* Sto.
Rep. i. 4, p. 1059. *Diog.* 198
mentions a treatise against
Arcesilaus.

[5] Here may be noted the
objection mentioned by *Sext.*
Math. viii. 463; Pyrh. ii. 186 :
The Sceptics cannot deny the
possibility of arguing without
proving their assertion and
thereby practically admitting
the possibility. Also another
one urged by Antipater against

ally took up their stand on one point, which was this, that, unless the knowledge of truth were possible, it would be impossible to act on fixed principles and convictions.[1] Thus, as a last bulwark against doubt, practical needs are resorted to.

The same result is obtained from a special inquiry into the nature of the standard of truth. If the question is raised, How are true perceptions distinguished from false ones? the immediate reply given by the Stoics is, that a true perception is one which represents a real object as it really is.[2] You are no

---

Carneades (*Cic.* Acad. ii. 9, 28; 34, 109): He who asserts that nothing can be known with certainty must, at least, believe that he can with certainty know this. The replies of the Sceptics to these objections, and the way they turned them in their own favour, will be found in *Sext.* Math. l. c. and vii. 433.

[1] *Plut.* Sto. Rep. 10 (see p. 66, 1); *Ibid.* 47, 12: καὶ μὴν ἕν γε τοῖς πρὸς τοὺς Ἀκαδημαϊκοὺς ἀγῶσιν ὁ πλεῖστος αὐτῷ τε Χρυσίππῳ καὶ Ἀντιπάτρῳ πόνος γέγονε περὶ τοῦ μήτε πράττειν μήτε ὁρμᾶν ἀσυγκαταθέτως, ἀλλὰ πλάσματα λέγειν καὶ κενὰς ὑποθέσεις τοὺς ἀξιοῦντας οἰκείας φαντασίας γενομένης εὐθὺς ὁρμᾶν μὴ εἴξαντας μηδὲ συγκατατιθεμένους. *Ibid.* adv. Col. 26, 3, p. 1122: τὴν δὲ περὶ πάντων ἐποχὴν οὐδ' οἱ πολλὰ πραγματευσάμενοι καὶ κατατείναντες εἰς τοῦτο συγγράμματα καὶ λόγους ἐκίνησαν · ἀλλ' ἐκ τῆς Στοᾶς αὐτῆς τελευτῶντες ὥσπερ Γοργόνα τὴν ἀπραξίαν ἐπάγοντες ἀπηγόρευσαν. *Epict.* (Arrian. Diss. i. 27, 15) quietly suppresses a Sceptic by saying: οὐκ ἄγω σχολὴν πρὸς

ταῦτα. Following also the Stoic line, *Cic.* Acad. ii. 10–12, makes Antiochus argue that Scepticism makes all action impossible.

[2] In *Sext.* Math. vii. 244, ἀληθεῖς φαντασίαι are, first of all, literally explained to be φαντασίαι, ὧν ἔστιν ἀληθῆ κατηγορίαν ποιήσασθαι · then, under the head of true φαντασίαι, the καταληπτικαὶ and οὐ καταληπτικαὶ are distinguished, i.e., notions which are accompanied by a clear impression of being true, and such as are not; and, in conclusion, φαντασία καταληπτικὴ is defined: ἡ ἀπὸ τοῦ ὑπάρχοντος καὶ κατ' αὐτὸ τὸ ὑπάρχον ἐναπομεμαγμένη καὶ ἐναπεσφραγισμένη, ὁποία οὐκ ἂν γένοιτο ἀπὸ μὴ ὑπάρχοντος. This definition is afterwards more fully explained. The same explanation is given *Ibid.* 402 and 426; viii. 85; Pyrrh. ii. 4; iii. 242; *Augustin*, c. Acad. ii. 5, 11; *Cic.* Acad. ii. 6, 18. *Diog.* vii. 46: τῆς δὲ φαντασίας τὴν μὲν καταληπτικὴν τὴν δὲ ἀκατάληπτον · καταληπτικὴν μὲν, ἣν κριτήριον εἶναι τῶν πραγμάτων φασί, τὴν γινομένην ἀπὸ

further with this answer, and the question has again
to be asked, How may it be known that a perception
faithfully represents a reality? The Stoics can only
reply by pointing to a relative, but not to an absolute, test—the degree of strength with which certain
perceptions force themselves on our notice. By itself
a perception does not necessarily carry conviction or
assent (συγκατάθεσις); for there can be no assent
until the faculty of judgment is directed towards the
perception, either for the purpose of allowing or of
rejecting it, truth and error residing in judgment.
Assent therefore, generally speaking, rests with us, as
does also the power of decision; and a wise man differs from a fool quite as much by conviction as by
action.[1] Some of our perceptions are, however, of

ὑπάρχοντος κατ᾽ αὐτὸ τὸ ὕπαρχον
ἐναπεσφραγισμένην καὶ ἐναπομε-
μαγμένην· ἀκατάληπτον δὲ τὴν μὴ
ἀπὸ ὑπάρχοντος, ἢ ἀπὸ ὑπάρχοντος
μὲν, μὴ κατ᾽ αὐτὸ δὲ τὸ ὑπάρχον,
τὴν μὴ τρανῆ μηδὲ ἔκτυπον. Ibid.
50.

[1] Sext. Math. viii. 397: ἔστι
μὲν οὖν ἡ ἀπόδειξις, ὡς ἔστι παρ᾽
αὐτῶν ἀκούειν, καταληπτικῆς φαντασίας συγκατάθεσις, ἥτις διπλοῦν
ἔοικεν εἶναι πρᾶγμα καὶ τὸ μέν τι
ἔχειν ἀκούσιον, τὸ δὲ ἑκούσιον καὶ
ἐπὶ τῇ ἡμετέρᾳ κρίσει κείμενον. τὸ
μὲν γὰρ φαντασιωθῆναι ἀβούλητον
ἦν καὶ οὐκ ἐπὶ τῷ πάσχοντι ἔκειτο
ἀλλ᾽ ἐπὶ τῷ φαντασιοῦντι·τὸ οὑτωσὶ
διατεθῆναι . . . τὸ δὲ συγκατα-
θέσθαι τούτῳ τῷ κινήματι ἔκειτο
ἐπὶ τῷ παραδεχομένῳ τὴν φαντασίαν. Diog. vii. 51; Cic. Acad.
i. 14, 40: [Zeno] ad hæc quæ
visa sunt, et quasi accepta sensibus assensionem adjungit animorum: quam esse vult in nobis

positam et voluntariam. Ibid.
ii. 12, 37; De Fato, 19, 43,
Chrysippus affirms: visum ob-
jectum imprimet illud quidem
et quasi signabit in animo suam
speciem sed assensio nostra erit
in potestate. Plut. Sto. Rep.
47, 1: τὴν γὰρ φαντασίαν βουλό-
μενος [ὁ Χρύσιππος] οὐκ οὖσαν
αὐτοτελῆ τῆς συγκαταθέσεως
αἰτίαν ἀποδεικνύειν εἴρηκεν ὅτι·
βλάψουσιν οἱ σοφοὶ ψευδεῖς φαντασίας ἐμποιοῦντες, ἂν αἱ φαντασίαι
ποιῶσιν αὐτοτελῶς τὰς συγκαταθέσεις, κ.τ.λ. Id. 13: αὖθις δέ
φησι Χρύσιππος, καὶ τὸν θεὸν
ψευδεῖς ἐμποιεῖν φαντασίας καὶ
τὸν σοφὸν .., ἡμᾶς δὲ φαύλους
ὄντας συγκατατίθεσθαι ταῖς τοιαύταις φαντασίαις. Id. Fragm.
De An. 2: οὐχ ἡ ψυχὴ τρέπει
ἑαυτὴν εἰς τὴν τῶν πραγμάτων
κατάληψιν καὶ ἀπάτην, κατὰ τοὺς
ἀπὸ τῆς στοᾶς. Epictet. in Gell.
N.A. xix. 1, 15: visa animi, quas

such a kind that they at once oblige us to bestow on
them assent, compelling us not only to regard them
as probable, but also as true[1] and corresponding with
the actual nature of things. Such perceptions produce in us that strength of conviction which the
Stoics call a conception; they are therefore termed
conceptional perceptions. Whenever a perception
forces itself upon us in this irresistible form, we are
no longer dealing with a fiction of the imagination,
but with something real; but whenever the strength
of conviction is wanting, we cannot be sure of the
truth of our perception. Or, expressing the same
idea in the language of Stoicism, conceptional or irresistible perceptions, φαντασίαι καταληπτικαὶ, are
the standard of truth.[2] The test of irresistibility

φαντασίας philosophi appellant
. . . non voluntatis sunt neque
arbitrariæ, sed vi quadam sua
inferunt sese hominibus nos-
citandæ; probationes autem,
quas συγκαταθέσεις vocant, quibus eadem visa noscuntur ac
dijundicantur, voluntariæ sunt
fiuntque hominum arbitratu:
the difference between a wise
man and a fool consists in
συγκατατίθεσθαι and προσεπιδοξά-
ζειν. The freedom of approba-
tion must, of course, be so
understood in harmony with
Stoic doctrine of the freedom
of the will.

[1] On the difference between
the conception of εὔλογον and
that of καταληπτικὴ φαντασία,
consisting as it does in the fact
that the latter alone is unerring,
see *Athen.* viii. 354, e; *Diog.*
vii. 177.

[2] Compare besides p. 87, 2,

Cic. Acad. i. 11, 41: [Zeno]
visis (= φαντασίαις) non omnibus
adjungebat fidem, sed iis solum,
quæ propriam quandam habe-
rent declarationem earum rerum, quæ viderentur: id autem
visum, cum ipsum per se cer-
neretur, comprehensibile (καταληπτικὴ φαντασία). *Ibid.* ii.
12, 38: ut enim necesse est
lancem in libra ponderibus im-
positis deprimi, sic animum
perspicuis cedere . . . non potest objectam rem perspicuam
non approbare. Conf. Fin. v.
26, 76: percipiendi vis ita de-
finitur a Stoicis, ut negent
quidquam posse percipi nisi
tale rerum, quale falsum esse
non possit. *Diog.* vii. 54;
Sext. Math. vii. 227: κριτήριον
τοίνυν φασὶν ἀληθείας εἶναι οἱ
ἄνδρες οὗτοι τὴν καταληπτικὴν
φαντασίαν. It was a deviation
from the older Stoic teaching,

CHAP.
V.

(γ) Pri-
mary con-
ceptions a
standard
as well as
irresistible
percep-
tions.

(κατάληψις) was, in the first place, understood to apply to sensations from without, such sensations, according to the Stoic view, alone supplying the material for knowledge. An equal degree of certainty was, however, attached to terms deduced from originally true data, either by the universal and natural exercise of thought, or by scientific processes of proof. Now, since among these derivative terms some—the primary conceptions (κοιναὶ ἔννοιαι), for instance—serve as the basis for deriving others, it may in a certain sense be asserted that sensation and primary conceptions are both standards of truth.[1] In strict accuracy, neither sensation nor primary conceptions (πρόληψεις) can be called standards. The

to refuse, as the later Stoics did, to allow a conceptional notion to be considered a test of truth, except with the proviso that no argument could be adduced against its truth. *Sext.* 253 : ἀλλὰ γὰρ οἱ μὲν ἀρχαιότεροι τῶν Στωϊκῶν κριτήριόν φασιν εἶναι τῆς ἀληθείας τὴν καταληπτικὴν ταύτην φαντασίαν· οἱ δὲ νεώτεροι προσετίθεσαν καὶ τὸ μηδὲν ἔχουσαν ἔνστημα, since cases could be imagined in which a faulty view presented itself with the full force of truth. This was equivalent to overthrowing the whole doctrine of a criterion ; for how could it be known in any particular case that there was not a negative instance ? But it is quite in harmony with the Stoic teaching for a later Stoic (*Ibid.* 257) to say of conceptional perception : αὕτη γὰρ ἐναργὴς οὖσα καὶ πληκτικὴ μονονουχὶ τῶν τριχῶν, φασι, λαμβά-

νεται κατασπῶσα ἡμᾶς εἰς συγκατάθεσιν καὶ ἄλλου μηδενὸς δεομένη εἰς τὸ τοιαύτῃ προσπίπτειν, κ.τ.λ. Hence *Simpl.* Phys. 20, b : ἀνῄρουν τὰ ἄλλα . . . πλὴν τὰ ἐναργῆ.

[1] *Diog.* vii. 54 : κριτήριον δὲ τῆς ἀληθείας φασὶ τυγχάνειν τὴν καταληπτικὴν φαντασίαν, τουτέστι τὴν ἀπὸ ὑπάρχοντος, καθά φησι Χρύσιππος ἐν τῇ δωδεκάτῃ τῶν φυσικῶν καὶ Ἀντίπατρος καὶ Ἀπολλόδωρος. ὁ μὲν γὰρ Βοηθὸς κριτήρια πλείονα ἀπολείπει, νοῦν καὶ αἴσθησιν καὶ ὄρεξιν καὶ ἐπιστήμην (this looks like an approximation to the teaching of the Peripatetics) ; ὁ δὲ Χρύσιππος διαφερόμενος πρὸς αὐτὸν ἐν τῷ πρώτῳ περὶ λόγου εἶναι αἴσθησιν καὶ πρόληψιν ... ἄλλοι δέ τινες τῶν ἀρχαιοτέρων Στωϊκῶν τὸν ὀρθὸν λόγον κριτήριον ἀπολείπουσιν, ὡς ὁ Ποσειδώνιος ἐν τῷ περὶ κριτηρίου φησίν. See above p. 76.

real standard, whereby the truth of a perception is ascertained, consists in the power, inherent in certain perceptions, of carrying conviction—τὸ καταληπτικὸν —a power which belongs, in the first place, to sensations, whether of objects without or within, and, in the next place, to primary conceptions formed from them in a natural way—κοιναὶ ἔννοιαι or προλήψεις. On the other hand, conceptions and terms formed artificially can only have their truth established by being subjected to a scientific process of proof. How, after these statements, the Stoics could attribute a greater strength of conviction to artificial than to primary conceptions; [1] how they could raise doubts as to the trustworthiness of simple sensations,[2] is one of the paradoxes of the Stoic system, proving the existence, as in so many other systems, of a double current of thought. There is, on the one hand, a seeking for what is innate and original, a going back to nature, an aversion to everything artificial and of human device, inherited by Stoicism from its ancestral Cynicism. On the other hand, there is a desire to supplement the Cynic appeal to nature by a higher culture, and to assign scientific reasons for truths which the Cynics laid down as self-evident.

The latter tendency will alone explain the care

---

[1] See above p. 82, 1.
[2] See above p. 89, 2, and *Cic.* Acad. ii. 31, 101 : neque eos (the Academicians) contra sensus aliter dicimus, ac Stoici, qui multa falsa esse dicunt, longeque aliter se habere ac sensibus videantur. Chrysippus had inquired into the truth of the perceptions of the senses, and of the notions derived from them, in his treatise περὶ συνηθείας, without, however, satisfactorily answering the objections which he quoted against the theory. See p. 46, 2.

and precision which the Stoics devoted to studying
the forms and rules which govern intellectual processes. Attention to this branch of study may be
noticed in Zeno and his immediate successors at the
first separation of Stoicism from Cynicism.[1] Aristo
is the only Stoic who is opposed to it, his whole
habit of mind being purely that of a Cynic. In
Chrysippus, however, it attained its greatest development, and by Chrysippus the formal logic of
the Stoics attained scientific completeness. In later
times, in proportion as Stoicism reverted to its original Cynical type, and in connection therewith appealed to the immediate suggestions of the mind, it
lost its interest in logic, as may be observed in
Musonius, Epictetus, and others. For the present,
however, let it suffice to consider the logic of Chrysippus, as far as that is known to us.

*C. Formal
logic.
(1) Utter-
ance in
general.*

The term formal logic is here used to express
those investigations which the Stoics included under
the doctrine of utterance.[2] The common object
of those inquiries is that which is thought, or, as
the Stoics called it, that which is uttered ($\lambda \varepsilon \kappa \tau \acute{o} \nu$),
understanding thereby the substance of thought—
thought regarded by itself as a distinct something,
differing alike from the external object to which it
refers, from the sound by which it is expressed, and
from the power of mind which produces it. For
this reason, they maintain that only utterance is
not material; things are always material; even the
process of thought consists in a material change

[1] See p. 60.   [2] See p. 73, 3.

within the soul, and an uttered word, in a certain movement of the atmosphere.[1]   A question is here

[1] See *Sext.* Math. viii. 11 : οἱ ἀπὸ τῆς στοᾶς, τρία φάμενοι συζυγεῖν ἀλλήλοις, τό τε σημαινόμενον καὶ τὸ σημαῖνον καὶ τὸ τυγχάνον. ὧν σημαῖνον μὲν εἶναι τὴν φωνὴν ... σημαινόμενον δὲ αὐτὸ τὸ πρᾶγμα τὸ ὑπ᾿ αὐτῆς δηλούμενον ... τυγχάνον δὲ τὸ ἐκτὸς ὑποκείμενον ... τούτων δὲ δύο μὲν εἶναι σώματα, καθάπερ τὴν φωνὴν καὶ τὸ τυγχάνον, ἓν δὲ ἀσώματον, ὥσπερ τὸ σημαινόμενον πρᾶγμα καὶ λεκτόν. *Sen.* Ep. 117, 13, giving it expressly as the teaching of the Stoics, not as his own :. Sunt, inquit, naturæ corporum ... has deinde sequuntur motus animorum enuntiativi corporum —for instance, I see Cato walk —corpus est, quod video. . . . Dico deinde : Cato ambulat. Non corpus est, inquit, quod nunc loquor, sed enuntiativum quiddam de corpore, quod alii effatum vocant, alii enuntiatum, alii edoctum.   Compare also on the λεκτόν *Sext.* Math. viii. 70 (above p. 83, 2) ; Pyrrh. iii. 52. Various arguments are used by the Stoics to prove that the voice as opposed to utterance (λεκτὸν) is material, as has been said, p. 74, 5. Illustrative of the distinction between utterance and the process of thought is the assertion (in *Sext.* Pyrrh. ii. 81) that certainty as being a definite condition of the soul is material, but that truth itself is not material : λέγεται διαφέρειν τῆς ἀληθείας τὸ ἀληθὲς τριχῶς, οὐσίᾳ, συστάσει, δυνάμει· οὐσίᾳ μὲν, ἐπεὶ τὸ μὲν ἀληθὲς ἀσώματόν ἐστιν, ἀξίωμα γάρ ἐστι καὶ λεκτὸν, ἡ δὲ ἀλήθεια σῶμα, ἔστι

γὰρ ἐπιστήμη πάντων ἀληθῶν ἀποφαντικὴ, ἡ δὲ ἐπιστήμη πὼς ἔχον ἡγεμονικόν (*Id.* Math. vii. 38, a similar statement is expressly attributed to a Stoic) ; likewise a similar statement which *Sen.* Ep. 117, discusses, and at length declares to be a mere quibble, but not till after a lengthy refutation : sapientiam bonum esse, sapere bonum non esse. The statement rests on the assertion that nothing can be a good which does not make itself felt, and nothing can make itself felt which is not material ; wisdom is material, because it is mens perfecta, but sapere is incorporale et accidens alteri, i.e. sapientiæ.   Accordingly, λεκτὸν (as *Ammon.* De Inter. 15, b, remarks) is a μέσον τοῦ τε νοήματος καὶ τοῦ πράγματος· if, however, νόημα be taken to express the thought itself, and not the process of thinking, it becomes identical with λεκτόν. Conf. *Simpl.* Cat. 3, a, Basil. : τὰ δὲ λεγόμενα καὶ λεκτὰ τὰ νοήματά ἐστιν, ὡς καὶ τοῖς Στωϊκοῖς ἐδόκει.   In *Plut.* Plac. iv. 11, 4, a definition of νόημα or ἐννόημα is given similar to that of λεκτὸν in *Sext.* Math. viii. 70 : φάντασμα διάνοιας λογικοῦ ζώου. See above p. 84, 4.   The statement, however, of *Philop.* Anal. Pr. lx. a, Schol. in Ar. 170, a, 2, cannot be true, that the Stoics called things τυγχάνοντα, thoughts ἐκφορικὰ, and sounds λεκτά, whereas ἐκφορικὸν may be used of thoughts in the same sense as λεκτόν.

CHAP.
V.

suggested in passing, which should not be lost sight of, viz. How far was it correct for the Stoics to speak of thoughts as existing, seeing they are not material, since, according to their teaching, reality only belongs to material things? [1]

Utterance may be either perfect or imperfect. It is perfect when it contains a proposition ; imperfect when the proposition is incomplete.[2] The portion of logic, therefore, which treats of utterance falls into two parts, devoted respectively to the consideration of complete and incomplete expressions.

(2) *In-complete expression.*

(a) *The grammar of words.*

In the section devoted to incomplete expressions, much is found which we should include under grammar rather than under logic. Thus all incomplete expressions are divided into two groups—one group

---

[1] See p. 84, 4. This question was raised in the Stoic School itself ; at least Sextus, not hesitating to attack the Stoic teaching from this side (Math. viii. 262), speaks of an ἀνήνυτος μάχη in reference to the ὕπαρξις of λεκτὰ, and he remarks (viii. 258) : ὁρῶμεν δὲ ὡς εἰσί τινες οἱ ἀνῃρηκότες τὴν ὕπαρξιν τῶν λεκτῶν, καὶ οὐχ οἱ ἑτερόδοξοι μόνον, οἷον οἱ Ἐπικούρειοι, ἀλλὰ καὶ οἱ Στωϊκοὶ, ὡς οἱ περὶ τὸν Βασιλείδην, οἷς ἔδοξε μηδὲν εἶναι ἀσώματον. Probably the question was first raised by later Stoics, when pressed by their opponents. Basilides was the teacher of Marcus Aurelius. Otherwise the existence of λεκτὰ was spoken of as quite natural.

[2] *Sext.* Math. viii. 70, see above p. 83, 2 : τῶν δὲ λεκτῶν τὰ μὲν ἐλλιπῆ καλοῦσι τὰ δὲ αὐτο-

τελῆ. Various kinds of propositions are then enumerated as being αὐτοτελῆ. Following the same authority, (Diocles ? see *Diog.* 48) *Diog.* 63, says : φασὶ δὲ τὸ λεκτὸν εἶναι τὸ κατὰ φαντασίαν λογικὴν ὑφιστάμενον. τῶν δὲ λεκτῶν τὰ μὲν λέγουσιν εἶναι αὐτοτελῆ οἱ Στωϊκοὶ, τὰ δὲ ἐλλιπῆ. ἐλλιπῆ μὲν οὖν ἔστι τὰ ἀναπάρτιστον ἔχοντα τὴν ἐκφορὰν, οἷον Γράφει· ἐπιζητοῦμεν γὰρ, Τίς ; αὐτοτελῆ δ' ἐστὶ τὰ ἀπηρτισμένην ἔχοντα τὴν ἐκφορὰν, οἷον Γράφει Σωκράτης. *Prantl* in saying, p. 438, that the Stoics divide judgments (ἀξιώματα) into complete and incomplete, is inaccurate. Only λεκτὰ are so divided, but λεκτὸν has a wider meaning than that of a logical judgment. ἀξιώματα are only one form of λεκτὰ αὐτοτελῆ.

including proper names and adjectives, the other including verbs.[1] These two groups are used respectively to express what is essential and what is accidental,[2] and are again divided into a number of subdivisions and varieties.[3] To this part of logic

---

[1] *Plut.* Qu. Plat. x. 1, 2, p. 1008. A judgment (πρότασις or ἀξίωμα) ἐξ ὀνόματος καὶ ῥήματος συνέστηκεν, ὧν τὸ μὲν‿πτῶσιν οἱ διαλεκτικοὶ, τὸ δὲ κατηγόρημα καλοῦσιν. The terms πτῶσις and κατηγόρημα belonging to the Stoic terminology, the Stoics must be meant by οἱ διαλεκτικοί. In the first class of words they distinguish ὄνομα and προσηγορία, limiting ὄνομα to proper names, and understanding by προσηγορία all general terms, whether substantives or adjectives (*Diog.* 58; *Bekker's* Anecd. ii. 842). According to *Stob.* Ecl. i. 332, πτῶσις was only used to express προσηγορία. *Diog.* 192, mentions two books of Chrysippus περὶ τῶν προσηγορικῶν. For the meaning of κατηγόρημα or ῥῆμα, the verb, consult *Diog.* 58 and 64; *Sext.* Pyrrh. iii. 14; *Cic.* Tusc. iv. 9, 21; *Porphyr.* in Ammon. De Inter. 37, a. According to *Apollon.* De Construct. i. 8, ῥῆμα was used in strict accuracy only for the infinitive, other forms being called κατηγορήματα.

[2] The distinction between ὄνομα and κατηγόρημα was somewhat bluntly referred to this logical and metaphysical antithesis by the Stoics, as may be seen in *Stob.* Ecl. i. 336 · αἴτιον δ' ὁ Ζήνων φησὶν εἶναι δι' ὃ, οὗ δὲ αἴτιον συμβεβηκός· καὶ τὸ μὲν αἴτιον σῶμα, οὗ δὲ αἴτιον κατηγόρημα. . . . Ποσειδώνιος . . . τὸ μὲν αἴτιον ὂν καὶ σῶμα, οὗ δὲ αἴτιον

οὔτε ὂν οὔτε σῶμα, ἀλλὰ συμβεβηκὸς καὶ κατηγόρημα. Hence for the latter the names σύμβαμα and παρασύμβαμα. See following note.

[3] In nouns the cases were distinguished, the nominative, according to *Ammon.* l. c. being called ὄνομα, and the other five cases πτώσεις · a statement, however, which does not agree with the usual use of those terms. In *Diog.* 65, the cases (γενικὴ, δοτικὴ, αἰτιατικὴ) are called πλάγιαι πτώσεις. Chrysippus wrote a distinct treatise on the five cases, *Diog.* 192. Similar were the divisions of the κατηγόρημα. According to *Diog.* 65, the Stoics distinguished between transitive verbs (ὀρθὰ), such as ὁρᾷ, διαλέγεται· passive verbs (ὕπτια), such as ὁρῶμαι· neuter verbs (οὐδέτερα), such as φρονεῖν, περιπατεῖν· and verbs which, with a passive form, do not express a passive relation (ἀντιπεπονθότα), κείρεσθαι, πείθεσθαι, &c. Consult on this point *Philo.* De Cherub. 121, c; *Orig.* C. Cels. vi. 57. On the ὀρθὰ and ὕπτια, also *Dionys.* Thrax. § 15, p. 886, Bekk.; *Simpl.* Categ. 79, a, ζ; *Diog.* 191; and respecting all three divisions, *Lersch.* ii. 196; *Steinthal*, Gesch. der Sprachw. i. 294. They also distinguished between σύμβαμα and παρασύμβαμα—a verb, when used with a nominative, being called σύμβαμα or κατηγόρημα, and

investigations into the formation and division of
conceptions, and the doctrine of the categories, properly belong ; but it cannot be said with certainty
what place they occupy in the logic of the Stoics.[1]

Certain it is that these researches introduced little
new matter ; all that is known of the Stoic views in
reference to the formation, the mutual relation and
the analysis of conceptions, differing only from the
corresponding parts in the teaching of Aristotle by
the change of a few expressions, and a slightly
altered order of treatment.[2]

παρασύμβαμα when used with an
oblique case ; περιπατεῖ is a σύμβαμα, μεταμέλει a παρασύμβαμα,
περιπατεῖrequiring a nominative
(Σωκράτης), μεταμέλει requiring
a dative (Σωκράτει). If an oblique case was necessary to complete a sentence, besides the
subject, the verb was called
ἔλαττον ἢ σύμβαμα or ἔλαττον ἢ
κατηγόρημα, as in the sentence
Πλάτων φιλεῖ, such, for instance,
is φιλεῖ, for these words only
make a complete sentence by
the addition of an object thus:
Πλάτων φιλεῖ Δίωνα. If this was
necessary with a παρασύμβαμα,
it was called ἔλαττον ἢ παρασύμβαμα ; such, for instance, is
the word μέλει, for to complete
the sentence it is not enough
to say Σωκράτει μέλει, but the object must be added, as in the sentence: Σωκράτει μεταμέλει Ἀλκι-
βιάδους. This difference is explained by Porphyr. in Ammon.
l. c., 36, b, whom Lersch. ii.
31, misunderstanding, blames.
See Diog. 64 where the text is
evidentlycorrupt. Withoutgreat
temerity we mightsubstitute for

the meaningless οἷον τὸ διὰ πέ-
τρας πλεῖν—τὰ δὲ παρασύμβαματα,
which at least gives a better
meaning than the proposals of
R. Schmidt, Sto. Gramm. 66, 91,
and Lersch. l. c. 33. Apollon.
De Const. iii. 32, p. 299 ; Bekk.;
Suid. σύμβαμα (very inaccurate);
Priscian, xviii. p. 1118, who, in
his equally inaccurate account,
has ἀσυμβάματα. The example
which Lucian. Vit. Auct. 21
employs to laugh at the Stoic
hair-splitting anent σύμβαμα
and παρασύμβαμα, of course
proves nothing.

[1] There is nothing whatever
on record which serves to show
the position held by the categories. By several, definition
and division were treated of
most improperly under the head
of language.

[2] According to Diog. 60,
Bekker, Anecd. ii. 647, ὅρος was
defined by Chrysippus as ἰδίου
(which must be read in Diog.
in place of καὶ) ἀπόδοσις · by
Antipater as λόγος κατ’ ἀνάλυσιν
(Anecd. ἀνάγκην) ἀπαρτιζόντως
ἐκφερόμενος, i.e. a proposition in

Of greater importance is the Stoic doctrine of the categories.[1] In this branch of logic, the Stoics again follow Aristotle, but not without deviating from him in three points. Aristotle referred his categories to no higher conception regarding them severally as

which the subject and the collective predicates may be interchanged. Ὁρισμὸς gives in detail what ὄνομα gives collectively (*Simpl.* Categ. 16, β). An imperfect ὅρος is called ὑπογραφή. Instead of the Aristotelian τί ἦν εἶναι, the Stoics were content with the τί ἦν of Antisthenes (*Alex.* Top. 24, m). Like Prodicus, they laid great stress on distinguishing accurately the conceptions of words of similar meanings, χαρά, τέρψις, ἡδονή, εὐφροσύνη (*Alex.* Top. 96). The relation of γένος to εἶδος is also explained : γένος is defined to be the summing up of many thoughts (ἀναφαιρέτων ἐννοημάτων · which might mean thoughts which, as integral parts of a conception, cannot be separated from it ; only this explanation would not agree with what follows, according to which one would more likely think of the different species included in the genus. *Prantl* p. 422 suggests ἀναφορητῶν, which, however, requires explanation) ; εἶδος as τὸ ὑπὸ τοῦ γένους περιεχόμενον (*Diog.* 60). γενικώτατον is δ γένος ὂν γένος οὐκ ἔχει· εἰδικώτατον δ εἶδος ὂν εἶδος οὐκ ἔχει (*Diog.* 61 ; conf. *Sext.* Pyrrh. i. 138). As to διαίρεσις, ὑποδιαίρεσις, and ἀντιδιαίρεσις (division into contradictories) nothing new is stated; but μερισμὸς has a special notice

(*Diog.* 61). Lastly, if *Sext.* Pyrrh. ii. 213 (the previous definition of dialectic is found (as was stated on p. 73, 3), in *Alcinous* Isag. 3, and he also mentions c. 5 three of the four kinds of division, instead of the fourth he gives two others), refers to the Stoics, four kinds of division are enumerated. The reference of the 8 διαιρέσεις mentioned by *Prantl*, p. 423, on the authority of *Bekker's* Anecd. ii. 679 to a Stoic source is much more doubtful. There is a little that is new in the Stoic discussion of Opposition, and the same may be said of what *Simpl.* (Categ. 100, β and δ ; 101, ε ; 102, β) quotes from Chrysippus (περὶ τῶν κατὰ στέρησιν λεγομένων) on the subject of στέρησις and ἕξις. Conf. *Diog.* vii. 190.

[1] See *Petersen*, Philos. Chrysipp. Fund. pp. 36–144, invaluable for its careful collection of authorities, but in its attempt to build the Stoic system on the categories giving way to many capricious combinations. *Trendelenburg*, Hist. Beitr. i. 217; *Prantl*, Gesch. der Logik, i. 426. Our authorities for the knowledge of the Stoic doctrine of the categories are besides a few notices on other writers principally *Simplicius*, on the Categories, and *Plotinus*, Ennead. vi. 1, 25–30.

class-conceptions; the Stoics referred them all to one higher conception. Aristotle enumerated ten categories; the Stoics thought that they could do with four,[1] which four only partially coincide with those of Aristotle. Aristotle placed the categories side by side, as co-ordinate, so that no object could come under a second category in the same respect in which it came under the first one;[2] the Stoics placed them one under the other, as subordinate, so that every preceding category is more accurately determined by the next succeeding one.

(a) Highest Conception— an indefinite Something.

The highest conception of all was apparently by the older Stoics declared to be the conception of Being. Since, however, speaking strictly, only what is material can be said to have any being, and many of our notions refer to incorporeal and therefore unreal objects, the conception of Something[3]

[1] The Stoics attack the Aristotelian categories for being too numerous, and endeavoured to show that they do not include every kind of expression (as if, rejoined *Simplicius*, Categ. 5, α, this was the point at all). Compare *Simpl.* Categ. 5, α; 15, δ; 16, δ, who quotes these as objections raised by Athenodorus and Cornutus, the former living in the time of Augustus, the latter in the reign of Nero. Observations of these writers on some of the Aristotelian categories are given, *Ibid.* 47, ζ, 91, α.

[2] That such was the intended position of the Aristotelian categories appears by the way in which they were introduced, no less than by the inquiry (Phys. v. 2) into the various kinds of motion—this inquiry being entirely based on the idea of their co-ordination.

[3] It will thus be understood how the ancients could at one time speak of ὄν, at another of τί, as being the highest conception of the Stoics. The former is found in *Diog.* 61: γενικώτατον δέ ἐστιν ὃ γένος ὃν γένος οὐκ ἔχει, οἷον τὸ ὄν. *Sen.* Ep. 58, 8: Nunc autem genus illud primum quærimus, ex quo ceteræ species suspensæ sunt, a quo nascitur omnis divisio, quo universa comprehensa sunt; after noticing the distinction between what is material and what is immaterial, he proceeds: quid

was in later times put in the place of the conception
of Being. This indefinite Something comprehends
alike what is material and what is not material—in
other words, what has being and what has not being;
and the Stoics appear to have made this contrast
the basis of a real division of things.[1] When it
becomes a question, however, of formal elementary
conceptions or categories, other points are emphasised
having no connection with the division into things
material and things not material. Of this kind are the

ergo erit, ex quo hæc dedu-
cantur? illud . . . quod est [τὸ
ὂν] . . . quod est aut corporale
est aut incorporale. Hoc ergo
genus est primum et antiquissi-
mum et, ut ita dicam, generale
[τὸ γενικώτατον]. It is, however, more usual to find τί.
Thus *Plotin.* Enn. vi. 1, 25 : κοινὸν τὶ καὶ ἐπὶ πάντων ἓν γένος
λαμβάνουσι. *Alex. Aphrod.* Top.
155 ; Schol. 278, b, 20 : οὕτω
δεικνύοις ἂν ὅτι μὴ καλῶς τὸ τὶ οἱ
ἀπὸ στοᾶς γένος τοῦ ὄντος (τὶ as
the genus, of which ὂν is a
species) τίθενται· εἰ γὰρ τὶ, δῆλον
ὅτι καὶ ὂν . . . ἀλλ᾽ ἐκεῖνοι νο-
μοθετήσαντες αὐτοῖς τὸ ὂν κατὰ
σωμάτων μόνων λέγεσθαι διαφεύ-
γοιεν ἂν τὸ ἠπορημένον· διὰ τοῦτο
γὰρ τὸ τὶ γενικώτερον αὐτοῦ φασιν
εἶναι κατηγορούμενον οὐ κατὰ σωμάτων μόνον ἀλλὰ καὶ ἀσωμάτων.
Schol. in Arist. 34, b, 11. *Sext.*
Pyrrh. ii. 86 : τὸ τὶ, ὅπερ φασὶν
εἶναι πάντων γενικώτατον. Math.
x. 234 : The Stoics affirm τῶν
τινῶν τὰ μὲν εἶναι σώματα τὰ δὲ
ἀσώματα. *Sen.* l. c. 13 : Stoici volunt superponere huic etiam-
nunc aliud genus magis principale . . . primum genus Stoicis

quibusdam videtur quid, for in
rerum, inquiunt, natura quaedam
sunt, quaedam non sunt : examples of the latter are centaurs, giants, and similar notions of unreal things. Ritter,
iii. 566, remarks, with justice,
that the older teaching must
have placed the conception of
Being at the head ; otherwise
the objection could not have
been raised, that what has not
being is thus made an object of
thought. Probably the change
was made by Chrysippus, although it is not definitely proved
by *Stob.* Ecl. i. 390. *Petersen*
confuses the two views, in
thinking (p. 146) that the
Stoics divided Something into
Being and Not Being, subdivid-
ing Being again into what is
material and what is not material. In other respects, too,
he confounds the Stoic teaching with the consequences,
whereby *Plotinus* l. c. and *Plut.*
Comm. Not. 30, sought to refute
it.

[1] See previous note and p.
92, 2.

four highest conceptions,[1]—all subordinate to the conception of Something, viz. *subject-matter* or *substance* (τὸ ὑποκείμενον), *property* or *form* (τὸ ποιὸν), *variety* (τὸ πῶς ἔχον), and *variety of relation* (τὸ πρός τί πῶς ἔχον).[2]

(β) Category of subject-matter or substance.

The first of these categories [3] denotes the subject-matter of things in themselves (τὸ ὑποκείμενον), the material of which they are made, irrespective of any and every quality,[4] the something which underlies all definite being, and which alone has a substantial value.[5] Following Aristotle, the Stoics

[1] The Stoics appear to have regarded them as γενικώτατα or πρῶτα γένη, rather than as categories. Conf. *Simpl.* Categ. 16, δ (in other places as 51, β; 79, β, he is speaking for himself and not of the Stoic categories): *Marc. Aurel.* vi. 14; κατηγορία did not suit them so well because of their use of κατηγόρημα. See p. 95, 1.

[2] *Simpl.* 16, δ: οἱ δέ γε Στωϊκοὶ εἰς ἐλάττονα συστέλλειν ἐξιοῦσι τὸν τῶν πρώτων γενῶν ἀριθμόν . . . ποιοῦνται γὰρ τὴν τομὴν εἰς τέσσαρα· εἰς ὑποκείμενα καὶ ποιὰ καὶ πῶς ἔχοντα καὶ πρὸς τί πῶς ἔχοντα. *Plot.* En. vi. 1, 25; *Plut.* Comm. Not. 44, 6. p. 1083.

[3] Instead of ὑποκείμενον, the Aristotelian category of being, οὐσία, was substituted by some, not only without the School, but also by Posidonius, who in *Stob.* Ecl. i. 434 distinguishes οὐσία and ποιὸς the change of the one and the other. Similarly his fellow-disciple Mnesarchus.

[4] *Porphyr.* in Simpl. 12, δ: ἥ τε γὰρ ἄποιος ὕλη . . . πρῶτόν

ἐστι τοῦ ὑποκειμένου σημαινόμενον. *Plot.* 588, B : ὑποκείμενα μὲν γὰρ πρῶτα τάξαντες καὶ τὴν ὕλην ἐνταῦθα τῶν ἄλλων προτάξαντες. *Galen.* Qu. Qual. S. Incorp. 6, xix. 478 : λέγουσι μόνην τὴν πρώτην ὕλην ἀΐδιον τὴν ἄποιον. Compare following note. It would seem to follow, as a matter of course, from the Stoic belief in immaterial properties, see p. 106, 4, that the Stoics also believed in immaterial substances (*Petersen*, 60); but contradicting as this would their belief that reality only belongs to material things, and being mentioned by no authority, although obviously so open to the criticism of opponents, it is safer to suppose that they never went so far as to state the belief in words.

[5] *Simpl.* 44, δ: ἔοικε Στωϊκῇ τινι συνηθείᾳ συνεπέσθαι, οὐδὲν ἄλλο ἢ τὸ ὑποκείμενον εἶναι νομίζων, τὰς δὲ περὶ αὐτὸ διαφορὰς ἀνυποστάτους ἡγούμενος. *Diog.* 150. *Stob.* Ecl. i. 322 (see below 101, 2) and 324 : ἔφησε δὲ ὁ Ποσειδώνιος τὴν τῶν ὅλων οὐσίαν

distinguish,[1] in this category of matter, between matter in general, or universal matter, and the particular matter or material out of which individual things are made. The former alone is incapable of being increased or diminished. Far otherwise is the material of which particular things are made. This can be increased and diminished, and, indeed, is ever undergoing change; so much so, that the only feature which continues the same during the whole term of its existence[2] constituting its identity, is its quality.

καὶ ὕλην ἄποιον καὶ ἄμορφον εἶναι, καθ' ὅσον οὐδὲν ἀποτεταγμένον ἴδιον ἔχει σχῆμα οὐδὲ ποιότητα κατ' αὐτήν [καθ' αὐτὴν] · ἀεὶ δ' ἔν τινι σχήματι καὶ ποιότητι εἶναι. διαφέρειν δὲ τὴν οὐσίαν τῆς ὕλης, τὴν οὖσαν κατὰ τὴν ὑπόστασιν, ἐπινοίᾳ μόνον. *Simpl.* Phys. 50: τὸ ἄποιον σῶμα τὴν πρωτίστην ὕλην εἶναί φασιν. Further particulars on matter hereafter.

[1] *Porphyr.* in Simpl. Cat. 12, δ: διττόν ἐστι τὸ ὑποκείμενον οὐ μόνον κατὰ τοὺς ἀπὸ τῆς στοᾶς ἀλλὰ κατὰ τοὺς πρεσβυτέρους. *Dexipp.* See following note.

[2] *Diog.* 150: οὐσίαν δέ φασι τῶν ὄντων ἁπάντων τὴν πρώτην ὕλην. So thought Zeno and Chrysippus: ὕλη δέ ἐστιν ἐξ ἧς ὁτιδηποτοῦν γίνεται. καλεῖται δὲ διχῶς οὐσία τε καὶ ὕλη, ἥ τε τῶν πάντων καὶ ἡ τῶν ἐπὶ μέρος. ἡ μὲν οὖν τῶν ὅλων οὔτε πλείων οὔτε ἐλάττων γίνεται, ἡ δὲ τῶν ἐπὶ μέρους καὶ πλείων καὶ ἐλάττων. *Stob.* Ecl. i. 322: (Ζήνωνος·) οὐσίαν δὲ εἶναι τὴν τῶν ὄντων πάντων πρώτην ὕλην, ταύτην πᾶσαν ἀίδιον καὶ οὔτε πλείω γιγνομένην οὔτε ἐλάττω, τὰ δὲ μέρη

ταύτης οὐκ ἀεὶ ταὐτὰ διαμένειν, ἀλλὰ διαιρεῖσθαι καὶ συγχεῖσθαι. The same was held by Chrysippus, according to *Stob.* Ecl. i. 432, who says: Posidonius held that there were four varieties of change, those κατὰ διαίρεσιν, κατ' ἀλλοίωσιν (water to air), κατὰ σύγχυσιν (chemical combination), κατ' ἀνάλυσιν, the latter also called τὴν ἐξ ὅλων μεταβολήν. τούτων δὲ τὴν κατ' ἀλλοίωσιν περὶ τὴν οὐσίαν γίγνεσθαι (the elements, according to the Stoics, changing into each other) τὰς δὲ ἄλλας τρεῖς περὶ τοὺς ποιοὺς λεγομένους τοὺς ἐπὶ τῆς οὐσίας γιγνομένους. ἀκολούθως δὲ τούτοις καὶ τὰς γενέσεις συμβαίνειν. τὴν γὰρ οὐσίαν οὔτ' αὔξεσθαι οὔτε μειοῦσθαι . . . ἐπὶ δὲ τῶν ἰδίως ποιῶν (which may be understood, not of individual properties, but of individually determined things) οἶον Δίωνος καὶ Θέωνος, καὶ αὐξήσεις καὶ μειώσεις γίγνεσθαι. (These words are explained by *Prantl*, 432, thus: qualitative determination admits increase or decrease of intensity; but the use of the

(γ) *The
category of
property
or form.*

The second category, that of property[1] or form,
comprises all those essential attributes, by means of

terms αὔξησις and μείωσις, and
indeed the whole context no
less than the passage quoted
from Diogenes, prove that they
refer rather to the increase or
diminution of substance in the
individual thing.) διὸ καὶ παρα-
μένειν τὴν ἑκάστου ποιότητα ἀπὸ
τῆς γενέσεως μέχρι τῆς ἀναιρέσεως.
... ἐπὶ δὲ τῶν ἰδίως ποιῶν δύο
μὲν εἶναί φασι τὰ δεκτικὰ μόρια
(individual things have two
component parts, which are
capable of change), τὸ μέν τι
κατὰ τὴν τῆς οὐσίας ὑπόστασιν τὸ
δέ τι κατὰ τὴν τοῦ ποίου. τὸ γὰρ
[ἰδίως ποιὸν] ὡς πολλάκις λέγομεν
τὴν αὔξησιν καὶ τὴν μείωσιν ἐπιδέ-
χεσθαι. *Porphyr.* See previous
note. *Dexipp.* in Cat. 31, 15,
Speng.: ὡς ἔστι τὸ ὑποκείμενον
διττὸν, οὐ μόνον κατὰ τοὺς ἀπὸ τῆς
στοᾶς ἀλλὰ καὶ κατὰ τοὺς πρεσβυτέρους, ἐν μὲν τὸ λεγόμενον πρῶτον ὑποκείμενον, ὡς ἡ ἄποιος ὕλη
... δεύτερον δὲ ὑποκείμενον τὸ
ποιὸν ἢ κοινῶς ἢ ἰδίως ὑφίσταται,
ὑποκείμενον γὰρ καὶ ὁ χαλκὸς καὶ
ὁ Σωκράτης. *Plut.* Comm. Not.
44, 4, p. 1083 (the Stoics assert)
ὡς δύο ὄντων ἡμῶν ἕκαστός ἐστιν ὑποκείμενα, τὸ μὲν οὐσία, τὸ δὲ [ποιόν].
καὶ τὸ μὲν ἀεὶ ῥεῖ καὶ φέρεται, μήτ'
αὐξόμενον μήτε μειούμενον, μήτε
ὅλως οἷόν ἐστι διαμένον, τὸ δὲ
διαμένει καὶ αὐξάνεται καὶ μειοῦται
καὶ πάντα πάσχει τἀναντία θατέρῳ
συμπεφυκὸς καὶ συνηρμοσμένον καὶ
συγκεχυμένον, καὶ τῆς διαφορᾶς τῇ
αἰσθήσει μηδαμοῦ παρέχον ἅψασθαι.
The latter is the individual
thing itself, the former the material thereof, in reference to
which Plutarch had just said:
τὰ λήμματα συγχωροῦσιν οὗτοι,

τὰς [μὲν] ἐν μέρει πάσας οὐσίας
ῥεῖν καὶ φέρεσθαι, τὰ μὲν ἐξ αὐτῶν
μεθείσας, τὰ δὲ ποθὲν ἐπιόντα
προσδεχομένας· οἷς δὲ πρόσεισι
καὶ ἄπεισιν ἀριθμοῖς καὶ πλήθεσιν,
ταῦτα μὴ διαμένειν, ἀλλ' ἕτερα
γίγνεσθαι ταῖς εἰρημέναις προσό-
δοις, ἐξαλλαγὴν τῆς οὐσίας λαμ-
βανούσης. That of this perpetually changing material it
should be said μήτ' αὐξόμενον
μήτε μειούμενον may appear
strange; but the meaning is
this: it can only be said of an
individual thing that it increases and diminishes in so
far as it remains as one and
the same subject, an ἰδίως ποιὸν
during the change; but the
material itself, which is ever
changing, cannot be regarded
as the one identical subject of
increase and diminution. This
idea is expanded by *Alex.
Aphro.* Quæst. Nat. I. 5.

[1] ποιὸν or ποιότης, and also
ποιὸς (sc. λόγος). According to
Simpl. 55, a, many Stoics assign
a threefold meaning to ποιόν.
The first, which is also the most
extensive meaning, includes
every kind of quality, whether
essential or accidental—the πὼς
ἔχον as well as the ποιόν. In
the second meaning ποιὸν is
used to express *permanent* qualities, including those which are
derivative and non-essential—
the σχέσεις. In the third and
narrowest sense it expresses
τοὺς ἀπαρτίζοντας (κατὰ τὴν ἐκφορὰν) καὶ ἐμμόνως ὄντας κατὰ
διαφορὰν ποιοὺς, i.e. those qualities which faithfully represent
essential attributes in their

which a definite character is impressed on matter otherwise indeterminate.[1] If the definite character

distinctive features. The substantive ποιότης is only used in the last sense.

[1] *Simpl.* 57, ε (the passage is fully discussed by *Petersen*, 85, and *Trendelenburg*, 223): οἱ δὲ Στωϊκοὶ τὸ κοινὸν τῆς ποιότητος τὸ ἐπὶ τῶν σωμάτων λέγουσι διαφορὰν εἶναι οὐσίας οὐκ ἀποδιαληπτὴν (separable, i.e., from matter) καθ᾽ ἑαυτὴν, ἀλλ᾽ εἰς ἓν νόημα καὶ ἰδιότητα [sc. μίαν] ἀπολήγουσαν οὔτε χρόνῳ οὔτε ἰσχύϊ εἰδοποιουμένην, ἀλλὰ τῇ ἐξ αὐτῆς τοιουτότητι, καθ᾽ ἣν ποιοῦ ὑφίσταται γένεσις. In place of ἓν νόημα *Petersen*, 85, with the approval of *Trendelenburg* and *Prantl* (433, 96), reads ἐννόημα. To me, *Brandis* Schol. 69, a, 32, appears to retain it with reason, the meaning being that ποιότης constitutes no independent unity, but only a unity of conception. Non-essential qualities were by the Stoics excluded from the category of ποιὸν, and reckoned under that of πὼς ἔχον.

The same distinction between what is essential and what is not essential is indicated in the terms ἕξις and σχέσις· ποιότητες, or essential properties, being called essential forms (ἕξεις or ἐκτά); non-essential qualities being called features or varieties (σχέσεις). See *Simpl.* 54, γ; 55, ε. In determining essential attributes, these, according to *Simpl.* 61, β (Schol. in Arist. 70, b, 43), are declared to be essential, not when they happen to be permanent, but when they spring from

the nature of the object to which they belong : τὰς μὲν γὰρ σχέσεις ταῖς ἐπικτήτοις καταστάσεσι χαρακτηρίζεσθαι τὰς δὲ ἕξεις ταῖς ἐξ ἑαυτῶν ἐνεργείαις. A more limited meaning, that of local position, is given to σχέσις in *Stob.* Ecl. i. 410.

The distinction between ἕνωσις and συναφὴ also belongs here. Only that, the oneness of which depends on an essential quality is ἡνωμένον· everything else is either συνημμένον or ἐκ διεστώτων. *Sext.* Math. ix. 78 (also in vii. 102) : τῶν τε σωμάτων τὰ μέν ἐστιν ἡνωμένα τὰ δὲ ἐκ συναπτομένων τὰ δὲ ἐκ διεστώτων· ἡνωμένα μὲν οὖν ἐστι τὰ ὑπὸ μιᾶς ἕξεως κρατούμενα, καθάπερ φυτὰ καὶ ζῷα· συνάφεια applies to chains, houses, ships, &c. ; combination ἐκ διεστώτων to flocks and armies. *Seneca*, Ep. 102, 6, Nat. Qu. ii. 2, says the same. Conf. *Alex.* De Mixt. 143 : ἀνάγκη δὲ τὸ ἓν σῶμα ὑπὸ μιᾶς ὥς φασιν ἕξεως συνελέσθαι [l. συνέχεσθαι]. *Simpl.* 55, ε : τὰς γὰρ ποιότητας ἐκτὰ λέγοντες οὗτοι [οἱ Στωϊκοὶ] ἐπὶ τῶν ἡνωμένων μόνων ἐκτὰ ἀπολείπουσιν· ἐπὶ δὲ τῶν κατὰ συναφὴν, οἷον νεὼς, καὶ ἐπὶ τῶν κατὰ διάστασιν, οἷον στρατοῦ, μηδὲν εἶναι ἐκτὸν μηδὲ εὑρίσκεσθαι πνευματικόν τι ἣν ἐπ᾽ αὐτῶν μηδὲ ἕνα λόγον ἔχον ὥστε ἐπί τινα ὑπόστασιν ἐλθεῖν μιᾶς ἕξεως.

Those ἕξεις which admit of no increase or diminution (ἐπίτασις, and ἄνεσις) are called διαθέσεις or *permanent forms*. Virtues, for instance, which, according to the Stoics, always exist in a perfect form where

be one which belongs to a group or class, it is called
a common quality—κοινῶς ποιόν·—or, if it be something peculiar and distinctive, it is called a distinctive
quality—ἰδίως ποιόν.[1] Properties therefore combined
with matter constitute the special materials out of
which individual things are made;[2] and quality in
this combination (ποιόν), corresponds, as Trendelenburg has well shown,[3] with the form (εἶδος) of
Aristotle.[4] It may, in fact, like that, be described

they exist at all, are διαθέσεις,
but arts are only ἕξεις. *Simpl.*
Categ. 61, β ; 72, δ ; 73, β ; Schol.
in Arist. 70, b, 28 ; 76, a, 12,
24 ; *Stob.* Ecl. ii. 98 and 128.
Conf. *Petersen* 91. A different
view was taken by Aristotle
of the relations of these expressions.
  [1] *Syrian.* on Arist. Metaph.
21, p. 90 in *Petersen*: καὶ οἱ Στωϊκοὶ
δὲ τοὺς κοινοὺς ποιοὺς πρὸ τῶν ἰδίων
ποιῶν ἀποτίθενται. *Stob.* Ecl. i.
434 ; see above p. 101, 2. *Simpl.*
De An. 61, a, explains ἰδίως ποιὸς
by ἀτομωθὲν εἶδος. *Diog.* vii.
138 ; *Plut.* C. Not. 36, 3.
  [2] Besides the passages already
quoted in note 2 on p. 101, from
Plutarch and Stobæus, see *Sext.*
Pyrrh. i. 57 : τὰ κιρνάμενα (the
intermingling materials,—the
question here is the possibility
of mingling) ἐξ οὐσίας καὶ ποιοτήτων συγκεῖσθαί φασιν. *Por-
phyry* in *Simpl.* Categ. 12, δ
contests this view himself.
The Stoics, therefore, clearly
distinguish ἕξις, or *essential
form,* from the subject to which
it belongs ; and Philo must
have been following the Stoics
when he said (Nom. Mutat.
1063, D) : ἕξεις γὰρ τῶν κατ'

αὐτὰς ποιῶν ἀμείνους, ὡς μουσικὴ
μουσικοῦ, κ.τ.λ. They also distinguish between a thing and
its οὐσία. *Stob.* Ecl. i. 436 : μὴ
εἶναί τε ταὐτὸν τό τι ποιὸν ἰδίως
καὶ τὴν οὐσίαν ἐξ ἧς ἔστι τοῦτο, μὴ
μέντοι γε μηδ' ἕτερον, ἀλλὰ μόνον
οὐ ταὐτὸν, διὰ τὸ καὶ μέρος εἶναι
τῆς οὐσίας καὶ τὸν αὐτὸν ἐπέχειν
τόπον, τὰ δ' ἕτερα τινῶν λεγόμενα
δεῖν καὶ τόπῳ κεχωρίσθαι καὶ μηδ'
ἐν μέρει θεωρεῖσθαι. Conf. *Sext.*
Pyrrh. iii. 170 ; Math. ix. 336 :
οἱ δὲ Στωϊκοὶ οὔτε ἕτερον τοῦ ὅλου
τὸ μέρος οὔτε τὸ αὐτό φασιν
ὑπάρχειν · and *Seneca,* Ep. 313,
4. Mnesarchus, a fellow disciple of Posidonius, accordingly
compares the relation of an
individual thing to its (οὐσία)
with that of a statue to the
material of which it is composed. Since the ἰδίως ποιὸς
distinguishes a thing from
every other, there follows as a
matter of course, what is asserted circumstantially and in
detail by Chrysippus (in *Philo,*
Incorrupt. M. 951, B), ὅτι δύο
εἰδοποιοὺς [= ἰδίως ποιοὺς] ἐπὶ τῆς
αὐτῆς οὐσίας ἀμήχανον συστῆ-
ναι.
  [3] L. c. 222.
  [4] This may be seen from the

as the active and efficient part of a thing.[1] Aristotle's form, however, expresses only the non-material side of a thing, whereas quality is regarded by the Stoics as something material—in fact, as an air-current.[2] Hence the mode in which a quality is conceived to reside in matter is that of an intermingling of elements.[3] The same theory of intermingling applies of course to the union of several properties in one and the same matter,[4] and likewise to the combination of

passages quoted in note 2 on the previous page.

[1] *Plut.* St. Rep. 43, 4, p. 1054: τὴν ὕλην ἀργὸν ἐξ ἑαυτῆς καὶ ἀκίνητον ὑποκεῖσθαι ταῖς ποιότησιν ἀποφαίνουσι, τὰς δὲ ποιότητας πνεύματα οὔσας καὶ τόνους ἀερώδεις οἷς ἂν ἐγγένωνται μέρεσι τῆς ὕλης εἰδοποιεῖν ἕκαστα καὶ σχηματίζειν. It is a carrying out of the Stoic teaching (as *Simpl.* 57, ε, remarks) for Plotinus to reduce ποιότης to the class-conception of δύναμις (Enn. vi. 1, 10, 574, β). But the Stoic definition of δύναμις (quoted by *Simpl.* 58, α—ἡ πλειόνων ἐποιστικὴ συμπτωμάτων, with the additional words καὶ κατακρατοῦσα τῶν ἐνεργειῶν—does not directly refer to ποιότης. Ποιότης may also be connected with the λόγος σπερματικός. See *Plotin.* i. 29, 593, A: εἰ δὲ τὰ ποιὰ ὕλην ποιὰν λέγοιεν, πρῶτον μὲν οἱ λόγοι αὐτοῖς ἔνυλοι ἀλλ' οὐκ ἐν ὕλῃ γενόμενοι σύνθετόν τι ποιήσουσιν . . . οὐκ ἄρα αὐτοὶ εἴδη οὐδὲ λόγοι. *Diog.* vii. 148: ἔστι δὲ φύσις ἕξις [=ποιότης] ἐξ αὑτῆς κινουμένη, κατὰ σπερματικοὺς λόγους ἀποτελοῦσά τε καὶ συνέχουσα τὰ ἐξ αὑτῆς, κ.τ.λ.

[2] *Plut.* Ibid. § 2: (Χρύσιππος)

ἐν τοῖς περὶ ἕξεων οὐδὲν ἄλλο τὰς ἕξεις πλὴν ἀέρας εἶναί φησιν· ὑπὸ τούτων γὰρ συνέχεται τὰ σώματα, καὶ τοῦ ποιὸν ἕκαστον εἶναι αἴτιος ὁ συνέχων ἀήρ ἐστιν, ὃν σκληρότητα μὲν ἐν σιδήρῳ, πυκνότητα δ' ἐν λίθῳ, λευκότητα δ' ἐν ἀργύρῳ καλοῦσιν. *Simpl.* 69, γ: ἡ τῶν Στωϊκῶν δόξα λεγόντων, σώματα εἶναι τὰ σχήματα ὥσπερ τὰ ἄλλα ποιά. Ibid. 67, ε; 56, δ: πῶς δὲ καὶ πνευματικὴ ἡ οὐσία ἔσται τῶν σωματικῶν ποιοτήτων αὐτοῦ τοῦ πνεύματος συνθέτου ὄντος, κ.τ.λ.

[3] *Alex. Aphr.* De An. 143, b: πῶς δὲ σωζόντων ἐστὶ τὴν περὶ κράσεως κοινὴν πρόληψιν τὸ λέγειν καὶ τὴν ἕξιν τοῖς ἔχουσιν αὐτὴν μεμίχθαι καὶ τὴν φύσιν τοῖς φυτοῖς καὶ τὸ φῶς τῷ ἀέρι καὶ τὴν ψυχὴν τῷ σώματι. Ibid. 144, α, the saying is quoted against the Stoics: μεμίχθαι τῇ ὕλῃ τὸν θεόν.

[4] *Plut.* C. Not. 36, 3: λέγουσιν οὗτοι καὶ πλάττουσιν ἐπὶ μιᾶς οὐσίας δύο ἰδίως γενέσθαι ποίους (this follows from their hypothesis, but it is distinctly denied by Chrysippus *in thesis*. See p. 104, 2) καὶ τὴν αὐτὴν οὐσίαν ἕνα ποιὸν ἰδίως ἔχουσαν ἐπιόντος ἑτέρου δέχεσθαι καὶ διαφυλάττειν ὁμοίως ἀμφοτέρους.

CHAP.
V.

several attributes to produce a single conception of quality.[1] In all cases the relation is supposed to be a materialistic one, and is explained by the doctrine of the mutual interpenetration of material things.[2] This explanation, indeed, could not apply to every kind of attributes. Unable to dispense entirely with things not material,[3] the Stoics were obliged to admit the existence of attributes belonging to immaterial things, these attributes being, of course, themselves not material.[4] What idea they formed to themselves

[1] *Simpl.* 70, ε: καὶ οἱ Στωϊκοὶ δὲ ποιότητας ποιοτήτων ποιοῦσιν ἑαυτῶν (? ἐκτῶν) ποιοῦντες ἐκτὰς ἕξεις [1. ἐκτὰ καὶ ἕξεις or ἕξεις only]. The context shows that the meaning of these words is that given above. The conception of a property is compounded of several attributes, and, therefore, a property of several subordinate properties. If λευκὸν is a χρῶμα, the διακριτικὸν ὄψεως is the ἕξις, or form of λευκόν.

[2] This follows of necessity, quite independently of the above quoted language of Alexander, from the Stoic doctrine of the material nature of properties and of the mingling of materials. For if that intermingling of materials in which each one retains its properties (μῖξις and κρᾶσις in contrast to chemical combination παράθεσις and σύγχυσις) is defined to be the complete interpenetration of one material by another, without passing into a third (*Stob.* Ecl. i. 376; *Alex.* De Mixt. 142, a; *Plut.* C. Not. 37, 2); if, moreover, properties are

said to be material; and in all cases when they are combined, each property retains its own peculiarity, and yet is inherent in the subject-matter and in every other property belonging to the same subject-matter; it follows that this relation can only be explained by supposing a mutual interpenetration of properties with each other and with their subject-matter.

[3] The proof of this will be given subsequently. Meantime compare the remarks, p. 92, 2; 94, 1 on the λεκτόν.

[4] *Simpl.* 56, δ, and 54, β: οἱ δὲ Στωϊκοὶ τῶν μὲν σωμάτων σωματικὰς, τῶν δὲ ἀσωμάτων ἀσωμάτους εἶναι λέγουσι τὰς ποιότητας. Only the σωματικαὶ ποιότητες are πνεύματα, see p. 105, 2; incorporeal properties are called ἐκτὰ, to distinguish them from ἕξεις (essential forms). *Dexipp.* in Cat. 61, 17, Speng.: θαυμάζω δὲ τῶν Στωϊκῶν χωριζόντων τὰς ἕξεις ἀπὸ τῶν ἐκτῶν· ἀσώματα γὰρ μὴ παραδεχόμενοι καθ' ἑαυτὰ, ὅταν ἐρεσχελεῖν δεόν ᾖ ἐπὶ τὰς τοιαύτας διαλήψεις ἔρχονται. But this use of terms appears not to have

of these incorporeal attributes, when reality was considered to belong only to things corporeal, it is, of
course, impossible for us to determine.[1]

The two remaining categories include everything
which may be excluded from the conception of a
thing on the ground of being either non-essential or
accidental. In so far as such things belong to the
object taken by itself alone, they come under the
category of variety (πὼς ἔχον); but when they belong
to it, because of its relation to something else, they
come under the category of variety of relation (πρὸς
τί πως ἔχον). Variety includes all accidental qualities, which can be assigned to any object independently of its relation to any other object.[2] Size,
colour, place, time, action, passion, possession, motion, state, in short, all the Aristotelian categories,
with the exception of substance, whenever they apply
to an object independently of its relation to other
objects, belong to the category of variety[3] (πὼς ἔχον).

CHAP.
V.

(δ) *The
categories
of variety
and
variety of
relation.*

---

been universal among the Stoics
(*Simpl.* Categ. 54, γ), with
whom different views prevailed
touching the extent of the conception of ἐκτόν. According to
this passage it was Antipater
who wished to include under
ἐκτὰ, the κοινὰ συμπτώματα
σωμάτων καὶ ἀσωμάτων.

[1] Conf. *Simpl.* 57, ε, who
after giving the definition of
quality, quoted p. 103, 1, continues: ἐν δὲ τούτοις, εἰ μὴ οἷόν
τε κατὰ τὸν ἐκείνων λόγον κοινὸν
εἶναι σύμπτωμα σωμάτων τε καὶ
ἀσωμάτων, οὐκέτι ἔσται γένος ἢ
ποιότης, ἀλλ᾽ ἑτέρως μὲν ἐπὶ τῶν

σωμάτων ἑτέρως δὲ ἐπὶ τῶν ἀσωμάτων αὕτη ὑφέστηκε.

[2] *Simpl.* 44, δ: ὁ δὲ τὴν
στάσιν καὶ τὴν κάθισιν μὴ προσ-
ποιούμενος (including sc. τοῖς
οὖσιν) ἔοικε Στωϊκῇ τινι συνηθείᾳ
συνέπεσθαι οὐδὲν ἄλλο ἢ τὸ
ὑποκείμενον εἶναι νομίζων, τὰς δὲ
περὶ αὐτὸ διαφορὰς ἀνυποστάτους
ἡγούμενος καὶ πὼς ἔχοντα αὐτὰ
ἀποκαλῶν ὡς ἐν τοῖς ὑποκειμένοις
ἔχοντα αὐτὸ τοῦτο τὸ πὼς ἔχειν.

[3] *Dexipp.* in Cat. 41, 20,
Speng.: εἰ δέ τις εἰς τὸ πὼς ἔχον
συντάττοι τὰς πλείστας κατη-
γορίας, ὥσπερ οἱ Στωϊκοὶ ποιοῦσιν.
Plotin. vi. 1, 30, 594, A: πῶς δὲ

On the other hand, those features and states which are purely relative—such as right and left, sonship and fatherhood, &c.—come under the category of variety of relation (πρός τί πως ἔχον); a category from which the simple notion of relation (πρὸς τὶ) must be distinguished. Simple relation (πρὸς τὶ) is not spoken of as a distinct category, since it includes not only accidental relations, but also those essential properties (ποιὰ) which presuppose a definite relation to something else—such as knowledge and perception.[1]

ἐν τὸ πὼς ἔχον, πολλῆς διαφορᾶς ἐν αὐτοῖς οὔσης; πῶς γὰρ τὸ τρίπηχυ καὶ τὸ λευκὸν εἰς ἐν [γένος θετέον], τοῦ μὲν ποσοῦ τοῦ δὲ ποιοῦ ὄντος; πῶς δὲ τὸ ποτὲ καὶ τὸ ποῦ; πῶς δὲ ὅλως πὼς ἔχοντα τὸ χθὲς καὶ τὸ πέρυσι καὶ τὸ ἐν Λυκείῳ καὶ ἐν ᾿Ακαδηγίᾳ; καὶ ὅλως πῶς δὲ ὁ χρόνος πὼς ἔχον; ... τὸ δὲ ποιεῖν πὼς πὼς ἔχον ... καὶ ὁ πάσχον οὐ πὼς ἔχον ... ἴσως δ᾽ ἂν μόνον ἁρμόσει ἐπὶ τοῦ κεῖσθαι τὸ πὼς ἔχον καὶ ἐπὶ τοῦ ἔχειν · ἐπὶ δὲ τοῦ ἔχειν οὐ πὼς ἔχον ἀλλὰ ἔχον. Simpl. Categ. 94, ε: The Stoics included ἔχειν under πὼς ἔχον. In saying as Simpl. 16, δ, does that the Stoics omitted ποσὸν, time, and place, it must be meant that they did not treat these conceptions as separate categories. What they did with them Simpl. explains l. c. εἰ γὰρ τὸ πὼς ἔχον νομίζουσιν αὐτοῖς τὰ τοιαῦτα περιλαμβάνειν. Trendelenburg, 229, with justice, observes that, wherever the species-forming difference lies in ποσὸν as in mathematical conceptions, there ποσὸν comes under ποιόν.

[1] Simpl. 42, ε: οἱ δὲ Στωϊκοὶ ἀνθ᾽ ἑνὸς γένους δύο κατὰ τὸν τόπον τοῦτον ἀριθμοῦνται, τὰ μὲν ἐν τοῖς πρός τι τιθέντες, τὰ δ᾽ ἐν τοῖς πρός τί πως ἔχουσι, καὶ τὰ μὲν πρός τι ἀντιδιαιροῦντες τοῖς καθ᾽ αὐτὰ, τὰ δὲ πρός τί πως ἔχοντα τοῖς κατὰ διαφοράν. (Ibid. 44, β: οἱ Στωϊκοὶ νομίζουσι πάσης τῆς κατὰ διαφορὰν ἰδιότητος ἀπηλλάχθαι τὰ πρός τί πως ἔχοντα.) Sweet and bitter belong to τὰ πρός τι · to the other class belong δεξιὸς, πατὴρ, &c., κατὰ διαφορὰν δέ φασι τὰ κατά τι εἶδος χαρακτηριζόμενα. Every καθ᾽ αὐτὸ is also κατὰ διαφορὰν (determined as to quality), and every πρός τί πως ἔχον is also a πρός τι, but not conversely. Conf. 43, β. εἰ δὲ δεῖ σαφέστερον μεταλαβεῖν τὰ λεγόμενα, πρός τι μὲν λέγουσιν ὅσα κατ᾽ οἰκεῖον χαρακτῆρα διακείμενά πως ἀπονεύει πρὸς ἕτερον (or, according to the definition in Sext. Math. viii. 454: πρός τι ἐστὶ τὸ πρὸς ἑτέρῳ νοούμενον), πρός τι δέ πως ἔχοντα ὅσα πέφυκε συμβαίνειν τινὶ καὶ μὴ συμβαίνειν ἄνευ τῆς περὶ αὐτὰ μεταβολῆς καὶ ἀλλοιώσεως μετὰ τοῦ πρὸς τὸ ἐκτὸς

The relation of these four categories to one another is such, that each preceding category is included in the one next following, and receives from it a more definite character.[1] Substance never occurs in reality without property, but has always some definite quality to give it a character. On the other hand, property is never met with alone, but always in connection with some subject-matter.[2] Variety presupposes some definite substance, and variety of relation supposes the existence of variety.[3] It will hereafter be

ἀποβλέπειν, ὥστε ὅταν μὲν κατὰ διαφοράν τι διακείμενον πρὸς ἕτερον νεύσῃ, πρός τι μόνον τοῦτο ἔσται, ὡς ἡ ἕξις καὶ ἡ ἐπιστήμη καὶ ἡ αἴσθησις· ὅταν δὲ μὴ κατὰ τὴν ἐνοῦσαν διαφορὰν κατὰ ψιλὴν δὲ τὴν πρὸς ἕτερον σχέσιν θεωρῆται, πρός τί πως ἔχοντα ἔσται· ὁ γὰρ υἱὸς καὶ ὁ δεξιὸς ἔξωθεν τινῶν προσδεόντα, πρὸς τὴν ὑπόστασιν· διὸ καὶ μηδεμιᾶς γινομένης περὶ αὐτὰ μεταβολῆς γένοιτ' ἂν οὐκέτι πατ-ὴρ, τοῦ υἱοῦ ἀποθανόντος, ὁ δὲ δεξιὸς τοῦ παρακειμένου μεταστάντος· τὸ δὲ γλυκὺ καὶ πικρὸν οὐκ ἂν ἀλλοῖα γένοιτο εἰ μὴ συμμεταβάλλοι καὶ ἡ περὶ αὐτὰ δύναμις. In this sense, therefore, πρός τι belongs to ποιόν, being composed (as *Simpl.* 43, a, says) of ποιόν and πρός τι. On the other hand, πρός τί πως ἔχον only expresses, to quote *Herbart*, an accidental relation. *Prantl's* quotation (I. 437, 108) from *Simpl.* 44, β, we have no special reason to refer to the Stoics.

[1] *Trendelenburg*, 220, considers that these genera are in so far subordinate to one another, that the previous one continues in the next, but with

the addition of a fresh determination; a better name for the second category would be ὑποκείμενα ποιά· for the third, ὑποκείμενα ποιά πως ἔχοντα· for the fourth, ὑποκείμενα ποιά πρός τί πως ἔχοντα. In support of this, he refers to *Simpl.* 43, a: ἔπεται δὲ αὐτοῖς κἀκεῖνο ἄτοπον τὸ σύνθετα ποιεῖν τὰ γένη ἐκ προτέρων τινῶν καὶ δευτέρων ὡς τὸ πρός τι ἐκ ποιοῦ καὶ τοῦ πρός τι. *Plut.* C. Not. 44, 6: τέτταρά γε ποιοῦσιν ὑποκείμενα περὶ ἕκαστον, μᾶλλον δὲ τέτταρα ἕκαστον ἡμῶν. *Plot.* Enn. vi. 1, 29, 593, A: ἄτοπος ἡ διαίρεσις . . . ἐν θατέρῳ τῶν εἰδῶν τὸ ἕτερον τιθεῖσα, ὥσπερ ἂν [εἴ] τις διαιρῶν τὴν ἐπιστήμην τὴν μὲν γραμματικὴν λέγοι, τὴν δὲ γραμματικὴν καὶ ἄλλο τι· if ποιά are to be ὕλη ποιά, they are composed of ὕλη and εἶδος or λόγος. See p. 48, 2.

[2] See p. 103, 1.

[3] See p. 107, 2; *Plotin.* vi. 1, 30: Why are πῶς ἔχοντα enumerated as a third category, since πάντα περὶ τὴν ὕλην πῶς ἔχοντα; the Stoics would probably say that ποιά are περὶ τὴν ὕλην πῶς ἔχοντα, whereas the

CHAP.
V.

(3) Com-
plete ut-
terance.
(a) Judg-
ment.

seen how closely these deductions, and, indeed, the
whole doctrine of the categories, depend on the metaphysical peculiarities of the Stoic system.

Passing from incomplete to complete utterance,
we come, in the first place, to sentences or propositions,[1] all the various kinds of which, as they may be
deduced from the different forms of syntax, were enumerated by the Stoics with the greatest precision.[2]
Detailed information is, however, only forthcoming
in reference to the theory of judgment (ἀξίωμα),
which certainly occupied the greatest and most important place in their speculations. A judgment is
a perfect utterance, which is either true or false.[3]

πὼs ἔχοντα, in the strict sense
of the term, are περὶ τὰ ποιά.
Yet since the ποιά themselves
are nothing more than ὕλη πως
ἔχουσα, all categories must be
ultimately reduced to ὕλη.
  [1] Prantl, Gesch. d. Logik, i.
440–467.
  [2] In Diog. 66; Sext. Math.
viii. 70; Ammon. De Interp. 4,
a (Schol. in Arist. 93, a ; 22, b,
20) ; Simpl. Cat. 103, a ; Boëth.
De Interp. 315 ; Cramer, Anecd.
Oxon. iii. 267, conf. I. 104, a
distinction is drawn between
ἀξίωμα (a judgment), ἐρώτημα (a
direct question, requiring Yes
or No), πύσμα (an inquiry),
προστακτικὸν, ὁρκικὸν, ἀρατικὸν
(wishes), εὐκτικὸν (a prayer),
ὑποθετικὸν (a supposition), ἐκθε-
τικὸν (as ἐκκείσθω εὐθεῖα γραμμὴ),
προσαγορευτικὸν (an address),
θαυμαστικὸν, ψεκτικὸν, ἐπαπορη-
τικὸν, ἀφηγηματικὸν (explanatory
statements), ὅμοιον ἀξιώματι (a
judgment with something ap-
pended, as : ὡς Πριαμίδησιν

ἐμφερὴs ὁ βουκόλοs ! by Sextus
called Πλείον ἢ ἀξίωμα). Ammon.
in Waitz, Arist. Orig. i. 43,
speaks of ten forms of sentences
held by the Stoics, mentioning,
however, only two, προστακτικὸs
and ἐβκτικόs (so reads the MS.
Waitz suggests ἐφεκτικὸs, more
probably it is εὐκτικός). Diog.
191, mentions treatises of
Chrysippus on interrogatory
and hortatory sentences. On
the relation of an oath to ἀξίωμα
light is thrown by Simpl. l. c.,
also by Chrysippus' distinction
between ἀληθορκεῖν and εὐορκεῖν
ψευδορκεῖν and ἐπιορκεῖν in Stob.
Floril. 28, 15.
  [3] Diog. 65 : ἀξίωμα δέ ἐστιν ὃ
ἐστιν ἀληθὲs ἢ ψεῦδος. Questions
and other similar sentences are
neither true nor false (Ibid. 66
and 68). This definition of a
judgment is constantly referred
to, see p. 83, 2, by Simpl. Cat.
103, a ; Cic. Tusc. i. 7, 14 ; De
Fato, 10, 20 ; Gell. N. A. xvi. 8,
8; Schol. in Arist. 93, b, 35.

Judgments are divided into two classes: *simple* judgments, and *composite* judgments.[1] By a simple judgment the Stoics understood a judgment which is purely categorical.[2] Under the head of composite judgments are comprised hypothetical, corroborative, copulative, disjunctive, comparative, and causal judgments.[3] In the case of simple judgments, a greater or less definiteness of expression is substituted by the Stoics in the place of the ordinary difference in respect of quantity;[4] and with regard to quality, they

(*a*) *Simple judgment.*

The purport of the expression λόγος ἀποφαντικὸς, λεκτὸν ἀποφαντὸν (in *Diog.* 65; *Gell.* xvi. 8, 4; *Ammon.* De Interp. 4, a; Schol. in Arist. 93, b, 20) is the same.

[1] *Sext.* Math viii. 93 : τῶν γὰρ ἀξιωμάτων πρώτην σχεδὸν καὶ κυριωτάτην ἐκφέρουσι διαφορὰν οἱ διαλεκτικοὶ καθ᾽ ἣν τὰ μέν ἐστιν αὐτῶν ἁπλᾶ τὰ δ᾽ οὐχ ἁπλᾶ. *Ibid.* 95 and 108. *Diog.* 68 gives the definitions of both.

[2] *Sext.* l. c., by whom *Diog.* must be corrected, see p. 113, 3.

[3] *Diog.* 69 : ἐν δὲ τοῖς οὐχ ἁπλοῖς τὸ συνημμένον καὶ τὸ παρασυνημμένον καὶ τὸ συμπεπλεγμένον καὶ τὸ αἰτιῶδες καὶ τὸ διεζευγμένον καὶ τὸ διασαφοῦν τὸ μᾶλλον καὶ τὸ διασαφοῦν τὸ ἧττον. Further details presently respecting the συνημμένον and διεζευγμένον. For the παρασυνημμένον—a conditional sentence, the first part of which is introduced by ἐπειδὴ— see *Diog.* 71 and 74; for the συμπεπλεγμένον, the characteristic of which is the καὶ and καὶ, see *Diog.* 72; *Sext.* Math. viii. 124; *Gell.* N. A. xvi. 8 and 9; Ps. *Galen,* Εἰσαγ. διαλ. 13; *Dexipp.* in Cat. 27, 3, Speng. ;

(Schol. in Arist. 44, a, 9— *Prantl,* 446, says this passage is not quite correct; it only implies that the term συμπλοκὴ was confined to a copulative judgment); for the αἰτιῶδες, which is characterised by a διότι, and therefore is not identical with the παρασυνημμένον, *Diog.* 72 and 74; for the διασαφοῦν τὸ μᾶλλον and the διασαφοῦν τὸ ἧττον, *Diog.* 72 ; conf. *Cramer,* Anecd. Oxon. i. 188 ; *Apollon.* Synt. (*Bekker's* Anecd. ii.), 481. These are only some of the principal forms of composite judgments, their number being really indefinite. Chrysippus estimated that a million combinations might be formed with ten sentences. The celebrated mathematician, Hipparchus, however, proved that only 103,049 affirmative and 310,952 negative judgments could be formed with that material (*Plut.* Sto. Rep. 29, 5, p. 1047; Qu. Symp. viii. 9, 3, 11, p. 732).

[4] There is no notice of a division of judgments into general and particular. Instead of that, *Sext.* (Math. viii. 96) distinguishes ὡρισμένα as οὗτος

CHAP.
V.

not only make a distinction between affirmative and negative judgments,[1] but, following the various forms of language, they speak of judgments of general negation, judgments of particular negation, and judgments of double negation.[2] Only affirmative and negative judgments have a contradictory relation to one another; all other judgments stand to each other in the relation of contraries.[3] Of two proposi-

κάθηται, ἀόριστα as τὶς κάθηται, and μέσα as ἄνθρωπος κάθηται, Σωκράτης περιπατεῖ. When the subject stood in the nominative, ὡρισμένα were called παταγορευτικὰ (*Diog.* 70); the others κατηγορικά · a καταγορευτικὸν is οὖτος περιπατεῖ · a καπηγορικὸν, Δίων περιπατεῖ.

[1] An affirmative judgment was called καταφατικὸν, a negative ἀποφατικὸν, by Chrysippus in the fragment about to be quoted, and *Simpl.* Cat. 102, δ, ζ. *Apul.* Dogm. Plat. iii. 266, Oud. renders these terms by dedicativa and abdicativa. For the manner in which they expressed negative sentences, see *Boëth.* De Interp. 373; Schol. in Arist. 120.

[2] *Diog.* 69 gives an example of ἀρνητικὸν, οὐδεὶς περιπατεῖ · one of particular negation, στερητικὸν—ἀφιλάνθρωπός ἐστιν οὗτος · one of double negation, ὑπεραποφατικὸν—as, οὐχὶ ἡμέρα οὐκ ἐστί.

[3] *Sext.* Math. viii. 89; *Diog.* 73 : ἀντικείμενα are ὧν τὸ ἕτερον τοῦ ἑτέρου ἐστὶν ἀποφατικὸν or (according to the outward treatment of these determinations) ἀποφάσει πλεονάζει—as, It is day, and It is not day. Aristotle called such a contra-

dictory ἀντίφασις, a contrary ἐναντιότης, putting both under the class conception of ἀντικείμενα. The Stoics reserved ἀντικείμενα for contradictories (*Simpl.* Cat. 102, δ and 102, ζ, a Stoic discussion intended to show that the conception of ἐνάντιον is not applicable to negative sentences and conceptions), which is after all only a difference in terminology. 'Εναντίον they also call μαχόμενον (*Apollon.* Synt. 484, Bekk.). Otherwise, following Aristotle, they distinguished between ἐναντίον and ἐναντίως ἔχον · ἐναντία are conceptions which are in plain and immediate contrast, such as φρόνησις and ἀφρόνησις · ἐναντίως ἔχοντα are those which are only contrasted by means of the ἐναντία, such as φρόνιμος and ἄφρων (*Simpl.* Categ. 98, γ). The former, therefore, apply to abstract, the latter to concrete notions. That every negative judgment has an affirmative judgment opposed to it is elaborately proved by a series of quotations from poets, each one of which is four times repeated in the fragment περὶ ἀποφατικῶν first edited by *Letronne* (Fragments inédits, Paris, 1838),

tions which are related as contradictories, according to the old rule, one must be true and the other false.[1]

Among composite judgments the most important are the hypothetical and the disjunctive. As regards the latter, next to no information has reached us.[2] A hypothetical judgment (συνημμένον) is a judgment consisting of two clauses, connected by the conjunction ' if,' and related to one another as cause and effect; the former being called the *leading* (ἡγούμενον), and the latter the *concluding* or *inferential* clause (λῆγον).[3] In the correctness of the inference the truth of a hypothetical judgment consists.

(β) Composite judgments.

---

and subsequently emended, explained, and with a great degree of probability referred to Chrysippus by Bergk (De Chrysippi libro περὶ ἀποφατικῶν, Cassel, 1841, Gymn. progr.). In explaining the fragment *Prantl*, Gesch. d. Log. I. 451 appears to have hit the truth in one point, where Bergk is not satisfied.

[1] *Simpl.* Categ. 103, β ; *Cic.* De Fato, 16, 37 ; N. De. i. 25, 70. Further particulars above p. 83, 2 ; 110, 3.

[2] Viz. that the members of a disjunction, as well as their contradictory opposites, must also be contraries (adversa or pugnantia), and that from the truth of the one the falsehood of the other follows. A disjunction which does not satisfy one or the other of these conditions is false (παραδιεζευγμένον). *Gell.* N. A. xvi. 8, 12; *Sext.* Pyrrh. ii. 191; *Alex.* Anal. Pr. 7, b.

[3] *Diog.* 71 ; *Sext.* Math. 109 ; Galen, De Simpl. Medicamen. ii. 16, vol. xi. 499 ; Ps. *Galen,* Εἰσαγ. διαλ. p. 15., The Stoics distinguish most unnecessarily, but quite in harmony with their ordinary formal punctiliousness, the case in which the leading clause is identical with the inferential clause (εἰ ἡμέρα ἐστὶν, ἡμέρα ἔστιν) and the case in which it is different (εἰ ἡμέρα ἐστὶν, φῶς ἔστιν). Conditional sentences of the first kind are called διφορούμενα συνημμένα. *Sext.* viii. 281 ; 294 ; and 466; Pyrrh. ii. 112 ; conf. viii. 95; *Diog.* 68. That in all these passages διφορούμενον must be read, and not διαφορούμενον, appears according to *Prantl's* (p. 445, 122) very true observation from the remarks of *Alex.* Top. 7, a ; Anal. Pr. 7, b, on διφορούμενοι συλλογισμοί.

Chap.
V.

As to the conditions upon which the accuracy of an inference rests, different opinions were entertained within the Stoic School itself.[1]   In as far as the

[1] *Sext.* Math. viii. 112; κοινῶς μὲν γάρ φασιν ἅπαντες οἱ Διαλεκτικοὶ ὑγιὲς εἶναι συνημμένον, ὅταν ἀκολουθῇ τῷ ἐν αὐτῷ ἡγουμένῳ τὸ ἐν αὐτῷ λῆγον. περὶ δὲ τοῦ πότε ἀκολουθεῖ καὶ πῶς, στασιά-ζουσι πρὸς ἀλλήλους καὶ μαχόμενα τῆς ἀκολουθίας ἐκτίθενται κριτήρια. *Cic.* Acad. ii. 47, 143 : In hoc ipso, quod in elementis dialectici docent, quomodo judicare oporteat, rerum falsumne sit, si quid ita connexum est, ut hoc : Si dies est, lucet ; quanta contentio est ! aliter Diodoro aliter Philoni, Chrysippo aliter placet. (The further remarks on the points of difference between Chrysippus and Cleanthes have no reference to hypothetical judgments.) The Philo here alluded to—the same Philo against whom Chrysippus wrote his treatises (*Diog.* vii. 191 and 194), the well-known dialectician, and pupil of Diodorus —had declared all conditional sentences to be right in which a false inferential clause is not drawn from a true leading clause. According to this view, conditional sentences would be right, with both clauses true, or both false, or with a false leading clause and true inferential clause (*Sext.* l. c. viii. 245 and 449 ; Pyrrh. ii. 110). According to *Sext.* Pyrrh. ii. 104, the view of Philo appears to have gained acceptance among the Stoics, perhaps through Zeno, for whose connection with Philo see *Diog.* vii. 16. But, in any case, the meaning appears to have been (*Diog.* vii. 81), that, in the cases mentioned, conditional sentences *may* be right, not that they must be right.

Others more appropriately judged of the correctness of conditional sentences by the connection of their clauses, either requiring, for a conditional sentence to be right, that the contradictory opposite (ἀντινείμενον) of the inferential clause should be irreconcileable with the leading clause, or that the inferential clause should be potentially (δυνάμει) contained in the leading clause (*Sext.* Pyrrh. ii. 111). The first of these requirements, which is mentioned by *Diog.* 73 as the only criterion of the Stoic School, was due to Chrysippus, who accordingly refused to allow sentences in which this was not the case to be expressed hypothetically (*Cic.* De Fato, 6, 12; 8, 15) : it was not right to say, Si quis natus est oriente canicula, is in mari non morietur; but, Non et natus est quis oriente canicula et is in mari morietur.

It may be observed, in connection with the enquiry into the accuracy of conditional sentences, that a true conditional sentence may become false in time. The sentence, If Dion is alive now, he will continue to live, is true at the present moment; but in the last moment of Dion's life it

leading clause states something, from the existence of
which an inference may be drawn as to the statement
in the concluding clause, it is also called an *indication* or *suggestive sign*.[1]

The modality of judgments, which engaged the
attention of Aristotle and his immediate pupils so
much, was likewise treated by the Stoics at considerable length ; but, from the sphere of these enquiries,
so much only is known to us as relates to possible and
necessary judgments,—being the outcome chiefly of
the contest between Chrysippus and the Megarian
Diodorus.[2] It is in itself of no great value. Great

will cease to be true. Such
sentences were called ἀπεριγρά-
φως μεταπίπτοντα, because the
time could not be previously
fixed when they would become
false (*Simpl.* Phys. 305, a).
Chrysippus also wrote on the με-
ταπίπτονα, according to *Dionys.*
Comp. Verb. p. 72 Schäfer. *Diog.*
vii. 105, mentions two treatises
of his on the subject, cha-
racterising them, however, as
spurious.

[1] According to *Sext.* Pyrrh.
ii. 100, Math. viii. 143 and 156,
the Stoics distinguished between σημεῖα ὑπομνηστικὰ and
σημεῖα ἐνδεικτικά. The definition
of the latter was ἐνδεικτικὸν
ἀξίωμα ἐν ὑγιεῖ συνημμένῳ καθη-
γούμενον (or προκαθηγούμενον)
ἐκκαλυπτικὸν τοῦ λήγοντος · the
ὑγιὲς συνημμένον being a sentence
with both the leading and inferential clauses true. *Sext.*
Pyrrh. ii. 101 ; 106 ; 115 ; Math.
viii. 249.

[2] Diodorus had said that
Only what is, or what will be,
is possible. The Stoics, and
in particular Chrysippus, define
δυνατὸν as what is capable of
being true (τὸ ἐπιδεκτικὸν τοῦ
ἀληθὲς εἶναι), if circumstances
do not prevent ; ἀδύνατον as ὃ
μή ἐστιν ἐπιδεκτικὸν τοῦ ἀληθὲς
εἶναι. From the δυνατὸν they
distinguish the οὐκ ἀναγκαῖον,
which is defined as ὃ καὶ ἀληθές
ἐστι καὶ ψεῦδος οἷόν τε εἶναι τῶν
ἐκτὸς μηδὲν ἐναντιουμένων (*Plut.*
Sto. Rep. 46, p. 1055 ; *Diog.* 75 ;
Boëth. De Interp. 374, Bas.
The same thing is also stated
in *Alex. Aphr.* De Fato, c. 10,
p. 30. δυνατὸν εἶναι γενέσθαι
τοῦτο δ' ὑπ' οὐδενὸς κωλύετα γενέσθαι κἂν μὴ γένηται.) On the
other hand, ἀναγκαῖον is, what
is both true and incapable of
being false, either in itself or
owing to other circumstances.
Diog. and *Boëth.* There was
probably anothe definition of

CHAP.
V.

value was, nevertheless, attached to it by the Stoics, in the hope thereby to escape the difficulties necessarily resulting from their views on freedom and necessity.[1]

(b) In-
ference.

In their theory of illation,[2] to which the Stoics attached special value, and on which they greatly prided themselves,[3] chief attention was paid to hypothetical and disjunctive inferences.[4] In regard to these forms of inference, the rules they laid down are well known :[5] and from these forms they invariably took their examples, even when treating of inference

οὐκ ἀναγκαῖον, as ὃ ψεῦδος οἷόν τε εἶναι τῶν ἐκτὸς μὴ ἐναντιουμένων· so that it might be said (*Boëth.* 429) that the οὐκ ἀναγκαῖον was partly possible and partly impossible, without contradicting (as *Boëth.* and *Prantl,* p. 463 believe) their other statement, that the δυνατὸν was partly necessary and partly not necessary. The conceptions of the Possible and the Not-necessary are thus made to overlap, the former including the Necessary and Not-necessary, the latter the Possible and the Not-possible.

To defend his definition of the Possible against the κυριεύων of Diodorus, Chrysippus denied the statement, δυνατῷ ἀδύνατον μὴ ἀκολουθεῖν, without exposing the confusion contained in it between sequence in time and causal relation (*Alex.* Anal. Pr. 57, b ; *Philop.* Anal. Pr. xlii. b ; Schol. in Arist. 163, a ; *Cic.* De Fato, 7, 13 ; Ep. ad Div. ix. 4). Cleanthes, Antipater, and Pan-

thoides preferred to attack another leading clause of Diodorus, the clause that Every past occurrence must necessarily be true (*Epictet.* Diss. ii. 19, 2 and 5). The Aristotelian position in reference to a disjunction, that When the disjunction refers to something future, the disjunction itself is true, without either clause being necessarily true, was not accepted by the Stoics (*Simpl.* Cat. 103, β).

[1] *Plut.* Sto. Rep. 46, p. 1055, justly insists on this point.

[2] *Prantl,* pp. 467–496.

[3] *Diog.* 45 ; *Sext.* Pyrrh. ii. 194, see above p. 65.

[4] Both were included by the Peripatetics under the term hypothetical. In the same way the Stoics include both among the five ἀναπόδεικτοι. See below p. 119, 2.

[5] Chain-argument seems to have been also treated of in the categorical form. See p. 120, 3.

in general.[1] According to Alexander,[2] the hypothetical and disjunctive forms were considered the only regular forms of inference,[3] the categorical form being considered correct in point of fact, but defective in proper syllogistic form.[4] In hypothetical infer-

CHAP.
V.

(a) *Hypothetical inference the original form.*

[1] As shown by *Prantl*, 468, 171 ; on *Diog*. 76 ; *Sext*. Pyrrh. ii. 135 ; *Apul*. Dogm. Plat. iii. 279, Oud. The latter rightly refers to the fact, that Chrysippus discussed the main forms of hypothetical inference at the very beginning of his doctrine of inference, *Sext*. Math. viii. 223.

[2] Anal. Pr. 87, b : δι' ὑποθέσεως δὲ ἄλλης, ὡς εἶπεν (*Arist*. Anal. Pr. i. 23, 41, a, 37) εἶεν ἂν καὶ οὓς οἱ νεώτεροι συλλογισμοὺς μόνους βούλονται λέγειν· οὗτοι δ' εἰσὶν οἱ διὰ τροπικοῦ, ὡς φασὶ, καὶ τῆς προλήψεως γινόμενοι, τοῦ τροπικοῦ ἢ συνημμένου (conditional) ὄντος ἢ διεζευγμένου (disjunctive) ἢ συμπεπλεγμένου (a copulative judgment suggesting partly hypothetical judgments like the συμπεπλεγμένον in *Sext*. Math. viii. 235, partly negative categorical judgments which have the force of hypothetical judgments, such as : it is not at the same time A and B. Conf. *Diog*. 80. *Sext*. Pyrrh. ii. 158 ; Math. viii. 226. *Cic*. De Fato, vi. 12). By the νεώτεροι, the Stoics must be meant, for the terminology is theirs ; and the Peripatetics, to whom it might otherwise apply, always considered the categorical to be the original form of judgment. See *Prantl*, 468, 172.

[3] Such an inference was called λόγος· when it was ex-

pressed in definite terms, for instance, If it is day, it is light. The arrangement of the clauses (which were designated by numbers, and not by letters, as the Peripatetics had done), was called τρόπος· for instance, εἰ τὸ πρῶτον, τὸ δεύτερον. A conclusion composed of both forms of expression was a λογότροπος· for instance, εἰ ζῇ Πλάτων, ἀναπνεῖ Πλάτων· ἀλλὰ μὴν τὸ πρῶτον· τὸ ἄρα δεύτερον. The premisses were called λήμματα (in contrast to ἀξίωμα which expresses a judgment independently of its position in a syllogism) ; or, more correctly, the major premiss was λῆμμα, the minor πρόσληψις (hence the particles δέ γε were προσληπτικὸς σύνδεσμος, *Apollon*. Synt. p. 518, Bekk.). The conclusion was ἐπιφορά, also ἐπιφορικοὶ σύνδεσμοί. *Ibid*. 519. The major premiss in a hypothetical syllogism was called τροπικὸν, its two clauses being called, respectively, ἡγούμενον (as by the Peripatetics) and λῆγον (by the Peripatetics ἑπόμενον). *Diog*. 76 ; *Sext*. Pyrrh. ii. 135 ; Math. viii. 301, 227 ; *Alex*. l. c. and p. 88, a ; 109, a ; 7, b ; *Philop*. Anal. Pr. lx. a ; Schol. in Arist. 170, a, 2 ; *Ammon*. on Anal. Pr. 24, b, 19 ; Arist. Orig. ed. Waitz, i. 45 ; *Apul*. Dog. Plat. iii. 279, Oud. ; Ps. *Galen*, Εἰσαγ. διαλ. p. 19.

[4] *Alex*. Anal. Pr. 116, b, after

ences a distinction was also made between such as are connected and such as are disconnected.[1]   In connected inferences the Stoics look principally at the greater or less accuracy of expression,[2] and partly at the difference between correctness of form and truth of matter.[3]   They also remarked that true conclusions do not always extend the field of knowledge; and that those which do frequently depend on reasons conclusive for the individual, but not on proofs universally acknowledged.[4]   The main point, however, to be considered in dividing inferences is their

mentioning ἀμεθόδως περαίνοντες συλλογισμοί, or inferences incomplete in point of form, such as : A = B, B = C, ∴ A = C, which is said to want as its major premiss : Two things which are equal to a third are equal to one another. On these ἀμεθόδως περαίνοντες of the Stoics see l. c. 8, a ; 22, b ; Alex. Top. 10, Ps. Galen, Eἰς. διάλ. 59. He then continues : οὓς ὅτι μὲν μὴ λέγουσι συλλογιστικῶς συνάγειν, ὑγιῶς λέγουσι [οἱ νεώτεροι] . . . ὅτι δὲ ἡγοῦνται ὁμοίους αὐτοὺς εἶναι τοῖς κατηγορικοῖς συλλογισμοῖς . . . τοῦ παντὸς διαμαρτάνουσιν.

[1] συνακτικοὶ or περαντικοὶ, and ἀσυνακτικοὶ or ἀπέραντοι, or ἀσυλλόγιστοι. Sext. Pyrrh. ii. 137 ; Math. viii. 303 and 428 ; Diog. 77.

[2] Syllogisms which are conclusive in point of fact, but wanting in precision of form, were called περαντικοί in the narrower sense ; those complete also in form, συλλογιστικοί. Diog. 78 ; Ps. Galen, Eἰσαγ. διαλ. 58.

[3] An inference is true (ἀλη-

θής) when not only the illation is correct (ὑγιὴς), but when the individual propositions, the premisses as well as the conclusion, are materially true. The λόγοι συνακτικοὶ may therefore be divided into true and false. Sext. Pyrrh. ii. 138 ; Math. viii. 310 and 412 ; Diog. 79.

[4] Sext. Pyrrh. ii. 140 and 135 ; Math. viii. 305 ; 313 ; and 411 : True forms of inference are divided into ἀποδεικτικοὶ and οὐκ ἀποδεικτικοί. ἀποδεικτικοὶ = οἱ διὰ προδήλων ἄδηλόν τι συνάγοντες· οὐκ ἀποδεικτικοὶ when this is not the case, as in the inference : If it is day, it is light—It is day, ∴ It is light ; for the conclusion, It is light, is known as well as it is known that It is day. The ἀποδεικτικοὶ may proceed either ἐφοδευτικῶς from the premisses to the conclusions, or ἐφοδευτικῶς ἅμα καὶ ἐκκαλυπτικῶς· ἐφοδευτικῶς when the premisses rest upon belief (πίστις and μνήμη) ; ἐκκαλυπτικῶς when they are based on a scientific necessity.

logical form.   There are, according to Chrysippus,[1]
who herein adopted the division of Theophrastus,
five original forms of hypothetical inference, the accuracy of which is beyond dispute, and to which all
other forms of inference may be referred and thereby
tested.[2] Yet even among these forms, importance is
attached to some in which the same sentence is repeated tautologically in the form of a conclusion,[3]
proving how mechanical and barren must have been
the formalism in which the Stoic logic so abounds.

The combination of these five simple forms of inference gives rise to the composite forms of inference,[4]
all of which may be again resolved into their simple
forms.[5] Among the composite forms of inference,

CHAP.
V.

(β) *The
five simple
forms of
hypotheti-
cal in-
ference.*

(γ) *Com-
posite
forms of
inference.*

---

[1] According to *Diog.* 79, *Sext.*
Pyrrh. ii. 157, others added
other forms of ἀναπόδεικτοι.
Cic., in adding a sixth and
seventh (Top. 14, 57), must
have been following these authorities.

[2] Consult, on these five ἀναπόδεικτοι of Chrysippus (which
need not be given here more at
length, being absolutely identical with those of Theophrastus) *Diog.* 79–81 (on p. 79 we
must read συλλογιστικῶν for
συλλογισμῶν. See p. 118, 2);
Sext. Pyrrh. ii. 156–159; 201;
Math. viii. 223–227; *Cic.* Top.
13; *Simpl.* Phys. 123, b; Ps.
Galen, Εἰσαγ. διαλ. 17; *Prantl,*
473, 182; on the πέμπτος ἀνα-
πόδεικτος διὰ πλειόνων *Sext.* Pyrrh.
i. 69; *Cleomed.* Meteora, pp.
41 and 47; *Prantl,* p. 475.

[3] Two such cases are distinguished, one in which all three
clauses, the other in which the

conclusion and minor premiss
are identical. The first class are
called διφορούμενοι· If it is day, it
is day; It is day, ∴ It is day. The
second class, ἀδιαφόρως περαίνον-
τες· It is either day or night;
It is day, ∴ It is day.   The
latter term is, however, applied
to both kinds. See *Alex.* Anal.
Pr. 7, a; 53, b; Top. 7; Schol.
in Arist. 294, b, 25; *Cic.* Acad.
ii. 30, 96; *Prantl,* 476, 185.

[4] *Cic.* Top. 15, 57 : ex his
modis conclusiones innumera-
biles nascuntur. *Sext.* Math.
viii. 228, in which passage it is
striking that ἀναπόδεικτοι should
be divided into ἁπλοῖ and οὐχ
ἁπλοῖ. It has been suggested
that ἀποδεικτικῶν should be substituted for ἀναποδείκτων, but it
is also possible that the latter
word may be used in a narrow
as well as in a wider sense.

[5] *Diog.* 78 : συλλογιστικοὶ [λό-
γοι] μὲν οὖν εἰσιν οἱ ἤτοι ἀναπό-

those composed of similar parts are distinguished from those composed of dissimilar parts;[1] in the treatment of the former, however, such a useless formality is displayed, that it is hard to say what meaning the Stoics attached to them.[2] If two or more inferences, the conclusion of one of which is the first premiss of the other, are so combined that the judgment which constitutes the conclusion and premiss at once is omitted in each case, the result is a Sorites or Chain-inference. The rules prescribed by the Peripatetics for the Chain-inference were developed by the Stoics with a minuteness far transcending all the requirements of science.[3] With these

δεικτοι ὄντες ἢ ἀναγόμενοι ἐπὶ τοὺς ἀναποδείκτους κατά τι τῶν θεμάτων ἢ τινά. According to *Galen*, Hipp. et Plat. ii. 3, p. 224, Chrysippus had taken great pains in resolving the composite forms of inference (*Diog.* 190 and 194). Antipater suggested still simpler modes.

[1] *Sext.* 229–243, borrowing the example used by Ænesidemus, but no doubt following the Stoic treatment. *Prantl*, 479. Such a composite inference is that mentioned by *Sextus* l. c. 281.

[2] *Sext.*; *Prantl*, p. 478.

[3] *Alex.* on Anal. Pr. i. 25, 42, b, 5, after speaking of the Sorites, continues (p. 94, b): ἐν τῇ τοιαύτῃ τῶν προτάσεων συνεχείᾳ τό τε συνθετικόν ἐστι θεώρημα . . . καὶ οἱ καλούμενοι ὑπὸ τῶν νεωτέρων ἐπιβάλλοντές τε καὶ ἐπιβαλλόμενοι. The συνθετικὸν θεώρημα (or chain-argument), the meaning of which is next investigated, must be a Peripa-

tetic expression. The same meaning must attach to ἐπιβάλλοντές τε καὶ ἐπιβαλλόμενοι, which are to be found ἐν ταῖς συνεχῶς λαμβανομέναις προτάσεσι χωρὶς τῶν συμπερασμάτων· for instance, A is a property of B, B of C, C of D; ∴ A is a property of D. ἐπιβαλλόμενος means the inference, the conclusion of which is omitted; ἐπιβάλλων, the one with the omitted premiss. These inferences may be in either of the three Aristotelian figures κατὰ τὸ παραδεδομένον συνθετικὸν θεώρημα. ὃ οἱ μὲν περὶ Ἀριστοτέλην τῇ χρείᾳ παραμετρήσαντες παρέδοσαν, ἐφ᾽ ὅσον αὐτὴ ἀπῇτει, οἱ δὲ ἀπὸ τῆς τοῦ [στοᾶς] παρ᾽ ἐκείνων λαβόντες καὶ διελόντες ἐποίησαν ἐξ αὐτοῦ τὸ καλούμενον παρ᾽ αὐτοῖς δεύτερον καὶ τρίτον θέμα καὶ τέταρτον, ἀμελήσαντες μὲν τοῦ χρησίμου, πᾶν δὲ τὸ ὁπωσοῦν δυνάμενον λέγεσθαι ἐν τῇ τοιαύτῃ θεωρίᾳ, κᾶν ἄχρηστος ᾖ, ἐπεξελθόντες τε καὶ ζηλώσαντες. Reference is made to the same

composite forms of inference Antipater contrasted
other forms having only a single premiss,[1] but it was
an addition to the field of logic of very doubtful
worth. On a few other points connected with the
Stoic theory of illation, we have very imperfect information.[2] The loss, however, is not to be regretted,
seeing that in what we already possess there is conclusive evidence that the objections brought against
the Stoic logic were really well deserved. It was in-

CHAP.
V.

(δ) In-
ference
from a sin-
gle pre-
miss.

thing in *Simpl.* De Cœlo; Schol.
in Arist. 483, b, 26 : ἡ δὲ τοιαύτη
ἀνάλυσις τοῦ λόγου, ἡ τὸ συμ-
πέρασμα λαμβάνουσα καὶ προσλαμ-
βάνουσα ἄλλην πρότασιν, κατὰ τὸ
τρίτον λεγόμενον παρὰ τοῖς Στωϊκοῖς θέμα περαίνεται, the rule of
which is, that when a third proposition can be concluded from
the conclusion of an inference
and a second proposition, that
third proposition can be concluded also from the premisses
of the inference and the second
proposition. Both these passages appear to have escaped
the notice of *Prantl* in his
summing up, otherwise so accurate. Or else the πρῶτον,
δεύτερον, τρίτον and τέταρτον θέμα
mentioned by *Galen*, Hipp. et
Plat. ii. 3, vol. v. 224. *Alex.*
Anal. Pr. 53, b, would hardly
suggest to him the various
forms of the ἀναπόδεικτοι instead
of the formulae for the resolution of composite conclusions.
The expressions διὰ δύο τροπικῶν,
διὰ τριῶν τροπικῶν, and the title
of a treatise of Chrysippus περὶ
τοῦ διὰ τριῶν (sc. τροπικῶν or
λημμάτων conf. p. 117, 3) in
Diog. vii. 191 ; (*Galen*, l. c. ;
Sext. Pyrrh. ii. 2), appear to

refer to such composite inferences.

[1] Called μονολήμματοι συλλογισμοί. Such were ἡμέρα ἔστι,
φῶς ἄρα ἔστιν· and ἀναπνεῖς, ζῆς
ἄρα. See *Alex.* Top. 6, 274 ;
Anal. Pr. 7, a, 8, a ; *Sext.* Pyrrh.
ii. 167 ; Math. viii. 443 ; *Apul.*
Dogm. Plat. iii. 272, Oud. ;
Prantl, 477, 186.

[2] Compare the remarks of
Prantl, 481, on *Sext.* Pyrrh. ii.
2 ; *Alex.* Anal. Pr. 53, b ; *Galen,*
l. c. ; Ps. *Galen,* Εἰσαγ. διαλ.
57. If Posidonius, according
to the latter passage, calls analogical conclusions συνακτι-
κοὺς κατὰ δύναμιν ἀξιώματος, and
the Stoics also, according to
Schol. in Hermog. Rhet. Gr. ed.
Walz, vii. 6, 764, spoke of a κατὰ
δύναμιν τροπικὸν, we have already
met with the same thing, p.
119, 1, where an analogical conclusion was included in the
ἀμεθόδως περαίνοντες, which, by
the addition of an ἀξίωμα, can
be changed into regular conclusions. In the doctrine of
proof the τόπος παράδοξος was
also treated of, according to
Prokl. in Euclid, 103, being
probably suggested by the ethical paradoxes of the Stoics.

CHAP.
V.

(c) *Refutation of fallacies.*

deed a petty carefulness to trace, as they did, even the most worthless logical forms[1] to the end.

Next to describing the inferences which were valid, another subject engaged the careful attention of the Stoics, and afforded an opportunity for vindicating their dialectical subtlety. This was no other than the enumeration and refutation of false inferences,[2] and in particular the exposing of the many fallacies which had become current since the age of the Sophists and Megarians. In this department, too, as might be expected, Chrysippus led the way.[3] Not that Chrysippus was always able to overcome the difficulties that arose; witness his remarkable attitude towards the Chain-inferences, from which he thought to escape by withholding judgment.[4] The fallacies, however, to which the Stoics devoted their attention, and the way in which they met them, need not occupy our attention further.[5]

---

[1] Conf. *Alex.* Anal. Pr. 95, a; *Galen.* See above p. 120, 3. According to Ps. *Galen*, l. c. p. 58, Chrysippus wrote these treatises on Συλλογιστικαὶ ἄχρηστοι.

[2] *Diog.* 186, mentions fallacies due to Chrysippus, which can only have been raised for the purpose of being refuted.

[3] The list of his writings contains a number of treatises on fallacies, among them no less than five on the ψευδόμενος.

[4] *Cic.* Acad. ii. 29, 93 : Placet enim Chrysippo, cum gradatim interrogetur, verbi causa, tria pauca sint, anne multa, aliquanto prius, quam ad multa perveniat, quiescere, id est, quod

ab iis dicitur ἡσυχάζειν. The same remark is made by *Sext.* Math. vii. 416; Pyrrh. ii. 253. The same argument was employed against other fallacies (*Simpl.* Cat. 6, γ). With this λόγος ἡσυχάζων (*Diog.* 198), *Prantl*, p. 489, connects ἀργὸς λόγος (*Cic.* De Fato, 12, 28), regarding the one as the practical application of the other, but apparently without reason. The ἀργὸς λόγος, by means of which the Stoic fatalism was reduced ad absurdum, could not of course commend itself to Chrysippus, nor is it attributed to him.

[5] *Prantl*, pp. 485–496.

In all these enquiries the Stoics were striving to
find firm ground for a scientific process of proof.
Great as was the value which they attached to such
a process, they nevertheless admitted, as Aristotle had
done before, that everything could not be proved.
Here, then, was the weak point. Instead, however,
of filling up this weak point by means of induction,
and endeavouring to obtain a more complete theory
of induction, they were content with conjectural data,
sometimes carrying their own truth in themselves, at
other times leaving it to be established by the truth
of their inferences.[1] Thus, their theory of method,
like their theory of knowledge, ended by an ultimate
appeal to what is directly certain.

No very high estimate can therefore be formed of
the formal logic of the Stoics. Incomplete as is our
knowledge of that logic, still what is known is enough
to determine the judgment absolutely. That the
greatest care was expended by the Stoics since the
time of Chrysippus in tracing into their minutest
ramifications, and referring to a fixed type, the forms
of intellectual procedure, we see indeed. At the same
time, we see that the real business of logic was lost
sight of in the process, the business of portraying
the operations of thought, and giving its laws, whilst

CHAP.
V.

D. *Esti-
mate of
Stoic
Logic.*
(1) *Its
short-
comings.*

(2) *Its
value.*

---

[1] *Sext.* Math. viii. 367: ἀλλ'
οὐ δεῖ, φασὶ, πάντων ἀπόδειξιν
αἰτεῖν, τινὰ δὲ καὶ ἐξ ὑποθέσεως
λαμβάνειν, ἐπεὶ οὐ δυνήσεται προ-
βαίνειν ἡμῖν ὁ λόγος, ἐὰν μὴ δοθῇ
τι πιστὸν ἐξ αὑτοῦ τυγχάνειν.
Ibid. 375: ἀλλ' εἰώθασιν ὑποτυγ-
χάνοντες λέγειν ὅτι πίστις ἐστὶ
τοῦ ἐρρῶσθαι τὴν ὑπόθεσιν τὸ
ἀληθὲς εὑρίσκεσθαι ἐκεῖνο τὸ τοῖς
ἐξ ὑποθέσεως ληφθεῖσιν ἐπιφερό-
μενον· εἰ γὰρ τὸ τούτοις ἀκολουθοῦν ἐστιν ὑγιὲς, κἀκεῖνα οἷς ἀκο-
λυυθεῖ ἀληθῆ καὶ ἀναμφίλεκτα
καθέστηκεν.

the most useless trifling with forms was recklessly indulged in. No discoveries of importance can have been made even as to the logical forms of thought, or they would not have been passed over by writers ever on the alert to note the slightest derivations from the Aristotelian logic. Hence the whole contribution of the Stoics in the field of logic consists in this,— in clothing the logic of the Peripatetics with a new terminology, and developing certain parts of it with painful minuteness, whilst other parts were wholly neglected. Thus it fared with the part treating of inference. Assuredly it. was no improvement for Chrysippus to regard the hypothetical rather than the categorical as the original form of inference. Making every allowance for the extension of the field of logic, in scientific precision it lost more than it gained by the labours of Chrysippus. The history of philosophy cannot pass over in silence this branch of the Stoic system, so carefully cultivated by the Stoics themselves, and so characteristic of their intellectual attitude. Yet, when all has been said, the Stoic logic is only an outpost of their system, and the care which was lavished on it since the time of Chrysippus indicates the decline of intellectual originality.

CHAPTER VI.

THE STUDY OF NATURE. FUNDAMENTAL POSITIONS.

OF far more importance in the Stoic system than the study of logic was the study of nature. This branch of learning, notwithstanding an appeal to older views, was treated by them with more independence than any other. The subjects which it included may be divided under four heads, viz.: 1. Fundamental positions; 2. The course, character, and government of the universe; 3. Irrational nature; and 4. Man.[1]

The present chapter will be devoted to considering the first of these groups—the fundamental positions held by the Stoics in regard to nature; among

---

[1] Natural Science was divided by the Stoics themselves (*Diog.* 132): (1) εἰδικῶς into τόποι περὶ σωμάτων καὶ περὶ ἀρχῶν καὶ στοιχείων καὶ θεῶν καὶ περάτων καὶ τόπου καὶ κενοῦ· (2) γενικῶς into three divisions, περὶ κόσμου, περὶ στοιχείων, and the αἰτιολογικός. The first of these divisions covers ground which is partly peculiar to natural science and is shared by the mathematician (astronomy. Posidonius in *Simpl. Phys.* 64, b, discusses at length the difference between astronomy and natural science); and the third, ground which is shared by both the physician and the mathematician. The precise allotment of the subject into these divisions is not known. At best, it would be a very uncomfortable division.

A. *Mate-
rialism.*
(1) *Mean-
ing of the
Stoic ma-
terialism.*
(a) *Mate-
rial or cor-
poreal
objects.*

(α) *Reality
belongs to
material
objects
only.*

which three specially deserve notice—their Materialism; their Dynamical view of the world; and their
Pantheism.

Nothing appears more striking to a reader fresh
from the study of Plato or Aristotle than the startling
contrast presented thereto by the Materialism of the
Stoics. Whilst so far following Plato as to define a
real thing[1] to be anything possessing the capacity of
acting or being acted upon, the Stoics nevertheless
restricted the possession of this power to material
objects. Hence followed their conclusion that nothing real exists except what is material; or, if they
could not deny existence in some sense or other to
what is incorporeal, they were fain to assert that
essential and real Being only belongs to what is material, whereas of what is incorporeal only a certain
modified kind of Being can be predicated.[2] Follow-

[1] Soph. 247, D.

[2] *Plut.* Com. Not. 30, 2, p.
1073: ὄντα γὰρ μόνα τὰ σώματα
καλοῦσιν, ἐπειδὴ ὄντος τὸ ποιεῖν τι
καὶ πάσχειν. Plac. i. 11, 4: οἱ
Στωϊκοὶ πάντα τὰ αἴτια σωματικά·
πνεύματα γάρ. iv. 20: οἱ δὲ Στωϊκοὶ σῶμα τὴν φωνήν· πᾶν γὰρ τὸ
δρώμενον ἢ καὶ ποιοῦν σῶμα· ἡ δὲ
φωνὴ ποιεῖ καὶ δρᾷ . . . ἔτι πᾶν
τὸ κινοῦν καὶ ἐνοχλοῦν σῶμά ἐστιν
. . . ἔτι πᾶν τὸ κινούμενον σῶμά
ἐστιν. *Cic.* Acad. i. 11, 39:
[Zeno] nullo modo arbitrabatur
quidquam effici posse ab ea
[natura] quæ expers esset corporis . . . nec vero aut quod
efficeret aliquid aut quod efficeretur (more accurately: in
quo efficeretur aliquid. Conf.
Ritter, iii. 577) posse esse non
corpus. *Seneca*, see below p.
128, 1; 129, 1; *Stob.* Ecl. i. 336

(see p. 95, 2) and 338: Χρύσιππος
αἴτιον εἶναι λέγει δι' ὅ. καὶ τὸ
μὲν αἴτιον ὂν καὶ σῶμα, κ.τ.λ.
Ποσειδώνιος δὲ οὕτως. αἴτιον δ'
ἐστί τινος δι' ὃ ἐκεῖνο, ἢ τὸ ἀρχηγὸν ποιήσεως, καὶ τὸ μὲν αἴτιον ὂν
καὶ σῶμα, οὗ δὲ αἴτιον οὔτε ὂν οὔτε
σῶμα, ἀλλὰ συμβεβηκὸς καὶ κατηγόρημα. See p. 95, 1 and 2.
Diog. vii. 56: According to
Chrysippus, Diogenes (see
Simpl. Phys. 97, a), and others,
the voice is material, πᾶν γὰρ
τὸ ποιοῦν σῶμά ἐστι. *Ibid.* 150:
οὐσίαν δέ φασι τῶν ὄντων ἁπάντων
τὴν πρώτην ὕλην, ὡς καὶ Χρύσιππος ἐν τῇ πρώτῃ τῶν φυσικῶν καὶ
Ζήνων· ὕλη δέ ἐστιν, ἐξ ἧς ὁτιδηποτοῦν γίνεται . . . σῶμα δέ ἐστι
κατ' αὐτοὺς ἡ οὐσία. *Hippolyt.*
Refut. Haer. i. 21: σώματα δὲ
πάντα ὑπέθεντο, κ.τ.λ.

ing out this view, it was natural that they should
regard many things as corporeal which are not generally considered so; for instance, the soul and virtue.
Nevertheless, it would not be correct to say[1] that the
Stoics gave to the conception of matter or corporeity
a more extended meaning than it usually bears. For
they define a body to be that which has three dimensions,[2] and they also lay themselves out to prove how
things generally considered to be incorporeal may be
material in the strictest sense of the term. Thus,
besides upholding the corporeal character of all substances, including the human soul and God,[3] they
likewise assert that properties or forms are material:
all attributes by means of which one object is distinguished from another are produced by the existence of certain air-currents,[4] which, emanating from
the centre of an object, diffuse themselves to its
extremities, and having reached the surface, return
again to the centre to constitute the inward unity.[5]

(β) *Theory
of air-cur-
rents.*

[1] As do *Ritter*, iii. 577, and
Schleiermacher, Gesch. der
Philos. 129.
[2] *Diog.* vii. 135 : σῶμα δ' ἐστι
(φησὶν 'Απολλόδωρος ἐν τῇ φυσικῇ)
τὸ τριχῇ διαστατὸν, κ.τ.λ.
[3] See p. 98. The corporeal
nature of deity and the soul
will be subsequently discussed.
[4] See p. 105. *Sen.* Ep. 102, 7,
remarks, in reference to the
difference of ἡνωμένα · (see p.
103, 1): nullum bonum putamus
esse, quod ex distantibus constat : uno enim spiritu unum
bonum contineri ac regi debet,
unum esse unius boni principale.
Hence the objection raised in

Plut. Com. Not. 50, 1, p. 1085 :
τὰς ποιότητας οὐσίας καὶ σώματα
ποιοῦσιν, and *Ibid.* 44, 4, the
statement discussed on p. 101, 2.
[5] *Philo*, Qu. De S. Immut.
p. 298, D (the same in the
spurious treatise De Mundo, p.
1154, E): ἡ δὲ [ἕξις = ποιότης]
ἐστὶ πνεῦμα ἀντιστρέφον ἐφ' ἑαυτό.
ἄρχεται μὲν γὰρ ἀπὸ τῶν μέσων
ἐπὶ τὰ πέρατα τείνεσθαι, ψαῦσαν
δὲ ἄκρας ἐπιφανείας ἀνακάμπτει
πάλιν, ἄχρις ἂν ἐπὶ τὸν αὐτὸν ἀφί-
κηται τόπον, ἀφ' οὗ τὸ πρῶτον
ὡρμίσθη. ἕξεως ὁ συνεχὴς οὗτος
δίαυλος ἄφθαρτος, κ.τ.λ. Qu.
Mund. S. Incorr. 960, D [De
Mundo, 1169, A]: ἡ δ' [ἕξις] ἐστὶ

Nor was the theory of air-currents confined to bodily attributes. It was applied quite as much to mental attributes. Virtues and vices are said to be material,[1] and are deduced from the tension imparted to the soul by atmospheric substances therein subsisting.[2] For the same reason the Good is called a body, for according to the Stoics the Good is only a virtue, and

πνευματικὸς τόνος. There can be no doubt that Philo is describing the Stoic teaching in these passages. The same idea is also used to explain the connection between the soul and the body. The unity of the universe is proved by the fact that the Divine Spirit pervades it. Further particulars hereafter. Conf. *Alex. Aphr.* De Mixt. 142, a: ἡνῶσθαι μὲν ὑποτίθεται [Χρύσιππος] τὴν σύμπασαν οὐσίαν πνεύματός τινος διὰ πάσης αὐτῆς διήκοντος, ὑφ' οὗ συνάγεταί τε καὶ συμμένει καὶ σύμπαθές ἐστιν αὐτῷ τὸ πᾶν. (That must be the reading, the next sentence containing τῶν δὲ, κ.τ.λ. Conf. 143, b). *Alex.* 143, b, carefully denies the statement, that the all penetrating Breath keeps things together.
[1] *Plut.* Com. Not. 45. See p. 129, 3. *Sen.* Ep. 117, 2: Placet nostris, quod bonum sit, esse corpus, quia quod bonum est, facit: quidquid facit corpus est . . . sapientiam bonum esse dicunt: sequitur, ut necesse sit illam corporalem quoque dicere. Conf. p. 129, 1.
[2] This is the conception of τόνος, upon which the strength of the soul depends, as well as the strength of the body. *Clean-*

thes, in Plut. Sto. Rep. 7, 4, p. 1034: πληγὴ πυρὸς ὁ τόνος ἐστὶ κἂν ἱκανὸς ἐν τῇ ψυχῇ γένηται πρὸς τὸ ἐπιτελεῖν τὰ ἐπιβάλλοντα ἰσχὺς καλεῖται καὶ κράτος. *Stob.* Ecl. ii. 110: ὥσπερ ἰσχὺς τοῦ σώματος τόνος ἐστὶν ἱκανὸς ἐν νεύροις, οὕτω καὶ ἡ τῆς ψυχῆς ἰσχὺς τόνος ἐστὶν ἱκανὸς ἐν τῷ κρίνειν καὶ πράττειν καὶ μή. All properties may be classed under the same conception of tension. See p. 127, 5 and *Plut.* Com. Not. 49, 2, p. 1085: γῆν μὲν γὰρ ἴσασι καὶ ὕδωρ οὔτε αὐτὰ συνέχειν οὔτε ἕτερα, πνευματικῆς δὲ μετοχῇ, καὶ πυρώδους δυνάμεως τὴν ἑνότητα διαφυλάττειν· ἀέρα δὲ καὶ πῦρ αὐτῶν τ' εἶναι δι' εὐτονίαν ἐκτατικὰ καὶ τοῖς δυσὶν ἐκείνοις ἐγκεκραμένα τόνον παρέχειν καὶ τὸ μόνιμὸν καὶ οὐσιῶδες. Ps. *Censorin.* Fragm. c. 1, p. 75, Jahn: Initia rerum eadem elementa et principia dicuntur. Ea Stoici credunt tenorem atque materiam; tenorem, qui rarescente materia a medio tendat ad summum, eadem concrescente rursus a summo referatur ad medium. Here tenor or τόνος is made equivalent to πνεῦμα. Seneca, however, Nat. Qu. ii. 8, conf. vi. 21, endeavours to show that *intentio* belongs to *spiritus* more than to any other body.

virtue is a definite condition of that material which
constitutes the soul.[1] In the same sense also truth
is said to be material, personal and not independent
truth being of course meant,[2] that is to say, knowledge, or a property of the soul that knows. And
since according to the Stoics knowledge consists in
the presence of certain material elements within the
soul, truth in the sense of knowledge may be rightly
called something material. Even emotions, impulses,
notions and judgments, in so far as they are due to
material causes, the air-currents pouring into the
soul (πνεύματα), were regarded as material objects,
and for the same reason not only artistic skill but
individual actions were said to be corporeal.[3] Yet

[1] Sen. Ep. 106, 4: bonum
facit, prodest enim quod facit
corpus est: bonum agitat animum et quodammodo format et
continet, quæ propria sunt corporis. Quæ corporis bona sunt,
corpora sunt: ergo et quæ
animi sunt. Nam et hoc corpus. Bonum hominis necesse
est corpus sit, cum ipse sit cor-
poralis . . . si adfectus corpora
sunt et morbi animorum et
avaritia, crudelitas, indurata
vitia . . . ergo et malitia et
species ejus omnes . . . ergo et
bona. It is then specially remarked that the Good, i.e. virtue, works upon the body,
governing it and representing
itself therein.   Conf. p. 128, 1.
[2] Sext. Math. vii. 38: τὴν δὲ
ἀλήθειαν οἴονταί τινες, καὶ μάλιστα
οἱ ἀπὸ τῆς στοᾶς, διαφέρειν τἀλη-
θοῦς κατὰ τρεῖς τρόπους . . . οὐσίᾳ
μὲν παρ' ὅσον ἡ μὲν ἀλήθεια σῶμά
ἐστι τὸ δὲ ἀληθὲς ἀσώματον ὑπῆρ-

χε. καὶ εἰκότως, φασί. τουτὶ μὲν
γὰρ ἀξίωμά ἐστι, τὸ δὲ ἀξίωμα λεκτὸν, τὸ δὲ λεκτὸν ἀσώματον· ἀνά-
παλιν δὲ ἡ ἀλήθεια σῶμά ἐστιν
παρ' ὅσον ἐπιστήμη πάντων ἀληθῶν
ἀποφαντικὴ δοκεῖ τυγχάνειν· πᾶσα
δὲ ἐπιστήμη πῶς ἔχον ἐστὶν ἡγεμονικὸν . . . τὸ δὲ ἡγεμονικὸν
σῶμα κατὰ τούτους ὑπῆρχε. Similarly Pyrrh. ii. 81. See p. 92,
2.
[3] Plut. Com. Not. 45, 2,
p. 1084: ἄτοπον γὰρ εὖ μάλα, τὰς
ἀρετὰς καὶ τὰς κακίας, πρὸς δὲ
ταύταις τὰς τέχνας καὶ τὰς μνήμας
πάσας, ἔτι δὲ φαντασίας καὶ πάθη
καὶ ὁρμὰς καὶ συγκαταθέσεις
σώματα ποιουμένους ἐν μηδενὶ
φάναι κεῖσθαι, κ.τ.λ. . . . οἱ δ' οὐ
μόνον τὰς ἀρετὰς καὶ τὰς κακίας
ζῷα εἶναι λέγουσιν, οὐδὲ τὰ πάθη
μόνον, ὀργὰς καὶ φθόνους καὶ λύπας
καὶ ἐπιχαιρεκακίας, οὐδὲ καταλήψεις καὶ φαντασίας καὶ ἀγνοίας οὐδὲ
τὰς τέχνας ζῷα, τὴν σκυτοτομικὴν,
τὴν χαλκοτυπικήν· ἀλλὰ πρὸς

CHAP.
VI.

(γ) *The
causes of
actions
material.*

certain actions, such as walking and dancing, can hardly have been called bodies by the Stoics, any more than being wise was called a body;[1] but the objects which produced these actions, as indeed everything which makes itself felt, were considered to be corporeal. To us it appears most natural to refer these actions to the soul as their originating cause; but the Stoics, holding the theory of subject-matter and property, preferred to refer each such action to some special material as its cause, considering that an action is due to the presence of this material. The idealism of Plato was thus reproduced in a new form by the materialism of the Stoics.

τούτοις καὶ τὰς ἐνεργείας σώματα καὶ ζῷα ποιοῦσι, τὸν περίπατον ζῷον, τὴν ὄρχησιν, τὴν ὑπόθεσιν, τὴν προσαγόρευσιν, τὴν λοιδορίαν. Plutarch is here speaking as an opponent. Seneca, however (Ep. 106, 5), observes: Non puto te dubitaturum, an adfectus corpora sint . . . tanquam ira, amor, tristitia : si dubitas, vide an vultum nobis mutent: . . . Quid ergo? tam manifestas corpori notas credis imprimi, nisi a corpore? See p. 129, 1 ; Stob. Ecl. ii. 114 : The Stoics consider virtues to be substantially identical (τὰς αὐτὰς καθ' ὑπόστασιν) with (the leading part of the soul (ἡγεμονικὸν), and consequently to be, like it, σώματα and ζῷα. Seneca, Ep. 113, 1, speaks still more plainly : Desideras tibi scribi a me, quid sentiam de hac quaestione jactata apud nostros : an justitia, an fortitudo, prudentia ceteraeque virtutes animalia sint. . . . Me in alia sententia profiteor esse. . . . Quae sint ergo quae antiquos moverint, dicam. Animum constat animal esse. . . . Virtus autem nihil aliud est, quam animus quodammodo se habens : ergo animal est. Deinde : virtus agit aliquid : agi autem nihil sine impetu (ὁρμὴ) potest. If it is urged : Each individual will thus consist of an innumerable number of living beings, the reply is that these animalia are only parts of one animal, the soul ; they are accordingly not many (multa), but one and the same viewed from different sides : idem est animus et justus et prudens et fortis ad singulas virtutes quodammodo se habens. From the same letter, p. 23, we gather that Cleanthes explained ambulatio as spiritus a principali usque in pedes permissus, Chrysippus as principale itself.

[1] See p. 92, 2, the extract from *Sen.* Ep. 117.

Plato had said, a man is just and musical when he
participates in the *idea* of justice and music; the
Stoics said, a man is virtuous when the *material* producing virtue is in him; musical, when he has the
material producing music.

Moreover, these materials produce the phenomena
of life. Hence, not content with calling them bodies,
the Stoics actually went so far as to call them living
beings. It seems, however, quite as startling to hear
such things as day and night, and parts of the day
and parts of the night, months and years, even days
of the month and seasons of the year, called bodies.[1]
But by these singularly unhappy expressions Chrysippus appears to have meant little more than that
the realities corresponding to these names depend on
certain material conditions : by summer is meant a
certain state of the air when highly heated by the
sun ; by month the moon for a certain definite period
during which it gives light to the earth.[2] From all

CHAP.
VI.

(δ) *Wide
extension
of mate-
rial.*

---

[1] *Plut.* Com. Not. 45, 5,
p. 1084 : Χρυσίππου μνημονεύοντες
ἐν τῷ πρώτῳ τῶν φυσικῶν ζητη-
μάτων οὕτω προσάγοντος · οὐχ ἡ
μὲν νὺξ σῶμά ἐστιν, ἡ δ᾽ ἑσπέρα
καὶ ὁ ὀρθὸς καὶ τὸ μέσον τῆς νυκτὸς
σώματα οὐκ ἔστιν · οὐδὲ ἡ μὲν
ἡμέρα σῶμά ἐστιν,᾿ οὐχὶ δὲ καὶ ἡ
νουμηνία σῶμα, καὶ ἡ δεκάτη, καὶ
πεντεκαιδεκάτη καὶ ἡ τριακὰς καὶ ὁ
μὴν σῶμά ἐστι καὶ τὸ θέρος καὶ τὸ
φθινόπωρον καὶ ὁ ἐνιαντός.
[2] *Diog.* 151: χειμῶνα μὲν
εἶναί φασι τὸν ὑπὲρ γῆς ἀέρα κατε-
ψυγμένον διὰ τὴν τοῦ ἡλίου πρόσω
ἄφοδον, ἔαρ δὲ τὴν εὐκρασίαν τοῦ
ἀέρος κατὰ τὴν πρὸς ἡμᾶς πορείαν,
θέρος δὲ τὸν ὑπὲρ γῆς ἀέρα κατα-

θαλπόμενον, κ.τ.λ. *Stob.* Ecl. i.
260: Chrysippus defines ἔαρ
ἔτους ὥραν κεκραμένην ἐκ χειμῶνος
ἀπολήγοντος καὶ θέρους ἀρχομένου
. . . θέρος δὲ ὥραν τὴν μάλιστ᾽ ἀφ᾽
ἡλίου διακεκαυμένην · μετόπωρον δὲ
ὥραν ἔτους τὴν μετὰ θέρος μὲν πρὸ
χειμῶνος δὲ κεκραμένην · χειμῶνα
δὲ ὥραν ἔτους τὴν μάλιστα κατεψυγμένην, ἢ τὴν τῷ περὶ γῆν ἀέρι
κατεψυγμένην, *Ibid.*: According
to Empedocles and the Stoics,
the cause of winter is the preponderance of air, the cause of
summer the preponderance of
fire. *Ibid.* 556: μεὶς δ᾽ ἐστὶ, φησὶ
[Χρύσιππος] τὸ φαινόμενον τῆς σελήνης πρὸς ἡμᾶς, ἢ σελήνη μέρος

K 2

(b) The in-
corporeal
or non-
material.

(2) Causes
which pro-
duced the
Stoic ma-
terialism.

these examples one thing is clear, how impossible the Stoics found it to assign reality to what is not material.

In carrying out this theory, they could not, as might be expected, wholly succeed. Hence a Stoic could not deny that there are certain things which it is absurd to call material. Among such include empty space, place, time, and expression (λεκτόν).[1] Admitting these to be incorporeal, they still would not allow that they do not exist at all. This view belongs only to isolated members of the Stoic School, for which they must be held personally responsible.[2] How they could harmonise belief in incorporeal things with their tenet that existence alone belongs to what is material is not on record.

The question next before us is: What led the Stoics to this materialism? It might be supposed that their peculiar theory of knowledge based on sensation was the cause; but this theory did not preclude the possibility of advancing from the sensible to the super-sensible. It might quite as well be said that their theory of knowledge was a consequence of their materialism, and that they referred all know-ledge to sensation, because they could allow no real being to anything which is not material. The pro-bability therefore remains that their theory of know-

---

ἔχουσα φαινόμενον πρὸς ἡμᾶς.
Cleomedes, Meteora, 112, distinguishes four meanings of
μὴν. In the two first it means
something material; in the
others, as a definition of time,

something immaterial.
[1] *Diog.* vii. 140; *Stob.* Ecl. i.
392; *Sext.* Math. x. 218 and
237; viii. 11; vii. 38; *Pyrrh.*
ii. 81; iii. 52. See p. 92, 2.
[2] See p. 94, 1.

ledge and their materialistic view of nature both
indicate one and the same habit of mind, and that
both are due to the action of the same causes.

CHAP.
VI.

Nor will it do to seek for these causes in the influence exercised by the Peripatetic or pre-Socratic
philosophy on the Stoic School: At first sight, indeed,
it might appear that the Stoics had borrowed from
Heraclitus their materialism, together with their
other views on nature; or else it might seem to be
an expansion of the metaphysical notions of Plato
and Aristotle. For if Aristotle denied Plato's distinction of form and matter to such an extent that
he would hardly allow form to *exist* at all except in
union with matter, might it not appear to others
more logical to do away with their distinction in
thought, thus reducing form to a property of matter?
Were there not difficulties in the doctrine of a God
external to the world, of a passionless Reason; were
there not even difficulties in the antithesis of form
and matter, which Aristotle's system was powerless to
overcome? And had not Aristoxenus and Dicæarchus
before the time of Zeno, and Strato immediately after
his time, been led from the ground occupied by the
Peripatetics to materialistic views? And yet we
must pause before accepting this explanation. The
founder of Stoicism appears, from what is recorded of
his intellectual growth, to have been repelled by the
Peripatetic School more than by any other; nor is there
the least indication in the records of the Stoic teaching that that teaching resulted from a criticism of
the Aristotelian and Platonic views of a double origin

*(a) The
Stoic ma-
terialism
not an ex-
pansion of
Peripate-
tic views.*

*(b) The
Stoic ma-
terialism
not due to
Heracli-
tus.*

*(c) Prac-
tical turn
of the Stoic
philosophy
the cause.*

of things. Far from it, the proposition that everything capable of acting or being acted upon must be
material, appears with the Stoics as an independent
axiom needing no further proof.

The supposed connection between the Stoics and
Heraclitus, so far from explaining their materialistic
views, already presumes their existence. Yet long
before Zeno's time the philosophy of Heraclitus as a
living tradition had become extinct. No historical
connection therefore, or relation of original dependence, can possibly exist between the two, but at most
a subsequent perception of relationship can have
directed Zeno to Heraclitus. Zeno's own view of the
world was not a consequence, but the cause, of his
sympathy with Heraclitus. In short, neither the
Peripatetics nor Heraclitus can have given the first
impulse to Zeno's materialism, although they may
have helped in many ways to strengthen his views on
that subject, when already formed.

The real causes for these views must therefore be
sought elsewhere, and will be found in the central
idea of the whole system of the Stoics—the practical
character of their philosophy. From the first devoting themselves with all their energies to practical
enquiries, in their theory of nature the Stoics occupied the ground of common views, which know of no
real object excepting what is grossly sensible and corporeal. Their aim in speculation was to discover a
firm basis for human actions.[1] In action, however,
men are brought into direct and experimental contact

[1] See p. 66, 1.

with objects. The objects then presented to the senses are, we must know, regarded in their naked reality without concealment, nor is an opportunity afforded for doubting their real being. Their reality is proved practically, inasmuch as it affects us and offers itself for the exercise of our powers. In every such exercise of power, both subject and object are always material. Even when an impression is conveyed to the soul of man, the direct instrument is something material—the voice or the gesture. In the region of experience there are no such things as non-material impressions. This was the ground occupied by the Stoics: a real thing is what either acts on us, or is acted upon by us. Such a thing is naturally material; and the Stoics with their practical ideas not being able to soar above what is most obvious, declared that reality belongs only to the world of bodies.

CHAP.
VI.

Herefrom it would appear to follow that only individual perceptions are true, and that all general conceptions without exception must be false. If each notion (λεκτὸν) is incorporeal, and consequently unreal,[1] will not absence of reality in a much higher degree belong to the notion of what is general? Individual notions refer directly to perceptions, i.e. to something incorporeal; nevertheless they indirectly refer to the things perceived, i.e. to what is material. But general notions do not even indirectly refer to anything corporeal; they are pure fabrications of the mind, which have nothing real as their object.

(3) *Consequences of the Stoic materialism.* (a) *Individual perceptions alone true; yet a higher truth assigned to general conceptions.*

---

[1] See p. 93; 132, 1.

This the Stoics explicitly maintained.[1] To attribute notwithstanding to these general conceptions, to which no real objects correspond, a higher truth and certainty than belongs to the perceptions of individual objects, was a gross inconsistency, but one which the Stoic system made not the slightest attempt to overcome.

(b) Theory of universal intermingling.

The materialism of the Stoics likewise led to some remarkable assertions in the matter of natural science. If the attributes of things, the soul and even the powers of the soul, are all corporeal, the relation of attributes to their objects, of the soul to the body, of one body to another body, is that of *mutual intermingling.*[2] Moreover, inasmuch as the essential attributes of any definite material belong to every part of that material, and the soul resides in every part of the body, without the soul's being identical with the body, and without the attributes being identical with the material to which they belong, or with one another; it follows that one body may intermingle with another not only by occupying the vacant spaces in that body, but by interpenetrating all its parts, without, however, being fused into a homogeneous mass with it.[3] This view involves not only a denial of the impenetrability of matter, but it

[1] See p. 84, 4.
[2] See p. 105, 3.
[3] Let a piece of red-hot iron be taken, every part of which is heavy, hard, hot, &c. Not one of these attributes can be confounded with another, or with the iron itself, but each one runs through the whole iron. Now, if each attribute is due to the presence of some material producing it, there is no avoiding the conclusion that there must exist in the iron, and in each part of it, as many various materials as there are attributes, without any one of them losing its own identity.

further supposes that a smaller body when mingled
with a greater body will extend over the whole of the
latter. It is known as the Stoic theory of universal
intermingling (κρᾶσις δι᾽ ὅλων), and is alike different
from the ordinary view of mechanical mixture and
from that of chemical mixture. It differs from the
former in that every part of the one body is inter-
penetrated by every part of the other; from the
latter, because the bodies after mixture still retain
their own properties.[1] This peculiar theory, which

[1] *Diog.* vii. 151 : καὶ τὰς
κράσεις δὲ διόλου γίνεσθαι, καθά
φησιν ὁ Χρύσιππος ἐν τῇ τρίτῃ
τῶν φυσικῶν, καὶ μὴ κατὰ περι-
γραφὴν καὶ παράθεσιν · καὶ γὰρ εἰς
πέλαγος ὀλίγος οἶνος βληθεὶς ἐπὶ
πόσον ἀντιπαρεκταθήσεται εἶτα
συμφθαρήσεται. According to
Stob. Ecl. i. 374, the Stoics
more accurately distinguish
μῖξις, κρᾶσις, παράθεσις, σύγχυσις.
Παράθεσίς is σωμάτων συναφὴ κατὰ
τὰς ἐπιφανείας ; for instance, the
combination of various kinds
of grain. Μῖξις is δύο ἢ καὶ
πλειόνων σωμάτων ἀντιπαρέκτασις
δι᾽ ὅλων, ὑπομενουσῶν τῶν συμφυῶν
περὶ αὐτὰ ποιοτήτων ; for instance, the union of fire and
iron, of soul and body. Such a
union is called μῖξις in the case
of solid bodies, κρᾶσις in the
case of fluids. Σύγχυσις is δύο
ἢ καὶ πλειόνων ποιοτήτων περὶ τὰ
σώματα μεταβολὴ εἰς ἑτέρας δια-
φερούσης τούτων ποιότητος γένεσιν, as in the making up salves
and medicines. Very much in
the same way according to
Alex. Aphr. De Mixt. 142, a,
Chrysippus distinguished three
kinds of μῖξις : παράθεσις, or

union of substances, in which
each retains its οἰκεία οὐσία or
ποιότης κατὰ τὴν περιγραφήν ;
σύγχυσις, in which both substances, as well as attributes,
are destroyed (φθείρεσθαι),
giving rise to a third body ;
κρᾶσις = δύο ἢ καὶ πλειόνων τινῶν
σωμάτων ὅλων δι᾽ ὅλων ἀντιπαρέ-
κτασιν ἀλλήλοις οὕτως, ὥστε
σώζειν ἕκαστον αὐτῶν ἐν τῇ μίξει ·
τῇ τοιαύτῃ τήν τε οἰκείαν οὐσίαν
καὶ τὰς ἐν αὐτῇ ποιότητας. Materials thus united can be again
separated, but yet are they so
united : ὡς μηδὲν μόριον ἐν αὐτοῖς
εἶναι μὴ μετέχον πάντων τῶν ἐν τῷ
μίγματι.

For such a union to be possible, (1) it must be possible
for one body to penetrate every
part of another, without being
fused into a homogeneous mass.
Hence the expression σῶμα διὰ
σώματος ἀντιπαρήκειν, σῶμα σώματος εἶναι τόπον καὶ σῶμα χωρεῖν
διὰ σώματος κένυν μηδετέρου περιέ-
χοντος ἀλλὰ τοῦ πλήρους εἰς τὸ
πλῆρες ἐνδυομένου (*Plut.* C. Not.
37, 2, p. 1077 ; *Alex.* 142, b ;
Themist. Phys. 37 ; *Simpl.* Phys.
123, b ; *Hippolyt.* Refut. Haer.

is one of the much debated but distinctive features of the Stoic system,[1] cannot have been deduced from physical causes. On the contrary, the arguments by which Chrysippus supported it prove that it was ultimately the result of metaphysical considerations.[2]

i. 21); (2) it must be possible for the smaller body to extend over the whole size of the greater. This is affirmed by Chrysippus : οὐδὲν ἀπέχειν φάμενος, οἴνου σταλαγμὸν ἕνα κεράσαι τὴν θάλατταν, or even εἰς ὅλον τὸν κόσμον διατενεῖν τῇ κράσει τὸν σταλαγμόν (Plut. 10 ; Alex. 142, b ; Diog.). The greater body is said to help the smaller, by giving to it an extension of which it would not otherwise be capable. Nevertheless, the bodies so united need not necessarily occupy more space than was previously occupied by one of them (Alex. 142, b; Plotin. Enn. iv. 7, 8, p. 463, C. Fic. 860, 14, Cr.). The absurdities which this theory involves were already exposed by Arcesilaus (Plut. 7), and in detail by Alexander, Plutarch, Sextus, and Plotinus, by the latter in a whole treatise (Enn. ii. 7) περὶ τῆς δι' ὅλων κράτεως.

[1] Πολλὰ μὲν γὰρ λέγεται περὶ κράσεως καὶ σχεδὸν ἀνήνυτοι περὶ τοῦ προκειμένου σκέμματός εἰσι παρὰ τοῖς Δογματικοῖς στάσεις. Sext. Pyrrh. iii. 56. See previous note.

[2] According to Alex. 142, a, the following arguments were used by Chrysippus :—(1) The argument from κοιναὶ ἔννοιαι— our notion of κρᾶσις is different from that of σύγχυσις or παράθεσις. (2) Many bodies are

capable of extension, whilst retaining their own properties ; frankincense, for instance, when burnt, and gold. (3) The soul penetrates every part of the body, without losing its properties. So φύσις does in plants, and ἕξις does in all which it connects. (4) The same holds good of fire in red-hot metal, of fire and air in water and earth, of poisons and perfumes in things with which they are mixed, and of light, which penetrates air.

The first of these arguments clearly does not embody the real reason in the mind of Chrysippus ; it might, with equal justice, have been used to prove anything else. Just as little does the second ; for the phenomena to which it refers would be equally well explained on the theory of simple intermingling (παράθεσις) or complete (σύγχυσις) mixing. Nor does the fourth argument, taken independently of the theory of the corporeal nature of properties, necessarily lead to the idea of κρᾶσις as distinct from παράθεσις and σύγχυσις. For heat, according to the Peripatetic view, might be regarded as a property of what is hot, light as a definite property of a transparent body (conf. Alex. 143, a), παράθεσις and σύγχυσις sufficing for other

We have, moreover, all the less reason to doubt this fact, inasmuch as the materialistic undercurrent of the Stoic system affords for it the best explanation.

Although the stamp of materialism was sharply cut, and its application fearlessly made by the Stoics, they were yet far from holding the mechanical theory of nature, which appears to us to be a necessary consequence of strict materialism. The universe was explained on a dynamical theory; the notion of force was placed above the notion of matter. To matter, they held, alone belongs real existence; but the characteristic of real existence they sought in causation, in the capacity to act and to be acted upon.[1] This capacity belongs to matter only by virtue of certain inherent forces, which impart to it definite attributes. Let pure matter devoid of every attribute

things. Even the fact, greatly insisted upon by the Stoics, that things so mixed can be again separated into their component materials (*Alex.* 143, a; *Stob.* i. 378) was not conclusive. As long as the knowledge of the actual composition depended on isolated cases and crude experiments, like the one named by Stobæus (into a mixture of wine and water, put an oiled sponge, it will absorb the water and not the wine), and as long as the substantial change of elements, advocated by the Stoics as well as by the Peripatetics, was clung to, it was no difficult matter for an opponent to reply. On the other hand, the relation of the soul to the body, of property to subject-matter, of φύσις to φυτὸν, of God to the world, can hardly be otherwise explained than as Chrysippus did, if once material existence be assigned to the soul, to φύσις, to ἕξις, and to God. We have, therefore, here the real ground on which this theory of κρᾶσις was based; and Simplicius rightly deduces it herefrom (Phys. 123, b): τὸ δὲ σῶμα διὰ σώματος χωρεῖν οἱ μὲν ἀρχαῖοι ὡς ἐναργὲς ἄτοπον ἐλάμβανον, οἱ δὲ ἀπὸ τῆς στοᾶς ὕστερον προσήκαντο ὡς ἀκολουθοῦν ταῖς σφῶν αὐτῶν ὑποθέσεσιν . . . σώματα γὰρ λέγειν πάντα δοκοῦντες, καὶ τὰς ποιότητας καὶ τὴν ψυχήν, καὶ διὰ παντὸς ὁρῶντες τοῦ σώματος καὶ τὴν ψυχὴν χωροῦσαν καὶ τὰς ποιότητας ἐν ταῖς κράσεσι, συνεχώρουν σῶμα διὰ σώματος χωρεῖν.

[1] See p. 95, 2; 126, 1.

be considered, the matter which underlies all definite
materials, and out of which all things are made;[1] it
will be found to be purely passive, a something
subject to any change, able to assume any shape and
quality, but taken by itself devoid of quality, and
unable to produce any change whatsoever.[2] This
inert and powerless matter is first reduced into shape
by means of attributes,[3] all of which suppose tension
in the air-currents which produce them, and consequently suppose a force producing tension.[4] Even
the shape of bodies, and the place they occupy in
space is, according to the Stoics, something derivative, the consequence of tension; tension keeping the
different particles apart in one or the other particular
way.[5] Just as some modern physiologists construct
nature by putting together a sum of forces of attraction and repulsion, so the Stoics refer nature to two
forces, or, speaking more accurately, to a double kind
of motion—expansion and condensation. Expansion
works outwardly, condensation inwardly; condensation
produces being, or what is synonymous with it, mat-

---

[1] On ἄποιος ὕλη, as the universal ὑποκείμενον or οὐσία κοινὴ,
see p. 100. Sext. Math. x. 312: ἐξ
ἀποίου μὲν οὖν καὶ ἑνὸς σώματος
τὴν τῶν ὅλων ὑπεστήσαντο γένεσιν
οἱ Στωϊκοί. ἀρχὴ γὰρ τῶν ὄντων
κατ᾽ αὐτούς ἐστιν ἡ ἄποιος ὕλη καὶ
δι᾽ ὅλων τρεπτὴ, μεταβαλλούσης
τε ταύτης γίνεται τὰ τέσσαρα
στοιχεῖα, πῦρ, κ.τ.λ. Plut. C.
Not. 48, 2, p. 1085: ἡ ὕλη καθ᾽
αὑτὴν ἄλογος οὖσα καὶ ἄποιος.
M. Aurel. xii. 30: μία οὐσία
κοινὴ, κἂν διείργηται ἰδίως ποιοῖς
σώματι μυρίοις. Diog. 137: τὰ

δὴ τέτταρα στοιχεῖα εἶναι ὁμοῦ τὴν
ἄποιον οὐσίαν τὴν ὕλην.

[2] See p. 141, 2.

[3] Plut. Sto. Rep. 43. See p.
105, 1.

[4] See p. 105, 1 and 2; 127,
5; 128, 2.

[5] Simpl. Cat. 67, ε (Schol.
74, a, 10): τὸ τοίνυν σχῆμα οἱ
Στωϊκοὶ τὴν τάσιν παρέχεσθαι
λέγουσιν, ὥσπερ τὴν μεταξὺ τῶν
σημείων διάστασιν. διὸ καὶ εὐθεῖαν
ὁρίζονται γραμμὴν τὴν εἰς ἄκρον
τεταμένην.

ter; expansion gives rise to the attributes of things.[1]
Whilst, therefore, they assert that everything really
existing must be material, they still distinguish in
what is material two component parts—the part which
is acted upon, and the part which acts, or in other
words *matter* and *force*.[2]

The Stoics, however, would not agree with Plato (2) *The*
and Aristotle so far as to allow to formal and final *nature of*
causes a place side by side with this acting force or (a) *Force*
force.
efficient cause.   If in general anything may be called *limited to*
the notion
of efficient
cause.

[1] *Simpl.* Cat. 68, ε: οἱ δὲ
Στωϊκοὶ δύναμιν, ἢ μᾶλλον κίνησιν
τὴν μανωτικὴν καὶ πυκνωτικὴν
τίθενται, τὴν μὲν ἐπὶ τὰ ἔσω, τὴν
δὲ ἐπὶ τὰ ἔξω· καὶ τὴν μὲν τοῦ
εἶναι, τὴν δὲ τοῦ ποιὸν εἶναι νομίζουσιν αἰτίαν. *Nemes.* Nat. Hom.
c. 2, p. 29 : εἰ δὲ λέγοιεν, καθάπερ οἱ
Στωϊκοὶ, τονικήν τινα εἶναι κίνησιν
περὶ τὰ σώματα, εἰς τὸ ἔσω ἅμα
καὶ εἰς τὸ ἔξω κινουμένην, καὶ τὴν
μὲν εἰς τὸ ἔξω μεγεθῶν καὶ ποιότη-
των ἀποτελεστικὴν εἶναι, τὴν δὲ
εἰς τὸ ἔσω ἑνώσεως καὶ οὐσίας.
This remark is confirmed by
what is quoted, p. 128, 2 from
Censorinus, and by the language
of Plutarch (Def. Orac. c. 28,
Schl. p. 425), in reference to
Chrysippus : πολλάκις εἰρηκὼς,
ὅτι ταῖς εἰς τὸ αὑτῆς μέσον ἡ οὐσία
καὶ ταῖς ἀπὸ τοῦ αὑτῆς μέσον διοικεῖται καὶ συνέχεται κινήσεσι.

[2] *Diog.* vii. 134 : δοκεῖ δ'
αὑτοῖς ἀρχὰς εἶναι τῶν ὅλων δύο,
τὸ ποιοῦν καὶ τὸ πάσχον. τὸ μὲν
οὖν πάσχον εἶναι τὴν ἄποιον οὐσίαν
τὴν ὕλην, τὸ δὲ ποιοῦν τὸν ἐν αὑτῇ
λόγον τὸν θεόν. τοῦτον γὰρ ὄντα
ἀΐδιον διὰ πάσης αὑτῆς δημιουργεῖν
ἕκαστα. Such is the teaching
of Zeno, Cleanthes, Chrysippus,

Archedemus, and Posidonius.
Sext. Math. ix. 11 : οἱ ἀπὸ τῆς
στοᾶς δύο λέγοντες ἀρχὰς, θεὸν καὶ
ἄποιον ὕλην, τὸν μὲν θεὸν ποιεῖν
ὑπειλήφασι, τὴν δὲ ὕλην πάσχειν
τε καὶ τρέπεσθαι.   Similarly
Alex. Aph. De Mixt. 144 ;
Achill. Tat. Isag. c. 3, 124, E ;
Plut. Pl. Phil. i. 3, 39 ; *Stob.*
Ecl. i. 306; 322, according to the
passage quoted, p. 101, 2, from
Zeno respecting ὕλη : διὰ ταύτης
δὲ διαθεῖν τὸν τοῦ παντὸς λόγον ὃν
ἔνιοι εἱμαρμένην καλοῦσιν, οἷόνπερ
ἐν τῇ γόνῃ τὸ σπέρμα. *Sen.* Ep.
65, 2 : Dicunt, ut scis, Stoici
nostri, duo esse in rerum natura,
ex quibus omnia fiant : causam
et materiam. Materia jacet
iners, res ad omnia parata, ces-
satura si nemo moveat. Causa
autem, i.e. ratio, materiam
format et quɔcunque vult versat,
ex illa varia opera producit.
Esse ergo debet, unde fit aliquid,
deinde a qno fiat. Hoc causa
est, illud materia. *Ibid.* 23 :
Universa ex materia et ex Deo
constant . . . potentius autem
est ac pretiosius quod facit,
quod est Deus, quam materia
patiens Dei.

a cause which serves to bring about a definite result[1]
—and various kinds of causes may be distinguished,
according as they bring about this result directly or
indirectly, by themselves alone or by the help of
others[2]—in the highest sense there can be, according
to the Stoics, only one acting or efficient cause. The
form is due to the workman, and is therefore only a
part of the efficient cause. The type-form is only an
instrument, which the workman employs in his work.
The final cause or end-in-chief, in as far as it represents the workman's intention, is only an occasional
cause; in as far as it belongs to the work he is about,
it is not a cause at all, but a result. There can be
but one pure and unconditional cause, just as there

---

[1] *Sen.* Ep. 65, 11: Nam si,
quocumque remoto quid effici
non potest, id causam judicant
esse faciendi, &c. *Sext.* Math.
ix. 228 : εἰ αἴτιόν ἐστιν οὗ παρόν-
τος γίνεται τὸ ἀποτέλεσμα. This
appears to be the most general
Stoic definition. That given by
Sext. Pyrrh. iii. 14—τοῦτο, δι' ὃ
ἐνεργοῦν γίνεται τὸ ἀποτέλεσμα —
and by him said to express the
views of several schools, expresses a narrower conception
—the conception of efficient
cause, which, however, for a
Stoic, is the only essential
one.

[2] *Sext.* Pyrrh. iii. 15, distinguishes between συνεκτικὰ,
συναίτια, and σύνεργα αἴτια, all of
which are, however, subordinated to the δι' ὃ, which he is
there alone discussing. Seneca
l. c. maintains that, according
to the definition given above,

time, place, and motion, ought
to be reckoned as causes, since
nothing can be produced without these. He allows, however,
that a distinction must be made
between causa efficiens and
causa superveniens. This agrees
with what Cicero (De Fato,
18, 41) quotes from Chrysippus
relative to causæ perfectæ et
principales, and causæ adjuvantes et proximæ, and with
the Platonic and Aristotelian
distinction of αἴτιον δι' ὃ and οὗ
οὐκ ἄνευ. See *Zeller's* Philosophie der Griechen. In the
same way, *Plut.* Sto. Rep. 47,
4, p. 1056 distinguishes between
αἴτια αὐτοτελῆς and προκαταρ-
κτική, *Alex. Aph.* De Fato, 72,
blames the Stoics : σμῆνος γὰρ
αἰτίων καταλέγουσι, τὰ μὲν προκα-
ταρκτικὰ, τὰ δὲ συναίτια, τὰ δὲ
ἑκτικά, τὰ δὲ συνεκτικὰ, τὰ δὲ ἄλλο
τι. Conf. Orelli ad locum.

can be but one matter; and to this efficient cause everything that exists and everything that takes place must be referred.[1]

In attempting to form a more accurate notion of this efficient cause, the first point which deserves attention is, that the Stoics believed every kind of action ultimately to proceed from one source.   For how could the world be such a self-circumscribed unity, such a harmonious whole, unless it were governed by one and the same force?[2]   Again, as everything which acts is material, the highest efficient cause must likewise be considered material; and since all qualities and forces are produced by vapour-like or fiery elements, can it be otherwise with the highest acting force?[3]   Everywhere warmth is the cause of nourishment and growth, life and motion; all things have in themselves their own natural heat, and are preserved and kept in life by the heat of the sun.

(b) Character of this efficient cause.

---

[1] *Seneca*, l. c., after enumerating the four causes of Aristotle, to which the Platonic idea is added as a fifth, continues: This turba causarum embraces either too much or too little. Sed nos nunc primam et generalem quærimus causam. Hæc simplex esse debet, nam et materia simplex est. Quærimus quæ sit causa, ratio scilicet faciens, id est Deus. Ita enim, quæcumque retulistis, non sunt multæ et singulæ causæ, sed ex una pendent, ex ea, quæ faciet. Conf. *Stob.* Ecl. i. 336: αἴτιον δ' ὁ Ζήνων φησὶν εἶναι δι' ὃ . . . Χρύσιππος αἴτιον εἶναι λέγει δι' ὃ . . . Ποσειδώνιος δὲ οὕτως · αἴτιον δ' ἐστί τινος δι' ὃ ἐκεῖνο, ἢ τὸ πρῶτον ποιοῦν ἢ τὸ ἀρχηγὸν ποιήσεως.

[2] *Cic.* N. De. ii. 7, 19, after speaking of the consentiens, conspirans, continuata cognatio rerum (συμπάθεια τῶν ὅλων), continues: Hæc ita fieri omnibus inter se concinentibus mundi partibus profecto non possent, nisi ea uno divino et continuato spiritu continerentur. See *Sext.* Math. ix. 78. The same view is further expanded in *Sext.* Math. ix. 78. Conf. the quotation on p. 127, 5, from Alexander.

[3] According to the remarks, p. 105 and 126, this requires no proof.

What applies to parts of the world must apply to the world as a whole; hence heat or fire is the power to which the life and the existence of the world must be referred.[1]

This power must be further defined to be the soul of the world, the highest reason, a kind, beneficent, and philanthropic being; in short, deity. The universal belief and the universal worship of God prove this, as the Stoics think, beyond a doubt;[2] still more accurate investigation confirms it. Matter can never move or fashion itself; nothing but a power inherent as the soul is in man can produce these results.[3] The world would not be the most perfect and complete thing it is unless Reason were inherent therein;[4]

---

[1] *Cic.* N. D. ii. 9, 23 (conf. iii. 14, 35), gives it apparently as the view of Cleanthes, who alone is mentioned, 9, 24. All living things, plants, and animals, exist by heat : nam omne quod est calidum et igneum cietur et agitur motu suo. Digestion and circulation are the result of heat: ex quo intelligi debet, eam caloris naturam vim habere in se vitalem per omnem mundum pertinentem. Moreover: omnes partes mundi . . . calore fultæ sustinentur. There must be fire in earth and stones, else it could not be extracted therefrom. Water, especially fresh spring water, is warm, more particularly in winter, and as motion warms us, so the roll of the waves does the sea. From water likewise as it evaporates, air derives its heat. . . . Jam vero reliqua quarta pars mundi,

ea et ipsa tota natura fervida est, et cæteris naturis omnibus salutarem impertit et vitalem calorem. Ex quo concluditur, cum omnes mundi partes sustineantur calóre, mundum etiam ipsum simili parique natura in tanta diuturnitate servari : eoque magis quod intelligi debet, calidum illum atque igneum ita in omni fusum esse natura, ut in eo insit procreandi vis, &c.

[2] On the argument, ex consensu gentium, consult *Plut.* Sto. Rep. 38, 3 ; Com. Not. 32, 1 ; *Cic.* N. D. ii. 2, 5 ; *Seneca*, Benef. iv. 4 ; *Sext.* Math. ix. 123 and 131, where different varieties of it are given, even a particular one from Zeno.

[3] *Sext.* Math. ix. 75.

[4] *Cic.* N. D. iii. 9, 22 : Zeno enim ita concludit : quod ratione utitur, melius est, quam id, quod ratione non utitur. Nihil

nor could it contain any beings possessed of consciousness, unless it were conscious itself.[1] It could not produce creatures endowed with a soul and reason, unless it were itself endowed with a soul and reason.[2] Actions so far surpassing man's power could not exist, unless there were a cause for them in perfection equally surpassing that of man.[3] The subordination of means to ends which governs the world in every part down to the minutest details would be inexplicable, unless the world owed its origin to a reasonable creator.[4] The graduated rank of beings would be

autem mundo melius. Ratione igitur mundus utitur. The same, *ibid.* ii. 8, 21, and 12, 34. *Sext.* Math. ix. 104 : εἰ τὸ λογικὸν τοῦ μὴ λογικοῦ κρεῖττόν ἐστιν, οὐδὲν δέ γε κόσμου κρεῖττόν ἐστι, λογικὸν ἄρα ὁ κόσμος . . . τὸ γὰρ νοερὸν τοῦ μὴ νοεροῦ καὶ ἔμψυχον τοῦ μὴ ἐμψύχου κρεῖττόν ἐστιν· οὐδὲν δέ γε κόσμου κρεῖττον· νοερὸς ἄρα καὶ ἔμψυχός ἐστιν ὁ κόσμος. Likewise *Diog.* 142, says that Chrysippus, Apollodorus, and Posidonius agree that the world is ζῷον καὶ λογικὸν καὶ ἔμψυχον καὶ νοερόν· τὸ γὰρ ζῷον τοῦ μὴ ζῴου κρεῖττον· οὐδὲν δὲ τοῦ κόσμου κρεῖττον· ζῷον ἄρα ὁ κόσμος.

[1] *Cic.* N. D. ii. 8, 22 : Zeno affirms : Nullius sensu carentis pars aliqua potest esse sentiens. Mundi autem partes sentientes sunt. Non igitur caret sensu mundus.

[2] *Diog.* 143 : ἔμψυχον δὲ [τὸν κόσμον], ὡς δῆλον ἐκ τῆς ἡμετέρας ψυχῆς ἐκεῖθεν οὔσης ἀποσπάσματος. *Sext.* Math. ix. 101 : Ζήνων δὲ ὁ Κιττιεὺς ἀπὸ Ξενοφῶντος τὴν ἀφορμὴν λαβὼν οὑτωσὶ

συνερωτᾷ· τὸ προιέμενον σπέρμα λογικοῦ καὶ αὐτὸ λογικόν ἐστιν· ὁ δὲ κόσμος προίεται σπέρμα λογικοῦ, λογικὸν ἄρα ἐστὶν ὁ κόσμος. The same proof in *Sext.* Math. ix. 77 and 84 ; *Cic.* l. c. Conf. *ibid.* ii. 31, 79 ; 6, 18, where also the passage in Xenophon, Mem. i. 4, 8, quoted by *Sext.* ix. 94, is referred to.

[3] *Cic.* l. c. iii. 10, 25 : Is [Chrysippus] igitur : si aliquid est, inquit, quod homo efficere non possit, qui id efficit melior est homine. Homo autem hæc, quæ in mundo sunt, efficere non potest. Qui potuit igitur, is præstat homini. Homini autem præstare quis possit, nisi Deus ? Est igitur Deus. The same, only a little more fully, *ibid.* ii. 6, 16. To this argument, another favourite one of the Stoics, based on the fulfilment of prophecy, belongs.

[4] Cleanthes made use of arguments from final causes to prove the existence of God. Of this nature are all the four arguments which he employs in *Cic.* N. D. ii. 5, but particularly

incomplete, unless there were a highest Being of all whose moral and intellectual perfection cannot be surpassed.[1] Although this perfection belongs, in the first place, to the world as a whole,[2] nevertheless, as in everything consisting of many parts, so in the world the ruling part must be distinguished from other parts. It is *the* part from which all acting forces emanate and diffuse themselves over the world,[3] whether the seat of this efficient force be placed in the heaven, as was done by Zeno, Chrysippus, and the majority of the Stoics;[4] or in the sun, as by

the fourth, based on the regular order and beauty of heaven. A building cannot exist withou a builder; no more can the building of the world exist without a ruling spirit. Therewith Cicero connects the above-named argument of Chrysippus. The same writer, N. D. ii. 32–66, gives very fully the physical theological argument for the existence of providence, which is given in a shorter form by *Cleomedes*, Meteora, 1 ; *Seneca*, De Provid. i. 1, 2–4 ; Nat. Qu. i.; *Sext*. Math. ix. 111 ; conf. Ps. *Censorin.* Fragm. i. 2, p. 75, Jahn ; *Plut.* Plac. i. 6, 8 : belief in gods grows out of considering the world and its beauty, an argument also quoted by *Sext.* Math. ix. 26.

[1] See the expansion of this thought by Cleanthes (in *Sext.* Math. ix. 88–91) and the Stoics (in *Cic.* N. D. ii. 12, 33). Cicero distinguishes four kinds of beings—Plants, Animals, Men, and that being which is altogether reasonable and perfect deity.

[2] See p. 143, 2 ; 144, 1–4 ; 145, 1 and 2.

[3] *Sext.* Math. ix. 102, expanding Zeno's argument given, p. 145, 2 : πάσης γὰρ φύσεως καὶ ψυχῆς ἡ καταρχὴ τῆς κινήσεως γίνεσθαι δοκεῖ ἀπὸ ἡγεμονικοῦ καὶ πᾶσαι αἱ ἐπὶ τὰ μέρη τοῦ ὅλου ἐξαποστελλόμεναι δυνάμεις ὡς ἀπό τινος πηγῆς τοῦ ἡγεμονικοῦ ἐξαποστέλλονται. *Cic.* N. D. ii. 29 : according to Cleanthes, omnem enim naturam necesse est, quæ non solitaria sit, neque simplex, sed cum alio juncta atque connexa, habere aliquem in se principatum [= ἡγεμονικὸν] ut in homine mentem, &c. . . . Itaque necesse est illud etiam, in quo sit totius naturæ principatus, esse omnium optimum. See following note.

[4] *Cic.* Acad. ii. 41, 126 : Zenoni et reliquis fere Stoicis æther videtur summus Deus, mente præditus, qua omnia regantur. N. D. i. 14, 36 : (Zeno) æthera Deum dicit. 15, 39 : ignem præterea et eum, quem antea dixi, æthera (Chrysippus Deum dicit esse). *Diog.* vii.

DYNAMICAL VIEW OF NATURE. 147

Cleanthes;¹ or in the centre of the world, as by Archedemus.² This primary source of all life and motion, the highest Cause and the highest Reason, is God. God therefore and formless matter are the *two* ultimate grounds of things.³

CHAP.
VI.

138 : οὐρανὸς δέ ἐστιν ἡ ἐσχάτη περιφέρεια, ἐν ᾗ πᾶν ἵδρυται τὸ θεῖον. *Ibid.* 139 : τὸν ὅλον κόσμον ζῷον ὄντα καὶ ἔμψυχον καὶ λογικὸν ἔχειν ἡγεμονικὸν μὲν τὸν αἰθέρα, καθά φησιν ᾿Αντίπατρος . . . Χρύσιππος δ᾿ . . . καὶ Ποσειδώνιος . . . τὸν οὐρανόν φασι τὸ ἡγεμονικὸν τοῦ κόσμου. He continues : ὁ μέντοι Χρύσιππος διαφορώτεροι πάλιν τὸ καθαρώτερον τοῦ αἰθέρος ἐν ταὐτῷ [= τῷ οὐρανῷ] ὃ καὶ πρῶτον θεὸν λέγουσιν, αἰσθητικῶς ὥσπερ κεχωρηκέναι διὰ τῶν ἐν ἀέρι καὶ διὰ τῶν ζῴων ἁπάντων καὶ φυτῶν, διὰ δὲ τῆς γῆς αὐτῆς καθ᾿ ἕξιν. *Arius Didymus,* in Eus. Præp. Ev. xv. 15, 4 : Χρυσίππῳ δὲ [ἡγεμονικὸν τοῦ κόσμου εἶναι ἤρεσε] τὸν αἰθέρα τὸν καθαρώτατον καὶ εἰλικρινέστατον, ἅτε πάντων εὐκινητότατον ὄντα καὶ τὴν ὅλην περιάγοντα τοῦ κόσμου φύσιν. *Ibid.* xv. 20, 2 : According to the Stoics, the air surrounding sea and earth is the soul of the world. *Cornut.* Nat. De. 8 Os. : Zeus dwells in heaven, ἐπεὶ ἐκεῖ ἐστι τὸ κυριώτατον μέρος τῆς τοῦ κόσμου ψυχῆς. *Tertullian* (Apol. 47; Ad Nat. ii. 2, 4) inaccurately attributes to the Stoics the belief in a God external to nature.
¹ *Cic.* Acad. l. c.: Cleanthes . . . solem dominari et rerum potiri = κρατεῖν τῶν ὄντων putat. He speaks with less accuracy (*Krische,* Forsch. 428) in N. D. i. 14, 37 : ether he

considers the original deity; for this does not exclude the other. No doubt he identified αἰθήρ with calor (see p. 144, 1), believing that it emanated from the sun. *Diog.* 139: Κλεάνθης δὲ [τὸ ἡγεμονικόν φησι] τὸν ἥλιον. *Ar. Didymus,* l. c. ἡγεμονικὸν δὲ τοῦ κόσμου Κλεάνθει μὲν ἤρεσε τὸν ἥλιον εἶναι διὰ τὸ μέγιστον τῶν ἄστρων ὑπάρχειν καὶ πλεῖστα συμβάλλεσθαι πρὸς τὴν τῶν ὅλων διοίκησιν, κ.τ.λ. *Stob.* Ecl. i. 452; Ps. *Censorin.* Fragm. i. 4. According to *Epiphan.* Exp. Fidei. 1090, c, he called the sun the δᾳδοῦχος to the universe.
² *Stob.* l. c. : ᾿Αρχίδαμος (leg. with Cod. A ᾿Αρχέδημος) τὸ ἡγεμονικὸν τοῦ κόσμου ἐν γῇ ὑπάρχειν ἀπεφήνατο : the same statement without mentioning the name in Ar. Didymus, l. c. This reminds one somewhat of the Pythagorean doctrine of a central fire, and the view of Speusippus. The resemblance to the Pythagoreans is greater, if *Simpl.* De Cœlo, Schol. in Ar. 505, a, 45, is correct in saying Archedemus denied with the Pythagoreans that the earth was in the centre of the world.
³ See p. 141, 2; 143, 1. *Aristocles,* in Eus. Pr. Ev. xv. 14: στοιχεῖον εἶναί φασι [οἱ Στωϊκοὶ] τῶν ὄντων τὸ πῦρ, καθάπερ ῾Ηράκλειτος, τούτου δ᾿ ἀρχὰς ὕλην καὶ θεὸν, ὡς Πλάτων.

L 2

CHAP.
VI.

(3) *Deity.*
(a) *The
conception
of Deity
more ac-
curately
defined.*

The language used by the Stoics in reference to
the Deity at one time gives greater prominence to
the material, at another to the spiritual side of their
conception of God. As a rule, both are united in expressions which only cease to be startling when taken
in connection with Stoic views in general. God is
spoken of as being Fire, Ether, Air, most commonly
as being πνεῦμα or Atmospheric-Current, pervading
everything without exception, what is most base and
ugly, as well as what is most beautiful.[1] He is further
described[2] as the Soul, the Mind, or the Reason of

[1] Fuller particulars p. 144,
1; 146. *Hippolytus,* Refut.
Haer. i. 21: Chrysippus and
Zeno suppose ἀρχὴν μὲν θεὸν τῶν
πάντων, σῶμα ὄντα τὸ καθαρώτατον
(æther). *Diog.* 148: Antipater
calls the οὐσία θεοῦ ἀεροειδής.
Stob. Ecl. i. 60: Mnesarchus (a
pupil of Panætius) defines God
to be τὸν κόσμον τὴν πρώτην οὐσίαν ἔχοντα ἐπὶ πνεύματος. *Sext.*
Pyrrh. iii. 218: Στωϊκοὶ δὲ [λέ-
γουσι θεὸν]. πνεῦμα διῆκον καὶ διὰ
τῶν εἰδεχθῶν (the adverse).
Alex. Aphr. on Metaph. 995, b,
31 (Schol. in Ar. 607, a, 19):
τοῖς ἀπὸ τῆς στοᾶς ἔδοξεν ὁ θεὸς
καὶ τὸ ποιητικὸν αἴτιον ἐν τῇ ὕλῃ
εἶναι. *Ibid.* De Mix. 144, gives
them credit: πνεύματι ὡς διὰ
πάντων 'διήκοντι ἀνάπτειν τό τε
εἶναι ἑκάστου καὶ τὸ σώζεσθαι καὶ
συμμένειν. Compare the quotations p. 127, 5 and De An. 145:
[εἶναι θεῖον ὄντα, ὡς τοῖς ἀπὸ τῆς
στοᾶς ἔδοξεν. *Lucian,* Hermot.
81: ἀκούομεν δὲ αὐτοῦ λέγοντος,
ὡς καὶ ὁ θεὸς οὐκ ἐν οὐρανῷ ἐστιν,
ἀλλὰ διὰ πάντων πεφοίτηκεν, οἷον
ξύλων καὶ λίθων καὶ ζῴων, ἄχρι καὶ

τῶν ἀτιμωτάτων. *Tertullian,*
Ad Nation. ii. 4: Zeno makes
God penetrate the materia mun-
dialis, as honey does the honey-
combs. See p. 105, 3.
Clemens, Strom. v. 591, A:
φασὶ γὰρ σῶμα εἶναι τὸν θεὸν οἱ
Στωϊκοὶ καὶ πνεῦμα κατ' οὐσίαν,
ὥσπερ ἀμέλει καὶ τὴν ψυχήν. *Ibid.*
i. 295, ϲ: (οἱ Στωϊκοὶ) σῶμα ὄντα
τὸν θεὸν διὰ τῆς ἀτιμοτάτης ὕλης
πεφοιτηκέναι λέγουσιν οὐ καλῶς.
Protrept. 44, A: τοὺς ἀπὸ τῆς
στοᾶς, διὰ πάσης ὕλης, καὶ διὰ τῆς
ἀτιμοτάτης, τὸ θεῖον διήκειν λέγοντας. *Orig.* c. Cels. vi. 71:
τῶν Στωϊκῶν φασκόντων ὅτι ὁ θεὸς
πνεῦμά ἐστι διὰ πάντων διεληλυθὸς
καὶ πάντ' ἐν ἑαυτῷ περιεχόν. Opponents like Origen, l. c. and
i. 21, Alexander, De Mixt. l. c.
and Plutarch, Com. Not. 48,
naturally attack them for their
materialistic views.
[2] *Stob.* Ecl. i. 58. See following note. *Diog.* 138 (according
to Chrysippus and Posidonius):
τὸν δὴ κόσμον οἰκεῖσθαι κατὰ νοῦν
καὶ πρόνοιαν . . . εἰς ἅπαν αὐτοῦ
μέρος διήκοντος τοῦ νοῦ καθάπερ
ἐφ' ἡμῶν τῆς ψυχῆς. ἀλλ' ἤδη δι'

the world; as a united Whole, containing in Himself the germs of all things; as the Connecting

ὃν μὲν μᾶλλον, δι' ὧν δὲ ἧττον.
More popularly, *ibid.* 147: θεὸν
εἶναι ζῷον ἀθάνατον λογικὸν τέλειον
ἢ νοερὸν ἐν εὐδαιμονίᾳ, κακοῦ παντὸς ἀνεπίδεκτον, προνοητικὸν κόσμου τε καὶ τῶν ἐν κόσμῳ, μὴ εἶναι
μέντοι ἀνθρωπόμορφον. εἶναι δὲ
τὸν μὲν δημιουργὸν τῶν ὅλων καὶ
ὥσπερ πατέρα πάντων κοινῶς τε
καὶ τὸ μέρος αὐτοῦ τὸ διῆκον διὰ
πάντων, ὃ πολλαῖς προσηγορίαις
προσονομάζεσθαι κατὰ τὰς δυνάμεις.
Phæd. Nat. De. (*Philodem.* περὶ
εὐσεβείας) Col. 1 and *Cic.* Nat.
De. i. 15, 39, quoting from him:
According to Chrysippus, Zeus
is κοινὴ φύσις, εἱμαρμένη, ἀνάγκη,
κ.τ.λ. *Ibid.* Col. 3: He considered νόμος to be deity. *Cic.*
l.c.: legis perpetuæ et æternæ
vim . . . Jovem dicit esse.
Themist. De An. 72, b: τοῖς ἀπὸ
Ζήνωνος . . . διὰ πάσης οὐσίας
πεφοιτηκέναι τὸν θεὸν τιθεμένοις,
καὶ τοῦ μὲν εἶναι νοῦν, ποῦ δὲ ψυχὴν, ποῦ δὲ φύσιν, ποῦ δὲ ἕξιν.
Cic. Acad: ii. 37, 119: No Stoic
can doubt hunc mundum esse
sapientem, habere mentem,
quæ se et ipsum fabricata sit,
et omnia moderetur, moveat,
regat. *Id.* N. D. ii. 22, 58:
ipsius vero mundi . . . natura
non artificiosa solum sed plane
artifex ab eodem Zenone dicitur, consultrix et provida utilitatum opportunitatumque omnium. . . . As every nature
develops from its stock, sic
Natura mundi omnes motus
habet voluntarios conatusque
et appetitiones, quas ὁρμὰς
Græci vocant, et his consentaneas actiones sic adhibet ut
nosmet ipsi, qui animis move-

mur et sensibus, on which account the mens mundi is called
πρόνοια. *M. Aurel.* iv. 40: ὡς ἓν
ζῷον τὸν , κόσμον μίαν οὐσίαν καὶ
ψυχὴν μίαν ἐπέχον συνεχῶς
ἐπινοεῖν· πῶς εἰς αἴσθησιν μίαν τὴν
τούτου πάντα ἀναδίδοται καὶ πῶς
ὁρμῇ μιᾷ πάντα πράσσει. *Heraclit.*
Alleg. Hom. 72. *Tertullian,*
Apol. 21: Hunc enim (λόγον)
Zeno determinat factitatorem,
qui cuncta in dispositione formaverit, eundem et fatum
vocari et Deum et animum
Jovis et necessitatem omnium
rerum. Hæc Cleanthes in spiritum congerit, quem permeatorem universitatis affirmat.
Similarly *Lactant.* Inst. iv. 9,
1, 5. *Epiphan.* Haer. v. 1, p.
12: According to the Stoics,
God is νοῦς, residing in the
world as its soul, and permeating the μερικαὶ οὐσίαι. Zeus is
also spoken of as being the soul
of the world by *Cornutus,* Nat.
De. 2; by *Plut.* Sto. Rep. 39, 2,
p. 1052; and by Chrysippus,
ibid. 34, 5, p. 1050: ὅτι δ' ἡ
κοινὴ φύσις καὶ ὁ κοινὸς τῆς φύσεως λόγος εἱμαρμένη καὶ πρόνοια
καὶ Ζεύς ἐστιν οὐδὲ τοὺς ἀντίποδας
λέληθε· πανταχοῦ γὰρ ταῦτα θρυλεῖται ὑπ' αὐτῶν. *Stob.* Ecl. i.
178: Ζήνων . . . [τὴν εἱμαρμένην]
δύναμιν κινητικὴν τῆς ὕλης κατὰ
ταὐτὰ καὶ ὡσαύτως, ἥντινα μὴ διαφέρειν πρόνοιαν καὶ φύσιν καλεῖν.
Ar. Didymus, in Eus. Pr. Ev.
xv. 15, 2: God cares for man;
He is kind, beneficent, and loves
men. Zeus is called κόσμος as
αἴτιος τοῦ ζῆν, εἱμαρμένη, because
εἰρομένῳ λόγῳ διοικεῖ all things,
ἀδράστεια, ὅτι οὐδὲν ἔστιν αὐτὸν

element in all things; as Universal Law, Nature,
Destiny, Providence; as a perfect, happy, ever kind
and all-knowing Being; nor was it hard to show that
no conception could be formed of God without these
attributes.[1] Both kinds of expression are combined

ἀποδιδράσκειν, πρόνοια, ὅτι πρὸς
τὸ χρήσιμον οἰκονομεῖ ἕκαστα.
Aristocles (Ibid. xv. 14): Primary fire contains the causes
and λόγοι of all things; the
unchangeable law and destiny
of the world supplies their connection. *Sen.* Benef. iv. 7, 1:
Quid enim aliud est natura,
quam Deus et divina ratio toti
mundo et partibus ejus inserta?
. . . . Hunc eundem et fatum si
dixeris non mentieris. (Similarly Frag. 122 in *Lact.* Inst. ii.
8, 23). *Id.* Nat. Qu. ii. 45, 2:
God or Jupiter may be equally
well spoken of as Destiny, Providence, Nature, the World.
Stob. Ecl. i. 178: 'Αντίπατρος ὁ
Στωϊκὸς θεὸν ἀπεφήνατο τὴν εἱμαρμένην. Zeus is called κοινὸς νόμος by *Diog.* vii. 88; by Cleanthes at the end of his hymn
(*Stob.* Ecl. i. 34); likewise *Cic.*
N. D. i. 14, 36 says of Zeno:
Naturalem legem divinam esse
censet, eamque vim obtinere
recta imperantem prohibentem-
que contraria. *Plut.* C. Not.
32, 1; Sto. Rep. 38, 3 and 7
(here following Antipater): God
must be conceived of as μακάριος,
εὐποιητικὸς, φιλάνθρωπος, κηδε-
μονικός, ὠφέλιμος. *Muson.* (in
Stob. Floril. 117, 8): God is the
type of every virtue, μεγαλόφρων,
ἐνεργέτικος, φιλάνθρωπος, κ.τ.λ.
Sen. Ep. 24, 49: Quæ causa est
Dis benefaciendi? Natura.
Errat, si quis illas putat nocere

nolle: non possunt. Further
details respecting the beneficent
nature of the Gods in *Sen.*
Benef. i. 9; iv. 3–9 and 25–28;
Clement, i. 5, 7; Nat. Qu. v.
18, 13. On the divine omniscience; Ep.83, 1; V. Beat. 20, 5.
[1] According to *Cic.* N. D. ii.
30, 75, the Stoics divided the
argument as to God's providential care of the world into three
parts. The first part went to
establish that if there existed
Gods, there must also be a care
of the world; for Gods could
not exist without having something to do, and to care for the
world is the noblest thing that
can be done. If, moreover,
deity is the highest being, the
world must be governed by
deity. The same conclusion is
arrived at from the wisdom and
power of deity, which must
always busy itself with what is
best and highest. Lastly, it is
stated, that inasmuch as the
stars, heaven, the universe, and
all powers in the world are
divine, it is clear that everything must be governed by
divine reason. The second part
proved that the force and skill
of nature produced and sustains
all things. All the more reason
that a universe so skillfully
formed and so harmoniously
arranged must be directed by a
natura sentiens. And since, in
its parts, it could not be more

in the assertion that God is the fiery Reason of the World, the Mind in Matter, the reasonable Air-Current, penetrating all things, and assuming various names according to the material in which He resides, the artistically moulding Fire, containing in Himself the germs of everything, and producing according to an unalterable law the world and all that is therein.[1]

beautiful or adapted to its purpose, it must be true of it more than of any human work of art, that it owes its origin to a forming reason. The third part aims at proving, on physico-theological grounds, quanta sit admirabilitas cœlestium rerum atque terrestrium.

[1] *Stob.* Ecl. i. 58: Διογένης καὶ Κλεάνθης καὶ Οἰνοπίδης τὴν τοῦ κόσμου ψυχὴν [θεὸν λέγουσι] ... Ποσειδώνιος πνεῦμα νοερὸν καὶ πυρῶδες, οὐκ ἔχον μὲν μορφὴν μεταβάλλον δὲ εἰς ὃ βούλεται καὶ συνεξομοιούμενον πᾶσιν ... Ζήνων ὁ Στωϊκὸς νοῦν κόσμον πύρινον. *Ib.* 64; *Plut.* Plac. i. 8, 17: οἱ Στωϊκοὶ νοερὸν (*Plut.* κοινότερον) θεὸν ἀποφαίνονται πῦρ τεχνικὸν ὁδῷ βαδίζον ἐπὶ γενέσει κόσμου (a similar definition of nature is given by Zeno in *Cic.* Nat. De. ii. 22, 57) ἐμπεριειληφός τε πάντας τοὺς σπερματικοὺς λόγους, καθ' οὓς ἅπαντα (*Pl.* ἕκαστα) καθ' εἱμαρμένην γίνεται, καὶ πνεῦμα ἐνδιῆκον, δι' ὅλον τοῦ κόσμου, τὰς δὲ προσηγορίας μεταλαμβάνον διὰ τὰς τῆς ὕλης, δι' ἧς κεχώρηκε μεταλλάξεις. Following the same source, *Athenag.* Leg. pro Christ. c. 5, Schl: εἰ γὰρ ὁ μὲν θεὸς πῦρ τεχνικὸν, κ.τ.λ. (the same down to γίνεται) τὸ δὲ πνεῦμα αὐτοῦ διῆ-

κει δι' ὅλου τοῦ κόσμου· ὁ θεὸς εἷς κατ' αὐτοὺς, Ζεὺς μὲν κατὰ τὸ ζέον τῆς ὕλης ὀνομαζόμενος, Ἥρα δὲ κατὰ τὸν ἀέρα καὶ τὰ λοιπὰ καθ' ἕκαστον τῆς ὕλης μέρος, δι' ἧς κεχώρηκε, καλούμενος. The latter passage is explained by *Diog.* 147, who thus continues: Δία μὲν γάρ φασι δι' ὃν τὰ πάντα· Ζῆνα δὲ καλοῦσι παρ' ὅσον τοῦ ζῆν αἴτιός ἐστιν ἢ διὰ τοῦ ζῆν κεχώρηκεν. (This, too, in *Stob.* Ecl. i. 48.) Ἀθηνᾶν δὲ κατὰ τὴν εἰς αἰθέρα διάτασιν τοῦ ἡγεμονικοῦ αὐτοῦ. Ἥραν δὲ κατὰ τὴν εἰς ἀέρα. καὶ Ἥφαιστον κατὰ τὴν εἰς τὸ τεχνικὸν πῦρ. καὶ Ποσειδῶνα κατὰ τὴν εἰς τὸ ὑγρόν. καὶ Δήμητραν κατὰ τὴν εἰς γῆν· ὁμοίως δὲ καὶ τὰς ἄλλας προσηγορίας ἐχόμενοί τινος ὁμοιότητος ἀπέδοσαν. *Plut.* C. Not. 48, 2, p. 1085: τὸν θεὸν ... σῶμα νοερὸν καὶ νοῦν ἐν ὕλῃ ποιοῦντες. *M. Aurel.* 5, 32: τὸν διὰ τῆς οὐσίας διήκοντα λόγον, κ.τ.λ. *Porphyr.* in Eus. Pr. Ev. xv. 16, 1: τὸν δὲ θεὸν ... πῦρ νοερὸν εἰπόντες. *Orig.* c. Cels. vi. 71· κατὰ μὲν οὖν τοὺς ἀπὸ τῆς στοᾶς ... καὶ ὁ λόγος τοῦ θεοῦ ὁ μέχρι ἀνθρώπων καὶ τῶν ἐλαχίστων καταβαίνων οὐδὲν ἄλλο ἐστὶν ἢ πνεῦμα σωματικόν. The same combination of nature and mind in the conceptions of God is

As used in the Stoic system, these expressions generally mean one and the same thing. It is an unimportant difference whether the original cause is described as an Air-Current or as Ether, or as Heat or as Fire. It is an Air-Current, Air-Currents being, as we have already seen, the causes of the properties of things, giving them shape and connection. It is also Fire, for by fire is only meant the warm air, or the fiery fluid, which is sometimes called Ether, at other times Fire, at other times Heat,[1] and which is expressly distinguished from ordinary fire.[2] Moreover the terms, Soul of the world, Reason of the world, Nature, Universal Law, Providence, Destiny— all mean the same thing, the one primary force penetrating the whole world. Even the more abstract expressions, Law, Providence, Destiny, have with the Stoics an essentially gross meaning, implying not only the form according to which the world is arranged and governed, but also the essential substance of the world, as a power above everything particular

found in the hymn of Cleanthes (in *Stob.* Ecl. i. 30), Zeus being described as the ἀρχηγὸς φύσεως, who directs the κοινὸς λόγος ὃς διὰ πάντων φοιτᾷ, by means of πῦρ ἀείζωον.

[1] *Stob.* Ecl. i. 374: Chrysippus teaches εἶναι τὸ ὂν πνεῦμα κινοῦν ἑαυτὸ πρὸς ἑαυτὸ καὶ ἐξ ἑαυτοῦ, ἢ πνεῦμα ἑαυτὸ κινοῦν πρόσω καὶ ὀπίσω· πνεῦμα δὲ εἴληπται διὰ τὸ λέγεσθαι αὐτὸ ἀέρα εἶναι κινούμενον· ἀνάλογον δὲ γίγνεσθαι ἔπειτα [? perhaps: αὐτὸ, or: πυρὸς ἢ] αἰθερὸς, ὥστε καὶ εἰς κοινὸν λόγον πεσεῖν αὐτά. *Diog.* vii.

137: ἀνωτάτω μὲν οὖν εἶναι τὸ πῦρ ὃν δὴ αἰθέρα καλεῖσθαι.

[2] *Stob.* Ecl. i. 538, on the authority of Zeno; *Cic.* N. D. ii. 15, 40, on that of Cleanthes. Both state that the difference consists in this: Ordinary (ἄτεχνον) fire consumes things; but the πῦρ τεχνικὸν, which constitutes φύσις and ψυχὴ, preserves things. Heraclitus, too, in making primary fire the basis of things, did not mean flame, but warmth, which may be equally well described as atmospheric substance or as ψυχή.

and individual.[1] If Nature must be distinguished
from Destiny, and both of these notions again from
Zeus,[2] the distinction can only consist herein, that
the three conceptions describe one original Being at
different stages of His manifestation and growth.
Viewed as the whole of the world it is called Zeus;
viewed as the inner power in the world, Providence
or Destiny;[3] and to prove this identity at the close
of every period, so taught Chrysippus, Zeus goes back
into Providence.[4]

Upon closer examination, even the difference between the materialistic and idealistic description of
God vanishes. God, according to Stoic principles,
can only be invested with reality when He has a

[1] *Seneca,* De Benefic. iv. 7,
2 : God may also be called
fatum : nam cum fatum nihil
aliud sit quam series implexa
causarum, ille est prima omnium causa, ex qua ceteræ pendent. Nat. Qu. ii. 45, 1 : Vis
illum fatum vocare? Non erra-
bis. Hic est, ex quo suspensa
sunt omnia, causa causarum.
The same applies to the name
of providence and nature. See
p. 162, 2.

[2] *Stob.* Ecl. i. 178 (*Plut.*
Plac. i. 28, 5): Ποσειδώνιος [τὴν
εἱμαρμένην] τρίτην ἀπὸ Διός.
πρῶτον μὲν γὰρ εἶναι τὸν Δία, δεύτερον δὲ τὴν φύσιν, τρίτην δὲ τὴν
εἱμαρμένην. Conf. *Cic.* Divin, i.
55, 125, where prophecy is deduced, according to Posidonius,
(1) a Deo, (2) a fato, (3) a
natura. *Plut.* C. Not. 36, 5, p.
1077 : λέγει γοῦν Χρύσιππος, ἐοικέναι τῷ μὲν ἀνθρώπῳ τὸν Δία καὶ
τὸν κόσμον (instead of which

Heine, Stoic. De Fat. Doct. p.
25, apparently without reason,
conjectures : καὶ τῷ μὲν σώματι
τὸν κόσμον), τῇ δὲ ψυχῇ τὴν πρό-
νοιαν· ὅταν οὖν ἐκ πύρωσις γένηται
μόνον ἄφθαρτον ὄντα τὸν Δία τῶν
θεῶν ἀναχωρεῖν ἐπὶ τὴν πρόνοιαν,
εἶτα ὁμοῦ γενομένους ἐπὶ μιᾶς τῆς
τοῦ αἰθέρος οὐσίας διατελεῖν ἀμφοτέρους. To this maxim of Chrysippus, reference is made by
Philo, Incorrup. M. 951, B,
where, too, πρόνοια is equivalent to ψυχὴ τοῦ κόσμου.

[3] According to Chrysippus.
A different view is taken by
Posidonius. With him Zeus
stands for the original force,
φύσις for its first, and εἱμαρμένη
for its second production.

[4] *Plut.* l. c. *Sen.* Ep. 9, 16 :
Jovis, cum resoluto mundo et
Diis in unum confusis paullis-
per cessante natura acquiescit
sibi cogitationibus suis tradi-
tur.

material form.   Hence, when He is called the Soul,
the Mind, or the Reason of the world, this language
does not exclude, but rather presupposes, that these
conceptions have bodies; and such bodies the Stoics
thought to discern in that heated fluid which they at
one time call the all-penetrating Breath, at another
Ether, or primary Fire.[1]   Each of these two determinations appeared to them indispensable,[2] and both
became identical by assuming, as the Stoics did, that
the infinite character of the divine Reason depends on
the purity and lightness of the fiery material which
composes it.[3]   Seneca is therefore only following
out the principles of his school when he calls it quite
indifferent whether God is regarded as Destiny or as
an all-pervading Breath.[4]   Those who charge the

[1] Compare, besides what
has been already quoted, *Cic.*
Acad. i. 11, 39 : (Zeno) statuebat ignem esse ipsam naturam.
Diog. vii. 156: δοκεῖ δὲ αὐτοῖς
τὴν μὲν φύσιν εἶναι πῦρ τεχνικὸν
ὁδῷ βαδίζον εἰς γένεσιν, ὅπερ ἐστὶ
πνεῦμα πυροειδὲς καὶ τεχνοειδές.
Stob. Ecl. i. 180: Χρύσιππος
δύναμιν πνευματικὴν τὴν οὐσίαν
τῆς εἱμαρμένης τάξει τοῦ παντὸς
διοικητικήν ; or, according to
another definition : εἱμαρμένη
ἐστὶν ὁ τοῦ κόσμου λόγος, ἢ λόγος
τῶν ἐν τῷ κόσμῳ προνοίᾳ διοικουμένων, κ.τ.λ.   Instead of λόγος,
he also used ἀλήθεια, φύσις,
αἰτία, ἀνάγκη, &c.
[2] See p. 143.
[3] *Cic.* N. D. ii. 11, 30 : Atque
etiam mundi ille fervor purior,
perlucidior mobiliorque multo
ob easque causas aptior ad sensus commovendos quam hic

noster calor, quo hæc quæ nota
nobis sunt, retinentur et vigent.
Absurdum igitur est dicere,
cum homines bestiæque hoc
calore teneantur et propterea
moveantur ac sentiant, mundum
esse sine sensu, qui integro et
puro et libero eodemque acerrimo et mobilissimo ardore teneatur.   Conf. *Ar. Didymus*, in
the passage quoted, p. 146, 4,
p. 105, 127.
[4] Consol. ad Helvid. 8, 3 : Id
actum est, mihi crede, ab illo
quisquis formatio universi fuit,
sive ille Deus est potens omnium, sive incorporalis ratio
ingentium operum artifex, sive
divinus spiritus per omnia
maxima ac minima æquali in-
tentione [= τόνος] diffusus, sive
fatum et immutabilis causarum
inter se cohærentium series.
Conf. p. 153, 1.

Stoics with inconsistency for calling God at one time
Reason, at another Soul of the universe, at another
Destiny, at another Fire, Ether, or even the Universe,[1]
forget that they are attaching to these terms a meaning entirely different from that in which they were
used by the Stoics.[2]

The more the two sides of the conception of God
—the material and the ideal—are compared, the
clearer it becomes that there is no difference between
God and primary Matter. Both are one and the same
substance, which, when regarded as the universal
substratum, is known as undetermined matter; but
when conceived of as acting force, is called all-pervading Ether, all-warming Fire, all-penetrating Air,
Nature, Soul of the world, Reason of the world, Providence, Destiny, God. Matter and power, material
and form, are not, as with Aristotle, things radically
different, though united from all eternity. Far from
it, the forming force resides in matter as such; it is
in itself something material; it is identical with
Ether, or Fire-element, or Breath. Hence the difference between efficient and material cause, between
God and matter, resolves itself into the difference
between Breath and other elements. This difference,
too, is no original or ultimate difference. According

*(b) God
original
matter.*

---

[1] *Cic.* N. D. i. 14: Zeno calls
natural law divine, but he also
calls the Ether and the all-pervading Reason deity. (We
shall come back presently to
what he says as to the divinity
of the stars.) Cleanthes gives
the name of deity to the world,
reason, the soul of the world,
and ether; Chrysippus to reason, to the soul of the world, to
ruling reason, to communis
natura, destiny, fire, ether, the
universe, and eternal law.

[2] *Krische*, Forsch. i. 365.

CHAP.
VI.

to the Stoic teaching, every particular element has in process of time developed out of primary fire or God, and to God it will return at the end of every period of the world.[1] It is therefore only a derivative and passing difference with which we are here concerned. But taking the conception of Deity in its full meaning, it may be described as primary matter, as well as primary power. The sum total of all that is real is the divine Breath, moving forth from itself and returning to itself again.[2] Deity itself is primary fire, containing in itself in germ both God and matter;[3] the world in its original gaseous condition;[4] the Universal Substance changing into particular elements, and from them returning to itself again, which regarded in its real form as God includes at one time everything, at another only a part of real existence.[5]

C. *Pantheism.*
(1) *God identical with the world.*

From what has been said it follows that the Stoics admitted no essential difference between God and the world. Their system was therefore strictly pantheistic. The world is the sum of all real existence, and all real existence is originally contained in deity, which is at once the matter of everything and the creative force which moulds this matter into particu-

[1] See pp. 153, 2; 153, 4.
[2] *Chrysippus.* See p. 152, note 1.
[3] *Aristocles.* See p. 147, note 3.
[4] *Mnesarchus*, in Stob. i. 60. See p. 148, 1.
[5] *Orig.* c. Cels. iii. 75, p. 497, A: Στωϊκῶν θεὸν φθαρτὸν εἰσαγόντων καὶ τὴν οὐσίαν αὐτοῦ

λεγόντων σῶμα τρεπτὸν διόλου καὶ ἀλλοιωτὸν καὶ μεταβλητὸν καί ποτε πάντα φθειρόντων καὶ μόνον τὸν θεὸν καταλιπόντων. *Ibid.* iv. 14: ὁ τῶν Στωϊκῶν θεὸς ὅτε σῶμα τυγχάνων ὅτε μὲν ἡγεμονικὸν ἔχει τὴν ὅλην οὐσίαν ὅταν ἡ ἐκπύρωσις ᾖ· ὅτε δὲ ἐπὶ μέρους γίνεται αὐτῆς ὅταν ᾖ διακόσμησις.

PANTHEISM: GOD AND THE WORLD.

lar individual substances. We can, therefore, think
of nothing which is not either immediately deity or
a manifestation of deity. In point of essence, God
and the world are therefore the same; indeed, the
two conceptions are declared by the Stoics to be absolutely identical.[1] If they have nevertheless to be
distinguished, the distinction is only derivative and
partial. The same universal Being is called God
when it is regarded as a whole, World when it is regarded as progressive in one of the many forms

[1] Besides the quotations already given from Chrysippus
on p. 153, 2, and Cleanthes on
p. 155, 1, compare *Phædr.* Nat.
De. (*Philodem.* περὶ εὐσεβείας),
Col. 5 : Διογένης δ' ὁ Βαβυλώνιος
ἐν τῷ περὶ τῆς Ἀθηνᾶς τὸν κόσμον
γράφει τῷ Διὶ τὸν αὐτὸν ὑπάρχειν,
ἢ περιέχειν τὸν Δία καθάπερ ἄνθρωπον ψυχήν. *Cic.* N. De. ii.
17, 45 : Nothing corresponds
better to the idea of God, quam
ut primum hunc mundum, quo
nihil fieri excellentius potest,
animantem esse et Deum judi-
cem. *Ibid.* 13, 34 : Perfect
reason Deo tribuenda, id est
mundo. *Sen.* Nat. Qu. ii. 45, 3 ;
Vis illum vocare mundum ?
Non falleris. Ipse enim est
hoc quod vides totum, suis partibus inditus et se sustinens et
sua. *Ibid.* Prolog. 13 : Quid
est Deus? Mens universi.
Quid est Deus? Quod vides
totum et quod non vides totum.
Sic demum magnitudo sua illi
redditur, qua nihil majus ex-
cogitari potest, si solus est
omnia, opus suum et extra et
intra tenet. *Diog.* vii. 148 :
οὐσίαν δὲ θεοῦ Ζήνων μέν φησι τὸν

ὅλον κόσμον και τὸν οὐρανόν. *Ar.
Didym.* in Eus. Pr. Ev. xv. 15,
1 and 3 : ὅλον δὲ τὸν κόσμον σὺν
τοῖς ἑαυτοῦ μέρεσι προσαγορεύουσι
θεόν. . . . διὸ δὴ καὶ Ζεὺς λέγεται
ὁ κόσμος. *Orig.* c. Cels. v. 7 :
σαφῶς δὴ τὸν ὅλον κόσμον λέγουσιν εἶναι θεὸν Στωϊκοὶ μὲν τὸ
πρῶτον. The arguments given,
p. 144, for the existence of God
are based on the supposition
that God is the same as the
world. The existence of God
is proved by showing the rea-
sonableness of the world.
Aratus gives a poet's description of the Stoic pantheism at
the beginning of the Phænomena: Zeus is the being of
whom streets and markets, sea
and land, are full, whose offspring is man, and who, out of
regard for man, has appointed
signs in the heaven to regulate
the year. The same idea is
contained in the well-known
lines of Virgil, Georg. iv. 220;
Æn. vi. 724. The round figure
of the Stoic deity, *Sen.* Ep. 113,
22 ; De M. Claud. 8, 1, has also
reference to the world as God.
Conf. *Cic.* N. D. i. 17, 46.

assumed in the course of its development.   The difference, therefore, is tantamount to assigning a
difference of meaning to the term world, according as
it is used to express the whole of what exists, or only
the derivative part.[1]

(2) *Dif-*
ference be-
tween God
and the
world only
relative.

Still this distinction does not depend only upon
our way of looking at things, but it is founded in the
nature of things.   Primary force, as such, primary
fire, primary reason, constitute what is primarily God.
Things into which this primary substance has changed
itself are only divine in a derivative sense.   Hence
deity, which is ultimately identical with the whole
of the world, may again be described as a part of the
world, as the leading part (τὸ ἡγεμονικὸν), as the
Soul of the world, as the all-pervading fiery Breath.[2]

[1] *Stob.* Ecl. i. 444: κόσμον δ'
εἶναί φησιν ὁ Χρύσιππος σύστημα
ἐξ οὐρανοῦ καὶ γῆς καὶ τῶν ἐν τούτοις φύσεων · ἢ τὸ ἐκ θεῶν καὶ ἀνθρώπων σύστημα καὶ ἐκ τῶν ἕνεκα
τούτων γεγονότων.   λέγεται δ'
ἑτέρως κόσμος ὁ θεὸς, καθ' ὃν ἡ
διακόσμησις γίνεται καὶ τελειοῦται.
Diog. vii. 137 : λέγουσι δὲ κόσμον
τριχῶς · αὐτόν τε τὸν θεὸν τὸν ἐκ
τῆς ἁπάσης οὐσίας ἰδίως ποιὸν, ὃς
δὴ ἄφθαρτός ἐστι καὶ ἀγέννητος
δημιουργὸς ὢν τῆς διακοσμήσεως
κατὰ χρόνων τινὰς περιόδους ἀνα-
λίσκων εἰς ἑαυτὸν τὴν ἅπασαν
οὐσίαν καὶ πάλιν ἐξ ἑαυτοῦ γεννῶν.
καὶ αὐτὴν δὲ τὴν διακόσμησιν τῶν
ἀστέρων κόσμον εἶναι λέγουσι καὶ
τρίτον τὸ συνεστηκὸς ἐξ ἀμφοῖν.
καὶ ἔστι κόσμος ἢ (according to
the first meaning of the word) ὁ
ἰδίως ποιὸς τῆς τῶν ὅλων οὐσίας,
(universal substance in its definite quality) ἢ (second mean-

ing) ὥς φησι Ποσειδώνιος . . .
σύστημα ἐξ οὐρανοῦ καὶ γῆς καὶ
τῶν ἐν τούτοις φύσεων, ἢ (third
meaning) σύστημα ἐκ θεῶν καὶ
ἀνθρώπων καὶ τῶν ἕνεκα τούτων
γεγονότων.   *Ar. Didym.* in Eus.
Pr. Ev. xv. 15, 1 : κόσμος is the
name for τὸ ἐκ πάσης τῆς οὐσίας
ποιὸν, and for τὸ κατὰ τὴν διακόσμησιν τὴν τοιαύτην καὶ διάταξιν
ἔχον.   In the former sense, the
world is eternal, and the same
as God ; in the latter, created,
and subject to change.   Compare also the quotations from
the mathematician Diodorus,
in *Ach. Tat.* Isag. c. 6. p. 129,
b.

[2] See p. 148. The two ideas
blend into each other.   Thus
Seneca, Nat. Qu. Prol. 13, says
God must be the Reason of the
world and must also be the
universe itself ; and he con-

The distinction, however, is only a relative one. What is not immediately divine is nevertheless divine derivatively, as being a manifestation of primary fire; and if the soul of the world is not identical with the body, at least it pervades every part of that body.[1] It is a distinction, too, which applies only to a part of the conditions of the world. At the end of every period, the sum of all derivative things reverts to the unity of the divine Being, and the distinction between what is originally and what is derivatively divine, in other words, the distinction between God and the world, ceases.

Boëthus alone dissented from the pantheism of the Stoics by making a real distinction between God and the world. Agreeing with the other Stoics in considering deity to be an ethereal Substance,[2] he would not allow that it resided, as the Soul, within the whole world, and, consequently, he refused to call the world a living being.[3] Instead of doing this, he placed the seat of deity in the highest of the heavenly spheres, the sphere of the fixed stars, and made it operate upon the world from this abode.[4] The oppo-

(3) *Boëthus dissents from the pantheism of the Stoics.*

---

tinues: Quid ergo interest inter naturam Dei et nostram? Nostri melior pars animus est, in illo nulla pars extra animum est. Totus est ratio, &c.

[1] The connection of the two, like the connection between soul and body, and the argument quoted by Tertullian from Zeno on p. 148, 1, is a κρᾶσις δι' ὅλων. See p. 135.

[2] *Stob.* Ecl. i. 60 : Βόηθος τὸν αἰθέρα θεὸν ἀπεφήνατο.

[3] *Diog.* 143: Βόηθος δέ φησιν οὐκ εἶναι ζῷον τὸν κόσμον. The words of *Philo,* Incorrupt. M. 953, C—ψυχὴ δὲ τοῦ κόσμου κατὰ τοὺς ἀντιδοξοῦντας ὁ θεὸς—imply the same, but these words evidently are not taken from Boëthus.

[4] *Diog.* 148: Βόηθος δὲ ἐν τῇ περὶ φύσεως οὐσίαν θεοῦ τὴν τῶν ἀπλανῶν σφαῖραν· which must be understood in the same sense as the corresponding statements

site view detracted, in his eyes, from the unchangeable and exalted character of the divine Being. How
anxious he was to vindicate that character will also
be seen in the way in which he differed from his
fellow-Stoics in reference to the destruction of the
world.

of other Stoics: the ἡγεμονικὸν of
the world resides in the purest
part of the ether. Yet, inasmuch as the world is no living
being, nor is deity the soul of
the world, it must, according
to the view of Boëthus, act upon
it from without. This is expressly stated in *Philo*, Incorrup. M. 953, B, God is described
as the charioteer guiding the
world, and παριστάμενος the
stars and elements. But this
passage, beginning at καὶ μήποτ'
εἰκότως, is evidently Philo's
own expansion of what he has
just quoted from Boëthus.

CHAPTER VII.

THE STUDY OF NATURE. COURSE, CHARACTER, AND
GOVERNMENT OF THE UNIVERSE.

By virtue of a law inherent in nature, Primary
Being passes over into particular objects; for, involving as it does the conception of a forming and
creating force, it must as necessarily develope into a
universe, as a seed or ovum must develope into a
plant or animal.[1] Primary fire—so taught the Stoics,
following Heraclitus—first goes over into vapour,
then into moisture; one part of this moisture is pre-
cipitated in the form of earth, another remains as
water, whilst a third part evaporating constitutes
atmospheric air, and air, again, enkindles fire out of
itself. By the mutual play of these four elements
the world is formed,[2] built round the earth as a

CHAP.
VII.

A. *The
general
course of
the uni-
verse.*
(1) *Origin
of the
world.*

[1] *Diog.* vii. 136: κατ' ἀρχὰς
μὲν οὖν καθ' αὑτὸν ὄντα [τὸν θεὸν]
τρέπειν τὴν πᾶσαν οὐσίαν δι' ἀέρος
εἰς ὕδωρ· καὶ ὥσπερ ἐν τῇ γονῇ τὸ
σπέρμα περιέχεται, οὕτω καὶ τοῦτον σπερματικὸν λόγον ὄντα τοῦ
κόσμου τοιοῦδε ὑπολιπέσθαι ἐν τῷ
ὑγρῷ ἐνεργὸν αὑτῷ ποιοῦντα τὴν
ὕλην πρὸς τὴν τῶν ἑξῆς γένεσιν,
κ.τ.λ. *Seneca*, Nat. Quæst. iii.

13, 1: Fire will consume the
world: hunc evanidum con-
sidere, et nihil relinqui aliud in
rerum natura, igne restincto,
quam humorem. In hoc futuri
mundi spem latere. *Stob.* Ecl.
i. 372 and 414, 5. See pp. 161, 2;
164, 2.

[2] *Stob.* i. 370: Ζήνωνα δὲ οὕτως
ἀποφαίνεσθαι διαῤῥήδην· τοιαύτην

centre;[1] heat, as it is developed out of water,[2] moulding the chaotic mass.　By the separation of these

δεήσει εἶναι ἐν περιόδῳ τὴν τοῦ
ὅλου διακόσμησιν ἐκ τῆς οὐσίας.
ὅταν ἐκ πυρὸς τροπὴ εἰς ὕδωρ δι'
ἀέρος γένηται τὸ μέν τι ὑφίστασθαι
καὶ γῆν συνίστασθαι, ἐκ τοῦ λοιποῦ
δὲ τὸ μὲν διαμένειν ὕδωρ, ἐκ δὲ τοῦ
ἀτμιζομένου ἀέρα γίνεσθαι, ἔκ τινος
δὲ τοῦ ἀέρος πῦρ ἐξάπτειν.　*Diog.*
vii. 142 : γίνεσθαι δὲ τὸν κόσμον
ὅταν ἐκ πυρὸς ἡ οὐσία τραπῇ δι'
ἀέρος εἰς ὑγρότητα, εἶτα τὸ παχυ-
μερὲς αὐτοῦ συστὰν ἀποτελεσθῇ γῆ
τὸ δὲ λεπτομερὲς ἐξαερωθῇ καὶ
τοῦτ' ἐπιπλέον λεπτυνθὲν πῦρ ἀπο-
γεννήσῃ ; εἶτα κατὰ μίξιν ἐκ τούτων φυτά τε καὶ ζῷα καὶ ἄλλα γένη.
Chrys. in *Plut.* St. Rep. 41, 3,
p. 1053 : ἡ δὲ πυρὸς μεταβολὴ
ἐστι τοιαύτη · δι' ἀέρος εἰς ὕδωρ
τρέπεται · κἀκ' τούτου γῆς ὑφισ-
ταμένης ἀὴρ ἐνθυμιᾶται · λεπτυ-
νομένου δὲ τοῦ ἀέρος ὁ αἰθὴρ
περιχεῖται κύκλῳ.　The same
writer observes, in the Scholia
on Hesiod's Theogony, v. 459,
ὅτι καθύγρων ὄντων τῶν ὅλων καὶ
ὄμβρων καταφερομένων πολλῶν
τὴν ἔκκρισιν τούτων Κρόνον ὠνο-
μάσθαι. Conf. *Clemens,* Strom.
v. 599, C, and *Stob.* i. 312.

[1] *Stob.* Ecl. i. 442, also
affirms that the creation of the
universe begins with earth.

[2] *Stob.* l. c.: Κλεάνθης δὲ
οὕτω πῶς φησιν · ἐκφλογισθέντος
τοῦ παντὸς συνίζειν τὸ μέσον αὐτοῦ
πρῶτον, εἶτα τὰ ἐχόμενα ἀποσβέν-
νυσθαι δι' ὅλου. τοῦ δὲ παντὸς
ἐξυγρανθέντος, τὸ ἔσχατον τοῦ
πυρός, ἀντιτυπήσαντος αὐτῷ τοῦ
μέσου, τρέπεσθαι πάλιν εἰς τοὐναν-
τίον (the probable meaning is,
that the last remains of the
original fire begin a motion in
the opposite direction) εἶθ' οὕτω

τρεπόμενον ἄνω φησὶν αὔξεσθαι ·
καὶ ἄρχεσθαι διακοσμεῖν τὸ ὅλον,
καὶ τοιαύτην περίοδον ἀεὶ καὶ διακόσμησιν ποιουμένου τοῦ ἐν τῇ
τῶν ὅλων οὐσίᾳ τόνου (for this favourite expression of Cleanthes,
see p. 127, 5 ; 128, 2) μὴ παύεσθαι
[διακοσμούμενον τὸ ὅλον]. ὥσπερ
γὰρ ἑνός τινος τὰ μέρη πάντα
φύεται ἐκ σπερμάτων ἐν τοῖς καθήκουσι χρόνοις, οὕτω καὶ τοῦ ὅλου
τὰ μέρη, ὧν καὶ τὰ ζῷα καὶ τὰ
φυτὰ ὄντα τυγχάνει, ἐν τοῖς καθήκουσι χρόνοις φύεται.　καὶ ὥσπερ
τινὲς λόγοι τῶν μερῶν εἰς σπέρμα
συνιόντες μίγνυνται καὶ αὖθις δια-
κρίνονται γενομένων τῶν μερῶν,
οὕτως ἐξ ἑνός τε πάντα γίγνεσθαι
καὶ ἐκ πάντων εἰς ἓν συγκρίνεσθαι,
(conf. Heraclit. in vol. i. 467, 1),
ὁδῷ καὶ συμφώνως διεξιούσης τῆς
περιόδου.　A few further details
are supplied by *Macrob.* Sat. i.
17. The myth respecting the
birth of Apollo and Artemis is
referred to the formation of the
sun and moon. Namque post
chaos, ubi primum cœpit confusa　deformitas　in　rerum
formas et elementa nitescere,
terræque adhuc humida substantia in molli atque instabili
sede mutaret : convalescente
paullatim ætheres calore atque
inde seminibus in eam igneis
defluentibus (the connection of
Zeus, i.e., of Ether, with Leto,
the Earth) hæc sidera edita
esse credantur ; et solem maxima caloris vi in suprema rap-
tum ; lunam vero humidiore et
velut femineo sexu naturali
quodam pressam tepore infe-
riora tenuisse, tanquam ille
magis substantia patris con-

elements, a distinction between the active and the passive powers of nature—between the soul of the world and the body of the world—becomes apparent. The moisture into which the primary fire was first changed represents the body, just as the heat[1] latent in it represents the soul;[2] or, taking the later four-fold division of the elements, the two lower ones correspond to matter, the two higher ones to acting force.[3]

As the distinction between matter and force has

(2) *End of the world.*

stet, hæc matris. The statement that besides other things plants and animals had their origin in the intermingling of elements (*Stob.* and *Diog.*) must be understood in the sense of generatio æquivoca. *Lactant.* Inst. vii. 4, says the Stoics make men grow like sponges out of the earth, and *Sext.* Math. ix. 28, says the Stoics speak of the earth-born men of prehistoric ages.

[1] There must always be some remainder of heat or fire, as Cleanthes and Chrysippus avowed, or else there would be no active life-power from which a new creation could emanate. *Philo,* Incorrupt. M. 954, C, observes that, if the world were entirely consumed by fire at the ἐκπύρωσις, the fire itself would be extinguished, and no new world would be possible. διὸ καί τινες τῶν ἀπὸ τῆς στοᾶς . . . ἔφασαν, ὅτι μετὰ τὴν ἐκπύρωσιν, ἐπειδὰν ὁ νέος κόσμος μέλλῃ δημιουργεῖσθαι, σύμπαν μὲν τὸ πῦρ οὐ σβέννυται, ποσὴ δέ τις αὐτοῦ μοῖρα ὑπολείπεται.

[2] Chrys. in *Plut.* l. c. 41, 6:

διόλου μὲν γὰρ ὢν ὁ κόσμος πυρώδης εὐθὺς καὶ ψυχή ἐστιν ἑαυτοῦ καὶ ἡγεμονικόν. ὅτε δὲ μεταβαλὼν εἰς τὸ ὑγρὸν καὶ τὴν ἐναπολειφθεῖσαν ψυχὴν τρόπον τινὰ εἰς σῶμα καὶ ψυχὴν μετέβαλεν ὥστε συνεστάναι ἐκ τούτων, ἄλλον τινὰ ἔσχε λόγον.

[3] *Nemes.* Nat. Hom. C. 2, p. 72 : λέγουσι δὲ οἱ Στωϊκοὶ, τῶν στοιχείων τὰ μὲν εἶναι δραστικὰ τὰ δὲ παθητικά · δραστικὰ μὲν ἀέρα καὶ πῦρ, παθητικὰ δὲ γῆν καὶ ὕδωρ. *Plut.* Com. Not. 49, 2. See above p. 127, 5. From this passage a further insight is obtained into two points connected with the Stoic philosophy, which have been already discussed. It can no longer appear strange that the active power, or deity (and likewise the human soul) should at one time be called Fire, at another Air-Current, for both represent equally the acting force ; and the statement that properties are atmospheric currents—as, indeed, the whole distinction of subject-matter and property —follows from this view of things.

its origin in time, so it will also have an end in time.[1]
Matter which primary Being has separated from itself
to form its body is being gradually resolved into primary Being again; so that, at the end of the present
course of things, a general conflagration of the world
will restore all things to their original form, in which
everything derivative will have ceased to exist, and
pure Deity, or primary fire, will alone remain in its
original purity.[2]   This resolution of the world into

[1] The Stoics, according to
Diog. 141, where, however,
there is apparently a lacuna
in the text, prove that the
world (διακόσμησις, not κόσμος,
in the absolute sense, see p.
158, 1) will come to an end,
partly because it has come into
being, and partly by two not
very logical inferences : οὗ τὰ
[vulgo οὖ τε τὰ, *Cobet*: οὗτάτε]
μέρη φθαρτά ἐστι, καὶ τὸ ὅλον · τὰ
δὲ μέρη τοῦ κόσμου φθαρτὰ, εἰς
ἄλληλα γὰρ μεταβάλλει · φθαρτὸς
ἄρα ὁ κόσμος · and εἴ τι ἐπιδεικτόν
ἐστὶ τῆς ἐπὶ τὸ χεῖρον μεταβολῆς,
φθαρτόν ἐστι · καὶ ὁ κόσμος ἄρα ·
ἐξαυχμοῦται γὰρ καὶ ἐξυδατοῦται.
Conf. *Alex.* Meteora, 90. In
Plut. Sto. Rep. 44, 2, p. 1054,
Chrysippus asserts that the
οὐσία is immortal, but to κόσμος
belongs a ὥσπερ ἀφθαρσία.

[2] *Plut.* Sto. Rep. 39, 2, p.
1052 : [Χρύσιππος] ἐν τῷ πρώτῳ
περὶ προνοίας τὸν Δία, φησὶν,
αὔξεσθαι μέχρις ἂν εἰς αὐτὸν ἅπαντα
καταναλώσῃ. ἐπεὶ γὰρ ὁ θάνατος
μέν ἐστι ψυχῆς χωρισμὸς ἀπὸ τοῦ
σώματος, ἡ δὲ τοῦ κόσμου ψυχὴ οὐ
χωρίζεται μὲν, αὔξεται δὲ συνεχῶς
μέχρις ἂν εἰς αὐτὴν ἐξαναλώσῃ
τὴν ὕλην, οὐ ῥητέον ἀποθνήσκειν
τὸν κόσμον. Stob. Ecl. i. 414

(according to *Numenius*: see
Eus. Pr. Ev. xv. 18, 1) : Ζήνωνι
καὶ Κλεάνθει καὶ Χρυσίππῳ ἀρέσκει
τὴν οὐσίαν μεταβάλλειν οἶον εἰς
σπέρμα τὸ πῦρ (*Philo*, Incorrupt.
M. 956, B, expresses himself
against this description) καὶ
πάλιν ἐκ τούτου τοιαύτην ἀποτελεῖσθαι τὴν διακόσμησιν οἷα πρότερον ἦν.   Seneca, Consol. ad
Marciam, gives a graphic description of the end of the
world, which recalls the language of the Revelation. Compare, on the subject of ἐκπύρωσις,
Diog. vii. 142, 137 (see above
p. 158, 1); *Ar. Didym.* in Eus.
Pr. Ev. xv. 15, 1 : *Plut.* Com.
Not. 36 (see p. 153, 2); *Heraclit.* Alleg. Hom. c, 25, p. 53;
Cic. Acad. ii. 37, 119 ; N. D. ii.
46, 118 ; *Sen.* Consol. ad Polyb.
i. 2 ; *Alex. Aphr.* in Meteor. 90,
a. In the last-named passage,
it is urged by the Stoics, in
support of their view, that even
now large tracts of water are
dried up or else take the place
of dry land. *Simpl.* Phys. iii.
b ; De Cœlo; Schol. in Arist.
487, b, 35 and 489, a, 13 ;
Justin. Apol. i. 20 ; ii. 7; *Orig.*
c. Cels. iii. 75, 497, a ; vi. 71.
Since at the ἐκπύρωσις every-

fire or ether,[1] the Stoics thought, would take place, through the same intermediate stages as its generation from the primary fire.[2] Cleanthes, following his peculiar view as to the seat of the governing[3] force in the world, supposed that its destruction would come from the sun.[4]

No sooner, however, will everything have returned to its original unity,[5] and the course of the

CHAP.
VII.

(3) *Cycles in the world's course.*

thing is resolved into deity, *Plut.* C. Not. 17, 3, p. 1067, says: ὅταν ἐκπυρώσωσι τὸν κόσμον οὗτοι, κακὸν μὲν οὐδ᾽ ὁτιοῦν ἀπολείπεται, τὸ δ᾽ ὅλον φρόνιμόν ἐστι τηνικαῦτα καὶ σοφόν.

[1] *Numen.* in Eus. Pr. Ev. xv. 18, 1: ἀρέσκει δὲ τοῖς πρεσβυτάτοις τῶν ἀπὸ τῆς αἱρέσεως ταύτης, ἐξαγροῦσθαι πάντα κατὰ περιόδους τινὰς τὰς μεγίστας, εἰς πῦρ αἰθερῶδες ἀναλυομένων πάντων. According to *Philo,* Incorrup. M. 954, E, Cleanthes called this fire φλόξ, Chrysippus αὐγή. Respecting ἄνθραξ, φλόξ, αὐγή, see *ibid.* 953, E. The observations on p. 151 respecting the identity of πῦρ, πνεῦμα, αἰθὴρ apply here.

[2] This is, at least, the import of the general principle (assigned to Chrysippus by *Stob.* Ecl. i. 314) expressed by Heraclitus, that, in the resolution of earth and water into fire, the same steps intervene, in a retrograde order, as in their generation.

[3] See p. 147, 1.

[4] *Plut.* Com. Not. 31, 10: ἐπαγωνιζόμενος ὁ Κλεάνθης τῇ ἐκπυρώσει λέγει τὴν σελήνην καὶ τὰ λοιπὰ ἄστρα τὸν ἥλιον ἐξομοιῶσαι [leg. -εῖν] πάντα ἑαυτῷ καὶ μετα-

βαλεῖν εἰς ἑαυτόν.

[5] It is expressly asserted that everything, without exception, is liable to this destiny; neither the soul nor the Gods are exempt. Conf. *Sen.* Cons. ad Marc. 26, 7: Nos quoque felices animæ et æterna sortitæ (the words are put in the mouth of a dead man), cum Deo visum sit iterum ista moliri, labentibus cunctis et ipsæ parva ruinæ ingentis accessio in antiqua elementa vertemur. Chrysippus says of the Gods, in *Plut.* Sto. Rep. 38, 5: Some of the Gods have come into being and are perishable, others are eternal: Helios and Selene, and other similar deities, have come into being; Zeus is eternal. In *Philo,* Incorrupt. M. 950, A, *Orig.* c, Cels. iv. 68, *Plut.* Def. Oræ. 19, p. 420, Com. Not. 31, 5, p. 1075, it is objected that, at the general conflagration, the Gods will melt away, as though they were made of wax or tin. According to *Philodem.* περὶ θεῶν διαγωγῆς, Tab. i. 1, Vol. Hercul. vi. 1, even Zeno restricted the happy life of the Gods to certain lengthy periods of time.

world have come to an end, than the formation of a new world will begin,[1] so exactly corresponding with the previous world that every particular thing, every particular person, and every occurrence will recur in it,[2] precisely as they occurred in the world prece-

[1] *Arius*, in Eus. Pr. Ev. xv. 19 : ἐπὶ τοσοῦτο δὲ προελθὼν ὁ κοινὸς λόγος καὶ κοινὴ φύσις μεί- ζων καὶ πλείων γενομένη τέλος ἀναξηράνασα πάντα καὶ εἰς ἑαυτὴν ἀναλαβοῦσα ἐν τῇ πάσῃ οὐσίᾳ γίνεται (it occupies the room of the whole substance) ἐπανελ- θοῦσα εἰς τὸν πρῶτον ῥηθέντα λόγον καὶ εἰς ἀνάστασιν [? κατα- σιν—?] ἐκείνην τὴν ποιοῦσαν ἐνιαυτὸν τὸν μέγιστον, καθ᾽ ὃν ἀπ᾽ αὐτῆς μόνης εἰς αὐτὴν πάλιν γίνεται ἡ ἀποκατάστασις (the same in *Philop.* Gen. et Corr. B. ii. Schl. p. 70), ἐπανελθοῦσα δὲ διὰ τάξιν ἀφ᾽ οἵας διακοσμεῖν ὡσαύτως ἤρξατο κατὰ λόγον πάλιν τὴν αὐ- τὴν διεξαγωγὴν ποιεῖται. See p. 161. Accordiug to *Nemes.* Nat. Hom. c, 38, p. 147, conf. *Censorin.* Di. Nat. 18, 11, the ἐκπύρωσις takes place when all the planets have got back to the identical places which they oc- cupied at the beginning of the world, or, in other words, when a periodic year is complete. The length of a periodic year was estimated by Diogenes (*Plut.* Pl. i. 32, 2 ; *Stob.* Ecl. i. 264) at 365 periods, or 365 × 18,000 ordinary years. *Plut.* De Ei. ap. D. 9, g, E, p. 389 mentions the opinion, ὅπερ τρία πρὸς ἕν, τοῦτο τὴν διακόσμησιν χρόνῳ πρὸς τὴν ἐκπύρωσιν εἶναι. Inasmuch as it had been pre- viously said that the duration of κόρος (i. e. ἐκπύρωσις) was tne

longer, and that therefore Apollo, who represents the state of perfect unity was honoured nine months with the pæan, whilst Dionysus, torn to pieces by the Titans, the emblem of the present world of contraries, was only honoured for three with the dithyramb, some mistake seems to have crept in. Pro- bably we ought either to read ὅπερ πρὸς τρία ἕν, or to transpose the passage from διακόσμησιν to ἐκπύρωσιν.

[2] The belief in changing cycles is a common one in the older Greek philosophy. In particular, the Stoics found it in Heraclitus. The belief, how- ever, that each new world exactly represents the preceding one is first encountered among the Pythagoreans, and is closely connected with the theory of the migration of souls and a periodic year. Eudemus, in a passage which has generally been lost sight of in describing Pythagorean teaching, had taught (in *Simpl.* Phys. 173) : εἰ δέ τις πιστεύσειε τοῖς Πυθαγο- ρείοις, ὡς πάλιν τὰ αὐτὰ ἀριθμῷ κἀγὼ μυθολογήσω τὸ ῥαβδίον ἔχων ὑμῖν καθημένοις οὕτω καὶ τὰ ἄλλα πάντα ὁμοίως ἕξει, καὶ τὸν χρόνον εὔλογόν ἐστι τὸν αὐτὸν εἶναι (in that case the time must be the same as the present time). The Stoics appear to have borrowed this view from the Pytha-

ding. Hence the history of the world and of Deity
—as, indeed, with the eternity of matter and acting
force, must necessarily be the case—revolves in an
endless cycle through exactly the same stages.[1] Still

goreans (unless with other Orphic-Pythagorean views it was known to Heraclitus), and it commended itself to them as being in harmony with their theory of necessity. Hence they taught : μετὰ τὴν ἐκπύρωσιν πάλιν πάντα ταὐτὰ ἐν τῷ κόσμῳ γενέσθαι κατ᾽ ἀριθμὸν, ὡς καὶ τὸν ἰδίως ποιὸν πάλιν τὸν αὐτὸν τῷ πρόσθεν εἶναί τε καὶ γίνεσθαι ἐκείνῳ τῷ κόσμῳ (*Alex.* Anal. Pr. 58, b). τούτου δὲ οὕτως ἔχοντος, δῆλον, ὡς οὐδὲν ἀδύνατον, καὶ ἡμᾶς μετὰ τὸ τελευτῆσαι πάλιν περιόδων τινῶν εἰλημμένων χρόνον εἰς ὃν νῦν ἐσμεν καταστήσεσθαι σχῆμα (Chrysippus, περὶ Προνοίας, in *Lactant.* Inst. vii. 23. Conf. *Seneca,* Ep. 36, 10 : Veniet iterum qui nos in lucem reponat dies). This is to apply to every fact and to every occurrence in the new world, at the παλιγγενεσία or ἀποκατάστασις (as the return of a former age is called) : thus there will be another Socrates, who will marry another Xanthippe, and be accused by another Anytus and Meletus. Hence *M. Aurel.* vii. 19, xi. 1, deduces his adage, that nothing new happens under the sun. *Simpl.* Phys. 207, b ; *Philop.* Gen. et Corr. B. ii. Schl. p. 70 ; *Tatian.* c. Græc. c, 3, 245, d ; *Clemens,* Strom. v. 549, D ; *Orig.* c, Cels. iv. 68 ; v. 20 and 23 ; *Nemes.* l. c. ; *Plut.* Def. Or. 29, p. 425. Amongst other things, the Stoics raised the question, Whether the Socrates

who would appear in the future world would be numerically identical (εἷς ἀριθμῷ) with the present Socrates or not ? (*Simpl.* l. c.) the answer being, that they could not be numerically identical, since this would involve uninterrupted existence, but that they were alike without a difference (ἀπαράλλακτοι). Others, however, chiefly among the younger Stoics, appear to have held that there could be noticeable differences between the two. (*Orig.* v. 20, 592, c.) This remark appears to have given rise to the false notion (*Hippolyt.* Refut. Hær. i. 21 ; *Epiphan.* Hær. v. p. 12, b) that the Stoics believed in the transmigration of souls. The remark made by *Nemes.,* that the Gods know the whole course of the present world, from having survived the end of the former one, can only apply to one highest God, who, however, does not require such empirical knowledge. The other deities will not have survived the general conflagration.

[1] *Ar. Didym.* l. c. continues : τῶν τοιούτων περιόδων ἐξ ἀϊδίου γινομένων ἀκαταπαύστως. οὔτε γὰρ τῆς ἀρχῆς αἰτίαν καὶ [del.] πᾶσιν οἷόν τε γίνεσθαι, οὔτε τοῦ διοικοῦντος αὐτά. οὐσίαν τε γὰρ τοῖς γινομένοις ὑφεστάναι δεῖ πεφυκυῖαν ἀναδέχεσθαι τὰς μεταβολὰς πάσας καὶ τὸ δημιουργῆσον ἐξ αὐτῆς, κ.τ.λ. Conf. *Philop.* : ἀπορήσειε δ᾽ ἄν τις, ὥς φησιν

there were not wanting, even in comparatively early
times, members of the Stoic School who entertained
doubts on this teaching; and among the most distinguished of the later Stoics some gave it up altogether.[1] Besides the periodical destruction by fire,

'Αλέξανδρος, πρὸς 'Αριστοτέλη. εἰ
γὰρ ἡ ὕλη ἡ αὐτὴ ἀεὶ διαμένει,
ἔστι δὲ καὶ τὸ ποιητικὸν αἴτιον τὸ
αὐτὸ ἀεὶ, διὰ ποίαν αἰτίαν οὐχὶ
κατὰ περίοδόν τινα πλείονος χρόνου
ἐκ τῆς αὐτῆς ὕλης τὰ αὐτὰ πάλιν
κατ' ἀριθμὸν ὑπὸ τῶν αὐτῶν ἔσται;
ὅπερ τινές φασι κατὰ τὴν παλιγ-
γενέσιαν καὶ τὸν μέγαν ἐνιαυτὸν
' συμβαίνειν, ἐν ᾧ πάντων τῶν αὐτῶν
ἀποκατάστασις γίνεται. See *M.
Aurel.* v. 32.

[1] According to Philo (Incorrup. M. 947, C), besides
Posidonius and Panætius, his
instructor (*Diog.* vii. 142; *Stob.*
Ecl. i. 414), Boëthus asserted,
in opposition to the ordinary
Stoic teaching, the eternity of
the world. Philo adds that
this was also the ·view of Diogenes of Seleucia, in his later
years. Moreover, Zeno of
Tarsus, on the authority of
Numenius (in *Euseb.* Præp. Ev.
xv. 19, 2), considered that the
destruction of the world by fire
could not be proved (φασὶν
ἐπισχεῖν περὶ τῆς ἐκπυρώσεως τῶν
ὅλων). But these statements
are elsewhere contradicted.
Diogenes mentions Posidonius
as one who held the destruction
of the world by fire. The
testimony of Diogenes is confirmed by *Plut.* Pl. Phil. ii. 9, 3
(*Stob.* Ecl. i. 380; *Eus.* Pr.
Ev. xv. 40. See *Achill. Tatian,*
Isag. 131, c), who says that
Posidonius only allowed so

much empty space outside the
world as was necessary for the
world to be dissolved in at the
ἐκπύρωσις. The difference between his view and the older
Stoical view which Bake (Posidon. Rel. 58) deduces from
Stob. i. 432, is purely imaginary.
Antipater, according to Diogenes, also believed in a future
conflagration. Little importance can be attached to the
statement in *Cic.* N. D. ii. 46,
118, respecting Panætius, addu-
bitare dicebant; whereas the
words of *Stob.* are: πιθανωτέραν
νομίζει τὴν ἀϊδιότητα τοῦ κόσμου;
and those of *Diog.*: ἄφθαρτον
ἀπεφήνατο τὸν κόσμον.

Boëthus emphatically denied
the destruction of the world,
his chief reasons (in *Philo,* l. c.
952, c) being the following:—
(1) If the world were de-
stroyed, it would be a destruction without a cause, for
there is no cause, either within
or without, which could produce such an effect. (2) Of
the three modes of destruction,
those κατὰ διαίρεσιν, κατὰ ἀναίρε-
σιν τῆς ἐπεχούσης ποιότητος (as
in the crushing of a statue),
κατὰ σύγχυσιν (as in chemical
resolution), not one can apply
to the world. (3) If the world
ceased to exist, the action of
God on the world, in fact, His
activity would altogether cease.
(4) If everything were con-

periodical destructions by floods [1] were also assumed;
there being, however, a difference of opinion as to
whether the whole universe, or only the earth and its
inhabitants, were subject to these floods.[2]

sumed by fire, the fire must go
out for want of fuel. With
that, the possibility of a new
world is at an end.

The resolution of the world
into indefinite vacuum, attributed by *Plut.* Plac. ii. 9, 2, to
the Stoics in general, is no
doubt the same as the condensation and expansion of
matter. *Ritter,* iii. 599 and
703, supposes it to be a misapprehension of the real Stoic
teaching. How *Hegel,* Gesch.
d. Phil. ii. 391, and *Schleiermacher,* Gesch. d. Philos. p. 129,
in view of the passages quoted,
can absolutely deny that the
Stoics held a periodic destruction of the world, is hard to
comprehend.

[1] The flood and its causes
are fully discussed by *Sen.* Nat.
Qu. iii. 27–30. Rain, inroads
of the sea, earthquakes, are all
supposed to contribute. The
chief thing, however, is, that
such a destruction has been
ordained in the course of the
world. It comes cum fatalis
dies venerit, cum adfuerit illa
necessitas temporum (27, 1),
cum Deo visum, ordiri meliora,
vetera finiri (28, 7); it has
been fore-ordained from the
beginning (29, 2; 30, 1), and
is due, not only to the pressure
of the existing waters, but also
to their increase, and to a
changing of earth into water
(29, 4). The object of this

flood is to purge away the sins
of mankind, ut de integro totæ
rudes innoxiæque generentur
[res humanæ] nec supersit in
deteriora præceptor (29, 5);
peracto judicio generis humani
exstructisque pariter feris . . .
antiquus ordo revocabitur.
Omne ex integro animal gene-
rabitur dabiturque terris, homo
inscius scelerum : but this state
of innocence will not last long.
Seneca (29, 1) appeals to Bero-
sus, according to whom the
destruction of the world by fire
will take place when all the
planets are in the sign of the
Crab, its destruction by water
when they are in the sign of
the Capricorn.   Since these
signs correspond with the
summer and winter turns of
the sun, the language of Seneca agrees with that of *Censorin.*
Di. Nat. 18, 11, evidently quoted
from Varro, conf. *Jahn,* p. viii.:
Cujus anni hiems summa est
cataclysmus . . . æstas autem
ecpyrasis. Conf. *Heraclit.* Alleg.
Hom. c, 25, p. 53 : When one
element gains the supremacy
over the others, the course of
the world will come to an end,
by ἐκπύρωσις, if the element is
fire ; εἰ δ᾽ ἄθρουν ὕδωρ ἐκραγείη,
κατακλυσμῷ τὸν κόσμον ἀπολεῖσ-
θαι.

[2] For the former view, the
language of Heraclitus and
Censorinus tells, for the latter
that of Seneca.

Chap.
VII.

B. *Govern-
ment of the
world.*
(1) *Nature
of Destiny.*
(a) *Des-
tiny as
Provi-
dence.*

One point established by the generation and destruction of the world—the uncertainty of all particular things, and the unconditional dependence of
everything on a universal law and the course of the
universe—is throughout a leading one in the Stoic
enquiries into nature. All things in nature come
about by virtue of a natural and unchangeable connection of cause and effect, as the nature of the
universe and the general law require. This absolute necessity, regulating all Being and Becoming,
is expressed in the conception of Fate or Destiny
(ἡ εἱμαρμένη).[1] Viewed from the point of view of
natural science, Destiny is only another name for
primary Being, for the all-pervading, all-producing
Breath, for the artistic fire which is the Soul of the
world.[2] But again the activity of this Being being
always rational and according to law, Destiny may
also be described as the Reason of the World, as
universal Law, as the rational form of the world's

---

[1] *Diog.* vii. 149 : καθ' εἱμαρμένην δέ φασι τὰ πάντα γίνεσθαι
Χρύσιππος, κ.τ.λ. ἔστι δ' εἱμαρμένη αἰτία τῶν ὄντων εἱρομένη ἢ
λόγος καθ' ὃν ὁ κόσμος διεξάγεται.
A. Gell. vi. 2, 3 : (Chrysippus)
in . libro περὶ προνοίας quarto
εἱμαρμένην esse dicit φυσικήν
τινα σύνταξιν τῶν ὅλων ἐξ ἀϊδίου
τῶν ἑτέρων τοῖς ἑτέροις ἐπακο-
λουθούντων καὶ μετὰ πολὺ μὲν οὖν
ἀπαραβάτου οὔσης τῆς τοιαύτης
συμπλοκῆς. *Cic.* Divin. i. 55,
125 (according to Posidonius):
Fatum, or εἱμαρμένη, was called
ordinem seriemque causarum,
cum causa causæ nexa rem ex

se gignat. *Sen.* Nat. Qu. ii. 36 :
Quid enim intelligis fatum ?
existimo necessitatem rerum
omnium actionumque, quam
nulla vis rumpat. De Prov.
5, 8 : Irrevocabilis humana pariter ac divina cursus vehit.
Ille ipse omnium conditor et
rector scripsit quidem fata, sed
sequitur. Semper paret, semper
jussit.

[2] Conf. p. 152 and *Stob.*
Ecl. i. 180 (*Plut.* Plac. i. 28),
Χρύσιππος δύναμιν πνευματικὴν
τὴν οὐσίαν τῆς εἱμαρμένης τάξει
τοῦ παντὸς διοικητικήν.

course.[1] When regarded as the groundwork of natural formations, this primary Being or general Law is called Nature ; but when it appears as the cause of the orderly arrangement and development of the world, it is known as Providence ;[2] or in popular language it is called Zeus, or the will of Zeus ; and in this sense it is said that nothing happens without the will of Zeus.[3]

[1] Hence Chrysippus' definition (*Plut.* and *Stob.*): εἱμαρμένη ἐστὶν ὁ τοῦ κόσμου λόγος ἢ λόγος (*Plut.* νόμος) τῶν ἐν τῷ κόσμῳ προνοίᾳ διοικουμένων· ἢ λόγος καθ' ὃν τὰ μὲν γεγονότα γέγονε, τὰ δὲ γιγνόμενα γίγνεται, τὰ δὲ γενησόμενα γενήσεται. Instead of λόγος, Chrysippus also used ἀλήθεια, αἰτία, φύσις, ἀνάγκη. *Theodoret.* Cur. Gr. Aff. vi. 14, p. 87: Chrysippus assigns the same meaning to εἱμαρμένον and κατηναγκασμένον, explaining εἱμαρμένη to be κίνησις ἀΐδιος συνεχὴς καὶ τεταγμένη ; Zeno defines it (as *Stob.* i. 178, also says) as δύναμις κινητικὴ τῆς ὕλης ; also as φύσις or πρόνοια ; his successors as λόγος τῶν ἐν τῷ κόσμῳ προνοίᾳ διοικουμένων, or as εἱρμὸς αἰτίων. (The same in *Plut.* Plac. i. 28, 4. *Nemes.* Nat. Hom. c. 36, p. 143.) Even τύχη, he continues, is explained as a deity (or as *Simpl.* Phys. 74, b, has it as a θεῖον καὶ δαιμόνιον) ; but this supposes it to be essentially identical with εἱμαρμένη. Chrysippus in *Plut.* Sto. Rep. 34, 8, p. 1050: τῆς γὰρ κοινῆς φύσεως εἰς πάντα διατεινούσης δεήσει πᾶν τὸ ὁπωσοῦν γινόμενον ἐν τῷ ὅλῳ καὶ τῶν μορίων ὁτῳοῦν κατ' ἐκείνην γενέσθαι καὶ τὸν ἐκείνης λόγον κατὰ τὶ ἑξῆς ἀκωλύτως· διὰ τὸ μήτ' ἔξωθεν

εἶναι τὸ ἐνστησόμενον τῇ οἰκονομίᾳ μήτε τῶν μερῶν μηδὲν ἔχειν ὅπως κινηθήσεται ἢ σχήσει ἄλλως [ἢ] κατὰ τὴν κοινὴν φύσιν. *Cleanthes,* Hymn. (in *Stob.* Ecl. i. 30) v. 12, 18 ; *M. Aurel.* ii. 3. See p. 151, 1.

[2] It has been already demonstrated that all these ideas pass into one another.

[3] *Plut.* Com. Not. 34, 5, p. 1076 : εἰ δὲ, ὥς φησι Χρύσιππος, οὐδὲ τοὐλάχιστόν ἐστι τῶν μερῶν ἔχειν ἄλλως ἀλλ' ἢ κατὰ τὴν Διὸς βούλησιν, κ.τ.λ. Conf. Sto. Rep. 34, 2 : οὕτω δὲ τῆς τῶν ὅλων οἰκονομίας προαγούσης, ἀναγκαῖον κατὰ ταύτην, ὡς ἄν ποτ' ἔχωμεν, ἔχειν ἡμᾶς, εἴτε παρὰ φύσιν τὴν ἰδίαν νοσοῦντες, εἴτε πεπηρωμένοι, εἴτε γραμματικοὶ γεγονότες ἢ μουσικοὶ . . . κατὰ τοῦτον δὲ τὸν λόγον τὰ παραπλήσια ἐροῦμεν καὶ περὶ τῆς ἀρετῆς ἡμῶν καὶ περὶ τῆς κακίας καὶ τὸ ὅλον τῶν τεχνῶν καὶ τῶν ἀτεχνιῶν, ὡς ἔφην . . . οὐθὲν γὰρ ἔστιν ἄλλως τῶν κατὰ μέρος γενέσθαι, οὐδὲ τοὐλάχιστον, ἀλλ' ἢ κατὰ τὴν κοινὴν φύσιν καὶ κατὰ τὸν ἐκείνης λόγον, *Ibid.* 47, 4 and 8. *Cleanth.* Hymn v. 15 : οὐδέ τι γίγνεται ἔργον ἐπὶ χθονὶ σοῦ δίχα, δαῖμον, οὔτε κατ' αἰθέριον θεῖον πόλον οὔτ' ἐνὶ πόντῳ, πλὴν ὁπόσα ῥέζουσι κακοὶ σφετέρῃσιν ἀνοίαις.

CHAP.
VII.

(b) Destiny as generative reason.

In action as the creative force in nature, this universal Reason also bears the name of Generative Reason (λόγος σπερματικός). It bears this name more immediately in relation to the universe, not only as being the generating power by which all things are produced from primary fire as from seed according to an inner law, but because in the present condition of things all form and shape, all life and reason, grow out of it, in short, because primary fire and reason contain in themselves the germ of all things.[1] In the same sense, generative powers in the plural, or λόγοι σπερματικοὶ, are spoken of as belonging to Deity and Nature; and in treating of man, λόγοι σπερματικοὶ denote the generative powers as a part of the soul, and must be thought of as bearing the same relation to the individual soul as the generative powers of Nature do to the soul of nature.[2] By the term Generative Reason, therefore, must be understood the creative and forming forces in nature, which have collectively produced the universe, and particular exercises of which pro-

[1] See the quotations on p. 161, 1; 161, 2; 164, 2; 144, 1; 148; 145, 2, from *Diog.* vii. 136; *Stob.* Ecl. i. 372 and 414; *Cic.* N. D. ii.. 10, 28; 22, 58; *Sext.* Math. ix. 101: *M. Aurel.* iv. 14: ἐναφανισθήσῃ τῷ γεννήσαντι, μᾶλλον δὲ ἀναληφθήσῃ εἰς τὸν λόγον αὐτοῦ τὸν σπερματικὸν κατὰ μεταβολήν. *Ibid.* 21: αἱ ψυχαὶ . . . εἰς τὸν τῶν ὅλων σπερματικὸν λόγον ἀναλαμβανόμεναι.

[2] See on p. 151, 1, the definition of deity from *Stob.*

Plut. Athenag.; M. Aurel. ix. 1 : ὥρμησεν [ἡ φύσις] ἐπὶ τήνδε τὴν διακόσμησιν συλλαβοῦσά τινας λόγους τῶν ἐσομένων καὶ δυνάμεις γονίμους ἀφωρίσασα, κ.τ.λ. *Ibid.* vi. 24 : Alexander and his groom ἐλήφθησαν εἰς τοὺς αὐτοὺς τοῦ κόσμου σπερματικοὺς λόγους. *Diog.* vii. 148: ἔστι δὲ φύσις ἕξις ἐξ αὐτῆς κινουμένη κατὰ σπερματικοὺς λόγους, κ.τ.λ. *Ibid.* 157: μέρη δὲ ψυχῆς λέγουσιν ὀκτὼ, τὰς πέντε αἰσθήσεις καὶ τοὺς ἐν ἡμῖν σπερματικοὺς λόγους καὶ τὸ φωνητικὸν καὶ τὸ λογιστικόν.

duce individual things. These forces, agreeably with the ordinary Stoic speculations, are spoken of as the original *material*, or material germ of things. On the other hand, they also constitute the *form* of things—the law which determines their shape and qualities, the λόγος—only we must beware of trying to think of form apart from matter. Just as the igneous or etherial material of primary Being is in itself the same as the forming and creating element in things, the Reason of the world or the Soul of nature; so in the seeds of individual things, the atmospheric substance, in which the Stoics thought the generative power (σπέρμα) alone resides,[1] is in itself the germ out of which the corresponding thing is-produced by virtue of an inherent law.[2] The inward form is the only permanent element in things amid the perpetual change of materials.[3] It constitutes the identity of the universe; and whereas matter is constantly changing from one form to another,[4] the universal law of the process alone continues·unchangeably the same.

All parts of the Stoic system lead so unmistakeably to the conclusion, not only that the world as a whole is governed by Providence, but that every

(2) Arguments in favour of Providence.

[1] As the primary fire or ether is called the seed of the world (p. 161, 1), so, according to Chrysippus (in *Diog.* 159), the σπέρμα in the seed of plants and animals is a πνεῦμα κατ' οὐσίαν.

[2] σπερματικὸς λόγος is also used to express the seed or the egg itself. Thus, in *Plut.*

Quæst. Conviv. ii. 3, 3 and 4, it is defined as γόνος ἐνδεὴς γενέσεως.

[3] See p. 101, 2.

[4] This is particularly manifest, not only in the history of the world, but also in the doctrine of the constant change of the elements.

(a) *Argument from the general convictions of mankind.*

(b) *Argument from the perfection of God.*

(c) *Argument from the theory of necessity.*

part of it is subject to the same unchangeable laws, that no definite arguments would appear necessary to establish this point. Nevertheless, the Stoics lost no opportunity of meeting objections to their views in the fullest manner.[1] In the true spirit of a Stoic, Chrysippus appealed to the general conviction of mankind, as expressed in the names used to denote fate and destiny,[2] and to the language of poetry.[3] Nor was it difficult to show[4] that a divine government of the world followed of necessity from the Stoic conception of the perfection of God. Besides, in proving the existence of a God by the argument drawn from the adaptation of means to ends, a providential government of the world was at the same time proved.[5] Chrysippus also thought to defend his theory of necessity in the same strictly logical manner. For must not every judgment be either true or false?[6] And does not this apply to judgments which refer to future events, as well as to others? Judgments, however, referring to the future can only

[1] *Heine,* Stoicorum de Fato Doctrina (Naumb. 1859), p. 29.

[2] Compare what the Peripatetic Diogenianus (in *Eus.* Pr. Ev. vi. 8, 7) and *Stob.* (Ecl. i. 180) observe on the derivations of εἱμαρμένη, πεπρωμένη, Χρεὼν (*Heine,* p. 32, 1, suggests on the strength of *Theodoret,* Cur. Gr. Affect. vi. 11, p. 87, 4, who transcribes the quotation from Eusebius τὸν χρόνον κατὰ τὸ χρεῶν. We ought rather to read, according to *Theod.* Gaisf. τὸ χρεὼν κατὰ τὸ χρέος), Μοῖραι, Κλωθώ: and the quotations p. 170. 1; 171, 1;

also Ps. *Arist.* De Mundo, c. 7. The argument for Providence, drawn from the consensus gentium in *Sen.* Benef. iv. 4, follows another tack.

[3] Homeric passages, which he was in the habit of quoting in *Eus.* l. c. 8, 1.

[4] See *Cic.* N. D. ii. 30, 76.

[5] The two are generally taken together. Compare the quotations on p. 145, 4.

[6] See p. 83, 2; 110, 3; Aristotle and the Peripatetics thought differently. See *Simpl.* Cat. 103, β.

be true when what they affirm must come to pass of necessity; they can only be false when what they affirm is impossible; and, accordingly, everything that takes place must follow of necessity from the causes which produce it.[1]

(d) *Argument from foreknowledge of God.*

The same process of reasoning, transferred only from the outer world to the inner world of mind, underlies the argument from the foreknowledge of God.[2] If in the former case it was handed down that whatever is true, before it comes to pass, is necessary, so in this case it is said to be necessary, if it can be truly known before it comes to pass.

(e) *Argument from the existence of divination.*

To this argument may be added a further one to which the Stoics attached great importance—the argument from the existence of divination.[3] If it is impossible to know beforehand with certainty what is accidental, it is also impossible to predict it.

(3) *The idea of Providence determined.*

But the real kernel of the Stoic fatalism is expressed in the maxim, that nothing can take place without a sufficient cause, nor, under given circumstances, can happen differently from what has happened.[4] This were as impossible, according to the

(a) *Providence as necessity.*

[1] *Cic.* De Fato, 10, 20.

[2] *Alex.* De Fato, p. 92, Orel.: τὸ δὲ λέγειν εὔλογον εἶναι τοὺς θεοὺς τὰ ἐσόμενα προειδέναι . . . καὶ τοῦτο λαμβάνοντας κατασκευάζειν πειρᾶσθαι δι' αὐτοῦ τὸ πάντα ἐξ ἀνάγκης τε γίνεσθαι καὶ καθ' εἱμαρμένην οὔτε ἀληθὲς οὔτε εὔλογον.

[3] *Cic.* N. D. ii. 65, 162; De Fato, 3, 5 (unfortunately the previous exposition is wanting); *Diogenian* (in *Eus.* Pr. Ev. iv.

3, 1): Chrysippus proves, by the existence of divination, that all things happen καθ' εἱμαρμένην; for divination would be impossible, unless things were foreordained. *Alex.* De Fato, c. 21, p. 96: οἱ δὲ ὑμνοῦντες τὴν μαντικὴν καὶ κατὰ τὸν αὐτῶν λόγον μόνον σώζεσθαι λέγοντες αὐτὴν καὶ ταύτῃ πίστει τοῦ πάντα καθ' εἱμαρμένην γίνεσθαι χρώμενοι, κ.τ.λ.

[4] *Plut.* De Fato, 11, p. 374:

CHAP.
VII.

Stoics, as for something to come out of nothing;[1]
were it possible, the unity of the world would be
at an end, consisting, as it does, in the chain-like
dependence of cause upon cause, and in the absolute necessity of every thing and of every change.[2]
The Stoic doctrine of necessity was the direct consequence of the Stoic pantheism. The divine power
which rules the world could not be the absolute uniting cause of all things, if there existed anything in
any sense independent of it, and unless one unchanging causal connection governed every thing.

(b) Provi-
dence di-
rected im-
mediately
to the uni-
verse, in-
directly to
indivi-
duals.

Hence divine Providence does not extend to individual things taken by themselves, but only in
their relation to the whole. Everything being in
every respect determined by this relation, and being
consequently subject to the general order of the

κατὰ δὲ τὸν ἐναντίον [λόγον] μάλιστα μὲν καὶ πρῶτον εἶναι δόξειε τὸ
μηδὲν ἀναιτίως γίγεσθαι, ἀλλὰ
κατὰ προηγουμένας αἰτίας· δεύτερον δὲ τὸ φύσει διοικεῖσθαι τόνδε
τὸν κόσμον, σύμπνουν καὶ συμπαθῆ
αὐτὸν αὑτῷ ὄντα. Then come
the considerations confirmatory
of that view—divination, the
wise man's acquiescence in the
course of the world, the maxim
that every judgment is either
true or false. Nemes. Nat. Hom.
c. 35, p. 139: εἰ γὰρ τῶν αὐτῶν
αἰτίων περιεστηκότων, ὥς φασιν
αὐτοί, πᾶσα ἀνάγκη τὰ αὐτὰ γίνεσθαι.

[1] Alex. De Fato, c. 22, p. 72:
ὅμοιόν τε εἶναί φασι καὶ ὁμοίως
ἀδύνατον τὸ ἀναιτίως τῷ γίνεσθαί
τι ἐκ μὴ ὄντος.

[2] Alex. l. c. p. 70: φασὶ δὴ τὸν
κόσμον τόνδε ἕνα ὄντα . . . καὶ

ὑπὸ φύσεως διοικούμενον ζωτικῆς
τε καὶ λογικῆς καὶ νοερᾶς ἔχειν
τὴν τῶν ὄντων διοίκησιν ἀΐδιον
κατὰ εἱρμόν τινα καὶ τάξιν προϊοῦ-
σαν; so that everything is connected as cause and effect, ἀλλὰ
παντί τε τῷ γινομένῳ ἕτερόν τι
ἐπακολουθεῖν, ἡρτημένον ἐξ αὐτοῦ
ἀπ' ἀνάγκης ὡς αἰτίου, καὶ πᾶν τὸ
γινόμενον ἔχειν τι πρὸ αὐτοῦ, ᾧ ὡς
αἰτίῳ συνήρτηται· μηδὲν γὰρ ἀναιτίως μήτε εἶναι μήτε γίνεσθαι τῶν
ἐν τῷ κόσμῳ διὰ τὸ μηδὲν εἶναι ἐν
αὐτῷ ἀπολελυμένον τε καὶ κεχωρι-
σμένον τῶν προγεγονότων ἁπάντων·
διασπᾶσθαι γὰρ καὶ διαιρεῖσθαι καὶ
μηκέτι τὸν κόσμον ἕνα μένειν ἀεί,
κατὰ μίαν τάξιν τε καὶ οἰκονομίαν
διοικούμενον, εἰ ἀναίτιός τις εἰσά-
γοιτο κίνησις. See Cic. Divin. i.
55, 125; De Fato, 4, 7; M. Aurel.
x. 5.

world, it follows that we may say that God cares not only for the universe, but for all individuals therein.[1] The converse of this may also be asserted with equal justice, viz. that God's care is directed to the whole, and not to individuals, and that it extends to things great, but not to things small.[2] Directly it always extends to the whole, only indirectly to individuals throughout the whole, in so far as they are contained therein, and their condition is determined by its condition.[3] The Stoic notion of Providence is therefore entirely based on a view of the universe as a whole; individual things and persons can only come into consideration as dependent parts of this whole.

The Stoics were thus involved in a difficulty which besets every theory of necessity—the difficulty of doing justice to the claims of morality, and of vindicating the existence of moral responsibility.

(c) Diffi-culties connected with the theory of necessity.

---

[1] In *Cic.* N. D. ii. 65, 164, the Stoic says: Nec vero universo generi hominum solum, sed etiam singulis a Diis immortalibus consuli et provideri solet.

[2] *Sen.* Nat. Qu. ii. 46 : Singulis non adest [Jupiter], et tamen vim et causam et manum omnibus dedit. *Cic.* N. D. 66, 167 : Magna Dii curant, parva negligunt. *Ibid.* iii. 35, 86 : At tamen minora Dii negligunt . . . ne in regnis quidem reges omnia minima curant. Sic enim dicitis.

[3] Cicero uses the following argument to show that the providential care of God extends to individuals :—If the Gods care for all men, they must care for those in our hemisphere, and, consequently, for the cities in our hemisphere, and for the men in each city. The argument may be superfluous, but it serves to show that the care of individuals was the result of God's care of the whole world. *M. Aurel.* vi. 44 : εἰ μὲν οὖν ἐβουλεύσαντο περὶ ἐμοῦ καὶ τῶν ἐμοὶ συμβῆναι ὀφειλόντων οἱ θεοὶ, καλῶς ἐβουλεύσαντο . . . εἰ δὲ μὴ ἐβουλεύσαντο κατ᾽ ἰδίαν περὶ ἐμοῦ, περί γε τῶν κοινῶν πάντως ἐβουλεύσαντο, οἷς κατ᾽ ἐπακολούθησιν καὶ ταῦτα συμβαίνοντα ἀσπάζεσθαι καὶ στέργειν ὀφείλω. Similarly, ix. 28. It will be seen that the Stoics consider that the existence of divination, which served as a proof of special providence, was caused by the connection of nature.

CHAP.
VII.

(a) State-
ment of
several
difficul-
ties.

This difficulty became for them all the more pressing
the higher those claims were advanced, and the more
severely they judged the great majority of their fellow-men.[1] To overcome it, Chrysippus appears to
have made most energetic efforts.[2] The existence
of chance he could not allow, it being his aim to
establish that what seems to be accidental has always
some hidden cause.[3] Nor would he allow that everything is necessary, since that can only be called necessary which depends on no external conditions,
and is therefore always true;[4] in other words, what
is eternal and unchangeable, not that which comes
to pass in time, however inevitable it may be.[5] And,
by a similar process of reasoning, he still tried to
rescue the idea of the Possible, little as that idea
accords with the Stoic system.[6]

[1] As *Alex.* c. 28, p. 88, fitly
observes.

[2] The great majority of the
Stoic answers to πολλὰ ζητήματα
φυσικά τε καὶ ἠθικὰ καὶ διαλεκτικὰ,
which (according to *Plut.* De
Fato, c. 3) were called forth by
the theory of destiny, in all
probability belong to him.

[3] See p. 171, 3, Chrysippus,
in *Plut.* Sto. Rep. 23, 2, p. 1045.
He assigned as a general reason τὸ γὰρ ἀναίτιον ὅλως ἀνύ-
παρκτον εἶναι καὶ τὸ αὐτόματον.
Hence the Stoic definition of
τύχη is αἰτία ἀπρονόητος καὶ ἄδη-
λος ἀνθρωπίνῳ λογισμῷ in *Plut.*
De Fato, c. 7, p. 572; Plac. i.
29, 3 (*Stob.* Ecl. i. 218); *Alex.*
De Fato, p. 24; *Simpl.* Phys.
74, 6. See p. 171, 1.

[4] *Alex.* l. c. The Stoics assert that things are possible
which do not take place, if in

themselves they can take place,
and διὰ τοῦτο φασὶ μηδὲ τὰ γενό-
μενα καθ' εἱμαρμένην, καίτοι ἀπαρα-
βάτως γινόμενα, ἐξ ἀνάγκης γίνεσθαι, ὅτι ἔστιν αὐτοῖς δυνατὸν
γενέσθαι καὶ τὸ ἀντικείμενον. *Cic.*
Top. 15, 59: Ex hoc genere
causarum ex æternitate penden-
tium fatum a Stoicis nectitur.

[5] *Alex.* De Fato, c. 10, p. 32;
Cic. De Fato, 17, 39; 18, 41,
and above, p. 115, 2. Hence
Plut. Plac. (similarly *Nemes.*
Nat. Hom. c. 39, p. 149): ἃ μὲν
γὰρ εἶναι κατ' ἀνάγκην, ἃ δὲ καθ'
εἱμαρμένην, ἃ δὲ κατὰ προαίρεσιν,
ἃ δὲ κατὰ τύχην, ἃ δὲ κατὰ τὸ
αὐτοματόν, which is evidently
more explicit than the language used by *Stob.* Ecl. i. 176,
and the statement of Theodoret on p. 171, 1.

[6] See p. 115, 2. Opponents
such as *Plut.* Sto. Rep. c. 46,

In reference to human actions, the Stoics could not allow the freedom of the will, in the proper sense of the term;[1] but they were of opinion that this did not prejudice the character of the will as a deciding-power. For was not one and the same all-determining power everywhere active, working in each particular being according to the law of its nature, in one way in organic beings, in another in inorganic beings, differently again in animals and plants, in rational and irrational creatures?[2] And albeit every action may be brought about by the co-operation of causes depending on the nature of things and the character of the agent, is it not still free, the resultant of our own impulses and decision?[3] Involuntary it would only be were it produced by external causes alone, without any co-operation, on the part of our wills, with external causes.[4] Moral

CHAP. VII.

(β) *Moral responsibility vindicated.*

and *Alex.*, pointed out how illusory this attempt was. According to the latter, he fell back on the simple result, maintaining that, in the case of things happening καθ' εἱμαρμένην, there is nothing to prevent the opposite from coming about, so far as the causes which prevent this from happening are unknown to us.

[1] See above, p. 171, 3.

[2] *Chrysipp.* in *Gell.* N. A. vii. 2, 6; *Alex.* De Fato, c. 36, p. 112.

[3] *Gell.* l. c.; *Alex.* c. 13; *Nemes.* Nat. Hom. c. 35, p. 138, 140. *Alex.* c. 33 (on which see *Heine*, p. 43), gives a long argument, concluding with the words: πᾶν τὸ καθ' ὁρμὴν γινό-

μενον ἐπὶ τοῖς οὕτως ἐνεργοῦσιν εἶναι. *Nemes.* appeals to Chrysippus, and also to Philopator, a Stoic of the second century, A.D. Of him he remarks, that he has consistently attributed τὸ ἐφ' ἡμῖν to lifeless objects.

[4] *Cic.* De Fato, 18, 41: In order to avoid necessitas, or to uphold fate, Chrysippus distinguishes causæ principales et perfectæ from causæ adjuvantes, his meaning being that everything happens according to fate, not causis perfectis et principalibus, sed causis adjuvantibus. Conf. *Cic.* Top. 15, 59. Although these causes may not be in our power, still it is our will which assents to the impressions received. Œnomaus

responsibility, according to the Stoics, depends only on freedom of the will. What emanates from my will is my action, no matter whether it be possible for me to act differently or not.[1] Praise and blame, rewards and punishment, only express the judgment of society relative to the character of certain persons or actions.[2] Whether they could have been different, or not, is irrelevant. Otherwise virtue and vice must be set down as things not in our power, for which, consequently, we are not responsible, seeing that when a man is once virtuous or vicious, he cannot be otherwise;[3] and the highest perfection, that of the Gods, is absolutely unchangeable.[4] Chrysippus[5] even endeavoured to show, not only that his whole theory of destiny was in harmony with the claims of morality and moral responsibility, but that it presupposed their existence. The arrangement of the universe, he argued, involves law, and law involves the distinction between what is conventionally right and what is conventionally wrong, between what deserves praise and what deserves blame.[6]

(in *Eus.* Pr. Ev. vi. 7, 3 and 10) charges Chrysippus with making a ἡμίδουλον of the will, because he laid so great a stress on its freedom.

[1] *Gell.* vii. 2, 13 ; *Cic.* l. c.

[2] *Alex.* c. 34, p. 106, puts in the mouth of the Stoics : τὰ μὲν τῶν ζῴων ἐνεργήσει μόνον, τὰ δὲ πράξει τὰ λογικὰ, καὶ τὰ μὲν ἁμαρτήσεται, τὰ δὲ κατορθώσει. ταῦτα γὰρ τούτοις κατὰ φύσιν μὲν, ὄντων δὲ καὶ ἁμαρτημάτων καὶ κατορθωμάτων, καὶ τῶν τοιαύτων φύσεων καὶ

ποιοτήτων μὴ ἀγνοουμένων, καὶ ἔπαινοι μὲν καὶ ψόγοι καὶ τιμαὶ καὶ κολάσεις.

[3] *Alex.* c. 26, p. 82.

[4] *Alex.* c. 32, p. 102.

[5] The arguments usual among the Stoics in after times may, with great probability, be referred to Chrysippus.

[6] *Alex.* c. 35: λέγουσι γάρ· οὐκ ἔστι τοιαύτη μὲν ἡ εἱμαρμένη, οὐκ ἔστι δὲ πεπρωμένη· (It never happens that there is a εἱμαρμένη but not a πεπρωμένη) οὐδὲ ἔστι

Moreover, it is impossible to think of destiny with- out thinking of the world, or to think of the world
without thinking of the Gods, who are supremely
good. Hence the idea of destiny involves also that
of goodness, which again includes the contrast between virtue and vice, between what is praiseworthy
and what is blameworthy.¹ If his opponents objected that, if everything is determined by destiny, individual action is superfluous, since what
has been once foreordained must happen, come what
may, Chrysippus replied:—There is a distinction
to be made between simple and complex predestination; the consequences of human actions being
simply results of those actions, those consequences
are therefore quite as much foreordained as the
actions themselves.²

CHAP.
VII.

πεπρωμένη, οὐκ ἔστι δὲ αἶσα· οὐδὲ
ἔστι μὲν αἶσα, οὐκ [οὐδὲ] ἔστι δὲ
νέμεσις· οὐκ ἔστι μὲν νέμεσις, οὐκ
ἔστι δὲ νόμος· οὐδὲ ἔστι μὲν νόμος,
οὐκ ἔστι δὲ λόγος ὀρθὸς προστακτικὸς μὲν ὧν ποιητέον ἀπαγορευτικὸς
δὲ ὧν οὐ ποιητέον· ἀλλὰ ἀπαγορεύε-
ται μὲν τὰ ἁμαρτανόμενα, προστάτ-
τεται δὲ τὰ κατορθώματα · οὐκ ἄρα
ἔστι μὲν τοιαύτη ἡ εἱμαρμένη, οὐκ
ἔστι δὲ ἁμαρτήματα καὶ κατορθώ-
ματα· ἀλλ' εἰ ἔστιν ἁμαρτήματα
καὶ κατορθώματα, ἔστιν ἀρετὴ καὶ
κακία· εἰ δὲ ταῦτα, ἔστι καλὸν καὶ
αἰσχρόν· ἀλλὰ τὸ μὲν καλὸν ἐπαι-
νετόν, τὸ δὲ αἰσχρὸν ψεκτόν· οὐκ
ἄρα ἔστι τοιαύτη μὲν ἡ εἱμαρμένη,
οὐκ ἔστι δὲ ἐπαινετὸν καὶ ψεκτόν.
What is praiseworthy deserves
τιμή or γέρως ἀξίωσις, and what
is blameworthy merits κόλασις
or ἐπανόρθωσις.
¹ *Alex.* c. 37, p. 118: A

second argument ἀπὸ τῆς αὐτῆς
παλαίστρας is the following :—
οὐ πάντα μὲν ἔστι καθ' εἱμαρμένην,
οὐκ ἔστι δὲ ἀκώλυτος καὶ ἀπαρεμ-
πόδιστος ἡ τοῦ κόσμου διοίκησις·
οὐδὲ ἔστι μὲν τοῦτο, οὐκ ἔστι δὲ
κόσμος· οὐδὲ ἔστι μὲν κόσμος, οὐκ
εἰσὶ δὲ θεοί · (for κόσμος, according to the definitions of Chrysippus, is the whole, including
gods and men. See p. 158, 1)
εἰ δέ εἰσι θεοὶ, εἰσὶν ἀγαθοὶ οἱ θεοί·
ἀλλ' εἰ τοῦτο, ἔστιν ἀρετή · ἀλλ' εἰ
ἔστιν ἀρετή, ἔστι φρόνησις· ἀλλ'
εἰ τοῦτο ἔστιν ἡ ἐπιστήμη ποιητέων τε καὶ οὐ ποιητέων· ἀλλὰ
ποιητέα μὲν ἔστι τὰ κατορθώματα,
οὐ ποιητέα δὲ τὰ ἁμαρτήματα, κ.τ λ.
οὐκ ἄρα πάντα μὲν γίνεται καθ'
εἱμαρμένην, οὐκ ἔστι δὲ γεραίρειν
καὶ ἐπανορθοῦν.
² *Cic.* De Fato, 12, 28 ; *Diogenian.* (in *Eus.* Pr. Ev. vi. 8,

CHAP.
VII.

From all these observations, it appears that the Stoics never intended to allow man to hold a different position, in regard to destiny, from that held by other beings. All the actions of man—in fact his destiny—are decided by his relation to things : one individual only differs from another in that one acts on his own impulse, and agreeably with his own feelings, whereas another, under compulsion and against his will, conforms to the eternal law of the world.[1]

C. *Nature of the world.*

Everything in the world being produced by one and the same divine power, the world, as regards its structure, is an organic whole, in respect of its

16) ; *Sen.* Nat. Qu. ii. 37. Things which were determined by the co-operation of destiny alone Chrysippus called συγκαθειμαρμένα (confatalia). The argument by which he was confuted, which *Prantl*, Gesch. d. Log. i. 489, erroneously attributes to the Stoics themselves, went by the name of ἀργὸς λόγος (ignava ratio). Besides the ἀργὸς λόγος, *Plut.* De Fato, c. 11, p. 574, mentions the θερίζων and the λόγος παρὰ τὴν εἱμαρμένην as fallacies which could only be refuted on the ground of the freedom of the will. The last-named one, perhaps, turned on the idea (Œnomaus, in *Eus.* Pr. Ev. vi. 7, 12) that man might frustrate destiny if he neglected to do what was necessary to produce the foreordained results. According to *Ammon.* De Inter. 106, a, *Lucian*, Vit. Auct. 22, the θερίζων was as follows:— Either you will reap or you will not reap: it is therefore

incorrect to say, *perhaps* you will reap.

[1] *Sen.* (after Cleanthes, whose verses in *Epictet.* Man. 52) Ep. 107, 11 : Ducunt volentem fata, nolentem trahunt. *Hippolyt.* Refut. Hær. i. 21, has put it very plainly : τὸ καθ' εἱμαρμένην εἶναι πάντη διεβεβαιώσαντο παραδείγματι χρησάμενοι τοιούτῳ, ὅτι ὥσπερ ὀχήματος ἐὰν ᾖ ἐξηρτημένος κύων, ἐὰν μὲν βούληται ἕπεσθαι, καὶ ἕλκεται καὶ ἕπεται ἑκὼν . . . ἐὰν δὲ μὴ βούληται ἕπεσθαι, πάντως ἀναγκασθήσεται, τὸ αὐτὸ δήπου καὶ ἐπὶ τῶν ἀνθρώπων· καὶ μὴ βουλόμενοι γὰρ ἀκολουθεῖν ἀναγκασθήσονται πάντως εἰς τὸ πεπρωμένον εἰσελθεῖν. The same idea is expanded by *M. Aurel.* vi. 42: All must work for the whole, ἐκ περιουσίας δὲ καὶ ὁ μεμφόμενος καὶ ὁ ἀντιβαίνειν πειρώμενος καὶ ἀναιρεῖν τὰ γινόμενα, καὶ γὰρ τοῦ τοιούτου ἐχρῇζεν ὁ κόσμος. It is man's business to take care that he acts a dignified part in the common labour.

constitution perfect. The unity of the world, a
doctrine distinguishing the Stoics from the Epicureans, followed as a corollary from the unity of primary substance and of primary force.[1] It was further
proved by the intimate connection, or, as the Stoics
called it, the sympathy of all its parts, and, in particular, by the coincidence of the phenomena of
earth and heaven.[2] Its perfection followed generally

CHAP.
VII.

(1) *Its
unity and
perfec-
tions.*

---

[1] After all that has been
said, this needs no further con-
firmation. Conversely, the
unity of the forming power is
concluded from the unity of
the world. See p. 143, 1, 2.
Conf. *Plut.* Def. Orac. 29, p.
425. *M. Aurel.* vi. 38 : πάντα
ἀλλήλοις ἐπιπέπλεκται καὶ πάντα
κατὰ τοῦτο φίλα ἀλλήλοις ἐστί
. . . τοῦτο δὲ διὰ τὴν τονικὴν
κίνησιν καὶ σύμπνοιαν καὶ τὴν
ἔνωσιν τῆς οὐσίας. *Ibid.* vii. 9.

[2] *Sext.* Math. ix. 78 : τῶν
σωμάτων τὰ μέν ἐστιν ἡνωμένα,
τὰ δὲ ἐκ συναπτομένων, τὰ δὲ ἐκ
διεστώτων . . . ἐπεὶ οὖν καὶ ὁ
κόσμος σῶμά ἐστιν, ἤτοι ἡνω-
μένον ἐστὶ σῶμα ἢ ἐκ συναπτομένων ἢ ἐκ διεστώτων· οὔτε δὲ ἐκ
συναπτομένων οὔτε ἐκ διεστώτων,
ὡς δείκνυμεν ἐκ τῶν περὶ αὐτὸν
συμπαθειῶν· κατὰ γὰρ τὰς τῆς
σελήνης αὐξήσεις καὶ φθίσεις πολλὰ
τῶν τε ἐπιγείων ζῴων καὶ θαλασσίων
φθίνει τε καὶ αὔξεται, ἀμπώτεις τε
καὶ πλημμυρίδες (ebb and flood),
περί τινα μέρη τῆς θαλάσσης γίνονται. In the same way, atmospheric changes coincide with
the setting and rising of the
stars : ἐξ ὧν συμφανές, ὅτι ἡνω-
μένον τι σῶμα καθέστηκεν ὁ κόσμος,
ἐπὶ μὲν γὰρ τῶν ἐκ συναπτομένων
ἢ διεστώτων οὐ συμπάσχει τὰ μέρη

ἀλλήλοις. *Diog.* vii. 140 : ἐν δὲ
τῷ κόσμῳ μηδὲν εἶναι κενὸν ἀλλ'
ἡνῶσθαι αὐτόν, τοῦτο γὰρ ἀναγ-
κάζειν τὴν τῶν οὐρανίων πρὸς τὰ
ἐπίγεια σύμπνοιαν καὶ συντονίαν.
Ibid. 143 : ὅτι θ' εἷς ἐστι Ζήνων
φησὶν ἐν τῷ περὶ τοῦ ὅλου καὶ
Χρύσιππος καὶ Ἀπολλόδωρος . . .
καὶ Ποσειδώνιος. *Alex.* De Mixt.
142, a, see p. 127, 5 ; *Cic.* N. D.
ii. 7, 19 ; *Epictet.* Diss. i. 14, 2 :
οὐ δοκεῖ σοι, ἔφη, ἡνῶσθαι τὰ
πάντα ; Δοκεῖ, ἔφη· τί δέ ; συμπα-
θεῖν τὰ ἐπίγεια τοῖς οὐρανίοις οὐ
δοκεῖ σοι ; Δοκεῖ, ἔφη. Cicero
mentions the changes in animals and plants corresponding
to the changes of seasons, the
phases of the moon, and the
greater or less nearness of the
sun. *M. Aurel.* iv. 40. From
all these passages we gather
what the question really was.
It was not only whether other
worlds were possible, besides
the one which we know from
observation, but whether the
heavenly bodies visible were in
any essential way connected
with the earth, so as to form
an organic whole (ζῷον, *Diog.*
vii. 143).

The Stoic conception of συμπάθεια was not used to denote
the magic connection which it

from a consideration of their fundamental principles.[1] But the Stoics made use of many arguments
in support of it, appealing, after the example of
preceding philosophers, sometimes to its beauty, and,
at other times, to the adaptation of means to ends.[2]
An appeal to the former is the assertion of Chrysippus, that nature made many creatures for the
sake of beauty, the peacock, for instance, for the
sake of its tail[3];—and the dictum of Marcus Aurelius, that what is purely subsidiary and subservient
to no purpose, even what is ugly or frightful in
nature, has peculiar attractions of its own;[4] and the

expresses in ordinary parlance,
but the natural coincidence between phenomena belonging to
the different parts of the world,
the consensus, concentus, cognatio, conjunctio, or continuatio
naturæ (*Cic.* N. D. iii. 11, 28 ;
Divin. ii. 15, 34 ; 69, 142). In
this sense, *M. Aurel.* ix. 9, observes that like is attracted
by like; fire is attracted upwards, earth downwards; beasts
and men seek out each other's
society; even amongst the highest existences, the stars, there
exists a ἔνωσις ἐκ διεστηκότων, a
συμπάθεια ἐν διεστῶσι. Even the
last remark does not go beyond
the conception of a natural connection; nevertheless, it paves
the way for the later Neoplatonic idea of sympathy, as no
longer a physical connection,
but as an influence felt at a
distance by virtue of a connection of soul.

[1] *M. Aurel.* vi. 1 : ἡ τῶν ὅλων
οὐσία (the matter of the world)
εὐπειθὴς καὶ εὐτρεπής· ὁ δὲ ταύτην

διοικῶν λόγος οὐδεμίαν ἐν ἑαυτῷ
αἰτίαν ἔχει τοῦ κακοποιεῖν· κακίαν
γὰρ οὐκ ἔχει, οὐδέ τι κακῶς ποιεῖ,
οὐδὲ βλάπτεταί τι ὑπ᾽ ἐκείνου.
πάντα δὲ κατ᾽ ἐκεῖνον γίνεται καὶ
περαίνεται.
[2] *Diog.* 149 : ταύτην δὲ [τὴν
φύσιν] καὶ τοῦ συμφέροντος στοχάζεσθαι καὶ ἡδονῆς, ὡς δῆλον ἐκ τῆς
τοῦ ἀνθρώπου δημιουργίας.
[3] *Plut.* St. Rep. 21, 3, p.
1044 : εἰπὼν [Χρύσιππος] ὅτι . . .
φιλοκαλεῖν . . . τὴν φύσιν τῇ
ποικιλίᾳ χαίρουσαν εἰκός ἐστι,
ταῦτα κατὰ λέξιν εἴρηκε· γένηιτο
δ᾽ ἂν μάλιστα τούτου ἔμφασις ἐπὶ
τῆς κέρκου τοῦ ταώ. Conf. the
Stoic in *Cic.* Fin. ii. 5, 18 : Jam
membrorum . . . alia videntur
propter eorum usum a natura
esse donata . . . alia autem
nullam ob utilitatem, quasi ad
quendam ornatum, ut cauda
pavoni, plumæ versicolores co-
lumbis, viris mammæ atque
barba.
[4] *M. Aurel.* iii. 2 : It is there
proved by examples, ὅτι καὶ τὰ
ἐπιγινόμενα τοῖς φύσει γιγνομένοις

same kind of consideration may have led to the
Stoic assertion, that no two things in nature are altogether alike.[1] Their chief argument, however, for the
beauty of the world, was based on the shape, the
size, and the colour of the heavenly structure.[2]

The other line of argument is followed not so
much in individual expressions. But owing no
doubt to the same reason—the predominantly practical character of its treatment of things—the Stoic
view of nature, like the Socratic, has ever an
eye on the adaptation of means to ends in the
world. As, on the one hand, this adaptation of
means to ends is the most convincing proof of
the existence of deity, so, on the other hand, by it,
more than by anything else, the divine government of the world makes itself manifest.[3] Like
Socrates, however, they took a very superficial view
of the adaptation of means to ends, arguing that
everything in the world was created for the benefit of
some other thing—plants for the support of animals,
animals for the support and the service of man,[4]

ἔχει τι εὔχαρι καὶ ἐπαγωγὸν . . .
σχεδὸν οὐδὲν οὐχὶ καὶ τῶν κατ'
ἐπακολούθησιν συμβαινόντων ἡδεώς
πως διασυνίστασθαι.

[1] *Cic.* Acad. ii. 26, 85 ; *Sen.*
Ep. 113, 16. The latter includes
this variety of natural objects
among the facts, which must
fill us with admiration for the
divine artifices.

[2] *Plut.* Plac. i. 6, 2 : καλὸς δὲ
ὁ κόσμος· δῆλον δ' ἐκ τοῦ σχήματος καὶ τοῦ χρώματος καὶ τοῦ
μεγέθους καὶ τῆς περὶ τὸν κόσμον
τῶν ἀστέρων ποικιλίας ; the world

has the most perfect form, that
of a globe, with a sky the most
perfect in colour, &c.

[3] See the passages quoted
p. 145, 4, particularly *Cic.* N. D.
ii. 32.

[4] *Plut.* (in *Porphyr.* De
Abstin. iii. 32) : ἀλλ' ἐκεῖνο νὴ
Δία τοῦ Χρυσίππου πιθανὸν ἦν, ὡς
ἡμᾶς αὐτῶν καὶ ἀλλήλων οἱ θεοὶ
χάριν ἐποιήσαντο, ἡμῶν δὲ τὰ ζῷα,
συμπολεμεῖν μὲν ἵππους καὶ συνθη-
ρεύειν κύνας, ἀνδρείας δὲ γυμνάσια
παρδάλεις καὶ ἄρκτους καὶ λέοντας,
κ.τ.λ. *Cic.* N. D. ii. 14, 37 :

the world for the benefit of Gods and men[1]—not unfrequently degenerating into the ridiculous and pedantic, in their endeavours to trace the special end for which each thing existed.[2] But, in asking

Scite enim Chrysippus: ut clypei causa involucrum, vaginam autem gladii, sic præter mundum cætera omnia aliorum causa esse generata, ut eas fruges et fructus, quas terra gignit, animantium causa, animantes autem hominum, ut equum vehendi causa, arandi bovem, venandi et custodiendi canem. *Id.* Off. i. 7, 22: Placet Stoicis, quæ in terris gignantur ad usum hominum omnia creari.

[1] *Cic.* Fin. iii. 20, 67: Præclare enim Chrysippus, cetera nata esse hominum causa et Deorum, eos autem communitatis et societatis suæ. N. D. ii. 53, 133, in describing the Stoic teaching: Why has the universe been made? Not for the sake of plants or animals, but for the sake of rational beings, Gods and men. It is then shown (c. 54-61), by an appeal to the structure of man's body, and his mental qualities, how God has provided for the wants of man; and the argument concludes with the words, Omnia, quæ sint in hoc mundo, quibus utantur homines, hominum causa facta esse et parata. Just as a city, and what is therein, exists for the use of the inhabitants, so the world is intended for the use of Gods and men. Even the stars quanquam etiam ad mundi cohærentiam pertinent, tamen et spectaculum hominibus præ-

bent. The earth with its plants and animals was created for the service of man. In *Orig.* c. Cels. iv. 74, p. 559, the Stoics assert that Providence created all things for the sake of rational beings; *M. Aurel.* v. 16 and 30; *Gell.* vii. 1, 1. Hence the definition of κόσμος quoted on p. 158, 1.

[2] Chrysippus (in *Plut.* Sto. Rep. 32, 1, p. 1049) shows how useful fowls are; the horse is intended for riding, the ox for ploughing, the dog for hunting. The pig, Cleanthes thought (*Clemens*, Strom. vii. 718, B), was made to sustain man, and endowed with a soul, in place of salt, to prevent its corrupting (*Cic.* N. D. ii. 64, 160; Fin. v. 13, 38; *Plut.* Qu. Conviv. v. 10, 3 and 6, p. 685; *Porphyr.* De Abstin. iii. 20); oysters and birds for the same purpose also (*Porphyr.* l. c.). In the same way, he spoke of the value of mice and bugs, see p. 189, 1. The Stoic in *Cic.* N. D. ii. 63, 158, following in the same track, declares that sheep only exist for the purpose of clothing, dogs for guarding and helping man, fishes for eating, and birds of prey for divers uses. *Epictet.* Diss. ii. 8, 7, in the same spirit, speaks of asses being intended to carry burdens; for this purpose he must be able to walk, and in order to walk, must possess the power of imagination.

the further question, For what purpose do Gods and
men exist? they could not help being at length
brought beyond the idea of a relative end to the
idea of an end-in-itself. The end for which Gods
and men exist is that of mutual society.[1] Or, expressing the same idea in language more philosophical, the end of man is the contemplation and
imitation of the world; man has only importance
as being a part of a whole; only this whole is perfect and an end-in-itself.[2]

The greater the importance attached by the
Stoics to the perfection of the world, the less were
they able to avoid the difficult problem of recon-
ciling the various forms of evil in the world. By
the attention which, following the example of Plato,
they gave to this question, they may be said to be
the real creators of the moral theory of the world.[3]
The character of this moral theory was already
determined by their system. Subordinating individuals, as that system did, to the law of the whole,
it met the charges preferred against the evil found
in the world by the general maxim, that imperfection in details is necessary for the perfection of the
whole.[4] This maxim, however, might be explained

*(2) Moral
theory of
the world.*

---

[1] See p. 186, 1.
[2] *Cic.* N. D. ii. 14, 37 : Ipse
autem homo ortus est ad mundum contemplandum et imitan-
dum, nullo modo perfectus, sed
est quædam particula perfecti.
Sed mundus quoniam omnia
complexus est, nec est quidquam, quod non insit in eo,
perfectus undique est.

[3] We gather this from the
comparatively full accounts of
the Stoic theory of the moral
government of the world. *Plut.*
Sto. Rep. 37, 1, p. 1051, says
that Chrysippus wrote several
treatises περὶ τοῦ μηδὲν ἐγκλητὸν
εἶναι μηδὲ μεμπτὸν κόσμῳ.
[4] See p. 187, 2, and Chrysippus (in *Plut.* Sto. Rep. 44, 6):

in several ways, according to the meaning assigned
to the term necessary. If necessity was taken to be
physical, the existence of evil was excused as being
a natural necessity, from which not even deity could
grant exemption. If, on the other hand, the necessity was not a physical one, but one arising from the
relation of means to ends, evil was justified as a condition or necessary means for bringing about good.
Both views are combined in the three chief questions
involved in the moral theory of the world : the existence of physical evil, the existence of moral
evil, and the relation of outward circumstances to
morality.

*(a) Exist-
ence of
physical
evil.*

The existence of physical evil gave the Stoics
little trouble, since they refused to regard it as an
evil at all, as will be seen in treating of their ethical
system. It was enough for them to refer evils of
this kind—diseases, for instance—to natural causes,·
and to regard them as the inevitable consequences
of causes framed by nature to serve a definite purpose.[1] Still, they did not fail to point out that

τέλεον μὲν ὁ κόσμος σῶμά ἐστιν,
οὐ τέλεα δὲ τὰ κόσμου μέρη τῷ
πρὸς τὸ ὅλον πως ἔχειν καὶ μὴ καθ'
αὑτὰ εἶναι. Compare also the
statement in *Plut.* Solert. An.
c. 2, 9, p. 960, that animals
must be irrational, because the
irrational must be contrasted
with the rational.

[1] *Gell.* vii. [vi.] 1, 7: Chrysippus, in his treatise περὶ προνοίας,
discussed, amongst other things,
the question, εἰ αἱ τῶν ἀνθρώπων
νόσοι κατὰ φύσιν γίνονται. Existimat autem non fuisse hoc

principale naturæ consilium,
ut faceret homines morbis ob-
noxios . . . sed cum multa
inquit atque magna gigneret
pareretque aptissima et utilis-
sima, alia quoque simul agnata
sunt incommoda iis ipsis, quæ
faciebat cohærentia: eaque non
per naturam sed per sequelas
quasdam necessarias facta dicit,
quod ipse appellat κατὰ παρακο-
λούθησιν. . . . Proinde morbi
quoque et ægritudines partæ
sunt dum salus paritur. *M.
Aurel.* vi. 36: All evils are

many things only become evil by a perverted use,[1]   CHAP.
and that other things, ordinarily regarded as evil,   VII.
are of the greatest value.[2]

Greater difficulty was found by the Stoics as by   (b) *Exist-*
others to beset the attempt to justify the existence   *ence of moral evil.*
of moral evil—the difficulty being enhanced by the
extent and degree of moral evil in the world[3] according to their views. By their theory of necessity
they were prevented from rolling the responsibility
for moral evil from natural law or deity on to man.
If, nevertheless, they did not altogether exclude this
course, inasmuch as they refused to allow to deity any
participation in evil, and referred evil to the free will
and intention of man,[4] they only acted like other

ἐπιγεννήματα τῶν σεμνῶν καὶ
καλῶν. *Plut.* An. Procr. c. 6
and 9, p. 1015 : αὐτοὶ δὲ (the
Stoics) κακίαν καὶ κακοδαιμονίαν
τοσαύτην . . . κατ᾽ ἐπακολούθησιν
γεγονέναι λέγουσιν. *Sen.* Nat.
Qu. vi. 3, 1.

[1] *Sen.* Nat. Qu. v. 18, 4 and
13 : Non ideo non sunt ista
natura bona, si vitio male
utentium nocent . . . si bene-
ficia naturæ utentium pravitate
perpendimus, nihil non nostro
malo accepimus.

[2] Chrysippus (in *Plut.* St.
Rep. 21, 4) remarks that bugs do
us good service by preventing
us from sleeping too long, and
mice warn us not to leave
things about. He also observes
(*Ibid.* 32, 2) that wars are as
useful as colonies, by preventing
over-population. See the quotations, p. 185, 4 ; 186, 2. *M.
Aurel.* viii. 50, makes a similar
remark in regard to weeds. In

the house of nature all the
waste has its uses.

[3] A circumstance which
Plut. Com. Not. 19, p. 1067,
dexterously uses against the
Stoics.

[4] *Cleanthes,* Hymn. v. 17
(see p. 171, 3) ; *Plut.* St. Rep.
33, 2 : Chrysippus affirms, ὡς
τῶν αἰσχρῶν τὸ θεῖον παραίτιον
γίνεσθαι οὐκ εὔλογόν ἐστιν, law is
innocent of crime, God of impiety. *Id.* (in *Gell.* vii. 2, 7) :
Quanquam ita sit, ut ratione
quadam necessaria et principali
coacta atque connexa sint fato
omnia, ingenia tamen ipsa men-
tium nostrarum perinde sunt
fato obnoxia, ut proprietas
eorum est ipsa et qualitas . . .
sua sævitate et voluntario impetu in assidua delicta, et
in errores se ruunt. Hence
Cleanthes continues, in a passage quoted in Greek by Gellius ;
ὡς τῶν βλαβῶν ἑκάστοις παρ᾽

systems of necessity, in not treating this solution as
final.[1] The real solution which they gave to the
difficulty was partly by asserting that even the deity
is not able to keep human nature free from faults,[2]
and partly by the consideration that the existence of
evil is necessary, as a counterpart and supplement to
good,[3] and that, in the long run, evil would be turned
by the deity into good.[4]

αὐτοῖς γινομένων καὶ καθ' ὁρμὴν
αὐτῶν ἁμαρτανόντων τε καὶ βλαπ-
τομένων καὶ κατὰ τὴν αὐτῶν διάνοιαν καὶ πρόθεσιν. In *Plut.* Sto.
Rep. 47, 13, p. 1057, Chrysippus
says that, even if the Gods
make false representations to
man, it is man's fault if he
follows those representations.
Conf. *Epictet.* Ench. c. 27:
ὥσπερ σκοπὸς πρὸς τὸ ἀποτυγχεῖν
οὐ τίθεται, οὕτως οὐδὲ κακοῦ φύσις
(evil in itself) ἐν κόσμῳ γίνεται.
Id. Diss. i. 6, 40. Such observations bear out in some
degree the statement of *Plut.*
Plac. ii. 27. 3, that, according
to the Stoics, τὰ μὲν εἱμάρθαι, τὰ
δὲ ἀνειμάρθαι. See above p. 179,
3, 4.

Chrysippus recognised
this; and hence he says (in
Gell.): It has been also decreed by destiny that the bad
should do wrong.

[2] Chrysippus in *Plut.* Sto.
Rep. 36, 1: κακίαν δὲ καθόλου
ἆραι οὔτε δυνατόν ἐστιν οὔτ' ἔχει
καλῶς ἀρθῆναι. *Id.* (in *Gell.*
vii. 1, 10): As diseases spring
from human nature, sic hercle
inquit dum virtus hominibus
per consilium naturæ gignitur
vitia ibidem per affinitatem
contrariam nata sunt.

[3] Chrysippus in *Plut.* Sto.

Rep. 35, 3 (C. Not. 13, 2):
γίνεται γὰρ αὐτή πως [ἡ κακία]
κατὰ τὸν τῆς φύσεως λόγον καὶ
ἵνα οὕτως εἴπω οὐκ ἀχρήστως γίνεται πρὸς τὰ ὅλα, οὐδὲ γὰρ ἂν
τἀγαθὸν ἦν. C. Not. 14, 1: As
in a comedy, what is absurd
contributes to the effect of the
whole, οὕτω ψέξειας ἂν αὐτὴν ἐφ'
ἑαυτῆς τὴν κακίαν· τοῖς δ' ἄλλοις
οὐκ ἀχρηστός ἐστιν. Similarly
M. Aurel. vi. 42. *Gell.* vii.
1, 2: (Chrysippus) nihil est
prorsus istis, inquit, insubidius,
qui opinantur, bona esse po-
tuisse, si non essent ibidem
mala: nam cum bona malis
contraria sint, utraque necessum
est opposita inter se et quasi
mutuo adverso quæque fulta
nixu (Heraclitus' ἀντίξουν συμ-
φέρον) consistere: nullum adeo
contrarium est sine contrario
altero. Without injustice,
cowardice, &c., we could not
know what justice and valour
are. If there were no evil,
φρόνησις as ἐπιστήμη ἀγαθῶν καὶ
κακῶν would be impossible
(*Plut.* C. Not. 16, 2, p. 1066).

[4] *Cleanthes,* Hymn. 18:
ἀλλὰ σὺ καὶ τὰ περισσὰ ἐπίστασαι
ἄρτια θεῖκαι
καὶ κοσμεῖν τὰ ἄκοσμα, καὶ οὐ φίλα
σοὶ φίλα ἐστίν·

The third point in the moral theory of the world, the connection between moral worth and happiness, engaged all the subtlety of Chrysippus and his followers. To deny any connection between them would have been to contradict their ordinary views of the relation of means to ends. Besides, they were prepared to regard a portion of our outward ills as divine judgments.[1] Still there were facts which could not be reconciled with this view—the misfortunes of the virtuous, the good fortune of the vicious—and which required explanation. The task of explaining these facts appears to have involved the Stoics in considerable embarrassment, nor were their answers altogether satisfactory.[2] But, in the spirit of their sys-

---

ὦδε γὰρ εἰς ἓν ἅπαντα συνήρμοκας
ἐσθλὰ κακοῖσιν
ὥσθ᾽ ἕνα γίγνεσθαι πάντων λόγον
αἰὲν ἐόντα.

[1] *Plut.* Sto. Rep. 35, 1 : τὸν θεὸν κολάζειν φησὶ τὴν κακίαν καὶ πολλὰ ποιεῖν ἐπὶ κολάσει τῶν πονηρῶν . . . ποτὲ μὲν τὰ δύσχρηστα συμβαίνειν φησὶ τοῖς ἀγαθοῖς οὐχ ὥσπερ τοῖς φαύλοις κολάσεως χάριν ἀλλὰ κατ᾽ ἄλλην οἰκονομίαν ὥσπερ ἐν ταῖς πόλεσιν . . . [τὰ κακὰ] ἀπονέμεται κατὰ τὸν τοῦ Διὸς λόγον ἤτοι ἐπὶ κολάσει ἢ κατ᾽ ἄλλην ἔχουσάν πως πρὸς τὰ ὅλα οἰκονομίαν. *Id.* 15, 2 : ταῦτά φησι τοὺς θεοὺς ποιεῖν ὅπως τῶν πονηρῶν κολαζομένων οἱ λοιποὶ παραδείγμασι τούτοις χρώμενοι ἧττον ἐπιχειρῶσι τοιοῦτόν τι ποιεῖν. At the beginning of the same chapter, the ordinary views of divine punishment had been treated with ridicule. Conf. Quæst. Rom. 51, p. 277.

[2] Thus Chrysippus (in *Plut.*

St. Rep. 37, 2) in answer to the question, How the misfortune of the virtuous is to be explained, says: πότερον ἀμελουμένων τινῶν καθάπερ ἐν οἰκίαις μείζοσι παραπίπτει τινὰ πίτυρα καὶ ποσοὶ πυροί τινες τῶν ὅλων εὖ οἰκονομουμένων· ἢ διὰ τὸ καθίστασθαι ἐπὶ τῶν τοιούτων δαιμόνια φαῦλα ἐν οἷς τῷ ὄντι γίνονται ἐγκλητέαι ἀμέλειαι; Similarly the Stoic in *Cic.* N. D. ii. 66: Magna Dii curant, parva negligunt,—hardly satisfactory explanations for any theory of necessity. It is still more unsatisfactory to hear Seneca (Benef. iv. 32) justifying the unmerited good fortune of the wicked as due to the nobility of their ancestors. The reason assigned by Chrysippus (in *Plut.*)—πολὺ καὶ τὸ τῆς ἀνάγκης μεμῖχθαι—does not quite harmonise with *Plut.* C. Not. 34, 2 : οὐ γὰρ ἢ γε ὕλη τὸ κακὸν ἐξ

tem, only one explanation was possible : no real evil
could happen to the virtuous, no real good fortune
could fall to the lot of the vicious.[1] Apparent misfortune will therefore be regarded by the wise man
partly as a natural consequence, partly as a whole-
some exercise of his moral powers ;[2] there is nothing
which is not matter for rational action : everything
that happens, when rightly considered, contributes
to our good; nothing that is secured by moral depravity is in itself desirable.[3] With this view, it

ἑαυτῆς παρέσχηκεν, ἄποιος γάρ
ἐστι καὶ πάσας ὅσας δέχεται διαφορὰς ὑπὸ τοῦ κινοῦντος αὐτὴν καὶ
σχηματίζοντος ἔσχεν. Just as
little does Seneca's—Non potest artifex mutare materiam
(De Prov. 5, 9)—agree with his
lavish encomia on the arrangement and perfection of the
world. For, according to the
Stoics, matter is ultimately
identical with reason and deity.
These contradictions do not,
however, justify the doubt expressed by *Heine*, Stoic. de
Fato Doct. 46, that Seneca is
here not speaking as a Stoic.
For Chrysippus says very much
the same thing. See p. 190,
1, 2.

[1] *M. Aurel.* ix. 16 : οὐκ ἐν
πείσει, ἀλλ' ἐνεργείᾳ, τὸ τοῦ λογικοῦ ζῴου κακὸν καὶ ἀγαθόν, ὥσπερ
οὐδὲ ἡ ἀρετὴ καὶ κακία αὐτοῦ ἐν
πείσει, ἀλλὰ ἐνεργείᾳ.

[2] *M. Aurel.* viii. 35 : ὃν
τρόπον ἐκείνη [ἡ φύσις] πᾶν τὸ
ἐνιστάμενον καὶ ἀντιβαῖνον ἐπι-
περιτρέπει καὶ κατατάσσει εἰς τὴν
εἱμαρμένην καὶ μέρος ἑαυτῆς ποιεῖ,
οὕτως καὶ τὸ λογικὸν ζῷον δύναται
πᾶν κώλυμα ὕλην ἑαυτοῦ ποιεῖν

καὶ χρῆσθαι αὐτῷ ἐφ' οἷον ἂν καὶ
ὥρμησεν.

[3] Seneca's treatise, De Providentia, is occupied with expanding this thought. In this
treatise, the arguments by which
the outward misfortunes of
good men are harmonised with
the divine government of the
world are : (1) The wise man
cannot really meet with misfortune : he cannot receive at
the hands of fortune what he
does not, on moral grounds,
assign to himself (c. 2, 6). (2)
Misfortune, therefore, is an
unlooked-for exercise of his
powers, a divine instrument of
training ; a hero in conflict
with fortune is a spectaculum
Deo dignum (c. 1, 2–4. Conf.
Ep. 85, 39). (3) The misfortunes of the righteous show
that external conditions are
neither a good nor an evil (c. 5).
(4) Everything is a natural
consequence of natural causes
(c. 5). Similar explanations in
Epictet. Diss. iii. 17; i. 6, 37;
i. 24, 1 ; *Stob.* Ecl. i. 132 ; *M.
Aurel.* iv. 49 ; vii. 68 and 54 ;
x. 33.

was possible to connect a belief in divine punishment, by saying that what to a good man is an exercise of his powers, is a real misfortune and consequently a punishment to a bad man; but we are
not informed whether the scattered notes in Chrysippus really bear out this meaning.

The whole investigation is one involving much
doubt and inconsistency. Natural considerations frequently intertwine with considerations based on the
adaptation of means to ends; the divine power is
oftentimes treated as a will working towards a definite purpose, at one time arranging all things for
the best with unlimited power, at another time according to an unchangeable law of nature;[1] but all
these inconsistencies and defects belong to other
moral theories of the world, quite as much as they
belong to that of the Stoics.

---

[1] *Philodem.* περὶ θεῶν διαγωγῆς, col. 8, Vol. Herc. vi. 53:
ἰδιωτικῶς ἄπαντος αὐτῷ [θεῷ]
δύναμιν ἀναθέντες, ὅταν ὑπὸ τῶν
ἐλέγχων πιέζωνται, τότε κατα-
φεύγουσιν ἐπὶ τὸ διὰ τοῦτο φάσκειν
τὰ συναπτόμενα (what is suitable)
μὴ ποιεῖν, ὅτι οὐ πάντα δύναται.

CHAPTER VIII.

IRRATIONAL NATURE.   THE ELEMENTS.   THE UNIVERSE.

CHAP.
VIII.

A. *The
most gene-
ral ideas
on nature.*

TURNING now from the questions which have hitherto
engaged our attention to natural science in the
stricter sense of the term, we must first touch upon
a few characteristic questions affecting the general
conditions of all existence. Yet even here the Stoics
hold little that is of a distinctive character. The
matter or substance of which all things are made is
corporeal.[1] All that is corporeal is infinitely divi-
sible, although it is never infinitely divided.[2] At the
same time, all things are exposed to the action of
change, since one material is constantly going over
into another.[3] Herein the Stoics following Aristotle, in contrast to the mechanical theory of nature,[4]

[1] See above, p. 126 ; 101, 2 ;
Diog. 135. Conf. *Stob.* Ecl.
i. 410.
[2] In *Diog.* 150, there is no
difference made between Apollodorus and Chrysippus. *Stob.*
Ecl. i. 344 ; *Plut.* C. Not. 38, 3,
p. 1079 ; *Sext.* Math. x. 142.
Similarly Aristotle.
[3] *Plut.* Plac. i. 9, 2 : οἱ Στωϊκοὶ
τρεπτὴν καὶ ἀλλοιωτὴν καὶ μετα-
βλητὴν καὶ ῥευστὴν ὅλην δι' ὅλου τὴν
ὕλην. *Diog.* 150. *Sen.* Nat. Qu. iii.

101, 3 : Fiunt omnia ex omnibus,
ex aqua aër, ex aëre aqua, ignis
ex aëre, ex igne aër . . . ex
aqua terra fit, cur non aqua fiat
e terra ? . . . omnium elemen-
torum in alternum recursus
sunt. Similarly *Epictet.* in
Stob. Floril. 108, 60. Conf. p.
101, 2 ; 198, 3. This is borrowed
not only from Heraclitus, but
also from Aristotle.
[4] They only called the first
kind κίνησις. Aristotle under-

distinguish change in quality from mere motion in
space. They enumerate several varieties of each
kind.[1] Nevertheless, they look upon motion in space
as the primary form of motion.[2] Moreover, under
the conception of motion, they include action and
suffering.[3] The condition of all action is contact;[4]
and since the motions of different objects in nature
are due to various causes, and have a variety of
characters, the various kinds of action must be distinguished which correspond with them.[5] In all

stood by κίνησις every form of
change.

[1] *Stob.* Ecl. i. 404, 408, gives
definitions of κίνησις, of φορὰ,
and of μονὴ, taken from Chrysippus and Apollodorus. *Simpl.*
Categ. 110, β (Schol. in Arist.
92, 6, 30. Respecting the kinds
of μεταβολὴ see the extracts
from Posidonius on p. 101, 2)
distinguishes between μένειν,
ἠρεμεῖν, ἡσυχάζειν, ἀκινητεῖν, but
this is rather a matter of language. *Simpl.* Cat. 78. β, relates that the Stoics differed
from the Peripatetics in explaining Motion as an incomplete energy, and discusses
their assertion that κινεῖσθαι is
a wider, κινεῖν a narrower, idea.

[2] *Simpl.* Phys. 310, b : οἱ δὲ
ἀπὸ τῆς στοᾶς κατὰ πᾶσαν κίνησιν
ἔλεγον ὑπεῖναι τὴν τοπικὴν, ἢ
κατὰ μέγαλα διαστήματα ἢ κατὰ
λόγῳ θεωρητὰ ὑφισταμένην.

[3] *Simpl.* Categ. 78, β (Schol.
78, a, 23) : Plotinus and others
introduce into the Aristotelian
doctrine the Stoic view : τὸ
κοινὸν τοῦ ποιεῖν καὶ πάσχειν εἶναι
τὰς κινήσεις.

[4] *Simpl.* l. c. 77, β ; Schol.

77, b, 33. Simplicius himself
contradicts this statement. It
had, however, been already advanced by Aristotle.

[5] *Simpl.* l. c. 78, β (Schol.
78, a, 28) : The Stoics who, according to p. 84, ε, Schol. 79,
a, 16, very fully discussed the
categories, made the following
διαφοραὶ γενῶν : τὸ ἐξ αὐτῶν κινεῖσθαι, ὡς ἡ μάχαιρα τὸ τέμνειν ἐκ
τῆς οἰκείας ἔχει κατασκευῆς—τὸ
δι' ἑαυτοῦ ἐνεργεῖν τὴν κίνησιν, ὡς
αἱ φύσεις καὶ αἱ ἰατρικαὶ δυνάμεις
τὴν ποίησιν ὑπεργάζονται ; for
instance, the seed, in developing into a plant—τὸ ἀφ'
ἑαυτοῦ ποιεῖν, or ἀπὸ ἰδίας ὁρμῆς
ποιεῖν, one species of which is
τὸ ἀπὸ λογικῆς ὁρμῆς—τὸ κατ'
ἀρετὴν ἐνεργεῖν. It is, in short,
the application to a particular
case of the distinction which
will be subsequently met with
of ἕξις, φύσις, ψυχὴ, and ψυχὴ
λογική. The celebrated gram-
matical distinction of ὀρθὰ and
ὕπτια mentioned p. 95, 3 is connected with the distinction
between ποιεῖν and πάσχειν.
Conf. *Simpl.* p. 79, α, ζ; Schol.
78, b, 17 and 30.

these statements there is hardly a perceptible deviation from Aristotle.

Of a more peculiar character are the views of the Stoics as to the intermingling of substances, to which reference has already been made.[1] Even with regard to Time and Space, they found some innovations on Aristotle's theory to be necessary. Space (τόπος), according to their view, is the room occupied by a body,[2] the distance enclosed within the limits of a body.[3] From Space they distinguish the Empty. The Empty is not met with in the universe, but beyond the universe it extends indefinitely.[4] And hence they assert that Space is limited, like the world of matter, and that the Empty is unlimited.[5] Nay, not only Space, but Time also, is by them set

---

[1] See page 135.

[2] *Stob.* Ecl. i. 382 : Ζήνων καὶ οἱ ἀπ' αὐτοῦ ἐντὸς μὲν τοῦ κόσμου μηδὲν εἶναι κενὸν ἔξω δ' αὐτοῦ ἄπειρον (conf. *Themist.* Phys. 40, b ; *Plut.* Plac. i. 18, 4 ; *ibid.* c. 20, beginning οἱ Στωικοὶ καὶ Ἐπίκουρος). διαφέρειν δὲ κενὸν τόπον χώραν· καὶ τὸ μὲν κενὸν εἶναι ἐρημίαν σώματος, τὸν δὲ τόπον τὸ ἐπεχόμενον ὑπὸ σώματος, τὴν δὲ χώραν τὸ ἐκ μέρους ἐπεχόμενον (*Plut.* adds, like a half-empty vessel). *Stob.* i. 390 : Chrysippus defined τόπος = τὸ κατεχόμενον δι' ὅλου ὑπὸ ὄντος, ἢ τὸ οἷον κατέχεσθαι ὑπὸ ὄντος καὶ δι' ὅλου κατεχόμενον εἴτε ὑπὸ τινὸς εἴτε ὑπὸ τινῶν. If, however, only one portion of the οἷόν τε κατέχεσθαι ὑπὸ ὄντος is really filled, the whole is neither κενὸν nor τόπος, but ἕτερόν τι οὐκ ὠνομασμένον, which may possibly be called χώρα. Hence τόπος corresponds to a full, κενὸν to an empty, χώρα to a half-empty, vessel. *Sext.* Math. x. 3, Pyrrh. iii. 124, speaks to the same effect. *Cleomed.* Meteor. p. 2, 4 ; *Simpl.* Categ. 91, δ. According to the Stoics, παρυφίσταται τοῖς σώμασιν ὁ τόπος καὶ τὸν ὅρον ἀπ' αὐτῶν προσλαμβάνει τὸν μέχι τοσοῦδε, καθόσον συμπληροῦνται [-οῦται] ὑπὸ τῶν σωμάτων.

[3] The Stoic idea of space is so understood by *Themist.* Phys. 38, b ; *Simpl.* Phys. 133, a.

[4] See previous note and in *Diog.* 140 (where, however, instead of ἀσώματον δὲ, we should read κενὸν δὲ) definitions of κενόν.

[5] *Stob.* Ecl. i. 392, quoting Chrysippus.

down as immaterial;[1] and yet to the conception of
Time a meaning as concrete as possible is assigned,
in order that Time may have a real value. Zeno
defined Time as the extension of motion; Chrysippus
defines it, more definitely, as the extension of the
motion of the world.[2] The Stoics affirm the infinite
divisibility of Time and Space,[3] but do not appear
to have instituted any deep researches into this
point.

In expanding their views on the origin of the
world, the Stoics begin with the doctrine of the
four elements,[4] a doctrine which, since the time of
Aristotle and Plato, was the one universally accepted. They even refer this doctrine to Heraclitus,

---

[1] See p. 131, 2.

[2] *Simpl.* Categ. 88, ζ. Schol.
80, a, 6 : τῶν δὲ Στωϊκῶν Ζήνων
μὲν πάσης ἁπλῶς κινήσεως διάστημα τὸν χρόνον εἶπε(conf. *Plut.*
Plat. Quæst. viii. 4, 3) Χρύσιππος
δὲ διάστημα τῆς τοῦ κόσμου κινήσεως. Conf. *Ibid.* 89, a, β ;
Simpl. Phys. 165, a. More full
is *Stob.* Ecl. i. 260 : ὁ δὲ Χρύσιππος χρόνον εἶναι κινήσεως διάστημα καθ' ὃ ποτε λέγεται μέτρον
τάχους τε καὶ βραδύτητος, ἢ τὸ
παρακολουθοῦν διάστημα τῇ τοῦ
κόσμου κινήσει. The passages
quoted by *Stob.* Ibid. 250 (*Plut.*
Plac. i. 22, 2), 254, 256, 258,
and *Diog.* 141, from Zeno,
Chrysippus, Apollodorus, and
Posidonius, are in agreement
with this. In the same places
occur several other observations
on Time, which are, however,
of no importance, such as that
Time as a whole, and likewise
the past and the future are un-

limited, the present is limited ;
the present cannot be accurately determined, it is the
boundary between the past and
the future (Archedemus in
Plut. C. Not. 38, 6, p. 1081),
lying partly in the one, partly
in the other (Chrysippus, *ibid.*
38, 8).

[3] *Sext.* Math. x. 142 ; *Plut.*
Com. Not. 41, p. 1081 ; *Stob.* i.
260.

[4] For the conception of
στοιχεῖον, which is also that of
Aristotle (Metaph i. 3, 938, b, 8),
and its difference from that of
ἀρχή, see *Diog.* 134 ; 136. The
difference, however, is not
always observed. Chrysippus
(in *Stob.* Ecl. i. 312) distinguishes three meanings of
στοιχεῖον. In one sense, it is
fire ; in another, the four elements ; in the third, any material out of which something is
made.

wishing, above all things, to follow his teaching on
natural science.[1] On a previous occasion, the order
and the stages have been pointed out, according to
which primary fire developed into these elements in
the formation of the world.[2] In the same order,
these elements now go over one into the other. And
yet, in this constant transformation of materials, in
the perpetual change of form to which primary matter is subject, in this flux of all its parts, the unity
of the whole still remains untouched.[3] The distinctive characteristic of fire is heat; that of air is cold;

[1] *Lassalle*, Heraclitus, ii.
84.

[2] See p. 161. As is there
stated, primary fire first goes
over into water δι' ἀέρος (i. e.
after first going over into air,
not passing through air as an
already existing medium, as
Lassalle, Heracl. ii. 86 inaccurately says), and water goes
over into the three other elements. In this process there
is, however, a difficulty. Fire
is said to derive its origin from
water, and yet a portion of
primary fire must have existed
from the beginning, as the soul
of the world. Nor is it correct
to say, that *actual* fire is never
obtained from water in the
formation of the upper elements (as *Lassalle*, p. 88, does).

[3] Chrysippus, in *Stob.* Ecl. i.
312: πρώτης μὲν γιγνομένης τῆς
ἐκ πυρὸς κατὰ σύστασιν εἰς ἀέρα
μεταβολῆς, δευτέρας δ' ἀπὸ τούτου
εἰς ὕδωρ, τρίτης δ' ἔτι μᾶλλον κατὰ
τὸ ἀνάλογον συνισταμένου τοῦ ὕδατος εἰς γῆν, πάλιν δὲ ἀπὸ ταύτης
διαλυομένης καὶ διαχεομένης πρώτη

μὲν γίγνεται χύσις εἰς ὕδωρ, δεύ-
τερα δὲ ἐξ ὕδατος εἰς ἀέρα, τρίτη
δὲ καὶ ἐσχάτη εἰς πῦρ. On account of this constant change,
primary matter is called (*Ibid.*
316, where, however, the text
is obviously corrupt, and therefore only partially intelligible)
ἡ ἀρχὴ καὶ ὁ λόγος καὶ ἡ ἀΐδιος
δύναμις . . . εἰς αὐτήν τε πάντα
καταναλίσκουσα καὶ τὸ [ἐξ] αὐτῆς
πάλιν ἀποκαθιστᾶσα τεταγμένως
καὶ ὁδῷ. Epictet. in *Stob.* Floril.
108, 60: Not only mankind and
animals are undergoing perpetual changes, ἀλλὰ καὶ τὰ
θεῖα, καὶ νὴ Δι' αὐτὰ τὰ τέτταρα
στοιχεῖα ἄνω καὶ κάτω τρέπεται
καὶ μεταβάλλει· καὶ γῆ τε ὕδωρ
γίνεται καὶ ὕδωρ ἀὴρ, οὗτος δὲ
πάλιν εἰς αἰθέρα μεταβάλλει· καὶ
ὁ αὐτὸς τρόπος τῆς μεταβολῆς
ἄνωθεν κάτω. On the flux of
things, see also *M. Aurel.* ii. 3;
vii. 19; ix. 19; 28. *Cic.* N. D.
ii. 33, 84: Et cum quatuor sint
genera corporum, vicissitudine
eorum mundi continuata (= συν-
εχής; conf. *Sen.* Nat. Qu. ii. 2,
2, continuatio est partium inter

that of water, moisture; dryness that of the earth.[1]
These essential qualities, however, are not always
found in the elements to which they belong in a pure
state,[2] and hence every element has several forms
and varieties.[3] Among the four essential qualities
of the elements, Aristotle had already singled out
two, viz. heat and cold, as the two active ones, calling dryness and moisture the passive ones. The
Stoics do the same, only more avowedly. They consider the two elements to which these qualities properly belong to be the seats of all active force, and
distinguish them from the other two elements, as
the soul is distinguished from the body.[4] In their

se non intermissa conjunctio)
natura est. Nam ex terra
aqua, ex aqua oritur aër, ex
aëre æther: deinde retrorsum
vicissim ex æthere aër, ex aëre
aqua, ex aqua terra infima. Sic
natura his, ex quibus omnia
constant, sursum, deorsum,
ultro citroque commeantibus
mundi partium conjunctio continetur. See p. 194, 3.

[1] *Diog.* 137: εἶναι δὲ τὸ μὲν
πῦρ τὸ θερμὸν, τὸ δ' ὕδωρ τὸ ὑγρὸν,
τόν τ' ἀέρα τὸ ψυχρὸν καὶ τὴν γῆν
τὸ ξηρόν. *Plut.* Sto. Rep. 43, 1,
p. 1053. The air is, according
to Chrysippus, φύσει ζοφερὸς and
πρώτως ψυχρός. *Id.* De Primo
Frig. 9, 1; 17, 1, p. 948, 952;
Galen, Simpl. Medic. ii. 20,
vol. xi. 510. *Sen.* Nat. Qu. iii.
10; i. 4 : Aër . . . frigidus per
se et obscurus . . . natura enim
aëris gelida est. Conf. *Cic.*
N. D. ii. 10, 26. Of the four
properties by the pairing of
which elements arise, even
Aristotle had attributed one to

each element as its distinguishing feature, assigning cold
to water, moisture to air.
[2] Thus the upper portion of
the air, owing to its proximity
to the region of fire and the
stars (*Sen.* Nat. Qu. iii. 10), is
the warmest, the driest, and
the rarest; but yet owing to
the evaporation of the earth
and the radiation of heat,
warmer than the middle, which
in point of dryness and density,
is between the two, but exceeds
both in cold. See p. 146, 4.
[3] Chrysippus, in *Stob.* i. 314 :
λέγεσθαι δὲ πῦρ τὸ πυρῶδες πᾶν
καὶ ἀέρα τὸ ἀερῶδες καὶ ὁμοίως τὰ
λοιπά. Thus *Philo,* Incorrupt.
M. 953, E, who is clearly following the Stoics, distinguishes
three kinds of fire : ἄνθραξ,
φλὸξ, αὐγή. He seems, however,
only to refer to terrestrial fire,
which, after all, forms only one
small portion of fire.
[4] Pp. 128, 2; 148, 2; 151, 1;
163, 2.

materialistic system, the finer materials as opposed to the coarser, occupy the place of incorporeal forces.

The relative density of the elements also determines their place in the universe. Fire and air are light; water and earth are heavy. Fire and air move away from the centre of the universe;[1] water and earth are drawn thereto;[2] and thus, from above to below—or, what is the same thing, from without to within—the four layers of fire, air, water, and earth are formed.[3] The fire on the circumference

[1] This statement must be taken with such modification as the unity of the world renders necessary. If the upper elements were to move altogether away from the centre, the world would go to pieces. Hence the meaning can only be this : that the difference of natural motions can only take place within the enclosure holding the elements together, and so far a natural motion towards the centre can be attributed to all bodies as a distinctive feature, anterior to the contrast between heaviness and lightness. Conf. Chrysippus, in *Plut.* Sto. Rep. 44, 6, p. 1054 : The striving of all the parts of the world is to keep together, not to go asunder. οὕτω δὲ τοῦ ὅλου τεινομένου εἰς ταὐτὸ καὶ κινουμένου καὶ τῶν μορίων ταύτην τὴν κίνησιν ἐχόντων ἐκ τῆς τοῦ σώματος φύσεως, πιθανὸν, πᾶσι τοῖς σώμασιν εἶναι τὴν πρώτην κατὰ φύσιν κίνησιν πρὸς τὸ τοῦ κόσμου μέσον, τῷ μὲν κόσμῳ οὕτωσὶ κινουμένῳ πρὸς αὐτὸν, τοῖς δὲ μέρεσιν ὡς ἂν μέρεσιν οὖσιν. *Achill. Tat.* Isag. 132, A : The

Stoics maintain that the world continues in empty space, ἐπεὶ πάντα αὐτοῦ τὰ μέρη ἐπὶ τὸ μέσον νένευκε. The same reason is assigned by *Cleomedes*, Meteor. p. 5.

[2] *Stob.* Ecl. i. 346 (*Plut.* Pl. i. 12, 4). Zeno, *Ibid.* 406 : οὐ πάντως δὲ σῶμα βάρος ἔχειν, ἀλλ' ἀβαρῆ εἶναι ἀέρα καὶ πῦρ . . . φύσει γὰρ ἀνώφοιτα ταῦτ' εἶναι διὰ τὸ μηδενὸς μετέχειν βάρους. *Plut.* Sto. Rep. 42, p. 1053 : In the treatise περὶ κινήσεως, Chrysippus calls fire ἀβαρὲς and ἀνωφερὲς καὶ τούτῳ παραπλησίως τὸν ἀέρα, τοῦ μὲν ὕδατος τῇ γῇ μᾶλλον προσνεμομένου, τοῦ δ' ἀέρος, τῷ πυρί. (So too in *Ach. Tat.* Isag. i. 4 in Pet. Doctr. Temp. iii. 75.) On the other hand, in his Φυσικαὶ τέχναι, he inclines to the view that air in itself is neither heavy nor light, which however can only mean that it is neither absolutely, being heavy compared with fire, and light compared with water and earth.

[3] *Diog.* 137 : ἀνωτάτω μὲν οὖν εἶναι τὸ πῦρ ὃ δὴ αἰθέρα καλεῖσθαι,

goes by the name of Ether.[1] Its most remote portion was called by Zeno Heaven;[2] and it differs from earthly fire not only by its greater purity,[3] but also because the motion of earthly fire is in a straight line, whereas the motion of the Ether is circular.[4] A radical difference between these two kinds of fire, which Aristotle supposed to exist, because of this difference of motion, the Stoics did not feel it necessary to admit.[5] They could always maintain that, when beyond the limits of its proper locality, fire tried to return to it as quickly as possible,

ἐν ᾧ πρώτην τὴν τῶν ἀπλανῶν σφαῖραν γεννᾶσθαι, εἶτα τὴν τῶν πλανωμένων. μεθ᾽ ἣν τὸν ἀέρα, εἶτα τὸ ὕδωρ, ὑποστάθμην δὲ πάντων τὴν γῆν, μέσην ἁπάντων οὖσαν. *Ibid.* 156; see p. 202, 3. To these main masses, all other smaller masses of the same element in different parts of the world are attracted, because all seek to reach their natural place. Conf. *M. Aurel.* ix. 9.

[1] *Sen.* Nat. Qu. vi. 16, 2 (totum hoc cœlum, quod igneus æther, mundi summa pars claudit), and p. 198, 3, where the same thing is called πῦρ by Stobæus, æther by Cicero. See p. 146, 4. The same thing is meant by Zeno, where he says (*Stob.* Ecl. i. 538, 554, and Cleanthes says the same in *Cic.* N. D. ii. 15, 40. *Ach. Tat.* Isag. 133, c) that the stars are made of fire; not, however, of πῦρ ἄτεχνον, but of πῦρ τεχνικὸν. which appears in plants as φύσις, in animals as ψυχή. See p. 201, 5.

[2] In *Ach. Tat.* Isag. 130, A, he defines οὐρανὸς as αἰθέρος τὸ ἔσχατον, ἐξ οὗ καὶ ἐν ᾧ ἐστὶ πάντα ἐμφανῶς. Similarly *Diog.* 138; *Cleomed.* Met. p. 7. Otherwise the term is used in a wider sense.

[3] See p. 146, 4.

[4] *Stob.* i. 346: τὸ μὲν περίγειον φῶς κατ᾽ εὐθεῖαν, τὸ δ᾽ αἰθέριον περιφερῶς κινεῖται. See p. 202, 3. It is only of terrestrial fire that Zeno can (*Stob.* Ecl. i. 356) say, it moves in a straight line. Cleanthes even attributed to the stars the spherical shape, which on the strength of this passage he attributes to it. See *Plut.* Plac. ii. 14, 2; *Stob.* i. 516; *Ach. Tat.* Isag. 133, B.

[5] They denied it, according to *Orig.* c. Cels. iv. 56. *Cic.* Acad. i. 11, 39, says : Zeno dispensed with a quinta natura, being satisfied with four elements : statuebat enim ignem esse ipsam naturam, quæquæque gignerit, et mentem atque sensus.

whereas within those limits it moved in the form of
a circle.

Taking this view of the elements, the Stoics did
not deviate to any very great extent, in their ideas
of the World, from Aristotle and the views which
were generally entertained. In the centre of the
Universe reposes the globe of the earth;[1] around
it is water, above the water is air. These three
strata form the kernel of the world, which is in a
state of repose,[2] and around these the Ether revolves
in a circle, together with the stars which are set
therein. At the top, in one stratum, are all the
fixed stars; under the stratum containing the fixed
stars are the planets, in seven different strata—
Saturn, Jupiter, Mars, Mercury, Venus, then the
Sun, and in the lowest stratum, bordering on the
region of air, is the Moon.[3] Thus the world con-

[1] The spherical shape of the
earth is a matter of course, and
is mentioned by *Ach. Tat.* Isag.
126, C ; *Plut.* Plac. iii. 10, 1 ;
9, 3. *Cleom.* Met. p. 40, gives
an elaborate proof of it, for the
most part taken from Posidonius.

[2] *Heraclit.* Alleg. Hom. c. 36,
and *Diog.* 145, also affirm that
the earth is in the centre, *un-
moved.* The reason for this
fact is stated by *Stob.* i. 408, to
be its weight. Further proofs
in *Cleomed.* Met. p. 47.

[3] *Stob.* Ecl. i. 446 : τοῦ δὲ
. . . κόσμου τὸ μὲν εἶναι περιφερόμενον περὶ τὸ μέσον, τὸ δ'
ὑπομένον, περιφερόμενον μὲν τὸν
αἰθέρα, ὑπομένον δὲ τὴν γῆν καὶ τὰ
ἐπ' αὐτῆς ὑγρὰ καὶ τὸν ἀέρα. The

earth is the natural framework,
and, as it were, the skeleton of
the world. Around it water
has been poured, out of which
the more exalted spots project
as islands. For what is called
continent is also an island :
ἀπὸ δὲ τοῦ ὕδατος τὸν ἀέρα
ἐξῆφθαι καθάπερ ἐξατμισθέντα
σφαιρικῶς καὶ περικεχύσθαι, ἐκ δὲ
τούτου τὸν αἰθέρα ἀραιότατόν τε
καὶ εἰλικρινέστατον. It moves in
circular form round the world.
Then follows what is given in
the text as to the stars, next
to which comes the stratum of
air, then that of water, and
lastly, in the centre, the earth.
Conf. *Achil. Tat.* Isag. 126, B,
see p. 200, 3. The language of
Cleomed. Met. c. 3, p. 6, is

sists, as with Aristotle, of a globe containing many
strata, one joining the other.[1] That it cannot be
unlimited, as Democritus and Epicurus maintain,
follows from the very nature of body.[2] The space
within the world is fully occupied by the material
of the world, without a vacant space being anywhere
left.[3] Outside the world, however, is an empty place,
or else how—the Stoics asked—would there be a
place into which the world could be resolved at the
general conflagration?[4] Moreover, this empty place
must be unlimited; for how can there be a limit, or
any kind of boundary, to that which is immaterial
and non-existent?[5] But although the world is in

somewhat divergent. He places
the sun amongst the planets,
between Mars and Venus. That
Archidemus also refused to allow
the earth a place in the centre
has been already stated, p. 147,
2. The language of *Ach. Tat.*
Isag. c. 7, 131, B, is ambiguous:
As the circumference originates
from the centre, so according
to the Stoics the outer circle
originates from the earth; when
compared with the quotations
on p. 161, 2 ; 162, 1.

[1] *Stob.* i. 356 ; *Plut.* Plac. ii.
2, 1; i. 6, 3; *Diog.* 140; *Cleomed.*
Met. pp. 39 and 46; *Heraclit.*
Alleg. Hom. c. 46. *Ibid.* on the
perfection of this form and its
adaptation for motion. Comparing *Achil. Tat.* Isag. 130, C,
Plut. Plac. ii. 2, 1 (*Galen.*
Hist. Phil. c. 11), with the passages on p. 201, note 4, it appears probable that Cleanthes
believed in a spherical form of
the earth. According to *Ach.*

Tat. Isag. 152, A, who probably
has the Stoics in view, the axis
of the world consists of a current of air passing through the
centre. On the division of the
heaven into five parallel circles,
and that of the earth into five
zones, conf. *Diog.* 155 ; *Strabo*,
ii. 2, 3, p. 95.

[2] *Stob.* i. 392 ; *Simpl.* Phys.
iii. 6 ; *Diog.* 143 and 150.

[3] *Diog.* 140 ; *Stob.* i. 382 ;
Plut. Plac. i. 18, 4 ; *Sext.* Math.
vii. 214; *Theodoret*, Cur. Gr. Aff.
iv. 14, p. 58 ; *Hippolyt.* Refut.
Hær. i. 21. *Sen.* Nat. Qu. ii. 7,
observes that motion is possible
by means of ἀντιπερίστασις,
without supposing the existence
of empty space. A number of
arguments against the existence of empty space may be
found in *Cleomed.* Met. p. 4.

[4] See p. 168, 1 ; *Cleomed.*
Met. 2 and 5.

[5] Chrysippus, in *Stob.* i. 392 :
The Empty and the Non-Mate-

CHAP.
VIII.

empty space, it does not move, for the half of its
component elements being heavy, and the other half
light, as a whole it is neither heavy nor light.[1]

(1) *Stars.* The stars are spherical masses,[2] consisting of fire ;
but the fire is not in all cases equally pure,[3] and is
sustained, as Heraclitus taught, by evaporations from

rial is unlimited. ὥσπερ γὰρ
τὸ μηδὲν οὐδέν ἐστι πέρας, οὕτω
καὶ τοῦ μηδενὸς, οἷόν ἐστι τὸ
κενόν. The Empty could only
be bounded by being filled. To
the same effect, *Cleomed.* p. 6.
On the unlimited beyond the
world, see *Diog.* 140 and 143;
Stob. i. 260 and 382 ; *Plut.* Sto.
Rep. 44, 1, p. 1054 ; C. Not. 30,
2, p. 1073 ; Plac. i. 18, 4 ; ii. 9,
2 ; *Theodoret*, l. c. and p. 196, 2.
That Posidonius denied the in-
finity of the Empty has been
already stated, p. 168, 1. Chrysippus, in affirming that the
world occupies the centre of
space, was therefore contradicting himself, as *Plut.* Def.
Or. 28, p. 425, Sto. Rep. 44, 2,
observe.
   [1] *Achil. Tat.* Isag. 126, A;
132, A, see p. 200, 1 ; *Stob.*
i. 408.   According to *Stob.*
i. 442, *Plut.* C. Not. 30, 2 and
10, p. 1073, Plac. ii. 1, 6 ; i. 5,
1, *Diog.* 143, *Sext.* Math. ix.
332, *Ach. Tat.* 129, D, the Stoics
had various names for the
world, according as the Empty
was included or excluded in
the conception. Including the
Empty, it is called τὸ πᾶν ;
without it, ὅλον (τὸ ὅλον, τὰ
ὅλα, frequently occurs with the
Stoics). The πᾶν, it was said,
is neither material nor immaterial, since it consists of both.
Plut. C. Not. l. c.

   [2] *Diog.* 145 ; *Plut.* Plac. ii.
14, 1 ; 22, 3 ; 27,1 ; *Stob.* i. 516;
540 ; 554 ; *Ach. Tat.* 133, D.
Compare the reference to
Cleanthes on p. 201, 4, with
which, however, the statement
in *Stob.* i. 554, that he considered the moon πιλοειδής
(ball-like — the MSS. have
πηλοειδῆ) does not agree.
   [3] According to *Cic.* N. D.
ii. 15, 40, *Diog.* 144, *Stob.* Ecl.
i. 314 ; 519 ; 538 ; 554 ; 565,
Plut. Fac. Lun. 5, 1 ; 21, 13,
p. 921, 935, Plac. ii. 25, 3 ;
30, 3, *Galen*, Hist. Phil. 15,
Philo, De Somn. 587, B, *Achil.
Tat.* Isag. 124, D ; 133, C, and
above p. 200, 3 ; 162, 2, the
stars generally consist of fire,
or, more accurately, of πῦρ
τεχνικὸν, or Ether. The purest
fire is in the sun. The moon is
a compound of dull fire and air,
or, as it is said, is more earth-
like, since (as *Plin.* Hist. Nat.
ii. 9, 46, without doubt after
Stoic teaching, observes) owing
to its proximity to the earth, it
takes up earthy particles in
vapour. Perhaps it was owing
to this fact that it was said to
receive its light from the sun
(*Diog.* 145) which, according to
Posidonius in *Plut.* Fac. Lun.
16, 12, p. 929, *Cleomed.* Met.
p. 106, not only illuminates its
surface, but penetrates some
depth. *Cleomed.* 100, believes

the earth and from water.[1] With this process of
sustentation the motion of the stars is brought into
connection, their orbit extending over the space in
which they obtain their nutriment.[2] Not only the
sun, but the moon also, was believed to be larger
than the earth.[3] Plato and Aristotle had already held

that, besides the light of the
sun, it has also a light of its
own.

[1] *Diog.* 145; *Stob.* i. 532;
538; 554; Floril. 17, 43; *Plut.*
De Is. 41, p. 367; Sto. Rep. 39,
1; Qu. Conv. viii. 8, 2, 4; Plac.
ii. 17, 2; 20, 3; 23, 5; *Galen,*
Hist. Phil. 14; *Porphyr.* Antr.
Nymph. c. 11; *Cic.* N. D. iii.
14, 37; ii. 15, 40; 46, 118; *Sen.*
Nat. Qu. vi. 16, 2; *Heraclit.*
Alleg. Hom. c. 36, p. 74 and 56,
p. 117; most of whom affirm
that the sun is sustained by
vapours from the sea, the moon
by those of fresh water, and
the other stars by vapours from
the earth. The stars are also
said to owe their origin to such
vapours. Chrysippus, in *Plut.*
Sto. Rep. 41, 3, adds to the
passage quoted p. 161, 2; οἱ δ'
ἀστέρες ἐκ θαλάσσης μετὰ τοῦ
ἡλίου ἀνάπτονται. *Plut.* Ibid. 2:
ἔμψυχον ἡγεῖται τὸν ἥλιον, πύρινον
ὄντα καὶ γεγενημένον ἐκ τῆς ἀνα-
θυμιάσεως εἰς πῦρ μεταβαλούσης.
Id. C. Not. 46, 2, p. 1084:
γεγονέναι δὲ καὶ τὸν ἥλιον ἔμψυχον
λέγουσι τοῦ ὑγροῦ μεταβάλλοντος
εἰς πῦρ νοερόν.

[2] *Stob.* i. 532; *Cic.* l. c.;
Macrob. Sat. i. 23, quoting
Cleanthes and Macrobius; *Plut.*
Plac. ii. 23, 5. Diogenes of
Apollonia had already expressed
similar views. Further par-
ticulars as to the courses of the

stars without anything very
peculiar in *Stob.* i. 448; 538;
Plut. Pl. ii. 15, 2; 16, 1; *Diog.*
144; *Cleomed.* Meteor. i. 3.
Eclipses are also discussed by
Diog. 145; *Stob.* i. 538; 560;
Plut. Fac. Lun. 19, 12, p. 932;
Plac. ii. 29, 5; *Cleomed.* pp. 106
and 115, nor is there anything
remarkable. Quite in the ordinary way are some observations of Posidonius and Chrysippus given in *Stob.* i. 518;
Achil. Tat. Isag. 132, B; 165, C.
The information—quoted from
Posidonius by *Cleomed.* Meteor,
51; *Procl.* in Tim. 277, E:
Strabo, ii. 5, 14, p. 119—respecting observations of Cano-
bus have no bearing on our
present enquiry.

[3] *Stob.* i. 554 (*Plut.* Pl. ii.
26, 1). This statement, however, appears only to be true of
the sun, to which, indeed, it is
confined by *Diog.* 144. That
the sun is much larger than
the earth, Posidonius proved;
not only because its light extends over the whole heaven,
but also because of the spherical
form of the earth's shadow in
eclipses of the moon. *Diog.*
l. c.; *Macrob.* Somn. i. 20;
Heracl. Alleg. Hom. c. 46;
Cleomed. Met. ii. 2. According
to *Cleomed.* p. 79, he allowed to
it an orbit 10,000 times as
large as the circumference of

CHAP.
VIII.

that the stars are living rational divine beings ; and the same view was entertained by the Stoics, not only because of the wonderful regularity of their motion and orbits, but also from the very nature of the material of which they consist.[1] The earth, likewise, is filled by an animating soul; or else how could it supply plants with animation, and afford nutriment to the stars?[2] Upon the oneness of the soul, which permeates all its parts, depends, in the opinion of the Stoics, the oneness of the universe.

(2) *Meteorology.*

Most thoroughly, however, did the Stoics—and, in particular, Posidonius[3]—devote themselves to in-

---

the earth, with a diameter of four million stadia. The Stoic, in *Cic.* N. D. ii. 40, 103, only calls the moon half that size ; and *Cleomed.* p. 97, probably following Posidonius, calls it considerably smaller than the earth. The other stars, according to Cleomed. p. 96, are some of them as large as, and others larger than the sun. Posidonius, according to *Plin.* His. N. ii. 23, 85, estimated the moon's distance from the earth at two millions, and the sun's distance from the moon at 500 million stadia. He estimated the earth's circumference at 240,000, according to *Cleomed.*; at 180,000 according to *Strabo,* ii. 2, 2, p. 95.

[1] Conf. *Stob.* i. 66; 441; 518; 532; 538; 554; Floril. 17, 43 ; *Plut.* Sto. Rep. 39, 1 ; 41, 2 ; C. Not. 46, 2 ; Plac. ii. 20, 3; *Diog.* 145 ; *Phædr.* Nat. De. (*Philodem.* περὶ εὐσεβείας) Col. 3 ; *Cic.* N. D. i. 14, 36 and 50 ; ii. 15, 39 and 42 ; 16, 43 ; 21,

54 ; Acad. ii. 37, 110; *Porphyr.* l. c.; *Achill. Tat.* Isag. c. 13, p. 134, A. Hence, in several of these passages, the sun is called after Cleanthes and Chrysippus a νοερὸν ἄναμμα (or ἔξαμμα) ἐκ θαλάσσης.

[2] *Sen.* Nat. Qu. vi. 16, discusses the point at length. See also the quotations on p. 144, 1, from *Cic.* N. D. ii. 9, and on p. 151, 1, from *Diog.* 147.

[3] *Diog.* vii. 152 and 138, mentions a treatise of his, called μετεωρολογικὴ or μετεωρολογικὴ στοιχείωσις ; also, vii. 135, a treatise περὶ μετεώρων, in several books. Alexander, in *Simpl.* Phys. 64, 6, speaks of an ἐξήγησις μετεωρολογικῶν, which, judging by the title, may be a commentary on Aristotle's meteorology. Geminus had made an extract from this book, a long portion of which on the relation of astronomy and natural science is there given. Whether these various titles really belong to these different treatises is not

vestigating those problems, which may be summed up under the name of meteorology. This portion, however, of their enquiries is of little value as illustrating their philosophical tenets. It may therefore suffice to mention in a note the objects which it included, and the sources whence information may be obtained.¹ The same treatment may apply to

clear. Posidonius is probably the author of most of the later statements about the Stoic meteorology. He appears also to be the chief authority for Seneca's Naturales Quæstiones, in which he is frequently named (i. 5, 10; 13; ii. 26, 4; 54, 1; iv. 3, 2; vi. 21, 2; 24, 6; vii. 20, 2; 4), particularly ˙in his meteorological treatises.

¹ On the Milky Way, which Posidonius, agreeing with Aristotle, looked upon as a collection of fiery vapours, see *Stob.* i. 576; *Plut.* Plac. iii. 1, 10; *Macrob.* Somn. Scip. i. 15. On the comets, which are explained in a similar way, *Stob.* i. 580 (Plac. iii. 2, 8.—Whether the Diogenes mentioned here who looked upon comets as real stars is Diogenes the Stoic, or Diogenes of Apollonia, is not clear. The former is more probable, Boëthus having been just before mentioned); Arrian, in *Stob.* i. 584; *Diog.* vii. 152; and, particularly, *Sen.* Nat. Qu. vii. We learn from the latter that Zeno held (vii. 19–21; 30, 2), with Anaxagoras and Democritus, that comets are formed by several stars uniting; whereas the majority of the Stoics — and, amongst their number, Panætius and Posi-

donius (further particulars in Schol. in Arat. v. 1091)—considered them passing phenomena. Even Seneca declared for the opinion that they are stars. On the phenomena of light and fire, called πωγωνίαι, δοκοὶ, etc., see Arrian in *Stob.* i. 584; *Sen.* Nat. Qu. i. 1, 14; 15, 4. On σέλας, consult *Diog.* 153; *Sen.* i. 15; on halo (ἅλως), *Sen.* i. 2; *Alex. Aphr.* Meteorol. 116; on the rainbow, *Diog.* 152; *Sen.* i. 3–8; on *virgæ* and *parhelia*, *Sen.* i. 9–13; Schol. in Arat. v. 880 (Posidonius); on storms, lightning, thunder, summer lightning, cyclones, and siroccos, *Stob.* i. 596; 598 (Plac. iii. 3, 4); *Arrian,* Ibid. 602; *Sen.* ii. 12–31; 51–58 (c. 54, the view of Posidonius); ii. 1, 3; *Diog.* 153; on rain, sleet, hail, snow, *Diog.* 153; *Sen.* iv. 3–12; on earthquakes, *Diog.* 154; Plac. iii. 15, 2; *Sen.* vi. 4–31 (particularly c. 16; 21, 2); also *Strabo,* ii. 3, 6, p. 102; on winds, Plac. iii. 7, 2; *Sen.* v. 1–17; *Strabo,* i. 2, 21, p. 29; iii. 2, 5, p. 144; on waterspouts, *Sen.* iii. 1–26; the Nile floods, *Ibid.* iv. 1; *Strabo,* xvii. 1, 5, p. 790; *Cleomed.* Meteor. p. 32; on tides, *Strabo,* i. 3, 12, p. 55; iii. 3, 3, p. 153; 5, 8, p. 73; on seasons, p. 111, 2.

CHAP.
VIII.

(3) *Plants and animals.*

the few maxims laid down by the Stoics on the subject of inorganic nature which have come down to us.[1] Nor need we mention here the somewhat copious writings of Posidonius,[2] on the subjects of geography, history, and mathematics.

Little attention was devoted by the Stoics to the world of plants and animals. About this fact there can be no doubt, since we neither hear of any treatises by the Stoics on this subject, nor do they appear to have advanced any peculiar views. The most prominent point is, that they divided all things in nature into four classes—the class of inorganic beings, the class of plants, that of animals, and that of rational beings. In beings belonging to the first class a simple quality (ἕξις) constitutes the bond of union; in those of the second class, a forming power (φύσις); in those of the third class, a soul; and in those of the fourth class, a rational soul.[3] By means of this divi-

---

[1] Thus colours are explained as being πρῶτοι σχηματισμοὶ τῆς ὕλης (*Stob.* i. 364; Plac. i. 15, 5); and sounds are spoken of as undulations in the air by *Plut.* Plac. iv. 19, 5; *Diog.* 158.

[2] Conf. *Bake,* Posidonii Rhod. Reliquiæ, pp. 87–184; *Müller,* Fragm. Hist. Græc. iii. 245.

[3] *Sext.* Math. ix. 81: τῶν ἡνωμένων (on ἕνωσις see p. 103, 1) σωμάτων τὰ μὲν ὑπὸ ψιλῆς ἕξεως συνέχεται, τὰ δὲ ὑπὸ φύσεως, τὰ δὲ ὑπὸ ψυχῆς· καὶ ἕξεως μὲν ὡς λίθοι καὶ ξύλα, φύσεως δὲ, καθάπερ τὰ φυτὰ, ψυχῆς δὲ τὰ ζῷα. *Plut.* Virt. Mor. c. 12, p. 451: καθόλου δὲ τῶν ὄντων αὐτοί τέ φασι καὶ δῆλόν ἐστιν ὅτι τὰ

μὲν ἕξει διοικεῖται τὰ δὲ φύσει, τὰ δὲ ἀλόγῳ ψυχῇ, τὰ δὲ καὶ λόγον ἐχούσῃ καὶ διάνοιαν. *Themist.* De An. 72, b; *M. Aurel.* vi. 14; *Philo,* Qu. De. S. Immut. 298, D; De Mundo, 1154, E; Leg. Alleg. 1091, D; Incorrupt. M. 947, A; *Plotin.* Enn. iv. 7, 8, p. 463, C, Bas. 861, Cr. (Otherwise *Cic.* N. D. ii. 12, 33. See p. 146, 1). Respecting the difference of φύσις and ψυχή, φύσις is said to consist of a moister, colder, and denser πνεῦμα than ψυχή; but, on this point, see *Plut.* Sto. Rep. 41, 1; Com. Not. 46, 2; *Galen,* Hipp. et Plat. v. 3. Vol. v. 521. Qu. Animi Mores, c. 4. Vol. iv. 783. In *Diog.* 139, ἕξις and νοῦς as the

sion, the various branches of a science of nature were mapped out, based on a gradually-increasing development of the powers of life. But no serious attempt was made by the Stoics to work out this thought. With the single exception of man, we know exceedingly little of their views on organic beings.[1]

highest and lowest links in the series, are contrasted. *Ibid.* 156, there is a definition of φύσις = πῦρ τεχνικὸν ὁδῷ βαδίζον εἰς γένεσιν; and (148) another = ἕξις ἐξ αὑτῆς κινουμένη κατὰ σπερματικοὺς λόγους ἀποτελοῦσά τε καὶ συνέχουσα τὰ ἐξ αὑτῆς ἐν ὡρισμένοις χρόνοις καὶ τοιαῦτα δρῶσα ἀφ' οἵων ἀπεκρίθη. It hardly need be repeated that the force is one and the same, which at one time appears as ἕξις, at another as φύσις. Conf. *Diog.* 138; *Themist.* l. c.; *Sext. Math.* ix. 84.

[1] The belief that blood circulates in the veins, spiritus in the arteries (*Sen. Nat. Qu.* ii. 15, 1), which was shared by the Peripatetics, deserves to be mentioned here, *Sen. Nat. Qu.* ii. 15, 1; also the explanations of sleep, death, and age in *Plut. Plac.* v. 23, 4; 30, 5; the assertion that animals are not only deficient in reason (on this point see *Plut. Solert. An.* 2, 9; 6, 1; 11, 2, pp. 960, 963, 967), but also (according to Chrysippus in *Galen*, Hippoc. et Plat. iii. 3; v. 1, 6. Vol. v. 309, 429, 431, 476) in emotions (or as *Galen* also says in θυμὸς and ἐπιθυμία), even in man the emotions being connected with the rational soul. Posidonius, however, denied this statement (*Galen*, p. 476), and Chrysippus believed that animals had a ἡγεμονικόν. (*Chalcid* in Tim. p. 148, b.) He even discovered in the scent of dogs traces of an unconscious inference. *Sext. Pyrrh.* i. 69. See also p. 225, 2.

CHAPTER IX.

THE STUDY OF NATURE. MAN.

CHAP. IX.

A. The soul. (1) Materialistic nature of the soul.

THE Stoic teaching becomes peculiarly interesting, when it treats of Man; and the line it here follows was decided by the tone of the whole system. On the one hand, the Stoic materialism could not fail to show itself most unmistakeably in the department of anthropology; on the other hand, the conviction that all actions must be referred to active powers, and all the several active powers to one original power, could not be held without leading to a belief in the oneness and in the regulating power of the soul. Not only does it follow, as a corollary from the materialistic view of the world, that the soul must be in its nature corporeal, but the Stoics took pains to uphold this view by special arguments. Whatever, they said, influences the body, and is by it influenced in turn, whatever is united with the body and again separated from it, must be corporeal. How, then, can the soul be other than corporeal? [1]

[1] Cleanthes, in *Nemes.* Nat. Hom. p. 33, and *Tert.* De An. c. 5 : οὐδὲν ἀσώματον συμπάσχει σώματι οὐδὲ ἀσωμάτῳ σῶμα ἀλλὰ σῶμα σώματι· συμπάσχει δὲ ἡ ψυχὴ τῷ σώματι νοσοῦντι καὶ τεμνομένῳ καὶ τὸ σῶμα τῇ ψυχῇ· αἰσχυνομένης γοῦν ἐρυθρὸν γίνεται

Whatever has extension in three dimensions is corporeal; and this is the case with the soul, since it extends in three directions over the whole body.[1] Moreover, thought and motion are due to animal life.[2] Animal life is nurtured and kept in health by the breath of life.[3] Experience also proves that mental qualities are propagated by natural generation, and that they must be consequently connected with a corporeal substratum.[4] As, therefore, the mind is nothing but fiery breath, so the human soul is described by the Stoics sometimes as fire, sometimes as breath, at other times, more accurately, as warm breath, diffused throughout the body, and forming a bond of union for the body,[5] in the very same way

καὶ φοβουμένης ὠχρόν· σῶμα ἄρα ἡ ψυχή. Chrysippus in *Nemes.* p. 34: ὁ θάνατός ἐστι χωρισμὸς ψυχῆς ἀπὸ σώματος· οὐδὲν δὲ ἀσώματον ἀπὸ σώματος χωρίζεται· οὐδὲ γὰρ ἐφάπτεται σώματος ἀσώματον· ἡ δὲ ψυχὴ καὶ ἐφάπτεται καὶ χωρίζεται τοῦ σώματος· σῶμα ἄρα ἡ ψυχή. The same is said by Tertullian.

[1] *Nemes.* Nat. Hom. c. 2, p. 30.

[2] *Diog.* 157; *Cic.* N. D. ii. 14, 36.

[3] Zeno, in *Tertull.* l. c., and very nearly the same in *Chalcid.* in Tim. p. 306 Meurs.: Quo digresso animal emoritur: consito autem spiritu digresso animal emoritur: ergo consitus spiritus corpus est, consitus autem spiritus anima est: ergo corpus est anima. Chrysippus in *Chalcid.* l. c.

[4] Cleanthes, in *Nemes.* l. c. 32: οὐ μόνον ὅμοιοι τοῖς γονεῦσι

γινόμεθα, κατὰ τὸ σῶμα, ἀλλὰ καὶ κατὰ τὴν ψυχήν. τοῖς πάθεσι, τοῖς ἤθεσι, ταῖς διαθέσεσι· σώματος δὲ τὸ ὅμοιον καὶ ἀνόμοιον, οὐχὶ δὲ ἀσώματον· σῶμα ἄρα ἡ ψυχή. The same in Tertullian, l. c.

[5] Chrysippus in *Galen*, Hipp. et Plat. iii. 1. Vol. v. 287: ἡ ψυχὴ πνεῦμά ἐστι σύμφυτον ἡμῖν συνεχὲς παντὶ τῷ σώματι διῆκον. *Zeno. Macrob.* Somn. i. 14: Zenon [dixit animam] concretum corpori spiritum . . . Boëthos (probably the Stoic, not the Peripatetic of the first century, is meant) ex aëre et igne [*sc.* constare]. Diog. in *Galen*, ii. 8, p. 282: τὸ κινοῦν τὸν ἄνθρωπον τὰς κατὰ προαίρεσιν κινήσεις ψυχική τίς ἐστιν ἀναθυμίασις. *Cic.* Nat. D. iii. 14, 36; Tusc. i. 9, 19; 18, 42: Zeno considers the soul to be fire; Panætius believes that it is burning air. *Diog. L.* vii. 156, on the authority of Zeno, Antipater, Posidonius,

that the soul of the world is diffused throughout
the world, and forms a bond of union for the world.[1]
This warm breath was believed to be connected with
the blood; and hence the soul was said to be fed by
vapours from the blood, just as the stars are fed by
vapours from the earth.[2]

The same hypothesis was also used to explain the
origin of the soul. One part of the soul was believed
to be transmitted to the young in the seed.[3] From

says that it is πνεῦμα σύμφυτον,
πνεῦμα ἔνθερμον. *Stob.* Ecl. i.
796 (*Plut.* Plac. iv. 3, 3). *Cornut.* N. D. p. 8: καὶ γὰρ αἱ ἡμέ-
τεραι ψυχαὶ πῦρ εἰσι. Ar. Didymus, in *Eus.* Pr. Ev. xv. 20, 1 :
Zeno calls the soul αἴσθησιν ἢ
ἀναθυμίασιν (should be αἰσθητι-
κὴν ἀναθυμίασιν, conf. § 2 and
Ps. *Plut.* Vit. Hom. c. 127 : τὴν
ψυχὴν οἱ Στωϊκοὶ ὁρίζονται πνεῦμα
συμφυὲς καὶ ἀναθυμίασιν αἰσθη-
τικὴν ἀναπτομένην ἀπὸ τῶν ἐν
σώματι ὑγρῶν). Longin. in *Eus.*
Ibid. 21, 1 and 3. *Alex.* De An.
127, b : οἱ ἀπὸ τῆς στοᾶς πνεῦμα
αὐτὴν λέγοντες εἶναι συγκείμενόν
πως ἔκ τε πυρὸς καὶ ἀέρος. Since,
however, every πνεῦμα is not a
soul, a soul is stated to be
πνεῦμα πῶς ἔχον (*Plotin.* Enn.
iv. 7, 4, p. 458, E) ; and the distinctive quality of the soul-
element is its greater warmth
and rarity. See *Plut.* Sto. Rep.
41, 2, p. 1052 : Chrysippus considers the ψυχὴ to be ἀραιότερον
πνεῦμα τῆς φύσεως καὶ λεπτομερέ-
στερον. Similarly, *Galen*, Qu.
An. Mores, c. 4. Vol. iv. 783 :
The Stoics say that both φύσις
and ψυχὴ is πνεῦμα, but that the
πνεῦμα is thick and cold in
φύσις, dry and warm in ψυχή.

[1] *Chrysippus.* See previous
note. This diffusion is further
explained by Iamb. in *Stob.* Ecl.
i. 870 and 874, *Themist.* De
Anim. f. 68, a, *Plotin.* iv. 7, 8,
p. 463, c, as being κρᾶσις, i.e. an
intermingling of elements. That
the soul forms the bond of
union for the body, and not
vice versâ, was a point vindicated by the Stoics against the
Epicureans. Posid. in *Achil.
Tat.* Isag. c. 13, p. 133, E ; *Sext.*
Math. ix. 72.

[2] *Galen.* Hippocr. et Plat. ii.
8, p. 282, on the authority of
Zeno, Cleanthes, Chrysippus,
and Diogenes ; Longin. in *Eus.*
Pr. Ev. xv. 21, 3 ; *M. Aurel.* v.
33 ; vi. 15 ; Ps. *Plut.* Vit. Hom.
127.

[3] Zeno described the seed as
πνεῦμα μεθ᾽ ὑγροῦ ψυχῆς μέρος καὶ
ἀπόσπασμα . . . μίγμα τῶν τῆς
ψυχῆς μερῶν (Arius Didymus, in
Eus. Pr. Ev. xv. 20, 1), or as
σύμμιγμα καὶ κέρασμα τῶν τῆς
ψυχῆς δυνάμεων (*Plut.* Coh. Ir.
15). Similarly Chrysip. in
Diog. 159, Conf. *Tertullian*, De
An. c. 27. According to Sphærus,
in *Diog.* 159, the seed is formed
by separation from all parts of
the body, and can consequently

the part so transmitted there arises, by development
within the womb, first the soul of a plant; and this
becomes the soul of a living creature after birth by
the action of the outer air.[1] This view led to the
further hypothesis that the seàt of the soul must be
in the breast, not in the brain; since not only breath
and warm blood, but also the voice, the immediate
expression of thought, comes from the breast.[2]

Nor is this further hypothesis out of harmony
with the notions otherwise entertained by them as to

produce all, as Democritus had
already said. Panætius (in *Cic.*
Tusc. i. 31, 79) proves, from
the mental similarity between
parents and children, that the
soul comes into existence by
generation. For the mother's
share in producing the soul, see
Ar. Did. l. c. See above p.
127, 5.

[1] *Plut.* Sto. Rep. 41, 1 and 8,
p. 1052; C. Not. 46, 2, p. 1084.
De Primo Frig. 2, 5, p. 946: οἱ
Στωϊκοὶ καὶ τὸ πνεῦμα λέγουσιν
ἐν τοῖς σώμασι τῶν βρεφῶν τῇ
περιψύξει στομοῦσθαι καὶ μεταβάλλον ἐκ φύσεως γενέσθαι ψυχήν.
Similarly, *Plotin.* Enn. iv. 7, 8,
p. 463, c; Conf. *Hippolyt.* Refut. Hær. c. 21, p. 40; *Tertull.*
De An. c. 25. Plutarch (Plac.
v. 16, 2; 17, 1; 24, 1) draws
attention to the inconsistency
of saying that the animal soul,
which is warmer and rarer than
the vegetable soul, has been
developed thereout by cooling
and condensation.

[2] On this point, the Stoics
were not altogether agreed.
Some (not all, as *Plut.* Pl. Phil.
iv. 21, 5, asserts) made the
brain the seat of the soul, in
proof of which they appealed
to the story of the birth of
Pallas. *Sext.* Math. ix. 119;
Diog. in *Phædr.* Fragm. De
Nat. De. col. 6. Conf. *Krische,*
Forschungen, i. 488, and Chrysip. in *Galen,* l. c. iii. 8, p. 349.
It appears, however, from *Galen,*
l. c. i. 6, ii. 2 and 5, iii. 1, pp.
185, 214, 241, 287, *Tertull.* De
An. c. 15, that the most distinguished Stoics—Zeno, Chrysippus, Diogenes, and Apollodorus—decided in favour of the
heart. The chief proof is, that
the voice does not come from
the hollow of the skull, but
from the breast. Chrysippus
was aware of the weakness of
this proof, but still did not
shrink from using it. *Galen,*
l. c. p. 254, 261. At the same
time, he also appealed to the
fact (ii. 7, 268; iii. 1, 290, c. 5,
321, c. 7, 335, 343; iv. 1, 362)
that, by universal assent, supported by numerous passages
from the poets, the motions of
the will and the feelings proceed from the heart.

the nature of man. Plato and Aristotle had already
fixed on the heart as the central organ of the lower
powers, having assigned the brain to reason, with
the view of distinguishing the rational from the
mere animal soul.[1] When, therefore, the Stoics as-
similated man's rational activity to the activity of
the senses, deducing both from one and the same
source, it was natural that they would depart from
Aristotle's view. Accordingly, the various parts of
the soul were supposed to discharge themselves from
their centre in the heart into the several organs, in
the form of atmospheric-currents. Seven such parts
were enumerated, besides the dominant part or
reason, which was also called ἡγεμονικὸν, διανο-
ητικὸν, λογιστικὸν, or λογισμὸς. These seven parts
consist of the five senses, the power of reproduction,
and the power of speech;[2] and, following out their
view of the close relation of speech and thought,[3]

---

[1] Aristotle had assigned no
particular organ of the body to
reason.

[2] *Plut.* Plac. iv. 4, 2. Ibid.
c. 21 : The Stoics consider the
ἡγεμονικὸν to be the highest part
of the soul; it begets the φαντασίαι, συγκαταθέσεις, αἰσθήσεις,
and ὁρμαί, and is by them called
λογισμός; from it the seven
divisions of the soul reach to
the body, like the arms of a
cuttle-fish, and are therefore
collectively defined as πνεῦμα
διατεῖνον ἀπὸ τοῦ ἡγεμονικοῦ
(μέχρις ὀφθαλμῶν, ὤτων, μυκ-
τήρων, γλώττης, ἐπιφανείας, παρυ-
στάτων, φάρυγγος γλώττης καὶ
τῶν οἰκείων ὀργάνων). *Galen,*
l. c. iii. 1, 287. See p. 215, 2 ;

Diog. 110 and 157 ; Porphyr.
and Iamblich. in *Stob.* i. 836,
874, and 878 ; *Chalcid.* in Tim.
307 ; Nicomachus, in *Iambl.*
Theol. Arith. p. 50. But there
was no universal agreement
among the Stoics on this subject. According to *Tertull.* De
An. 14, Zeno only admitted
three divisions of the soul,
whilst some among the later
Stoics enumerated as many as
ten ; Panætius only held six,
and Posidonius went still further away from the view current among the Stoics. The remarks of *Stob.* i. 828, probably
refer to the Peripatetic Aristo.

[3] See p. 73, 2.

great importance was attached to the power of
speech.[1] At the same time, the Stoics upheld the
oneness of the substance of the soul with greater
vigour than either Plato or Aristotle had done.
Reason, or τὸ ἡγεμονικὸν, is with them the primary
power, of which all other powers are only parts, or
derivative powers.[2] Even feeling and desire are
derived from it, in direct contradiction to the teaching of Plato and Aristotle;[3] and this power was

---

[1] Conf. *Cleanth.* Hymn. 4 :
ἐκ σοῦ γὰρ γένος ἐσμὲν ἰῆς μίμημα
λαχόντες
μοῦνοι, ὅσα ζώει τε καὶ ἕρπει θνητ'
ἐπὶ γαῖαν.
[2] See p. 214, 2 and Chrys.
in *Galen*, l. c. iii. 1, p. 287.
Conf. p. 211, 5 : ταύτης οὖν [τῆς
ψυχῆς] τῶν μερῶν ἐκάστῳ διατε-
ταγμένον [ων] μορίῳ, τὸ διῆκον
αὐτῆς εἰς τὴν τραχεῖαν ἀρτηρίαν
φωνὴν εἶναι, τὸ δὲ εἰς ὀφθαλμοὺς
ὄψιν, κ.τ.λ. καὶ τὸ εἰς ὄρχεις,
ἕτερόν τιν' ἔχον τοιοῦτον λόγον,
σπερματικὸν, εἰς ὃ δὲ συμβαίνει
πάντα ταῦτα, ἐν τῇ καρδίᾳ εἶναι,
μέρος ὂν αὐτῆς τὸ ἡγεμονικόν.
Plut. Plac. iv. 4, 2 : τοῦ ἡγεμονικοῦ ἀφ' οὗ ταῦτα πάντα ἐπιτέ-
τακται [=τατοι] διὰ τῶν οἰκείων
ὀργάνων προσφερῶς ταῖς τοῦ πολύ-
ποδος πλεκτάναις. Conf. *Sext.*
Math. ix. 102. *Alex. Aphr.*
(De An. 146) therefore denies
the Stoical assertion, that the
ψυχικὴ δύναμις is only one, and
that every activity of the
soul is only the action of the
πῶς ἔχον ἡγεμονικόν. Conversely
Tertullian, De An. 14, speaking
quite after the manner of a
Stoic, says: Hujusmodi autem
non tam partes animæ habe-
buntur, quam vires et efficaciæ

et operæ . . . non enim membra sunt substantiæ animalis,
sed ingenia (capacities). Iambl.
in *Stob.* i. 874 : The powers of
the soul bear, according to the
Stoics, the same relation to the
soul that qualities have to the
substance ; and their difference
is partly owing to the diffusion
of the πνεύματα, of which they
consist, in different parts of
the body, partly to the union of
several qualities in one subject-
matter, the latter being necessary, for ἡγεμονικὸν to include
φαντασία, συγκατάθεσις, ὁρμὴ,
and λόγος.
[3] *Plut.* Virt. Mort. c. 3, p.
441, speaking of Zeno, Aristo,
and Chrysippus : νομίζουσιν οὐκ
εἶναι τὸ παθητικὸν καὶ ἄλογον δια-
φορᾷ τινι καὶ φύσει ψυχῆς τοῦ
λογικοῦ διακεκριμένον, ἀλλὰ τὸ
αὐτὸ τῆς ψυχῆς μέρος, ὃ δὴ καλοῦσι διάνοιαν καὶ ἡγεμονικὸν,
δι'όλου τρεπόμενον καὶ μεταβάλλον
ἔν τε τοῖς πάθεσι καὶ ταῖς κατὰ
ἕξιν ἢ διάθεσιν μεταβολαῖς κακίαν
τε γίνεσθαι καὶ ἀρετὴν καὶ μηδὲν
ἔχειν ἄλογον ἐν ἑαυτῷ. Plac.
Phil. iv. 21, 1. *Galen*, l. c. iv.
1, p. 364 : Chrysippus sometimes speaks as if he admitted
a distinct δύναμις ἐπιθυμητικὴ or

B. *The in-
dividual
soul and
the soul of
the uni-
verse.*

declared to be the seat of personal identity, a point
on which former philosophers had refrained from
expressing any opinion.[1]

The individual soul bears the same relation to
the soul of the universe that a part does to the
whole. The human soul is not only a part, as are all
other living powers, of the universal power of life,
but, because it possesses reason, it has a special relationship to the Divine Being [2]—a relationship which

θυμοειδής; at other times, as if
he denied it. The latter is
clearly his meaning. *Ibid.* v.
6, 476 : ὁ δὲ Χρύσιππος οὐθ' ἕτερον
εἶναι νομίζει τὸ παθητικὸν τῆς ψυχῆς τοῦ λογιστικοῦ καὶ τῶν ἀλόγων
ζῴων ἀφαιρεῖται τὰ πάθη. See p.
209, 1. Iamb. in *Stob.* Ecl. i.
890; *Diog.* vii. 159. *Orig.* c.
Cels. v. 47 : τοὺς ἀπὸ τῆς στοᾶς
ἀρνουμένους τὸ τριμερὲς τῆς ψυχῆς.
Posidonius (in *Galen*, l. c. 6,
476) endeavours to prove that
Cleanthes held a different view,
by a passage in which he con-
trasts θυμὸς with λόγος—but
this is confounding a rhetorical
flourish with a philosophic
view.

[1] Chrys. (in *Galen*, ii. 2,
215): οὕτως δὲ καὶ τὸ ἐγὼ λέγομεν
κατὰ τοῦτο (the primary power
in the breast) δεικνύντες αὑτοὺς
ἐν τῷ ἀποφαίνεσθαι τὴν διάνοιαν
εἶναι.

[2] *Cleanthes*, v. 4, p. 215, 1.
Epictet. Diss. i. 14, 6 : αἱ ψυχαὶ
συναφεῖς τῷ θεῷ ἅτε αὐτοῦ μόρια
οὖσαι καὶ ἀποσπάσματα. *Id.* ii.
8, 11. *M. Aurel.* ii. 4, v. 27,
calls the soul μέρος ἀπόρροια,
ἀπόσπασμα θεοῦ; and, xii. 26,
even calls the human νοῦς θεός.
Sen. Ep. 41, 2 : Sacer intra nos

spiritus sedet . . . in unoquo-
que virorum bonorum, quis Deus
incertum est, habitat Deus. *Id.*
Ep. 66, 12 : Ratio autem nihil
aliud est quam in corpus humanum pars divini spiritus
mersa. Consequently, reason,
thought, and virtue are of the
same nature in the human soul
as in the soul of the universe,
as Iambl. in *Stob.* Ecl. i. 886,
states as a Stoic view. From
this relationship to God, Posidonius deduces in a well-known
simile (see p. 84, 1) the soul's
capacity for studying nature,
and Cicero (De Leg. i. 8, 24)
the universality of a belief in
God. All souls, as being parts
of the divine mind, may be collectively regarded as one soul
or reason. *Marc. Aurel.* ix. 8 :
εἰς μὲν τὰ ἄλογα ζῷα μία ψυχὴ
δήρηται· εἰς δὲ τὰ λογικὰ μία
λογικὴ ψυχὴ μεμέρισται. xii. 30 :
ἐν φῶς ἠλίου, κἂν διείρηται τοίχοις,
ὄρεσιν, ἄλλοις μυρίοις· μία οὐσία
κοινὴ, κἂν διείργηται ἰδίως ποιοῖς
σώμασι μυρίοις· μία ψυχὴ, κἂν
φύσεσι διείρηται μυρίαις καὶ ἰδίαις
περιγραφαῖς. This oneness, however, must, as the comparison
shows, be understood in the
sense of the Stoic realism : the

becomes closer in proportion as we allow greater play to the divine element in ourselves, i. e. to reason.[1] On this very account, however, the soul cannot escape the law of the Divine Being, in the shape of general necessity, or destiny. It is a mere delusion to suppose that the soul possesses a freedom independent of the world's course. The human will, like everything else in the world, is bound into the indissoluble chain of natural causes, and that irrespectively of our knowing by what causes the will is decided or not. Its freedom consists only in that, instead of being ruled from without, it obeys the call of its own nature, external circumstances concurring.[2] To this power of self-determination, however, the greatest value is attached. Not only are our actions due to it to such an extent that only because of it can they be considered ours,[3] but even our judgments are, as the Stoics thought, dependent on it. The soul itself inclining towards truth or error, our convictions are quite as much in our power as our actions:[4] both are alike the necessary result of our will. And just as the individual soul does not possess activity independently of the universal soul, no more can the individual soul escape the law of destiny. It, too, at the end of the world's course, will be resolved into the primary substance, into the Divine Being,

---

universal soul, in the sense of etherial substance, is the element of which individual souls consist. See also *Marc. Aurel.* viii. 54.

[1] In this sense, *Sen.* Ep. 31, 11, calls the animus rectus,

bonus, magnus, a Deus in corpore humano hospitans.

[2] Further particulars, p. 174, 180, 189.

[3] See p. 179.

[4] See p. 88, 1.

CHAP.
IX.

The only point about which the Stoics were undecided was, whether all souls would last until that
time as separate souls, which was the view of Cleanthes, or only the souls of the wise, as Chrysippus
held.[1]

[1] *Diog.* 156; *Plut.* N. P.
Suav. Viv. 31, 2, p. 1107; Plac.
iv. 7. 2; Ar. Didymus, in *Eus.*
Præp. Ev. xv. 20, 3; *Sen.* Consol. ad Marc. c. 26, 7; Ep. 102,
22; 117, 6; *Cic.* Tusc. i. 31, 77.
Seneca (ad Polyb. 9, 2; Ep. 65,
24; 71, 16; 36, 9, and in *Tertull.* De An. c. 42; Resurr.
Carn. c. 1) and M. Aure-
lius (iii. 3; vii. 32; viii. 25, 58)
are only speaking κατ᾽ ἄνθρωπον,
in seeming to doubt a future
life after death, in order to dis-
pel the fear of death in every
case. It is, however, a mistake
of *Tiedemann* (Sto. Phil. ii. 155)
to suppose that they, in many
passages (*Sen.* Ep. 71, 102, *M.
Aur.* ii. 17; v. 4, 13), supposed
the immediate dissolution of
the soul after death. It is, on
the contrary, clear, from *M.
Aurel.* iv. 14, 21, that the soul
lives some time after death,
and is not resolved into the
world-soul till the general conflagration. But even this is
a variation from the ordinary
view of the Stoics. According
to *Seneca* (Consol. ad Marcum)
the souls of the good, as in the
doctrine of purgatory, undergo
a purification, before they are
admitted to the ranks of the
blessed; and here this purification is no doubt required on
physical grounds. When the
soul is purified, both in substance and morals, it rises up
to the ether, and there, according to M. Aurelius, united to
the σπερματικὸς λόγος τῶν ὅλων,
it lives, according to the common view, until the end of the
world. The ether is also allotted to the blessed, for their
residence, by *Cic.* Tusc. i. 18,
42; *Lactant.* Inst. vii. 20; *Plut.*
N. P. Suav. Vivi. 31, 2, p. 1107.
The souls, as Cicero remarks,
penetrating the thick lower air,
mount to heaven, until they
reach an atmosphere (the juncti
ex anima tenui et ardore solis
temperato ignes) congenial with
their own nature. Here they
naturally stop, and are fed by
the same elements as the stars.
According to Chrysippus (in
Eustath. on Il. xxiii. 65), they
there assume the spherical
shape of the stars. According
to *Tertull.* De An. 54, conf.
Lucan. Phars. ix. 5, their place
is under the moon. Zeno, in
speaking of the islands of the
blest (*Lact.* Inst. vii. 7, 20),
probably only desired to enlist
popular opinion in his own
favour. The souls of the foolish
and bad also last some time
after death; only, as being
weaker, they do not last until
the end of the world (*Ar. Did.*;
Theodoret. Cur. Gr. Affec. v. 23,
p. 73); and meantime, as it is
distinctly asserted by *Sen.* Ep.
117, 6, *Tertullian,* and *Lactantius,* they are punished in the

The effects of the Stoic principles appear unmistakeably in the above statements. They, however, pervade the whole body of the Stoical views on man.[1] From one point of view, the theory of necessity, and the denial of everlasting life after death, seem quite unintelligible in a system the moral tone of which is so high; yet the connection of these theories with the Stoic ethics is very intimate. These theories commended themselves to the Stoics, as they have done in later times to Spinoza and Schleiermacher, because they corresponded with their fundamental view of morality, according to which the individual can only be regarded as the instrument of reason in general, as a dependent portion of the collective universe. Moreover, since the Stoics admitted a future existence—of limited, but yet indefinite, length—the same practical results followed from their belief as from the current belief in immortality. The statements of Seneca,[2] that this life is a prelude to a better; that the body is a lodging-house, from which the soul will return to its own home; his joy in looking forward to the day which will rend the bonds of the body asunder,

CHAP.
IX.
———
C. *Free-
dom and
immor-
tality.*

nether world. Tertullian in placing a portion of the souls of the foolish in the region of the earth, and there allowing them to be instructed by the wise, is probably referring to the purification mentioned by Seneca. For the supposed transmigration of souls see p. 166, 2.

[1] The peculiar notion mentioned by Seneca (Ep. 57, 7) as belonging to the Stoics—animam hominis magno pondere extriti permanere non posse et statim spargi, quia non fuerit illi exitus liber—was not required by their principles, as Seneca already observed. It belongs, in fact, only to individual members of that School.

[2] Conf. *Baur*, Seneca und Paulus in Hilgenfeld's Zeitschrift für wissensch. Theol. i. 2, 221.

which he, in common with the early Christians, calls
the birthday of eternal life;[1] his description of the
peace of the eternity there awaiting us, of the freedom and bliss of the heavenly life, of the light of
knowledge which will there be shed on all the secrets
of nature;[2] his language on the future recognition
and happy society of souls made perfect;[3] his seeing in death a great day of judgment, when sentence

[1] Ep. 102, 22 : Cum venerit
dies ille, qui mixtum hoc divini
humanique secernat, corpus
hic, ubi inveni, relinquam, ipse
me Dis reddam . . . per has
mortalis vitæ moras illi meliori
vitæ longiorique proluditur. As
a child in its mother's womb,
sic per hoc spatium, quod ab
infantia patet in senectutem,
in alium maturescimus partum.
All we possess, and the body
itself, is only the baggage,
which we neither brought into
the world, nor can carry away
with us. Dies iste, quem tanquam extremum reformidas,
æterni natalis est. Ep. 120,
14 : The body is breve hos-
pitium, which a noble soul does
not fear to lose. Scit enim, quo
exiturus sit, qui, unde venerit,
meminit. Conf. Ep. 65, 16.
[2] Consol. ad Marc. 24, 3 :
Imago dumtaxat filii tui periit
. . . ipse quidem æternus me-
liorisque nunc status est, de-
spoliatus oneribus alienis et
sibi relictus. The body is only
a vessel, enveloping the soul in
darkness : nititur illo, unde
dimissus est ; ibi illum æterna
requies manet. Ibid. 26, 7 : Nos
quoque felices animæ et æternæ
sortitæ. Ibid. 19, 6 : Excessit

filius tuus terminos intra quos
servitur : excepit illum magna
et æterna pax. No fear or care,
no desire, envy, or compassion
disturbs him. Ibid. 26, 5.
Consol. ad Polyb. 9, 3, 8 : Nunc
animus fratris mei velut ex
diutino carcere emissus, tandem
sui juris et arbitrii, gestit et
rerum naturæ spectaculo fruitur
. . . fruitur nunc aperto et
libero cœlo . . . et nunc illic
libere vagatur omniaque rerum
naturæ bona cum summa vo-
luntate perspicit. Ep. 79, 12 :
Tunc animus noster habebit,
quod gratuletur sibi, cum emissus his tenebris . . . totum
diem admiserit, et cœlo red-
ditus suo fuerit. Ep. 102, 28 :
Aliquando naturæ tibi arcana
retegentur, discutietur ista
caligo et lux undique clara
percutiet, which Seneca then
further expands.
[3] In Consol. ad Marc. 25, 1,
Seneca describes how, the time
of purification ended, the deceased one inter felices currit
animas (the addition : excepit
illum cœtus sacer *Hanse* rightly
treats as a gloss) and how his
grandfather shows him the hall
of heaven. Ibid. 26, 3.

will be pronounced on every one;[1] his making
the thought of a future life the great stimulus to
moral conduct here;[2] even the way in which he
consoles himself for the destruction of the soul by
the thought that it will live again in another form
hereafter[3]—all contain nothing at variance with
the Stoic teaching, however near they may approach
to Platonic or even Christian modes of thought.[4]

[1] Ep. 26, 4: Velut adpro-
pinquet experimentum et ille
laturus sententiam de omnibus
annis meis dies . . . quo, re-
motis strophis ac fucis, de me
judicaturus sum. Compare the
hora decretoria, Ep. 102, 24.

[2] Ep. 102, 29: Hæc cogi-
tatio (that of heaven and a
future life) nihil sordidum
animo subsidere sinit, nihil
humile, nihil crudele. Deos
rerum omnium esse testes ait:
illis nos adprobari, illis in
futurum parari jubet et æterni-
tatem menti proponere.

[3] Ep. 36, 10: Mors . . . in-
termittit vitam, non eripit:
veniet iterum qui nos in lucem
reponat dies, quem multi re-
cusarent, nisi oblitos reduceret.
Sed postea diligentius docebo
omnia, quæ videntur perire,
mutari. Æquo animo debet
rediturus exire. The souls cannot return, according to the
Stoic teaching, until after the
general conflagration; and that
is on the supposition that the
same persons will be found in
the future world as in the present. See p. 166, 2. As long
as the latter lasts, the better
souls continue to exist, and
only the particles of the body

are employed for fresh bodies.
Accordingly, the passage just
quoted, and also Ep. 71, 13,
must refer to the physical side
of death, or else to the return
of personality after the conflagration of the world.

[4] Besides the definitions of
αἴσθησις in *Diog.* 52, and the
remark that impressions are
made on the organs of sense,
but that the seat of feeling is
in the ἡγεμονικὸν (*Plut.* Plac. iv.
23, 1), the following statements
may be mentioned: In the process of seeing, the ὁρατικὸν
πνεῦμα, coming into the eyes
from the ἡγεμονικὸν, gives a
spherical form to the air before
the eye, by virtue of its τονικὴ
κίνησις (on τόνος, see p. 128, 2),
and, by means of the sphere of
air, comes in contact with
things; and since by this process rays of light emanate from
the eye, darkness must be
visible. *Diog.* 158; *Alex. Aph.*
De Anim. 149; *Plut.* Plac. iv.
15. The process of hearing is
due to the spherical undulations of the air, which com-
municate their motion to the
ear. *Diog.* 158; *Plut.* Plac. iv.
19, 5. On the voice, called also
φωνᾶεν, see *Plut.* Plac. iv. 20, 2;

Seneca merely expanded the teaching of his School
in one particular direction, in which it harmonises
most closely with Platonism ; and, of all the Stoics,
Seneca was the most distinctly Platonic.

Excepting the two points which have been discussed at an earlier time,[1] and one other point relating to the origin of ideas and emotions, which will
be considered subsequently, little is on record relating to the psychological views of the Stoics.

21, 4; *Diog.* 55, and above
p. 214, 2; 74, 5. Disease is
caused by changes in the πνεῦμα,
Diog. 158 ; sleep ἐκλυομένου τοῦ
αἰσθητικοῦ τόνου περὶ τὸ ἡγεμονικόν, *Diog.* 158 ; *Tertull.* De An.
43 ; and in a similar way, death
ἐκλυομένου τοῦ τόνου καὶ παριε-
μένου, Iambl. (in *Stob.* Ecl. i.
922), who, however, does not
mention the Stoics by name. In
the case of man, the ex-
tinguishing of the power of
life is only a liberation of
rational souls.
[1] Page 77.

CHAPTER X.

ETHICS.   THE GENERAL PRINCIPLES OF THE STOIC
ETHICS.   ABSTRACT THEORY OF MORALITY.

WHATEVER attention the Stoics paid to the study of
nature and to logic, the real kernel of their system
lies, as has been already observed, in their Ethics ;
even natural science, that 'most divine part of philosophy,' being only pursued as an intellectual preparation for Ethics. In the domain of Ethics the true
spirit of the Stoic system may therefore be expected
to appear, and it may be anticipated that this subject will be treated by them with special care. Nor
is this expectation a vain one ; for here the springs
of information flowing freely give ample data respecting the Stoic doctrine of morality. Nevertheless, respecting the formal grouping of these data
only vague and contradictory statements are forthcoming. Moreover, the Stoics appear to have been
so unequal in their treatment, and so little afraid of
repetitions, that it is hardly possible to obtain a
complete survey of their whole system by following
any one of the traditional divisions.[1]

CHAP.
X.

---

[1] The chief passage in *Diog.*
vii. 84, is as follows : τὸ δὲ ἠθικὸν μέρος τῆς φιλοσοφίας διαιροῦ-
σιν εἴς τε τὸν περὶ ὁρμῆς καὶ εἰς

Proceeding to group the materials in such a way
as to give the clearest insight into the peculiarities

τὸν περὶ ἀγαθῶν καὶ κακῶν τόπον
καὶ τὸν περὶ παθῶν καὶ περὶ ἀρετῆς
καὶ περὶ τέλους περί τε τῆς πρώτης
ἀξίας καὶ τῶν πράξεων καὶ περὶ τῶν
καθηκόντων προτροπῶν τε καὶ ἀποτροπῶν. καὶ οὕτω δ' ὑποδιαιροῦσιν
οἱ περὶ Χρύσιππον καὶ Ἀρχέδημον
καὶ Ζήνωνα τὸν Ταρσέα καὶ Ἀπολ-
λόδωρον καὶ Διογένην καὶ Ἀντί-
πατρον καὶ Ποσειδώνιον· ὁ μὲν
γὰρ Κιττιεὺς Ζήνων καὶ ὁ Κλεάνθης
ὡς ἂν ἀρχαιότεροι ἀφελέστερον
περὶ τῶν πραγμάτων διέλαβον.
There may be doubts as to the
punctuation, and, consequently,
as to the sense, of the first sentence; but the form of expression seems to imply that
the five first portions contain
main divisions, and the six
following subdivisions. The
ethics of Chrysippus and his
followers would therefore be
divided into the following main
divisions: περὶ ὁρμῆς, περὶ ἀγαθῶν
καὶ κακῶν, περὶ παθῶν; but it
would be hard to assign to these
divisions their respective subdivisions. The statement of
Epictetus, Diss. iii. 2, agrees in
part with this division. He distinguishes in his introduction
to virtue three τόποι: ὁ περὶ τὰς
ὀρέξεις καὶ τὰς ἐκκλίσεις, called
also ὁ περὶ τὰ πάθη; ὁ περὶ τὰς
ὁρμὰς καὶ ἀφορμὰς καὶ ἁπλῶς ὁ
περὶ τὸ καθῆκον; and, lastly, ὁ
περὶ τὴν ἀναξαπατησίαν καὶ ἀνει-
καιότητα καὶ ὅλως ὁ περὶ τὰς συγκαταθέσεις. The first of these
divisions would correspond to
the third of Diogenes, the
second to his first; but the
division περὶ ἀγαθῶν καὶ κακῶν
does not harmonise with the

third of Epictetus (which, according to what follows, rather
refers to the critical confirma-
tion of moral principles not
specially mentioned by Diogenes), but rather with his first
division treating of ὀρέξεις and
ἐκκλίσεις. Stobæus again differs
from either. In his survey of
the Stoic ethics (Ecl. ii. c. 5),
he first, p. 90, treats of what is
good, evil, and indifferent, of
what is desirable and de-
testable, of the end-in-chief,
and of happiness, in this section discussing at length the doctrine of virtue. He then goes on,
p. 158, to consider the καθῆκον,
the impulses, p. 166, and the
emotions (πάθη, as being one
kind of impulse), appending
thereto, p. 186, a discussion on
friendship; and, concluding,
p. 192 to 242, with a long treatise on ἐνεργήματα (κατορθώματα, ἁμαρτήματα, οὐδέτερα), the
greater portion of which is devoted to describing the wise
man and the fool. Turning to
Sen. Ep. 95, 65, it is stated, on
the authority of Posidonius, that
not only præceptio, but also
suasio, consolatio, and exhorta-
tio, and, moreover, causarum
inquisitio (which, however, can
hardly have been called etymo-
logia by Posidonius, as Hanse
reads but ætiologia) and etho-
logia, description of moral
states, are necessary. In Ep.
89, 14, the parts of moral
science are more accurately
given as three; the first determining the value of things, the
second treating de actionibus,

and connection of the Stoic principles, the first distinction to be made will be one between morality in
general and particular points in morality. In considering morality in general, those statements which
give the abstract theory of morals will be distinguished from those which modify it with a view to
meet practical wants. The former again may be
grouped round three points :—the enquiry into the
highest good, that into the nature of virtue, and
that relating to the wise man.

The enquiry into the destiny and end of man
turns, with the Stoics, as it did with all moral philosophers since the time of Socrates, about the fundamental conception of the good, and the ingredients
necessary to make up the highest good or happiness.[1] Happiness, they consider, can only be sought
in rational activity or virtue. Speaking more ex-

A. *The
highest
good.*
(1) *Nature
of the
highest
good.*

the third de impetu, περὶ ὁρμῆς.
Two of these parts coincide
indeed with those of Diogenes,
but this is not the case with
the third, which is only one of
the subdivisions in Diogenes
(περὶ τῶν πράξεων); and even
Seneca's first part more nearly
agrees with one of these (περὶ
τῆς πρώτης ἀξίας). Unfortunately, Seneca does not mention
his authorities ; and, accordingly, we are not sure whether
his division is a genuine Stoical
division. A similar division
will be subsequently met with
in the eclectic Academician
Eudorus (living under Au-
gustus). None of the divisions
quoted agree with the three

problems proposed by *Cic.* Off.
ii. 5, 18, or the three sections
enumerated by *Epict.* Enchir.
c. 51 (76), in which Petersen
(Phil. Chrys. Fund. p. 260) recognises Seneca's three main
divisions of Ethics. In the
midst of such contending authorities it seems impossible to
establish the main division of
the Stoic Ethics. One thing
alone is clear, that they were
themselves not agreed on the
subject. *Petersen's* attempt,
l. c. p. 258, appears to me a
failure.

[1] *Stob.* Ecl. ii. 138 : τέλος δέ
φασιν εἶναι τὸ εὐδαιμονεῖν, οὗ
ἕνεκα πάντα πράττεται, αὐτὸ δὲ
πράττεται μὲν, οὐδενὸς δὲ ἕνεκα.

Q

CHAP.
X.

plicitly,[1] the primary impulse of every being is towards self-preservation and self-gratification.[2] It follows that every being pursues those things which are most suited to its nature,[3] and that such things

[1] *Diog,* vii. 85; *Cic.* Fin. iii. 5; *Gell.* N. A. xii. 5, 7. ' That the two latter writers follow one and the same authority appears partly from their literal agreement with each other, and partly from their adopting a uniform method in refuting the Epicurean statement, that the desire for pleasure is the primary impulse. That authority is probably the treatise of Chrysipɟ us περὶ τέλους, since it is distinctly referred to by Diogenes. *Plut.* Sto. Rep. 12, 4, quotes from it: ὡς οἰκειούμεθα πρὸς αὐτοὺς εὐθὺς γενόμενοι καὶ τὰ μέρη καὶ τὰ ἔκγονα ἑαυτῶν. The difference mentioned by *Alex. Aphr.* De An. 154—that at one time self-love, at another the preservation of one's own nature, is the impulse—is unimportant.

[2] *Diog.* vii. 85 : τὴν δὲ πρώτην ὁρμήν φασι τὸ ζῷον ἴσχειν ἐπὶ τὸ τηρεῖν ἑαυτὸ, οἰκειούσης αὐτῷ [αὐτῷ] τῆς φύσεως ἀπ' ἀρχῆς, καθά φησιν ὁ Χρύσιππος ἐν τῷ πρώτῳ περὶ τελῶν, πρῶτον οἰκεῖον εἶναι λέγων παντὶ ζῴῳ τὴν αὐτοῦ σύστασιν καὶ τὴν ταύτης συνείδησιν. οὔτε γὰρ ἀλλοτριῶσαι εἰκὸς ἦν αὐτοῦ [Cobet incorrectly αὐτὸ] τὸ ζῷον, οὔτε ποιῆσαι ἂν [l. ποιησᾶσαν sc. τὴν φύσιν] αὐτὸ μήτ' ἀλλοτριῶσαι μήτ' οὐκ [must evidently be struck out] οἰκειῶσαι. ἀπολείπεται τοίνυν λέγειν συστησαμένην αὐτὸ οἰκείως πρὸς ἑαυτό· οὕτω γὰρ τά τε βλάπτοντα διω-

θεῖται καὶ τὰ οἰκεῖα προσίεται. Similarly, *Cic.* l. c. 5, 16. Antisthenes had already reduced the conception of the good to that of οἰκεῖον, without the fuller explanation. Here the Academic theory of life according to nature, which had been enunciated by Polemo, Zeno's teacher, is combined therewith. Some difficulty was nevertheless caused by the question whether all living creatures possess a consciousness (συνείδησις, sensus) of their own nature; without such a consciousness, natural self-love seemed to the Stoics impossible. They thought, however, that this question (according to *Sen.* Ep. 121, 5, conf. *Cic.* l. c.) could be answered in the affirmative without hesitation, appealing for evidence to the instinctive activities by which children and animals govern their bodily motions, guard themselves from dangers, and pursue what is to their interest, without denying that the ideas which children and animals have of themselves are very indistinct, that they only know their own constitution, but not its true conception (constitutionis finitio *Sen.* ꝑ. 11). Constitutio, or σύστασις, was defined by the Stoics, *Sen.* p. 10, as principale animi quodam modo se habens erga corpus.

[3] *Cic.* Fin. iii. 5, 17; 6, 20.

only have for it a value (ἀξία). Hence the highest
good—the end-in-chief,[1] or happiness—can only be
found in what is conformable to nature.[2] Nothing,
however, can be conformable to nature for any individual thing, unless it be in harmony with the course
of law of the universe,[3] or with the universal reason of
the world ; nor, in the case of a conscious and reasonable being, unless it proceeds from a recognition
of this general law—in short, from rational intelligence.[4] In every enquiry into what is conformable

---

[1] The terms are here treated
as synonymous, without regard
to the hair splitting with which
the Stoics distinguished (*Stob.*
Ecl. ii. 136) three meanings of
τέλος, between τέλος and σκόπος.
[2] *Stob.* ii. 134 and 138;
Diog. vii. 88 ; 94 ; *Plut.* C. Not.
27, 9 ; *Cic.* Fin. iii. 7, 26 ; 10,
33 ; *Sen.* V. Beat. 3, 3 ; conf.
Ep. 118, 8; *Sext.* Pyrrh. iii. 171 ;
Math. xi. 30. In *Stob.* ii. 78
and 96, formal definitions are
given of ἀγαθὸν, τέλος, and
εὐδαιμονία. The latter is generally paraphrased by εὔροια βίου,
as Zeno had defined it. Various
formulæ for the conception of
a life according to nature are
given by Cleanthes, Antipater,
Archedemus, Diogenes, Panætius, Posidonius, and others in
Clem. Alex. Strom. ii. 416;
Stob. 134 ; and *Diog.*, all apparently taken from the same
source.
[3] *Diog.* vii. 88 : διόπερ τέλος
γίνεται τὸ ἀκολούθως τῇ φύσει
ζῆν · ὅπερ ἐστὶ κατά τε τὴν αὑτοῦ
καὶ κατὰ τὴν τῶν ὅλων, οὐδὲν
ἐνεργοῦντας ὧν ἀπαγορεύειν εἴωθεν
ὁ νόμος ὁ κοινὸς ὅσπερ ἐστὶν ὁ

ὀρθὸς λόγος διὰ πάντων ἐρχόμενος
ὁ αὐτὸς ὢν τῷ Διΐ . . . εἶναι δ᾽
αὐτὸ τοῦτο τὴν τοῦ εὐδαίμονος
ἀρετὴν καὶ εὔροιαν βίου, ὅταν
πάντα πράττηται κατὰ τὴν συμφω-
νίαν τοῦ παρ᾽ ἑκάστῳ δαίμονος πρὸς
τὴν τοῦ τῶν ὅλων διοικητοῦ βούλησιν.
[4] *Stob.* ii. 160 (conf. 158):
διττῶς θεωρεῖσθαι τήν τε ἐν τοῖς
λογικοῖς γιγνομένην ὁρμὴν καὶ τὴν
ἐν τοῖς ἀλόγοις ζᾴοις. *Diog.* 86 :
Plants are moved by nature
without impulse, animals by
means of impulse. In the case
of animals, therefore, τὸ κατὰ
τὴν φύσιν is the same as τὸ κατὰ
τὴν ὁρμήν. In rational creatures,
reason controls impulse ; and
accordance with nature means
accordance with reason. In
Galen. Hippoc. et Plat. v. 2,
p. 460, Chrysippus says : ἡμᾶς
οἰκειοῦσθαι πρὸς μόνον τὸ καλόν.
M. Aurel. vii. 11 : τῷ λογικῷ ζῴῳ
ἡ αὐτὴ πρᾶξις κατὰ φύσιν ἐστὶ καὶ
κατὰ λόγον. Hence the definition
of a virtuous life, or a life according to nature : ζῆν κατ᾽ ἐμ-
πειρίαν τῶν φύσει συμβαινόντων
(Chrysippus, in *Stob.* 134 ; *Diog.*
87 ; *Clem.* l. c.; also Diogenes,

CHAP.
X.

to nature, all turns upon agreement with the essential constitution of the being, and this essential constitution consists, in the case of man, simply in reason.[1] One and the same thing, therefore, is always meant, whether, with Zeno, life according to nature is spoken of as being in harmony with oneself, or whether, following Cleanthes, it is simply said to be the agreement of life with nature, and whether, in the latter case, φύσις is taken to mean the world at large, or is limited to human nature in particular.[2] In every case the meaning is, that the

Antipater, Archedemus, Posidonius); and that of the good: τὸ τέλειον κατὰ φύσιν λογικοῦ ὡς λογικοῦ (*Diog.* 94).

[1] *Sen.* Ep. 121, 14: Omne animal primum constitutioni suæ conciliari : hominis autem constitutionem rationalem esse : et ideo conciliari hominem sibi non tanquam animali sed tanquam rationali. Ea enim parte sibi carus est homo, qua homo est. *Id.* Ep. 92, 1 : The body is subservient to the soul, and the irrational part of the soul to the rational part. Hence it follows: In hoc uno positam esse beatam vitam, ut in nobis ratio perfecta sit. Similarly, Ep. 76, 8. *M. Aurel.* vi. 44 : συμφέρει δὲ ἑκάστῳ τὸ κατὰ τὴν ἑαυτοῦ κατασκευὴν καὶ φύσιν · ἡ δὲ ἐμὴ φύσις λογικὴ καὶ πολιτική. Conf. viii. 7 and 12.

[2] According to *Stob.* ii. 132, *Diog.* vii. 89, the ancient Stoics were not altogether agreed as to the terms in which they would express their theory. Zeno, for instance, is said by Stobæus to have defined τέλος = ὁμολογουμένως ζῆν ; Cleanthes first added the words τῇ φύσει, and Chry-

sippus and his followers augmented the formula by several additions. *Diog.* 87 attributes the words τῇ φύσει to Zeno, adding, however, 89, that Chrysippus understood by φύσις, τήν τε κοινὴν καὶ ἰδίως τὴν ἀνθρωπίνην, whereas Cleanthes understood τὴν κοίνην μόνην οὐκέτι δὲ καὶ τὴν ἐπὶ μέρους. These differences are, however, not important. The simple expression ὁμολογουμένως ζῆν means, without doubt, ἀκόλουθον ἐν βίῳ, the ζῆν καθ' ἕνα λόγον καὶ σύμφωνον (*Stob.* ii. 132 and 158), the ὁμολογία παντὸς τοῦ βίου (*Diog.* vii. 89), the vita sibi concors, the concordia animi (*Sen.* Ep. 89, 15 ; V. Be. 8, 6), the unum hominem agere, which, according to *Sen.* Ep. 120, 22, is only found in a wise man—in a word, the even tenour of life and consistency. Nevertheless, this consistency is only possible when individual actions accord with the requirements of the character of the agent. Accordingly, *Stob.* ii. 158, places ἀκολούθως τῇ ἑαυτῶν φύσει by the side of ἀκόλουθον ἐν βίῳ. Cleanthes

life of the individual approximates to or falls short
of the goal of happiness, exactly in proportion as it
approaches to or departs from the universal law of
the world and the particular rational nature of man.
In a word, a rational life, an agreement with the
general course of the world, constitutes virtue. The
principle of the Stoic morality might therefore be
briefly expressed in the sentence: Only virtue is
good, and happiness consists exclusively in virtue.[1]
If, however, following Socrates, the good is defined
as being what is useful,[2] then the sentence would

therefore, in adding to the expression ὁμολογουμένως the words τῇ φύσει, which, however, according to *Diog.* 87, Zeno had done before him, was only going back to the next condition of ὁμολογουμένως ζῆν. We can, however, hardly believe with Diogenes that Cleanthes understood by φύσις only nature in general, but not human nature. He may have alluded in express terms to κοινὴ φύσις or κοινὸς νόμος only, with the praise of which his well-known hymn ends, but it cannot have been his intention to exclude human nature, which is only a particular form of nature in general. Chrysippus therefore only expanded, but did not contradict, the teaching of his master.

[1] *Diog.* vii. 30; 94; 101; *Stob.* ii. 200; 138; *Sext,* Pyrrh. iii. 169; Math. xi. 184; *Cic.* Tusc. ii. 25, 61; Fin. iv. 16, 45; Acad. i. 10; Parad. 1; *Sen.* Benef. vii. 2, 1; Ep. 71, 4; 74, 1; 76, 11; 85, 17; 120, 3; 118, 10, where the relation of the conceptions honestum bo-

num, secundum naturam is specially considered. To prove their position, the Stoics make use of the chain-argument, of which they are generally fond. Thus Chrysippus (in *Plut.* Sto. Rep. 13, 11) : τὸ ἀγαθὸν αἱρετόν· τὸ δ' αἱρετὸν ἀρεστόν· τὸ δ' ἀρεστὸν ἐπαινετόν· τὸ δ' ἐπαινετὸν καλόν. (The same in *Cic.* Fin. iii. 8, 27, and iv. 18, 50, where I would suggest the reading validius instead of vitiosius.) Again: τὸ ἀγαθὸν χαρτόν· τὸ δὲ χαρτὸν σεμνόν· τὸ δὲ σεμνὸν καλόν. (The same somewhat expanded in *Cic.* Tusc. v. 15, 43.) *Stob.* ii. 126: πᾶν ἀγαθὸν αἱρετὸν εἶναι, ἀρεστὸν γὰρ καὶ δοκιμαστὸν καὶ ἐπαινετὸν ὑπάρχειν· πᾶν δὲ κακὸν φευκτόν. Another sorites of the same kind in *Sen.* Ep. 85, 2.

[2] *Stob.* ii. 78; 94; *Diog.* vii. 94 and 98; *Sext.* Pyrrh. iii. 169; Math. xi. 22, 25, and 30. According to *Cic.* Fin. iii. 10, 33, Diogenes reconciled this definition with the definition of the good and the perfect quoted on p. 227, 4, by observing that the useful is a motus aut status natura absoluti.

CHAP.
X.

run thus: Only Virtue is useful; advantage cannot be distinguished from duty, whilst to a bad man nothing is useful,[1] since, in the case of a rational being, good and evil does not depend on what happens to him, but simply on his own conduct.[2] A view of life is here presented to us in which happiness coincides with virtue, the good and the useful with duty and reason. There is neither any good independently of virtue, nor is there in virtue and for virtue any evil.

(2) The good and evil.

The Stoics accordingly refused to admit the ordinary distinction, sanctioned by popular opinion and the majority of philosophers, between various kinds and degrees of good; nor would they allow bodily advantages and external circumstances to be included among good things, together with mental and moral qualities. A certain distinction between goods they did not indeed deny, and various kinds of goods are mentioned by them in their formal division of goods.[3] But these distinctions amount,

[1] Sext. 1. c. Stob. ii. 188: μηδένα φαῦλον μήτε ὠφελεῖσθαι μήτε ὠφελεῖν. εἶναι γὰρ τὸ ὠφελεῖν ἴσχειν κατ' ἀρετὴν, καὶ τὸ ὠφελεῖσθαι κινεῖσθαι κατ' ἀρετήν. Ibid. ii. 202; Plut. Sto. Rep. 12; Com. Not. 20, 1; Cic. Off. ii. 3, 10; iii. 3, 11; 7, 34.
[2] M. Aurel. ix. 16.
[3] See Diog. 94; Stob. ii. 96; 124; 130; 136; Sext. Pyrrh. iii. 169; Math. xi. 22; Cic. Fin. iii. 16, 55; Sen. Ep. 66, 5. Good is here defined to be either ὠφέλεια or οὐχ ἕτερον ὠφελείας (inseparably connected

with ὠφέλεια, the good in itself, just as the virtuous man is connected with virtue, which is a part of himself. See Sextus l. c. and above p. 104, 2), or, what is the same thing, ἀρετὴ ἢ τὸ μετέχον ἀρετῆς. (Sext. Math. xi. 184.) A distinction is made between three kinds of good: τὸ ὑφ' οὗ ἢ ἀφ' οὗ ἔστιν ὠφελεῖσθαι, τὸ καθ' ὃ συμβαίνει ὠφελεῖσθαι, τὸ οἷόν τε ὠφελεῖν. Under the first head comes virtue, under the second virtuous actions, under the third, besides the two others, virtuous

in the end, to no more than this, that whilst some goods are good and useful in themselves, others are only subsidiary to them. The existence of several equally primary goods appears to the Stoics to be at variance with the conception of the good. That only is a good, according to their view, which has an unconditional value. That which has a value only in comparison with something else, or as leading to something else, does not deserve to be called a good. The difference between what is good and what is not good is not only a difference of degree, but also one of kind ; and what is not a good *per se* can never

subjects—men, Gods, and demons. A second division of goods (*Diog., Sext.* iii. 181, *Stob.*) is into goods of the soul, external goods, the possession of virtuous friends and a virtuous country, and such as are neither (τὸ αὑτὸν ἑαυτῷ εἶναι σπουδαῖον καὶ εὐδαίμονα, virtue and happiness considered as the relation of the individual to himself, as his own possessions). Goods of the soul are then divided into διαθέσεις (virtues), ἕξεις (or ἐπιτηδεύματα, as instances of which *Stob.* ii. 100, 128, quotes μαντικὴ and φιλογεωμετρία, &c., these are not so unchangeable as peculiarities of character, and are therefore only ἕξεις, p. 103, 1), and those which are neither ἕξεις nor διάθεσεις—actions themselves. A third division of goods (*Diog., Cic.* l. c., *Stob.* 80, 100, 114) distinguishes τελικὰ or δι' αὑτὰ αἱρετὰ (moral actions), ποιητικὰ (friends and the services they render), τελικὰ and ποιητικὰ (virtues themselves) ; fourthly and fifthly, μικτὰ (as εὐτεκνία and εὐγηρία), and ἁπλᾶ or ἄμικτα (such as science), and the ἀεὶ παρόντα (virtues), and οὐκ ἀεὶ παρόντα (οἷον χαρὰ, περιπάτησις). The corresponding divisions of evil are given by Diogenes and Stobæus. The latter (ii. 126 and 136) enumerates, in addition, the ἀγαθὰ ἐν κινήσει (χαρὸ, &c.) and ἐν σχέσει (εὔτακτος ἡσυχία, &c.), the latter being partially ἐν ἕξει ; the ἀγαθὰ καθ' αὑτὰ (virtues) and πρὸς τί πως ἔχοντα (honour, benevolence, friendship) ; the goods which are necessary for happiness (virtues), and those which are not necessary (χαρὰ, ἐπιτηδεύματα). Seneca's list is far more limited, although it professes to be more general. He mentions, prima bona, tanquam gaudium, pax, salus patriæ ; secunda, in materia infelici expressa, tanquam tormentorum patientia ; tertia, tanquam modestus incessus.

be a good under any circumstances.[1] The same remarks apply to evil. That which is not in itself
an evil can never become so from its relation to
something else. Hence only that which is absolutely
good, or virtue, can be considered a good; and only
that which is absolutely bad, or a vice,[2] can be considered an evil. All other things, however great
their influence may be on our state, belong to a class
of things neither good nor evil, but indifferent, or
ἀδιάφορα.[3] Neither health, nor riches, nor honour,
not even life itself, is a good; and just as little are
the opposite states—poverty, sickness, disgrace, and
death—evils.[4] Both are in themselves indifferent,

---

[1] *Cic.* Fin. iii. 10, 33: Ego
assentior Diogeni, qui bonum
definiet id quod esset natura
absolutum [αὐτοτελὲς] . . . hoc
autem ipsum bonum non accessione neque crescendo aut cum
ceteris comparando sed propria
vi et sentimus et appellamus
bonum. Ut enim mel, etsi dul-
cissimum est, suo tamen pro-
prio genere saporis, non com-
paratione cum aliis, dulce esse
sentitur, sic bonum hoc de quo
agimus est illud quidem plurimi
æstimandum, sed ea æstimatio
genere valet non magnitudine,
&c.

[2] *Sen.* Benef. vii. 2, 1: Nec
malum esse ullum nisi turpe,
nec bonum nisi honestum.
Alex. Aph. De Fat. c. 28, p. 88:
ἡ μὲν ἀρετή τε καὶ ἡ κακία μόναι
κατ' αὐτοὺς ἡ μὲν ἀγαθὸν ἡ δὲ
κακόν. See p. 229; 233, 1.

[3] *Sext.* Math. xi. 61, after
giving two irrelevant definitions of ἀδιάφορον: κατὰ τρίτον

δὲ καὶ τελευταῖον τρόπον φασὶν
ἀδιάφορον τὸ μήτε πρὸς εὐδαιμονίαν
μήτε πρὸς κακοδαιμονίαν συλλαμ-
βανόμενον. To this category belong external goods, health,
&c. ᾧ γὰρ ἔστιν εὖ καὶ κακῶς
χρῆσθαι, τοῦτ' ἂν εἴη ἀδιάφορον·
διὰ παντὸς δ' ἀρετῇ μὲν κακῶς,
κακίᾳ δὲ κακῶς, ὑγιείᾳ δὲ καὶ τοῖς
περὶ σώματι ποτὲ μὲν εὖ ποτὲ δὲ
κακῶς ἔστι χρῆσθαι. Similarly,
Pyrrh. iii. 177, and *Diog.* 102,
who defines οὐδέτερα as ὅσα μήτ'
ὠφελεῖ μήτε βλάπτει. *Stob.* ii.
142: ἀδιάφορον = τὸ μήτε ἀγαθὸν
μήτε κακὸν, καὶ τὸ μήτε αἱρετὸν
μήτε φευκτόν. *Plut.* Sto. Rep.
31, 1: ᾧ γὰρ ἔστιν εὖ χρήσασθαι
καὶ κακῶς τοῦτό φασι μήτ' ἀγαθὸν
εἶναι μήτε κακόν.

[4] Zeno (in *Sen.* Ep. 82, 9)
proves this of death by a process of reasoning, the accuracy
of which he appears to have
mistrusted: Nullum malum
gloriosum est: mors autem
gloriosa est (there is a glorious

a material which may either be employed for good or else for evil.[1]

The Academicians and Peripatetics were most vigorously attacked by the Stoics for including among goods external things which are dependent on chance. For how can that be a good under any circumstances, which bears no relation to man's moral nature, and is even frequently obtained at the cost of morality?[2] If virtue renders a man happy,

death): ergo mors non est malum. In general, two considerations are prominent in the Stoic treatment of this subject: that what is according to nature cannot be an evil, and that life taken by itself is not a good. Other arguments, however, for diminishing the fear of death are not despised. See *Sen.* Ep 30, 4; 77, 11, 82, 8; Cons. ad Marc. 19, 3; *M. Aurel.* ix. 3; viii. 58. And other passages quoted in *Baumhauer's* Vet. Philosoph. Doctr. De Morte Voluntaria, p. 211.

[1] Chrysippus (in *Plut.* Sto. Rep. 15, 4): All virtue is done away with, ἂν ἢ τὴν ἡδονὴν ἢ τὴν ὑγίειαν ἤ τι τῶν ἄλλων, ὃ μὴ καλόν ἐστιν, ἀγαθὸν ἀπολίπωμεν. *Id.* (in *Plut.* C. Not. 5, 2): ἐν τῷ κατ᾽ ἀρετὴν βιοῦν μόνον ἐστὶ τὸ εὐδαιμόνως, τῶν ἄλλων οὐδὲν ὄντων πρὸς ἡμᾶς οὐδ᾽ εἰς τοῦτο συνεργούντων. Similarly, Sto. Rep. 17, 2. *Sen.* Vit. Be. 4, 3: The only good is honestas, the only evil turpitudo, cetera vilis turba rerum, nec detrahens quicquam beatæ vitæ nec adjiciens. *Id.* Ep. 66, 14: There is no difference between the wise man's joy and the firmness with which

he endures pains, quantum ad ipsas virtutes, plurimum inter illa, in quibus virtus utraque ostenditur . . . virtutem materia non mutat. Ep. 71, 21: Bona ista aut mala non efficit materia, sed virtus. Ep. 85, 39: Tu illum [sapientem] premi putas malis? Utitur. *Id.* Ep. 44; 120, 3; *Plut.* C. Not. 4, 1; Sto. Rep. 18, 5; 31, 1; Chrysippus, in Ps. *Plut.* De Nobil. 12, 2; *Diog.* 102; *Stob.* ii. 90; *Sext.* Pyrrh. iii. 181; *Alex. Aphr.* Top. 43 and 107.

[2] *Sext.* Math. xi. 61. See above, p. 232, 3. *Diog.* 103: The good can only do good, and never do harm; οὐ μᾶλλον δ᾽ ὠφελεῖ ἢ βλάπτει ὁ πλοῦτος καὶ ἡ ὑγίεια· οὐκ ἄρ᾽ ἀγαθὸν οὔτε πλοῦτος οὔθ᾽ ὑγίεια. Again: ᾧ ἔστιν εὖ καὶ κακῶς χρῆσθαι, τοῦτ᾽ οὐκ ἔστιν ἀγαθόν· πλούτῳ δὲ καὶ ὑγιείᾳ ἔστιν εὖ καὶ κακῶς χρῆσθαι, κ.τ.λ. In *Sen.* Ep. 87, 11, instead of the proposition, that nothing is a good except virtue, the following arguments are given as traditional among the Stoics (interrogationes nostrorum), apparently taken from Posidonius (see p. 31, 35, 38): (1) Quod bonum est, bonos

it must render him perfectly happy in himself, since no one can be happy who is not happy altogether. If, on the other hand, anything which is not in man's power were allowed an influence on his happiness, it would detract from the absolute worth of virtue, and man would never be able to attain to that imperturbable serenity of mind without which no happiness is conceivable.[1]

facit: fortuita bonum non faciunt: ergo non sunt bona. (Similarly in *M. Aurel.* ii. 11, iv. 8: Whatever does no moral harm, does no harm to human life.) (2) Quod contemptissimo cuique contingere ac turpissimo potest, bonum non est; opes autem et lenoni et lenistæ contingunt: ergo, &c. (So, too. *Marc. Aurelius,* v. 10.) (3) Bonum ex malo non fit: divitiæ fiunt, fiunt autem ex avaritia: ergo, &c. (Conf. *Alex. Aphr.* Top. 107: τὸ διὰ κακοῦ γιγνόμενον οὐκ ἔστιν ἀγαθόν· πλοῦτος δὲ καὶ διὰ πορνοβοσκίας κακοῦ ὄντος γίνεται, κ.τ.λ.) (4) Quod dum consequi volumus in multa mala incidimus, id bonum non est: dum divitias autem consequi volumus, in multa mala incidimus, &c. (5) Quæ neque magnitudinem animo dant nec fiduciam nec securitatem, contra autem insolentiam, tumorem, arrogantiam creant, mala sunt: a fortuitis autem (previously, not only riches but health had been included in this class) in hæc impellimur: ergo non sunt bona. That riches are not a good is proved by Diogenes (in *Cic.* Fin. iii. 15, 49); that poverty and pain are no evils is

proved by the argument, quoted in *Sen.* Ep. 85, 30: Quod malum est nocet: quod nocet deteriorem facit. Dolor et paupertas deteriorem non faciunt: ergo mala non sunt. The Stoic proposition is also established from a theological point of view. Nature, says *M. Aurel.* ii. 11, ix. 1, could never have allowed that good and evil should equally fall to the lot of the good and the bad; consequently, what both enjoy equally—life and death, honour and dishonour, pleasure and trouble, riches and poverty— can neither be good nor evil. On the value of fame, see *id.* iv. 19.

[1] This view is compared with the Academician in *Cic.* Tusc. v. 13, 39; 18, 51; *Sen.* Ep. 85, 18; 71, 18; 92, 14. In the last passage, the notion that happiness can be increased by external goods, and is consequently capable of degrees, is refuted by arguments such as, 4, 24: Quid potest desiderare is, cui omnia honesta contingunt? ... et quid stultius turpiusve, quam bonum rationalis animi ex irrationalibus nectere? ... non intenditur virtus, ergo ne beata quidem vita, quæ ex

Least of all, however, according to the Stoic view, can pleasure be considered a good, or be regarded, as by Epicurus, as the ultimate and highest object in life. He who places pleasure on the throne makes a slave of virtue;[1] he who considers pleasure a good ignores the real conception of the good and the peculiar value of virtue;[2] he appeals to feelings, rather than to actions;[3] he requires reasonable creatures to

---

virtute est. Conf. Ep. 72, 7: Cui aliquid accedere potest, id imperfectum est.

[1] Cleanthes expands this notion, in rhetorical language, in *Cic.* Fin. ii. 21, 69. Conf. *Sen.* Benef. iv. 2, 2: [Virtus] non est virtus si sequi potest. Primæ partes ejus sunt : ducere debet, imperare, summo loco stare : tu illam jubes signum petere. *Id.* Vit. Be. 11, 2; 13, 5; 14, 1.

[2] Compare on this subject, the words of Chrysippus on p. 233, 1, quoted by *Plut.* Sto. Rep. 15, and, for their explanation, *Sen.* Benef. iv. 2, 4: Non indignor, quod post voluptatem ponitur virtus, sed quod omnino cum voluptate conferatur contemptrix ejus et hostis et longissime ab illa resiliens. *Id.* Vit. Be. 15, 1: Pars honesti non potest esse nisi honestum, nec summum bonum habebit sinceritatem suam, si aliquid in se viderit dissimile meliori. According to *Plut.* 15, 3 ; 13, 3, Com. Not. 25, 2, this statement of Chrysippus is at variance with another statement of his, in which he says : If pleasure be declared to be a good, but not

the highest good, justice (the Peripatetic view) might perhaps still be safe, since, in comparison with pleasure, it may be regarded as the higher good. Still, this was only a preliminary and tentative concession, which Chrysippus subsequently proved could not be admitted, inasmuch as it was out of harmony with the true conception of the good, and changed the difference in kind (on which see p. 232, 1) between virtue and other things into a simple difference in degree. Plutarch (Sto. Rep. 15, 6), with more reason, blames Chrysippus for asserting against Aristotle that, if pleasure be regarded as the highest good, justice becomes impossible, but not other virtues ; for how could a Stoic, of all philosophers, make such a distinction between virtues ? Evidently the zeal of controversy has here carried away the philosopher beyond the point at which his own principles would bear him out.

[3] *M. Aurel.* vi. 15 : ὁ μὲν φιλόδοξος ἀλλοτρίαν ἐνέργειαν ἴδιον ἀγαθὸν ὑπολαμβάνει · ὁ δὲ φιλήδονος ἰδίαν πεῖσιν · ὁ δὲ νοῦν

pursue what is unreasonable, and souls nearly allied to God to go after the enjoyments of the lower animals.[1] Pleasure must never be the object of our pursuit, not even in the sense that true pleasure is invariably involved in virtue. That it no doubt is.[2] It is true that there is always a peculiar satisfaction, and a quiet cheerfulness and peace of mind, in moral conduct, just as in immoral conduct there is a lack of inward peace; and in this sense it may be said that the wise man alone knows what true and lasting pleasure is.[3] But even the pleasure afforded by moral excellence ought never to be an object, but only a natural consequence, of virtuous conduct; otherwise the independent value of virtue is impaired.[4]

ἔχων ἰδίαν πρᾶξιν. Conf. ix. 16 : οὐκ ἐν πείσει, ἀλλ᾽ ἐνεργείᾳ, τὸ τοῦ λογικοῦ πολιτικοῦ ζῴου κακὸν καὶ ἀγαθόν.

[1] Sen. Ep. 92, 6–10 ; Vit. Beat. 5, 4 ; 9, 4 ; Posidonius, in Sen. Ep. 92, 10.

[2] Taking the expression in its strict meaning, it is hardly allowed by the Stoics, when they speak accurately. Understanding by ἡδονή an emotion, i.e. something contrary to nature and blameworthy, they assert that the wise man feels delight (χαρὰ, gaudium), but not pleasure (ἡδονή, lætitia, voluptas). See Sen. Ep. 59, 2 ; Diog. 116 ; Alex. Aphr. Top. 96 ; the last-named giving definitions of χαρὰ, ἡδονὴ, τέρψις, εὐφροσύνη.

[3] Sen. Ep. 23, 2; 27, 3; 59, 2 ; 14 ; 72, 8 ; Vit. Be. 3, 4 ; 4, 4 ; De Ira, ii. 6, 2.

[4] Diog. 94 : Virtue is a good ; ἐπιγεννήματα δὲ τήν τε χαρὰν καὶ τὴν εὐφροσύνην καὶ τὰ παραπλήσια. Sen. Benef. iv. 2, 3 : It is a question utrum virtus summi boni causa sit, an ipsa summum bonum. Seneca, of course, says the latter. Conf. De Vit. Be. 4, 5 : The wise man takes pleasure in peace of mind and cheerfulness, non ut bonis, sed ut ex bono suo ortis. Ibid. 9, 1 : Non, si voluptatem præstatura virtus est, ideo propter hanc petitur . . . voluptas non est merces nec causa virtutis, sed accessio, nec quia delectat placet, sed si placet et delectat. The highest good consists only in mental perfection and health, in ipso judicio et habitu optimæ mentis, in the sanitas et libertas animi, which desires nothing but virtue ; ipsa pretium sui. Ibid. 15, 2 : Ne

Nor may pleasure be placed side by side with
virtue, as a part of the highest good, or be declared
to be inseparable from virtue. Pleasure and virtue
are different in essence and kind. Pleasure may be
immoral, and moral conduct may go hand in hand
with difficulties and pains. Pleasure is found among
the worst of men, virtue only amongst the good;
virtue is dignified, untiring, imperturbable; pleasure
is grovelling, effeminate, fleeting. Those who look
upon pleasure as a good are the slaves of pleasure;
those in whom virtue reigns supreme control pleasure, and hold it in check.[1] In no sense, therefore,
ought any weight to be allowed to pleasure in a
question of morals: pleasure is not an end in view,
but only the result of an action;[2] not a good, but
something absolutely indifferent. The only point on
which the Stoics are not unanimous is, whether every
pleasure is contrary to nature,[3] as the stern Cleanthes

gaudium quidem, quod ex virtute oritur, quamvis bonum sit,
absoluti tamen boni pars est,
non magis quam lætitia et
tranquillitas . . . sunt enim
ista bona, sed consequentia
summum bonum, non consum-
mantia. Here, too, belongs
the statement in *Stob.* ii. 184,
188 (conf. *M. Aurel.* vii. 74):
πάντα τὸν ὀντινοῦν ὠφελοῦντα
ἴσην ὠφέλειαν ἀπολαμβάνειν παρ'
αὐτὸ τοῦτο, for the reasons
stated, p. 230, 1.
  [1] *Sen.* Vit. Be. c. 7 and
10–12; *M. Aurel.* viii. 10.
Among the Stoic arguments
against identifying pleasure
and pain with good and evil,

may be placed the inference in
Clem. Strom. iv. 483, c, which
bears great similarity to the
third argument, quoted on
p. 233, 2 : If thirst be painful,
and it be pleasant to quench
thirst, thirst must be the cause
of this pleasure ; ἀγαθοῦ δὲ ποιητικὸν τὸ κακὸν οὐκ ἂν γένοιτο, κ.τ.λ.
  [2] *Diog.* 85 : ὃ δὲ λέγουσί
τινες, πρὸς ἡδονὴν γίγνεσθαι τὴν
πρώτην ὁρμὴν τοῖς ζῴοις, ψεῦδος
ἀποφαίνουσιν. ἐπιγέννημα γάρ
φασιν, εἰ ἄρα ἐστὶν, ἡδονὴν εἶναι,
ὅταν αὐτὴ καθ' αὑτὴν ἡ φύσις
ἐπιζητήσασα τὰ ἐναρμόζοντα τῇ
συστάσει ἀπολάβῃ.
  [3] Taking pleasure in its
widest sense. In its more re-

CHAP.
X.

asserted, in the spirit of Cynicism, or whether there is such a thing as a natural and desirable pleasure.[1] Virtue, on the other hand, needs no extraneous additions, but contains in itself all the conditions of happiness.[2] The reward of virtuous conduct, like the punishment of wickedness, consists only in the character of those actions, one being according to nature, the other contrary to nature.[3] And so unconditional is this self-sufficiency of virtue,[4] that the

stricted sense, they reject ἡδονή, understanding thereby a particular emotion. See p. 236, 2.

[1] *Sext.* Math. xi. 73 : τὴν ἡδονὴν ὁ μὲν Ἐπίκουρος ἀγαθὸν εἶναί φησιν· ὁ δὲ εἰπὼν 'μανείην μᾶλλον ἢ ἡσθείην' (Antisthenes) κακόν· οἱ δὲ ἀπὸ τῆς στοᾶς ἀδιάφορον καὶ οὐ προηγμένον. ἀλλὰ Κλεάνθης μὲν μήτε κατὰ φύσιν αὐτὴν εἶναι μήτε ἀξίαν ἔχειν αὐτὴν ἐν τῷ βίῳ, καθάπερ δὲ τὸ κάλλυντρον κατὰ φύσιν μὴ εἶναι· ὁ δὲ Ἀρχέδημος κατὰ φύσιν μὲν εἶναι ὡς τὰς ἐν μασχάλῃ τρίχας, οὐχὶ δὲ καὶ ἀξίαν ἔχειν. Παναίτιος δὲ τινὰ μὲν κατὰ φύσιν ὑπάρχειν τινὰ δὲ παρὰ φύσιν.

[2] Accordingly, it is also defined to be τέχνη εὐδαιμονίας ποιητική. *Alex. Aphr.* De An. 156, b.

[3] *Diog.* 89 : τήν τ' ἀρετὴν διάθεσιν εἶναι ὁμολογουμένην καὶ αὐτὴν δι' αὑτὴν εἶναι αἱρετήν, οὐ διά τινα φόβον ἢ ἐλπίδα ἤ τι τῶν ἔξωθεν· ἐν αὐτῇ τ' εἶναι τὴν εὐδαιμονίαν, ἅτ' οὔσῃ [-ης] ψύχῃ [-ης] πεποιημένῃ [-ης] πρὸς ὁμολογίαν παντὸς τοῦ βίου. *Sen.* De Clem. i. 1, 1: Quamvis enim recte factorum verus fructus sit fecisse, nec ullum virtutum pretium dignum illis extra ipsas sit. *Id.* Ep. 81, 19. Ep. 94, 19 : Æquitatem

per se expetendam nec metu nos ad illam cogi nec mercede conduci. Non esse justum cui quicquam in hac virtute placet praeter ipsam. *Id.* Ep. 87, 24 : Maximum scelerum supplicium in ipsis est. Benef. iv. 12 : Quid reddat beneficium ? dic tu mihi, quid reddat justitia, &c. ; si quicquam praeter ipsas, ipsas non expetis. *M. Aurel.* ix. 42 : τί γὰρ πλέον θέλεις εὖ ποιήσας ἄνθρωπον ; οὐκ ἀρκῇ τούτῳ, ὅτι κατὰ φύσιν τὴν σήν τι ἔπραξας, ἀλλὰ τούτου μισθὸν ζητεῖς ; When man does good, πεποίηκε πρὸς ὃ κατεσκεύασται καὶ ἔχει τὸ ἑαυτοῦ. *Id.* vii. 73 ; viii. 2. See pp. 230, 1 ; 236, 4.

[4] *Diog.* vii. 127 : αὐτάρκη εἶναι τὴν ἀρετὴν πρὸς εὐδαιμονίαν. *Cic.* Parad. 2; *Sen.* Ep. 74, 1 : Qui omne bonum honesto circumscripsit, intra se felix est. This αὐτάρκεια is even asserted of individual virtues, by virtue of the connection between them all. Of φρόνησις, for instance, in *Sen.* Ep. 85, 2, it is said : Qui prudens est, et temperans est. Qui temperans, est et constans. Qui constans est, imperturbatus est. Qui imperturbatus est, sine tristitia

happiness which it affords is not increased by length of time.[1] Rational self-control being here recognised as the only good, man makes himself thereby independent of all external circumstances, absolutely free, and inwardly satisfied.[2]

The happiness of the virtuous man—and this is a very distinctive feature of Stoicism—is thus far more negative than positive. It consists more in independence and peace of mind than in the enjoyment which moral conduct brings with it. In mental disquietude—says Cicero, speaking as a Stoic—consists misery; in composure, happiness. How can he be deficient in happiness, he enquires, whom courage preserves from care and fear, and self-control guards from passionate pleasure and desire?[3] How can he fail to be absolutely happy who is in no way dependent on fortune, but simply and solely on himself?[4] To be free from disquietude, says Seneca, is the

est. Qui sine tristitia est, beatus est. Ergo prudens est beatus, et prudentia ad vitam beatam satis est. Similarly in respect of bravery (*ibid.* 24). This αὐτάρκεια of virtue was naturally a chief point of attack for an opponent. It is assailed by *Alex. Aphr.* De An. 156, on the ground that neither the things which the Stoics declare to be natural and desirable (προηγμένα), nor, on the other hand, the natural conditions of virtuous action, can be without effect on happiness, and that it will not do to speak of the latter as only negative conditions (ὧν᾽οὐκ ἄνευ). See *Plut.* C. Not. 4, and 11, 1.

[1] *Plut.* Stô. Rep. 26; C. Not. 8, 4, where Chrysippus is charged with at one time denying that happiness is augmented by length of time, and at another declaring momentary wisdom and happiness to be worthless. *Cic.* Fin. iii. 14, 45; *Sen.* Ep. 74, 27; 93, 6; Benef. v. 17, 6; *M. Aurel.* xii. 35. The Stoics are, on this point, at variance with Aristotle.

[2] This view is frequently expressed by the Stoics of the Roman period, Seneca, Epictetus, and M. Aurelius. Proofs will be found subsequently.

[3] Tusc. v. 15, 43; 14, 42.

[4] Parad. 2.

peculiar privilege of the wise ; [1] the advantage which
is gained from philosophy is, that of living without
fear, and rising superior to the troubles of life.[2] Far
more emphatically, however, than by any isolated
expressions is this negative view of moral aims supported by the whole character of the Stoic ethics,
the one doctrine of the apathy of the wise man
sufficiently proving that freedom from disturbances,
an unconditional assurance, and self-dependence, are
the points on which these philosophers lay especial
value.

(5) *The
highest
good as
law.*

The Good, in as far as it is based on the general
arrangement of the world, to which the individual is
subordinate, appears to man in the character of *Law.*
This law being, however, the law of his own nature,
the Good becomes the natural object of man's desire,
and suits his natural impulse. The former view,
which was never unfamiliar to moral philosophy, was
cultivated by the Stoics with peculiar zeal ; [3] and
this view of morality forms one of the points on
which Stoicism subsequently came into contact, partly
with Roman jurisprudence, partly with the ethics of
the Jews and Christians. Moreover, as the Stoics
considered that the Reason which governs the world

[1] De Const. 13, 5 ; 75, 18 :
Expectant nos, si ex hac aliquando fæce in illud evadimus
sublime et excelsum, tranquillitas animi et expulsis
erroribus absoluta libertas.
Quæris, quæ sit ista? Non
homines timere, non Deos. Nec
turpia velle nec nimia. In se
ipsum habere maximam po-

testatem : inæstimabile bonum
est, suum fieri.
[2] Ep. 29, 12 : Quid ergo
. . . philosophia præstabit ?
Scilicet ut malis tibi placere,
quam populo, . . . ut sine metu
Deorum hominumque vivas, ut
aut vincas mala aut finias.
[3] See *Krische*, Forschungen,
368 and 475.

is the general Law of all beings,[1] so they recognised
in the moral demands of reason the positive and
negative aspects of the Law of God.[2] Human law
comes into existence when man becomes aware of
the divine law, and recognises its claims on him.[3]
Civil and moral law are, therefore, commands absolutely imperative on every rational being.[4] No man
can feel himself to be a rational being without at
the same time feeling himself pledged to be moral.[5]

---

[1] See p. 148, 2.

[2] νόμος, according to the
Stoic definition (*Stob.* Ecl. ii.
190, 204 ; Floril. 44, 12, and in
the fragment of Chrysippus
quoted by *Marcian* in Digest.
i. 3, 2, and the Scholiast of
Hermogenes in *Spengel*, Συναγ.
τεχν. 177,*Krische*, Forsch. 475)
= λόγος ὀρθὸς προστακτικὸς μὲν
τῶν ποιητέων, ἀπαγορευτικὸς δὲ τῶν
οὐ ποιητέων. It is therefore σπου-
δαῖόν τι or ἀστεῖον, something of
moral value, imposing duties
on man. The ultimate source
of this λόγος must be looked
for in the λόγος κοινὸς, the
divine or world reason. The
general law is, according to
Diog. vii. 88, who here (according to the passage quoted
from *Cic.* N. D. i. 15, 40 on p.
148, 2, is apparently following
Chrysippus) = ὁ ὀρθὸς λόγος διὰ
πάντων ἐρχόμενος, ὁ αὐτὸς ὢν τῷ
Διΐ. It is the ratio summa
insita in natura, quæ jubet ea
quæ facienda sunt, prohibetque
contraria (*Cic.* Legg. i. 6, 18,
conf. the quotation from *Cic.*
N. D. i. 14, 36, respecting Zeus
on p. 150). According to *Cic.*
Legg. ii. 4, 8 and 10, it is no

human creation sed æternum
quiddam, quod universum mundum regeret imperandi pro-
hibendique sapientia, the mens
omnia ratione aut cogentis aut
vetantis Dei, the ratio recta
summi Jovis (conf. Fin. iv. 5,
11, in the fragment in *Lact.*
Inst. vi. 8). It is, accordingly
as Chrysippus l. c. says in the
words of Pindar. (*Plato*, Georg.
484, B), πάντων βασιλεὺς θείων τε
καὶ ἀνθρωπίνων πραγμάτων.

[3] *Cic.* Leg. i. 6, 18 ; ii. 4,8 ;
5, 11.

[4] Or as *Stob.* ii. 184, expresses it, δίκαιον is φύσει καὶ μὴ
θέσει.

[5] This is proved by *Cic.*
Legg. i. 12, 33, in a chain-
argument clearly borrowed
from the Stoics : Quibus ratio
a natura data est, iisdem etiam
recta ratio data est. Ergo et
lex, quæ est recta ratio in
jubendo et vetando. Si lex,
jus quoque. At omnibus ratio.
Jus igitur datum est omnibus.
Upon this conception of law is
based the Stoic definition of
κατόρθωμα as εὐνόμημα, that of
ἁμάρτημα as ἀνόμημα.

Obedience, therefore, to this law is imposed upon man, not only by external authority, but by virtue of his own nature. The good is for him an object of pursuit—the natural object of man's will; on the other hand, evil is that against which his will revolts.[1] The former arouses his desire (ὁρμή), the latter his aversion (ἀφορμή):[2] and thus the demands of

[1] The good alone, or virtue, is αἱρετόν; evil is φευκτόν. See p. 229, 1; 238, 3, and Stob. Ecl. ii. 202. αἱρετὸν is, however, Ibid. 126, 132, ὃ αἵρεσιν εὔλογον κινεῖ, or, more accurately, τὸ ὁρμῆς αὐτοτελοῦς κινητικόν; and αἱρετὸν is accordingly distinguished from ληπτόν—αἱρετὸν being what is morally good, ληπτὸν being everything which has value, including external goods. The Stoics make a further distinction (according to Stob. ii. 140 and 194) with unnecessary subtlety between αἱρετὸν and αἱρετέον, and similarly between ὀρεκτὸν and ὀρεκτέον, ὑπομενετὸν and ὑπομενετέον, using the first form to express the good in itself (for instance, φρόνησις), the latter to express the possession of the good (for instance, φρονεῖν).

[2] ὁρμὴ is defined by Stob. ii. 160, as φορὰ ψυχῆς ἐπί τι; ἀφορμή, which is contrasted therewith in Epict. Enchirid. 2, 2 Diss. iii. 2, 2, 22, 36, as (according to the most probable correction of the text) φορὰ διανοίας ἀπό τινος. See p. 243, 3. A further distinction (connecting herewith what may be otherwise gathered from the statements of Stobæus respecting the Stoic doctrine of impulses) is made between the impulses of reasonable beings and beings devoid of reason. It is only in the case of reasonable beings that it can be said that impulse is called forth by the idea of a thing as something which has to be done (φαντασία ὁρμητικὴ τοῦ καθηκόντος); that every impulse contains an affirmative judgment in itself (συγκατάθεσις), to which has been superadded a κινητικόν; συγκατάθεσις applying to particular propositions (those in which truth and falsehood consist. See p. 110, 3; 83, 2), whereas ὁρμὴ applies to κατηγορήματα (i. e. activities expressed by verbs. See p. 95, 1 and 2), since every impulse and every desire aims at the possession of a good. Ὁρμὴ λογικὴ is defined to be φορὰ διανοίας ἐπί τι τῶν ἐν τῷ πράττειν, and is also called ὁρμὴ πρακτικὴ (only a rational being being capable of πρᾶξις). If the φορὰ διανοίας refers to something future, the ὁρμὴ becomes an ὄρεξις, for which the text twice reads ὅρουσις. Among the varieties of ὁρμὴ πρακτικὴ, Stob. enumerates πρόθεσις, ἐπιβολὴ, παρασκευὴ, ἐγχείρησις, αἵρεσις, πρόθεσις, βούλησις, θέλησις, the definitions of which he gives, passing then to the doctrine of

morality, besides arising from the natural impulse
of a reasonable being, are, at the same time, also
an object towards which his desires are naturally
directed.[1]

However simple this state of things may be to
a purely rational being, it must be remembered that
man is not purely rational.[2] He has, therefore, irrational as well as rational impulses.[3] He is not

CHAP.
X.

B. *Emo-
tions and
virtue.*
(1) *The
emotions.*
(a) *Their
nature.*

emotions, these being also a
kind of ὁρμή. It appears, therefore, that activities of feeling
and will are included in the
conception of the ὁρμή, as will be
subsequently seen more fully in
the doctrine of emotions, the
conception of which likewise
includes both.

[1] *Stob.* ii. 116, similarly
108 : πάντας γὰρ ἀνθρώπους
ἀφορμὰς ἔχειν ἐκ φύσεως πρὸς
ἀρετὴν καὶ οἰονεὶ τὸ [1. τὸν] τῶν
ἡμιαμβειαίων λόγον ἔχειν κατὰ τὸν
Κλεάνθην, ὅθεν ἀτελεῖς μὲν ὄντας
εἶναι φαύλους, τελειωθέντας δὲ
σπουδαίους. *Diog.* 89, see p. 238,
3 : The soul rests on the
harmony of life with itself
(virtue) ; extraneous influences
corrupt it, ἐπεὶ ἡ φύσις ἀφορμὰς
δίδωσιν ἀδιαστρόφους. *Sen.* Ep.
108, 8 : Facile est auditorem
concitare ad cupiditatem recti :
omnibus enim natura fundamenta dedit semenque vir-
tutis.

[2] The one point, according
to *Cic.* N. D. ii. 12, 34, which
distinguishes man from God
is, that God is absolutely
rational and by nature good
and wise.

[3] Chrysippus (in *Galen.* De
Hippocr. et Plat. iv. 2, vol. v.

368 Kühn) : τὸ λογικὸν ζῷον
ἀκολουθητικὸν φύσει ἐστὶ τῷ λόγῳ
καὶ κατὰ τὸν λόγον ὡς ἂν ἡγεμόνα
πρακτικόν · πολλάκις μέντοι καὶ
ἄλλως φέρεται ἐπί τινα καὶ ἀπό
τινων (for so we must punctuate,
the reference being to ὁρμὴ
and ἀφορμὴ, according to the
definition, p. 242, 2) ἀπειθῶς τῷ
λόγῳ, ὠθούμενον ἐπὶ πλεῖον, κ.τ.λ.
From this, it appears that
Chrysippus' definition of ὁρμὴ
(in *Plut.* Sto. Rep. 11, 6 = τοῦ
ἀνθρώπου λόγος προστακτικὸς
αὐτῷ τοῦ ποιεῖν) must not be
understood (as in *Baumhauer's*
Vet. Philos. Doct. De morte
voluntaria, p. 74) to imply
that man has only rational,
and no irrational impulses.
Chrysippus, in the passage
quoted, must either be referring
to that impulse which is peculiar to man, and is according
to his nature ; or else λόγος
must be taken in its more extended meaning of notion or
idea, for all impulses are based
on judgments, see p. 242, 2 ;
and it is clear, from *Cic.* Fin.
iii. 7, 23 ('as our limbs are
given to us for a definite purpose, so ὁρμὴ is given for some
definite object, and not for
every kind of use '), that ὁρμὴ

originally virtuous, but he becomes virtuous by
overcoming his emotions. Emotion or passion[1] is
a movement of mind contrary to reason and nature,
an impulse transgressing the right mean.[2] The
Peripatetic notion, that certain emotions are in accordance with nature, was stoutly denied by the
Stoics.[3] The seat of the emotions—and, indeed, of
all impulses and every activity of the soul[4]—is in
man's reason, the ἡγεμονικόν.[5] Emotion is that state
of the ἡγεμονικὸν in which it is hurried into what
is contrary to nature by excess of impulse Like
virtue, it is due to a change taking place simulta-

is not in itself rational, but
first becomes rational by the
direction given to it by man.

[1] The term emotion is used
to express πάθος, although the
terms of modern psychology
are more or less inadequate to
express the ancient ideas, as
Cic. Fin. iii. 10, 35, already
observed.

[2] *Diog.* vii. 110 : ἔστι δὲ αὐτὸ
τὸ πάθος κατὰ Ζήνωνα ἡ ἄλογος
καὶ παρὰ φύσιν ψυχῆς κίνησις ἢ
ὁρμὴ πλεονάζουσα. The same
definitions are found in *Stob.* ii.
36, 166, with this difference,
that ἀπειθὴς τῷ αἱροῦντι λόγῳ
stands in place of ἄλογος, as in
Marc. Aurel. ii. 5. *Cic.* Tusc.
iii. 11, 24 ; iv. 6, 11 ; 21, 47 ;
Chrysippus in *Galen.* De Hipp.
et Plat. iv. 2, 4 ; v. 2, 4, vol. v.
368, 385, 432, 458 Kühn., and
Id. in *Plut.* Virt. Mor. 10,
Schl. p. 450 ; *Sen.* Ep. 75, 12.
A similar definition is attributed to Aristotle by *Stob.* ii.
36, but it is no longer to be
found in his extant writings.

If it was in one of the lost
books (*Heeren* suggests in the
treatise περὶ παθῶν ὀργῆς *Diog.*
v. 23), was that book genuine ?

[3] *Cic.* Acad. i. 10, 39 : Cumque eas perturbationes [πάθη]
antiqui naturales esse dicerent
et rationis expertes aliaque in
parte animi cupiditatem, alia
rationem collocarent, ne his
quidem assentiebatur [Zeno].
Nam et perturbationes voluntarias esse putabat, opinion-
isque judicio suscipi, et omnium
perturbationum arbitrabatur
esse matrem immoderatam
quandam intemperantiam. Fin.
iii. 10, 35 : Nec vero perturbationes animorum . . . vi aliqua
naturali moventur. Tusc. iv.
28, 60 : Ipsas perturbationes
per se esse vitiosas nec habere
quidquam aut naturale aut ne-
cessarium.

[4] See p. 215, 3 ; 242, 2.

[5] Chrysippus, in *Galen.* iii.
7, p. 335 ; v. 1 and 6, p. 476
and above, p. 215, 3.

neously, not to the effect of a separate extraneous force.[1] Imagination, therefore, alone calls it into being, as it does impulse in general.[2] All emotions arise from a fault in judgment, from a false notion of good and evil, and may therefore be called in so many words, judgments or opinions;[3]—avarice, for instance, is a wrong opinion as to the value of money,[4] fear is a wrong opinion as regards future, trouble as regards present ills.[5] Still, as appears from the general view of the Stoics respecting impulses,[6] this language does not imply that emotion is only a theoretical condition. On the contrary, the effects of a faulty imagination—the feelings and motions of will, to which it gives rise—are expressly included in its

---

[1] *Plut.* Virt. Mor. 3, p. 441 (the first part of this passage has been already quoted, p. 215, 3, the continuation being) λέγεσθαι δὲ [τὸ ἡγεμονικὸν] ἄλογον, ὅταν τῷ πλεονάζοντι τῆς ὁρμῆς ἰσχυρῷ γενομένῳ καὶ κρατήσαντι πρός τι τῶν ἀτόπων παρὰ τὸν αἱροῦντα λόγον ἐκφέρηται· καὶ γὰρ τὸ πάθος, κ.τ.λ. See below, note 3.

[2] See p. 242, 2.

[3] *Diog.* vii. 111: δοκεῖ δ' αὐτοῖς τὰ πάθη κρίσεις εἶναι, καθά φησι Χρύσιππος ἐν τῷ περὶ παθῶν. *Plut.* Virt. Mor. c. 3, p. 441: τὸ πάθος εἶναι λόγον πονηρὸν καὶ ἀκόλαστον ἐκ φαύλης καὶ διημαρτημένης κρίσεως σφοδρότητα καὶ ῥώμην προσλαβόντα. *Stob.* ii. 168 : ἐπὶ πάντων δὲ τῶν τῆς ψυχῆς παθῶν ἐπὶ δόξας αὐτὰ λέγουσιν εἶναι [instead of which read πάντων . . . παθῶν δόξας αἰτίας

λέγ. εἶν.], παραλαμβάνεσθαι [add δὲ] τὴν δόξαν ἀντὶ τῆς ἀσθενοῦς ὑπολήψεως. Conf. *Cic.* Tusc. iv. 7, 14 : Sed omnes perturbationes judicio censent fieri et opinione . . . opinationem autem volunt esse imbecillam assensionem. *Id.* iii. 11, 24 : Est ergo causa omnis in opinione, nec vero ægritudinis solum sed etiam reliquarum omnium perturbationum? Fin. iii. 10, 35 : Perturbationes autem nulla naturæ vi commoventur ; omniaque ea sunt opiniones ac judicia levitatis. Acad. i. 10. See p. 244, 3.

[4] *Diog.* l. c.

[5] *Cic.* Tusc. iii. 11, 25 ; iv. 7, 14. Posidon. (in *Galen.* iv. 7, p. 416) : Chrysippus defined apprehension (ἄτη) as δόξα πρόσφατος κακοῦ παρουσίας.

[6] See p. 242, 1.

CHAP.
X.

conception;[1] nor is it credible, as Galenus states,[2] that this was only done by Zeno, and not by Chrysippus.[3] The Stoics, therefore, notwithstanding their

[1] *Cic.* Tusc. iv. 7, 15: Sed quæ judicia quasque opiniones perturbationum esse dixi, non in eis perturbationes solum positas esse dicunt, verum illa etiam, quæ efficiuntur perturbationibus, ut ægritudo quasi morsum quendam doloris efficiat: metus recessum quendam animi et fugam: lætitia profusam hilaritatem; libido effrenatam appetentiam. *Galen.* Hipp. et Plat. iv. 3, p. 377: (Ζήνωνι καὶ πολλοῖς ἄλλοις τῶν Στωϊκῶν) οἳ οὐ τὰς κρίσεις αὐτὰς τῆς ψυχῆς, ἀλλὰ καὶ [should perhaps be struck out], τὰς ἐπὶ ταύταις ἀλόγους συστολὰς καὶ ταπεινώσεις καὶ δείξεις [both for δείξεις, and for λήξεις in the passage about to be quoted from Plutarch, *Thurot.* Etudes sur Aristote, p. 249, suggests δέσεις · δήξεις is more probable, confirmed too by Cicero's morsus doloris] ἐπάρσεις τε καὶ διαχύσεις ὑπολαμβάνουσιν εἶναι τὰ τῆς ψυχῆς πάθη. *Plut.* Virt. Mor. 10, p. 449: τὰς ἐπιτάσεις τῶν παθῶν καὶ τὰς σφοδρότητας οὔ φασι γίνεσθαι κατὰ τὴν κρίσιν, ἐν ᾗ τὸ ἁμαρτητικόν, ἀλλὰ τὰς λήξεις [δήξεις] καὶ τὰς συστολὰς καὶ τὸ ἧττον τῷ ἀλόγῳ δεχομένας. The same results are involved in the definitions of emotion already given, p. 244, 2. In reference to this pathological action of representations, one kind of emotions was defined (*Stob.* ii. 170; *Cic.* Tusc. iv. 7, 14) as δόξα πρόσφατος, or opinio recens boni (or mali) præsentis,

πρόσφατον being κινητικὸν συστολῆς ἀλόγου ἢ ὑπάρσεως.
[2] De Hipp. et Plat. v. 1, p. 429: Χρύσιππος μὲν οὖν ἐν τῷ πρώτῳ περὶ παθῶν ἀποδεικνύναι πειρᾶται, κρίσεις τινὰς εἶναι τοῦ λογιστικοῦ τὰ πάθη, Ζήνων δ' οὐ τὰς κρίσεις αὐτὰς, ἀλλὰ τὰς ἐπιγιγνομένας αὐταῖς συστολὰς καὶ λύσεις, ἐπάρσεις τε καὶ τὰς πτώσεις τῆς ψυχῆς ἐνόμιζεν εἶναι τὰ πάθη. Conf. iv. 2, p. 367, and 3, p. 377.
[3] *Diog.* 111 (see above, p. 245, 3, and the definition quoted on p. 245, 5) confirms the view that, in the passage referred to by Galenus, Chrysippus explained the emotions to be κρίσεις. Elsewhere Galenus asserts (iv. 2, p. 367) that he called λύπη a μείωσις ἐπὶ φευκτῷ δοκοῦντι ; ἡδονὴ, an ἔπαρσις ἐφ' αἱρετῷ δοκοῦντι ὑπάρχειν ; and charges him (iv. 6, p. 403), quoting passages in support of the charge, with deducing emotions from ἀτονία and ἀσθένεια ψυχῆς. That Chrysippus agreed with Zeno in his definition of emotion, has already been stated (p. 244, 2). No doubt, too, with an eye to Chrysippus, Stobæus also (ii. 166) defines emotion as πτοία (violent mental motion), the words used being πᾶσαν πτοίαν πάθος εἶναι καὶ πάλιν πάθος πτοίαν ; and, in Galenus (iv. 5, p. 392), Chrysippus says : οἰκείως δὲ τῷ τῶν παθῶν ἀποδίδοται καὶ ἡ πτοία κατὰ τὸ ἐνσεβοβημένον τοῦτο καὶ φερόμεναν εἰκῆ. Chrys-

theory of necessity, did not originally assent to the
Socratic dictum, that no one does wrong voluntarily,[1]
although younger members of the School may have
used it as an excuse for human faults,[2] fearing lest,
in allowing the freedom of emotions, they·should
give up their moral inadmissibility and the possibility of overcoming them.[3] Nay more, as all that

ippus even repeatedly insists
on the difference between
emotion and error—error being
due to deficient knowledge,
emotion to opposition to the
claims of reason, to a disturbance of the natural relation
of the impulses (τὴν φυσικὴν
τῶν ὁρμῶν συμμετρίαν ὑπερβαίνειν).
He shows that both Zeno's definitions come to this (*Galen.*
iv. 2, p. 368 and iv. 4, p. 385 ;
Stob. ii. 170), and elsewhere
explains (*Plut.* Vir. Mor. 10,
p. 450) how emotion takes
away consideration, and im-
pels to irrational conduct. The
quotations on p. 246, 1 from
Cicero and Stobæus are an
explanation of positions of
Chrysippus, of which Chrysippus is himself the source. And
were he not directly the source,
Galenus (iv. 4, p. 390) observes
that the view of Chrysippus on
the emotions was generally held
in the Stoic School after his
time. In designating the emotions κρίσεις, Chrysippus cannot therefore have intended
thereby to exclude the emotions of impulse and feeling.
All that he meant was, that
emotions, as they arise in the
individual soul (we should say
as conditions of consciousness),
are called forth by imagina-

tion. This is clear from the
fact that the modes in which
the pathological character of
emotions displays itself are appealed to as evidence. See
his words in *Galen.* iv. 6,
p. 409, τῷ [1. τό] τε γὰρ θυμῷ
φέρεσθαι καὶ ἐξεστηκέναι καὶ οὐ
παρ' ἑπυτοῖς οὐδ' ἐν ἑαυτοῖς εἶναι
καὶ πάνθ' ὅσα τοιαῦτα φανερῶς
μαρτυρεῖ τῷ κρίσεις εἶναι τὰ πάθη
κἂν τῇ λογικῇ δυνάμει τῆς ψυχῆς
συνίστασθαι καθάπερ καὶ τὰ οὕτως
ἔχοντα. On the other hand,
Zeno never denied the influence
of imagination on emotion, as
is perfectly clear from the expression of Galenus, quoted
pp. 246, 2 ; 246, 1.

[1] *Stob.* Ecl. ii. 190 (Floril.
46, 50) : The wise man, according to the Stoic teaching, exercises no indulgence ; for indulgence would suppose τὸν ἡμαρ-
τηκότα μὴ παρ' αὑτὸν ἡμαρτηκέναι
πάντων ἁμαρτανόντων παρὰ τὴν
ἰδίαν κακίαν.

[2] *Epictet.* Diss. i. 18, 1-7 ;
28, 1-10 ; ii. 26 ; *M. Aurel.* ii.
1 ; iv. 3; viii. 14 ; xi. 18 ; xii. 12.

[3] This motive can be best
gathered from the passages in
Cicero already quoted, p. 244,
3, and from *Sen.* De Ira, ii. 2,
1 : Anger can do nothing by itself, but only animo adpro-
bante . . . nam si invitis nobis

proceeds from our will and impulse is by them declared to be voluntary,[1] so too emotions are also in
our power; and, as in the case of every other conviction,[2] so in the case of convictions out of which emotions arise, it is for us to say whether we will yield or
withhold assent.[3] Just as little would they allow
that only instruction is needed in order to overcome
emotions; for all emotions arise, as they say, from
lack of self-control,[4] and differ from errors in that they
assert themselves and oppose our better intelligence.[5]
How irregular and irrational impulses arise in reason
was a point which the Stoics never made any serious
attempt to explain.

nascitur, nunquam rationi suc-
cumbet. Omnes enim motus
qui non voluntate nostra fiunt
invicti et inevitabiles sunt,
&c.

[1] See p. 179, 3, 4.
[2] See p. 88, 1.
[3] *Cic.* Acad. i. 10, 39: Perturbationes voluntarias esse.
Tusc. iv. 7, 14: Emotions proceed from judgment; itaque
eas definiunt pressius, ut intel-
ligatur non modo quam vitiosæ,
sed etiam quam in nostra sunt
potestate, upon which follow
the definitions quoted, p. 246,
1.

[4] *Cic.* Tusc. iv. 9, 22: Omnium autem affectionum fon-
tem esse dicunt intemperantiam (ἀκράτεια) quæ est a tota
mente et a recta ratione de-
fectio sic aversa a præscriptione
rationis ut nullo modo adpeti-
tiones anima nec regi nec contineri queant.

[5] *Stob.* Ecl. ii. 170, probably

from Chrysippus, of whom similar remarks were quoted, p. 246,
3: πᾶν γὰρ πάθος βιάστικόν ἐστιν,
ὡς καὶ πολλάκις ὁρῶντας τοὺς ἐν
τοῖς πάθεσιν ὄντας ὅτι συμφέρει
τόδε οὐ ποιεῖν, ὑπὸ τῆς σφοδρότη-
τος ἐκφερομένους . . . ἀνάγεσθαι
πρὸς τὸ ποιεῖν αὐτὸ . . . πάντες
δ' οἱ ἐν τοῖς πάθεσιν ὄντες ἀπο-
στρέφονται τὸν λόγον, οὐ παραπλησίως δὲ τοῖς ἐξηπατημένοις ἐν
ὁτωοῦν, ἀλλ' ἰδιαζόντως. οἱ μὲν
γὰρ ἠπατημένοι . . . διδαχθέντες
. . . ἀφίστανται τῆς κρίσεως· οἱ
δ' ἐν τοῖς πάθεσιν ὄντες, κἂν μά-
θωσι κἂν μεταδιδαχθῶσιν, ὅτι οὐ
δεῖ λυπεῖσθαι ἢ φοβεῖσθαι ἢ ὅλως
ἐν τοῖς πάθεσιν εἶναι τῆς ψυχῆς,
ὅμως οὐκ ἀφίστανται τούτων ἀλλ'
ἄγονται ὑπὸ τῶν παθῶν εἰς τὸ ὑπὸ
τούτων κρατεῖσθαι τυραννίδος. A
different view is taken by
Epictet. Diss. i. 28, 8, who à
propos of Medea remarks: ἐξηπά-
τηται· δεῖξον αὐτῇ ἐναργῶς, ὅτι
ἐξηπάτηται, καὶ οὐ ποιήσει.

Emotions being called forth by imagination, their peculiar character depends on the kind of imagination which produces them. Now, all our impulses are directed to what is good and evil, and consist either in pursuing what appears to us to be a good, or in avoiding what appears to us to be an evil.[1] This good and this evil is sometimes a present, and sometimes a future object. Hence there result four chief classes of faulty imagination, and, corresponding with them, four classes of emotions. From an irrational opinion as to what is good there arises *pleasure*, when it refers to things present; *desire*, when it refers to things future. A faulty opinion of present evils produces *care*; of future evils, *fear*.[2] Zeno had already distinguished these four principal varieties of emotions.[3] The same division was adopted by his pupil Aristo,[4] and afterwards became quite general. Yet the vagueness, already mentioned, appears in the Stoic system in the definition of individual emotions. By some, particularly by Chrysippus, the essence of these emotions is placed in the imagination which causes them; by others, in the state of mind which the imagination produces.[5] The four principal

[1] See p. 242, 2. The same idea is expressed in applying the terms αἱρετὸν and φευκτὸν to good and evil (*Stob.* ii. 126 and 142; see p. 229, 1, and 232, 3).

[2] *Stob.* ii. 166; *Cic.* Tusc. iii. 11; iv. 7, 14; 15, 43; Fin. iii. 10, 35.

[3] According to *Diog.* 110, this distinction was found in the treatise περὶ παθῶν.

[4] In *Clem.* Strom. ii. 407, A, the words being πρὸς ὅλον τὸ τετράχορδον, ἡδονὴν, λύπην, φόβον, ἐπιθυμίαν, πολλῆς δεῖ τῆς ἀσκήσεως καὶ μάχης.

[5] The definition of λύπη or ἄση (Cicero ægritudo) as δόξα πρόσφατος κακοῦ παρουσίας is explicitly referred to Chrysippus (more at length in *Cic.* Tusc. iv. 7, 14: Opinio recens mali præsentis, in quo demitti con-

classes of emotions were again subdivided into numerous subordinate classes, in the enumeration of which
the Stoic philosophers appear to have been more
guided by the use of language than by psychology.[1]

In treating the subject of emotions in general,
far less importance was attached by the Stoics to
psychological accuracy than to considerations of
moral worth. That the result could not be very satis-

trahique animo rectum esse
videatur), as also the definition
of φιλαργυρία = ὑπόληψις τοῦ τὸ
ἀργύριον καλὸν εἶναι. See p. 254,
4, 5. In like manner μέθη, ἀκολασία, and the other passions,
were, according to *Diog.* 110,
defined. To Chrysippus also
belong the definitions—quoted
Tusc. iv. 7, 14 ; iii. 11, 25—of
ἡδονή (lætitia, voluptas ges-
tiens) = opinio recens boni præsentis, in quo efferri rectum
videatur ; of fear = opinio im-
pendentis mali quod intolera-
bile esse videatur, agreeing
with the προσδοκία κακοῦ of *Diog.*
112 ; of desire (cupiditas, libido,
ἐπιθυμία) = opinio venturi boni,
quod sit ex usu jam præsens
esse atque adesse. It is, however, more common to hear
λύπη (*Diog.* 111 ; *Stob.* 172 :
Cic. Tusc. iii. 11) described as
συστολὴ ψυχῆς ἀπειθὴς λόγῳ,
more briefly συστολὴ ἄλογος,
fear as ἔκκλισις ἀπειθὴς λόγῳ,
ἡδονή even according to *Alex.
Aphr.* top. 96, as ἄλογος ἔπαρσις
ἐφ᾽ αἱρέτῳ δοκοῦντι ὑπάρχειν, two
different translations of which
are given by *Cic.* l. c. and Fin.
ii. 4, 13, ἐπιθυμία as ὄρεξις ἀπειθὴς λόγῳ, or immoderata appe-
titio opinati magni boni. The

latter definitions appear to belong to Zeno. They were probably appropriated by Chrysippus, and the additions made
which are found in Stobæus.

[1] Further particulars may
be gathered from *Diog.* vii.
111 ; *Stob.* ii. 174. Both include under λύπη sub-divisions
as ἔλεος, φθόνος, ζῆλος, ζηλο-
τυπία, ἄχθος, ἀνία, ὀδύνη. Diogenes adds ἐνόχλησις and σύγχυσις ; Stobæus πένθος, ἄχος,
ἄση. Both include under φόβος,
δεῖμα, ὄκνος, αἰσχύνη, ἔκπληξις,
θόρυβος, ἀγωνία ; Stobæus adds
δέος and δεισιδαιμονία. Under
ἡδονή, Diogenes includes κή-
λησις, ἐπιχαιρεκακίαι, τέρψις, διά-
χυσις ; Stobæus, ἐπιχαιρεκακίαι,
ἀσμενισμοὶ, γοητεῖαι καὶ τὰ ὅμοια.
Under ἐπιθυμία, Diogenes places
σπάνις, μῖσος, φιλονεικία, ὀργὴ,
ἔρως, μῆνις, θυμός ; Stobæus,
ὀργὴ καὶ τὰ εἴδη αὐτῆς (θυμὸς,
χόλος, μῆνις, κότος, πικρία,
κ.τ.λ.), ἔρωτες σφοδροὶ, πόθοι,
ἵμεροι, φιληδονίαι, φιλοπλουτίαι,
φιλοδοξίαι. Definitions for all
these terms—which, without
doubt, belong to Chrysippus—
may be found in the writers
named. Greek lexicographers
may obtain many useful hints
from Stoic definitions.

factory, follows from what has been already stated.[1]
Emotions are impulses, overstepping natural limits,
upsetting the proper balance of the soul's powers,
contradicting reason—in a word, they are failures,
disturbances of mental health, and, if indulged in,
become chronic diseases of the soul.[2] Hence a Stoic

[1] *Plut.* Vir. Mor. 10, p. 449: πᾶν μὲν γὰρ πάθος ἁμαρτία κατ' αὐτούς ἐστιν καὶ πᾶς ὁ λυπούμενος ἢ φοβούμενος ἢ ἐπιθυμῶν ἁμαρτάνει. The Stoics are therefore anxious to make a marked distinction in the expressions for emotions and the permitted mental affections, between pleasure and joy, see p. 236, 2, fear and precaution (εὐλαβεία), desire and will (βούλησις, *Diog.* 116; cupere et velle, *Sen.* Ep. 116,1), αἰσχύνη and αἰδὼς (*Plut.* Vit. Pud. c. 2, p. 529).

[2] On this favourite proposition of the Stoics, consult *Diog.* 115; *Stob.* ii. 182; *Cic.* Tusc. iv. 10; whose remarkable agreement with Stobæus seems to point to a common source of information directly or indirectly drawn upon by both; iii. 10, 23; *Galen.* Hipp. et Plat. v. 2; *Sen.* Ep. 75,11. According to these passages, the Stoics distinguish between simple emotions and diseases of the soul. Emotions, in the language of Seneca, are motus animi improbabiles soluti et concitati. If they are frequently repeated and neglected, then inveterata vitia et dura, or diseases, ensue. Disease of the soul is therefore defined as δόξα ἐπιθυμίας ἐρρυηκυῖα εἰς ἕξιν καὶ ἐνεσκιρρωμένη καθ᾽ ἣν ὑπολαμ-

βάνουσι τὰ μὴ αἱρετὰ σφόδρα αἱρετὰ εἶναι (*Stob.* translations of the definition in Cicero and Seneca). The opposite of such a δόξα, or a confusion arising from false fear, is an opinio vehemens inhærens atque insita de re non fugienda tanquam fugienda—such as hatred of womankind, hatred of mankind, &c. If the fault is caused by some weakness which prevents our acting up to our better knowledge, the diseased states of the soul are called ἀῤῥωστήματα, egrotationes (*Diog.*; *Stob.*; *Cic.* Tus. iv. 13, 29); but this distinction is, of course, very uncertain. The same fault is at one time classed among νόσοι, at another among ἀῤῥωστήματα; and Cicero (11, 24; 13, 29) repeatedly observes that the two can only be distinguished in thought. Moreover, just as there are certain predispositions (ἐνεμπτωσίαι) for bodily diseases, so within the sphere of mind there are εὐκαταφορίαι εἰς πάθος. *Diog.*, *Stob.*, *Cic.* 12. The distinction between vitia and morbi (*Cic.* 13) naturally coincides with the distinction between emotions and diseases. The former are caused by conduct at variance with principles, by inconstantia et repugnantia, like-

demands their entire suppression: true virtue can only exist where this process has succeeded. As being contrary to nature and symptoms of disease, the wise man must be wholly free from them.[1] When we have once learnt to value things according to their real worth, and to discover everywhere nature's unchanging law, nothing will induce us to yield to emotion.[2] Hence the teaching of Plato and Aristotle, requiring emotions to be regulated, but not uprooted, was attacked in the most vigorous manner by these philosophers. A moderate evil, they say, always remains an evil. What is faulty and opposed to reason, ought never to be tolerated, not even in the smallest degree.[3] On the other hand, when

wise vitiositas in a habitus in tota vita inconstans; the latter consist in corruptio opinionum. It is not consistent with this view to call κακίαι, διαθέσεις; and νόσοι, as well as ἀρρωστήματα and εὐκαταφορίαι, ἕξεις (*Stob.* ii. 100, on the difference between ἕξις and διάθεσις. see 102, 1); and, accordingly, Heine suggests (De Font. Tuscul. Dis.: Weimar; 1863, p. 18) that, on this point, Cicero may have given inaccurate information. The unwise who are near wisdom are free from disease of the soul, but not from emotions (*Sen., Cic.*). The points of comparison between diseases of the body and those of the soul were investigated by Chrysippus with excessive care. Posidonius contradicted him, however, in part (*Galen*, l. c., *Cic.* 10, 23; 12, 27); but their differences are not of interest to us.

[1] *Cic.* Acad. i. 10, 38: Cumque perturbationem animi illi [superiores] ex homine non tollerent . . . sed eam contraherent in angustumque deducerent: hic omnibus his quasi morbis voluit carere sapientem. *Ibid.* ii. 43, 135. We shall find subsequently that the mental affections, which cause emotions, are allowed to be unavoidable.

[2] *Cic.* Tusc. iv. 17, 37.

[3] *Cic.* Tusc. iii. 10, 22: Omne enim malum, etiam mediocre, magnum est. Nos autem id agimus, ut id in sapiente nullum sit omnino. *Ibid.* iv. 17, 39: Modum tu adhibes vitio? An vitium nullum est non parere rationi? *Ibid.* 18, 42: Nihil interest, utrum moderatas perturbationes approbent, an moderatam injustitiam, &c. Qui enim vitiis modum apponit, is partem suscipit vitiorum.

an emotion is regulated by and subordinated to reason, it ceases to be an emotion, the term emotion
only applying to violent impulses, which are opposed
to reason.[1] The statement of the Peripatetics, that
certain emotions are not only admissible, but are
useful and necessary, appears of course to the Stoics
altogether wrong.[2] To them, only what is morally
good appears to be useful: emotions are, under all
circumstances, faults; and were an emotion to be
useful, virtue would be advanced by means of what
is wrong.[3] The right relation, therefore, towards
emotions—indeed, the only one morally tenable—is
an attitude of absolute hostility. The wise man
must be emotionless.[4] Pain he may feel, but, not
regarding it as an evil, he will suffer no affliction,
and know no fear.[5] He may be slandered and ill-
treated, but he cannot be injured or degraded.[6] Being

Sen. Ep. 85, 5, says that moderation of emotions is equivalent to modice insaniendum,
modice ægrotandum. Ep. 116,
1: Ego non video, quomodo
salubris esse aut utilis possit
ulla mediocritas morbi.

[1] *Sen.* De Ira, i. 9, 2; particularly with reference to
anger, conf. Ep. 85, 10.

[2] Full details are given by
Cic. Tusc. iv. 19–26; Off. i. 25,
88; *Sen.* De Ira, i. 5, 21; ii.
12; particularly with regard to
the use of anger.

[3] In the same spirit *Sen.* i.
9, 1; 10, 2, meets the assertion
that valour cannot dispense
with anger by saying: Nunquam virtus vitio adjuvanda
est se contenta . . . absit hoc

a virtute malum, ut unquam
ratio ad vitia confugiat.

[4] *Diog.* vii. 117: φασὶ δὲ καὶ
ἀπαθῆ εἶναι τὸν σόφον, διὰ τὸ
ἀνέμπτωτον (faultless) εἶναι.
From the apathy of the wise
man, absence of feeling and
severity, which are faults, must
be distinguished.

[5] Chrysippus (in *Stob.*
Floril. vii. 21): ἀλγεῖν μὲν τὸν
σόφον μὴ βασανίζεσθαι δέ· μὴ γὰρ
ἐνδιδόναι τῇ ψυχῇ. *Sen.* De Prov.
6, 6; Ep. 85, 29; *Cic.* Tusc. ii.
12, 29; 25, 61; iii. 11, 25.

[6] *Plut.* Sto. Rep. 20, 12;
Musonius (in *Stob.* Floril. 19,
16); *Sen.* De Const. 2; 3; 5; 7;
12. The second title of this treatise is: nec injuriam nec con-
tumeliam accipere sapientem.

untouched by honour and dishonour, he has no vanity.
To anger[1] he never yields, not needing this irrational
impulse, not even for valour and the championship
of right. But he also feels no pity,[2] and exercises
no indulgence.[3] For how can he pity others for
what he would not himself consider an evil? How
can he yield to a diseased excitement for the sake
of others, which he would not tolerate for his own
sake? If justice calls for punishment, feelings will
not betray him into forgiveness. We shall subsequently have an opportunity for learning the further
application of these principles.

(2) *Idea
of virtue.*
(a) *Posi-
tive and
negative
aspects.*

Virtue is thus negatively defined as the being
exempt from emotions, as apathy;[4] but there is also
a positive side supplementing this barely negative
view. Looking at the *matter* of virtuous action, this
may be said to consist in subordination to the general law of nature, looking at its *manner*, in rational
self-control.[5] Virtue is exclusively a matter of reason[6]—in short, it is nothing else, but rightly-ordered
reason.[7] To speak more explicitly, virtue contains

---

[1] See 253, 2 and 3 and *Cic.*
Tusc. iii. 9, 19.

[2] *Cic.* Tusc. iii. 9, 20; *Sen.*
De Clem. ii. 5; *Diog.* vii. 123.

[3] *Stob.* Ecl. ii. 190; Floril.
46, 50; *Sen.* l. c. 5, 2; 7; *Diog.*
l. c.; *Gell.* N. A. xiv. 4, 4.

[4] Ps. *Plut.* V. Hom. 134: οἱ
μὲν οὖν Στωϊκοὶ τὴν ἀρετὴν τίθενται ἐν τῇ ἀπαθείᾳ.

[5] See p. 193. *Alex. Aphr.*
De An. 156, b. Virtue consists
in ἐκλογὴ τῶν κατὰ φύσιν. *Diog.*
vii. 89 (conf. *Plut.* Aud. Po. c.

6, p. 24): τήν τ' ἀρετὴν διάθεσιν
εἶναι ὁμολογουμένην.

[6] *Cic.* Acad. i. 10, 38: Cumque superiores (Aristotle and
others) non omnem virtutem
in ratione esse dicerent, sed
quasdam virtutes natura aut
more perfectas: hic [Zeno]
omnes in ratione ponebat.

[7] *Cic.* Tusc. iv. 15, 34: Ipsa
virtus brevissime recta ratio
dici potest. Conf. *Sen.* Ep.
113, 2: Virtus autem nihil
aliud est quam animus quodam-

in itself two elements—one practical, the other speculative. At the root, and as a condition of all rational conduct, lies, according to the Stoics, right knowledge ; and on this point they are at one with the well-known Socratic doctrine, and with the teaching of the Cynics and Megarians. Natural virtue, or virtue acquired only by exercise, they reject altogether, defining virtue, after the manner of Socrates, as knowledge, vice as ignorance,[1] and insisting on the necessity of learning virtue.[2] Even the avowed enemy of all speculative enquiry, Aristo of Chios, was on this point at one with the rest of the School. All virtues were by him referred to wisdom,[3] and, consequently, he denied the claims of most to be virtues at all.[4]

But, however closely the Stoics cling to the idea that all virtue is based on knowledge, and is in itself nothing else but knowledge, they are not content with knowledge, or with placing knowledge above

modo se habens, and the remarks, p. 128, 1 ; 129, 3.

[1] The proof of this will be found subsequently in the Stoic definitions of various virtues and vices. Compare preliminarily 254, 6 and *Diog.* vii. 93 : εἶναι δ' ἀγνοίας τὰς κακίας, ὧν αἱ ἀρεταὶ ἐπιστῆμαι. *Stob.* Ecl. ii. 108 : ταύτας μὲν οὖν τὰς ῥηθείσας ἀρετὰς τελείας εἶναι λέγουσι περὶ τὸν βίον καὶ συνεστηκέναι ἐκ θεωρημάτων. It is not opposed to these statements for *Stob.* ii. 92 and 110, to distinguish other virtues besides those which are τέχναι and ἐπιστῆμαι; nor for Hecato in (*Diog.* vii. 90) to divide vir-

tues into ἐπιστημονικαὶ καὶ θεωρητικαὶ (σύστασιν ἔχουσαι τῶν θεωρημάτων) and ἀθεώρητοι; for by the latter must be understood not the virtuous actions themselves, but only the states resulting from them—health of soul, strength of will, and the like. On the health of the soul, in its relation to virtue, see *Cic.* Tusc. iv. 13, 30.

[2] *Diog.* vii. 91 (following Cleanthes, Chrysippus and others) ; Ps. *Plut.* V. Hom. 144.

[3] See p. 260, 3.

[4] *Plut.* Stu. Rep. 7 ; *Diog.* vii. 161 ; *Galen*, vii. 2, p. 595.

practical activity, as Plato and Aristotle had done.
As we have seen already that, with them, knowledge
was only a means towards rational conduct,[1] so it is
expressly mentioned, as a deviation from the teaching of the School, that Herillus of Carthage, Zeno's
pupil, declared knowledge to be the end of life,
and the only unconditional good.[2] Virtue may, it is
true, be called knowledge, but it is, at the same time,
essentially health and strength of mind, a right state
of the soul agreeing with its proper nature;[3] and it
is required of man that he should never desist from
labouring and contributing towards the common
good.[4] Thus, according to Stoic principles, virtue
is such a combination of theory and practice, in
which action is invariably based on intellectual
knowledge, but, at the same time, knowledge finds

---

[1] See p. 56.

[2] See p. 58, 2. *Diog.* vii.
165, conf. 37 : "Ηρίλλος δὲ ὁ
Καρχηδόνιος τέλος εἶπε τὴν ἐπιστήμην, ὅπερ ἐστὶ ζῆν ἀεὶ πάντα
ἀναφέροντα πρὸς τὸ μετ' ἐπιστήμης ζῆν καὶ μὴ τῇ ἀγνοίᾳ διαβε-
βλημένον. εἶναι δὲ τὴν ἐπιστήμην
ἕξιν ἐν φαντασιῶν προσδέξει ἀμετάπτωτον ὑπὸ λόγου. On the
definition, see p. 82, 1.

[3] Cleanthes (in *Plut.* Sto.
Rep. 7) : When τόνος, on which
see p. 128, 2, is found in the
soul in a proper degree, ἰσχὺς
καλεῖται καὶ κράτος · ἡ δ' ἰσχὺς
αὕτη καὶ τὸ κράτος ὅταν μὲν ἐπὶ
τοῖς ἐπιφανέσιν ἐμμενετέοις ἐγγένηται ἐγκράτειά ἐστι, κ.τ.λ. In
the same way, Chrysippus (according to *Galen*, Hipp. et Plat.
iv. 6, p. 403) deduced what is

good in our conduct from
εὐτονία and ἰσχύς ; what is bad,
from ἀτονία καὶ ἀσθένεια τῆς ψυχῆς ; and (*ibid.* vii. 1, p. 590)
he referred the differences of
individual virtues to changes
in quality within the soul. By
Aristo, p. 220, 1, virtue is defined as health ; by *Stob.* ii.
104, as διάθεσις ψυχῆς σύμφωνος
αὑτῇ ; by *Diog.* 89, as διάθεσις
ὁμολογουμένη.

[4] *Sen.* De Otio, i. (28) 4 :
Stoici nostri dicunt : usque ad
ultimum vitæ finem in actu
erimus, non desinemus communi bono operam dare, &c.
Nos sumus, apud quos usque eo
nihil ante mortem otiosum est,
ut, si res patitur, non sit ipsa
mors otiosa.

its object in moral conduct—it is, in short, power of will based on rational understanding.[1] Nor yet must this definition be taken to imply that moral knowledge precedes will, and is only subsequently referred to will, nor conversely that the will only uses knowledge as a subsidiary instrument. In the eyes of a Stoic, knowledge and will are not only inseparable, but they are one and the same thing. Virtue cannot be conceived without knowledge, nor knowledge without virtue.[2] The one, quite as much as the other, is a right quality of the soul, or, speaking more correctly, is the rightly-endowed soul,— reason, when it is as it ought to be.[3] Hence virtue may be described, with equal propriety, either as knowledge or as strength of mind ; and it is irrelevant to inquire which of these two elements is anterior in point of time.

But how are we to reconcile with this view the Stoic teaching of a plurality of virtues and their mutual relations ? As the common root from which they spring, Zeno, following Aristotle, regarded understanding, Cleanthes, strength of mind, Aristo, at one time health, at another the knowledge of good and evil.[4] Later teachers, after the time of Chry-

CHAP.
X.

(*b*) *The virtues severally.*

---

[1] This will appear from the definitions of virtue about to follow.

[2] See pp. 59, 1 ; 56, 2.

[3] See p. 254, 7. *Sen.* Ep. 65, 6, after describing a great and noble soul, adds : Talis animus virtus est.

[4] *Plut.* Vir. Mor. 2 : 'Αρίστων δὲ ὁ Χῖος τῇ μὲν οὐσίᾳ μίαν καὶ

αὐτὸς ἀρετὴν ἐποίει καὶ ὑγίειαν ὠνόμαζε, κ.τ.λ. *Id.* on Zeno, see p. 260, 3, and Cleanthes, p. 236, 3. According to Galenus, Aristo defined the one virtue to be the knowledge of good and evil (Hipp. et Plat. v. 5, p. 468) : κάλλιον οὖν 'Αρίστων ὁ Χῖος, οὔτε πολλὰς εἶναι τὰς ἀρετὰς τῆς ψυχῆς ἀποφηνάμενος, ἀλλὰ μίαν,

sippus, thought that it consisted in knowledge or
wisdom, understanding by wisdom absolute knowledge, the knowing all things, human and divine.[1]
From this common root, a multiplicity of virtues
was supposed to proceed, which, after Plato's example,
are grouped under four principal virtues[2]—intelli-

ἣν ἐπιστήμην ἀγαθῶν τε καὶ κακῶν
εἶναί φησιν. vii. 2, p. 595.
νομίσας γοῦν ὁ Ἀρίστων, μίαν
εἶναι τῆς ψυχῆς δύναμιν, ᾗ λογιζό-
μεθα, καὶ τὴν ἀρετὴν τῆς ψυχῆς
ἔθετο μίαν, ἐπιστήμην ἀγαθῶν καὶ
κακῶν. The statement that
Aristo made health of soul
consist in a right view of good
and evil agrees with the language of Plutarch. Perhaps
Zeno had already defined
φρόνησις as ἐπιστήμη ἀγαθῶν καὶ
κακῶν.
[1] Conf. p. 255, 1. Cic. De
Off. i. 43, 153 : Princepsque omnium virtutum est illa sapientia, quam σοφίαν Græci vocant:
prudentiam enim, quam Græci
φρόνησιν dicunt, aliam quandam
intelligimus : quæ est rerum
expetendarum fugiendarumque
scientia. Illa autem scientia,
quam principem dixi, rerum
est divinarum atque human-
arum scientia. A similar definition of wisdom, amplified
by the words, nosse divina et
humana et horum causas, is
found Ibid. ii. 2, 5. Sen. Ep.
85, 5; Plut. Plac. Procem. 2 ;
Strabo, i. 1, 1. It may probably be referred to Chrysippus ;
and it was no doubt Chrysippus who settled the distinction
between σοφία and φρόνησις, in
the Stoic school, although
Aristo had preceded him in
distinguishing them. Explain-

ing particular virtues as spring-
ing from the essence of virtue,
with the addition of a differen-
tial quality, he needed separate
terms to express generic and
specific virtue. In Zeno's definition too, as later writers
would have it (Plut. Vir. Mat.
2), to φρόνησις was given the
meaning of ἐπιστήμη.
[2] ἀρεταὶ πρῶται. Diog. 92 ;
Stob. ii. 104. In stating that
Posidonius counted four—
Cleanthes, Chrysippus, and Antipater more than four—virtues,
Diogenes can only mean that
the latter enumerated the
subdivisions, whereas Posidonius confined himself to the
four main heads of the four
cardinal virtues. Besides this
division of virtues, another,
threefold, division is also met
with, see p. 56, 2 ; 57, 1, that
into logical, physical, and
ethical virtues. In other words,
the whole of philosophy and
likewise its parts are brought
under the notion of virtue ;
but it is not stated how this
threefold division is to harmonise with the previous four-
fold one. A twofold division,
made by Panætius and referred
to by Seneca (Ep. 94, 45)—
that into theroretical and practical virtues—is an approximation to the ethics of the Peripatetics.

gence, bravery, justice, self-control.[1] Intelligence consists in knowing what is good and bad, and what is neither the one nor the other, the indifferent;[2] bravery, in knowing what to choose, what not to avoid, and what neither to choose nor to avoid; or, substituting the corresponding personal attitude for knowledge, bravery is fearless obedience to the law of reason, both in boldness and endurance.[3] Self-control consists in knowing what to choose, and what to eschew, and what neither to choose nor eschew;[4] justice, in knowing how to give to everyone what is his due.[5] In a corresponding manner, the principal

---

[1] The scheme was in vogue before Zeno's time. See *Plut.* Sto. Rep. 7, 1, and the quotations, p. 260, 3.

[2] ἐπιστήμη ἀγαθῶν καὶ κακῶν καὶ οὐδετέρων, or ἑκάστων ὧν ποιητέον καὶ οὐ ποιητέον καὶ οὐδετέρων. *Stob.* 102. Stobæus adds, that the definition needs to be completed by the words, occurring in the definition of every virtue, φύσει πολιτικοῦ ζῴου. But this is superfluous, for only in the case of such a being can the terms good and evil apply. *Diog.* 92; *Sext.* Math. xi. 170 and 246; *Cic.* l. c.

[3] ἐπιστήμη δεινῶν καὶ οὐ δεινῶν καὶ οὐδετέρων (*Stob.* 104); ἐπιστήμη ὧν αἱρετέον καὶ ὧν εὐλαβητέον καὶ οὐδετέρων (*Diog.*); ἐπιστήμη ὧν χρὴ θαρρεῖν ἢ μὴ θαρρεῖν (*Galen.* Hipp. et Plat. vii. 2, 597). *Cic.* Tusc. iv. 24, 53, conf. v. 14, 41: (Chrysippus) fortitudo est, inquit, scientia perferendarum rerum, vel affectio animi in patiendo ac perferendo, summæ legi parens

sine timore. The last-named characteristic appears still more strongly in the definition attributed to the Stoics by *Cic.* Off. i. 19, 62: Virtus propugnans pro æquitate.

[4] ἐπιστήμη αἱρετῶν καὶ φευκτῶν καὶ οὐδετέρων. *Stob.* 102. The definition of φρόνησις in Cicero is the same, word for word. See p. 258, 1; that of valour in Diogenes is not very different. Since all duties refer to ποιητέα and οὐ ποιητέα, the definitions of the remaining virtues must necessarily agree with those of φρόνησις.

[5] ἐπιστήμη ἀπονεμητικὴ τῆς ἀξίας ἑκάστῳ, in *Stob. Id.* p. 104, further enumerates the points of difference between the four virtues: intelligence refers to καθήκοντα, self-control to impulses, valour to ὑπομοναί, justice to ἀπονεμήσεις. See also the distinctive peculiarities of the four virtues in *Stob.* 112. Below, p. 263.

CHAP.
X.

faults are traced back to the conception of igno-rance.[1] Probably all these definitions belong to Chrysippus.[2] Other definitions are attributed to his predecessors,[3] some more, others less, agreeing with him in respect of their conception of virtue. Within these limits, a great number of individual virtues were distinguished, their differences and precise shades of meaning being worked out with all the pedantry which characterised Chrysippus.[4] The de-

[1] *Diog.* 93 ; *Stob.* 104. The πρῶται κακίαι are : ἀφροσύνη, δει-λία, ἀκολασία, ἀδικία. The de-finition of ἀφροσύνη is ἄγνοια ἀγαθῶν καὶ κακῶν καὶ οὐδετέρων. See p. 255, 1.

[2] This follows from the fact that the conception of ἐπιστήμη is the basis in all. See p. 258, 1.

[3] Of Zeno, *Plut.* Vir. Mor. 2, p. 441, says: ὁριζόμενος τὴν φρόνησιν ἐν μὲν ἀπονεμητέοις δι-καιοσύνην· ἐν δ' αἱρετέοις σωφρο-σύνην· ἐν δ' ὑπομενετέοις ἀνδρίαν. The like in regard to justice in Sto. Rep. 7, 2. On the other hand valour is here termed φρόνησις ἐν ἐνεργητέοις. He also says, p. 440, that, according to Aristo, ἡ ἀρετὴ ποιητέα μὲν ἐπι-σκοποῦσα καὶ μὴ ποιητέα κέκληται φρόνησις· ἐπιθυμίαν δὲ κοσμοῦσα καὶ τὸ μέτρων καὶ τὸ εὔκαιρον ἐν ἡδοναῖς ὁρίζουσα, σωφροσύνη· κοινωνήμασι δὲ καὶ συμβολαίοις ὁμιλοῦσα τοῖς πρὸς ἑτέρους, δι-καιοσύνη. Further particulars as to Aristo may be found in *Galen.* Hipp. et Plat. vii. 2, p. 595: Since the soul has only one power, the power of thought, it can only have one virtue, the ἐπιστήμη ἀγαθῶν καὶ κακῶν.

ὅταν μὲν οὖν αἱρεῖσθαί τε δέῃ τἀγαθὰ καὶ φεύγειν τὰ κακά, τὴν ἐπιστήμην τήνδε καλεῖ σωφροσύ-νην· ὅταν δὲ πράττειν μὲν τἀγαθά, μὴ πράττειν δὲ τὰ κακά, φρόνησιν· ἀνδρείαν δὲ ὅταν τὰ μὲν θαρρῇ, τὰ δὲ φεύγῃ· ὅταν δὲ τὸ κατ' ἀξίαν ἑκάστῳ νέμῃ, δικαιοσύνην· ἑνὶ δὲ λόγῳ, γινώσκουσα μὲν ἡ ψυχὴ χωρὶς τοῦ πράττειν τἀγαθά τε καὶ κακὰ σοφία τ' ἐστὶ καὶ ἐπιστήμη, πρὸς δὲ τὰς πράξεις ἀφικνουμένη τὰς κατὰ τὸν βίον ὀνόματα πλείω λαμβάνει τὰ προειρημένα. We know, from *Plut.* Sto. Rep. 7, 4, see p. 256, 3, that, according to Cleanthes, strength of mind, ὅταν μὲν ἐπὶ τοῖς ἐπιφανέσιν ἐμ-μενετέοις ἐγγένηται, ἐγκράτειά ἐστιν· ὅταν δ' ἐν τοῖς ὑπομενε-τέοις, ἀνδρεία· περὶ τὰς ἀξίας δὲ, δικαιοσύνη· περὶ τὰς αἱρέσεις καὶ ἐκκλίσεις, σωφροσύνη. With him, too, if Plutarch's account is ac-curate, ἐγκράτεια, or persever-ance, takes the place of φρόνησις. *Cic.* Tusc. iv. 24, 53, quotes no less than three definitions of bravery given by Sphærus. See p. 259, 3.

[4] *Plut.* Vir. Mor. 2, p. 441, charges him with creating a σμῆνος ἀρετῶν οὐ σύνηθες οὐδὲ γνώριμον, and forming a χαριεν-

finitions of a portion or them have been preserved by Diogenes and Stobæus.[1] In a similar way, too, the Stoics carried their classification of errors into the minutest details.[2]

The importance attaching to this division of virtues, the ultimate basis on which it rests, and the relation which they bear, both to one another and to the common essence of virtue, are topics upon which Zeno never entered. Plutarch, at least, blames him[3] for treating virtues as many, and yet inseparable, and at the same time for finding in all only certain manifestations of the understanding. Aristo attempted to settle this point more precisely. According to his view, virtue is in itself only one; in speaking of many virtues, we only refer to the variety of objects with which that one virtue has to

τότης, ἐσθλότης. μεγαλότης, καλό-της, ἐπιδεξιότης, εὐαπαντησία, εὐ-τραπελία, after the anology of πραότης, ἀνδρεία, &c. In *Stob.* ii. 118, among the Stoic virtues, is found an ἐρωτική as ἐπιστήμη νέων θήρας εὐφυῶν, &c., and a συμποτικὴ as ἐπιστήμη τοῦ πῶς δεῖ ἐξάγεσθαι τὰ συμπόσια καὶ τοῦ πῶς δεῖ συμπίνειν. An ἐρωτικὴ and συμποτικὴ ἀρετὴ are also mentioned by *Philodem.* De Mus. col. 15. According to *Athen.* 162, b (Vol. Herc. i.), Per-sæus, in his συμποτικοὶ διάλογοι, had discussed συμποτικὴ at length; and since, according to the Stoics (*Sen.* Ep. 123, 15: *Stob.* l. c.), none but the wise know how to live aright and how to drink aright, these arts belong to a complete treatment of wisdom.

[1] *Stob.* 106, includes under φρόνησις, εὐβουλία, εὐλογιστία, ἀγχίνοια, νουνέχεια, εὐμηχανία; under σωφροσύνη, εὐταξία, κοσ-μιότης, αἰδημοσύνη, ἐγκράτεια; under ἀνδρεία, καρτερία, θαρραλιό-της, μεγαλοψυχία, εὐψυχία, φιλο-πονία; under δικαιοσύνη, εὐσέ-βεια (on which *Diog.* 119), χρηστότης, εὐκοινωνησία, εὐσυν-αλλαξία. *Diog.* 126, is slightly different. Stobæus gives the definitions of all these virtues, and Diogenes of some. By Stobæus, they are generally described as ἐπιστῆμαι; by Dio-genes, as ἕξεις or διαθέσεις. Otherwise, the definitions are the same. A definition of εὐ-ταξία is given by *Cic.* Off. i. 40, 142.

[2] *Diog.* 93; *Stob.* 104.

[3] *Sto. Rep.* 7.

do.¹ The difference of one virtue from another is not one of inward quality, but depends on the external conditions under which they are manifested; it only expresses a definite relation to something else, or, as Herbart would say, an accidental aspect.² The same view would seem to be indicated by the manner in which Cleanthes determines the relations of the principal virtues to one another.³ It was, however, opposed by Chrysippus. The assumption of many virtues he believed rested upon an inward difference;⁴ each definite virtue, as also each definite fault, becoming what it does by a peculiar change in character of the soul itself;⁵ in short, for a particular virtue to come into being, it is not enough that the constituent element of all virtue should be directed towards a particular object, but

¹ Plut. Vir. Mor. 2 : 'Αρίστων δὲ ὁ Χῖος τῇ μὲν οὐσίᾳ μίαν καὶ αὐτὸς ἀρετὴν ἐποίει καὶ ὑγίειαν ὠνόμαζε· τῷ δὲ πρός τι διαφόρους καὶ πλείονας, ὡς εἴ τις ἐθέλοι τὴν ὅρασιν ἡμῶν λευκῶν μὲν ἀντιλαμβανομένην λευκοθέαν καλεῖν, μελάνων δὲ μελανθέαν ἤ τι τοιοῦτον ἕτερον. καὶ γὰρ ἡ ἀρετὴ, κ.τ.λ. See p. 260, 3. καθάπερ τὸ μαχαίριον ἕν μέν ἐστιν, ἄλλοτε δὲ ἄλλο διαιρεῖ· καὶ τὸ πῦρ ἐνεργεῖ περὶ ὕλας διαφόρους μιᾷ φύσει χρώμενον.
² Galen. Hipp. et Plat. vii. 1, p. 590 : νομίζει γὰρ ὁ ἀνὴρ ἐκεῖνος, μίαν οὖσαν τὴν ἀρετὴν ὀνόμασι πλείοσιν ὀνομάζεσθαι κατὰ τὴν πρός τι σχέσιν. Conf. note 5 and Diog. vii. 161 : ἀρετάς τ' οὔτε πολλὰς εἰσῆγεν, ὡς ὁ Ζήνων, οὔτε μίαν πολλοῖς ὀνόμασι καλου-

μένην, ὡς οἱ Μεγαρικοὶ, ἀλλὰ καὶ [l. κατὰ] τὸ πρός τί πως ἔχειν (scil. πολλοῖς ὀνόμασι καλουμένην).
³ See p. 260, 3.
⁴ Their distinguishing features fall under the category of ποιὸν, to use Stoic terms, not under that of πρός τί πως ἔχον, as Aristo maintained.
⁵ Galenus l. c. continues: ὁ τοίνυν Χρύσιππος δείκνυσιν, οὐκ ἐν τῇ πρός τι σχέσει γενόμενον τὸ πλῆθος τῶν ἀρετῶν τε καὶ κακιῶν, ἀλλ' ἐν ταῖς οἰκείαις οὐσίαις ὑπαλλαττομέναις κατὰ τὰς ποιότητας. Plut. Sto. Rep. 7, 3 : Χρύσιππος, 'Αρίστωνι μὲν ἐγκαλῶν, ὅτι μιᾶς ἀρετῆς σχέσεις ἔλεγε τὰς ἄλλας εἶναι. Id. Vir. Mor. 2 : Χρύσιππος δὲ κατὰ τὸ ποιὸν ἀρετὴν ἰδίᾳ ποιότητι συνίστασθαι νομίζων.

to the common element must be superadded a further characteristic element, or differentia; the several
virtues being related to one another, as the various
species of one genus.

All virtues have, however, one and the same end,
which they compass in different ways, and all presuppose the same moral tone and conviction,[1] which is
only to be found where it is to be found perfect, and
ceases to exist the moment it is deprived of one of its
component parts.[2] They are, indeed, distinct from one
another, each one having its own end, towards which it
is primarily directed; but, at the same time, they again
coalesce, inasmuch as none can pursue its own end without pursuing that of the others at the same time.[3] Ac-

[1] *Stob.* ii. 110: πάσας δὲ τὰς
ἀρετὰς, ὅσαι ἐπιστῆμαί εἰσι καὶ
τέχναι (compare on this additions p. 255, 1) κοινά τε θεωρήματα ἔχειν καὶ τέλος, ὡς εἴρηται
(p. 108—the same is more fully
given by Panetius, p. 112), τὸ
αὐτὸ, διὸ καὶ ἀχωρίστους εἶναι·
τὸν γὰρ μίαν ἔχοντα πάσας ἔχειν,
καὶ τὸν κατὰ μίαν πράττοντα κατὰ
πάσας πράττειν. *Diog.* 125: τὰς
δ' ἀρετὰς λέγουσιν ἀντακολουθεῖν
ἀλλήλαις καὶ τὸν μίαν ἔχοντα
πάσας ἔχειν· εἶναι γὰρ αὐτῶν τὰ
θεωρήματα κοινά, as Chrysippus,
Apollodorus, and Hecato assert.
τὸν γὰρ ἐνάρετον θεωρητικόν τ'
εἶναι καὶ πρακτικὸν τῶν ποιητέων.
τὰ δὲ ποιητέα καὶ αἱρετέα ἐστὶ
καὶ ὑπομενητέα καὶ ἀπονεμητέα,
knowledge and action including
all the four principal instincts.
[2] *Cic.* Parad. 3, 1 : Una virtus est, consentiens cum ratione
et perpetua constantia. Nihil
huic addi potest, quo magis

virtus sit; nihil demi, ut virtus
nomen relinquatur. Conf. *Sen.*
Ep. 66, 9. See p. 267.
[3] *Stob.* 112 (conf. *Diog.* 126):
διαφέρειν δ' ἀλλήλων τοῖς κεφα-
λαίοις. φρονήσεως γὰρ εἶναι κε-
φάλαια τὸ μὲν θεωρεῖν καὶ πράττειν
ὃ ποιητέον προηγουμένως, κατὰ δὲ
τὸν δεύτερον λόγον τὸ θεωρεῖν καὶ
ἃ δεῖ ἀπονέμειν, χάριν τοῦ ἀδιαπτώτως πράττειν ὃ ποιητέον· τῆς
δὲ σωφροσύνης ἴδιον κεφάλαιόν
ἐστι τὸ παρέχεσθαι τὰς ὁρμὰς εὐ-
σταθεῖς καὶ θεωρεῖν αὐτὰς προηγουμένως, κατὰ δὲ τὸν δεύτερον λόγον
τὰ ὑπὸ τὰς ἄλλας ἀρετὰς, ἕνεκα
τοῦ ἀδιαπτώτως ἐν ταῖς ὁρμαῖς ἀνα-
στρέφεσθαι. Similarly of bravery, which has for its basis
πᾶν ὃ δεῖ ὑπομένειν; and of justice, which has τὸ κατ' ἀξίαν
ἑκάστῳ. *Plut.* Alex. Virt. 11 :
The Stoics teach that μία μὲν
ἀρετὴ πρωταγωνιστεῖ πράξεως
ἑκάστης, παρακαλεῖ δὲ τὰς ἄλλας
καὶ συντείνει πρὸς τὸ τέλος.

cordingly, no part of virtue can be separated from its other parts. Where one virtue exists, the rest are also to be found, and where there is one fault, there all is faulty. Even each single virtuous action contains all other virtues, the moral tone of which it comes including in itself all the rest.[1] What makes virtue virtue, and vice vice, is simply and solely the intention.[2] The will, although it may lack the means of execution, is worth quite as much as the deed;[3] a wicked desire is quite as criminal as the gratification of that desire.[4] Hence only that action can be called virtuous which is not only good in itself, but which proceeds from willing the good; and although, in the

---

[1] *Stob.* 116 : φασὶ δὲ καὶ πάντα ποιεῖν τὸν σόφον κατὰ πάσας τὰς ἀρετάς· πᾶσαν γὰρ πρᾶξιν τελείαν αὐτοῦ εἶναι. *Plut.* Sto. Rep. 27, 1, conf. *Alex.* Virt. l. c.: τὰς ἀρετάς φησι [Χρύσιππος] ἀντακολουθεῖν ἀλλήλαις, οὐ μόνον τῷ τὸν μίαν ἔχοντα πάσας ἔχειν, ἀλλὰ καὶ τῷ τὸν κατὰ μίαν ὁτιοῦν ἐνεργοῦντα κατὰ πάσας ἐνεργεῖν· οὔτ᾽ ἄνδρα φησὶ τέλειον εἶναι τὸν μὴ πάσας ἔχοντα τὰς ἀρετὰς, οὔτε πρᾶξιν τελείαν, ἥτις οὐ κατὰ πάσας πράττεται τὰς ἀρετάς. If Chrysippus allowed, as Plutarch states, that the brave man does not always act bravely, nor the bad man always like a coward, it was a confession to which he was driven by experience, contrary to Stoic principles.

[2] *Cic.* Acad. i. 10, 38 : Nec virtutis usum modo [Zeno dicebat] ut superiores (whom the Stoic evidently wrongs), sed ipsum habitum per se esse præclarum. *Id.* Parad. 3, 1 : Nec enim peccata rerum eventu sed

vitiis hominum metienda sunt. *Sen.* Benef. vi. 11, 3 : Voluntas est, quæ apud nos ponit officium, which Cleanthes then proceeds to illustrate by a parable of two slaves, one of whom diligently seeks for the man whom he is sent to find but without success, whilst the other taking it easy accidently comes across him. *Ibid.* i. 5, 2 : A benefaction is only ipsa tribuentis voluntas. 6, 1 : Non quid fiat aut quid detur refert, sed qua mente.

[3] Compare also the paradoxical statement—Qui libenter beneficium accepit, reddidit—which *Sen.* l. c. ii. 31, 1, justifies by saying : Cum omnia ad animum referamus, fecit quisque quantum voluit.

[4] Cleanthes, in *Stob.* Floril. 6, 19:
ὅστις ἐπιθυμῶν ἀνέχετ᾽ αἰσχροῦ πράγματος
οὗτος ποιήσει τοῦτ᾽ ἐὰν καιρὸν λάβῃ.

first instance, the difference between the discharge and the neglect of duty (κατόρθωμα and ἁμάρτημι) depends on the real agreement or disagreement of our actions with the moral law,[1] yet that alone can be said to be a true and perfect discharge of duty which arises from a morally perfect character.[2]

[1] On the notions of κατόρθωμα and ἁμάρτημα, see *Plut.* Sto. Rep. 11, 1: τὸ κατόρθωμά φασι νόμου προστάγμα εἶναι, τὸ δ᾽ ἁμάρτημα νόμου ἀπαγόρευμα. To a bad man, law only gives prohibitions, and not commands: οὐ γὰρ δύναται κατορθοῦν. Chrysippus, *Ibid.* 15, 10 : πᾶν κατόρθωμα καὶ εὐνόμημα καὶ δικαιοπράγημά ἐστι. *Stob.* ii. 192: ἔτι δὲ τῶν ἐνεργημάτων φασὶ τὰ μὲν εἶναι κατορθώματα, τὰ δ᾽ ἁμαρτήματα, τὰ δ᾽ οὐδέτερα (examples of the latter are speaking, giving, &c.) . . . πάντα δὲ τὰ κατορθώματα δικαιοπραγήματα εἶναι καὶ εὐνοήματα καὶ εὐτακτήματα, κ.τ.λ. τὰ δὲ ἁμαρτήματα ἐκ τῶν ἀντικειμένων ἀδικήματα καὶ ἀνομήματα καὶ ἀτακτήματα.

[2] It is to this view that the distinction between κατόρθωμα and καθῆκον refers from the one side. A καθῆκον (the conceptions of which will be subsequently more fully discussed) is, in general, any discharge of duty, or rational action; κατόρθωμα only refers to a perfect discharge of duty, or to a virtuous course of conduct. Conf. *Stob.* 158 : τῶν δὲ καθηκόντων τὰ μὲν εἶναί φασι τέλεια, ἃ δὴ καὶ κατορθώματα λέγεσθαι. κατορθώματα δ᾽ εἶναι τὰ κατ᾽ ἀρετὴν ἐνεργήματα . . . τὸ δὲ καθῆκον τελειωθὲν κατόρθωμα γίνεσθαι. Similarly, 184: A κατόρθωμα is a καθῆκον πάντας ἐπέχον τοὺς ἀριθμούς. *Cic.* Fin. iii. 18, 59 : Quoniam enim videmus esse quiddam, quod recte factum appellemus, id autem est perfectum officium ; erit autem etiam inchoatum ; ut, si juste depositum reddere in rec e factis sit, in officiis (καθήκοντα) ponatur depositum reddere. Off. i. 3, 8: Et medium quoddam officium dicitur et perfectum ; the former is called κατόρθωμα, the latter καθῆκον. A virtuous action can only be done by one who has a virtuous intention, i.e. by a wise man. *Cic.* Fin. iv. 6, 15 : If we understand by a life according to nature, what is rational, rectum est, quod κατόρθωμα dicebas, contingitque sapienti soli. Off. iii. 3, 14 : Illud autem officium, quod rectum idem [Stoici] appellant, perfectum atque absolutum est, et, ut iidem dicunt, omnes numeros habet, nec præter sapientem, cadere in quenquam potest. Off. iii. 4, 16 : When the Decii and Scipios are called brave, Fabricius and Aristides just, Cato and Lælius wise, the wisdom and virtue of the wise man are not attributed to them in the strict sense of the term : sed ex mediorum officiorum frequentia similitudinem quandam gerebant speciemque sapientum.

Such a character, the Stoics held, must either exist altogether, or not at all; for virtue is an indivisible whole, which we cannot possess in part, but must either have or not have.[1] He who has a right intention, and a right appreciation of good and evil, is virtuous; he who has not these requisites is lacking in virtue; there is no third alternative. Virtue admits neither of increase nor diminution,[2] and there is no mean between virtue and vice.[3] This being

---

[1] See p. 263, 2.

[2] In *Simpl.* Categ. 61, β (Schol. in Arist. 70, b, 28), the Stoics say: τὰς μὲν ἕξεις ἐπιτείνεσθαι δύνασθαι καὶ ἀνίεσθαι· τὰς δὲ διαθέσεις ἀνεπιτάτους εἶναι καὶ ἀνέτους. Thus straightness is, for instance, a διάθεσις, and no mere ἕξις. οὑτωσὶ δὲ καὶ τὰς ἀρετὰς διαθέσεις εἶναι, οὐ κατὰ τὸ μόνιμον ἰδίωμα, ἀλλὰ κατὰ τὸ ἀνεπίτατον καὶ ἀνεπίδεκτον τοῦ μᾶλλον· τὰς δὲ τέχνας, ἤτοι δυσκινήτους οὔσας ἢ μὴ (add οὐκ) εἶναι διαθέσεις. Conf. p. 103, 1. *Ibid.* 72, δ (Schol. 76, a, 12): τῶν Στωϊκῶν, οἵτινες διελόμενοι χωρὶς τὰς ἀρετὰς ἀπὸ τῶν μέσων τεχνῶν ταύτας οὔτε ἐπιτείνεσθαι λέγουσιν οὔτε ἀνίεσθαι, τὰς δὲ μέσας τέχνας καὶ ἐπίτασιν καὶ ἄνεσιν δέχεσθαι φασίν. Simpl. (73, a. Schol. 76, a, 24) replies: This would be true, if virtue consisted only in theoretical conviction: such a conviction must be either true or false, and does not admit of more or less truth (for the same line of argument, see p. 267, 1); but it is otherwise where it is a matter for exercise. It may be remarked, in passing, that a further distinction was made between ἀρετὴ and τέχνη—the one being preceded by an ἀξιόλογος προκοπὴ, the other by a simple ἐπιτηδειότης (*Simpl.* Categ. 62, β; Schol. 71, a, 38). There is also a definition of τέχνη attributed by Olympiodorus, in Gorg. 53 (Jahrb. für. Philol. See Supplementb. xiv. 239), to Zeno, Cleanthes, and Chrysippus; to Zeno in *Sext.* Pyrrh. iii. 241; Math. vii. 109 and 373; more fully in *Lucian*, Paras. c. 4, Conf. *Cic.* Acad. ii. 7, 22.

[3] *Diog.* vii. 127: ἀρέσκει δὲ αὐτοῖς μηδὲν μέσον εἶναι ἀρετῆς καὶ κακίας· τῶν Περιπατητικῶν μεταξὺ ἀρετῆς καὶ κακίας εἶναι λεγόντων τὴν προκοπήν· ὡς γὰρ δεῖν, φασιν, ἢ ὀρθὸν εἶναι ξύλον ἢ στρεβλὸν, οὕτως ἢ δίκαιον ἢ ἄδικον· οὔτε δὲ δικαιότερον οὔτε ἀδικώτερον, καὶ ἐπὶ τῶν ἄλλων ὁμοίως. Similarly, *Sen.* Ep. 71, 18: Quod summum bonum est supra se gradum non habet . . . hoc nec remitti nec intendi posse, non magis, quam regulam, qua rectum probari solet, flectes. Quicquid ex illa mutaveris injuria est recti. *Stob.* ii. 116: ἀρετῆς δὲ καὶ κακίας οὐδὲν εἶναι μεταξύ.

the case, and the value of an action depending wholly on the intention, it follows, necessarily, that virtue admits of no degrees. If the intention must be either good or bad, the same must be true of actions; and if a good intention or virtue has in it nothing bad, and a bad intention has in it nothing good, the same is true of actions. A good action is unconditionally praiseworthy; a bad one, unconditionally blameworthy, the former being only found where virtue exists pure and entire; the latter, only where there is no virtue at all. All good actions are, on the one hand, according to the well-known paradox, equally good; all bad actions, on the other, of equal moral worth. The standard of moral judgment is an absolute one; and when conduct does not altogether conform to this standard, it falls short of it altogether.[1]

[1] The much-discussed paradox (*Cic.* Parad. 3; Fin. iv. 27; *Diog.* 101 and 120; *Stob.* 218; *Plut.* Sto. Rep. 13, 1; *Sext.* Math. vii. 422; *Sen.* Ep. 66, 5) is this: ὅτι ἴσα τὰ ἁμαρτήματα καὶ τὰ κατορθώματα. It was, according to *Diog.*, supported, on the one hand, by the proposition, πᾶν ἀγαθὸν ἐπ' ἄκρον εἶναι αἱρετὸν καὶ μήτε ἄνεσιν μήτε ἐπίτασιν δέχεσθαι; on the other hand, by the remark, to which *Sext.* and *Simpl.* in Categ., Schol. in Arist. 76, a, 30, refer: If truth and falsehood admit of no difference of degree, the same must be true of the errors of our conduct. A man is not at the mark, no matter whether he is one or a hundred stadia away. Similarly, Stobæus: The Stoics declare all errors to be ἴσα, although not ὅμοια· πᾶν γὰρ τὸ ψεῦδος ἐπίσης ψεῦδος συμβέβηκεν· (a statement quoted as Stoical by *Alex.* in Metaph. p. 258, 3 Bon. 667, a, 19 Brand) every ἁμαρτία is the result of a διάψευσις. It is, however, impossible for κατορθώματα not to be equal to one another, if vices are equal; πάντα γάρ ἐστι τέλεια, διόπερ οὔτ' ἐλλείπειν οὔθ' ὑπερέχειν δύναιτ' ἂν ἀλλήλων. Cicero and Seneca devoted particular attention to this enquiry. The investigations of Cicero in the Paradoxa result in bringing him to the passage quoted p. 263, 2, from which it follows that nothing can be recto rectius, nor

CHAP.
X.

C. *The
wise man.*
(1) *Wis-
dom and
folly.*

From what has been said, it follows that there can be but one thorough moral distinction for all mankind, the distinction between the virtuous and the vicious; and that within each of these classes there can be no difference in degree. He who possesses virtue possesses it whole and entire; he who lacks it lacks it altogether; and whether he is near or far from possessing it is a matter of no moment. He who is only a hand-breadth below the surface of

bono melius. The equality of faults is a corollary from the equality of virtues; it also follows from the consideration that whatever is forbidden at all is equally forbidden. De Fin.: It is said, all faults are equal, quia nec honesto quidquam honestius nec turpi turpius. Seneca (Ep. 66, 5) raises the question, How, notwithstanding the difference between goods (see p. 230, 3 end), can all be equal in value? and at once replies : Is virtue—or, what is the same thing, a rightly-moulded soul—the only primary good? Virtue, indeed, admits of various forms, according to the activities imposed on it, but can neither be increased nor diminished ; Decrescere enim summum bonum non potest, nec virtuti ire retro licet. It cannot increase, quando incrementum maximo non est : nihil invenies rectius recto, non magis quam verius vero, quam temperato temperatius. All virtue consists in modo, in certa mensura. Quid accedere perfecto potest? Nihil, aut perfectum non erat, cui

accesset : ergo ne virtuti quidem, cui si quid adjici potest, defuit . . . ergo virtutes inter se pares sunt et opera virtutis et omnes homines, quibus illæ contigere . . . una inducitur humanis virtutibus regula. Una enim est ratio recta simplexque. Nihil est divino divinius, cœlesti cœlestius. Mortalia minuuntur . . . crescunt, &c.; divinorum una natura est. Ratio autem nihil aliud est, quam in corpus humanum pars divini spiritus mersa . . . nullum porro inter divina discrimen est : ergo nec inter bona. *Ibid.* 32 : Omnes virtutes rationes sunt : rationes sunt rectæ: si rectæ sunt, et pares sunt. Qualis ratio est, tales et actiones sunt : ergo omnes pares sunt : ceterum magna habebunt discrimina variante materia, etc. On the same ground, *Seneca*, Ep. 71, defended the equality of all goods and of all good actions, in particular p. 18, where to the quotation given, p. 266, 3, the words are added : Si rectior ipsa [virtus] non potest fieri, ne quæ ab illa quidem fiunt, alia aliis rectiora sunt.

the water will be drowned just as surely as one who is five hundred fathoms deep; he who is blind sees equally little whether he will recover his sight to-morrow or never.[1] The whole of mankind are thus divided by the Stoics into two classes—those who are wise and those who are foolish;[2] and these two classes are treated by them as mutually exclusive, each one being complete in itself. Among the wise no folly, among the foolish no wisdom of any kind, is possible.[3] The wise man is absolutely free from faults and mistakes: all that he does is right; in him all virtues centre; he has a right opinion on every subject, and never a wrong one, nor, indeed, ever what is merely

---

[1] *Plut.* C. *Not.* 10, 4 : ναί, φασίν· ἀλλὰ ὥσπερ ὁ πῆχυν ἀπέχων ἐν θαλάττῃ τῆς ἐπιφανείας οὐδὲν ἧττον πνίγεται τοῦ καταδεδυκότος ὀργυίας πεντακοσίας, οὕτως οὐδὲ οἱ πελάζοντες ἀρετῇ τῶν μακρὰν ὄντων ἧττόν εἰσιν ἐν κακίᾳ· καὶ καθάπερ οἱ τυφλοὶ τυφλοί εἰσι κἂν ὀλίγον ὕστερον ἀναβλέπειν μέλλωσιν, οὕτως οἱ προκόπτοντες ἄχρις οὗ τὴν ἀρετὴν ἀναλάβωσιν ἀνόητοι καὶ μοχθηροὶ διαμένουσιν. *Diog.* 127 (see p. 266, 3). *Stob.* ii. 236 : πάντων τε τῶν ἁμαρτημάτων ἴσων ὄντων καὶ τῶν κατορθωμάτων καὶ τοὺς ἄφρονας ἐπίσης πάντας ἄφρονας εἶναι τὴν αὐτὴν καὶ ἴσην ἔχοντας διάθεσιν. *Cic.* Fin. iii. 14, 48 : Consentaneum est his quæ dicta sunt, ratione illorum, qui illum bonorum finem quod appellamus extremum quod ultimum crescere putent posse, iisdem placere, esse alium alio etiam sapientiorem, itemque alium magis alio vel peccare vel recte facere. Quod nobis non licet dicere, qui crescere bonorum finem non putamus. Then follow the same comparisons as in Plutarch. *Sen.* Ep. 66, 10 : As all virtues are equal, so are omnes homines quibus illæ contigere. Ep. 79, 8 : What is perfect admits of no increase; quicunque fuerint sapientes pares erunt et æquales.

[2] *Stob.* ii. 198 : ἀρέσκει γὰρ τῷ τε Ζήνωνι καὶ τοῖς ἀπ' αὐτοῦ Στωϊκοῖς φιλοσόφοις, δύο γένη τῶν ἀνθρώπων εἶναι, τὸ μὲν τῶν σπουδαίων τὸ δὲ τῶν φαύλων· καὶ τὸ μὲν τῶν σπουδαίων διὰ παντὸς τοῦ βίου χρῆσθαι ταῖς ἀρεταῖς τὸ δὲ τῶν φαύλων ταῖς κακίαις.

[3] *Plut.* Aud. Poet. 7, p. 25 : μήτε τι φαῦλον ἀρετῇ προσεῖναι μήτε κακίᾳ χρηστὸν ἀξιοῦσιν, ἀλλὰ πάντως μὲν ἐν πᾶσιν ἁμαρτωλὸν εἶναι τὸν ἁμαρτῆ, περὶ πάντα δ' αὖ κατορθοῦν τὸν ἀστεῖον.

an opinion. The bad man, on the contrary, can do
nothing aright: he has every kind of vice; he has
no right knowledge, and is altogether rude, violent,
cruel, and ungrateful.[1]

The Stoics delight in insisting upon the perfection of the wise man, and contrasting with it the
absolute faultiness of the foolish man, in a series of
paradoxical assertions.[2] The wise man only is free,
because he only uses his will to control himself;[3] he
only is beautiful, because only virtue is beautiful and
attractive;[4] he only is rich and happy (εὐτυχὴς),
because goods of the soul are the most valuable, true
riches consisting in being independent of wants.[5]
Nay, more, he is absolutely rich, since he who has a
right view of everything has everything in his intellectual treasury,[6] and he who makes the right use
of everything bears to everything the relation of
owner.[7] The wise only know how to obey, and they
also only know how to govern; they only are therefore kings, generals, pilots;[8] they only are orators,

[1] *Stob.* Ecl. ii. 116; 120;
196; 198; 220; 232; *Diog.* vii.
117; 125; *Cic.* Acad. i. 10, 38;
ii. 20, 66; *Plut.* Sto. Rep. 11,
1; *Sen.* Benef. iv. 26; *Sext.*
Math. vii. 434.

[2] Compare the collection of
expressions respecting the wise
and unwise in *Baumhauer*, Vet.
Phil. Doct. De Mort. Volunt.
p. 169.

[3] *Diog.* 121; 32; *Cic.* Acad.
ii. 44, 136. Parad. 5: ὅτι μόνος
ὁ σοφὸς ἐλεύθερος καὶ πᾶς ἄφρων
δοῦλος.

[4] *Plut.* C. Not. 28, 1; *Cic.*
Acad. l. c.; *Sext.* Math. xi. 170.

[5] *Cic.* Parad. 6; Acad. l. c.;
Cleanthes, in *Stob.* Floril. 94,
28; *Sext.* l. c.; *Alex. Aphr.*
Top. 79.

[6] *Sen.* Benef. vii. 3, 2; 6, 3;
8, 1.

[7] *Cic.* Acad. l. c.; *Diog.* vii.
125.

[8] *Cic.* l. c.; *Diog.* vii. 122;
Stob. ii. 206; *Plut.* Arat. 23.
On all the points discussed,
Plut. C. Not. 3, 2; De Adul.
16, p. 58; Tran. An. 12, p. 472;
Ps. *Plut.* De Nobil. 17, 2; *Cic.*
Fin. iii. 22, 75; *Hor.* Ep. i. 1,
106; Sat. i. 3, 124.

poets, and prophets;[1] and since their view of the
Gods and their worship of the Gods is the true one
only, only amongst them can true piety be found—
they are the only priests and friends of heaven; all
foolish men, on the contrary, being impious, profane,
and enemies of the Gods.[2] Only the wise man is
capable of feeling gratitude, love, and friendship,[3]
he only is capable of receiving a benefit, nothing
being of use or advantage to the foolish man.[4]
To sum up, the wise man is absolutely perfect, absolutely free from passion and want, absolutely
happy;[5] as the Stoics conclusively assert, he in no
way falls short of the happiness of Zeus,[6] since time,
the only point in which he differs from Zeus, does
not augment happiness at all.[7] On the other hand,
the foolish man is altogether foolish, unhappy, and
perverse; or, in the expressive language of the Stoics,

---

[1] *Plut.* Tran. An. 12; *Cic.*
Divin. ii. 63, 129; *Stob.* ii. 122;
conf. Ps. *Plut.* Vit. Hom. 143.

[2] *Stob.* ii. 122 and 216;
Diog. 119; *Sen.* Provid. i. 5.
Philodemus, περὶ θεῶν διαγωγῆς
(Vol. Hercul. vi. 29), quotes a
Stoic saying that the wise are
the friends of heaven, and
heaven of the wise.

[3] *Sen.* Ep. 81, 11; *Stob.* ii.
118.

[4] *Sen.* Benef. v. 12, 3; *Plut.*
Sto. Rep. 12, 1; C. Not. 20, 1;
and above, p. 230, 1.

[5] *Stob.* ii. 196; *Plut.* Stoic.
Abs. Poët. Dic. 1, 4.

[6] Chrysippus, in *Plut.* Sto.
Rep. 13, 2; Com. Not. 33, 2;
Stob. ii. 198. *Seneca*, Prov. i.
5 : Bonus ipse tempore tantum

a Deo differt. *Ibid.* 6, 4 :
Jupiter says to the virtuous :
Hoc est, quo Deum antecedatis :
ille extra patientiam malorum
est, vos supra patientiam. Ep.
73, 11; De Const. 8, 2; *Cic.*
N. D. ii. 61, 153; *Epictet.* Diss.
i. 12, 26; Man. 15; *Horat.*
Ep. i. 1, 106.

[7] See p. 239, 1 ; *Sen.* Ep. 53,
11 : Non multo te Di ante-
cedent . . . diutius erunt. At
mehercule magni artificis est
clausisse totum in exiguo.
Tantum sapienti sua, quantum
Deo omnis ætas patet. 73, 13 :
Jupiter quo antecedit virum
bonum ? Diutius bonus est :
sapiens nihilo se minoris æsti-
mat, quod virtutes ejus spatio
breviore clauduntur.

every foolish man is a madman, he being a madman
who has no knowledge of himself, nor of what most
closely affects him.[1]

This assertion was all the more sweeping, since
the Stoics recognised neither virtue nor wisdom
outside their own system or one closely related to it,
holding at the same time a most unfavourable opinion of the moral condition of their fellow-men.
That their opinion should be unfavourable was inevitable from their point of view. A system which
sets up its own moral ideal against the current notions so sharply as that of the Stoics can only be the
offspring of a thorough disapproval of existing circumstances, and must, on the other hand, contribute
thereto. According to the Stoic standard, by far
the majority, indeed, almost the whole of mankind,
belong to the class of the foolish ; were all foolish
people equally and altogether bad, mankind must
have seemed to them to be a sea of corruption and
vice, from which, at best, but a few swimmers emerge
at spots widely apart.[2] Man passes his life—such
had already been the complaint of Cleanthes [3]—in
wickedness. Only here and there does one, in the

---

[1] πᾶς ἄφρων μαίνεται. *Cic.*
Parad. 4 ; Tusc. iii. 5, 10 ; *Diog.*
vii. 124 ; *Stob.* Ecl. ii. 124 ;
Horat. Sat. ii. 3, 43.

[2] The Peripatetic Diogenianus raises the objection (in
Eus. Præp. Ev. vi. 8, 10):
πῶς οὖν οὐδένα φῇς ἄνθρωπον, ὃς
οὐχὶ μαίνεσθαί σοι δοκεῖ κατ᾽ ἴσον
Ὀρέστῃ καὶ Ἀλκμαίωνι, πλὴν τοῦ
σοφοῦ ; ἕνα δὲ ἢ δύο μόνους φῇς

σόφους γεγονέναι. Similarly
Plut. Sto. Rep. 31, 5.
[3] *Sext.* Math. ix. 90 in the
argument quoted, p. 146, 1 :
Man cannot be the most perfect
being, οῖυν εὐθέως, ὅτι διὰ κακίας
πορεύεται τὸν πάντα χρόνον, εἰ δὲ
μή γε. τὸν πλεῖστον · καὶ γὰρ εἴ
ποτε περιγένοιτο ἀρετῆς, ὀψὲ καὶ
πρὸς ταῖς τοῦ βίου δυσμαῖς περι-
γίνεται.

evening of life, after many wanderings, attain to virtue. And that this was the common opinion among the successors of Cleanthes, is witnessed by their constant complaints of the depravity of the foolish, and of the rare occurrence of a wise man.[1]

No one probably has expressed this opinion more frequently or more strongly than Seneca. We are wicked, he says; we have been wicked; we shall be wicked. Our ancestors complained of the decline of morals; we complain of their decline; and posterity will utter the very same complaint. The limits within which morality oscillates are not far apart; the modes in which vice shows itself change, but its power remains the same.[2] All men are wicked; and he who has as yet done nothing wicked is at least in a condition to do it. All are thankless, avaricious, cowardly, impious; all are mad.[3] We have all done wrong—one in a less, the other in a greater degree; and we shall all do wrong to the end of the chapter.[4] One drives the other into folly, and the foolish are too numerous to allow the individual to improve.[5]

---

[1] This point will be again considered in the next chapter. Compare at present *Sext.* Math. ix. 133, who says: εἰσὶν ἄρα σοφοί· ὅπερ οὐκ ἤρεσκε τοῖς ἀπὸ τῆς Στοᾶς, μεχρὶ τοῦ νῦν ἀνευρέτου ὄντος κατ᾽ αὐτοὺς τοῦ σοφοῦ. *Alex. Aphrod.* De Fat. 28, p. 90 : τῶν δὲ ἀνθρώπων οἱ πλεῖστοι κακοί, μᾶλλον δὲ ἀγαθὸς μὲν εἶς ἢ δεύτερος ὑπ᾽ αὐτῶν γεγονέναι μυθεύεται, ὥσπερ τι παράδοξον ζῷον καὶ παρὰ φύσιν, σπανιώτερον τοῦ Φοίνικος . . . οἱ δὲ πάντες κακοὶ καὶ ἐπίσης ἀλλήλοις τοιοῦτοι,

ὡς μηδὲν διαφέρειν ἄλλον ἄλλου, μαίνεσθαι δὲ ὁμοίως πάντας. *Philodem.* De Mus. (Vol. Herc. i.), col. 11, 18 : The Stoic cannot take his stand upon the opinion of the majority (consensus gentium), since he has declared it to be profane and impious.

[2] Benef. i. 10, 1–3.

[3] De Ira, iii. 26, 4; Benef. v. 17, 3.

[4] De Clemen. i. 6, 3; De Ira, ii. 28, 1; iii. 27, 3.

[5] Ep. 41, 9; Vit. Be. i. 4.

T

He who would be angry with the vices of men, instead of pitying their faults, would never stop. So great is the amount of iniquity![1]

No doubt the age in which Seneca lived afforded ample occasion for such effusions, but his predecessors must have found similar occasions in their own days. Indeed, all the principles of the Stoic School, when consistently developed, made it impossible to consider the great majority of men as anything else but a mass of fools and sinners. From this sweeping verdict, even the most distinguished names were not excluded. If asked for examples of wisdom, they would point to Socrates, Diogenes, Antisthenes,[2] and, in later times, to Cato;[3] but not only would they deny philosophic virtue, as Plato had done before them, to the greatest statesmen and heroes of early times, but they would deny to them all and every kind of virtue.[4] Even the admission that general faults belong to some in a lower degree than to

---

[1] See the pathetic description, De Ira, ii. 8–10, amongst other passages the following: Ferarum iste conventus est: . . . certatur ingenti quidem nequitiæ certamine: major quotidie peccandi cupiditas, minor verecundia est, &c.

[2] *Diog.* vii. 91: τεκμήριον δὲ τοῦ ὑπαρκτὴν εἶναι τὴν ἀρετὴν φησιν ὁ Ποσειδώνιος ἐν τῷ πρώτῳ τοῦ ἠθικοῦ λόγῳ τὸ γενέσθαι ἐν προκοπῇ τοὺς περὶ Σωκράτην, Διογένην καὶ 'Αντισθένην. The limitation likewise contained herein will be presently discussed. *Epictet.* Man. 15, mentions Heraclitus as well as Diogenes

as θεῖοι.

[3] See the immoderate language of praise of his admirer *Sen.* De Const. 7, 1: The wise man is no unreal ideal, although, like everything else that is great, he is seldom met with; ceterum hic ipse M. Cato vereor ne supra nostrum exemplar sit. *Ibid.* 2, 1: Catonem autem certius exemplar sapientis viri nobis Deos immortales dedisse quam Ulixen et Herculem prioribus sæculis.

[4] *Plutarch*, Prof. in Virt. 2, p. 76; *Cic.* Off. iii. 4, 16, p. 265, 2.

others can hardly be reconciled with their principle of the equality of all who are not wise.[1]

The two moral states being thus at opposite poles, a gradual transition from one to the other is, of course, out of the question. There may be a progress from folly and wickedness in the direction of wisdom,[2] but the actual passage from one to the other must be momentary and instantaneous.[3] Those who are still progressing belong, without exception, to the class of the foolish;[4] and one who has lately become wise is in the first moment unconscious of his new state.[5]

---

[1] *Sen.* Benef. iv. 27, 2 : Itaque errant illi, qui interrogant Stoicos : quid ergo ? Achilles timidus est ? quid ergo ? Aristides, cui justitia nomen dedit, injustus est ? &c. Non hoc dicimus, sic omnia vitia esse in omnibus, quomodo in quibusdam singula eminent : sed malum ac stultum nullo vitio vacare . . . omnia in omnibus vitia sunt, sed non omnia in singulis extant (*i.e.*, all points are not equally prominent in each one). It hardly requires to be noticed how nearly this view coincides with that of Augustine on the virtues of the heathen, how close a resemblance the Stoic doctrine of folly bears to the Christian doctrine of the unregenerate, and how the contrast between wisdom and folly corresponds to that between the faithful and unbelievers.

[2] *Plut.* C. N. 10, 1 ; Prof. in Virt. 12, p. 82 ; *Sen.* Ep. 75, 8.

[3] *Plut.* C. Not. 9 ; Stoic.

Abs. Poët. Dic. 2. The Stoics are here ridiculed because, according to their view, a man may go to bed ugly, poor, vicious, miserable, and rise the next morning wise, virtuous, rich, happy, and a king. In Prof. in Virt. 1, p. 75, a saying of Zeno's is given, that it is possible to tell by a dream whether we are advancing in virtue.

[4] See p. 266, 3 ; *Plut.* Prof. in Virt. 1 ; Com. Not. 10, 2 ; see p. 269, 1 ; *Sen.* Ep. 75, 8.

[5] *Plut.* C. Not. 9, 1 : τῆς ἀρετῆς καὶ τῆς εὐδαιμονίας παραγινομένης πολλάκις οὐδ᾽ αἰσθάνεσθαι τὸν κτησάμενον οἴονται διαλεληθέναι δ᾽ αὐτὸν ὅτι μικρῷ πρόσθεν ἀθλιώτατος ὢν καὶ ἀχρονέστατος νῦν ὁμοῦ φρόνιμος καὶ μακάριος γέγονεν. So Sto. Rep. 19, 3. In explanation of these words, *Ritter*, iii. 657, aptly refers to *Stob.* ii. 234 (γίγνεσθαι δὲ καὶ διαλεληθότα τινὰ σοφὸν νομίζουσι κατὰ τοὺς πρώτους χρόνους), and *Philo*, De Agric. p. 325 : Those yet inexperienced

The transition takes place so rapidly, and his former state affords so few points of contact with the one on which he has newly entered, that the mind does not keep pace with the change, and only becomes conscious of it by subsequent experience.

In this picture of the wise man, the moral idealism of the Stoic system attained its zenith. A virtuous will appears here so completely sundered from all outward conditions of life, so wholly free from all the trammels of natural existence, and the individual has become so completely the organ of universal law, that it may be asked, What right has such a being to call himself a person? How can such a being be imagined as a man living among fellowmen? Nor was this question unknown to the Stoics themselves. Unless they were willing to allow that their theory was practically impossible, and their ideal scientifically untenable, how could they escape the necessity of showing that it might be reconciled with the wants of human life and the conditions of reality? Let the attempt be once made, however, and withal they would be forced to look for some means of adapting it to those very feelings and opi-

---

in wisdom παρὰ τοῖς φιλοσόφοις διαλεληθότες εἶναι λέγονται σοφοί· τοὺς γὰρ ἄχρι σοφίας ἄκρας ἐληλακότας καὶ τῶν ὅρων αὐτῆς ἄρτι πρῶτον ἀψαμένους ἀμήχανον εἰδέναι, φασί, τὴν ἑαυτῶν τελείωσιν. μὴ γὰρ κατὰ τὸν αὐτὸν χρόνον ἄμφω συνίστασθαι τήν τε πρὸς τὸ πέρας ἄφιξιν καὶ τὴν τῆς ἀφίξεως κατάληψιν, ἀλλ᾽ εἶναι μεθόριον ἄγνοιαν, κ.τ.λ. *Sen.* Ep. 75, 9,

likewise investigates the same point, but ranges those who have not yet attained the consciousness of perfection among advancers, but not among the wise. *Prantl's* conjecture (Gesch. d. Logik, i. 490, 210), that the σοφὸς διαλεληθὼς is connected with the fallacy known as διαλανθάνων, appears to be questionable.

nions towards which their animosity had formerly been so great. Nor could the attempt be long delayed. Daily a greater value was attached to the practical working of their system, and to its agreement with general opinion. If, therefore, the original direction of Stoic morality aimed at the absolute and unconditional submission of the individual to the law of the universe, still, in developing that theory, the rights of the individual asserted themselves unmistakeably. From this confluence of opposite currents arose a deviation from the rigid type of the Stoic system, some varieties of which, in the direction of the ordinary view of life, deserve now further consideration.

CHAPTER XI.

THE STOIC THEORY OF MORALS AS MODIFIED BY
PRACTICAL NEEDS.

CHAP.
XI.

A. *Things
to be pre-
ferred and
eschewed.*

THE Stoic theory of Ethics is entirely rooted in the
proposition, that only virtue is a good and only vice
an evil. This proposition, however, frequently brought
the Stoics into collision with current views ; nor was
it without its difficulties for their own system. In
the first place, virtue is made to depend for its existence upon certain conditions, and to lead to certain results, from which it is inseparable. These
results, we have already seen,[1] were included by the
Stoics in the list of goods. Moreover, virtue is
said to be the only good, because only what is according to nature is a good, and rational conduct is for
man the only thing according to nature. But can
this be so absolutely and unconditionally stated ?
According to the Stoic teaching the instinct of self-
preservation being the primary impulse, does not
this instinct manifestly include the preservation and
advancement of outward life ? The Stoics, therefore, could not help including physical goods and
activities among things according to nature—for in-

[1] See p. 230, 3.

stance, health, a right enjoyment of the senses, and such like.[1] Practically, too, the same admission was forced upon them by the consideration[2] that, if there is no difference in value between things in them- selves, rational choice—and, indeed, all acting on motives—is impossible. At the same time, they re- ject the notion that what is first according to nature must therefore be perfect or good, just as in theory they allow that the source of knowledge, but not truth itself, is derived from the senses. When man has once recognised the universal law of action, he will, according to their view, think little of what is sensuous and individual, only considering it an in- strument in the service of virtue and reason.[3]

---

[1] *Cic.* Fin. iii. 5, 17. *Gell.* N. A. xii. 5, 7: The primary objects of natural self-love are the πρῶτα κατὰ φύσιν ; and self- love consists mainly in this : Ut omnibus corporis sui com- modis gauderet [unusquisque], ab incommodis omnibus abhor- reret. *Stob.* Ecl. ii. 142: Some things are according to nature, others contrary to nature, others neither one nor the other. Health, strength, and such like, are among things according to nature. *Ibid.* p. 148 : τῶν δὲ κατὰ φύσιν ἀδιαφόρων ὄντων τὰ μέν ἐστι πρῶτα κατὰ φύσιν τὰ δὲ κατὰ μετοχήν. πρῶτα μέν ἐστι κατὰ φύσιν κίνησις ἢ σχέσις κατὰ τοὺς σπερματικοὺς λόγους γινομένη, οἷον ὑγιεία καὶ αἴσθησις, λεγὼ δὲ τὴν κατάληψιν καὶ ἰσχύν. κατὰ μετοχὴν δὲ . . . οἷον χεὶρ ἀρτία καὶ σῶμα ὑγιαῖνον καὶ αἰσθήσεις μὴ πεπηρωμέναι. ὁμοίως δὲ καὶ τῶν παρὰ φύσιν κατ'

ἀνάλογον. Conf. *Ibid.* p. 60, where the enumeration of the πρῶτα κατὰ φύσιν is also in the Stoic sense, and above, p. 225. [2] *Cic.* Fin. iii. 15, 50 : Dein- ceps explicatur differentia re- rum : quam si non ullam esse diceremus, confunderetur om- nis vita, ut ab Aristone : nec ullum sapientis munus aut opus inveniretur, cum inter res eas, quæ ad vitam degendam per- tinerent, nihil omnino interes- set neque ullum delectum adhiberi oporteret. The same argument was used by the Stoa against the theoretical ἀδιαφορία of the Sceptics (see above, p. 37, 1), with which the practical ἀδιαφορία of Aristo, differing only in name from the ἀπαραξία of the Sceptics, is most closely connected, Aristo declining to Scepticism. See p. 61, 1. [3] *Cic.* Fin. iii. 6, 21 : Prima est enim conciliatio [οἰκείωσις]

Still, it would be difficult to say how this can be possible. The contemporary opponents of the Stoics already took exception to the way in which the first demands of nature were excluded from the aims of a life [1] according to nature; and we, too, cannot suppress a feeling of perplexity at being told that all duties aim at attaining what is primarily according to nature, but that what is according to nature must not be looked upon as the aim of our actions; [2] since not that which is simply according to nature, but the rational choice and combination of what is according to nature constitutes the good.[3] Even if the Stoics pretend to dispose of this difficulty, they could not, at least, fail to see that whatever contri-

hominis ad ea quæ sunt secundum naturam, simul autem cepit intelligentiam vel notionem potius, quam appellant ἔννοιαν illi, viditque rerum agendarum ordinem et ut ita dicam concordiam, multo eam pluris æstimavit quam omnia illa quæ primum dilexerat: atque ita cognitione et ratione collegit ut statueret in eo collocatum summum illud hominis per se laudandum et expetendum bonum . . . cum igitur in eo sit id bonum, quo referenda sint omnia . . . quamquam post oritur, tamen id solum vi sua et dignitate expetendum est, eorum autem quæ sunt prima naturæ propter se nihil expetendum, &c. Similarly Gell. l. c.

[1] Plut. Com. Not. 4; Cic. Fin. iv. 17; v. 24, 72; 29, 89.

[2] Cic. Fin. iii. 6, 22: Ut

recte dici possit, omnia officia eo referri, ut adipiscamur principia naturæ: nec tamen ut hoc sit bonorum ultimum, propterea quod non inest in primis naturæ conciliationibus honesta actio. Consequens enim est et post oritur.

[3] Plut. C. Not. 26, 2: εἰ γὰρ αὐτὰ μὲν [τὰ] πρῶτα κατὰ φύσιν ἀγαθὰ μή ἐστιν, ἡ δ' εὐλόγιστος ἐκλογὴ καὶ λῆψις αὐτῶν καὶ τὸ πάντα τὰ παρ' ἑαυτὸν ποιεῖν ἕκαστον ἕνεκα τοῦ τυγχάνειν τῶν πρώτων κατὰ φύσιν, κ.τ.λ. εἴπερ γὰρ οἴωνται, μὴ στοχαζομένους μηδ' ἐφιεμένους τοῦ τυχεῖν ἐκεῖνον τὸ τέλος ἔχειν, ἀλλ' οὗ δεῖ ἐκεῖνα ἀναφέρεσθαι, τὴν τούτων ἐκλογὴν, καὶ μὴ ταῦτα. τέλος μὲν γὰρ τὸ ἐκλέγεσθαι καὶ λαμβάνειν ἐκεῖνα φρονίμως· ἐκεῖνα δ' αὐτὰ καὶ τὸ τυγχάνειν αὐτῶν οὐ τέλος, ἀλλ' ὥσπερ ὕλη τις ὑπόκειται τὸν ἐκλεκτικὴν ἀξίαν ἔχουσα. Cic. See p. 279, 3.

butes to bodily well-being must have a certain positive value, and must be desirable in all cases in
which no higher good suffers in consequence ; and,
conversely, that whatever is opposed to bodily well-
being, when higher duties are not involved, must
have a negative value (ἀπαξία), and, consequently,
deserve to be avoided.[1] Such objects and actions
they would not, however, allow to be included in the
class of goods which are absolutely valuable ;[2] and
it was therefore a blending of the Stoic with the
Peripatetic teaching when Herillus, the fellow-student of Cleanthes, enumerated bodily and outward
goods as secondary and subsidiary aims besides virtue.[3]

Nor yet were the Stoics minded to follow the contemporary philosopher, Aristo of Chios (who in this
point, too, endeavoured to place their School on the
platform of the Cynic philosophy), in denying any
difference in value between things morally indifferent[4] and in making the highest aim in life

(2) *Classes
of things
indif-
ferent.*

[1] *Cic.* l. c. 6, 20 ; *Plut.* l. c.;
Stob. ii. 142 ; *Diog.* vii. 105.

[2] See p. 232. *Stob.* ii. 132 :
διαφέρειν δὲ λέγουσιν αἱρετὸν καὶ
ληπτὸν . . . καὶ καθόλου τὸ ἀγαθὸν τοῦ ἀξίαν ἔχοντος.

[3] *Diog.* vii. 165 : Herillus
taught διαφέρειν τέλος καὶ ὑποτε-
λίδα· (On this expression compare *Stob.* ii. 60) τῆς μὲν γὰρ καὶ
τοὺς μὴ σοφοὺς στοχάζεσθαι, τοῦ
δὲ μόνον τὸν σοφόν. Hence *Cic.*
Fin. iv. 15, 40, raises the objection, Facit enim ille duo se-
juncta ultima bonorum, because
he neither despises external
things, nor connects them with
the ultimate aim. *Diog.* l. c.,

however, says that he taught τὰ
μεταξὺ ἀρετῆς καὶ κακίας ἀδιάφορα
εἶναι ; and *Cic.* Off. i. 2, 6, mentions him, together with Pyrrho
and Aristo, as an upholder of
ἀδιαφορία. It would appear
from these passages that Herillus was not far removed from
true Stoicism. According to
Cic. Fin. ii. 13, 43 (conf. Offic.),
he had no followers after the
time of Chrysippus.

[4] *Cic.* Legg. i. 21, 55 : Si, ut
Chius Aristo dixit, solum bonum
esse diceret quod honestum
esset malumque quod turpe,
ceteras res omnes plane pares
ac ne minimum quidem utrum

consist in indifference to all external things.[1] Their virtue bearing, in comparison with the Cynic virtue, the more positive character of an energetic will, they required even for the outward circumstances and conditions of this activity some definite relation which should regulate the choosing or rejecting— in short, the practical decision. Accordingly, they divided things indifferent into three classes. To the first class belong all those things which, from a moral or absolute point of view, are neither good nor evil, but yet which have a certain value; no matter whether this value belongs to them properly, because they are in harmony with human nature, or whether it belongs to them improperly, because they are means for advancing moral and natural life, or whether it belongs to them on both grounds. The second class includes everything which, either by itself or in its relation to higher aims, is opposed to nature and harmful; the third, things which, even

adessent an abessent interesse. *Ibid.* 13, 38. Fin. iv. 17, 47: Ut Aristonis esset explosa sententia dicentis, nihil differre aliud ab alio nec esse res ullas præter virtutes et vitia intra quas quidquam omnino interesset. *Ibid.* ii. 13, 43; iii. 3, 11; 15, 50; iv. 16, 43; 25, 68; v. 25, 73; Acad. ii. 42, 130; Offic. Fragm. Hortens. (in *Nonn.* Præfract.); *Diog.* vii. 160; *Sext.* Math. xi. 64. *Cic.* usually places Aristo together with Pyrrho.

[1] *Diog.* l. c.: τέλος ἔφησεν εἶναι τὸ ἀδιαφόρως ἔχοντα ζῆν πρὸς τὰ μεταξὺ ἀρετῆς καὶ κακίας

μηδὲ ἡντινοῦν ἐν αὐτοῖς παραλλαγὴν ἀπολείποντα ἀλλ' ἐπίσης ἐπὶ πάντων ἔχοντα. *Cic.* Acad. l. c.: Huic summum bonum est in his rebus (the morally adiaphora) neutram in partem moveri: quæ ἀδιαφορία ab ipso dicitur. Chrysippus, in *Plut.* C. Not. 27, 2: Indifference to that which is neither good nor bad presupposes the idea of the good, and yet, according to Aristo, the good only consists in that state of indifference. *Stob.* i. 920; *Clem.* Strom. ii. 416, c. See *Cic.* Fin. iv. 25, 68, for Chrysippus' attack on this ἀδιαφορ α.

in this conditional sense, have neither positive nor negative value. The first class bears the name of things preferential (προηγμένον), or things desirable ; the second is the class of things to be eschewed (ἀποπροηγμένον) ; the third is the class of things intermediate.[1] The latter is called, in the strict sense, indifferent ἀδιάφορον.[2] It includes not only what is really indifferent, but whatever has such a slight negative or positive value that it neither enkindles desire nor aversion. Hence the terms προηγμένον and ἀποπροηγμένον are defined to mean respectively that which has an appreciable positive or negative value.[3] Under things preferential, the Stoics include partly mental qualities and conditions, such as

---

[1] *Diog.* vii. 105: τῶν ἀδιαφόρων τὰ μὲν λέγουσι προηγμένα
τὰ δὲ ἀποπροηγμένα. προηγμένα
μὲν τὰ ἔχοντα ἀξίαν· ἀποπροηγμένα δὲ τὰ ἀπαξίαν ἔχοντα. By
ἀξία, the three meanings of
which are discussed, they understand here μέσην τινὰ δύναμιν
ἢ χρείαν συμβαλλομένην πρὸς τὸν
κατὰ φύσιν βίον. 107 : τῶν προηγ-
μένων τὰ μὲν δι' αὑτὰ προῆκται,
τὰ δὲ δι' ἕτερα, τὰ δὲ δι' αὑτὰ καὶ
δι' ἕτερα . . . δι' αὑτὰ μὲν ὅτι
κατὰ φύσιν ἐστί. δι' ἕτερα δὲ ὅτι
περιποιεῖ χρείας οὐκ ὀλίγας.
ὁμοίως δὲ ἔχει καὶ ἀποπροηγμένον
κατὰ τὸν ἐναντίον λόγον. Essentially the same account, only
somewhat fuller, in *Stob.* Ecl.
ii. 142. Conf. *Cic.* Acad. i. 10,
36 ; Fin. iii. 15, 50 ; iv. 26, 72 ;
Sext. Pyrrh. iii. 191 ; Math. xi.
60 ; *Alex.* Aphr. De An. 157.
Zeno (in *Stob.* 156 ; *Cic.* Fin.
iii. 16, 52) explains the conception προηγμένον, and its distinc-

tion from ἀγαθόν: προηγμένον δ'
εἶναι λέγουσιν, ὃ ἀδιάφορον ὂν ἐκ-
λεγόμεθα κατὰ προηγούμενον λόγον
. . . οὐδὲν δὲ τῶν ἀγαθῶν εἶναι
προηγμένον, διὰ τὸ τὴν μεγίστην
ἀξίαν αὐτὰ ἔχειν. τὸ δὲ προηγμένον, τὴν δευτέραν χώραν καὶ ἀξίαν
ἔχον, συνεγγίζειν πως τῇ των
ἀγαθῶν φύσει· οὐδὲ γὰρ ἐν αὐλῇ
τὸν προηγούμενον εἶναι τὸν βασιλέα,
ἀλλὰ τὸν μετ' αὐτὸν τεταγμένον.
[2] *Stob.* ii. 142 : ἀδιάφορα δ'
εἶναι λέγουσι τὰ μεταξὺ τῶν ἀγαθῶν καὶ τῶν κακῶν, διχῶς τὸ ἀδιάφορον νοεῖσθαι φάμενοι, καθ' ἕνα
μὲν τρόπον τὸ μήτε ἀγαθὸν μήτε
κακὸν καὶ τὸ μήτε αἱρετὸν μήτε
φευκτόν· καθ' ἕτερον δὲ τὸ μήτε
ὁρμῆς μήτε ἀφορμῆς κινητικόν—τὰ
καθάπαξ ἀδιάφορα. Similarly
Diog. vii. 104. *Sext.* M. vi. 60,
distinguishes a third meaning.
It is, however, only a subdivi-
sion of the second.
[3] *Stob.* ii. 144, 156 ; *Sext.* P.
iii. 191 ; M. xi. 62.

CHAP.
XI.

talents and skill, even progress towards virtue, in as far as it is not yet virtue; partly bodily advantage—beauty, strength, health, life itself; partly external goods—riches, honour, noble birth, relations, &c. Under things to be eschewed, they understand the opposite things and conditions; under things indifferent, whatever has no appreciable influence on our choice, such as the question whether the number of hairs on the head is even or uneven; whether I pick up a piece of waste paper from the floor, or leave it; whether one piece of money or another is used in

(3) Collision of modified and abstract theory.

payment of a debt.[1] Yet they made a rigid difference between the purely relative value of things preferential, and the absolute value of things morally good. Only the latter were really allowed to be called good, because they only, under all circumstances, are useful and necessary. Of things morally indifferent, on the other hand, the best may, under certain circumstances, be bad, and the worst—sickness, poverty, and the like—may, under certain circumstances, be useful.[2] Just as little would they allow that the independence of the wise man suffered by the recognition outside himself of a class of things preferential. For the wise man, said Chrysippus,[3] uses such things

[1] *Diog.* vii. 106; *Stob.* ii. 142; *Cic.* Fin. iii. 15, 51; *Sext.* l. c.; *Plut.* Sto. Rep. 30. The Stoics were not altogether agreed as to whether fame after death belonged to things to be desired. According to *Cic.* Fin. iii. 17, 57, Chrysippus and Diogenes denied it; whereas the younger Stoics, pressed by the Academician Carneades, allowed it. *Sen.* Ep. 102, 3, even quotes it as a Stoic maxim that posthumous fame is a good. But probably bonum is here inaccurately used for προηγμένον.

[2] *Cic.* Fin. iii. 10, 34; 16, 52; *Sext.* M. xi. 62. See p. 232 and 283, 2.

[3] *Sen.* Ep. 9, 14: Sapientem

without requiring them. Nevertheless, the admission of classes of things to be preferred and to be declined obviously undermines their doctrine of the good. Between what is good and what is· evil, a third group is introduced, of doubtful character; and since we have seen the term ἀδιάφορον was only in its more extended meaning applied to this group, it became impossible for them to refuse to apply the term good to things desirable,[1] or to exclude unconditionally from the highest good many of the things which they were in the habit of pronouncing indifferent.[2] Nor was this concession merely the yielding of a term, as will appear when particular instances are considered. Not only may Seneca[3] be heard, in Aristotelian manner, defending external possessions as aids to virtue—not only Hecato, and even Diogenes, uttering ambiguous sentences as to permitted

---

nulla re egere [δεῖσθαι], et tamen multis illi rebus opus esse [χρῆναι].

[1] *Plut.* Sto. Rep. 30, 4 : ἐν δὲ τῷ πρώτῳ περὶ ἀγαθῶν τρόπον τινὰ συγχωρεῖ καὶ δίδωσι τοῖς βουλομένοις τὰ προηγμένα καλεῖν ἀγαθὰ καὶ κακὰ τἀναντία ταύταις ταῖς λέξεσιν · ἔστι, εἴ τις βούλεται, κατὰ τὰς τοιαύτας παραλλαγὰς (with reference to the greatness of the difference between προηγμένον and ἀποπροηγμένον) τὸ μὲν ἀγαθὸν αὐτῶν λέγειν τὸ δὲ κακὸν . . . ἐν μὲν τοῖς σημαινομένοις οὐ διαπίπτοντος αὐτοῦ τὰ δ' ἄλλα στοχαζομένου τῆς κατὰ τὰς ὀνομασίας συνηθείας. See p. 284, 1 ; *Cic.* Fin. iv. 25, 68, and the previous remarks on the division of goods, p. 230, 3. *Diog.*

103, says that Posidonius included bodily and external advantages among the ἀγαθά. In *Sen.* Ep. 87, 35, he, however, expressly proves that they are not goods.

[2] *Sen.* Ep. 95, 5 : Antipater quoque inter magnos sectæ hujus auctores aliquid se tribuere dicit externis (namely for the perfection of the highest good), sed exiguum admodum. Seneca here declaims, in the spirit of strict Stoicism, against such a heresy, but he himself says (De Vit. Be. 22, 5) : Apud me divitiæ aliquem locum habent, only not summum et postremum. But what philosopher would have said they had this ?

[3] De Vit. Bea. 21.

and forbidden gains [1]—not only Panætius giving expression to much that falls short of Stoic severity [2]—
but even Chrysippus avows that in his opinion it is
silly not to desire health, wealth, and freedom from
pain,[3] and that a statesman may treat honour and
wealth as real goods; [4] adding that the whole Stoic
School agrees with him in thinking it no disparagement for a wise man to follow a profession which lay
under a stigma in the common opinion of Greece.[5]
He did not even hesitate to assert that it is better
to live irrationally than not to live at all.[6] It is

---

[1] *Cic.* Off. iii. 12, 51; 13, 55;
23, 91; 15, 63; 23, 89. Diogenes of Seleucia says that it
is permitted to circulate base
money, knowingly to conceal
defects in a purchase from the
purchaser, and such like. Hecato of Rhodes, a pupil of Panætius, thinks that not only will
a wise man look after his property by means lawful and
right, but he believes that in a
famine he will prefer to let his
slaves starve, to maintaining
them at too great a sacrifice.

[2] According to *Cic.* Off. ii.
14, 51, he would allow an at-
torney to ignore truth, provided
his assertions were at least
probable.

[3] *Plut.* Sto. Rep. 30, 2.

[4] *Ibid.* 5.

[5] According to *Plut.* Sto.
Rep. 20, 3 and 7 and 10 ; 30, 3,
Diog. vii. 188, *Stob.* ii. 224, the
Stoics, following Chrysippus,
admit three ways of earning
an honest livelihood—by teaching, by courting the rich, by
serving states and princes. The
first and the last were no longer

condemned in the Alexandrian
period, as they had been before,
but still they were in bad repute, and the second was particularly so. Still more at
variance with Greek customs
was the course advocated by
Chrysippus (in *Plut.* Sto. Rep.
30): καὶ κυβιστήσειν τρὶς ἐπὶ τούτῳ λαβόντα τάλαντον. Chrysippus himself (in *Diog.*) enumerates the objections to the
modes of life just named, and,
in general, to all trading for
money, but his objections cannot have appeared to him conclusive.

[6] *Plut.* Sto. Rep. 18, 1 and
3. Com. Not. 12, 4: λυσιτελεῖ
ζῆν ἄφρονα μᾶλλον ἢ μὴ βιοῦν κἂν
μηδέποτε μέλλῃ φρονήσειν ; or, as
it is expressed, 11, 8: Heraclitus and Pherecydes would have
done well to renounce their
wisdom, if they could thereby
have got rid of their sickness.
A prudent man would rather be
a fool in human shape than a
wise man in the shape of a
beast.

impossible to conceal the fact that, in attempting to
adapt their system to general opinion and to the
conditions of practical life, the Stoics were driven
into admissions strongly at variance with their previous theories. It may hence be gathered with certainty that, in laying down those theories, they had
overstrained a point.

By means of this doctrine of things to be preferred and things to be eschewed, a further addition
was made to the conception of duty. Under duty,
or what is proper,[1] we have already seen, the Stoics
understand rational action in general, which becomes
good conduct, or κατόρθωμα, by being done with a
right intention.[2] The conception of duty, therefore,
contains in itself the conception of virtuous conduct,
and is used primarily to express what is good or
rational. Now, however, duty appears to have a
twofold meaning, in consequence of the twofold characters of things desirable and things good. If the
good were the only permitted object of desire, there
would, of course, be but one duty—that of realising
the good; and the various actions which contribute
to this result would only be distinguished by their
being employed on a different material, but not in
respect of their moral value. But if, besides what
is absolutely good, there are things relatively good,
things not to be desired absolutely, but only in cases
in which they may be pursued without detriment to
the absolute good or virtue—if, moreover, besides

B. *Perfect
and inter-
mediate
duties.*

---

[1] καθῆκον, an expression introduced by Zeno, according to
Diog. 108.   [2] See p. 265,

vice, as the absolute evil, there are also relative evils,
which we have reason to avoid in the same cases—
the extent of our duties is increased likewise; a
number of conditional duties are placed by the side
of duties unconditional, differing from the latter in
that they aim at pursuing things to be preferred,
and avoiding things to be eschewed. From this
platform, all that accords with nature is regarded as
proper, or a duty in the more extended sense of the
term; and the conception of propriety is extended
to include plants and animals.[1] Proper and dutiful
actions are then divided into those which are always
such and those which are only such under peculiar
circumstances—the former being called *perfect*, the
latter *intermediate* duties;[2] and it is stated, as a

[1] *Diog.* 107 : καθῆκον φασὶν
εἶναι ὃ πραχθὲν εὔλογόν τιν' ἴσχει
ἀπυλογισμὸν οἷον τὸ ἀκόλουθον ἐν
τῇ ζωῇ (the same in Cicero),
ὅπερ καὶ ἐπὶ τὰ φυτὰ καὶ ζῷα δια-
τείνει· ὁρᾶσθαι γὰρ κἀπὶ τούτων
καθήκοντα. *Stob.* 158: ὁρίζεται
δὲ τὸ καθῆκον τὸ ἀκόλουθον ἐν
ζωῇ, ὃ πραχθὲν εὔλογον ἀπολογίαν
ἔχει· παρὰ τὸ καθῆκον δὲ ἐναντίως.
τοῦτο διατείνει καὶ εἰς τὰ ἄλογα
τῶν ζῴων, ἐνεργεῖ γάρ τι κἀκεῖνα
ἀκολούθως τῇ ἑαυτῶν φύσει· ἐπὶ
δὲ τῶν λογικῶν ζῴων οὕτως ἀποδίδοται, τὸ ἀκόλουθον ἐν βίῳ. καθῆκον is, in general, what is according to nature, with which
ἀκόλουθον coincides. (See p.
228, 2.) See *Diog.* 108: ἐνέργημα
δ' αὐτὸ [τὸ καθῆκον] εἶναι ταῖς
κατὰ φύσιν κατασκευαῖς οἰκεῖον.
[2] *Diog.* vii. 109 : τῶν καθηκόντων τὰ μὲν ἀεὶ καθήκει τὰ δὲ οὐκ
ἀεί· καὶ ἀεὶ μὲν καθήκει τὸ κατ'

ἀρετὴν ζῆν· οὐκ ἀεὶ δὲ τὸ ἐρωτᾶν
τὸ ἀποκρίνεσθαι καὶ περιπατεῖν καὶ
τὰ ὅμοια. *Cic.* Fin. iii. 17, 58 :
Est autem officium quod ita
factum est, ut ejus facti proba-
bilis ratio reddi possit. Ex
quo intelligitur, officium medium quoddam esse, quod neque
in bonis ponatur neque in contrariis . . . quoniam enim videmus, &c. (see p. 265, 2) . . .
quoniamque non dubium est,
quin in iis quæ media dicimus
sit aliud sumendum aliud re-
jiciendum, quidquid ita fit aut
dicitur communi officio continetur. Also Off. i. 3, 8. Acad.
i. 10, 37. Corresponding to
προηγμένον and ἀποπροηγμένον,
Zeno placed officium and contra
officium, as media quædam between recte factum and pecca-
tum. *Stob.* ii. 158: τῶν δὲ
καθηκόντων τὰ μὲν εἶναί φασι

peculiarity of the latter, that, owing to circumstances, a course of conduct may become a duty
which would not have been a duty without those
peculiar circumstances.[1] In the wider sense of the
term, every action is proper or according with duty
which consists in the choice of a thing to be pre-
ferred ($\pi\rho o\eta\gamma\mu\acute{e}\nu o\nu$) and in avoiding a thing to be
eschewed. On the other hand, a perfect duty is only
fulfilled by virtuous action. A virtuous life and a
wish to do good constitutes the only perfect duty.[2]

τέλεια, ἃ δὴ καὶ κατορθώματα
λέγεσθαι . . . οὐκ εἶναι δὲ κατορθώματα τὰ μὴ οὕτως ἔχοντα, ἃ δὴ
οὐδὲ τέλεια, καθήκοντα προσαγο-
ρεύουσιν, ἀλλὰ μέσα, οἷον τὸ γα-
μεῖν, τὸ πρεσβεύειν, τὸ διαλέγεσθαι, τὰ τούτοις ὅμοια.

[1] *Stob.* 160. *Diog.* l. c.: τὰ
μὲν εἶναι καθήκοντα ἄνευ περιστάσεως, τὰ δὲ περιστατικά. καὶ
ἄνευ μὲν περιστάσεως τάδε, ὑγείας
ἐπιμελεῖσθαι καὶ αἰσθητηρίων καὶ
τὰ ὅμοια· κατὰ παρίστασιν δὲ τὸ
πηροῦν ἑαυτὸν καὶ τὴν κτῆσιν διαρ-
ριπτεῖν. ἀνάλογον δὲ καὶ τῶν
παρὰ τὸ καθῆκον. This distinction, of course, only applies to
μέσον καθῆκον. The unconditional duty of virtuous life cannot be abrogated by any circumstances

[2] Compare, on this point,
besides the quotations on p.
265, 2, *Diog.* 108 : τῶν γὰρ καθ'
ὁρμὴν ἐνεργουμένων τὰ μὲν καθήκοντα εἶναι, τὰ δὲ παρὰ τὸ καθῆκον, τὰ δ' οὔτε καθήκοντα οὔτε
παρὰ τὸ κοθῆκον. καθήκοντα
μὲν οὖν εἶναι ὅσα ὁ λόγος αἱρεῖ
(demands; see p. 244, 2,
the αἱρῶν λόγος) ποιεῖν. ὡς ἔχει τὸ
γονεῖς τιμᾶν, ἀδελφοὺς, πατρίδα,

συμπεριφέρεσθαι φίλοις · παρὰ τὸ
καθῆκον δὲ ὅσα μὴ αἱρεῖ λόγος,
e.g. neglect of parents ; οὔτε δὲ
καθήκοντα οὔτε παρὰ τὸ καθῆκον,
ὅσα οὔθ' αἱρεῖ λόγος πράττειν οὔτ'
ἀπαγορεύει, οἷον κάρφος ἀνελέσθαι,
κ.τ.λ. Combining with this the
passage previously quoted, it
appears that καθῆκον includes
not only actions which aim at a
moral good, but those which
aim at a simple προηγμένον; and,
in view of the latter, καθῆκον is
included among things intermediate, or ἀδιάφορα in its more
extended meaning. *Cic.*; see
p. 288, 2. *Stob.* 158, says that
those καθήκοντα which are at
the same time κατορθώματα, are
οὐδὲ τέλεια. ἀλλὰ μέσα . . . παρα-
μετρεῖσθαι δὲ τὸ μέσον καθῆκον
ἀδιαφόροις τισὶ καλουμένοις δὲ
παρὰ φύσιν καὶ κατὰ φύσιν, τοιαύτην δ' εὐφυΐαν προσφερομένοις,
ὥστ' εἰ μὴ λαμβάνοιμεν αὐτὰ ἢ
διωθούμεθα ἀπερισπάστως (if,
without particular occasion, or
as *Diog.* 109 observes, ἄνευ περιστάσεως—see previous note—
we despise or reject them) μὴ
εὐδαιμονεῖν.

Some confusion is introduced into this teaching by the fact that in setting up the standard for distinguishing perfect from imperfect duties, the Stoics sometimes look at the real, sometimes at the personal value, of actions, without keeping these two aspects distinct. They therefore use the terms perfect and imperfect sometimes to express the difference between conditional and unconditional duties; at other times, to express that between morality and law.[1] Far worse than the formal defect is the grouping in this division under the conception of duty things of the most varied moral character. If once things which have only a conditional value are admitted into the circle of duties, what is there to prevent their being defended in the practical application of the Stoic teaching, on grounds altogether repugnant to the legitimate consequences of the Stoic principles?

C. *Emotions.*
(1) *Permitted affections.*

In accordance with these admissions, the Stoic system sought in another respect to meet facts and practical wants by abating somewhat from the austerity of its demands. Consistently carried out, those demands require the unconditional extirpation of the whole sensuous nature, such as was originally expressed by the demand for apathy. But just as the stricter Stoic theory of the good was modified by the admission of προηγμένα, so this demand was modified in two ways; the first elements at least of the forbidden emotions were allowed under other names; and whilst emotions were still forbidden,

---

[1] In the latter sense καθῆκον and κατόρθωμα have been already discussed, p. 264.

certain mental affections were permitted, and even declared to be desirable. Taking the first point, it was allowed by the Stoics that the wise man feels pain, and that at certain things he does not remain wholly calm.[1] They appealed to this admission to show that their system was not identical with that of the Cynics.[2] For men to be entirely free from all such mental affections cannot be required, but only that he refuse assent to them, and do not suffer them to obtain the mastery.[3] In illustration of the other point, they propounded their doctrine of εὐπάθειαι, or rational dispositions, which, as distinct from emotions, are to be found in the wise man, and in the wise man only. Of these rational dispositions, they distinguish three chief varieties, besides several subordinate varieties.[4] Although this

---

[1] *Sen.* De Ira, i. 16, 7: When the wise man sees anything revolting, non . . . tangetur animus ejus eritque solito commotior? Fateor, sentiet levem quendam tenuemque motum. Nam, ut dixit Zeno, in sapientis quoque animo etiam cum vulnus sanatum est, cicatrix manet. *Id.* ii. 2; Ep. 57, 3; De Const. 10, 4; *Stob.* Floril. 7, 21; *Plut.* C. Not. 25, 5; Epictet. in *Gell.* N. A. xix. 1, 17. Conf. p. 253, 5, 6.

[2] *Sen.* Brevit. Vit. c. 14, 2: Hominis naturam cum Stoicis vincere cum Cynicis excedere. Similarly Ep. 9, 3: Hoc inter nos et illos (Stilpo and the Cynics in general) interest: noster sapiens vincit quidem incommodum omne, sed sentit: illorum ne sentit quidem.

[3] Conf. *Sen.* De Ira, ii. 2-4, particularly the quotation in *Gell.* from Epictetus: Even the wise man is apt, at terrible occurrences, paulisper moveri et contrahi et pallescere, non opinione alicujus mali percepta, sed quibusdam motibus rapidis et inconsultis, officium mentis atque rationis prævertentibus. But what distinguishes him from the foolish man is that only the foolish man and not the wise man assents (συγκατατίθεται, προσεπιδοξόζει) to such impressions (φαντασίαι).

[4] *Diog.* vii. 115: εἶναι δὲ καὶ εὐπαθείας φασὶ τρεῖς, χαρὰν, εὐλάβειαν, βούλησιν· καὶ τὴν μὲν χαρὰν ἐναντίαν φασὶν εἶναι τῇ ἡδονῇ οὖσαν εὔλογον ἔπαρσιν· τὴν δὲ εὐλάβειαν τῷ φόβῳ οὖσαν εὔλογον ἔκκλισιν· τῇ δὲ ἐπιθυμίᾳ

CHAP.
XI.

(2) Modi-
fication of
apathy.

admission was intended to vindicate the absence
of emotions in the wise man, since the permitted
feelings are not emotions, still it made the boundary-
line between emotions and feelings so uncertain that
in practice the sharply-defined contrast between the
wise and the foolish threatened wellnigh to disappear altogether.

This danger appears more imminent when we
observe the perplexity in which the Stoics were placed
when asked to point out the wise man in experience.
For not only do opponents asseverate that, according to their own confession, no one, or as good as no
one, can be found in actual history who altogether
deserves that high title,[1] but even their own admissions agree therewith.[2] They dare to describe even
Socrates, Diogenes, and Antisthenes as not completely
virtuous, but only as travellers towards virtue.[3] It was
of little avail to point to Hercules or Ulysses,[4] or,

ἐναντίαν φασὶν εἶναι τὴν βούλησιν
οὖσαν εὔλογον ὄρεξιν. Subdivisions of βούλησις are : εὔνοια,
εὐμένεια, ἀσπασμὸς, ἀγάπησις; of
εὐλάβεια : αἰδὼς, ἀγνεiά ; of χαρά:
τέρψις, εὐφροσύνη, εὐθυμία. The
same three εὐπάθειαι are mentioned by Cic. Tusc. iv. 6, 12,
with the remark that they only
belong to the wise. See Stob.
92, and Sen. Ep. 59, 14; 72, 4
and 8, respecting the wise man's
cheerfulness.
[1] Besides the quotations,
p. 271, see Plut. Sto. Rep. 31,
5 : καὶ μὴν οὔθ' αὐτὸν ὁ Χρύσιππος
ἀποφαίνει σπουδαῖον, οὔτε τινὰ τῶν
αὐτοῦ γνωρίμων ἢ καθηγεμόνων.
Cic. Acad. ii. 47, 145 ; Quintil.
Inst. xii. 1, 18.

[2] Sen. Tranq. An. 7, 4 : Ubi
enim istum invenies, quem tot
seculis quærimus ? (the wise
man.) Ep. 42, 1 : Scis quem
nunc virum bonum dicam?
Hujus secundæ notæ. Nam ille
alter fortasse tanquam phœnix
semel anno quingentesimo nascitur, see p. 273, 1, just as
everything great is rare. But
compare p. 274, 3.
[3] Cic. Fin. iv. 20, 56, and
p. 274, 2.
[4] Hos enim (says Sen. De
Const. 2, 1, of the two named)
Stoici nostri sapientes pronun-
tiaverunt, invictos laboribus,
etc. Further particulars in
Heraclit. Alleg. Hom. c. 33
and 70.

with Posidonius,[1] to the mythical golden age, in which the wise are said to have ruled. The pictures of those heroes would have to be changed altogether, to bring them into harmony with the wise men of the Stoics; and Posidonius might be easily disposed of on Stoic principles, by the rejoinder that virtue and wisdom are things of free exercise, and, since free exercise was wanting in the case of the first men, their condition can only have been a state of unconscious ignorance, and not one of perfection.[2] If, in reality, there are no wise men, the division of men into wise and foolish falls at once to the ground : all mankind belong to the fools; the conception of the wise man is an unreal fancy. It becomes all the more difficult to maintain the assertion that all fools are equally foolish, and all the wise are equally wise. If, instead of producing real wisdom, philosophy can only produce a progress in that direction, still it will hardly take such a modest estimate of its own success as to allow that there is no real distinction between a zealous student and a bigoted despiser of its doctrines.

It was therefore natural that the Stoics, notwithstanding their own maxims, found themselves compelled to recognise differences among the bad and

(3) *The state of progress.*

---

[1] *Sen.* Ep. 90, 5. To these wise men of the old world Posidonius traced back all kinds of useful discoveries. Posidonius is probably meant by the 'younger Stoics' (*Sext. Math.* ix. 28), who say that they introduced belief in the Gods.

[2] *Sen.* l. c. 44 : Non dat natura virtutem, ars est bonum fieri . . . ignorantia rerum innocentes erant . . . virtus non contingit animo nisi instituto et edocto et ad summum adsidua exercitatione perducto. Ad hoc quidem, sed sine hoc nascimus, &c.

differences among the good. In reference to their
system these differences were, indeed, made to depend in the case of the bad upon the greater or
less difficulty of healing the moral defects, or, in the
case of the good, upon qualities morally indifferent.[1]
It was also natural that they should so nearly identify the state of προκοπὴ—or progress towards wisdom, the only really existing state—with wisdom that
it could hardly be distinguished therefrom. If there
is a stage of progress at which a man is free from
all emotions, discharges all his duties, knows all that
is necessary, and is even secure against the danger of
relapse,[2] such a stage cannot be distinguished from
wisdom, either by its want of experience or by the

---

[1] *Stob.* Ecl. ii. 236 : ἴσων δὲ
ὄντων τῶν ἁμαρτημάτων εἶναί τινας
ἐν αὐτοῖς διαφορὰς, καθόσον τὰ μὲν
αὐτῶν ἀπὸ σκληρᾶς καὶ δυσιάτου
διαθέσεως γίγνεται, τὰ δ' οὔ. (See
p. 251, 2, for the difference
between emotion and disease of
the soul.) καὶ τῶν σπουδαίων γε
ἄλλους ἄλλων προτρεπτικωτέρους
γίγνεσθαι καὶ πιστικωτέρους ἔτι δὲ
καὶ ἀγχινουστέρους, κατὰ τὰ μέσα
τὰ ἐμπεριλαμβανόμενα τῶν ἐπιτά-
σεων συμβαινουσῶν, i. e., virtuous
men are not all equally secure.
These differences of degree do
not, however, apply to wisdom
(nor on the other hand to folly),
which admits of no increase,
but only to such properties as
are included in the whole moral
state, but are not themselves
of moral nature. See *Cic.* Fin.
iv. 20, 56, and p. 275, 1.

[2] *Stob.* Serm. 7, 21 : ὁ δ' ἐπ'
ἄκρον, φησὶ [Χρύσιππος] προκόπ-

τῶν ἅπαντα πάντως ἀποδίδωσι τὰ
καθήκοντα καὶ οὐδὲν παραλείπει ·
τὸν δὲ τούτου βίον οὐκ εἶναί πω
φησὶν εὐδαίμονα ἀλλ' ἐπιγίγνεσθαι
αὐτῷ τὴν εὐδαιμονίαν ὅταν αἱ μέσαι
πράξεις αὗται προσλάβωσι τὸ βέβαιον καὶ ἑκτικὸν καὶ ἰδίαν πῆξίν
τινα λάβωσιν. Chrysippus was
probably the author of the division of *progressers* into three
classes, which is discussed by
Sen. Ep. 75, 8. Of those who
have reached the highest stage
it is said, omnes jam affectus
et vitia posuerunt, quæ erant
complectenda didicerunt, sed
illis adhuc inexperta fiducia
est. Bonum suum nondum in
usu habent. Jam tamen in illa
quæ fugerunt recidere non possunt, jam ibi sunt unde non est
retro lapsus, sed hoc illis de se
nondum liquet et . . . scire se
nesciunt.

absence of a clear knowledge of oneself. For has it
not been frequently asserted that happiness is not
increased by length of time, and that the wise man
is at first not conscious of his wisdom?[1] If, however, the highest stage of approximation to wisdom
is supposed still to fall short of wisdom, because it
is not sure of its continuance, and though free from
mental diseases, it is not free from emotions,[2] how,
it may be asked, do these passing emotions differ
from the mental affections which are found in the
wise man? Is there any real distinction between
them? If the progressing candidate has attained
to freedom from diseased mental states, is the danger
of a relapse very great? Besides, the Stoics were by
no means agreed that the really wise man is free from
all danger, Cleanthes holding with the Cynics that
virtue can never be lost; Chrysippus admitting that,
in certain cases, it is defectible.[3] After all this

---

[1] See pp. 239, 1; 271, 7.

[2] *Sen.* Ep. 75, 10 : Quidam
hoc proficientium genus de quo
locutus sum ita complectuntur,
ut illos dicant jam effugisse
morbos animi, affectus nondum
(on this distinction, see p. 251,
2), et adhuc in lubrico stare,
quia nemo sit extra periculum
malitiæ nisi qui totam eam ex-
cussit. The same view is upheld by *Sen.* Ep. 72, 6.

[3] *Diog.* vii. 127 ; τὴν ἀρετὴν
Χρύσιππος μὲν ἀποβλητὴν, Κλεάνθης δὲ ἀναπόβλητον · ὁ μὲν, ἀποβλητὴν, διὰ μέθην καὶ μελαγχο-
λίαν · ὁ δὲ, ἀναπόβλητον, διὰ
βεβαίους καταλήψεις. The latter
view was that of the Cynics.
Although departed from by

Chrysippus, it belongs to those
points in which the original
relation of Stoicism to Cynicism was weakened by him.
Sen. Ep. 72, 6, speaking in the
tone of Cleanthes, says that
elsewhere he considered a candidate of the first class secure
against relapses. On the contrary, *Simpl.* Categ. 102, *a, β*
(Schol. in Arist. 86, a, 48 ;
b, 30), says first that the Stoics
declared virtue to be indefectible, but subsequently limits
this assertion by saying that,
ἐν καιροῖς (the reading κάροις is
better) καὶ μελαγχολίαις, virtue,
together with the whole rational
life (λογικὴ ἕξις), is lost, and
succeeded, not indeed by vice,

CHAP.
XI.

admission is only one among many traits which prove
that the Stoics were obliged to abate from the original severity of their demands.

but by a ἕξις μέση. A similar
question is, Whether the wise
man can become mad? which
is answered in the negative by
Diog. vii. 118, though not without some modifying clauses.
Alex. Aphr. De An. 156, b, also
combats the view that the wise
man will act virtuously when
in a frenzy.

CHAPTER XII.

APPLIED MORAL SCIENCE.

ALL that has hitherto been stated had regard to the general principles only of the Stoics touching the end and the conditions of moral action.   Whether the mere exposition of principles be enough, or whether the practical application of these principles to the special relations of life does not also form part of moral science—was a question as to which the Stoic School was not originally unanimous.   Aristo, on this as on other points a Cynic, was of opinion that this whole branch of moral science was useless and un- necessary ; the philosopher must confine himself ex- clusively to things which have a practical value, the fundamental points of morality.[1]   Within the Stoic School, however, this view did not gain much

[1] Further particulars have been already given, p. 61. Seneca (Ep. 95, 1) calls the subject of applied ethics, which Aristo rejected, paraenetice, or pars praeceptiva. Sextus speaks of two τόποι—a παραινετικὸς and a ὑποθετικός. Both terms, how- ever, appear to denote the same thing ; for ὑποθετικὸς is defined by Muson. in *Stob.* Floril. 117, 8, as παραινετικός. He who is himself insufficiently educated will do well ζητῶν λόγων ἀκούειν ὑποθετικῶν παρὰ τῶν πεποιημένων ἔργον εἰδέναι τίνα μέν βλαβερὰ τίνα δὲ ὠφέλιμα ἀνθρώποις. ὑπο- θετικὸς τόπος is therefore iden- tical with the suasio of Posi- donius (in *Sen.* Ep. 95, 65). See p. 223, note 1.

support. Even Cleanthes, otherwise agreeing with Aristo, would not deny the value of an application of theory to details, provided the connection of these details with general principles be not lost sight of.[1] Nor can there be any doubt that, after the time of Chrysippus, details engrossed much of the attention of the Stoic philosophers. Posidonius enumerates, as belonging to the province of moral philosophy, precept, exhortation, and advice.[2] His teacher, Panætius, had discussed the hortatory side of morality[3] in three books on duties, imitated by Cicero's well-known treatise.[4] The division of ethics attributed to Diogenes,[5] and by him referred to Chrysippus, leaves a place for such discussions ;[6] and, not to mention Aristo's opposition thereto, which supposes the existence of applied moral science, the example of his fellow-student Persæus, whose precepts for a banquet[7] have been already referred to, proves how

[1] *Sen.* Ep. 94, 4 : Cleanthes utilem quidem judicat et hanc partem, sed imbecillam nisi ab universo fluit, nisi decreta ipsa philosophiæ et capita cognovit.

[2] See p. 223, 1.

[3] See *Cic.* Off. i. 2, 7 ; 3, 9 ; iii. 2, 7. Cicero himself said that he chiefly followed Panætius (περὶ τῶν καθηκόντων), not as a mere translator, but correctione quadam adhibita. See p. 300, 2.

[4] *Cic.* Off. i. 3, 7 : Omnis de officio duplex est quæstio : unum genus est, quod pertinet ad finem bonorum : alterum, quod positum est in præceptis, quibus in omnes partes usus vitæ conformari possit. He would de-

vote his attention to officia, quorum præcepta traduntur. Cicero then goes fully into particulars. He treats of amusement and occupation (i. 29, 103) ; of the peculiar duties of the young and the old, of officials, citizens, foreigners (i. 34) ; of outward appearance, gait, conversation (i. 36) ; of the means of winning others (ii. 6, 21). Panætius must have given a similar treatment to the subject.

[5] See p. 223, 1.

[6] Particularly in the portions treating περὶ τῶν καθηκόντων and περὶ προτροπῶν τε καὶ ἀποτροπῶν.

[7] See p. 272, 2.

early practical ethics had obtained a footing within
the Stoic School. Moreover, the elaborate theory of
virtue propounded by Chrysippus and his followers [1]
can hardly have failed to include many of the principal occurrences in life. Thus a number of particular precepts are known to us, which are partly
quoted by other writers as belonging to the Stoics,
and are partly to be found in the pages of Seneca,
Epictetus, and Marcus Aurelius, and in Cicero's treatise on duties. Indeed, the Stoics were the first who
went at all deeply into the subject of casuistry.[2] At
a later epoch, when more general questions had been
settled by Chrysippus, the preference for particular
enquiries on the domain of applied moral science
appears to have increased among the Stoics.[3] Probably, however, none but the later members of
the School advanced the unscientific assertion [4]
that we ought to confine ourselves to precepts for

[1] See p. 260, 4, and 261, 1.

[2] According to *Cic.* Off. i.
2 ; 7, Ad Att. xvi. 11, Panætius,
in the third chief division of
his treatise on duties, intended
to discuss cases of collision between apparent interest and
duty, but his intentions were
never carried out. It appears,
however, from Off. i. 45, 159 ;
iii. 12, 50 ; 13, 55 ; 23, 89, that
these cases were frequently
discussed, not only by the
pupils of Panætius, Posidonius,
and Hecato, but by Diogenes
of Seleucia and Antipater of
Tarsus.

[3] The treatise of Panætius
appears to have been used as a
chief authority, not only by

Cicero, but by others. Antipater of Tyre, a cotemporary
of Cicero, had added dis-
cussions on the care of health
and wealth (*Cic.* Off. ii. 24, 86) ;
and Hecato, in his treatise on
duties, had added further
casuistical investigations (*Cic.*
iii. 23, 89). Brutus, too, who,
like his teacher Antiochus, was
devoted to a moderate Stoicism,
and of whom *Sen.* Ep. 95, 45,
reports that he had laid down
rules for the relations of
parents, children, and brothers
in his treatise περὶ τοῦ καθή-
κοντος, may have followed
Panætius.

[4] *Sen.* Ep. 94, 1 ; 95, 1.

particular cases, since only these have any practical
value.

In this extension of the moral theory, besides
the longing for scientific completeness, the endeavour may also be observed to subordinate all sides
of human activity to moral considerations. In the
virtuous man, as the Stoics held, everything becomes
virtue;[1] and hence everything is included in moral
philosophy. Thereby, without doubt, the Stoic School
contributed in no small degree towards settling and
defining moral ideas, not only for its immediate con-
temporaries, but also for all subsequent times. Nevertheless, the more the teaching of the School entered
into the details of every-day life, the more impossible
it became to prevent practical considerations from
overriding the natural severity of Stoic principles,
or to keep the strictness of scientific procedure from
yielding to the less accurate bias of experience.

The order and division which the Stoics adopted
for discussing details in the hortatory part of moral
science are not known to us; nor, indeed, is it known
whether that order was uniform in all cases.[2] It

[1] *Stob.* ii. 128: ἐν ἕξει (not
only ἐν σχέσει, see p. 230) δὲ οὐ
μόνας εἶναι τὰς ἀρετὰς ἀλλὰ καὶ
τὰς ἄλλας τέχνας τὰς ἐν τῷ σπουδαίῳ ἀνδρί, ἀλλοιωθείσας ὑπὸ τῆς
ἀρετῆς καὶ γενομένας ἀμεταπτώ-
τους, οἱονεὶ γὰρ ἀρετὰς γίγνεσθαι.

[2] The treatise of Panætius—
we learn from *Cic.* Off. i. 3, 9;
iii. 2, 7; 7, 33—discussed its
subject first from the platform
of duty, and then from that of

interest. The third part, which
Panætius proposed to himself—
the collision between duty and
interest—was never fully carried out. Cicero adds discussions on two questions, which
of two conflicting duties and
which of two conflicting interests must be preferred (i. 3,
10, c. 43; ii. 25). Otherwise
he appears in his two first
books to follow the order of
Panætius.

will be most convenient for the purpose of our present description to distinguish, in the first place, those points which refer to the moral activity of the individual as such, and afterwards to go on to those which relate to social life. Subsequently, the teaching of the Stoics on the relation of man to the course of the world and to necessity will engage our attention.

It was consistent with the whole tone of the Stoic system to devote, in ethics, more attention to the conduct and duties of the individual than had been done by previous philosophy. Not that previous philosophers had altogether ignored this side. Indeed, Aristotle, in his investigations into individual virtue, had been led to enquire carefully into individual morality. Still, with Aristotle, the influence of classic antiquity on the border-land of which he stands was sufficiently strong to throw the individual into the background as compared with the community, and to subordinate ethics to politics. In the post-Aristotelian philosophy, this relation was exactly reversed. With the decline of public life in Greece, intellectual interest in the state declined also ; and, in equal degree, the personality of the individual and circumstances of private life came into prominence. This feature may be already noticed in some of the older Schools, for instance, in the Academy and Peripatetic School. The Peripatetic, in particular, had already, in the time of its first adherents, travelled far on the road which the founder had struck out. Among the Stoics, the same

A. *The individual.*
(1) *Importance attached to the individual.*

feature was required by the whole spirit of their system. If happiness depends upon man's internal state only, nothing external having power to affect it, the science which professes to lead man to happiness must primarily busy itself with man's moral activity. It can only consider human society in as far as action for society forms part of the moral duty of the individual. Hence, in the Stoic philosophy, researches into the duties of the individual occupy a large space, there being a corresponding subordination of politics. These duties form the subject of by far the greater part of the applied moral science of the Stoics; and how minutely they entered in that study into possible details has been already set forth.[1] At the same time, the scientific harvest resulting from these researches is by no means in proportion to their extent.

Confining our attention to form some idea of the treatise of Panætius on duties to the two first books of Cicero's work, De Officiis, after a few introductory remarks, we find morality as such (honestum) described, according to the scheme of the four cardinal virtues (i. 5–42). In discussing the first of these, intelligence, love of research is recommended, and useless subtlety is deprecated. Justice and injustice are next discussed,

[1] See pp. 260, 298. Amongst other things, as we learn from the fragment in *Athen.* xiii. 565, a, Chrysippus discussed at length the question of shaving; and *Alex. Aphr.* Top. 26, quotes, in illustration of the useless enquiries of the Stoics, ἐν τοῖς περὶ καθηκόντων, an enquiry whether it is proper to take the largest portion before one's father at table, and whether it is proper to cross the legs in the school of a philosopher.

in all their various forms, due regard being had to the cases of ordinary occurrence in life. Liberality, kindness, and benevolence are treated as subdivisions of justice; and this leads to a consideration of human society in all its various forms (c. 16–18, 60). Next, turning to bravery (18, 61), the philosopher draws attention to the fact that bravery is inseparably connected with justice. He then describes it partly as it appears in the forms of magnanimity and endurance, regardless of external circumstances, partly in the form of energetic courage; and, in so doing, he discusses various questions which suggest themselves, such as the nature of true and false courage, military and civil courage, and the exclusion of anger from valour. Lastly, the object of the fourth chief virtue (c. 27) is described, in general terms, as what is proper (decorum, πρέπον), and the corresponding state as propriety, both in controlling the impulses of the senses, in jest and play, and in the whole personal bearing. The peculiar demands are discussed made by individual nature, by time of life, by civil position. Even outward proprieties—of speech and conversation, of domestic arrangement, tact in behaviour,[1] honourable and dishonourable modes of life—do not escape attention.[2]

In the second book of his work, Cicero considers the relation of interest to duty; and having proved,

---

[1] εὐταξία, εὐκαιρία, talis ordo actionum ut in vita omnia sint apta inter se et convenientia. i. 40, 142; 144.

[2] i. 43. We omit Cicero's treatise, this section not being found in Panætius.

at length,[1] that most that is advantageous and disadvantageous is brought on us by other men, he turns to the means by which we may gain the support of others, and by which affection, trust, and admiration may be secured. He reviews various kinds of services for individuals and the state, and embraces, at the same time, the opportunity of giving vent to his grudge against despotism and republican court of the people. The principles on which this review is conducted are such that objection can rarely be taken to them from the platform of modern morality. Yet unmistakeably the Stoic bias is present in the conception and support of the rules of life, and particularly in the definitions of various virtues, few of the moral judgments, however, are other than might have been expressed from the platform of the Platonic and Aristotelian ethics.[2] The same remark holds good of some other points on record, by means of which the Stoics gave a further expansion to their picture of the wise man.[3] Revolting as their tenets at times appear, there is yet little in their application that deviated from the moral ideas generally current.

[1] Panætius still more diffusively, 5, 16.

[2] Such, for instance, as the prohibition against being angry with enemies (i. 25, 88), which recalls at once the difference of the Stoics and Peripatetics on the admissibility of emotions. See p. 252.

[3] *Diog.* 117, says: The σόφος or σπουδαῖος is free from vanity (ἄτυφος), is earnest (αὐστηρὸς), frank (ἀκίβδηλος), and with no inclination to pretence. He stands aloof from the affairs of life (ἀπράγμων), lest he should do anything contrary to duty. See p. 323, 1. *Stob.* ii. 240, says: The wise man is gentle (πρᾶος), quiet (ἡσύχιος), and considerate (κόσμιος), never exciting angry feelings against others, never deferring what he has to do.

More peculiar, and at the same time more startling, is another feature about the Stoics. Let not too much be made of the fact that they, under certain circumstances, permitted a lie.[1] Were not Socrates and Plato, at least, of the same opinion? And, to be frank, we must admit that, although in this respect moral theories are strict enough, yet practice is commonly far too lax now. Very repulsive, however, are many assertions attributed to the Stoics, respecting the attitude of the wise man to the so-called intermediate things. Was not this very independence of externals, this indifference to everything but the moral state, which found expression in the doctrine of things indifferent and of the wise

---

[1] Chrysippus, in *Plut.* Sto. Rep. 47, 1: βλάψουσιν οἱ σοφοὶ ψευδεῖς φαντασίας ἐμποιοῦντες, ἂν αἱ φαντασίαι ποιῶσιν αὐτοτελῶς τὰς συγκαταθέσεις· πολλάκις γὰρ οἱ σοφοὶ ψεύδει χρῶνται πρὸς τοὺς φαύλους καὶ φαντασίαν παριστᾶσι πιθανήν, οὐ μὴν αἰτίαν τῆς συγκαταθέσεως· ἐπεὶ καὶ τῆς ὑπολήψεως αἰτία τῆς ψευδοῦς ἔσται καὶ τῆς ἀπάτης. *Stob.* ii. 230: μὴ ψεύδεσθαι τὸν σόφον ἀλλ' ἐν πᾶσιν ἀληθεύειν· οὐ γὰρ ἐν τῷ λέγειν τι ψεῦδος τὸ ψεύδεσθαι ὑπάρχειν, ἀλλ' ἐν τῷ διαψευστῶς τὸ ψεῦδος λέγειν καὶ ἐπὶ ἀπάτῃ τῶν πλησίον. τῷ μέντοι ψεύδει ποτὲ συγχρήσασθαι [1.—σεσθαι] νομίζουσιν αὐτὸν κατὰ πολλοὺς τρόπους ἄνευ συγκαταθέσεως· καὶ γὰρ κατὰ στρατηγίαν πρὸς τῶν ἀντιπάλων, καὶ κατὰ ἡν τοῦ συμφέροντος προόρασιν (which, however, may not be translated as *Ritter* iii. 662 does 'for the sake of advantage'; it rather refers to such cases as those mentioned by *Xen.* Mem. iv. 2, 17, and *Plato*, Rep. ii. 382, c. 389, B; iv. 459, C, in which the interests of another or of the community require deception) καὶ κατ' ἄλλας οἰκονομίας τοῦ βίου πολλάς. In accordance with this passage, too, the statement of Procl. in *Alcib.* (Op. ed. Cous. iii. 64)—that the Stoics differ from their predecessors in that they reject all lies— must be explained: οὔτε γὰρ ἐξαπατᾶν ἔστι δικαίως κατ' αὐτοὺς οὔτε βιάζεσθαι οὔτε ἀποστερεῖν, ἀλλ' ἑκάττη τῶν πράξεων τούτων ἀπὸ μοχθηρᾶς πρόεισιν ἕξεως καὶ ἄδικός ἐστιν. The point here in dispute is simply verbal; the Stoics were, in reality, at one with Plato, in not calling permitted falsehood untruth or deceit only for the reasons quoted by Chrysippus and Stobæus.

man's apathy, at the root of that onesidedness of life
and principle which is so prominent in the Cynic
School, the parent School of the Stoics? Granting
that in the Stoic School this onesidedness was toned
down and supplemented by other elements, still the
tendency thereto was too deeply rooted from its origin, and too closely bound up with its fundamental
view of life, to be ever properly eradicated. It did
not require, indeed, a Cynic life from its members;
nay, more, it even avowed that, except in rare cases,
such a life ought not to be followed ;[1] still the Cynic's
life was its ideal ; and when it asserted that it was not
necessary for a wise man to be a Cynic, it implied
that, if once a Cynic, he would always be a Cynic.[2]
Stoicism took for its patterns [3] Antisthenes and Diogenes quite as much as Socrates; even those who
held with Seneca,[4] that a philosopher ought to accommodate himself to prevailing customs, and, from
regard to others, do what he would not himself approve, did not therefore cease to bestow their highest
admiration on Diogenes's independence of wants, with

[1] *Cic.* Fin. iii. 20, 68 : Cy-
nicorum autem rationem atque
vitam alii cadere in sapientem
dicunt, si quis ejusmodi forte
casus inciderit, ut id faciendum
sit, alii nullo modo. The latter
must, however, have been in a
minority.

[2] *Diog.* 121 : κυνιεῖν τ᾿ αὐτὸν
[τὸν σοφόν] · εἶναι γὰρ τὸν κυνι-
σμὸν σύντομον ἐπ᾿ ἀρετὴν ὁδὸν, ὡς
Ἀπολλόδωρος [on whom, see p.
51, 1] ἐν τῇ ἠθικῇ. Stob. 238 :
κυνιεῖν τε τὸν σοφὸν λέγουσιν,
ἴσον τῷ ἐπιμένειν τῷ κυνισμῷ, οὐ

μὴν σοφὸν ὄντ᾿ ἂν ἄρξασθαι τοῦ
κυνισμοῦ.

[3] See p. 274, 2. According
to the epigrams of Timon, in
Diog. vii. 16, *Athen.* iv. 158, a,
Sext. Math. xi. 172, Zeno's
School must have presented a
very Cynical appearance. Probably, the description is partially true of the earlier history
of that School ; still I would
attach no great value to it as
illustrating the system.

[4] Ep. 5, 1; 103, 5 ; Fr. 19,
in *Lactant.* Inst. iii. 15.

all its eccentricities.[1] More consistent thinkers even approximated to Cynicism in their moral precepts,[2] and in later times a School of younger Cynics actually grew out of the Stoic School.

Bearing, as the Stoics did, so close a relationship to the Cynics, it cannot astonish us to find amongst them many instances of the most revolting traits in Cynicism—the contempt for cultured habits, the violation of right feelings—fully justifying the righteous indignation of their opponents. Chrysippus regarded many things as perfectly harmless in which the religious feeling of Greece saw pollution,[3] in defence of his opinion pleading the example of animals, to show that they were according to nature. The care for deceased relatives he not only proposed to limit to the simplest mode of burial, but would have it altogether put in the background; and he even made the horrible suggestion, which he described in full, of using for purposes of nourishment the flesh of amputated limbs and the corpses of even the nearest relatives.[4] Great offence, too, was given by

(b) In-stances of Cynicism.

[1] See, on this point, Tranq. An. 8, 4; Benef. v. 4, 3; 6, 1; Ep. 90, 14. *Sen.* Ep. 29, 1, does not, however, agree with the Stoic custom of sowing exhortations broadcast.

[2] As may be seen in Musonius and Epictetus.

[3] *Plut.* Sto. Rep. 22 (the question being as to the pollution of the temples by the contact with the dead or lying-in women or unclean foods); in other cases indeed, as Plu-

tarch objects, he would not allow these considerations.

[4] Besides *Diog.* vii. 188, and *Sext.* Pyrrh. iii. 207, see Chrysippus's own words, in *Sext.* Pyrrh. iii. 247 (Math. xi. 193). The majority of the Stoics appear to have limited cannibalism to cases of extreme necessity. See *Diog.* 121. Chrysippus had probably been speaking, in the context, of the different modes of treating the dead among various nations

the Stoics, and, in particular, by Chrysippus, by their treatment of the relations of the sexes to each other; nor can it be denied that some of their utterances on this subject sound exceedingly insidious. The Cynic assertion, that anything which is in itself allowed may be mentioned plainly and without a periphrasis, is also attributed to the Stoics.[1] By his proposals for the dress of women, Zeno offended against propriety and modesty,[2] and both he and Chrysippus advocated community of wives for their state of wise men.[3] It is, moreover, asserted that the Stoics raised no objection to the prevalent profligacy and the trade in unchastity,[4] nor to the still worse vice of unnatural crime.[5] Even marriage among the nearest relatives was found quite according to nature by the leaders of the School;[6] and the atrocious shamelessness of Diogenes found supporters in Chrysippus,[7] perhaps, too, in Zeno.[8]

(c) Cynicism a theoretical consequence of Stoic principles.

It would, however, be doing the Stoics a great injustice to take these statements for more than mere theoretical conclusions drawn from the prin-

(*Cic.* Tusc. i. 45, 108), intending to prove that no uniformity of practice prevailed.

[1] *Cic.* Off. i. 35, 128, with the limitation: Cynici aut si qui fuerunt Stoici pæne Cynici.

[2] *Diog.* vii. 33 : καὶ ἐσθῆτι δὲ τῇ αὐτῇ κελεύει χρῆσθαι καὶ ἄνδρας καὶ γυναῖκας καὶ μηδὲν μόριον ἀποκεκρύφθαι. The latter act is only conditional, and allowed in certain cases, such as for purposes of gymnastics.

[3] *Diog.* 33; 131.

[4] *Sext.* Pyrrh. iii. 201.

[5] *Sext.* Pyrrh. iii. 200 ; 245 ; Math. xi. 190 ; *Clement.* Homil. v. 18.

[6] *Sext.* Pyrrh. i. 160 ; iii. 205 ; 246 ; Math. xi. 191 ; *Plut.* Sto. Rep. 22 ; *Clement.* Hom. v. 18.

[7] *Plut.* l. c. 21, 1.

[8] Sextus, however (Pyrrh. iii. 206), attributes to him, as the representative of the School, what properly only belongs to Chrysippus : τό τε αἰσχρουργεῖν . . . ὁ Ζήνων οὐκ ἀποδοκιμάζει.

ciples to which they were pledged. The moral character of Zeno, Cleanthes, and Chrysippus is quite
above suspicion. It seems, therefore, strange that
they should have felt themselves compelled to admit
in theory what strikes the natural feeling with horror.
It cannot, however, be unconditionally accepted that
the statements laid to their charge imply as they used
them all that historians find in them. Far from it; of
some of their statements it may not only be said that
they do not justify conduct recognised to be immoral,
but that they are directed against actions customarily
allowed, the argument being, that between such
actions and actions admittedly immoral there is no
real difference. This remark applies, in particular, to
Zeno's language on unnatural vice.[1] It was not,
therefore, in opposition to the older Stoics, or in denial of their maxim, that love is permitted to a wise
man,[2] that the younger Stoics condemned most explicitly any and every form of unchastity, and, in
particular, the worst form of all, unnatural vice.[3]

[1] His words (*Sext.* Math. xi.
190; Pyrrh. iii. 245; *Plut.* Qu.
Con. iii. 6, 1, 6) are as follows:
διαμηρίζειν δὲ μηδὲν μᾶλλον μηδὲ
ἧσσον παιδικὰ ἢ μὴ παιδικὰ μηδὲ
θήλεα ἢ ἄρσενα· οὐ γὰρ ἄλλα παιδικοῖς ἢ μὴ παιδικοῖς οὐδὲ θηλείαις
ἢ ἄρρεσιν, ἀλλὰ τὰ αὐτὰ πρέπει τε
καὶ πρέποντά ἐστι; and: διαμεμή-
ρικας τὸν ἐρώμενον; οὐκ ἔγωγε·
πότερον οὖν ἐπεθύμησας αὐτὸν δια-
μηρίσαι; καὶ μάλα. ἀλλὰ ἐπεθύμησας παρασχεῖν σοι αὐτὸν ἢ
ἐφοβήθης κελεῦσαι; μὰ Δί'. ἀλλ'
ἐκέλευσας; καὶ μάλα. εἶτ' οὐχ
ὑπηρέτησέ σοι; οὐ γάρ. The
form of expression is certainly
very Cynic-like, but the meaning is not what Sextus supposes.
Zeno's object is not to justify
unnatural vice, but to show
that those who allow any form
of unchastity cannot forbid this
form, and that the wish and
the attempt are morally on a
par with the deed.

[2] See the following note.

[3] Musonius, in *Stob.* Serm. 6,
61 (conf. *Cic.* Fin. iii. 20, 68):
Ne amores quidem sanctos
alienos a sapiente esse volunt.
According to *Diog.* vii. 129,
Stob. ii. 238, love is only directed to beauty of soul. By *Diog.*,

In the same way, the language permitting marriage between those nearest of kin, when examined, is very much milder than it seems.[1] And Zeno's proposition for a community of wives may be fairly laid to the charge of Plato, and excused by all the charitable excuses of which Plato is allowed the benefit.[2]

Still, taking the most unprejudiced view of the Stoic propositions, enough remains to raise an extreme dislike to them, unless they could, without difficulty, be deduced from the fundamental principles of their system. A moral theory which makes such a sharp distinction between what is without and what is within, which regards the latter alone as essential, the former as altogether indifferent, which

Stob., Alex. Aphr. Top. 75, and Cic. Tusc. iv. 34, 72, it is defined to be ἐπιβολὴ φιλοποιίας διὰ κάλλος ἐμφαινόμενον; and, according to Plut. C. Not. 28, ἔμφασις κάλλους is an incentive to love; but these statements are guarded by adding that the bad and irrational are ugly, and the wise are beautiful. It was probably in imitation of Plat. Sym. 203, E, that the Stoics nevertheless stated τοὺς ἐρασθέντας αἰσχρῶν παύεσθαι καλῶν γενομένων. Love is excited by a sensation of εὐφυΐα πρὸς ἀρετὴν, its object being to develope this capacity into real virtue. Until this end has been attained, the loved one is still foolish, and therefore ugly. When it has been attained, the striving, in which Eros consists, has reached its object, and the love of the teacher to his pupil goes over into friendship between equals.

[1] Conf. Orig. c. Cels. iv. 45: The Stoics made good and evil depend alone on the intention, and declared external actions, independent of intentions, to be indifferent: εἶπον οὖν ἐν τῷ περὶ ἀδιαφόρων τόπῳ ὅτι τῷ ἰδίῳ λόγῳ (the action taken by itself) θυγατράσι μίγνυσθαι ἀδιάφορόν ἐστιν, εἰ καὶ μὴ χρὴ ἐν ταῖς καθεστώσαις πολιτείαις τὸ τοιοῦτον ποιεῖν. καὶ ὑποθέσεως χάριν . . . παρειλήφασι τὸν σοφὸν μετὰ τῆς θυγατρὸς μόνης καταλελειμμένον παντὸς τοῦ τῶν ἀνθρώπων γένους διεφθαρμένου, καὶ ζητοῦσιν εἰ καθηκόντως ὁ πατὴρ συνελεύσεται τῇ θυγατρὶ ὑπὲρ τοῦ μὴ ἀπολέσθαι . . . τὸ πᾶν τῶν ἀνθρώπων γένος.

[2] How strictly he respected chastity and modesty in women is proved by the fragment, preserved by Clem. Pædag. iii. 253, c, respecting the dress and conduct of maidens.

attaches no value to anything except virtuous intention, and places the highest value in being independent of everything—such a moral theory must of necessity prove wanting, whenever the business of morality consists in using the senses as instruments for expressing the mind, and in raising natural impulses to the sphere of free will. If its prominent feature is to allow less to the senses than naturally belongs to them, there is a danger that, in particular cases, in which intentions are not so obvious, the moral importance of actions will often be ignored, and those actions treated as indifferent.

The same observation will have to be made with regard to other positions which the Stoics laid down in reference to social relations. Not that it was their intention to detach man from his natural relation to other men. On the contrary, they held that the further man carries the work of moral improvement in himself, the stronger he will feel drawn to society. By the introduction of the idea of society, opposite tendencies arise in their ethics—one towards individual independence, the other in the direction of a well-ordered social life. The former tendency is the earlier one, and continues throughout to predominate ; still, the latter was not surreptitiously introduced—nay, more, it was the logical result of the Stoic principles, and to the eye of an Epicurean must have seemed a distinctive feature of Stoicism. In attributing absolute value only to rational thought and will, Stoicism had declared man to be independent of everything external, and, consequently, of

B. *Social
relations.*

(1) *Origin
and use of
society.*
(*a*) *Origin
of social
claims.*

his fellow-men. But since this value only attaches to *rational* thought and intention, the freedom of the individual at once involves the recognition of the community, and brings with it the requirement that everyone must subordinate his own ends to the ends and needs of the community. Rational conduct and thought can only then exist when the conduct of the individual is in harmony with general law; and this is the same for all rational beings. All rational beings must therefore aim at the same end, and recognise themselves subject to the same law. All must feel themselves portions of one connected whole. Man must not live for himself, but for society.

The connection between the individual and society was clearly set forth by the Stoics. The desire for society, they hold, is immediately involved in reason. By the aid of reason, man feels himself a part of a whole, and, consequently, bound to subordinate his own interests to the interests of the whole.[1] Like having always an attraction for like, this remark holds true of everything endowed with reason, since the rational soul is in all cases identical. From the consciousness of this unity, the desire for society at once arises in individuals endowed with reason.[2] They

[1] *Cic.* Fin. iii. 19, 64: Mundum autem censent regi numine Deorum eumque esse quasi communem urbem et civitatem hominum et Deorum; et unumquemque nostrum ejus mundi esse partem, ex quo illud consequi, ut communem utilitatem nostræ anteponamus.

[2] *M. Aurel.* ix. 9; xii. 30.

Sen. Ep. 95, 52: The whole world is a unit; membra sumus corporis magni. Natura nos cognatos edidit. Hence mutual love, love of society, justice, and fairness. Ep. 48, 2: Alteri vivas oportet, si vis tibi vivere. Hæc societas . . . nos homines hominibus miscet et judicat aliquod esse commune jus generis humani.

are all in the service of reason; there is, therefore, for all, but one right course and one law,[1] and they all contribute to the general welfare in obeying this law. The wise man, as a Stoic expresses it, is never a private man.[2]

At other times, social relations were explained by the theory of final causes.[3] Whilst everything else exists only for the sake of what is endowed with reason, individual beings endowed with reason exist for the sake of each other. Their social connection is therefore a direct natural command.[4] Towards animals we never stand in a position to exercise justice, nor yet towards ourselves.[5] Justice can only be exercised towards other men and towards God.[6] On the

[1] *Cic.* Legg. 12, 33 : Quibus enim ratio a natura data est, iisdem etiam recta ratio data est : ergo et lex, quæ est recta ratio in jubendo et vetando (see p. 241, 2): si lex, jus quoque. At omnibus ratio. Jus igitur datum est omnibus. *Ibid.* 7, 23 : Est igitur . . . prima homini cum Deo rationis societas. Inter quos autem ratio, inter eosdem etiam recta ratio communis est. Quæ cum sit lex, lege quoque consociati homines cum Diis putandi sumus. Inter quos porro est communio legis, inter eos communio juris est. Quibus autem hæc sunt inter eos communio, et civitatis ejusdem habendi sunt. Ps.-*Plut.* V. Hom. 119 : The Stoics teach ἕνα μὲν εἶναι τὸν κόσμον, συμπολιτεύεσθαι δὲ ἐν αὐτῷ θεοὺς καὶ ἀνθρώπους, δικαιοσύνης μετέχοντας φύσει.

[2] *Cic.* Tus. iv. 23, 51.

[3] *Cic.* Fin. iii. 20, 67 ; Off.

i. 7, 22 ; *Sen.* Clement. i. 3, 2 ; Benef. vii. 1, 7 ; *M. Aurel.* v. 16, 30 ; vii. 55 ; viii. 59 ; ix. 1 ; xi. 18 ; *Diog.* vii. 129 ; *Sext.* Math. ix. 131.

[4] Hence, according to *Cic.* Fin. iii. 21, 69, not only ὠφελήματα and βλάμματα (moral good and evil), but εὐχρηστήματα and δυσχρηστήματα (other advantages and disadvantages) are common to all men.

[5] According to *Plut.* Sto. Rep. 16, Chrysippus denied that a man could wrong himself. If, in other passages, he seems to assert the contrary, this apparent inconsistency is probably due to the double meaning of ἀδικεῖν, which sometimes means 'to wrong,' at others, simply 'to harm.' Strictly speaking, a relation involving justice can only exist towards another. See *Cic.* on p. 315, 2.

[6] Towards the Gods, man stands, according to the above

combination of individuals and their mutual support rests all their power over nature. A single man by himself would be the most helpless of creatures.[1]

The consciousness of this connection between all rational beings finds ample expression in Marcus Aurelius, the last of the Stoics. The possession of reason is, with him, at once love of society (vi. 14; x. 2). Rational beings can only be treated on a social footing (κοινωνικῶς) (vi. 23), and can only feel happy themselves when working for the community (viii. 7); for all rational beings are related to one another (iii. 4), all form one social unit (πολιτικὸν σύστημα), of which each individual is an integral part (συμπληρωτικός) (ix. 23); one body, of which every indivdual is an organic member (μέλος) (ii. 1; vii. 13). Hence the social instinct is a primary instinct in man (vii. 55), every manifestation of which contributes, either directly or indirectly, to the good of the whole (ix. 23). Our fellow-men ought to be loved from the heart. They ought to be benefited, not for the sake of outward decency, but because the benefactor is penetrated with the joy of benevolence, and thereby benefits himself.[2] Whatever hinders union with others has a tendency

passages, in a relation involving justice. There is, therefore (Sext. ix. 131), a justice towards the Gods, of which piety (see p. 261, 1) is only a part.

[1] Sen. Benef. iv. 18.
[2] M. Aurel. vii. 13: If you

only consider yourself a part, and not a member, of human society, οὔπω ἀπὸ καρδίας φιλεῖς τοὺς ἀνθρώπους· οὔπω σε καταληπτικῶς εὐφραίνει τὸ εὐεργετεῖν· ἔτι ὡς πρέπον αὐτὸ ψιλὸν ποιεῖς· οὔπω ὡς αὐτὸν εὖ ποιῶν.

to separate the members from the body, from which
all derive their life (viii. 34); and he who estranges
himself from one of his fellow-men voluntarily severs
himself from the stock of mankind (xi. 8). We shall
presently see that the language used by the philosophic emperor is quite in harmony with the Stoic
principles.

In relation to our fellow-men, two fundamental (2) *Justice*
points are insisted on by the Stoics—the duty of *and*
mercy.
justice and the duty of mercy. Cicero, without
doubt following Panætius,[1] describes these two virtues as the bonds which keep human society together,[2] and, consequently, gives to each an elaborate
treatment.[3] In expanding these duties, the Stoics
were led by the fundamental principles of their system to most distracting consequences. On the one
hand, they required from their wise men that strict
justice which knows no pity and can make no allow-
ances;[4] and hence their ethical system had about it
an air of austerity, and an appearance of severity
and cruelty. On the other hand, their principle of
the natural connection of all mankind imposed on
them the practice of the most extended and unre-
served charity, of beneficence, gentleness, meekness,
of an unlimited benevolence, and a readiness to for-

---

[1] See p. 298, 3.
[2] Off. i. 7, 20: De tribus
autem reliquis [virtutibus, the
three others besides under-
standing] latissime patet ea
ratio, qua societas hominum
inter ipsos et vitæ quasi com-
munitas continetur, cujus partes
duæ sunt : justitia, in qua vir-

tutis splendor est maximus, ex
qua viri boni nominantur, et
huic conjuncta beneficentia,
quam eandem vel benignita-
tem vel liberalitatem appellari
licet.
[3] Off. i. 7-13; ii. 14-17.
[4] See p. 254, 2, 3.

give in all cases in which forgiveness is possible. This last aspect of the Stoic teaching appears principally in the later Stoics—in Seneca, Epictetus, Marcus Aurelius, and Musonius;[1] and it is quite possible that they may have given more prominence to it than their predecessors. But the fact is there, that this aspect is due, not only to the peculiar character of these individuals, but is based on the spirit and tone of the whole system.[2]

The question then naturally arises, how these two opposites may be reconciled—how stern justice may be harmonised with forgiveness and mercy. Seneca, who investigated the question fully, replies : Not severity, but only cruelty, is opposed to mercy; for no one virtue is opposed to another : a wise man will always help another in distress, but without sharing his emotion, without feeling misery or compassion ; he will not indulge, but he will spare, advise, and improve ; he will not remit punishments in cases in which he knows them to be deserved, but, from a sense of justice, he will take human weakness into consideration in allotting punishments, and make every possible allowance for circumstances.[3] Every difficulty is not, indeed, removed by these statements ; still, those which remain apply more to the Stoic demand for apathy than to the reconciliation of

---

[1] We shall subsequently have occasion to prove this in detail. It may here suffice to refer to the treatises of Seneca, De Beneficiis, De Clementia, and De Ira. On the value of mercy, he remarks (De Clem. i. 3, 2): Nullam ex omnibus virtutibus magis homini convenire, cum sit nulla humanior.

[2] Conf. Panætius, in *Cic.* Off. i. 25, 88.

[3] De Clem. ii. 5-8.

the two virtues which regulate our relations to our
fellow-men.[1]

The society for which all rational beings are intended will naturally be found to exist principally
among those who have become alive to their rational
nature and destiny—in other words, among the wise.
All who are wise and virtuous are friends, because
they agree in their views of life, and because they
all love one another's virtue.[2]   Thus every action of a wise man contributes to the well-being
of every other wise man—or, as the Stoics pointedly
express it, if a wise man only makes a rational movement with his finger, he does a service to all wise
men throughout the world.[3]   On the other hand,
only a wise man knows how to love properly; true
friendship only exists between wise men.[4]   Only the
wise man possesses the art of making friends,[5] since

CHAP.
XII.

(3)*Friend-
ship.*

[1] Among the points cha-
racteristic of Stoicism, the censure deserves notice which *Sen.*
(Ep. 7, 3; 95, 33; Tranq. An.
2, 13) passes on gladiatorial
shows and the Roman thirst
for war. (Ep. 95, 30.) The attitude of the Stoics to slavery and
the demand for love of enemies
will be considered hereafter.

[2] *Stob.* ii. 184 : τήν τε ὁμόνοιαν ἐπιστήμην εἶναι κοινῶν
ἀγαθῶν, διὸ καὶ τοὺς σπουδαίους
πάντας ὁμονοεῖν ἀλλήλοις διὰ τὸ
συμφωνεῖν ἐν τοῖς κατὰ τὸν βίον.
Cic. N. D. i. 44, 121 : Censent
autem [Stoici] sapientes sa-
pientibus etiam ignotis esse
amicos, nihil est enim virtute
amabilius. Quam qui adeptus
erit, ubicumque erit gentium, a

nobis diligetur. See Off. i. 17,
55. Conf. p. 309, 3.

[3] *Plut.* C. Not. 22, 2. The
same thought is expressed in
the statement (*ibid.* 33, 2) that
the wise man is as useful to
deity (the universe) as deity is
to him.

[4] *Sen.* Benef. vii. 12, 2 ; Ep.
81, 11; 123, 15 ; 9, 5; *Stob.* ii.
118; see p. 271, 3. *Diog.* 124.
According to *Diog.* 32, Zeno,
like Socrates, was blamed for
asserting that only the good
(ὐνουδαῖοι) among themselves
are fellow-citizens, friends, and
relations; whilst all the bad
are enemies and strangers.

[5] He is, as *Sen.* Ep. 9, 5,
puts it, faciendarum amicitia-
rum artifex.

CHAP.
XII.

love is only won by love.[1] If, however, true friendship is a union between the good and the wise, its
value is thereby at once established ; and hence it is
distinctly enumerated among goods by the Stoics.[2]

On this point, difficulties reappear. How can this
need of society be reconciled with the wise man's
freedom from wants ? If the wise man is self-suffi-
cient, how can another help him ? How can he stand
in need of such help ? The answers given by Seneca
are not satisfactory. To the first question, he replies,
that none but a wise man can give the right induce-
ment to a wise man to call into exercise his powers.[3]
He meets the second by saying, that a wise man suf-
fices himself for happiness, but not for life.[4] Everywhere the wise man finds inducements to virtuous
action ; if friendship is not a condition of happiness, it is not a good at all. Nor are his further
observations more satisfactory. The wise man, he
says,[5] does not *wish* to be without friends, but still

[1] Si vis amari, ama, says
Hecato, in *Sen.* Ep. 9, 6.

[2] We have already encountered friendship in the Stoic
list of goods. See p. 230, 3.
Stob. 186, says, more accurately,
that friendship, for the sake of
the commonwealth, is not a
good, διὰ τὸ μηδὲν ἐκ διεστηκότων
ἀγαθὸν εἶναι ; on the other hand,
friendship, in the sense of
friendly relations to others,
belongs to external goods ; in
the sense of a friendly disposition merely, it belongs to
intellectual goods. On the
value of friendship, *Sen.* 99, 3.
Friendship is defined as κοινωνία
βίου (*Stob.* 130) ; κοινωνία τῶν

κατὰ τὸν βίον, χρωμένων ἡμῶν
τοῖς φίλοις ὡς ἑαυτοῖς (*Diog.*
124). Similar definitions are
given by *Stob.* of varieties of
friendship : γνωριμότης, συνήθεια,
κ.τ.λ. On the absolute community of goods among friends,
see *Sen.* Ep. 47, 2 ; 3, 2 ; Benef.
vii. 4, 1 ; 12, 1.

[3] Ep. 109, 3 and 11.

[4] Ep. 9, 13 : Se contentus
est sapiens ad beate vivendum,
non ad vivendum. Ad hoc
enim multis illi rebus opus
est, ad illud tantum animo
sano et erecto et despiciente
fortunam.

[5] Ep. 9, 5.

he *can* be without friends. But the question is not whether he *can* be, but whether he can be without loss of happiness. If the question so put is answered in the negative, it follows that the wise man is not altogether self-sufficing ; if in the affirmative—and a wise man, as Seneca affirms, will bear the loss of a friend with calmness, because he comforts himself with the thought that he can have another at any moment—then friendship is not worth much. Moreover, if a wise man can help another by communicating to him information and method, since no wise man is omniscient,[1] we ask, Is not a wise man, if not in possession of all knowledge, at least in possession of all knowledge contributing to virtue and happiness ? If it be added, that what one learns from another he learns by his own powers, and is consequently himself helping himself, does not this addition still overlook the fact that the teacher's activity is the condition of the learner's ? True and beautiful as is the language of Seneca : Friendship has its value in itself alone; every wise man must wish to find those like himself ; the good have a natural love for the good ; the wise man needs a friend, not to have a nurse in sickness and an assistant in trouble, but to have someone whom he can tend and assist, and for whom he can live and die[2]—nevertheless, this language does not meet the critical objection, that one who requires the help of another, be it only to have an object for his moral activity, cannot be wholly dependent on himself. If friendship, according to a

---

[1] *Sen.* Ep. 109, 5. [2] Ep. 109, 13 ; 9, 8 ; 10, 12 ; 18.

CHAP.
XII.

previously-quoted distinction,[1] belongs to external
goods, it makes man, in a certain sense, dependent
on externals.   If its essence is placed in an inward
disposition of friendliness, such a disposition depends
on the existence of those for whom it can be felt.
Besides, it involves the necessity of being recipro-
cated, and of finding expression in outward conduct,
to such an extent that it is quite subversive of the
absolute independence of the individual.

(4) *The family and political life.*

Nor yet is the friendship of the wise the only form
of society which appeared to the Stoics necessary
and essential.   If man is intended [2] to associate with
his fellow-men in a society regulated by justice and
law, how can he withdraw from the most common
institution—the state?   If virtue does not consist
in idle contemplation, but in action, how dare he
lose the opportunity of promoting good and repres-
sing evil by taking part in political life? [3]   If laws

[1] See p. 318, 2.
[2] *Stob.* ii. 208 : τὸν γὰρ νόμον εἶναι, καθάπερ εἴπομεν, σπουδαῖον, ὁμοίως δὲ καὶ τὴν πόλιν.   ἱκανῶς δὲ καὶ Κλεάνθης περὶ τὸ σπουδαῖον εἶναι τὴν πόλιν λόγον ἠρώτησε τοῦτον· πόλις μὲν εἰ (wrongly struck out by Meineke) ἔστιν οἰκητήριον κατασκεύασμα εἰς ὃ καταφεύγοντας ἔστι δίκην δοῦναι καὶ λαβεῖν, οὐκ ἀστεῖον δὴ πόλις ἐστίν; Floril. 44, 12.   See pp. 223 ; 241, 3.
[3] *Plut.* Sto. Rep. 2, 3 : Chry-sippus recommends political life, placing βίος σχολαστικὸς on the same footing with βίος ἡδονικός.   *Diog.* vii. 121 : πολι-τεύεσθαί φασιν τὸν σοφὸν ἂν μή τι κωλύῃ, ὥς φησι Χρύσιππος ἐν

πρώτῳ περὶ βίων · καὶ γὰρ κακίαν ἐφέξειν καὶ ἐπ' ἀρετὴν ἐφορμήσειν.   *Sen.* De Ot. 3, 2 : Epicurus ait : non accedet ad rempublicam sapiens, nisi si quid intervenerit. Zenon ait : accedet ad rempub-licam, nisi si quid impedierit. *Cic.* Fin. iii. 20, 68 : Since man exists for the sake of other men, consentaneum est huic naturæ, ut sapiens velit gerere et administrare rempublicam : atque, ut e natura vivat, uxorem adjungere et velle ex ea liberos procreare.   *Stob.* ii. 184 : τό τε δίκαιόν φασι φύσει εἶναι καὶ μὴ θέσει.   ἑπόμενον δὲ τούτοις ὑπάρ-χειν καὶ τὸ πολιτεύεσθαι τὸν σοφὸν . . . καὶ τὸ νομοθετεῖν τε καὶ παι-δεύειν ἀνθρώπους, κ.τ.λ.

further the well-being and security of the citizens, if they advance virtue and happiness, how can the wise man fail to regard them as beautiful and praiseworthy?[1] For the same reason, matrimony will command his respect. He will neither deny himself a union so natural and intimate, nor will he deprive the state of relays of men nor society of the sight of well-ordered family life.[2] Hence, in their writings and precepts, the Stoics paid great attention to the state and to domestic life.[3] In marriage they required chastity, and moderation. Love was to be a matter of reason, not of emotion—not a yielding to personal attractions, nor a seeking sensual gratification.[4] As

CHAP.
XII.

[1] *Cic.* Legg. ii. 5, 11.

[2] *Diog. Ibid.* : καὶ γαμήσειν, ὡς ὁ Ζήνων φησὶν ἐν πολιτείᾳ, καὶ παιδοποιήσεσθαι. *Ibid.* 120 : The Stoics consider love towards children, parents, and kindred to be according to nature. Chrysippus (in *Hieron.* Ad. Jovin. i. 191) : The wise man will marry, lest he offend Zeus Γαμήλιος and Γενέθλιος. Antipater (whether the well-known pupil of Diogenes of Seleucia, or the younger Stoic Antipater of Tyre mentioned by *Cic.* Off. ii. 24, 86, is not stated) in *Stob.* Floril. 67, 25 : Wife and child are necessary to give completeness to civil and domestic life ; a citizen owes children to his country, and family love is the purest. Musonius (*Ibid.* 67, 20, Conf. 75, 15) : A philosopher ought to be a pattern in married life, as in every other natural relation, and discharge his duties as a citizen by

founding a family ; love for wife and children is the deepest love.

[3] *Plut.* Sto. Rep. 2. 1 : ἐπεὶ τοίνυν πολλὰ μὲν, ὡς ἐν λόγοις, αὐτῷ Ζήνωνι, πολλὰ δὲ Κλεάνθει, πλεῖστα δὲ Χρυσίππῳ γεγραμμένα τυγχάνει περὶ πολιτείας καὶ τοῦ ἄρχεσθαι καὶ ἄρχειν καὶ δικάζειν καὶ ῥητορεύειν. Conf. the titles in *Diog.* vii. 4 ; 166 ; 175 ; 178. Diogenes's list contains no political writings of Chrysippus. It is, however, known to be incomplete ; for *Diog.* vii. 34 ; 131, quotes Chrysippus's treatise περὶ πολιτείας, a treatise also quoted by *Plut.* Sto. Rep. 21 (1, 3, 5). According to *Cic.* Legg. iii. 6, 14, Diogenes and Panætius were the only Stoics before his time who had entered into particulars respecting legislation, though others might have written much on politics.

[4] Conf. the fragment of *Sen.* De Matrimonio, in *Hieron.* Ad.

to their views on the constitution of a state, we
know [1] that they prefer a mixed constitution, compounded of the three simple forms, without objecting
to other forms of government. The wise man, according to Chrysippus, will not despise the calling
of a prince, if his interest so require, and, if he cannot govern himself, will reside at the court and in
the camp of princes, particularly of good princes.[2]

The ideal of the Stoics, however, was not realised
in any one of the existing forms of government, but
in that polity of the wise which Zeno described, undoubtedly when a Cynic,[3] but which was fully set
forth by Chrysippus [4]—a state without marriage, or
family, or temples, or courts, or public schools, or
coins [5]—a state excluding no other states, because all
differences of nationality have been merged in a
common brotherhood of all men.[6] Such an ideal may
show that, for the Stoic philosophers, there could be
no hearty sympathy with the state or the family, their
ideal state being, in truth, no longer a state. Indeed,

Jovin. i. 191, Fr. 81 Haase,
which, like the Essenes, requires absolute abstinence from
pregnant women. A few un-
important fragments are also
preserved by Chrysippus's treatise on the education of children. See *Quintil.* Inst. i. 11,
17; 1, 4 and 16; 3, 14; 10, 32;
Baguet, De Chrys. (Annal.
Lovan. iv. p. 335). He is re-
proached by Posidonius (*Galen.*
Hipp. et Plat. v. 1, p. 465) for
neglecting the first germs of
education, particularly those
previous to birth.

[1] *Diog.* vii. 131.
[2] *Plut.* Sto. Rep. 20, 3–5;
7; 30, 3; C. Not. 7, 6.
[3] *Diog.* vii. 4.
[4] *Diog.* vii. 131.
[5] *Diog.* 33: κοιιάς τε γὰρ
γυναῖκας δογματίζειν ὁμοίως ἐν τῇ
Πολιτείᾳ καὶ κατὰ τοὺς διακοσίους
στίχους, μήθ' ἱερὰ μήτε δικαστήρια
μήτε γυμνάσια ἐν ταῖς πόλεσιν
οἰκοδομεῖσθαι . . . νόμισμα δ' οὔτ'
ἀλλαγῆς ἕνεκεν οἴεσθαι δεῖν κατασκευάζειν οὔτ' ἀποδημίας. *Ibid.*
131.
[6] *Plut.* Alex. Virt. i. 6, p. 329.

the whole tone of Stoicism, and still more, the circumstances of the times to which it owed its rise
and growth, were against such a sympathy. If Plato
could find no scope for a philosopher in the political
institutions of his time, how could a Stoic, seeking
as he did for happiness more exclusively in seclusion
from the world, contrasting, too, the wise man more
sharply with the multitude of fools, and living for
the most part under political circumstances far less
favourable than Plato had enjoyed? To him the
private life of a philosopher must have seemed beyond compare more attractive than a public career.
An intelligent man, taking advice from Chrysippus,[1]
avoids business; he withdraws to peaceful retirement; and, though he may consider it his duty not
to stand aloof from public life, still he can only ac-
tively take a part in it in states which present an
appreciable progress towards perfection.[2] But where
could such states be found? Did not Chrysippus state
it as his conviction that a statesman must either
displease the Gods or displease the people?[3] And
did not later Stoics accordingly advise philosophers
not to intermeddle at all in civil matters?[4] Labour

[1] *Plut.* Sto. Rep. 20, 1: οἶμαι
γὰρ ἔγωγε τὸν φρόνιμον καὶ ἀπρά-
γμονα εἶναι καὶ ὀλιγοπράγμονα καὶ
τὰ αὑτοῦ πράττειν, ὁμοίως τῆς τε
αὐτοπραγίας καὶ ὀλιγοπράγμοσύνης
ἀστείων ὄντων . . . τῷ γὰρ ὄντι φαίνεται ὁ κατὰ τὴν ἡσυχίαν βίος ἀκιν-
δυνόν τε καὶ ἀσφαλὲς ἔχειν, κ.τ.λ.
[2] *Stob.* Ecl. ii. 186: πολιτεύεσθαι τὸν σοφὸν καὶ μάλιστα ἐν
ταῖς τοιαύταις πολιτείαις ταῖς

ἐμφαινούσαις τινὰ προκοπὴν πρὸς
τὰς τελείας πολιτείας.
[3] *Stob.* Floril. 45, 29 : In
answer to the question, why he
withdrew from public life, he
replied : διότι εἰ μὲν πονηρὰ πολι-
τεύεται [—σεται], τοῖς θεοῖς ἀπα-
ρέσει, εἰ δὲ χρηστά, τοῖς πολίταις.
[4] *Sen.* Ep. 29, 11 : Quis enim
placere potest populo, cui placet
virtus ? malis artibus popularis

for the commonwealth is only then a duty when there is no obstacle to such labour; but, as a matter of fact, there is always some obstacle, and in particular, the condition of all existing states.[1] A philosopher who teaches and improves his fellow-men benefits the state quite as much as a warrior, an administrator, or a civil functionary.[2]

(b) Practical aversion to political life.

Following out this idea,[3] Epictetus dissuades from matrimony and the begetting of children. Allowing that the family relation may be admitted in a community of wise men, he is of opinion that it is otherwise under existing circumstances; for how can a true philosopher engage in connections and actions which withdraw him from the service of God? The last expression already implies that unfavourable times were not the only cause deterring this Stoic from caring for family or the state, but that the occupation in itself seemed to him a subordinate and limited one; this is even stated in plain terms by

---

favor quæritur. Similem te illi: facias oportet . . . conciliari nisi turpi ratione amor turpium non potest.

[1] *Sen.* De Ot. 3, 3, p. 320, 3: It needs a special cause for devoting oneself to private life. Causa autem illa late patet: si respublica corruptior est quam ut adjuvari possit, si occupata est malis . . . si parum habebit [sc. sapiens] auctoritatis aut virium nec illum admissura erat respublica, si valetudo illum impediet. *Ibid.* 8, 1: Negant nostri sapientem ad quamlibet rempublicam accessurum: quid

autem interest, quomodo sapiens ad otium veniat, utrum quia respublica illi deest, an quia ipse reipublicæ, si omnibus defutura respublica est. (So we ought to punctuate.) Semper autem deerit fastidiose quærentibus. Interrogo ad quam rempublicam sapiens sit accessurus. Ad Athenienslum, etc.? Si percensere singulas voluero, nullam inveniam, quæ sapientem aut quam sapiens pati possit. Similarly Athenodorus, in *Sen.* Tranq. An. 3, 2.

[2] *Athenodor.* l. c. 3, 3.

[3] Diss. iii. 22, 67.

Seneca and Epictetus : He who feels himself a citizen
of the world finds in an individual state a sphere far
too limited—he prefers devoting himself to the universe ; [1] man is no doubt intended to be active, but
the highest activity is intellectual research.[2] On the
subject of civil society, opinions were likely to vary,
according to the peculiarities and circumstances of
individuals. The philosopher on the throne was more
likely than the freedman Epictetus to feel himself
a citizen of Rome as well as a citizen of the world,[3]
and to lower the demands made on a philosophic
statesman.[4] At the same time, the line taken by the
Stoic philosophy cannot be ignored. A philosophy

CHAP.
XII.

[1] *Sen.* De Otio, 4, 1 : Duas
respublicas animo complecta-
mur, alteram magnam et vere
publicam, qua Di atque homines
continentur, in qua non ad hunc
angulum respicimus aut ad illum, sed terminòs civitatis nostræ cum sole metimur : alteram
cui nos adscripsit condicio nas-
cendi. Does it not seem like
reading Augustin's De Civitate
Dei ? Some serve the great,
others the small state ; some
serve both. Majori reipublicæ
et in otio deservire possumus,
immo vero nescio an in otio
melius. Ep. 68, 2 : Cum sapienti rempublicam ipso dignam
dedimus, id est mundum, non
est extra rempublicam etiamsi
recesserit : immo fortasse re-
licto uno angulo in majora
atque ampliora transit, &c.
Epict. Diss. iii. 22, 83 : Do you
ask whether a wise man will
busy himself with the state ?
What state could he greater
than the one about which he
does busy himself, not consulting the citizens of one city
alone for the purpose of obtaining information about the re-
venues of a state, and such like,
but the citizens of the world,
that with them he may converse of happiness and unhap-
piness, of freedom and slavery.
τηλικαύτην πολίτειαν πολιτευσα-
μένου ἀνθρώπου, σύ μοι πυνθάνῃ, εἰ
πολιτεύσεται ; πυθοῦ μου καὶ, εἰ
ἄρξει· πάλιν ἐρῶ σοι· μωρὲ, ποίαν
ἀρχὴν μείζονα ἧς ἄρχει ;

[2] *Sen.* De Otio, 5, 1 ; 7 ; 6, 4.

[3] *Marcus Aurelius*, vi. 44 :
πόλις καὶ πατρὶς ὡς μὲν 'Αντωνίῳ
μοι ἡ 'Ρώμη, ὡς δὲ ἀνθρώπῳ ὁ
κόσμος. τὰ ταῖς πόλεσιν οὖν τού-
ταις ὠφέλιμα μόνα ἐστί μοι ἀγαθά.
ii. 5 : πάσης ὥρας φρόντιζε στι-
βαρῶς ὡς 'Ρωμαῖος καὶ ἄρρην.

[4] *Ibid.* ix. 29 : ὅρμησον ἐὰν δι-
δῶται καὶ μὴ περιβλέπου εἴ τις
εἴσεται μηδὲ τὴν Πλάτωνος πολίτειαν ἔλπιζε, ἀλλὰ ἀρκοῦ εἰ τὸ
βραχύτατον πρόεισι.

which attaches moral value to the cultivation of intentions only, considering at the same time all external circumstances as indifferent, can hardly produce
a taste or a skill for overcoming those outward interests and circumstances with which a politician is
chiefly concerned. A system which regards the mass
of men as fools, which denies to them every healthy
endeavour and all true knowledge, can hardly bring
itself unreservedly to work for a state, the course
and institutions of which depend upon the majority
of its members, and are planned with a view to their
needs, prejudices, and customs. Undoubtedly, there
were able statesmen among the Stoics of the Roman
period ; but Rome, and not Stoicism, was the cause
of their statesmanship. Taken alone, Stoicism could
form excellent men, but hardly excellent statesmen.
And, looking to facts, not one of the old masters of
the School ever had or desired any public office.
Hence, when their opponents urged that retirement
was a violation of their principles,[1] Seneca could with
justice meet the charge by replying, that the true
meaning of their principles ought to be gathered
from their actual conduct.[2]

*(c) Citi-
zenship
of the
world.*

The positive substitute wherewith the Stoics
thought to replace the ordinary relations of civil
society was by a citizenship of the world. No preceding system had been able to overcome the difficulty of nationalities. Even Plato and Aristotle
shared the prejudice of the Greeks against foreigners.

[1] *Plut.* Sto. Rep. 2, 1.
[2] De Otio, 6, 5 ; Tranq. An. 1, 10.

The Cynics alone appear as the precursors of the Stoa, attaching slight value to the citizenship of any particular state, in comparison with citizenship of the world.[1] Still, with the Cynics, this idea had not attained to the historical importance which afterwards belonged to it ; nor was it used so much with a positive meaning, to express the essential oneness of all mankind, as, in a negative sense, to imply the philosopher's independence of country and home. From the Stoic philosophy it first received a definite meaning, and became generally called into service. The causes of this change may be sought, not only in the historical surroundings amongst which Stoicism grew up, but also in the person of its founder. Far easier was it for philosophy to overcome national dislikes, after the genial Macedonian conqueror had united the vigorous nationalities comprised within his monarchy, not only under a central government, but also in a common culture.[2] Hence the Stoic citizenship of the world may be appealed to, to prove the assertion, that philosophic Schools only reflect the existing facts of history. On the other hand, taking into account the bias given to a philosopher's teaching by his personal circumstances, Zeno, being only half a Greek, would be more ready to underestimate the distinction of Greek and barbarian than any one of his predecessors.

However much these two causes—and, in parti-

[1] See Socrates and Socratic Schools, p. 324.
[2] This connection is already indicated by Plutarch's grouping the Stoics and Alexander together.

cular, the first—must have contributed to bring about the Stoic ideal of a citizenship of the world, nevertheless the connection of this idea with the whole of their system is most obvious. If human society, as we have seen, has for its basis the identity of reason in individuals, what ground have we for limiting this society to a single nation, or feeling ourselves more nearly related to some men than to others? All men, apart from what they have made themselves by their own exertions, are equally near, since all equally participate in reason. All are members of one body ; for one and the same nature has fashioned them all from the same elements for the same destiny.[1] Or, as Epictetus expresses it in religious language,[2] all men are brethren, since all have in the same degree God for their father. Man, therefore, who and whatever else he may be, is the object of our solicitude, simply as being a man.[3] No hostility and illtreatment should quench our benevolence.[4] No

---

[1] *Sen.* Ep. 95, 52 ; *M. Aurel.* See p. 312, 2 ; 313.

[2] Diss. i. 13, 3. See p. 331, 2.

[3] *Sen.* Ep. 95, 52, continues after the quotation in p. 312, 2 : Ex illius [naturæ] constitutione miserius est nocere quam lædi. Ex illius imperio paratæ sint juvantis manus. Ille versus et in pectore et in ore sit: homo sum, nihil humani a me alienum puto. V. Be. 24, 3 : Hominibus prodesse natura me jubet, et servi liberine sint hi, ingenui an libertini, justæ libertatis an inter amicos datæ quid refert? Ubicumque homo est, ibi beneficii locus est. De Clem. i. 1,

3 : Nemo non, cui alia desint, hominis nomine apud me gratiosus est. De Ira, i. 5.

[4] *Sen.* De Otio, i. 4 : see p. 256, 4 : Stoici nostri dicunt . . . non desinemus communi bono operam dare, adjuvare singulos, opem ferre etiam inimicis. We shall subsequently meet with similar explanations from Musonius, Epictetus, and Marcus Aurelius. In particular, Seneca's treatise, De Ira, deserves to be mentioned here, and especially i. 5, 2 : Quid homine aliorum amantius ? quid ira infestius ? Homo in adjutorium mutuum genitus est, ira in exi-

one is so low but that he has claims on the love and justice of his fellow-men.[1] Even the slave is a man deserving our esteem, and able to claim from us his rights.[2]

Nor yet did the Stoics go so far in their recognition of the universal rights of mankind as to disapprove of slavery. Attaching in general little value to external circumstances,[3] they cared the less to run

tium. Hic congregari vult, illa discedere. Hic prodesse, illa nocere. Hic etiam ignotis succurrere, illa etiam carissimos perdere. *Ibid.* ii. 32, 1 : It is not so praiseworthy to return injury for injury, as benefit for benefit. Illic vinci turpe est, hic vincere. Inhumanum verbum est . . . ultio et talio. Magni animi est injurias despicere. Conf. *Cic.* Off. i. 25, 88 : Violent anger towards enemies must be blamed : nihil enim laudabilius, nihil magno et præclaro viro dignius placabilitate atque clementia. Even when severity is necessary, punishment ought not to be administered in anger, since such an emotion cannot be allowed at all. See p. 254, 1.

[1] *Sen.* Ep. 95, 52. See p. 328, 3. *Cic.* Off. i. 13, 41.

[2] *Cic.* l. c.: Even towards slaves, justice must be observed. Here, too, belongs the question, discussed at full by *Sen.* Benef. iii. 18–28, Whether a slave can do a kindness to his master ? He who denies that he can, says Seneca (18, 2), is ignarus juris humani. Refert enim cujus animi sit, qui præstat, non cujus status: nulli præclusa virtus est, omnibus patet, om-

nes admittit, omnes invitat, ingenuas, libertinos, servos, reges, exules. Non eligit domum nec censum, nudo homine contenta est. Slavery, he continues, does not affect the whole man. Only the body belongs to his lord ; his heart belongs to himself, c. 20. The duties of the slave have limits, and over against them stand certain definite rights (c. 21. Conf. De Clement. i. 18, 2). He enumerates many instances of self-sacrifice and magnanimity in slaves, and concludes by saying : Eadem omnibus principia eademque origo, nemo altero nobilior, nisi cui rectius ingenium . . . unus omnium parens mundus est . . . neminem despexeris . . . sive libertini ante vos habentur sive servi sive exterarum homines : erigite audacter animos, et quicquid in medio sordidi est transilite : expectat vos in summo magna nobilitas, &c. So Ep. 31, 11 ; V. Be. 24, 3. See p. 328, 3. Conf. Ep. 44 : Rank and birth are of no consequence, and p. 270, 3.

[3] Only the wise man is really free ; all who are not wise are fools.

CHAP.
XII.

counter to the social institutions and arrangements of their age. Still they could not wholly suppress a confession that slavery is unjust,[1] nor cease to aim at mitigating the evil both in theory and practice.[2] If all men are, as rational beings, equal, all men together form one community. Reason is the common law for all, and those who owe allegiance to one law are members of one state.[3] If the Stoics, therefore, compared the world, in its more extended sense, to a society, because of the connection of its parts,[4] they must, with far more reason, have allowed that the world, in the narrower sense of the term, including all rational beings, forms one community,[5]

[1] *Diog.* 122, at least, calls δεσποτεία, the possession and government of slaves, something bad.

[2] According to *Sen.* Benef. iii. 22, 1, *Cic.* l. c., Chrysippus had defined a slave, perpetuus mercenarius; and hence inferred that as such he ought to be treated : operam exigendam, justa præbenda. *Sen.* Ep. 47, expresses a very humane view of treating slaves, contrasting a man with a slave: servi sunt; immo homines. He regards a slave as a friend of lower rank, and, since all men stand under the same higher power, speaks of himself as conservus.

[3] *M. Aurel.* iv. 4 : εἰ τὸ νοερὸν ἡμῖν κοινόν, καὶ ὁ λόγος καθ' ὃν λογικοί ἐσμεν κοινός· εἰ τοῦτο, καὶ ὁ προστακτικὸς τῶν ποιητέων ἢ μὴ λόγος κοινός· εἰ τοῦτο, καὶ ὁ νόμος κοινός. εἰ τοῦτο, πολῖταί ἐσμεν· εἰ τοῦτο, πολιτεύματός τινος μετέχομεν· εἰ τοῦτο, ὁ κόσμος ὡσανεὶ πόλις ἐστί.

[4] See pp. 312, 1, 3 ; 325, 3,

and *Plut.* Com. Not. 34, 6, who makes the Stoics assert : τὸν κόσμον εἶναι πόλιν καὶ πολίτας τοὺς ἀστέρας. *M. Aurel.* x. 15 : ζῆσον . . . ὡς ἐν πόλει τῷ κόσμῳ. iv. 3 : ὁ κόσμος ὡσανεὶ πόλις.

[5] *M. Aurel.* iv. 4, and ii. 16. *Cic.* Fin. iii. 20, 67 : Chrysippus asserts that men exist for the sake of each other ; quoniamque ea natura esset hominis ut ei cum genere humano quasi civile jus intercederet, qui id conservaret, eum justum, qui migraret, injustum fore. Therefore, in the sequel : in urbe mundove communi. See 331, 2 and p. 312, 2. *Sen.* De Ira, ii. 31, 7 : Nefas est nocere patriæ: ergo civi quoque . . . ergo et homini, nam hic in majore tibi urbe civis est. Musonius (in *Stob.* Floril. 40, 9) : νομίζει [ὁ ἐπιεικὴς] εἶναι πολίτης τῆς τοῦ Διὸς πόλεως ἣ συνέστηκεν ἐξ ἀνθρώπων τε καὶ θεῶν. *Epict.* Diss. iii. 5, 26 ; Ar. Didym. in *Eus.* Pr. Ev. xv. 15, 4.

to which individual communities are related, as the
houses of a city are to the city collectively.[1] Wise
men, at least, if not others, will esteem this great
community, to which all men belong, far above any
particular community in which the accident of birth
has placed them.[2] They, at least, will direct their
efforts towards making all men feel themselves to be
citizens of one community; and, instead of framing
exclusive laws and constitutions, will try to live as
one family, under the common governance of reason.[3]
The platform of social propriety receives hereby a
universal width. Man, by withdrawing from the
outer world into the recesses of his own intellectual
and moral state, becomes enabled to recognise everywhere the same nature as his own, and to feel himself one with the universe, by sharing with it the
same nature and the same destiny.

But, as yet, the moral problem is not exhausted.

[1] M. Aurel. iii. 11 : ἄνθρωπον
πολίτην ὄντα πόλεως τῆς ἀνωτά-
της ἧς αἱ λοιπαὶ πόλεις ὥσπερ
οἰκίαι εἰσίν.
[2] Sen. De Ot. 4 ; Ep. 68, 2.
See p. 325, 1. Vit. B. 20, 3 and
5 : Unum me donavit omnibus
[natura rerum] et uni mihi
omnis . . . patriam meam esse
mundum sciam et præsides
Deos. Tranq. An. 4, 4 : Ideo
magno animo nos non unius
urbis mœnibus clusimus, sed in
totius orbis commercium emisi-
mus patriamque nobis mundum
professi sumus, ut liceret la-
tiorem virtuti campum dare.
Epict. Diss. iii. 22, 83. Ibid.
i. 9 : If the doctrine that man
is related to God is true, man

is neither an Athenian nor a
Corinthian, but simply κόσμιος
and υἱὸς Θεοῦ. Muson. l. c. :
Banishment is no evil, since
κοινὴ πατρὶς ἀνθρώπων ἁπάντων ὁ
κόσμος ἐστίν. It is, says Cic.
Parad. 2, no evil for those qui
omnem orbem terrarum unam
urbem esse ducunt.
[3] Plut. Alex. M. Virt. i. 6, p.
329 : καὶ μὴν ἡ πολὺ θαυμαζομένη
πολίτεια τοῦ τὴν Στωϊκῶν αἵρεσιν
καταβαλλομένου Ζήνωνος εἰς ἓν
τοῦτο συντείνει κεφάλαιον, ἵνα μὴ
κατὰ πόλεις μηδὲ κατὰ δήμους
οἰκῶμεν, ἰδίοις ἕκαστοι διωρισμένοι
δικαίοις, ἀλλὰ πάντας ἀνθρώπους
ἡγώμεθα δημότας καὶ πολίτας, εἷς
δὲ βίος ᾖ καὶ κόσμος, ὥσπερ ἀγέλης
συννόμου νόμῳ κοινῷ τρεφομένης.

C. *Man
and the
course of
the world.*

Reason, the same as man's, rules pure and complete in the universe ; and if it is the business of man to give play to reason in his own conduct, and to recognise it in that of others, it is also his duty to subordinate himself to collective reason, and to the course of the world, over which it presides. In conclusion, therefore, the relation of man to the course of the world must be considered.

(1) *Submission to
the course
of nature.*

Firmly as the principles of the Stoic ethics insist upon moral conduct, those ethics, judged, by their whole tone, cannot rest short of requiring an absolute resignation to the course of the universe. This requirement is based quite as much upon the historical surroundings of their system as upon its intellectual principles. How, in an age in which political freedom was stifled by the oppression of Macedonian, and subsequently of Roman dominion, even that of the Roman conquerors being suppressed under the despotism of imperialism, in which Might, like a living fate, crushed every attempt at independent action—how, in such an age, could those aiming at higher objects than mere personal gratification have any alternative but to resign themselves placidly to the course of circumstances which individuals and nations were alike powerless to control ? In making a dogma of fatalism, Stoicism was only following the current of the age. At the same time, as will be seen from what has been said, it was only following the necessary consequences of its own principles. All that is individual in the world being only the result of a general connection of cause and effect—

being only a carrying out of a universal law—what
remains possible, in the face of this absolute necessity, but to yield unconditionally? How can yielding be called a sacrifice, when the law to which we
yield is nothing less than the expression of reason?
Hence resignation to the world's course was a point
chiefly insisted upon in the Stoic doctrine of morality.
The verses of Cleanthes,[1] in which he submits without reserve to the leading of destiny, are a theme
repeatedly worked out by the writers of this School.
The virtuous man, they say, will honour God by re-
signing his will to the divine will; the divine will
he will think better than his own will; he will re-
member that under all circumstances we must follow
destiny, but that it is the wise man's prerogative to
follow of his own accord; that there is only one way
to happiness and independence—that of willing nothing except what is in the nature of things, and
what will realise itself independently of our will.[2]

---

[1] In *Epictet.* Man. c. 53;
more fully, *Ibid.* Diss. iv. 1,
131; 4, 34; and translated by
Sen. Ep. 107, 11. See p. 182, 1.
The verses are:

ἄγου δέ μ' ὦ Ζεῦ καὶ σύγ' ἡ Πεπρωμένη
ὅποι ποθ' ὑμῖν εἰμι διατεταγ-
μένος·
ὡς ἔψομαί γ' ἄοκνος· ἢν δὲ μὴ
θέλω
κακὸς γενόμενος οὐδὲν ἧττον ἔψο-
μαι.

[2] *Sen.* Prov. 5, 4 and 8: Boni
viri laborant, impendunt, im-
penduntur, et volentes quidem,
non trahuntur a fortuna, etc.
. . . Quid est boni viri? Præ-

bere se fato. Vit. Be. 15, 5:
Deum sequere. . . Quæ autem
dementia est, potius trahi quam
sequi? . . . Quicquid ex universi constitutione patiendum
est, magno excipiatur animo.
Ad hoc sacramentum adacti
sumus, ferre mortalia. . . In
regno nati sumus: Deo parere
libertas est. Ep. 97, 2: Non
pareo Deo, sed adsentior. Ex
animo illum, non quia necesse
est, sequor, etc. Ep. 74, 20; 70,
23; 107, 9. *Epictet.* Diss. ii.
16, 42: τόλμησον ἀναβλέψας πρὸς
τὸν θεὸν εἰπεῖν, ὅτι χρῶ μοι λοι-
πὸν εἰς ὃ ἂν θέλῃς· ὁμογνωμονῶ
σοι, σός εἰμι. οὐδὲν παραιτοῦμαι

Similar expressions are not wanting amongst other philosophers ; nevertheless, by the Stoic philosophy, the demand is pressed with particular force, and is closely connected with its whole view of the world. In resignation to destiny, the Stoic picture of the wise man is completed. Therewith is included that peace and happiness of mind, that gentleness and benevolence, that discharge of all duties, and that harmony of life, which together make up the Stoic definition of virtue.[1] Beginning by recognising the existence of a general law, morality ends by unconditionally submitting itself to the ordinances of that law.

The one case in which this resignation would give

τῶν σοι δοκούντων· ὅπου θέλεις, ἄγε. i. 12, 7 : The virtuous man submits his will to that of God, as a good citizen obeys the law. iv. 7, 20 : κρεῖττον γὰρ ἡγοῦμαι ὃ ὁ θεὸς ἐθέλει, ἢ [ὃ] ἐγώ. iv. 1, 131, in reference to the verses of Cleanthes : αὕτη ἡ ὁδὸς ἐπ᾽ ἐλευθερίαν ἄγει, αὕτη μόνη ἀπαλλαγὴ δουλείας. Man. 8 : θέλε γίνεσθαι τὰ γινόμενα ὡς γίνεται καὶ εὑρήσεις. Similarly Fragm. 134, in *Stob.* Floril. 108, 60. *M. Aurel.* x. 28 : μόνῳ τῷ λογικῷ ζῴῳ δέδοται τὸ ἑκουσίως ἕπεσθαι τοῖς γινομένοις· τὸ δὲ ἕπεσθαι ψιλὸν πᾶσιν ἀναγκαῖον. *Ibid.* viii. 45 ; x. 14.

[1] *Sen.* Ep. 120, 11, investigates the question, How does mankind arrive at the conception of virtue ? and replies, By the sight of virtuous men. Ostendit illam nobis ordo ejus et decor et constantia et omnium inter se actionum concordia et

magnitudo super omnia efferens sese. Hinc intellecta est illa beata vita, secundo defluens cursu, arbitrii sui tota. Quomodo ergo hoc ipsum nobis adparuit ? Dicam : Nunquam vir ille perfectus adeptusque virtutem fortunæ maledixit. Numquam accidentia tristis excepit. Civem esse se universi et militem credens labores velut imperatos subiit. Quicquid inciderat, non tanquam malum aspernatus est, et in se casu delatum, sed quasi delegatum sibi. . . . Necessario itaque magnus adparuit, qui nunquam malis ingemuit, nunquam de fato suo questus est : fecit multis intellectum sui et non aliter quam in tenebris lumen effulsit, advertitque in se omnium animos, cum esset placidus et lenis, humanis divinisque rebus pariter æquus, &c.

place to active resistance to destiny is when man is
placed in circumstances calling for unworthy action
or endurance.[1]   Strictly speaking, the first case can
never arise, since, from the Stoic platform, no state
of life can be imagined which might not serve as an
occasion for virtuous conduct. It does, however,
seem possible that even the wise man may be placed by
fortune in positions which are for him unendurable;
and in this case he is allowed to withdraw from them
by suicide.[2] The importance of this point in the
Stoic ethics will become manifest from the language
of Seneca, who asserts that the wise man's independence of externals depends, among other things, on
his being able to leave life at pleasure.[3] To Seneca,
the deed of the younger Cato appears not only praise-

---

[1] Conf. *Baumhauer*, Vet.
Phil. præcipue Stoicorum Doct.
de Mor. Volunt.: Ut. 1842, p.
220.

[2] *Diog.* vii. 130 : εὐλόγως τέ
φασιν ἐξάξειν ἑαυτὸν τοῦ βίου τὸν
σοφὸν (ἐξαγωγὴ) is the standing
expression with the Stoics for
suicide. Full references for
this and other expressions are
given by *Baumhauer*, p. 243.)
καὶ ὑπὲρ πατρίδος καὶ ὑπὲρ φίλων
κἂν ἐν σκληροτέρᾳ γένηται ἀλγη-
δόνι ἢ πηρώσεσιν ἢ νόσοις ἀνιάτοις.
Stob. Ecl. ii. 226. Conf. the
comœdian Sopater, in *Athen.*
iv. 160, who makes a master
threaten to sell his slave to
Zeno ἐπ' ἐξαγωγῇ.

[3] Ep. 12, 10 : Malum est in
necessitate vivere. Sed in necessitate vivere necessitas nulla
est. Quidni nulla sit ? Patent
undique ad libertatem viæ mul-

tæ, breves, faciles. Agamus
Deo gratias, quod nemo in vita
teneri potest. Calcare ipsas ne-
cessitates licet. *Id.* Prov. c. 5, 6,
makes the deity say : Contem-
nite mortem quæ vos aut finit
aut transfert. . . . Ante omnia
cavi, ne quis vos teneret invitos.
Patet exitus. . . . Nihil feci
facilius, quam mori. Prono
animam loco posui. Trahitur.
Attendite modo et videbitis,
quam brevis ad libertatem et
quam expedita ducat via, &c.
Conf. Ep. 70, 14 : He who denies
the right of committing suicide
non videt se libertatis viam
eludere. Nil melius æterna lex
fecit, quam quod unum in-
troitum nobis ad vitam dedit,
exitus multos. Ep. 65, 22 ;
117, 21 ; 120, 14 ; *M. Aurel.* v.
29 ; viii. 47 ; x. 8 and 32 ; iii. 1 ;
Epictet. Diss. i. 24, 20; iii. 24, 95.

worthy, but the crowning-point of success over destiny, the highest triumph of the human will.[1] By
the chief teachers of the Stoic School this doctrine
was carried into practice. Zeno, in old age, hung
himself, because he had broken his finger; Cleanthes,
for a still less cause, continued his abstinence till he
died of starvation, in order to traverse the whole
way to death; and, in later times, the example of
Zeno and Cleanthes was followed by Antipater.[2]

In these cases suicide appears not only as a way
of escape, possible under circumstances, but absolutely as the highest expression of moral freedom.
Whilst all are far from being advised to adopt this
course,[3] everyone is required to embrace the opportunity of dying with glory, when no higher duties
bind him to life.[4] Everyone is urged, in case of
need, to receive death at his own hand, as a pledge
of his independence. Nor are cases of need decided
by what really makes a man unhappy—moral vice
or folly. Vice and folly must be met by other means.
Death is no deliverance from them, since it makes
the bad no better. The one satisfactory reason which
the Stoics recognised for taking leave of life is, when

[1] De Prov. 2, 9; Ep. 71,
16.
[2] In the passages already
quoted, pp. 40, 2; 41, 1; 50,
2.
[3] See Epictetus's discussion
of suicide committed simply
in contempt of life (Diss. i. 9,
10), against which he brings to
bear the rule (in *Plato*, Phæd.
61, E.) to resign oneself to the

will of God. ii. 15, 4. Conf.
M. Aurel. v. 10.
[4] Muson. in *Stob*. Floril. 7,
24, says: ἅρπαζε τὸ καλῶς ἀποθνήσκειν ὅτε ἔξεστι, μὴ μετὰ μικ-
ρὸν τὸ μὲν ἀποθνήσκειν σοι παρῇ,
τὸ δὲ καλῶς μηκέτι ἐξῇ; and,
again: He who by living is of
use to many, ought not to
choose to die, unless by death
he can be of use to more.

circumstances over which we have no control make
continuance in life no longer desirable.[1]

Such circumstances may be found in the greatest
variety of things. Cato committed suicide because
of the downfall of the republic; Zeno, because of a
slight injury received. According to Seneca, it is a
sufficient reason for committing suicide to anticipate
merely a considerable disturbance in our actions and
peace of mind.[2] Weakness of age, incurable disease,
a weakening of the powers of the mind, a great degree of want, the tyranny of a despot from which
there is no escape, justify us—and even, under circumstances, oblige us—to have recourse to this
remedy.[3] Seneca, indeed, maintains that a philosopher should never commit suicide in order to escape
suffering, but only to withdraw from restrictions in
following out the aim of his life; but he is nevertheless of opinion that anyone may rightly choose an
easier mode of death instead of a more painful one
in prospect, thus avoiding a freak of destiny and
the cruelty of man.[4] Besides pain and sickness, Diogenes also mentions a case in which suicide becomes
a duty, for the sake of others.[5] According to another

---

[1] *M. Aurel.* v. 29: Even
here you may live as though
you were free from the body:
ἐὰν δὲ μὴ ἐπιτρέπωσι, τότε καὶ
τοῦ ζῆν ἔξιθι· οὕτως μέντοι, ὡς
μηδὲν κακὸν πάσχων.

[2] Ep. 70. See p. 338, 3.
Clem. Strom. iv. 485, A, likewise calls the restriction of rational action sufficiently de-
cisive reason: αὐτίκα εὔλογον

ἐξαγωγὴν τῷ σπουδαίῳ συγχωροῦσ.
καὶ οἱ φιλόσοφοι (i.e. the Stoics),
εἴ τις τοῦ πράσσειν αὐτὸν οὕτως
τηρήσειεν [1. οὕτω στερήσειεν],
ὡς μηκέτι ἀπολελεῖφθαι αὐτῷ μηδὲ
ἐλπίδα τῆς πράξεως.

[3] Ep. 58, 33; 98, 16; 17, 9;
De Ira, iii. 15, 3.

[4] See Ep. 58, 36, and 70, 11.

[5] See p. 335, 2.

CHAP.
XII.

authority,[1] five cases were enumerated by the Stoics in which it was allowed to put oneself to death; if, by so doing, a real service could be rendered to others, as in the case of sacrificing oneself for one's country; to avoid being compelled to do an unlawful action; otherwise, on the ground of poverty, chronic illness, or incipient weakness of mind.

In nearly all these cases, the things referred to belong to the class of things which were reckoned as indifferent by the Stoics; and hence arises the apparent paradox, with which their opponents immediately twitted them, that not absolute and moral evils, but only outward circumstances, are admitted as justifying suicide.[2] The paradox, however, loses its point when it is remembered that, to the Stoics, life and death are quite as much indifferent as all other external things.[3] To them, nothing really good

---

[1] Olympiod. in *Phædr.* 3 (Schol. in Arist. 7, b, 25). The favourite comparison of life to a banquet is here so carried out, that the five occasions for suicide are compared with five occasions for leaving a banquet.

[2] Plut. C. Not. 11, 1 : παρὰ τὴν ἔννοιάν ἐστιν, ἄνθρωπον ᾧ πάντα τἀγαθὰ πάρεστι καὶ μηδὲν ἐνδεῖ πρὸς εὐδαιμονίαν καὶ τὸ μακάριον, τούτῳ καθήκειν ἐξάγειν ἑαυτόν· ἔτι δὲ μᾶλλον, ᾧ μηθὲν ἀγαθόν ἐστι μηδ' ἔσται τὰ δὲ δεινὰ πάντα καὶ τὰ δυσχερῆ καὶ κακὰ πάρεστι καὶ πάρεσται διὰ τέλους, τούτῳ μὴ καθήκειν ἀπολέγεσθαι τὸν βίον ἂν μή τι νὴ Δία τῶν ἀδιαφόρων αὐτῷ προσγένηται. *Ibid.* 22, 7 ; 33, 3 ; Sto. Rep. 14, 3 ; *Alex. Aphr.* De An.156,b ; 158,b.

[3] Plut. Sto. Rep. 18, 5 : ἀλλ'

οὐδ' ὅλως, φασίν, οἴεται δεῖν Χρύσιππος οὔτε μονὴν ἐν τῷ βίῳ τοῖς ἀγαθοῖς, οὔτ' ἐξαγωγὴν τοῖς κακοῖς παραμετρεῖν, ἀλλὰ τοῖς μέσοις κατὰ φύσιν. διὸ καὶ τοῖς εὐδαιμονοῦσι γίνεται ποτὲ καθῆκον ἐξάγειν ἑαυτοὺς, καὶ μένειν αὖθις ἐν τῷ ζῆν τοῖς κακοδαιμονοῦσιν. *Ibid.* 14, 3. *Sen.* Ep. 70, 5 : Simul atque occurrunt molesta et tranquillitatem turbantia, emittet se. Nec hoc tantum in necessitate ultima facit, sed cum primum illi cœpit suspecta esse fortuna, diligenter circumspicit, numquid illo die desinendum sit. Nihil existimat sua referre, faciat finem an accipiat, tardius fiat an citius. Non tanquam de magno detrimento timet : nemo multum ex stillicidio potest perdere. Conf. 77, 6.

appears to be involved in the question of suicide,
but only a choice between two things morally indifferent—one of which, life, is only preferable to death,
the other, whilst the essential conditions for a life
according to nature are satisfied.[1] The philosopher,
therefore, says Seneca,[2] chooses his mode of death just
as he chooses a ship for a journey or a house to live
in. He leaves life as he would leave a banquet—
when it is time. He lays aside his body when it no
longer suits him, as he would lay aside worn-out
clothes ; and withdraws from life as he would withdraw from a house no longer weather-proof.[3]

A very different question, however, it is, whether
life can be treated in this way as something indifferent, and whether it is consistent with an unconditional resignation to the course of the world, to
evade by personal interposition, what destiny with
its unalterable laws has decreed for us. Stoicism
may, indeed, allow this course of action. But in so

[1] *Cic.* Fin. iii. 18, 60 : Sed
cum ab his [the media] omnia
proficiscantur officia, non sine
causa dicitur, ad ea referri omnes nostras cogitationes ; in his
et excessum e vita et in vita
mansionem. In quo enim plura
sunt, quæ secundum naturam
sunt, hujus officium est in vita
manere : in quo autem aut
sunt plura contraria aut fore
videntur, hujus officium est e
vita excedere. E quo apparet,
et sapientis esse aliquando officium excedere e vita, cum beatus sit, et stulti manere in vita,
cum sit miser. . . . Et quoniam
excedens e vita et manens

æque miser est [stultus], nec
diuturnitas magis ei vitam fugi-
endam facit, non sine causa dicitur, iis qui pluribus naturali-
bus frui possint esse in vita
manendum. *Stob.* 226 : The
good may have reasons for
leaving life, the bad for continuing in life, even though
they never should become wise:
οὔτε γὰρ τὴν ἀρετὴν κατέχειν ἐν
τῷ ζῆν, οὔτε τὴν κακίαν ἐκβάλλειν·
τοῖς δὲ καθήκουσι καὶ τοῖς παρὰ τὸ
καθῆκον μετρεῖσθαι τήν τε ζωὴν
καὶ τὸν θάνατον.

[2] Ep. 70, 11.

[3] Teles. in *Stob.* Floril. 5,
67, p. 127 Mein.

z 2

doing does it not betray how little it had succeeded in the attempt to combine, without contradiction, two main tendencies so different as that of individual independence and that of submission to the universe?

CHAPTER XIII.

THE RELATION OF THE STOIC PHILOSOPHY TO RELIGION.

It would be impossible to give a full account of the philosophy of the Stoics without treating of their theology; for no early system is so closely connected with religion as that of the Stoics. Founded as their whole view of the world is upon the idea of one Divine Being, begetting from Himself and containing in Himself all finite creatures, upholding them by His might, ruling them according to an unalterable law, and thus manifesting Himself everywhere, their philosophy bears a decidedly religious tone. Indeed, there is hardly a single prominent feature in the Stoic system which is not, more or less, connected with theology. A very considerable portion of that system, moreover, consists of strictly theological questions; such as arguments for the existence of deity, and for the rule of Providence; investigations into the nature of God, His government, and presence in the world; into the relation of human activity to the divine ordinances; and all the various questions connected with the terms freedom and necessity. The natural science of the Stoics begins by evolving things from God; it ends with

Chap.
XIII.
___

A. *General
connection
of Stoic-
ism and
religion.*

resolving them again into God. God is thus the beginning and end of the world's development. In like manner, their moral philosophy begins with the notion
of divine law, which, in the form of eternal reason,
controls the actions of men; and ends by requiring
submission to the will of God, and resignation to the
course of the universe. A religious sanction is thus
given to all moral duties. All virtuous actions are
a fulfilment of the divine will and the divine law.
That citizenship of the world, in particular, which
constitutes the highest point in the Stoic morality,
is connected with the notion of a common relationship of all men to God. Again, that inward repose
of the philosopher, those feelings of freedom and
independence, on which so much stress was laid, rest
principally on the conviction that man is related to
God. In a word, Stoicism is not only a system of
philosophy, but also a system of religion. As such
it was regarded by its first adherents, witness the
fragments of Cleanthes;[1] and as such it afforded, in
later times, together with Platonism, to the best
and most cultivated men, wherever the influence of
Greek culture extended, a substitute for declining
natural religion, a satisfaction for religious cravings,
and a support for moral life.

[1] The well-known hymn to
Zeus, in *Stob.* Ecl. i. 30, and
the verses quoted p. 333, 1.
Nor is the poetic form used by
Cleanthes without importance.
He asserted, at least according
to *Philodem.* De Mus. Vol. Herc.
i. col. 28 : ἀμείνονά γε εἶναι τὰ
ποιητικὰ καὶ μουσικὰ παραδείγματα

καὶ τοῦ λόγου τοῦ τῆς φιλοσοφίας,
ἱκανῶς μὲν ἐξαγγέλλειν δυναμένου
τὰ θεῖα καὶ ἀνθρώπινα, μὴ ἔχοντος
δὲ ψιλοῦ τῶν θείων μεγεθῶν λέξεις
οἰκείας. τὰ μέτρα καὶ τὰ μέλη καὶ
τοὺς ῥυθμοὺς ὡς μάλιστα προσικνεῖ-
σθαι πρὸς τὴν ἀλήθειαν τῆς τῶν
θείων θεωρίας.

This philosophic religion is quite independent of the traditional religion. The Stoic philosophy contains no feature of importance which we can pronounce with certainty to be taken from the popular faith. Even the true worship of God, according to their view, consists only in the mental effort to know God, and in a moral and pious life.[1] A really acceptable prayer can have no reference to external goods ; it can only have for its object a virtuous and devout mind.[2] Still, there were reasons which led the Stoics to seek a closer union with the popular faith. A system attaching so great an importance to popular opinion, particularly for proving the existence of God,[3] could not, without extreme danger to itself, declare the current opinions respecting the Gods to be erroneous. And again, the ethical platform of the Stoic philosophy imposed on its adherents the duty of upholding rather than overthrowing the popular creed—that creed forming a barrier against the

CHAP. XIII.

(1) *Connection of Stoicism with popular faith.*

---

[1] Compare the celebrated dictum of the Stoic in *Cic.* N. D. ii. 28, 71 : Cultus autem Deorum est optimus idemque castissimus plenissimusque pietatis, ut eos semper pura integra incorrupta et mente et voce veneremur ; and more particularly *Epict.* Man. 31, 1 : τῆς περὶ τοὺς θεοὺς εὐσεβείας ἴσθι ὅτι τὸ κυριώτατον ἐκεῖνό ἐστιν, ὀρθὰς ὑπολήψεις περὶ αὐτῶν ἔχειν . . . καὶ σαυτὸν εἰς τοῦτο κατατεταχέναι, τὸ πείθεσθαι αὐτοῖς καὶ εἴκειν ἐν πᾶσι τοῖς γινομένοις, κ.τ.λ.   *Id.* Diss. ii. 18, 19. Further particulars on p. 345, 2.

[2] *M. Aurel.* ix. 40 : We ought not to pray the Gods to give us something, or to protect us from something, but only to pray : διδόναι αὐτοὺς τὸ μήτε φοβεῖσθαί τι τούτων μήτε ἐπιθυμεῖν τινος τούτων. *Diog.* vii. 124 : We ought, in fact, only to pray for what is good.

[3] See p. 144, 2. *Sext.* Math. ix. 28, says that some of the younger Stoics (perhaps Posidonius, whose views on the primitive condition have been already mentioned, p. 293, 1) traced the belief in Gods back to the golden age.

344 *THE STOICS.*

CHAP.
XIII.

violence of human passions.[1] The practical value of
the popular faith may, then, be the cause of their
theological orthodoxy. Just as the Romans, long
after all faith in the Gods had been lost under the
influence of Greek culture,[2] still found it useful and
necessary to uphold the traditional faith, so the
Stoics may have feared that, were the worship of the
people's Gods to be suspended, that respect for God
and the divine law on which they depended for the
support of their own moral tenets, would at the
same time be exterminated.

(2) *Free
criticism
of popular
belief.*

Meantime, they did not deny that much in the
popular belief would not harmonise with their principles; and that both the customary forms of religious worship, and also the mythical representations
of the Gods, were altogether untenable. So little did
they conceal their strictures, that it is clear that conviction, and not fear (there being no longer occasion
for fear), was the cause of their leaning towards tradition. Zeno spoke with contempt of the erection of
sacred edifices; for how can a thing be sacred which
is erected by builders and labourers?[3] Seneca denies the good of prayer.[4] He considers it absurd to

[1] In this spirit, *Epict.* Diss.
ii. 20, 32, blames those who
throw doubts on the popular
Gods, not considering that by
so doing they deprive many of
the preservatives from evil, the
very same argumentum ab utili
which is now frequently urged
against free criticism.

[2] Characteristic are the
utterances of the sceptic pon-

tifex Cotta, in *Cic.* N. D. i. 22,
61; iii. 2.

[3] *Plut.* Sto. Rep. 6, 1; *Diog.*
vii. 33. See p. 322, 5.

[4] Ep. 41, 1: Non sunt ad
cœlum elevandæ manus nec ex-
orandus ædituus, ut nos ad
aures simulacri, quasi magis
exaudiri possimus, admittat:
prope est a te Deus, tecum est,
intus est. Nat. Qu. ii. 35, 1:

entertain fear for the Gods, those ever-beneficent beings.[1] God he would have worshipped, not by sacrifices and ceremonies, but by purity of life ; not in temples of stone, but in the shrine of the heart.[2] Of images of the Gods, and the devotion paid to them, he speaks with strong disapprobation ;[3] of the

What is the meaning of expiations, if fate is unchangeable ? They are only ægræ mentis solatia. See p. 343, 2.

[1] Benef. iv. 19, 1 : Deos nemo sanus timet. Furor est enim metuere salutaria nec quisquam amat quos timet. Not only do the Gods not wish to do harm, but such is their nature that they cannot do harm. De Ira, ii. 27, 1 ; Benef. vii. 1, 7 ; Ep. 95, 49. It hardly needs remark, how greatly these statements are at variance with the Roman religion, in which fear holds such a prominent place.

[2] Ep. 95, 47 : Quomodo sint Di colendi, solet præcipi : accendere aliquem lucernas sabbatis prohibeamus, quoniam nec lumine Di egent et ne homines quidem delectantur fuligine. Vetemus salutationibus matutinis fungi et foribus adsidere templorum : humana ambitio istis officiis capitur : Deum colit, qui novit. Vetemus lintea et strigiles ferre et speculum tenere Junoni : non quærit ministros Deus. Quidni? Ipse humano generi ministrat, ubique et omnibus præsto est. . . . Primus est Deorum cultus Deos credere. Deinde reddere illis majestatem suam, reddere bonitatem, &c. Vis Deos propitiare? Bonus esto. Satis illos coluit,

quisquis imitatus est. Fr. 123 (in *Lactant.* Inst. vi. 25, 3) : Vultisne vos Deum cogitare magnum et placidum . . . non immolationibus et sanguine multo colendum—quæ enim ex trucidatione immerentium voluptas est ?—sed mente pura, bono honestoque proposito. Non templa illi congestis in altitudinem saxis extruenda sunt: in suo cuique consecrandus est pectore. Conf. Benef. vii. 7, 3 : The only worthy temple of God is the universe.

[3] In Fr. 120 (in *Lact.* ii. 2, 14), Seneca shows how absurd it is to pray and kneel before images, the makers of which are thought little of in their own profession. On this point he expressed his opinion with great severity in the treatise, De Superstitione, fragments of which *Augustin.* Civ. D. vi. 10, communicates (Fr. 31 Haase). The immortal Gods, he there says, are transformed into lifeless elements. They are clothed in the shape of men and beasts, and other most extraordinary appearances ; and are honoured as Gods, though, were they alive, they would be designated monsters. The manner, too, in which these Gods are honoured is most foolish and absurd ; such as by mortification and mutilation, stupid

CHAP.
XIII.

unworthy fables of mythology, with bitter ridicule;[1]
and he calls the popular Gods, without reserve, creations of superstition, whom the philosopher only in-
vokes because it is the custom so to do.[2] Moreover, the
Stoic in Cicero, and the elder authorities quoted by
him, allow that the popular beliefs and the songs of
the poets are full of superstition and foolish legends.[3]
Chrysippus is expressly said to have declared the distinction of sex among the Gods, and other features
in which they resemble men, to be childish fancies;[4]

and immoral plays, &c. The wise
man can only take part in such
acts tanquam legibus jussa, non
tanquam Diis grata. This view
of worship had been previously
set forth by Heraclitus, who
otherwise was so much admired
by the Stoics.

[1] Fr. 119 (in *Lact.* i. 16, 10):
Quid ergo est, quare apud poë-
tas salacissimus Jupiter desierit
liberos tollere? Utrum sexa-
genarius factus est, et illi lex
Papia fibulam imposuit? An
impetravit jus trium liberorum?
An . . . timet, ne quis sibi faciat, quod ipse Saturno? Similarly Fr. 39 (in *Augustin.* l. c.);
Brevit. Vit. 16, 5; Vit. Be. 26,
6, the ineptiæ poetarum which,
as in the stories of Jupiter's
many adulteries, give free rein
to sins.

[2] *Augustin.* l. c. Fr. 33: Quid
ergo tandem? Veriora tibi videntur T. Tatii aut Romuli aut
Tulli Hostilii somnia? Cloa-
cinam Tatius dedicavit Deam,
Picum Tiberinumque Romulus,
Hostilius Pavorem atque Pal-
lorem, teterrimos hominum adfectus. . . . Hæc numina potius

credes et cœlo recipies? Fr. 39:
Omnem istam ignobilem Deorum turbam, quam longo ævo
longa superstitio congessit, sic
adorabimus ut meminerimus
cultum ejus magis ad morem
quam ad rem pertinere.

[3] N. D. ii. 24, 63: Alia
quoque ex ratione et quidem
physica fluxit multitudo Deorum; qui induti specie humana
fabulas poëtis suppeditaverunt
hominum autem vitam superstitione omni referserunt. Atque
hic locus a Zenone tractatus
post a Cleanthe et Chrysippo
pluribus verbis explicatus est
. . . physica ratio non inelegans
inclusa est in impias fabulas.
Still stronger language is used
by the Stoic, c. 28, 70, respecting the commentitii et
ficti Dei, the superstitiones
pæne aniles, the futilitas sum-
maque levitas of their anthropomorphic legends.

[4] *Phædrus* (Philodemus), col.
2 of his fragment, according to
Petersen's restoration. Conf.
Cic. N. D. ii. 17, 45; *Diog.* vii.
147; both of whom assert that
the Stoics do not think of the

Zeno to have denied any real existence to the popular deities, transferring their names to natural objects;[1] and Aristo[2] is charged with having denied
shape and sensation to the Deity.[3]

The Stoics were, nevertheless. not disposed to let
the current beliefs quite fall through. Far from it,
they thought to discover real germs of truth in these
beliefs, however inadequate they were in form; and
they accordingly made it their business to give a relative vindication to the existing creed. Holding
that the name of God belongs, in its full and original sense, only to the one primary Being, they did
not hesitate to apply it, in a limited and derivative
sense, to all those objects by means of which the
divine power is especially manifested. Nay, more,
in consideration of man's relationship to God, they
found it not unreasonable to deduce from the primary Being Gods bearing a resemblance to men.[4]
Hence they distinguished, as Plato had done,

Gods as human in form; and
Lactant. De Ir. D. c. 18 : Stoici
negant habere ullam formam
Deum.

[1] The Epicurean in *Cic.* N.
D. i. 14, 36.

[2] *Cic.* l. c. 37. Conf. *Krische,*
Forschung. i. 406 and 415.

[3] *Clem.*, indeed, says (Strom.
vii. 720, D) : οὐδὲ αἰσθήσεων αὐτῷ
[τῷ θεῷ] δεῖ, καθάπερ ἤρεσε τοῖς
Στωϊκοῖς, μάλιστα ἀκοῆς καὶ ὄψεως·
μὴ γὰρ δύνασθαί ποτε ἑτέρως ἀντι-
λαμβάνεσθαι. But, according to
all accounts, this must be a misapprehension. Clement confounds what Stoic writers have
conditionally asserted, for the

purpose of disproving it, with
their real opinion. Conf. *Sext.*
Math. ix. 139.

[4] *Plut.* Plac. i. 6, 16, in a description of the Stoic theology,
evidently borrowed from a good
source : The Gods have been represented as being like men :
διότι τῶν μὲν ἁπάντων τὸ θεῖον
κυριώτατον, τῶν δὲ ζῴων ἄνθρωπος
κάλλιστον καὶ κεκοσμημένον ἀρετῇ
διαφόρως κατὰ τὴν τοῦ νοῦ συνί-
στασιν, (τὸ κράτιστον—probably
these words should be struck
out), τοῖς οὖν ἀριστεύουσι τὸ
κράτιστον ὁμοίως καὶ καλῶς ἔχειν
διενοήθησαν.

CHAP.
XIII.

between the eternal and immutable God and Gods created and transitory,[1] between God the Creator and Sovereign of the world, and subordinate Gods;[2] in other words, between the universal divine power as a Unity working in the world, and its individual parts and manifestations.[3] To the former they gave the name Zeus; to the latter, they applied the names of the other subordinate Gods.

(3) *The truth in Poly-theism.*

In this derivative sense, divinity was allowed to many beings by the Stoics, and, in particular, to the stars, which Plato had called created Gods, which Arsitotle had described as eternal divine beings, and the worship of which lay so near to the ancient cultus of nature. Not only by their lustre and effect on the senses, but far more by the regularity of their motions, do these stars prove that the material of which they consist is the purest, and that, of all created objects, they have the largest share in the divine reason.[4] And so seriously was this belief held by the Stoics, that a philosopher of the unwieldy piety of Cleanthes so far forgot himself as to charge Aristarchus of Samos, the discoverer of the earth's motion round the sun, the Galilæo of antiquity, with impiety for wishing to remove the hearth of the universe from its proper place.[5] This deification of the stars prepares us to find years, months, and seasons

---

[1] *Plut.* St. Rep. 38, 5; C. Not. 31, 5; Def. Orac. 19, p. 420.

[2] The numina, quæ singula adoramus et colimus, which are dependent on the Deus omnium Deorum, and whom ministros regni sui genuit. *Sen.* Fr. 26, 16 (in *Lact.* Inst. i. 5, 26).

[3] *Diog.* vii. 147.

[4] See p. 206, 1.

[5] *Plut.* De Fac. Lun. 6, 3.

called Gods,[1] as was done by Zeno, or at least by his School. Still, it must be remembered, that the Stoics referred these times and seasons to heavenly bodies, as their material embodiments.[2]

As the stars are the first manifestation, so the elements are the first particular forms of the Divine Being, and the most common materials for the exercise of the divine powers. It is, however, becoming that the all-pervading divine mind should not only be honoured in its primary state, but likewise in its various derivate forms, as air, water, earth, and elementary fire.[3]

All other things, too, which, by their utility to man, display in a high degree the beneficent power of God, appeared to the Stoics to deserve divine honours, those honours not being paid to the things themselves, but to the powers active within them. They did not, therefore, hesitate to give the names of Gods to fruits and wine, and other gifts of the Gods.[4]

How, then, could they escape the inference that among other beneficent beings, the heroes of antiquity, in particular, deserve religious honours, seeing that in these benefactors of mankind, of whom legend tells, the Divine Spirit did not show Himself under the lower form of a ἕξις, as in the elements,

---

[1] *Cic.* N. D. i. 14, 36.
[2] See p. 131.
[3] *Cic.* N. D. i. 15, 39; ii. 26 ; *Diog.* vii. 147.
[4] *Plut.* De Is. c. 66 ; *Cic.* l. c. ii. 23, 60 ; i. 15, 39, where this view is attributed,

in particular, to Zeno's pupil Persæus. *Krische* (Forschung. i. 442) reminds, with justice, of the assertion of Prodicus, that the ancients deified everything which was of use to man.

nor yet as simple φύσις, as in plants, but as a rational soul? Such deified men had, according to
the Stoic view—which, on this point, agrees with the
well-known theory of Euemerus—in a great measure,
contributed to swell the mass of the popular Gods;
nor had the Stoics themselves any objection to their
worship.[1] Add to this the personification of human
qualities and states of mind,[2] and it will be seen what

[1] *Phædr.* (Philodemus), Nat.
De. col. 3, and *Cic.* N. D. i. 15,
38, attribute this assertion specially to Persæus and Chrysippus. *Id.* ii. 24, 64, after speaking
of the deification of Hercules,
Bacchus, Romulus, &c., continues: Quorum cum remane-
rent animi atque æternitate
fruerentur, Dii rite sunt habiti,
cum et optimi essent et æterni.
Diog. vii. 151. See p. 351, 1.
[2] This is done in *Plut.* Plac.
i. 6, 9. Belief in the Gods, it is
there said, is held in three
forms—the physical, the mythical, and the form established
by law (theologia civilis). All
the Gods belong to seven classes,
εἴδη : (1) τὸ ἐκ τῶν φαινομένων καὶ
μετεώρων : the observation of the
stars, and their regularity of
movement, the changes of
season, &c., has conducted
many to faith; and, accordingly,
heaven and earth, sun and
moon, have been honoured. (2
and 3) τὸ βλάπτον καὶ ὠφελοῦν :
beneficent Beings are Zeus,
Here, Hermes, Demeter: baleful Beings are the Erinnyes,
Ares, &c. (4 and 5) πράγματα,
such as Ἐλπὶς, Δίκη, Εὐνομία ;
and πάθη, such as Ἔρως, Ἀφρο-
δίτη, Πόθος. (6) τὸ ὑπὸ τῶν
ποιητῶν πεπλασμένον (τὸ μυθικὸν),

such as the Gods invented by
Hesiod for the purpose of his
genealogies—Coios, Hyperion,
&c. (7) Men who are honoured
for their services to mankind—
Hercules, the Dioscuri, Dionysus. This list includes not
only things which deserve
divine honours, but all things
to which they have been actually given : hence it includes,
besides the purely mythical
Gods, things which the Stoics
can never have regarded as
Gods, such as the baleful Gods
and emotions, on which
see p. 345, 1 ; 346, 2. On the
other hand, they could raise no
objection to the worship of
personified virtues. In the
above list, the elementary Gods,
such as Here, are grouped, together with the Gods of fruits,
under the category of useful.
Another grouping was that followed by Dionysius (whether
the well-known pupil of Zeno
—see p. 44, 1—or some later
Stoic, is unknown), who, according to Tertullian (Ad Nat.
ii. 2, conf. c. 14), divided Gods
into three classes : the visible
—the sun and moon, for instance ; the invisible, or powers
of nature, such as Neptune
(that is, natural forces as they

ample opportunity the Stoics had for recognising everywhere in nature and in the world of man divine agencies and powers, and, consequently, Gods in the wider sense of the term.[1] When once it had been allowed that the name of God might be diverted from the Being to whom it properly belonged and applied, in a derivative sense, to what is impersonal and a mere manifestation of divine power, the door was opened to everything; and, with such concessions, the Stoic system could graft into itself even the most exceptional forms of polytheism.

With the worship of heroes is also connected the doctrine of demons.[2] The soul, according to the Stoic view already set forth, is of divine origin, a part of and emanation from God. Or, distinguishing more accurately in the soul one part from the rest, to reason only, as the governing part, this honour belongs. Now, since reason alone protects man from evil and conducts him to happiness—this, too, was the popular belief—reason may be described as the guardian spirit, or demon, in man. Not only by the younger members of the Stoic School, by Posidonius, Seneca, Epictetus, and Antoninus, are the popular notions of demons, as by Plato aforetime,[3]

(4) Doctrine of demons.

---

make themselves felt in the elements and in planets); and those *facti*, or deified men.

[1] *Plut.* Com. Not. 31, 5: ἀλλὰ Χρύσιππος καὶ Κλεάνθης, ἐμπεπληκότες, ὡς ἔπος εἰπεῖν, τῷ λόγῳ θεῶν τὸν οὐρανὸν, τὴν γῆν, τὸν ἀέρα, τὴν θάλατταν, οὐδένα τῶν τοσούτων ἄφθαρτον οὐδ' ἀΐδιον

ἀπολελοίπασι πλὴν μόνου τοῦ Διὸς, εἰς ὃν πάντας καταναλίσκουσι τοὺς ἄλλους.

[2] Conf. *Wachsmuth*, Die Ansichten der Stoiker über Mantik und Dämonen (Berl. 1860), pp. 29–39.

[3] Tim. 90, A.

explained in this sense,[1] but the same method is pursued by Chrysippus, who made εὐδαιμονία, or happiness, consist in a harmony of the demon in man (which, in this case, can only be his own will and understanding) with the will of God.[2] Little were the Stoics aware that, by such explanations, they were attributing to popular notions a meaning wholly foreign to them. But it does not therefore follow that they shared the popular belief in guardian spirits.[3] Their system, however, left room for be-

[1] Posid. in *Galen.* Hipp. et Plat. v. 6, p. 469: τὸ δὴ τῶν παθῶν αἴτιον, τουτέστι τῆς τε ἀνομολογίας καὶ τοῦ κακοδαίμονος βίου, τὸ μὴ κατὰ πᾶν ἔπεσθαι τῷ ἐν αὑτῷ δαίμονι συγγενεῖ τε ὄντι καὶ τὴν ὁμοίαν φύσιν ἔχοντι τῷ τὸν ὅλον κόσμον διοικοῦντι, τῷ δὲ χείρονι καὶ ζῳώδει ποτὲ συνεκκλίνοντας φέρεσθαι. Sen. Ep. 41, 2, according to the quotation, p. 344, 4: Sacer intra nos spiritus sedet, malorum bonorumque nostrorum observator et custos. His prout a nobis tractatus est, ita nos ipse tractat. Ep. 31, 11: Quid aliud voces hunc [animus rectus, bonus, magnus] quam Deum in corpore humano hospitantem? Just as Kant calls the moral idea, a primary notion which mankind has embraced, the moral tone a good spirit governing us. *Epict.* Diss. i. 14, 12: ἐπίτροπον [ὁ Ζεὺς] ἑκάστῳ παρέστησε τὸν ἑκάστου δαίμονα, καὶ παρέδωκε φυλάσσειν αὐτὸν αὐτῷ καὶ τοῦτον ἀκοίμητον καὶ ἀπαραλόγιστον. He who retires within himself is not alone, ἀλλ' ὁ θεὸς ἔνδον ἐστὶ καὶ ὁ ὑμέτερος δαίμων ἐστί. To

him each one has taken an oath of allegiance, as a soldier has to his sovereign, but ἐκεῖ μὲν ὀμνύουσιν, αὑτοῦ μὴ προτιμήσειν ἕτερον · ἐνταῦθα δ' αὑτοὺς ἁπάντων; so that, consequently, the demon is lost in the αὐτὸς within. *M. Aurel.* v. 27: ὁ δαίμων, ὃν ἑκάστῳ προστάτην καὶ ἡγεμόνα ὁ Ζεὺς ἔδωκεν, ἀπόσπασμα ἑαυτοῦ. οὗτος δέ ἐστιν ὁ ἑκάστου νοῦς καὶ λόγος. See ii. 13 and 17; iii. 3 ; Schl. 5, 6, 7, 12, 16 ; v. 10 ; viii. 45.

[2] See the passage quoted from *Diog.* vii. 88, on p. 227, 3. (*Diogenes* had only just before named Chrysippus περὶ τέλους, as source), which receives its explanation (if it needs one) from the above words of Posidonius.

[3] In this sense, the words of *Sen.* Ep. 110, 1, must be understood: Sepone in præsentia quæ quibusdam placent, unicuique nostrum pædagogum dari Deum, non quidem ordinarium, sed hunc inferioris notæ . . . ita tamen hoc seponas volo, ut memineris, majores nostros, qui crediderunt, Stoicos

lieving that, besides the human soul and the spirits
of the stars, other rational souls might exist, having
a definite work to perform in the world, subject to
the law of general necessity, and knit into the chain
of cause and effect. Nay, more, such beings might
even seem to them necessary for the completeness
of the universe.[1] What reason have we, then, to
express doubt, when we are told that the Stoics believed in the existence of demons, playing a part in
man and caring for him?[2] Is there anything extraordinary, from the Stoic platform, in holding that
some of these demons are by nature inclined to do
harm, and that these tormentors are used by the
deity for the punishment of the wicked,[3] especially

fuisse: singulis enim et Genium
et Junonem dederunt, i.e., the
old Romans, not the Stoics.

[1] Conf. *Sext.* Math. ix. 86.
Amongst other things, quoted
p. 146, 1, it is there said: If
living beings exist on the earth
and in the sea, there must be
νοερὰ ζῷα in the air, which is so
much purer ; and these are the
demons.

[2] *Diog.* vii. 151 : φασὶ δ' εἶναι
καί τινας δαίμονας ἀνθρώπων συμπάθειαν ἔχοντας, ἐπόπτας τῶν ἀν-
θρωπείων πραγμάτων· καὶ ἥρωας
τὰς ὑπολελειμμένας τῶν σπουδαίων
ψυχάς. *Plut.* De Is. 25, p. 360 :
Plato, Pythagoras, Xenocrates,
and Chrysippus hold, with the
old theologians (amongst whom
Wachsmuth, p. 32, 40, rightly
thinks of the Orphics), that the
demons are stronger than men,
from which the language used
of them by Chrysippus does not
follow. Def. Oracl. 19, p. 420 :

The Stoics believe demons to
be mortal. Plac. i. 8, 2 : Θαλῆς,
Πυθαγόρας, Πλάτων, οἱ Στωϊκοί,
δαίμονας ὑπάρχειν οὐσίας ψυχικάς.
A special treatise περὶ ἡρώων καὶ
δαιμόνων proceeded from the pen
of Posidonius, probably as was
his wont, containing more
learned than dogmatic statements, an extract from which is
given by *Macrob.* Sat. i. 23, containing the etymology of δαίμων.

[3] *Plut.* Quæst. Rom. 51, p.
277 : καθάπερ οἱ περὶ Χρύσιππον
οἴονται φιλόσοφοι φαῦλα δαιμόνια
περινοστεῖν, οἷς οἱ θεοὶ δημίοις
χρῶνται κολασταῖς ἐπὶ τοὺς ἀνο-
σίους καὶ ἀδίκους ἀνθρώπους. *Id.*
Def. Oracl. 17, p. 419 : φαύλους
. . . δαίμονας οὐκ Ἐμπεδοκλῆς
μόνον . . . ἀπέλιπεν, ἀλλὰ καὶ
Πλάτων καὶ Ξενοκράτης καὶ Χρύσιππος—a statement which, particularly as it is extended to
Plato, would prove little. The
baleful Gods of mythology (p.

when in such a strict system of necessity these demons could only work, like the powers of nature,
conformably with the laws of the universe and without disturbing those laws, occupying the same ground
as lightning, earthquakes, and drought? And yet
the language of Chrysippus, when speaking of evil
demons who neglect the duties entrusted to them,[1]
sounds as though it were only figurative and tentative language, not really meant. Besides, the later
Stoics made themselves merry over the Jewish and
Christian notions of demons and demoniacal possession.[2]

B. *The
Allegoris-
ing Spirit.*
(1) *Alle-
gorical
inter-
pretation
of myths.*

Yet, even, without accepting demons, there were
not wanting in the Stoic system objects to which the
popular beliefs could be referred, if it was necessary
to find in these beliefs some deeper meaning. Not
but that these beliefs were often so distorted in the
process of accommodation as to be no longer recognised. Thus a regular code of interpretation became necessary, by means of which a philosophic mind
might see its own thoughts in the utterances of com-
monplace thinkers. By the Stoics, as by their Jewish
and Christian followers, this code of interpretation
was found in the method of allegorical interpretation—a method which now received a most extended

350, 2) were explained as being
evil demons by those who did
not deny their existence altogether. Those demons, however, which purify the soul in
another world (*Sallust.* De
Mund. c. 19, p. 266, and whom
Villoisin on Cornutus, p. 553,
reminds of), are not borrowed

from Stoicism, but from Plato
(Rep. x. 615, E) and the Neo-
platonists.
  [1] *Plut.* Sto. Rep. 37, 2. See
p. 191, 2.
  [2] *Tertull.* Test. An. 3, after
speaking of demons, adds:
Aliqui Chrysippi sectator illu-
dit ea.

application, in order to bridge over the gulf between
the older and the more modern types of culture.[1]
Zeno, and still more Cleanthes, Chrysippus, and their
successors, sought to discover natural principles and
moral ideas—the λόγοι φυσικοὶ, or physicæ rationes,
in the Gods of popular belief and the stories of these
Gods,[2] supposing them to be represented in these
stories in a sensuous form.[3] In this attempt, they

---

[1] The Stoics are not the first
who resorted to allegorical explanations of myths. Just as
before philosophy had broken
away from mythology, a Pherecydes, an Empedocles, the
Pythagoreans had, whether con-
sciously or unconsciously, veiled
their thoughts in the language
of legend, and even subsequently Plato had used a veil of
poetry; so, now that the breach
between the two was open,
many attempts were made to
conceal its breadth, and individual beliefs were represented
as the real meaning of popular
beliefs, it being always supposed that the original framers
had an eye to this meaning.
Thus a twofold method of
treating the myths resulted—
that by natural explanation,
and that by allegorical interpretation. The former method
referred them to facts of history,
the latter to general truths,
whether moral or scientific;
and both methods agreed in
looking for a hidden meaning,
besides the literal one. This
method of treating myths had
been already encountered
among the older teachers, such
as Democritus, Metrodorus of

Lampsacus, and other followers
of Anaxagoras (according to
Hesych. even Agamemnon was
explained to be the ether). It
appears to have been a favourite
method in the time of the
Sophists (*Plato*, Theæt. 153, C;
Rep. ii. 378, D; Phædr. 229, C;
Crat., 407, A, to 530, C; Gorg.
493, A; *Xen.* Sym. 3, 6), as appears from Euripides and Herodotus. It follows naturally
from the view of Prodicus on
the origin of belief in the Gods.
Plato disapproved of it. Aristotle occasionally appealed to
it to note glimmers of truth in
popular notions without attributing to it any higher value.
The founder of cynicism and his
followers pursued it zealously.
From the Cynics the Stoics
appear to have derived it. They
carried it to a much greater
extent than any of their predecessors, and they, too, exercised a greater influence on
posterity than the Cynics.
[2] *Cic.* N. D. 24, 63; iii, 24,
63, see p. 346, 3.
[3] The definition of allegory ·
ὁ γὰρ ἄλλα μὲν ἀγορεύων τρόπος,
ἕτερα δὲ ὧν λέγει σημαίνων, ἐπω-
νύμως ἀλληγορία καλεῖται (*Heraclit.* Alleg. Hom. c. 5, p. 6).

clung to the poems of Homer and Hesiod, the Bible
of the Greeks,[1] without, however, excluding other
mythology from the sphere of their investigation.
One chief instrument which they, and modern lovers
of the symbolical after them, employed was that
capricious playing with etymologies of which so many
instances are on record.[2] Like most allegorisers, they
also laid down certain principles of interpretation
sensible enough theoretically,[3] but proving, by the
use which was made of them, that their scientific
appearance was only a blind to conceal the most
capricious vagaries. Approaching in some of their
explanations to the original bases of mythological
formation, they were still unable to shake off the

Accordingly, it includes every kind of symbolical expression. In earlier times, according to *Plut.* Aud. Po. c. 4, p. 19, it was termed ὑπόνοια, which term is found in *Plato*, Rep. ii. 378, D, conf. Io. 530, D; *Xen.* Symp. 3, 6.

[1] Zeno treated in this way all the poems of Homer and Hesiod (*Dio Chrysost.* Or. 53, p. 275; *Diog.* vii. 4; *Krische*, Forsch. 393), and so did Cleanthes (*Diog.* vii. 175; *Phædr.* [Philodem.] De Nat. De. col. 3; *Plut.* Aud. Po. 11, p. 31; De Fluv. 5, 3, p. 1003; *Krische*, 433) and Persæus. Chrysippus explained the stories in Homer, Hesiod, Orpheus, and Musæus (*Phædr.* col. 3; *Galen.* Hipp. et Plat. iii. 8, vol. v. 349, *Krische*, 391 and 479), and was followed by Diogenes (*Phæd.* col. 5; *Cic.*

N. D. i. 15, 41). Compare also *Plut.* Def. Orac. 12, p. 415, and respecting the theological literature of the Stoics *Villoisin* on Cornutus, p. xxxix. Among the Romans, the same method was followed by Varro (*Preller*, Röm. Myth. 29), and from his writings Heraclitus (living under Augustus) derived the material for his Homeric Allegories (edited by Mehler) and Cornutus, for his work on the nature of the Gods edited by Osann from Villoisin's papers.

[2] *Cic.* N. D. iii. 24, 63.

[3] *Corn.* c. 17, p. 80: δεῖ δὲ μὴ συγχεῖν τοὺς μύθους, μηδ' ἐξ ἑτέρου τὰ ὀνόματα ἐφ' ἕτερον μεταφέρειν, μηδ' εἴ τι προσεπλάσθη ταῖς κατ' αὐτοὺς παραδιδομέναις γενεαλογίαις ὑπὸ τῶν μὴ συνέντων ἃ αἰνίττονται κεχρημένων δ' αὐτοῖς ὡς τοῖς πλάσμασιν, ἀλόγως τίθεσθαι.

perverted notion that the originators of myths, fully
conscious of all their latent meanings, had framed
them as pictures to appeal to the senses;[1] and, in
innumerable cases, they resorted to explanations so
entirely without foundation that they would have
been impossible to anyone possessing a sound view
of nature and the origin of legends. To make theory
tally with practice, the founder of the School—
following Antisthenes, and setting an example afterwards repeated by both Jews and Christians—maintained that Homer only in some places expressed
himself according to truth, at other times according
to popular opinion.[2] Thus did Stoicism surround
itself with the necessary intruments for the most extended allegorical and dogmatic interpretation.

Proceeding further to enquire how this method
was applied to particular stories, the first point which
attracts attention is the contrast which they draw
between Zeus and the remaining Gods. From their
belief in one divine principle everywhere at work, it
followed as a corollary that this contrast, which elsewhere in Greek mythology was only a difference of
degree, was raised to a specific and absolute differ-

*(2) Inter-
pretation
of the
myths re-
specting
the gods.*

[1] Proofs may be found in
abundance in Heraclitus and
Cornutus. Conf. *Sen. Nat. Qu.*
ii. 45, 1 : The ancients did not
believe that Jupiter hurled his
thunderbolts broadcast ; sed
eundem, quem nos Jovem in-
telligunt, rectorem custodem-
que universi, animum ac spiritum mundi, &c.

[2] *Dio Chrysost.* Or. 53, p.

276, R. speaking of Zeno's commentaries on Homer, says : ὁ δὲ
Ζήνων οὐδὲν τῶν τοῦ Ὁμήρου
λέγει, ἀλλὰ διηγούμενος καὶ διδάσ-
κων, ὅτι τὰ μὲν κατὰ δόξαν, τὰ δὲ
κατὰ ἀλήθειαν γέγραφεν. . . .
ὁ δὲ λόγος οὗτος Ἀντισθένειός
ἐστι πρότερον . . . ἀλλ' ὁ μὲν οὐκ
ἐξειργάσατο αὐτὸν οὐδὲ κατὰ τῶν
ἐπὶ μέρους ἐδήλωσεν.

ence. Zeus was compared to other Gods as an incorruptible God to transitory divine beings. To the Stoics, as to their predecessor Heraclitus, Zeus is the one primary Being, who has engendered, and again absorbs into himself, all things and all Gods. He is the universe as a unity, the primary fire, the ether, the spirit of the world, the universal reason, the general law or destiny.[1] All other Gods, as being parts of the world, are only parts and manifestations of Zeus—only special names of the one God who has many names.[2] That part of Zeus which goes over into air is called Here ($\dot{a}\acute{\eta}\rho$); and its lower strata, full of vapours, Hades; that which becomes elementary fire is called Hephæstus; that which becomes water, Poseidon; that which becomes earth, Demeter, Hestia, and Rhea; lastly, that portion which remains in the upper region is called Athene in the more restricted sense. And since, according to the Stoics, the finer elements are the same as spirit, Zeus is not only the soul of the universe,

[1] Special references are hardly necessary after those already quoted, p. 148, 1; 153, 2; 164, 2; 165, 5. Conf. the hymn of *Cleanthes*; Chrysippus, in *Stob*. Ecl. i. 48; *Arat*. Phæn. Begin.; *Plut*. Aud. Poët. c. 11, p. 31; Varro, in *August*. Civ. D.-vii. 5; 6; 9; 28; Servius, in Georg. i. 5; *Heraclit*. c. 15, p. 31; c. 23, 49; c. 24, 50; *Corn*. pp. 7; 26; 35; 38, where Ζεὺς is derived from ζῆν or ζέειν and Διὸς from διὰ, ὅτι δι' αὐτὸν τὰ πάντα; conf. Villoisin and Osann on the passage of Cornutus, who give further authorities for the following in the notes on the respective passages. The same on Cornutus, p. 6, discuss the derivation of θεὸς from θέειν or τιθέναι; of αἰθὴρ from αἴθειν or ἀεὶ θέειν. A portion of these etymologies is well known to be Platonic.

[2] Πολυώνυμος, as he is called by Cleanthes v. 1. Conf. *Diog*. 147; *Corn*. c. 9 and 26. The further expansion of this idea may be found in the Neoplatonic doctrine.

but Athene, Reason, Intelligence, Providence.[1] The same Zeus appears in other respects as Hermes, Dionysus, Hercules.[2] The Homeric story of the binding and liberation of Zeus [3] points to the truth, already established in Providence, that the order of the world rests on the balance of the elements. The rise and succession of the elements is symbolised in the hanging of Here; [4] the arrangement of the spheres of the universe, in the golden chain, by which the Olympians thought to pull down Zeus.[5] The lameness of Hephæstus goes partly to prove the difference of the

---

[1] See *Diog.* l. c.; *Cic.* N. D. ii. 26, 66; *Phæd.* (Philodem.), Fragm. col. 2-5; *Heracl.* c. 25, p. 53. On Here, consult *Heracl.* c. 15 and 41, p. 85; *Corn.* c. 3; on Hephæstus, *Heracl.* c. 26, 55; 43, 91; *Corn.* c. 19, p. 98; *Plut.* De Is. c. 66, p. 377 (*Diog.* l. c. perhaps confounds as *Krische*, p. 399, supposes, common fire with πῦρ τεχνικὸν, but is it also possible that the artificial God of mythology may have been so explained now one way now another in the Stoic school, which is not always uniform in its interpretations); on Poseidon, *Heracl.* c. 7, 15; c. 18, 77; c. 46, 117; *Corn.* c. 12; *Plut.* De Is. c. 40, Schl. p. 367; on Hades, whom Cicero l. c. makes the representative of terrena vis; *Heracl.* c. 23, p. 50; c. 41, 87; *Corn.* 5; on Demeter and Hestia, *Corn.* c. 28, p. 156; *Plut.* l. c.; on Athene, *Heracl.* c. 19, 39; c. 28, 59; c. 61, 123; *Corn.* c. 20, 103. It is only by forced interpretation of a passage in

Homer, that (*Heraclit.* 25, 53) Athene is made to be earth. That even Zeno treated individual Gods in this way, as parts of one general divine power or Zeus, is rendered probable by *Krische*, Forsch. 399, by a comparison of *Phædr.* col. 5, with the passages quoted from Cicero and Diogenes.

[2] *Sen.* Benef. iv. 8, 1: Hunc [Jovem] et Liberum patrem et Herculem et Mercurium nostri putant. Liberum patrem, quia omnium parens sit. . . . Herculem, quia vis ejus invicta sit, quandoque lassata fuerit operibus editis, in ignem recessura. Mercurium, quia ratio penes illum est numerusque et ordo et scientia. The solution of Helios into Zeus (*Macrob.* Sat. i. 23) appears also to be of Stoic origin.

[3] *Heracl.* c. 25, 52. Conf. Il. t. 395.

[4] *Heracl.* c. 40, 83; Il. xv. 18.

[5] *Ibid.* c. 37, 73; Il. viii. 18.

earthly from the heavenly fire, and partly implies
that earthly fire can as little do without wood as the
lame without a wooden support; and if, in Homer,
Hephæstus is hurled down from heaven, the meaning
of the story is, that in ancient times men lighted
their fires by lightning from heaven and the rays of
the sun.[1] The connection of Here with Zeus [2] points
to the relation of the ether to the air surrounding
it; and the well-known occurrence on Mount Ida
was referred to the same event.[3] The still more
offensive scene in the Samian picture was expounded
by Chrysippus as meaning that the fertilising powers
(λόγοι σπερματικοὶ) of God are brought to bear upon
matter.[4] A similar meaning is found by Heraclitus in the story of Proteus,[5] and in that of the
shield of Achilles. If Hephæstus intended this shield
to be a representation of this world, what else is
thereby meant but that, by the influence of primary
fire, matter has been shaped into a world?[6]

[1] *Heracl.* c. 26, 54, who applies the same method of interpretation to the legend of
Prometheus (otherwise inter-
preted by *Corn.* c. 18, 96),
Corn. c. 19, 98. On the lameness
of Hephæstus, *Plut.* Fac. Lun.
5, 3, p. 922.

[2] According to Eustath. in
Il. p. 93, 46, probably following
a Stoic interpretation, Here is
the spouse of Zeus, because the
air is surrounded by the ether;
but does not agree with him,
because the two elements are
opposed to one another.

[3] *Heracl.* c. 39, 78 (conf.
Plut. Aud. Po. p. 19), where

this explanation is given very
fully. The occurrence on Mount
Ida is said to represent the
passage of winter into spring.
Here's tresses are the foliage
of trees, &c.

[4] See *Diog.* vii. 187; Prooem.
5; *Orig.* con. Cels. iv. 48;
Theophil. ad Autol. iii. 8, p.
122, c; *Clement.* Homil. v. 18.

[5] K. 64. Proteus, according
to this explanation, denotes
unformed matter; the forms
which he assumes denote the
four elements.

[6] See the description. Alleg.
Hom. 43–51, p. 90, of which
the above is a scanty abstract.

In a similar way, the Homeric theomachy was explained by many to mean a conjunction of the seven planets, which would involve the world in great trouble.[1] Heraclitus, however, gives the preference to an interpretation, half physical and half moral, which may have been already advanced by Cleanthes.[2] Ares and Aphrodite, rashness and profligacy, are opposed by Athene, or prudence ; Leto, forgetfulness, is attacked by Hermes, the revealing word ;[3] Apollo, the sun, by Poseidon, the God of the water, with whom, however, he comes to terms, because the sun is fed by the vapours of the water ; Artemis, the moon, is opposed by Here, the air, through which it passes, and which often obscures it ; Fluvius, or earthly water, by Hephæstus, or earthly fire.[4] That Apollo is the sun, and Artemis the moon, no one doubts ;[5] nor did it cause any difficulty to these

[1] According to *Heraclit.* 53, 112.

[2] We learn from Ps. *Plut.* De Fluv. 5, 3, p. 1003, that Cleanthes wrote a θεομαχία, a small fragment of which, containing a portion of the Prometheus legend in a later and evidently apologetically moulded form, is there preserved. The theomachy here explained by Cleanthes (for the Stoic appears to be the one here meant) appears not to be the Homeric one, but the struggle of the Gods with the Giants and Titans, identical with the book περὶ γιγάντων (*Diog.* vii. 175). Perhaps on this occasion he may have discussed the other. At any rate

the moral interpretation given by Heraclitus to Homer's θεομαχία is quite in the style of the interpretation of the legend of Hercules, probably borrowed from Cleanthes.

[3] Further particulars on Hermes, Alleg. Hom. c. 72, 141.

[4] Alleg. Hom. c. 54.

[5] Conf. *Heracl.* c. 6, p. 11 ; *Corn.* 32, p. 191 ; 34, 206 ; *Cic.* N. D. ii. 27, 68 ; *Phædr.* (Philodem.) Nat. De. col. 5 and 2. In *Phædrus*, too, col. 2 (τοὺς δὲ τὸν Ἀπόλλω), if ἥλιον seems too wild, perhaps φῶς should be substituted for τοὺς, for Apollo cannot well symbolise the earth.

mythologists to find the moon also in Athene.[1]
Many subtle discussions were set on foot by the
Stoics respecting the name, the form, and the attributes of these Gods, particularly by Cleanthes, for
whom the sun had particular importance,[2] as being
the seat of the power which rules the world.[3] The
stories of the birth of the Lotoides and the defeat
of the dragon Pytho are, according to Antipater,
symbolical of events which took place at the formation of the world, and the creation of the sun and
moon.[4] Others find in the descent of two Gods from

---

[1] *Plut.* Fac. Lun. 5, 2, p.
922. The Stoics address the
moon as Artemis and Athene.

[2] See p. 147, 1.

[3] The name Apollo is explained by Cleanthes, in *Macrob.* Sat. i. 17, ὡς ἀπ᾽ ἄλλων καὶ
ἄλλων τόπων τὰς ἀνατολὰς ποιουμένου; by Chrysippus, as derived
from α private and πολὺς, ὡς
οὐχὶ τῶν πολλῶν καὶ φαύλων
αὐσιῶν τοῦ πυρὸς ὄντα. The latter
explanation is quoted by *Plotin.*
v. 5, 6, p. 525, as Pythagorean,
and Chrysippus may have borrowed it thence, or the later
Pythagoreans from Chrysippus.
Cicero, in imitation, makes his
Stoic derive *sol* from *solus.* The
epithet of Apollo, Loxias, is
referred by Cleanthes to the
ἕλικες λοξαὶ of the sun's course,
or the ἀκτῖνες λοξαὶ of the sun ;
and by Œnopides, to the λοξὸς
κύκλος (the ecliptic). The
epithet Λύκιος is explained by
Cleanthes, quod veluti lupi pe-
cora rapiunt, ita ipse quoque
humorem eripit radiis ; Antipater, ἀπὸ τοῦ λευκαίνεσθαι πάντα
φωτίζοντος ἡλίου. In the same

author Macrobius found the
derivation of πύθιος from πύθειν
(because the sun's heat produces decay). Other explanations of these as well as of
other epithets of Apollo, of the
name of Artemis and her
epithets, of the attributes and
symbols of these Gods, are to be
found in abundance in *Cornutus*, c. 32, 34, and in *Macrobius*, l. c., who probably got the
most of them from Stoic sources.

[4] The first of these stories is
explained by *Macrob.* Sat. i. 17,
down to the most minute details, in the sense of the
cosmical views already given,
p. 162, 2, and likewise the
story of the slaying of the
Pytho, the dragon being taken
to represent the heavy vapours
of the marshy earth, which were
overcome by the sun's heat
(the arrows of Apollo). This
interpretation being expressly
attributed to Antipater by Macrobius, it appears probable
that the first one came from
the same source. Another likewise quoted by him according

Leto the simpler thought, that sun and moon came forth out of darkness.[1] In the same spirit, Heraclitus, without disparaging the original meaning of the story, sees in the swift-slaying arrows of Apollo a picture of devastating pestilence;[2] but then, in an extraordinary manner, misses the natural sense, in gathering from the Homeric story of Apollo's reconciliation (Il. i. 53) the lesson, that Achilles stayed the plague by the medical science which Chiron had taught him.[3]

Far more plausible is the explanation given of the dialogue of Athene with Achilles, and of Hermes with Ulysses. These dialogues are stated to be simply soliloquies of the two heroes respectively.[4] But the Stoic skill in interpretation appears in its fullest glory in supplying the etymological meanings of the various names and epithets which are attributed to Athene.[5] We learn, for instance, that the name Τριτογένεια refers to the three divisions of philosophy.[6]

to which the dragon represents the sun's course is perhaps also Stoical.

[1] *Cornutus*, c. 2, p. 10, points to this in explaining Leto as Ληθώ, and referring it to night, because everything is forgotten in sleep at night.

[2] c. 8, especially p. 16, 22, 28. *Ibid.* c. 12, p. 24, 28, the clang of Apollo's arrows is explained to be the harmony of the spheres.

[3] c. 15, p. 31.

[4] *Ibid.* c. 19, 72, p. 39, 141.

[5] See *Corn.* c. 20, 105, and *Villoisin's* notes on the passage. The most varied derivations of

Athene are given : from ἀθρεῖν by *Heracl.* c. 19, 40 ; Tzetz. in *Hesiod,*'Ερ. καὶ Ἡμε. 70 ; Etymol. Mag. 'Αθηνᾶ—from θῆλυς or θηλάζειν ('Αθήνη = ἀθήλη or ἀθηλᾶ = ἡ μὴ θηλάζουσα), by *Phædr.* Nat. D. col. 6 ; *Athenag.* Leg. pro. Christ. c. 17, p. 78—from θείνω, because virtue never allows itself to be beaten—from αἰθήρ + ναίω, so that 'Αθηναία = Αἰθεροναῖα.

[6] This explanation had been already given by Diogenes, according to *Phædr.* col. 6. Cornutus also mentions it (20, 108), but he prefers the derivation from τρεῖν.

Heraclitus discovers the same divisions in the three heads of Cerberus.[1] Chrysippus, in a diffuse manner, proves that the coming forth of the Goddess from the head of Zeus is not at variance with his view of the seat of reason.[2] It has been already observed that Dionysus means wine, and Demeter, fruit;[3] but, just as the latter was taken to represent the earth and its nutritious powers,[4] so Dionysus was further supposed to stand for the principle of natural life, the productive and sustaining breath of life;[5] and since this breath comes from the sun, according to Cleanthes, it was not difficult to find the sun represented by the God of wine.[6] Moreover, the stories of the birth of Dionysus, his being torn to pieces by Titans,

---

[1] c. 33, p. 69.

[2] It is to be found in *Galen.* Hipp. et Plat. iii. 8, p. 349–353, but, according to *Phædr.* (*Philodem.*) l. c., conf. *Cic.* N. D. I. 15, 41, was already put forward by Diogenes. For himself, he prefers the other explanation, according to which Athene comes forth from the head of Jupiter, because the air which she represents occupies the highest place in the universe. *Cornut.* c. 20, 103, leaves us to choose between this explanation and the assumption that the ancients regarded the head as the seat of the ἡγεμονικόν. *Heracl.* c. 19, 40, states the latter, *Eustath.* in Il. 93, 40, the former, as the reason.

[3] p. 349, 4, *Corn.* 30, p. 172.

[4] See p. 359, 1, *Plut.* De Is. c. 40, Schl. p. 367 : Demeter and Core are τὸ διὰ τῆς γῆς καὶ τῶν καρπων διῆκον πνεῦμα. *Phædr.*

col. 2 : τὴν Δήμητρα γῆν ἢ τὸ ἐν αὐτῇ γόνευμα [γόνιμον πνεῦμα]. On Demeter as γῆ μήτηρ or Δηὼ μήτηρ, see *Corn.* c. 28, p. 156, and *Villoison* on the passage.

[5] *Plut.* l. c. : Dionysus is τὸ γόνιμον πνεῦμα καὶ τρόφιμον.

[6] *Macrob.* Sat. i. 18 : Cleanthes derived the name Dionysus from διανύσαι, because the sun daily completes his course round the world. It is well known that, before and after his time, the identification of Apollo with Dionysus was common, and it is elaborately proved by Macrobius. *Servius*, too, on Georg. i. 5, says that the Stoics believed the sun, Apollo, and Bacchus—and likewise the moon, Diana, Ceres, Juno, and Proserpine—to be identical. Other etymologies of Διόνυσος are given by *Corn.* c. 30, 173.

his followers,[1] no less than the rape of Proserpine,[2] and the institution of agriculture,[3] and the names of the respective Gods, afforded ample material for the interpreting taste of the Stoics.

The Fates (μοῖραι), as their name already indicates, stand for the righteous and invariable rule of destiny;[4] the Graces (χάριτες), as to whose names, number, and qualities Chrysippus had given the fullest discussion,[5] represent the virtues of benevolence and gratitude;[6] the Muses, the divine origin of culture.[7] Ares is war;[8] Aphrodite, unrestrained pas-

---

[1] *Corn.* 30, discusses the point at large, referring both the story and the attributes of Dionysus to wine. He, and also *Heracl.* c. 35, p. 71, refer the story of Dionysus and Lycurgus to the vintage.

[2] *Corn.* c. 28, p. 163, who also refers the legend and worship of Demeter, in all particulars, to agriculture; and the rape of Persephone, to the sowing of fruits. Conf. *Cic.* N. D. ii. 26, 66. According to *Plut.* De Is. 66, p. 377, Cleanthes had already called Περσεφόνη, τὸ διὰ τῶν καρπῶν φερόμενον καὶ φονευόμενον πνεῦμα. A somewhat different explanation of the rape of Persephone is given in a passage of Mai's Mythograph vii. 4, p. 216, quoted by *Osann.* on Cornutus, p. 343.

[3] The legend of Triptolemus, which is explained by Cornutus, l. c. p 161, historically as referring to the discovery of agriculture by Triptolemus.

[4] Chrysippus, in *Stob.* i. 180; *Eus.* Pr. Ev. vi. 8, 7 (*Theodoret.* Cur. Gr. Aff. vi. 14, p. 87), see p. 171, 1. Conf.

Plut. Sto. Rep. 47, 5; *Corn.* c. 13, p. 38; and *Plato,* Rep. x. 617, c.

[5] According to *Sen.* Benef. i. 3, 8; 4, 4, he had filled a whole book, probably of a treatise not otherwise mentioned on kind deeds, with these ineptiæ—ita ut de ratione dandi accipiendi reddendique beneficii pauca admodum dicat, nec his fabulas, sed hæc fabulis inserit. A portion of these was made use of by Hecato in his work on this subject.

[6] Chrysippus, in *Phædr.* (Philodemus), col. 4. Further particulars in *Sen.* l. c., and *Corn.* 15, 55. Somewhat similar is the explanation of Λιταί (*Corn.* 12, 37; *Heracl.* 37, 75), which at best are only casual personifications.

[7] *Corn.* 14, 43, who, at the same time, mentions their names and number; *Philodem.* De Mus. Vol. Herc. i. col. 15; Erato indicating the importance of music for ἐρωτικὴ ἀρετή. *Ibid.* 10, 33, on the Erinnyes; 29, 171, on the Horoi.

[8] *Herac.* 31, 63; *Plu.* Am. 13, 15, p. 757.

sion, or, more generally, absence of control;[1] other interpreters, and among them Empedocles, consider Ares to represent the separating, Aphrodite the uniting, power of nature.[2] The stories of the two deities being wounded by Diomedes,[3] of their adulterous intrigues, and their being bound by Hephæstus,[4] are explained in various ways—morally, physically, technically, and historically.

In the case of another God, Pan, the idea of the Allnear was suggested simply by the name. His shaggy goat's feet were taken to represent the solid earth, and the human form of his upper limbs implied that the sovereign power in the world resides above.[5] To the Stoic without a misgiving as to these and similar explanations,[6] it was a matter of small

---

[1] *Heracl.* 28, 60; 30, 62, and above, p. 360.

[2] *Ibid.* 69, 136. In this sense, Aphrodite might be identified with Zeus, which was really done by *Phædr.* Nat. De. col. 1 : ἀνάλογον εὖν . . . θαι [Petersen suggests εὐνομεῖσθαι, but probably it should be ὀνομάζεσθαι] τὸν Δία καὶ τὴν κοινὴν πάντων φύσιν καὶ εἱμαρμένην καὶ ἀνάγκην καὶ τὴν αὐτὴν εἶναι καὶ Εὐνομίαν καὶ Δίκην καὶ Ὁμόνοιαν καὶ Εἰρήνην καὶ Ἀφροδίτην καὶ τὸ παραπλήσιον πᾶν.

[3] The story of Ares, νείατον ἐς κενεῶνα, means, according to *Heracl.* 31, 64, that Diomedes, ἐπὶ τὰ κενὰ τῆς τῶν ἀντεπάλων τάξεως παρεισελθών, defeated the enemy; that of Aphrodite (ἀφροσύνη, *ibid.* 30, 62), that, by his experience in war, he overcame the inexperienced troops of barbarians.

[4] In *Plut.* Aud. Po. c. 4, p. 19, the connection of Ares and Aphrodite is explained as meaning a conjunction of the two planets. *Heracl.* 69, 136, gives the alternative of referring this connection to the union of φιλία and νεῖκος, which produces harmony, or to the fact that brass (Ares) is moulded in the fire (Hephæstus) into objects of beauty (Aphrodite). The latter interpretation is given by *Corn.* 19, 102, who also explains the relation of Ares to Aphrodite to mean the union of strength and beauty.

[5] *Corn.* 27, 148; *Plut.* Krat. 408, c.

[6] His lewdness was said to indicate the fullness of the σπερματικοὶ λόγοι in nature; his sojourn in the wilderness, the solitariness of the world.

difficulty to make the Titan Ἰάπετος stand for language or Ἰάφετος, and Κοῖος for quality or ποιότης.[1]
Add to this the many more or less ingenious explanations of the well-known stories of Uranos and Cronos,[2] and we are still far from having exhausted the resources of the Stoic explanations of mythology. The most important attempts of this kind have, however, been sufficiently noticed.

Besides the legends of the Gods, the legends of the heroes attracted considerable attention in the Stoic Schools. Specially were the persons of Her-

(3) *Allegory applied to heroic myths.*

---

[1] *Corn.* 17, 91. Conf. *Osann* ad locum who points out similar interpretations, probably of Stoic origin, in the Scholia to the theogony, and also in Etymol. M.

[2] Besides the etymologies of οὐρανὸς in *Corn.* c. 1, and the observation of *Plut.* Pl. i. 6, 9, that heaven is the father of all things, because of its fertilising rains, and earth the mother, because she brings forth everything, the words in *Cic.* N. D. ii. 24, 63, on which *Krische*, Forsch. 397, deserve notice. It is there said, probably after Zeno : Uranos is the Ether, and was deprived of his vitality, because he did not need it for the work of begetting things. Cronos is Time (the same is said by *Heraclit.* c. 41, 86, who sees in Rhea the ever flowing motions), and consumes his children, just as Time does portions of time. Cronos was bound by Zeus, the unmeasured course of time having been bound by the courses of the

stars. A second explanation is given by *Corn.* 7, 21, after making (c. 3, 10) vain attempts at etymological interpretations of Cronos and Rhea. Cronos (from κραίνειν) stands for the order of nature, putting an end to the all too-violent atmospheric currents on earth, by diminishing the vapour-masses (compare the quotation from Chrysippus on p. 161, 2), and he is bound by Zeus, to represent that change in nature is limited. *Macrob.* Sat. i. 8 (betraying a Stoic pattern by Chrysippus's definition of time : certa dimensio quæ ex cœli conversione colligetur, conf. p. 197, 2), gives another explanation : Before the separation of elements, time was not ; after the seeds of all things had flowed from heaven down to the earth in sufficient quantity, and the elements had come into being, the process came to an end, and the different sexes were left to propagate animal life.

cules and Ulysses singled out, for the sake of illustrating the ideal of the wise man.[1] But here, too,
various modes of interpretation meet and cross. According to Cornutus,[2] the God Hercules must be distinguished from the hero of the same name—the
God being nothing less than Reason, ruling in the
world without a superior ;[3] and the grammarian
makes every effort to unlock with this key his history and attributes. Nevertheless, with all his respect for Cleanthes,[4] he could not accept that Stoic's
explanation of the twelve labours of Hercules. Heraclitus has probably preserved the chief points in
this explanation. Hercules is a teacher of mankind,
initiated into the heavenly wisdom. He overcomes
the wild bear, the lion, and the bull, i.e. the lusts
and passions of men ; he drives away the deer, i.e.
cowardice ; he purifies the stall of Augeas from filth,
i.e. he purifies the life of men from extravagances ;
he frightens away the birds, i.e. empty hopes ; and
burns to ashes the many-headed hydra of pleasure.
He brings the keeper of the nether world to light,
with his three heads—these heads representing the
three chief divisions of philosophy. In the same
way, the wounding of Here and Hades by Hercules
is explained. Here, the Goddess of the air represents the fog of ignorance, the three-barbed arrow

---

[1] See p. 292, 4, and *Sen.*
Benef. i. 13, 3.
[2] C. 31, 187.
[3] *Plut.* De Is. 44, Schl. p.
367 : He is τὸ πληκτικὸν καὶ
διαιρετικὸν πνεῦμα. *Sen.* Benef.
iv. 8, 1. See above, p. 359, 2,

and what *Villoison* quotes on
Cornutus, p. 366, from Schol.
Apollon. among the natural
philosophers, i. e., the Stoics,
Hercules symbolises strength
and intelligence.
[4] *Pers.* Sat. v. 63.

undeniably (so thought the Stoics) pointing to philosophy, with its threefold division, in its heavenly
flight. The laying prostrate of Hades by that arrow
implies that philosophy has access even to things
most secret.[1] The Odyssey is explained by Heraclitus in the same strain, he being apparently not the
first so to do.[2] In Ulysses you behold a pattern of
all virtues, and an enemy of all vices.[3] He flees from
the country of the Lotophagi, i.e. from wicked pleasures; he stays the wild rage of the Cyclopes; he
calms the winds, having first secured a prosperous
passage by his knowledge of the stars; the attractions of pleasure in the house of Circe he overcomes,
penetrates into the secrets of Hades, learns from the
Sirens the history of all times, saves himself from
the Charybdis of profligacy and the Scylla of shamelessness, and, in abstaining from the oxen of the sun,
overcomes sensuous desires. Such explanations may
suffice to show how the whole burden of the myths
was resolved into allegory by the Stoics, how little
they were conscious of foisting in foreign elements,
and how they degraded to mere symbols of philosophical ideas those very heroes on whose real existence
they continually insisted.

The Stoic theology has engaged a good deal of C. *Pro-*
our attention, not only because it is instructive to *phetic
powers.*
compare their views, in general and in detail, with
similar views advanced nowadays, but also because

[1] *Heraclit.* c. 33, p. 67, who,
in the introduction, expressly
refers to δοκιμώτατοι Στωϊκῶν.

[2] C. 70–75.
[3] C. 70–73, p. 137.

it forms a very characteristic and important part of their entire system. To us, much of it appears to be a mere worthless trifling; but, to the Stoics, these explanations were solemnly earnest. To them they seemed to be the only means of rescuing the people's faith, of meeting the severe charges brought against tradition and the works of the poets, on which a Greek had been fed from infancy.[1] Unable to break entirely with these traditions, they still would not sacrifice to them their scientific and moral convictions. Can we, then, wonder that they attempted the impossible, and sought to unite contradictions, or that such an attempt should land them in forced and artificial methods of interpretation?

(1) *Divination.*

Illustrative of the attitude of the Stoics towards positive religion are their views on divination.[2] The importance attached by them to the prophetic art appears in the diligence which the chiefs of this School devoted to discussing it. The ground for the later teaching having been prepared by Zeno and Cleanthes, Chrysippus gave the finishing touch to the Stoic dogmas on the subject.[3] Particular treatises

[1] Conf. the way in which *Heraclitus*, 74, 146, expresses himself as to Plato's and Epicurus's attacks upon Homer.

[2] Conf. *Wachsmuth's* treatise mentioned above, p. 351, 2.

[3] *Cic.* Divin. i. 3, 6. He there mentions two books of Chrysippus on divination, which are also referred to (as *Wachsmuth*, p. 12, shows) by *Diog.* vii. 149; *Varro* (in

Lactant. Inst. i. 6, 9); *Phot.* Amphiloch. Quæst. (*Montfauçon*, Bibl. Coisl. p. 347); *Philodemus*, περὶ θεῶν διαγωγῆς, Vol. Herc. vi. 49, col. 7, 33; and from which Cicero has borrowed Divin. i. 38, 82; ii. 17, 41; 49, 101; 15, 35; 63, 130; and perhaps De Fato, 7. Chrysippus also wrote a book, περὶ χρησμῶν (*Cic.* Divin. i. 19, 37; ii. 56, 115; 65, 134; *Suid.*

respecting divination were drawn up by Sphærus, Diogenes, Antipater, and, last of all, by Posidonius.[1] The subject was also fully treated by Boëthus, and by Panætius from a somewhat different side.[2] The common notions as to prognostics and oracles could not commend themselves to these philosophers, nor could they approve of common soothsaying. In a system so purely based on nature as theirs,[3] the supposition that God works for definite ends, after the manner of men, exceptionally announcing to one or the other a definite result—in short, the marvellous— was out of place. But to infer thence—as their op-

νεοττόs); and one περὶ ὀνείρων (*Cic.* Divin. i. 20, 39 ; ii. 70, 144 ; 61, 126 ; 63, 130 ; i. 27, 56 : *Suid.* τιμωροῦντος). In the former, he collected oracular responses ; in the latter, prophetic dreams.

[1] *Diog.* vii. 178, mentions a treatise of Sphærus περὶ μαντικῆς. *Cic.* (Divin. i. 3, 6 ; i. 38, 83 ; ii. 17, 41 ; 43, 90 ; 49, 101) mentions a treatise having the same title with that of Diogenes of Seleucia, and two books of Antipater περὶ μαντικῆς, in which many interpretations of dreams were given. The same writer (Divin. i. 3, 6 ; 20, 39 ; 38, 83 ; 54, 123 ; ii. 70, 144 ; 15, 35; 49, 101) mentions a treatise of Posidonius περὶ μαντικῆς, in five books, *Diog.* vii. 149 ; *Cic.* Divin. i. 3, 6 ; 30, 64 ; 55, 125 ; 57, 130 ; ii. 15, 35 ; 21, 47 ; De Fato, 3 ; *Boëth.* De Diis et Præsens (in Orelli's Cicero, v. 1) p. 395.

[2] Boëthus, in his commentary on Aratus, attempted to determine and explain the in-

dications of a storm. *Cic.* Divin. i. 8, 14 ; ii. 21, 47. On Panætius's objections to μαντικὴ a word will be presently said.

[3] *Cic.* Divin. i. 52, 118 : Non placet Stoicis, singulis jecorum fissis aut avium cautibus interesse Deum ; neque enim decorum est, nec Diis dignum, nec fieri ullo pacto potest. *Ibid.* 58, 132 : Nunc illa testabor, non me sortilegos, neque eos, qui quæstus causa hariolentur, ne psychomantia quidem . . agnoscere. Similarly in *Sen.* Nat. Qu. ii. 32, 2 (see p. 374, 3), the difference between the Stoic view and the ordinary one is stated to be this, that, according to the Stoics, auguries non quia significatura sunt fiant, but quia facta sunt significent. In c. 42, it is said to be an absurd belief that Jupiter should hurl bolts which as often hit the innocent as the guilty, an opinion invented ad coërcendos animos imperitorum.

ponents, the Epicureans, did—that the whole art of
divination is a delusion, was more than the Stoics
could do. The belief in an extraordinary care of
God for individual men was too comforting an idea
for them to renounce;[1] they not only appealed to
divination as the strongest proof of the existence of
Gods and the government of Providence,[2] but they
also drew the converse conclusion, that, if there be
Gods, there must also be divination, since the benevolence of the Gods would not allow them to refuse
to mankind so inestimable a gift.[3] The conception

[1] Conf. Diogenian, in *Eus.
Pr. Ev.* iv. 3, 5: τὸ χρειῶδες
αὐτῆς (divination) καὶ βιωφελὲς,
δι' ὃ καὶ μάλιστα Χρύσιππος δοκεῖ
ὑμνεῖν τὴν μαντικήν; and *M.
Aurel.* ix. 27; God cares even
for the wicked by means of
prophecies and by dreams.

[2] *Cic.* N. D. ii. 5, 13, where
among the four reasons from
which Cleanthes deduced belief in Gods, the first is præ-
sensio rerum futurarum, extraordinary natural phenomena
—pestilence, earthquakes, monsters, meteors, &c., being the
third. *Ibid.* 65, 165 : The
Stoic says of divination : Mihi
videtur vel maxime confirmare,
Deorum providentia consuli
rebus humanis, *Sext.* Math. ix.
132 : If there were no Gods, all
the varieties of divination
would be unmeaning ; these
are nevertheless universally admitted. *Cic.* Divin. i. 6, and the
quotations on p. 175, 3, 4.

[3] *Cic.* Divin. i. 5, 9 : Ego
enim sic existimo : si sint ea
genera divinandi vera, de quibus
accepimus quæque colimus, esse

Deos, vicissimque si Dii sint,
esse qui divinent. Arcem tu
quidem Stoicorum, inquam,
Quinte, defendis. *Ibid.* 38,
82 : Stoic proof of divination :
Si sunt Dii neque ante declarant
hominibus quæ futura sunt, aut
non diligunt homines, aut quid
eventurum sit ignorant, aut
existimant nihil interesse hominum, scire quid futurum sit,
aut non censent esse suæ majes-
tatis præsignificare hominibus
quæ sunt futura, aut ea ne ipsi
quidem Dii præsignificare possunt. At neque non diligunt
nos, &c. Non igitur sunt Dii
nec significant futura (οὐκ ἄρα
εἰσὶ μὲν θεοὶ οὐ προσημαίνουσι δὲ
—the well-known expression
of Chrysippus for εἰ θεοί εἰσιν,
οὐ προσημαίνουσι, conf. p. 114, 1);
sunt autem Dii : significant
ergo : et non, si significant,
nullas vias dant nobis ad signi-
ficationis scientiam, frustra
enim significarent : nec, si dant
vias, non est divinatio. Est
igitur divinatio. This proof,
says Cicero, was used by Chrysippus, Diogenes, Antipater.

of destiny, too, and the nature of man, appeared to
Posidonius to lead to the belief in divination;[1] if
all that happens is the outcome of an unbroken chain
of cause and effect, there must be signs indicating
the existence of causes, from which certain effects
result;[2] and if the soul of man is in its nature
divine, it must also possess the capacity, under circumstances, of observing what generally escapes its
notice.[3] Lest, however, the certainty of their belief
should suffer from lacking the support of experience,
the Stoics had collected a number of instances of
verified prophecies;[4] but with so little discrimina-
tion, that we could only wonder at their credulity,
did we not know the abject state of such historical
criticism as then existed, and the readiness with
which, in all ages, men believe whatever agrees with
their prejudices.[5]

In what way, then, can the two facts be com-

It may be easily recognised as
belonging to Chrysippus. *Cic.*
ii. 17, 41; 49, 101, again reverts
to the same proof. Conf. *id.*
i. 46, 104: Id ipsum est Deos
non putare, quæ ab iis signi-
ficantur, contemnere. *Diog.*
vii. 149: καὶ μὴν καὶ μαντικὴν
ὑφεστάναι πᾶσάν φασιν, εἰ καὶ
πρόνοιαν εἶναι. Some read ᾗ καὶ
πρόνοιαν εἶναι, in which case the
argument would be reversed,
not from providence to divination, but from divination to
providence.
[1] *Cic.* Div. i. 55, 125:
Primum mihi videtur, ut Posidonius facit, a Deo . . deinde a
fato, deinde a natura vis omnis
divinandi ratioque repetenda.

[2] *Cic.* l. c. 55, 126.
[3] *Ibid.* 57, 129.
[4] See p. 370, 3; 371, 1.
[5] *Cic.* Divin. i. 27, 56 (*Suid.*
τιμωροῦντος), ii. 65, 135 (*Suid.*
νεοττὸς), ii. 70, 144, quoting
from Chrysippus; i. 54, 123,
quoting from Antipater; i. 30,
64, De Fat. 3, 5, from Posidonius—gives instances of
stories to which the Stoics
attached great value, whilst
their opponents either pronounced the stories to be false,
or the prophecies to be deceptive, or their fulfilment to
be accidental (*Cic.* Divin. i.
19, 37; ii. 11, 27; 56, 115; De
Fato 3, 5).

*(2) Pro-
phecy ex-
plained by
a refer-
ence to
natural
causes.*

bined—the belief in prophecy, on the one hand, and,
on the other, the denial of unearthly omens arising
from an immediate divine influence? In answering this question, the Stoics adopted the only course
which their system allowed. The marvellous, which,
as such, they could not admit, was referred to natural
laws,[1] from which it was speculatively deduced. The
admirable Panætius is the only Stoic who is reported
as having maintained the independence of his judgment by denying omens, prophecy, and astrology.[2]
Just as in modern times Leibnitz and so many others
both before and after him thought to purge away
from the marvellous all that is accidental and superhuman, and to find in wonders links in the general
chain of natural causes, so, too, the Stoics, by assuming a natural connection between the token and
its fulfilment, made an effort to rescue omens and
divination, and to explain portents as the natural
symptoms of certain occurrences.[3] Nor did they con-

[1] Aristotle, in a somewhat
different sense, had explained
the marvellous by a reference
to natural causes, even allowing
the existence of presentiments
within certain limits.

[2] *Cic.* Divin. i. 3, 6, after
the passage quoted: Sed a
Stoicis vel princeps ejus disciplinæ Posidonii doctor disci-
pulus Antipatri degeneravit
Panætius, nec tamen ausus est
negare vim esse divinandi, sed
dubitare se dixit. *Ibid.* i. 7,
12; ii. 42, 88; Acad. ii. 33,
107; *Diog.* vii. 149; *Epiphan.*
Adv. Hær. Cicero appears to
have borrowed from Panætius,

as Wachsmuth rightly observes,
this denial of Astrology (Divin.
ii. 42–46), and he allows, c. 42,
88; 47, 97, that Panætius was
the only Stoic who rejected it.

[3] *Sen.* Nat. Quæ. ii. 32, 3:
Nimis illum [Deum] otiosum et
pusillæ rei ministrum facis, si
aliis somnia aliis exta, disponit.
Ista nihilominus divina ope ge-
runtur. Sed non a Deo pennæ
avium reguntur nec pecudum
viscera sub securi formantur.
Alia ratione fatorum series explicatur . . . quicquid fit alicujus
rei futuræ signum est . . . cujus
rei ordo est etiam prædictio est,
&c. *Cic.* Divin. i. 52, 118, after

fine themselves to cases in which the connection between the prophecy and the event can be proved.[1]
They insisted upon divination in cases in which it
cannot possibly be proved. The flight of birds and
the entrails of victims were stated to be natural
indications of coming events; and there was said to
be even a formal connection between the positions
of the stars and the individuals born under those
positions.[2] If it was urged, that in this case omens
must be far more numerous than they were supposed
to be, the Stoics answered, that omens were count-
less, but that only the meaning of a few was known
to men.[3] If the question were asked, how it is that,
in public sacrifices, the priest should always offer
those very animals whose entrails contained omens,
Chrysippus and his followers did not hesitate to affirm
that the same sympathy which exists between objects and omens also guides the sacrificer in the
choice of a victim.[4] And yet so bald was this hypo-

the passage quoted, p. 371, 3:
Sed ita a principio inchoatum
esse mundum, ut certis rebus
certa signa præcurrerent, alia
in extis, alia in avibus, &c.
Posidonius, *ibid.* 55, 125 (see
p. 373, 2). Nor was the meaning
otherwise, when portents (according to *Cic.* Divin. ii. 15,
33; 69, 142) were based on a
συμπάθεια τῆς φύσεως (on which
see p. 183, 2), an opponent not
without reason doubting whether it existed, for instance,
between a rent in the liver of
a victim and an advantageous
business, or between an egg in
a dream and treasure trove.

[1] As in the passage quoted
from Boëthus on p. 371, 2.
[2] Conf. p. 374, 2; 379, 1,
and *Cic.* Div. ii. 43, 90, according to whom Diogenes of
Seleucia conceded so much to
astrology as to allow that, from
the condition of the stars at
birth, it might be known quali
quisque natura et ad quam
quisque maxime rem aptus
futurus sit. More he would
not yield, because twins often
differ widely in their course of
life and destiny.
[3] *Sen.* Nat. Qu. ii 32, 5.
[4] *Cic.* l. c. ii. 15, 35: Chrysippus, Antipater, and Posi-

thesis, that they had, at the same time, a second answer in reserve, viz. that the corresponding change in the entrails did not take place until the victim had been chosen.[1] In support of such views, their only appeal was to the almighty power of God ; but, in making this appeal, the deduction of omens from natural causes was at an end.[2]

Nor, again, could the Stoics altogether quiet a suspicion that an unchangeable predestination of all events had rendered individual activity superfluous,[3] nor meet the objection[4] that, on the hypothesis of necessity, divination itself was unnecessary.[5] They quieted themselves, however, with the thought that divination, and the actions resulting from divination, are included among the causes foreordained by destiny.[6]

donius assert: Ad hostiam deligendam ducem esse vim quandam sentientem atque divinam, quæ tota confusa mundo sit, as was explained I. 52, 118.

[1] *Cic.* ii. 15, 35 : Illud vero multum etiam melius, quod . . . dicitur ab illis (conf. i. 52, 118): cum immolare quispiam velit, tum fieri extorum mutationem, ut aut absit aliquid, aut supersit : Deorum enim numini parere omnia. See p. 374, 3.

[2] *Cic.* i. 53, 120, defends auguries somewhat similarly by arguing: If an animal can move its limbs at pleasure, must not God have greater power over His? (his body according to them being the whole world).

[3] See p. 181.

[4] *Cic.* Divin. ii. 8, 20 ; Diogenian, in *Eus.* Pr. Ev. iv. 3, 5 ; *Alex. Aph.* De Fat. 31, p. 96.

[5] Upon the use of divination depends the whole argument for its reality, based on the divine kindness. *Cic.* i. 38, 83, and above, p. 372, 1.

[6] *Sen.* Nat. Qu. ii. 37, 2 ; 38, 2 : Effugiet pericula si expiaverit prædictas divinitus minas. At hoc quoque in fato est, ut expiet, &c. This answer probably came from Chrysippus, who, as it appears from *Cic.* Divin. ii. 63, 130, and *Philodem.* περὶ θεῶν διαγωγῆς, Vol. Herc. vi. col. 7, 33, defended the use of expiation. In the above quoted and more general form it is found in Alexander and Eusebius, probably also taken from Chrysippus, see p. 181.

Divination, accordingly, consists in the capacity
to read and interpret omens;[1] and this capacity is,
according to the Stoics, partly a natural gift, and
partly acquired by art and study.[2] The natural gift of
prophecy is based, as other philosophers had already
laid down,[3] on the relationship of the human soul to
God.[4] Sometimes it manifests itself in sleep, at other
times in ecstasy.[5] A taste for higher revelations will
be developed, in proportion as the soul is withdrawn
from the world of sense, and from all thought respecting things external.[6] The actual cause of the
prophetic gift was referred to influences coming to

[1] According to the definition
in *Sext.* Math. ix. 132, which
Cic. Divin. ii. 63, 130, attributes to Chrysippus, it is an
ἐπιστήμη (*Cic.* more accurately :
a vis = δύναμις, since besides scientific there is also a natural
divination), θεωρητικὴ καὶ ἐξηγη-
τικὴ τῶν ὑπὸ θεῶν ἀνθρώποις διδο-
μένων σημείων. *Stob.* Ecl. ii.
122 and 238; *Eus.* Pr. Ev. iv.
3, 5.

[2] *Plut.* Vit. Hom. 212, p.
1238 : [τῆς μαντικῆς] τὸ μὲν
τεχνικόν φασιν εἶναι οἱ Στωϊκοί.
οἷον ἱεροσκοπίαν καὶ οἰωνοὺς καὶ τὸ
περὶ φήμας καὶ κληδόνας καὶ σύμ-
βολα, ἅπερ συλλήβδην τεχνικὰ
προσηγόρευσαν· τὸ δὲ ἄτεχνον καὶ
ἀδίδακτον, τουτέστιν ἐνύπνια καὶ
ἐνθουσιασμούς. To the same
effect, *Cic.* Divin. i. 18, 34 ;
11. 11, 26.

[3] Conf. the fragment quoted
in 'Aristotle and the Peripatetics,' p. 300, which throws
light on old and well-known
views in the spirit of the
Platonic Aristotelian philo-

sophy, without, however, defending them.

[4] *Cic.* Divin. i. 30, 64; ii. 10,
26 : The naturale genus divinandi is, quod animos arriperet
aut exciperet extrinsecus a
divinitate, unde omnes animos
hausti aut acceptos aut libatos
haberemus. *Plut.* Plac. v. 1 ;
where, however, the words κατὰ
θειότητα τῆς ψυχῆς are only a
gloss on the preceding words
κατὰ τὸ ἔνθεον, κ.τ.λ. *Galen.*
Hist. Phil. p. 320.

[5] *Cic.* Divin. i. 50, 115, and
Plut. Compare the many
Stoic stories of dreams and
presentiments in *Cic.* i. 27, 56 ;
30, 64 ; ii. 65, 134 ; 70, 144.

[6] See besides the passages
just quoted, *Cic.* Divin. i. 49,
110 ; 50, 113 ; 51, 115 ; and in
particular i. 57. 129. Hence
the prophecies of the dying
(*ibid.* 30, 63, according to Posidonius ; conf. *Arist.* l. c.), and
the statement (*ibid.* 53, 121 ;
see p. 380, 1) that true dreams
come of innocent sleep.

the soul partly from God or the universal spirit diffused throughout the world,[1] and partly from the
souls which haunt the air or demons.[2] External
causes, however, contribute to put people in a state
of enthusiasm.[3]

Artificial soothsaying, or the art of divination,
depends upon observation and guess-work.[4] One
who could survey all causes in their effects on one
another would need no observation. Such a one
would be able to deduce the whole series of events
from the given causes. But God alone is able to do
this. Hence men must gather the knowledge of
future events from the indications by which their
coming is announced.[5] These indications may be of
every variety; and hence all possible forms of fore-
telling the future were allowed by the Stoics; the

---

[1] Conf. the quotations on
p. 375, 4, from *Cic.* Divin. ii.
10, 26 ; 15, 35 ; and his remarks
on the instinctus afflatusque
divinus. *Cic.* i. 18, 34.

[2] According to *Cic.* Divin. i.
30, 64, Posidonius thought prophetic dreams were realised in
one of three ways : uno, quod
prævideat animus ipse per sese,
quippe qui Deorum cognitione
teneatur ; altero, quod plenus
aër sit immortalium animorum,
in quibus tanquam insignitæ
notæ veritatis appareant ; tertio,
quod ipsi Dii cum dormientibus
colloquantur. Of these three
modes, not the first only, but
also the second, correspond with
the Stoic hypotheses. Indeed,
in *Stob.* Ecl. ii. 122, 238, μαντικὴ
is defined = ἐπιστήμη θεωρητικὴ
σημείων τῶν ἀπὸ θεῶν ἢ δαιμόνων
πρὸς ἀνθρώπινον βίον συντεινόντων.

Posidonius can only have spoken
of Gods in condescension to
popular views ; as a Stoic, he
would only know of that connection with the soul of the
universe which is referred to in
the first mode.

[3] Amongst such external
helps, the Stoic in *Cic.* Divin.
i. 50, 114 ; 36, 79, enumerates
the impression derived from
music, natural scenery, moun-
tains, woods, rivers, seas and
vapours arising from the earth.
But it is difficult to understand
how, on Stoic principles, he
can have attached value to
oracles (*ibid.* 18, 34) by lot or
justified them otherwise than
in the way mentioned on p.
375, 4.

[4] *Cic.* i. 18, 34 ; 33, 72.

[5] *Ibid.* i. 56, 127.

inspection of entrails, divination by lightning and other natural phenomena, by the flight of birds, and omens of every kind.[1] Some idea of the mass of superstition which the Stoics admitted and encouraged may be gathered from the first book of Cicero's treatise on divination. The explanation of these omens being, however, a matter of skill, individuals in this, as in every other art, may often go wrong in their interpretation.[2] To ensure against mistakes tradition is partly of use, establishing by manifold experiences the meaning of each omen ;[3] and the moral state of the prophet is quite as important for scientific divination as for the natural gift of prophecy. Purity of heart is one of the most essential conditions of prophetic success.

In all these questions the moral tone of Stoic piety is preserved, and great pains were taken by the Stoics to bring their belief in prophecy into harmony with their philosophic view of the world. Nevertheless, it is clear that success could neither be theirs in making this attempt, nor indeed in dealing with any other parts of the popular belief. Toiling with

[1] *Cicero*, ii. 11, 26, enumerates the above-named varieties, after having previously (i. 33) treated them separately. Similarly, Ps. *Plut.* V. Hom. 212. See above, p. 377, 2. *Stob.* Ecl. ii. 238, mentions tentatively, as varieties of μαντικὴ τό τε ὀνειροκριτικὸν, καὶ τὸ οἰωνοσκοπικὸν, καὶ θυτικόν. *Sext.* Math. ix. 132, says : If there were no Gods, there would be neither μαντικὴ nor θεοληπτικὴ, ἀστρομαντικὴ nor λογικὴ πρόρρησις δι' ὀνείρων. *Macrob.* Somn. Scip. i. 3, gives a theory of dreams ; but in how far it represents the views of the Stoics, it is impossible to say. *Sen.* Nat. Qu. ii: 39, i. 41, clearly distinguishes the discussion of natural omens from the doctrines of philosophy.

[2] *Cic.* i. 55, 124 ; 56, 128.
[3] *Ibid.* i 56, 127.

indefatigable zeal in an attempt so hopeless, they
proved at least the sincerity of their wish to reconcile religion and philosophy. But not less did they
disclose by these endeavours a misgiving that science,
which had put on so bold a face, was not in itself
sufficient, but needed support from the traditions of
religion, and from a belief in divine revelations.[1]
Probably we shall not be far wrong in referring to
this practical need the seeming vagaries of men
like Chrysippus, who, with the clearest intellectual
powers, could be blind to the folly of the methods
they adopted in defending untenable and antiquated
opinions. These vagaries show in Stoicism practical interests preponderating over science. They
also establish the connection of Stoicism with Schools
which doubted altogether the truth of the understanding, and thought to supplement it by divine
revelations. Thus the Stoic theory of divination is
the immediate forerunner of the Neopythagorean
and Neoplatonic doctrine of revelation.

[1] *Cic.* i. 53, 121: Ut igitur
qui se tradet quieti præparato
animo cum bonis cogitationibus tunc rebus (for instance,
nourishment; conf. c. 29, 60;
51, 115) ad tranquillitatem
accommodatis, certa et vera
cernit in somnis; sic castus
animus purusque vigilantis et
ad astrorum et ad avium re-
liquorumque signorum et ad
extorum veritatem est para-
tior.

CHAPTER XIV.

THE STOIC PHILOSOPHY AS A WHOLE AND ITS HISTO- RICAL POSITION.

HAVING now investigated the Stoic system in detail, we shall be in a position to pass a definite judgment on the scope of the Stoic philosophy, the import and the relation of its various parts, and its historical position. Its peculiar character manifests itself before all things in the three points to which attention was drawn at the very outset: [1]—its pre-eminently practical tone, the determining of this practical tendency by the notions of the good and virtue, the use of logic and natural science as a scientific basis therefor. Scientific knowledge is not, as we have seen, to the Stoics an end in itself, but only a means for producing a right moral attitude, all philosophical research standing directly or indirectly in the service of virtue. Both in its earlier as well as in the later days of its existence the Stoic School advocated this principle in the most determined and exclusive manner, nor was it even denied by Chrysippus, the chief representative of its science and learning.

CHAP. XIV.

A. *Inner connection of the Stoic system.*

[1] See p. 46.

If it be then asked what is the right moral attitude, the Stoics reply: action conformable to nature
and reason, in other words, virtue. Virtue, however,
implies two things. On the one hand it implies the
resignation of the individual to the universe, obedience to the universal law; on the other hand it
involves the harmony of man with himself, the dominion of his higher over his lower nature, of reason
over emotion, and the rising superior to every thing
which does not belong to his true nature. Both
statements may be reconciled, the law of morality
being addressed only to reasonable beings, and this
law being the law of their nature, and only to be
carried into execution by their own exertions. Still,
in the Stoic Ethics, two currents of thought may be
clearly distinguished, which from time to time come
into actual collision; the one requiring the individual
to live for the common good and for society, the
other impelling him to live for himself only, to emancipate himself from all that is not himself, and to
console himself with the feeling of virtue. The first
of these tendencies brings man to seek the society of
others; the second enables him to dispense with it.
From the former spring the virtues of justice, socia-
bility, love of man; from the latter, the inner freedom and happiness of the virtuous man. The former
culminates in citizenship of the world; the latter
in the self-sufficingness of the wise man. In as far
as virtue includes everything that can be required of
man, happiness depends on it alone; nothing is good
but virtue, nothing is evil but vice; all that is not

connected with the moral nature is indifferent. On the other hand, in as far as virtue is based on human nature, it stands on the same footing with all else that is conformable with nature. If its own peculiar value cannot be surrendered, no more can it be required that we should be indifferent to the latter, that it should not have for us some positive or negative value, or in some way affect our feelings. Therewith the doctrine of things indifferent and the wise man's freedom from emotions begins to totter. Lastly, if we look at the way in which virtue exists in man, we arrive at different results, according as we look at its essence or its manifestation. Virtue consisting in acting conformably with reason, and reason being one and undivided, it appears that virtue forms an undivided unity, and must, therefore, be possessed whole and entire or not at all. From this proposition the contrast of the wise and foolish man, with all its bluntness and extravagances, is only a legitimate consequence. Or, again, if we look at the conditions upon which owing to human nature the acquisition and possession of virtue depends, the conviction is inevitable that the wise man as drawn by the Stoics never occurs in reality. Hence the conclusion is undeniable that the contrast between wise men and fools is more uncertain than it at first appeared to be. Thus all the main features of the Stoic ethics may be simply deduced from the one fundamental notion, that rational action or virtue is the only good.

Not only does this view of ethics require a peculiar theory of the world to serve as its scientific basis, *(2) Scientific side of*

but it has a reflex action also, influencing alike the
tone and the results of theoretic enquiry. If the
duty of man is declared to consist in bringing his
actions into harmony with the laws of the universe,
it becomes also necessary that he should endeavour
himself to know the world and its laws. The more
his knowledge of the world increases, the greater
will be the value which he attaches to the forms of
scientific procedure. If, moreover, man is required
to be nothing more than an instrument of the universal law, it is only consistent to suppose an absolute regularity of procedure in the universe, an
unbroken connection of cause and effect, and ultimately to refer everything to one highest all-moving
cause, and to include everything under one primary
substance. If in human life the individual has no
rights as against the laws of the universe, so all that
is of individual occurrence in the world is powerless
against universal necessity. On the other hand, if
in the case of man everything turns upon his strength
of will, then likewise in the universe the acting power
must be regarded as the highest and most exalted.
There arises thus that view of the world as a series
of forces which constitutes one of the most peculiar
and penetrating characteristics of the Stoic view of
nature.[1] Lastly, if such an excessive importance is
attached to action and practice, as is here done,
that materialistic view of the world is suggested to
speculation, which finds its bluntest expression in
the Stoic Materialism and appeals to the senses.[2]

[1] See p. 139.   [2] See p. 132.

At the same time the Materialism of the Stoics is superseded and limited by the thought of the universe and of a divine all-penetrating power and reason, just as their appeal to the senses is by the demand for the formation of conceptions, and the general application of the process of demonstration ; the truth of knowledge itself is based on a practical postulate, and the greater or less certainty of the same is measured by the strength of personal conviction. If these elements proved too contradictory to be harmonised ; if the Materialism of the Stoics was at variance with their view of the world as a series of forces ; if appeals to the senses were obviously in conflict with logical method, it was at least thereby clearly established that a practical and not a purely intellectual interest lay at the root of their system.

Of course this statement must not be taken to mean that the Stoics first developed their ethical principles independently of their theory of the universe, and afterwards brought the two into connection with each other. On the contrary, it was by this peculiar connection of theory and practice that Stoicism itself first came into existence. The leading thought of Zeno consists in the attempt to vindicate the supremacy of virtue by a scientific knowledge of the laws of the world ; and he becomes the founder of a new School only by bringing to Cynicism those scientific ideas and aims which he had learned himself in the School of Polemo, Stilpo, and Diodorus, and otherwise gathered from a study of ancient phi-

(3) Connection of the moral and scientific elements.

losophy. These elements are not therefore accidentally brought together in Stoicism, but they are co-
extensive, and dependent one upon the other. As
in the natural science and theory of knowledge of
the Stoics, the experimental basis on which their system was built may be easily seen, so the peculiar
development of their ethics supposes all those positions respecting the universe and the powers therein
at work, which form the most important part of
their natural science. Only by a scientific treatment
of this kind was Stoicism at all able to improve upon
the onesidedness of the Cynic ethics, at least to the
extent in which it really did so, and to accommodate
itself to the wants of human nature, so far as to be
able to exercise an influence at large. Upon this union
only of ethics and metaphysics does that religious
attitude of the Stoic system repose, to which it owes
in a great measure its historical importance. Thereby only could it occupy so influential a position in an
age in which intellectual power was indeed declining,
but in which the interest for science was keen. But
that Stoic physics and metaphysics adopted this line,
and no other; that Zeno and his followers, who draw
on former systems for their own on the most extensive scale, borrowed from these systems these and no
other positions, and expanded them in this and no
other direction; these results are, doubtless, ultimately due to their moral attitude. All that bore
on the subject of ethics, and supported it, they
appropriated ; all that was opposed thereto they rejected. The Stoic system as such may owe its rise

to a union of ethical and speculative elements, in which both were more definitely determined by one another; still the ethical platform is the one on which its formation commences, and which primarily determined its course and results.

In order to obtain a more accurate notion of the rise of Stoicism, the premises on which it proceeds, and the grounds on which it is based, we must take a glance at its relations to preceding systems. The Stoics themselves deduced their philosophical pedigree directly from Antisthenes, and indirectly from Socrates.[1] Clear as is their connection with both these philosophers, it would nevertheless be a mistake to regard their teaching as a revival of Cynicism, still more to regard it as a simple following of Socrates. From both it undoubtedly borrowed much. The self-sufficiency of virtue, the distinction of things good, evil, and indifferent, the ideal picture of the wise man, the whole withdrawal from the outer world within the precincts of the mind, and the strength of moral will, are ideas taken from the Cynics. In the spirit of Cynicism, too, it explained general

B. *Relation of Stoicism to previous systems.*

(1) *Its relation to Socrates and the Cynics.*

---

[1] Whether Diogenes, in connecting the Stoics with the Cynics, was following a Stoic authority or not (vii.), is a moot point; nevertheless, the view comes to us from a time in which the relations of the two must have been well known, and the quotation from Posidonius on p. 274, 2, quite accords herewith. Not to mention others, *Diog.* vi. 14, speaking of Antisthenes, says : δοκεῖ δὲ καὶ τῆς ἀνδρωδεστάτης στωϊκῆς κατάρξαι . . . οὗτος ἡγήσατο καὶ τῆς Διογένους ἀπαθείας καὶ τῆς Κράτητος ἐγκρατείας καὶ τῆς Ζήνωνος καρτερίας, αὐτὸς ὑποθέμενος τῇ πόλει τὰ θεμέλια; and *Juvenal,* xiii. 121, calls the Stoic dogmas a Cynicis tunica (the common dress in distinction to the tribon) distantia.

ideas as simply names. Not to mention many
peculiarities of ethics, the contrasting of one God
with the many popular Gods, and the allegorical
explanation of myths, were likewise points borrowed
from Cynicism. The identification of virtue with
intelligence, the belief that virtue was one, and could
be imparted by teaching, were at once in the spirit
of Socrates and also in that of the Cynics. The argument for the existence of God based on the subordination of means to ends, the whole view of the
world as a system of means and ends, and the Stoic
theory of Providence, are views peculiarly Socratic ;[1]
and the Stoics followed Socrates in ethics by identifying the good and the useful.

And yet the greatness of the interval which sepa-
rates the Stoics even from the Cynics becomes at
once apparent on considering the relation of Aristo
to the rest of the Stoic School. In refusing to med-
dle with natural or mental science, or even with
ethical considerations at all, Aristo faithfully reflects
the principles of Antisthenes. In asserting the unity
of virtue to such an extent that all virtues are merged
in one, he was only repeating similar expressions of
Antisthenes. In denying any difference in value to
things morally indifferent, and in placing the highest
morality in this indifference, he was, according to
the older writers, reasserting a Cynic tenet.[2] Conversely, denying these statements as the great majority of Stoics did, the points are indicated in which

---

[1] *Krische*, Forschung. i. 363,   [2] On Aristo see p. 59 ; 260 ;
and above, p. 145, 2.   281.

Stoicism differed from Cynicism.[1]　In the feeling of moral independence, and in his invincible strength of will, the Cynic is opposed to the whole world; he needs for virtue no scientific knowledge of the world and its laws; he regards nothing external to himself; he allows nothing to influence his conduct, and attaches value to nothing; but, in consequence, he remains with his virtue confined to himself; virtue makes him independent of men and circumstances, but it has neither the will nor the power to interpose effectively in the affairs of life, and to infuse therein new moral notions. Likewise Stoicism insists upon the self-sufficiency of virtue quite as strongly, and will allow quite as little as Cynicism that anything except virtue can be a good in the strictest sense of the term. But in Stoicism the individual is not nearly so sharply opposed to the outer world as in Cynicism. The Stoic is too cultivated; he knows too well that he is a part of the universe to ignore the value of an intellectual view of the world, or to neglect the natural conditions of moral action, as things of no moment. What he aims at is not only a negation—independence from externals—but a positive position — life according to nature; and that life only he considers according to nature which is in harmony with the laws of the universe as well as with those of human nature. Hence Stoicism is

---

[1] Aristo cannot, therefore, be considered (as he is by *Krische*, Forsch. 411) the best representative of the original Stoic theory. On the contrry, he only represents a reaction of the Cynic element in Stoicism against the other component parts of this philosophy.

not only far in advance of Cynicism by its intellectual attitude, but its moral philosophy also breathes a freer and milder spirit. How deep-seated the difference between the two systems is, and how little Stoicism can be deduced from Cynicism as a philosophic system, will be at once seen; let only the principles of the Stoics on the necessity and value of scientific knowledge be compared with the sophistical assertions of Antisthenes, destructive of all knowledge; or the cultivated logical form of the intellectual edifice of the Stoics, with the chaotic condition of Cynic thought; or the careful metaphysical and psychological researches and the copious learning of the School of Chrysippus, with the Cynic contempt for all theory and all learned research.

In ethics, too, the difference of the two Schools is also fully apparent. Stoic morality recognises, at least conditionally, a positive and negative value in external things and circumstances; the Cynic allows absolutely no value. The former forbids affection contrary to reason, the latter any and every kind of affection.[1] The former throws back the individual upon human society, the latter isolates him. The former teaches citizenship of the world in a positive sense, requiring all to feel themselves one with their fellow-men; the latter in the negative sense, of feeling indifferent to home and family. The former has a pantheistic tone about it, due to the lively feeling of the connection between man and the universe, and a definite theological stamp owing to its taking a

[1] See p. 290.

stand by positive religion; the latter has a rationalistic character, owing to the enfranchisement of the wise man from the prejudices of popular belief, with which it has exclusively to do. In all these respects Stoicism preserved the original character of the Socratic philosophy far better than Cynicism, which only caricatured them. Still it departs from that character in two respects. In point of theory the Stoic doctrine received a systematic form and development such as Socrates never contemplated; and in natural science, it cultivated a field avoided by Socrates on principle, however much its doctrine of Providence, and its view of nature as a system of means subordinated to ends, may remind of Socrates. On the other hand, interest in science, although limited to the subject of ethics, is with Socrates far deeper and stronger than with the Stoics, the latter only pursuing scientific research as a means for solving moral problems. Hence the Socratic theory of a knowledge of conceptions, simple though it may sound, contained a fruitful germ of unexpanded speculations, in comparison with which all that the Stoics did is comparatively fragmentary. The Stoic ethics are not only more expanded and more carefully worked out in detail than those of Socrates, but they are also more logical in clinging to the principle of regarding virtue alone as an unconditional good. There are no concessions to current modes of thought, such as those of Socrates, who practically based his doctrine of morals upon utility. On the other hand, the moral science of the Stoics also falls

far short of the frankness and cheerfulness of the Socratic view of life. If in many respects it toned down the
asperities of Cynicism, still it appropriated its leading principles far too unreservedly to avoid accepting
a great number of its conclusions.

(2) *Rela-
tion to
Megarians
and He-
raclitus.*

Asking in the next place in how far the Stoics were
induced by other influences to change and extend
the platform of the Socratic philosophy, we have for
the practical tendency of their system, besides the
general tendency of the post-Aristotelian philosophy,
only to think of the example of Cynicism. Its speculative development, on the other hand, is partly
connected with the Megarians, partly with Heraclitus; to the Megarians the personal connection of
Zeno with Stilpo points, to Heraclitus the fact that
from him the Stoics themselves deduced their views
on natural science, unfolding them in commentaries
on his writings.[1]

(*a*) *The
Mega-
rians.*

Probably the Megarian influence must not be
rated too high. Zeno may have thence received
an impulse to that reasoning tone of mind which
appears with him in a preference for compressed
sharp-pointed syllogisms;[2] but in post-Aristote-

---

[1] Apart from the testimony
of Numenius (in *Eus.* Pr. Ev.
xiv. 5, 10), to which no great
value can be attached, the acquaintance of Zeno with Heraclitus is established by the fact
that not only the ethics, but
also the natural science of the
Stoic school owes its origin to
him. See pp. 40, 3; 62, 2, 3;
126, 2; 141, 2; 144, 4; 145, 1,
2; 146, 4; 148, 2; 151, 1. *Diog.*

mentions treatises of Cleanthes,
vii. 174; ix. 15, of Aristo, ix. 5,
of Sphærus (vii. 178; ix. 15)
treating of Heraclitus; and
Phædrus (Philodem.), Fragm.
col. 4, says that Chrysippus explained the old myths after the
manner of Heraclitus.

[2] Instances have often occurred. See p. 144, 4; 145, 1,
2; 232, 4. Conf. *Sen.* Ep.
83, 9.

lian times, contact with Megarians was no longer wanted for this, and the greatest reasoner among the Stoics, Chrysippus, appears not only in no personal relations to them, but his logic is throughout a simple continuation of that of Aristotle.

Far greater, and more generally recognised, is the importance of the influence which the doctrines of the natural philosopher of Ephesus exercised on the Stoics. A system which laid such emphasis on the subordination of everything individual to the law of the universe, which singled out universal reason from the flux of things as the one thing everlastingly and permanently the same—a system, too, so nearly related to their own, must have strongly commended itself to their notice, and offered them many points with which to connect their own. If the view of this teaching, that life is dependent for its existence on matter, is repulsive to us, it was otherwise to the Stoics, for whom this very theory possessed special attractions. Hence, with the exception of the three-fold division of the elements, there is hardly a single point in the Heraclitean theory of nature which the Stoics did not appropriate:—fire or ether as the primary element, the oneness of this element with universal reason, the law of the universe, destiny, God, the flux of things, the gradual change of the primary element into the four elements, and of these back to the primary element, the regular alternation of creation and conflagration in the world, the oneness and eternity of the universe, the description of the soul as fiery breath, the identification of the mind with the demon, the unconditional sovereignty of the universal law over individuals—these and many other points in the Stoic system, originally derived from Heraclitus,[1] prove how greatly this system is indebted to its predecessor.

Nor yet must it be forgotten that neither is there any analogy in Heraclitus to the reasoning forms of the Stoics, nor can their ethical views be referred to his few and undeveloped hints. Moreover, with all the importance attached to natural science, it is with the Stoics only subordinate to moral science; and the very fact that it is referred to Heraclitus as its author, proves how subordinate a position it held, and the want of any independent interest in the subject. Unmistakeable it also is that even in natural science the Stoics only partially follow Heraclitus, and that principles taken from Heraclitus often bear an altered meaning when wrought into the Stoic system. Omitting minor points, not only is the Stoic doctrine of nature in a formal point of view far more developed, and with regard to its extension, far more comprehensive, than the corresponding doctrine of Heraclitus, but the whole view of the world of the later system is by no means so completely identical with that of the earlier as might be supposed. The flux of things, which the Stoics teach equally with Heraclitus,[2] has not for them that overwhelming importance that it had for him. The

---

[1] Besides meteorological and other points of natural science, which the Stoics may have borrowed from Heraclitus, Heraclitus' attitude towards the popular faith also belongs here.

[2] See p. 101, 2.

matter of which the universe-consists may be always
going over into new forms, but, at the same time, it
is for them the permanent material and essence
of things.[1] Individual substances, too, are treated
by the Stoics as corporeally permanent.[2] Moreover,
from the material they distinguish the active principle, Reason or deity, far more definitely than Heraclitus had done, and the same distinction is carried
into individual things in contrast between matter
and quality. Thereby it becomes possible for them
to contrast much more sharply than their predecessor had done the reason of the world, and the blindly
working power of nature. Heraclitus, it would appear, confined his attention to observing nature and
describing its elementary meteorological processes.
But the natural science of the Stoics embodies the
idea of means working for ends. It sees its object
in referring the whole arrangement of the world to
man, and it pursues this line of thought exclusively,
neglecting in consequence proper science. Hence
the idea of sovereign reason or the universal law had
not the same meaning in the minds of both. Heraclitus sees this reason, primarily and chiefly, in the
ordinary sequence of natural phenomena, in the regularity of the course by which to each individual
phenomenon its place in the world, its extent and
duration is prescribed, in short, in the unchanging
coherence of nature. Without excluding this aspect

[1] See p. 100, 4, 5; 101, 2;
140, 1.
[2] As an illustration of the
difference, take Heraclitus'
statement of the daily extinction
of the sun, which every one
must admit would not have
been possible in the Stoic school.

in their proofs of the existence of God and the rule of Providence, the Stoics attach the chief importance to the serviceableness of the order of nature. The reason which rules the world appears in Heraclitus more as a natural power; in the Stoics, as intelligence working with a purpose. For Heraclitus Nature is the highest object, the object of independent and absolute interest; and hence the infinite Being is no more than the power which forms the world. The Stoics regard nature from the platform of humanity, as a means for the wellbeing and activity of man. Their deity accordingly does not work as a simple power of nature, but essentially as the wisdom which cares for the wellbeing of man. The highest conception in the system of Heraclitus is that of nature or destiny. Stoicism accepted this conception also, but at the same time developed it to the higher idea of Providence.

(3) *Connection with Aristotle.*

Shall we be wrong if we attribute this modification of the Heraclitean theory of nature by the Stoics partly to the influence of Socrates' and Plato's theory of final causes, but in a still greater degree to the influence of the Aristotelean philosophy? To Aristotle belongs properly the idea of matter without qualities, no less than the distinction between a material and a formal cause. Aristotle applied the idea of purpose to natural science far more extensively than any other system had done before; and although the mode in which the Stoics expressed this idea has more resemblance to the popular theological statements of Socrates and Plato than to

Aristotle, still the Stoic conception of a natural power working with a purpose, such as is contained in the idea of artificial fire and λόγοι σπερματικοὶ, is essentially Aristotelean. Even many positions which appear to be advanced in opposition to Aristotle were yet connected with him. Thus the existence of ether as a body distinct from the four elements is denied, and yet in point of fact it is asserted under a new name—that of artificial fire. The Peripatetic doctrine of the origin of the rational soul is contradicted by the Stoic theory of development, and yet the latter is based on a statement in Aristotle to the effect that the germ of the animal soul lies in the warm air [1] which surrounds the seed, warm air which Aristotle distinguishes from fire quite as carefully as Zeno and Cleanthes distinguished the two kinds of fire. Even the point of greatest divergence from Aristotelean teaching—the transformation of the human soul and the divine spirit into something corporeal—might yet be connected with Aristotle, and, indeed, the Peripatetic School here meets them for this very reason. Had not Aristotle described the ether as the most divine body, the stars formed out of it as divine and happy beings? Had he not brought down the acting and moving forces from a heavenly sphere to the region of earth? Had he not, as we have just seen, sought the germ of the soul in an ethereal matter? And might not others go a little further and arrive at materialistic views? and all the more so, seeing how hard it is to conceive

[1] πνεῦμα as with the Stoics.

the extra-mundane intelligence of Aristotle, at once
incorporeal, and yet touching and encircling the
world of matter, and in the human soul to harmonise personal unity with an origin in a reason coming
from above?

More directly had the Aristotelean speculations as
to the origin of notions and conceptions paved the
way for Stoicism. On this point the Stoics did little
more than omit (in conformity with their principles)
what their predecessor had said as to an original possession and immediate knowledge of truth. How
closely their formal logic adhered to that of Aristotle
has been remarked on an earlier occasion. Their
efforts were confined to building on Aristotelean
foundations, and even their additions have more reference to grammar than to logic. The actual influence of Peripatetic views on those of the Stoics
appears to have been least in the domain of ethics.
Here the crudeness of the Stoic conception of virtue, their entire suppression of emotions, their absolute exclusion of everything external from the circle
of moral goods, their antithesis between the wise and
the foolish man, their polemic against a purely speculative life, present a pointed contrast to the caution
and many-sidedness of Aristotle's moral theory, to
his careful weighing of current opinions and the possibility of carrying them out, to his recognition of
propriety in every shape and form, on the one hand,
and to the praise which he lavishes on a purely speculative life, on the other. In ethics, the formal
treatment of the ethical materials and the psycholo-

gical analysis of individual moral faculties, are the chief points on which the Stoics are indebted to Aristotle for instruction. On the other hand, in this province we must, on the contrary, look for traces of the teaching which Zeno received from Polemo, and, perhaps, from Xenocrates.

The speculative portions of Plato's teaching could offer no great attractions to such practical men and materialists as the Stoics, either in their original form or in the form which they assumed in the older Academy under Pythagorean influence. But, on the other hand, such points in Platonism as the Socratic building of virtue on knowledge, the comparative depreciation of external goods, the retreat from sensuality, the elevation and the purity of moral idealism, and, in the older Academy, the demand for life according to nature, the doctrine of the self-sufficingness of virtue, and the growing tendency to confine philosophy to practical issues—all these were questions for a Stoic full of interest. Unfounded as the notion of the later Eclectics is,[1] that the Stoic and Academician systems of morality were altogether the same, the Stoics, nevertheless, appear to have received impulses from the Academy which they carried out in a more determined spirit. Thus the theory of living according to nature belongs originally to the Academy, although the Stoics adopted it with a peculiar and somewhat different meaning. Besides moral doctrines, the attitude assumed by the

CHAP. XIV.

(4) *Connection with Plato.*

---

[1] So particularly Antiochus and also Cicero in many passages. See above, p. 39, 2.

older Academy towards positive religion may also
have had some influence on the orthodoxy of the
Stoics, their most decided representative, Cleanthes,
being in his whole philosophic character the counterpart of Xenocrates. Nor was the new Academy,
although later in its origin than Stoicism, without
important influence on that system, through the person of Chrysippus, but at first only of an indirect
kind, obliging the Stoics by its logical contradiction
to look about for a more logical basis for their system, and therewith to attempt a more systematic
expansion of their teaching.[1] Somewhat similar is
the case with Epicureanism, which by its strong opposition in the field of ethics contributed to impart
decision and accuracy to the Stoic doctrine, and,
perhaps, in the same way, may have helped to bring
it into existence.

C., The
Stoic
philosophy
as a whole.

(1) Its
historical
position.

By the aid of these remarks it now becomes possible to give a satisfactory account of the history of
Stoicism. Belonging to an age morally debased and
politically oppressed, its founder, Zeno, conceived the
idea of liberating himself and all who were able to
follow him from the degeneracy and slavery of the
age by means of a philosophy which, by purity and
strength of moral will, would procure independence
from all external things, and unruffled inward peace.
That his endeavours should have taken this practical
turn, that he should have proposed to himself not
knowledge as such, but the moral exercise of knowledge as the object to be realised, was in part due to

[1] See p. 46, 1, 2.

the personal character of the philosopher, and may
be in part referred to the general circumstances of
the times. On nobler and more serious minds, these
circumstances pressed too heavily not to call forth
opposition and resistance in place of listless contemplation. The sway of the Macedonian, and afterwards of the Roman Empire, was far too despotic to
allow the least prospect of open resistance. Nor must
it be overlooked that philosophy itself had reached a
pass at which satisfactory answers to speculative
problems were no longer forthcoming, and hence
attention was naturally directed to questions of
morals.

Haunted by this longing for virtue, Zeno must
have first felt attracted by that philosophy which had
at an earlier period cultivated a similar line with the
greatest decision, the Cynical, and what he doubtless
identified with the Cynical, the old Socratic teaching.[1]
Anxious, on the other hand, for a more positive meaning and scientific basis for virtue, he strove to appropriate from every system whatever agreed with the
bent of his own mind. By using all the labours of
his predecessors, and keeping his eye steadily fixed
upon the practical end of philosophy, he succeeded
in forming a new and more comprehensive system,
which was afterwards completed by Chrysippus. In
point of form this system was most indebted to the

[1] The story in *Diog.* vii. 3,
bears out this view, that Zeno
was first won for philosophy by
Xenophon's Memorabilia, and
that on asking who was the
representative of this line of
thought, was referred to Crates.
According to the quotations on
pp. 274, 2 ; 387, 1, the Cynics
were regarded in the Stoic
school as genuine followers of
Socrates.

Peripatetic philosophy; in point of matter, next to
its debt to the Cynics, which has been already mentioned, its chief obligation was to Heraclitus.   But
the moral theory of the Stoics was as little identical
with that of the Cynics, as the natural science of the
Stoics was with that of Heraclitus.   If the divergence was, in the first instance, due to the influence
of the Stoic principles, still the influence of the Peripatetic teaching is unmistakeable in the natural and
speculative science of the Stoics, and the influence
of the Academy in their moral science.   Stoicism
does not, therefore, appear simply as a continuation
of Cynicism, nor yet as an isolated innovation, but like
every other form of thought which marks an epoch,
it worked up into itself all previous materials, producing from their combination a new result.   In this
process of assimilation much that was beautiful and
full of meaning was omitted; everything was absorbed
that could be of use in the new career on which the
Greek mind was about to enter.

*(2) Its one-
sidedness.*

It was the fault of the age that it could no longer
come up to the many-sidedness of an Aristotle or a
Plato.   Stoicism, it is true, approximates thereto
more nearly than any other of the post-Aristotelean
systems.   But in its practical view of philosophy, in
its materialistic appeal to the senses, in its theoretical self-sufficiency, the wise man rising superior
to the weaknesses and wants of human nature ; in its
citizenship of the world, throwing political interests
into the background ; and in so many other traits it
is the fit exponent of an epoch in which the taste
for purely scientific research and the joyfulness of

practical creation was at an end, whilst amid the overthrow of states, and their freedom, the idea of humanity was rising to fuller recognition. Of such an age Stoicism represented most powerfully the moral and religious convictions, yet not without one-sidedness and exaggeration. By an exercise of the will and by rational understanding, man is to become free and happy. This aim was, however, pursued with such sternness that the natural conditions of human existence and the claims of individuality were ignored. To man, regarded as the organ of universal law, as little freedom of will was allowed by the Stoic natural science in face of the inexorable course of nature as freedom of action by the Stoic ethics in face of the demands of duty. The universal claims of morality were alone acknowledged; the right of the individual to act according to his peculiar character, and to develop that character, was as good as ignored. The individual, as such, dwindled into obscurity, whilst a high place in the world was assigned to mankind collectively. The individual was subordinated to the law of the whole, but by regarding nature as a system of means and ends, and introducing the belief in Providence and Prophecy, the universe was again subordinated to the interests of man—a view against which a more careful research has many objections to urge. In both respects Epicureanism is most decidedly contrasted with Stoicism, whilst it otherwise agreed with it in the general tone of its practical philosophy, and in its aim to make man independent of the outer world and happy in himself.

PART III.

THE EPICUREANS.

CHAPTER XV.

EPICURUS AND THE EPICUREAN SCHOOL.[1]

EPICURUS, the son of the Athenian Neocles,[2] was born in Samos[3] in the year 342 or 341 B.C.[4] His early education appears to have been neglected;[5]

---

[1] Consult, on this subject, the valuable treatise of *Steinhart*, in Ersch and Gruber's Encyclopædia, sect. i. vol. 35, pp. 459–477.

[2] *Diog.* x. i. He is frequently mentioned as an Athenian, belonging to the δῆμος Gargettos. *Diog.* l. c.; *Lucret.* Nat. Rer. vi. 1; *Cic.* Ad Fam. xv. 16; *Ælian*, V. H. iv. 13.

[3] *Diog.* i.; *Strabo*, xiv. 1, 18, p. 638. According to these authorities, and *Cic.* N. D. i. 26, 72, his father had gone there as a κληροῦχος. That this happened before his birth has been demonstrated by *Steinhart*, p. 461.

[4] Apollodorus (in *Diog.* x. 14) mentions 7 Gamelion, Ol. 109, 3, as the birthday of Epi-

curus. It was observed (Epicurus' will, *Diog.* 18) τῇ προτέρᾳ δεκάτῃ τοῦ Γαμηλιῶνος. Gamelion being the seventh month of the Attic year, the time of his birth must have been either early in 341 B.C., or the last days of 342 B.C.

[5] His father, according to Strabo, was a schoolmaster, and Epicurus had assisted him in teaching (Hermippus and Timon, in *Diog.* 2; *Athen.* xiii. 588, a). His mother is said to have earned money by repeating charms (καθαρμοί), and Epicurus to have assisted in this occupation (*Diog.* 4) Although the latter statement evidently comes from some hostile authority, it would seem that his circumstances in early

and his knowledge of previous philosophic systems was very superficial, even at the time when he first came forward as an independent teacher. Still he can hardly have been so entirely self-taught as he wished to appear at a later period in life. The names, at least, of the individuals are on record who instructed him in the systems of Democritus and Plato;[1] and although it is by no means an ascertained fact that he subsequently attended the lectures of Xenocrates,[2] on the occasion of a visit to Athens,[3] no doubt can be felt that he was

life were not favourable to a thoroughly scientific education. His language in disparagement of culture would lead us to this conclusion, even were the express testimony of *Sext.* Math. i. 1, wanting: ἐν πολλοῖς γὰρ ἀμαθὴς Ἐπίκουρος ἐλέγχεται, οὐδὲ ἐν ταῖς κοιναῖς ὁμιλίαις (in common expressions, conf. the censure passed on him by Dionysius of Halicarnassus and Aristophanes in *Diog.* 4, 13) καθαρεύων. *Cic.* Fin. i. 7, 26: Vellem equidem, aut ipse doctrinis fuisset instructior—est enim ... non satis politus in artibus, quas qui tenent eruditi appellantur—aut ne deterruisset alios a studiis. *Athen.* xiii. 588, a: ἐγκυκλίου παιδείας ἀμύητος ὤν.
[1] According to his own statement (*Diog.* 2), he was not more than fourteen (*Suid.* Ἐπικ. has twelve) years of age when he began to philosophise, i.e., to think about philosophical subjects; probably about chaos following the suggestion of Hesiod's verses. He subsequently boasted that he had

made himself what he was without a teacher, and refused to own his obligations to those shown to be his teachers. *Cic.* N. D. i. 26, 72; 33, 93; *Sext.* Math. i. 2, who mentions his disparagement of Nausiphanes; *Diog.* 8, 13; *Plut.* N. P. Suav. V. 18, 4; conf. *Sen.* Ep. 52, 3. It is, however, established that in his youth he enjoyed the instruction of Pamphilus and of that Nausiphanes, who is sometimes called a follower of Democritus, sometimes of Pyrrho (*Cic.*; *Sext.*; *Diog.* x. 8; 13; 14; ix. 64; 69; Procem. 15; *Suid.* Ἐπικ.; *Clem.* Strom. i. 301, D). The names of two other supposed instructors are also mentioned, Nausicydes and Praxiphanes (*Diog.* Procem. 15; x. 13), but they almost seem to be corruptions for Pamphilus and Nausiphanes.
[2] According to *Cic.* l. c., he denied the fact. Others, however, asserted it, and, among them, Demetrius of Magnesia. *Diog.* 13.
[3] Whither he came, in his

acquainted with the writings of previous philosophers, from whom he borrowed important parts of
his doctrine,[1] and, more particularly, with those of
Democritus.

After having been active as a teacher in several
Schools [2] in Asia Minor, he repaired to Athens about
the year 306 B.C.,[3] and there founded a School of his
own.[4] The meeting-place of this School was the
founder's garden,[5] and its centre of attraction was

eighteenth year, according to
Heraclides Lembus, in *Diog.* 1.
Conf. *Strabo*, l. c.: τραφῆναί
φασιν ἐνθάδε (in Samos) καὶ ἐν
Τέῳ καὶ ἐφηβεῦσαι 'Αθήνῃσι.

[1] According to Hermippus
(*Diog.* 2) Democritus first gave
him the impulse to pursue
philosophy; but this is only a
conjecture. Besides Democritus, Aristippus is also mentioned as a philosopher whose
doctrines he followed (*Diog.* 4).
Epicurus is even said to have
expressed a disparaging opinion
of Democritus (*Cic.* N. D. i.
33, 93; *Diog.* 8). Nor is this
denied by Diog. 9; but it probably only refers to particular
points, or it may have reference
to the attitude of later Epicureans, such as Colotes (*Plut.*
Adv. Col. 3, 3, p. 1108). *Plut.*
l. c., says, not only that Epicurus for a long time called
himself a follower of Democritus, but he also quotes passages from Leonteus and Metrodorus, attesting Epicurus'
respect for Democritus. *Philodem.* περὶ παρρησίας, Vol. Herc.
v. 2, col. 20, seems to refer to
expressions of Epicurus, excul-
pating certain mistakes of De-

mocritus. *Lucret.* iii. 370, v.
620, also speaks of Democritus
with great respect; and *Philodem.* De Mus. Vol. Herc. i. col.
36, calls him ἀνὴρ οὐ φυσιολογώ-
τατος μόνον τῶν ἀρχαίων ἀλλὰ
καὶ τῶν ἱστορουμενων οὐδενὸς ἧττον πολυπράγμων.

[2] *Diog.* 1, 15, mentions Colo-
phon, Mytilene, and Lampsacus.
Strabo, xiii. 1, 19, p. 589, also
affirms that Epicurus resided for
some time at Lampsacus, and
there made the acquaintance
of Idomeneus and Leonteus.

[3] *Diog.* 2, on the authority
of Heraclides and Sotion. According to him, Epicurus returned to Athens in the archonship of Anaxicrates, 307–6 B.C.
In that case the numbers must
be slightly reduced in the statement (*Diog.* 15) that he came
to Mytilene when 32, and taught
there and in Lampsacus for
five years.

[4] Not immediately, how-
ever, since *Diog.* 2, says, on the
authority of Heraclides: μέχρι
μέν τινος κατ' ἐπιμιξίαν τοῖς ἄλλοις φιλοσοφεῖν, ἔπειτ' ἰδίᾳ πως
τὴν ἀπ' αὐτοῦ κληθεῖσαν αἵρεσιν
συστήσασθαι.

[5] On this celebrated garden,

the founder himself, around whom a circle of friends gathered, knit together by a common set of principles, by a common affection for a master whom they almost worshipped, and by a common enjoyment of cultivated society.[1] Opponents charged the Epicureans with gross impropriety, because they admitted not only women,[2] but women of loose morality,[3] to this circle of philosophic culture; but in the then state of Greek society, such conduct does not appear extraordinary. Here Epicurus laboured for six and thirty years, and in this time succeeded in impressing such a definite stamp on his School as is now seen unchanged after the lapse of centuries. In the year 270 B.C.[4] he succumbed to disease, the pains and troubles of which he bore with great fortitude.[5] Out of the multitude of his writings[6] only a few have

after which the Epicureans were called οἱ ἀπὸ τῶν κήπων, see *Diog.* 10, 17; *Plin.* H. N. xix. 4, 51; *Cic.* Fin. i. 20, 65; v. 1, 3; Ad Fam. xiii. 1; *Sen.* Ep. 21, 10; *Steinhart*, p. 462, 45; 463, 72. Epicurus had purchased it for 80 minæ.

[1] This subject will be discussed at a later period.

[2] Such as Themista or Themisto, the wife of Leonteus (*Diog.* 5; 25; 26; *Clem.* Strom. iv. 522, D).

[3] *Diog.* 4; 6; 7; *Cleomed.* Meteor. p. 92, Balfor.; *Plut.* N. P. Suav. Vivi. 4, 8; 16, 1 and 6; Lat. Viv. 4, 2. The best-known among these ἑταῖραι is Leontion, who lived with Metrodorus, a pupil of Epicurus (*Diog.* 6; 23), and wrote with spirit against Theophrastus

(*Cic.* N. D. i. 33, 93; *Plut.* Hist. Nat. Præf. 29). Conf. *Diog.* 5; *Philodem.* περὶ παῤῥησίας, Vol. Herc. v. 2, Fr. 9. *Athen.* xiii. 593, b, tells a fine story of self-sacrifice of her daughter Danaë.

[4] Ol. 127, 2, in the archonship of Pytharatus, and in his seventy-second year. *Diog.* 15; *Cic.* De Fat. 9, 19.

[5] *Diog.* 15; 22; *Cic.* Ad Fam. vii. 26; Fin. ii. 30, 96; *Sen.* Ep. 66, 47; 92, 25. That he put an end to his own life (*Baumhauer*, Vet. Philo. Doct. De Mort. Volunt. 322), Hermippus (*Diog.* 15) by no means implies

[6] According to *Diog.* Pro. 16, x. 26, he was, next to Chrysippus, the most voluminous writer of the ancient philosophers, his writings filling 300

CHAP.
XV.

come down to us, and these are for the most part unimportant ones.[1] On the whole, these fragments [2] bear out the unfavourable opinions which opponents expressed with regard to his style.[3]

B. *Scholars of Epicurus.*

Among the numerous scholars of Epicurus [4] the best known are Metrodorus,[5] and Polyænus,[6] both of

rolls. The titles of his most esteemed works are given by *Diog.* 27. Conf. *Fabric.* Bibl. Græ. iii. 595, Harl.

[1] Three epistles in *Diog.* 35; 84; 122; and the κύριαι δόξαι, an epitome of his ethics, mentioned by *Cic.* N. D. i. 30, 85, and 139. Of his 37 books περὶ φύσεως, fragments of books 2 and 11 have been edited (Vol. Hercul. ii.).

[2] Fragments in *Diog.* 5; 7. Besides the testament and the letter to Idomeneus (*Diog.* 16-22), many individual expressions of Epicurus have been preserved by Seneca.

[3] Aristophanes (in *Diog.* 13) calls his style ἰδιωτικωτάτη. *Cleomed.* Meteor. p. 91, complains of his awkward and barbarous expressions, instancing: σαρκὸς εὐσταθῆ καταστήματα· τὰ περὶ ταύτης πιστὰ ἐλπίσματα· λιπάσμα ὀφθαλμῶν· ἱερὰ ἀνακραυγάσματα· γαργαλισμοὺς σώματος. In this respect, Chrysippus may be compared with him. See above, p. 48, 1.

[4] See *Fabric.* Bib. Gr. iii. 598 Harl. They were, no doubt, very numerous. *Diog.* x. 9, probably exaggerates their number in saying the friends of Epicurus would fill towns. *Cic.* Fin. i. 20, 65, speaks of magni greges amicorum. *Plut.* Lat. Viv. 3, 1, also mentions his friends in Asia and Egypt. In

Greece, however, on his own testimony, and that of Metrodorus (*Sen.* Ep. 79, 15), they attracted little notice.

[5] A native of Lampsacus (*Strabo*, xiii. 1, 19, p. 589), and, next to Epicurus, the most celebrated teacher of the School. *Cicero*, Fin. ii. 28, 92, calls him pæne alter Epicurus, and states (Fin. ii. 3, 7) that Epicurus gave him the name of a wise man (*Diog.* 18; *Sen.* Ep. 52, 3). Further particulars respecting him and his writings in *Diog.* x. 6; 18; 21-24; *Philodem.* De Vitiis, ix. (Vol. Herc. iii.), col. 12; 21; 27; *Athen.* vii. 279; *Plut.* N. P. Suav. Vivi. 7, 1; 12, 2; 16, 6 and 9; Adv. Col. 33, 2 and 6; *Sen.* Ep. 98, 9; 99, 25. Fragments of the letters are to be found in Plutarch, Seneca, and Philodemus. Whether the fragments of a treatise περὶ αἰσθητῶν in Vol. vi. of Vol. Hercul. belong to him, is very uncertain. According to *Diog.* 23, he died seven years before Epicurus, in his fifty-third year, and must therefore have been born 330 or 329 B.C. For the education of his children probably by Leontion, whom *Diog.* 23 calls παλλακή, and *Sen.* Fr. 45 in *Hiern.* Adv. Jovin. i. 191 calls his wife, provision is made by Epicurus in his will (*Diog.* 19, 21).

[6] Son of Athenodorus, like-

whom died before their master; Hermarchus,[1] upon whom the presidency of the School devolved after the death of Epicurus;[2] and Colotes,[3] against whom Plutarch, four hundred years later, wrote a treatise. Many others are also known, at least by name.[4] The

wise a native of Lampsacus (*Diog.* 24), a capital mathematician, according to *Cic.* Acad. ii. 33, 106; Fin. i. 6, 20. *Diog.* l. c., calls him ἐπιεικὴς καὶ φιλή- κοος; Metrodorus, in *Philodem.* περὶ παρρησίας (Vol. Her. V. a), col. 6, ἀποφθεγματίας. *Sen.* Ep. 6, 6, calls him, Metrodorus and Hermarchus, viros magnos. *Philodemus* (Vol. v. b), Fr. 49, praises his frankness towards his teacher. A son of his is also mentioned in Epicurus' will (*Diog.* 19), whose mother would appear to have been a courtesan, according to *Plut.* N. P. Suav. v. 16, 6.

[1] This individual's name, formerly written Hermachus, appears as Hermarchus in the modern editions of Diogenes, Cicero and Seneca. The latter form is now established beyond doubt by the Herculanian fragments from *Philodemus* (περὶ θεῶν διαγωγῆς, vol. vi. col. 13, 20; De Vitiis ix. vol. iii. col. 25, 1), and the inscription on a monument to him (Antiquitat. Hercul. V. 17). His birthplace was Mytilene, Agemarchus being his father. (*Diog.* 17, 15, 24.) *Diog.* 24, gives a list of his books. Epicurus (*Diog.* 20) describes him as one of his oldest and most faithful friends, in the words: μετὰ τοῦ συγκα- ταγεγηρακότος ἡμῖν ἐν φιλοσοφίᾳ. On his character, see *Sen.* Ep. 6, 6.

[2] According to what is stated in the testament of Epicurus. *Diog.* 16.

[3] Colotes, a native of Lampsacus. *Diog.* 25. Further particulars about him may be obtained from *Plut.* Adv. Col. 17, 5; 1, 1; N. P. Suav. Viv. 1, 1; *Macrob.* Somn. Scip. i. 2. Vol. Hercul. iv. Introd. in Polystor. p. iii.

[4] In particular, Neocles, Chairedemus, and Aristobulus, the brothers of Epicurus (*Diog.* 3, 28; *Plut.* N. P. Suav. Viv. 5, 3; where 'Αγαθόβουλος is evidently a copyist's error; 16, 3; De Lat. Viv. 3, 2); Idomeneus, a native of Lampsacus (*Diog.* 25; 22; 23; 5; *Plut.* Adv. Col. 18, 3; *Strabo*, xiii. 1, 19, p. 589; *Athen.* vii. 279; *Philodem.* περὶ παρρησίας. Fr. 72, Vol. Herc. v. 2; *Sen.* Ep. 21, 3 and 7; 22, 5; *Phot.* Lex.; and *Suid.* Πύθια καὶ Δήλια), from whose historical writings many fragments are quoted by *Müller*, Fragm. Hist. Gr. ii. 489; Leonteus, likewise a native of Lampsacus (*Diog.* 5; 25; *Plut.* Adv. Col. 3, 3; *Strabo*, l. c.); Herodotus (*Diog.* 4 and 34); Pythocles (*Diog.* 5 and 83; *Plut.* N. P. Suav. Vi. 12, 1; Adv. Col. 29, 2; *Philodem.* περὶ παρρησίας, Fr. 6); Apelles (*Plut.* N. P. Suav. Vi. 12, 1); Menœceus (*Diog.* 121); Nicanor (*Diog.* 20); Timocrates, the brother of Metrodorus, who afterwards fell out with Epi-

garden which Epicurus in his will left to the School[1] continued after his death to be the external rallying-point for his followers. Hermarchus was succeeded by Polystratus,[2] together with whom Hippoclides is also mentioned[3] as president. Hermarchus and Hippoclides were succeeded by Dionysius, and Dionysius again by Basilides.[4] Protarchus of Bargy-

curus (*Diog.* 4 and 6; 23 and 28; *Cic.* N. D. i. 33, 93; *Plut.* N. P. Suav. Vivi. 16, 9; Adv. Col. 32, 7; Comment. in *Hesiod.* Fr. 7, 1; *Philodem.* περὶ παρρη-σίας, Vol. Herc. v. a, col. 20). This Timocrates must not be confounded with the Athenian Timocrates, whom Epicurus appointed his heir, together with Amynomachus (*Diog.* 16; *Cic.* Fin. ii. 31, 101). Both the latter were probably pupils of Epicurus. Other names of pupils are: Mithras, a Syrian, an official under Lysimachus (*Diog.* 4 and 28; *Plut.* Adv. Col. 33, 2; N. P. Suav. Viv. 15, 5); Mys, a slave of Epicurus, on whom he bestowed liberty (*Diog.* 21; 3; 10; *Gell.* ii. 18, 8; *Macrob.* Sat. i. 11); the ladies mentioned on p. 407, 2, 3; likewise Anaxarchus, to whom Epicurus addressed a letter, and Timarchus, to whom Metrodorus addressed one (*Plut.* Adv. Col. 17 3); Hegesianax, who died early (*Plut.* N. P. Sua. Vi. 20, 5); the poet Menander, whose wondrous epigram on Epicurus is to be found in the anthology; and probably Dionysius ὁ μεταθέμενος. (See above p. 44, 1.)

[1] *Diog.* 16. In Cicero's time, the plot of ground, together with the tenement standing thereupon, and at that time in ruins (parietinæ), was in the hands of C. Memmius, a distinguished Roman, to whom Cicero wrote (Ad Fam. xiii. 1), conf. Ad Att. v. 11, begging him to restore it to the School. Whether he was successful is not known from *Sen.* Ep. 21, 10.

[2] *Diog.* 25, does not say that Polystratus was a personal disciple of Epicurus, but it seems probable. Fragments of a treatise of his περὶ ἀλόγου κατα-φρονήσεως in the fourth volume of Vol. Hercul.

[3] According to *Valer. Max.* i. 8, ext. 17, both these individuals were born on the same day, and passed their whole lives together with a common purse. Lysias, according to the older text of *Diog.* x. 25, was a cotemporary, at whose house Hermarchus died, as *Fabric.* Bibl. Gr. iii. 606 believes, and who is styled in *Athen.* v. 215, b, tyrant of Tarsus. *Cobet*, however, reads παραλύσει instead of παρὰ Λυσίᾳ.

[4] *Diog.* 25. The Dionysius referred to can hardly be Dionysius ὁ μεταθέμενος (see p. 44, 1), or Diogenes would have said so. Besides the chronology forbids such an assumption.

lium,[1] and his pupil, Demetrius the Laconian,[2] appear
to belong to the second century before Christ; but the
time in which these philosophers flourished cannot
be established with certainty; and the same remark
applies to several others whose names are on record.[3]

Before the middle of the second century B.C.
Epicureanism is said to have obtained a footing in
Rome.[4] It is certain that it was existing there not
long after. C. Amafinius is mentioned as the first
who paved the way for the spread of Epicurean doctrines by discussing them in Latin;[5] and it is stated

[1] *Strabo,* xiv. 2, 20, p. 658.
He is probably the Protarchus
whose sayings are quoted by
Simpl. Phys. 78, a; *Themist.*
Phys. 27, a.
[2] According to *Strabo,* l. c.,
Diog. 26, *Sext.* Empir. Pyrrh.
iii. 137, Math. viii. 348, x. 219,
Erotian, Lex. Hippocr. Κλαγγώ-
δη, Demetrius was one of the
most distinguished Epicureans.
Whether a treatise on mathematics, illegible fragments of
which are found in Hercula-
num (Vol. Herc. iv. Introd. in
Polystr. iii. 2), is his, or belongs
to another Demetrius men-
tioned by *Strabo,* xii. 3, 16,
p. 548, it is impossible to say.
[3] Both the Ptolemies of
Alexandria (*Diog.* 25); Diogenes of Tarsus (*Diog.* vi. 81;
x. 26; 97; 118; 136; 138);
Orion (*Diog.* 26); Timagoras
(*Cic.* Acad. ii. 25, 80); and
also Metrodorus of Stratonice,
who went over from Epicurus
to Carneades (*Diog.* 9)—a very
rare thing for an Epicurean to
do—may be named among his
pupils.

[4] According to *Athen.* xii.
547, a *Ælian,* V. H. ix. 12, two
Epicureans, Alcius and Philis-
cus, were banished from Rome,
in the consulate of L. Postumius (173 or 155 B.C.; see
Clinton's Fasti), because of
their evil influence on youth.
Although the story is obviously
taken from a hostile authority,
in *Suid.* (Ἐπίκουρος, T. 1, b, 419
Bern.) and is told with such ex-
aggerations as to inspire grave
mistrust—it can hardly be altogether without some foundation. *Plut.* N. P. Suav. V. 19,
4, says, that in some cities
severe laws were passed against
the Epicureans, and just at
that time there was a strong
feeling in Rome against innovations, witness the well-known
enquiry into the Bacchanalia
instituted 186 B.C.
[5] According to *Cic.* Tusc.
iv. 3, 6, Amafinius seems to
have come forward not long
after the philosophic embassy
of 156, B.C.; nor is this at
variance with *Lucr.* v. 336,
who claims primus cum primis

that these doctrines soon found many supporters, attracted partly by their merits, but more often by the simplicity and the ease with which they could be understood.[1]

Towards the close of the second century Apollodorus, one of the most voluminous writers on philosophy, taught at Athens.[2] His pupil, Zeno of Sidon, the most important among the Epicureans of that age, laboured for a long time successfully, both orally and in writing.[3] About the same time Phædrus is

to have set forth the Epicurean teaching in Latin. His works made a great impression at the time, according to *Cic.* l. c. (cujus libris editis commota multitudo contulit se ad eam potissimum disciplinam). According to Acad. i. 2, 5, he pursued natural science, carefully following the views of Epicurus. Cicero then complains of him and Rabirius, we know not which one is meant, nor whether he was an Epicurean, qui nulla arte adhibita de rebus ante oculos positis vulgari sermone disputant: nihil definiunt, nihil partiuntur, &c. Conf. Tusc. ii. 3, 7. Cassius, too (*Cic.* Ad Fam. xv. 12), calls him and Catius (see p. 414, 3) mali verborum interpretes.

[1] *Cic.* Tusc. iv. 3, 7: Post Amafinium autem multi ejusdem æmuli rationis multa cum scripsissent, Italiam totam occupaverunt, quodque maximum argumentum est non dici illa subtiliter, quod et tam facile ediscantur et ab indoctis probentur, id illi firmamentum esse disciplinæ putant. Conf.

in Fin. i. 7, 25, the question : Cur tam multi sint Epicurei ?

[2] Surnamed ὁ κηποτύραννος, the writer of more than 400 books. *Diog.* 25 ; 2 ; 13 ; vii. 181.

[3] *Diog.* vii. 35, x. 25, and Procl. in *Euclid.* 55, say that Zeno was a native of Sidon, and a pupil of Apollodorus ; nor can these statements be referred to an older Zeno, as some previous writers maintained, believing Apollodorus to be called in error a pupil of Epicurus by *Diog.* x. 25, instead of to the one mentioned by Cicero. For no trace of such a one exists ; and Diogenes vii. 35 would then have passed over the teacher of Cicero without notice who cannot possibly have been unknown to him. According to *Cic.* Acad. i. 12, 46, Zeno attended the lectures of Carneades and admired them ; and since Carneades died not later than 129 B.C., Zeno cannot have been born much later than 150 B.C. If, therefore, Zeno was really the successor of Apollodorus, the latter must be placed entirely in the second

heard of in Rome and Athens,[1] and at a little
later period Philodemus,[2] and Syro or Sciro in

century. But this fact is not
sufficiently established. Cicero,
in company with Atticus, attended his lectures (*Cic.* l. c.;
Fin. i. 5, 16; Tusc. iii. 17, 38.
In *Cic.* N. D. i. 21, 58, Cotta
says the same of himself), on
his first visit to Athens, 78 to
79 B.C.; conf. N. D. i. 34, 93;
but this cannot possibly be the
same Zeno or Xeno (as however
Krische, Forsch. 26 maintains)
whom *Cic.* Ad Att. v. 10, 11;
xvi. 3 mentions as living in 50
and 43 B.C. *Cic.* N. D. i. 21,
calls him princeps Epicureorum
(and Philo of Larissa, cory-
phæus Epicureorum); Tusc. l. c.,
acriculus senex, istorum (Epicureans) acutissimus. *Diog.* x.
25, calls him πολύγραφος ἀνήρ.
From Procl. in *Euclid.* 55; 59;
60, we hear of a treatise of
Zeno, in which he attacked the
validity of mathematical proofs.
Philodemus' treatise περὶ παῤῥησίας (Vol. Herc. · v. a) seems,
from the title, to have been an
abstract from Zeno. Cotemporary with Zeno was that
Aristio, or Athenio, who played
a part in Athens during the
Mithridatic war, and is sometimes called a Peripatetic, and
sometimes an Epicurean (*Plut.*
Sulla, 12; 14; 23). See *Zeller's*
Philosophie der Griechen, vol.
ii. b, 759, 2. Perhaps to the
time of his despotism the statement may be referred (*Demetrius* Magnes in *Athen.* xiii.
611, b) that the Stoic Theo-
timus, who wrote against Epicureus, was killed at the instance
of Zeno.

[1] Cicero (N. D. i. 33, 93;

Fin. i. 5, 16; v. 1, 3; Legg. i.
20, 53) had also studied under
him in Athens, and previously
in Rome, where Phædrus must
then have been residing (Ad
Fam. xiii. 1). He was old
when Cicero had, for the second
time, relations with him. According to Phlegon, in *Phot.*
Bibl. Cod. 97, p. 84, a, 17, he
was succeeded by Patron (Ol.
177, 3, or 70 B.C.) in the head-
ship of the School, after holding
it only for a very short time;
but this is not a well-ascertained
fact. Cicero, l. c., praises the
character of Phædrus. He calls
him nobilis philosophus (Philip.
v. 5, 13). It was supposed that
Cicero's description (N.D. i. 10,
25; 15, 41), and that the fragments first published by Drum-
mond (Herculanensia: London,
1810), and then by Petersen
(Phædri . . . de Nat. De.
Fragm.: Hamb. 1833), and
illustrated by Krische (Forschungen), were from a treatise
of Phædrus on the Gods, to
which perhaps *Cic.* Ad Att.
xiii. 39 refers. But Spengel
(from the Herculanean rolls,
Philodemu's περὶ εὐσεβείας. Abh.
d. Münch. Akad. Philos-philol.
Kl. x. 1, 127) and Sauppe (De
Philodemi libro . . ·. de pietate.
Gött. Lections verz. für Som-
mer, 1864) have shown that the
Neapolitan (Vol. Herc. Coll.
Alt. i. ii. 1862) editors are
right in regarding these fragments as the remains of a
treatise of Philodemus περὶ
εὐσεβείας.

[2] Philodemus (see Vol.
Herc. i. 1; *Gros,* Philod. Rhet.

Rome,[1] and Patro,[2] the successor of Phædrus, in Athens. The number of Epicureans at Rome, known to us chiefly by Cicero's writings,[3] is not small, no one of

cxii.; *Preller*, Allg. Encyclc. Sect. III. Bd. xxiii. 345) was a native of Gadara, in Cœle-Syria (*Strabo*, xvi. 2, 29, p. 759). He lived at Rome in Cicero's time, and is mentioned by Cicero as a learned and amiable man (Fin. ii. 35, 119; Or. in Pison. 28). Besides philosophic works, he also wrote poems (*Cic.* In Pis.; *Hor.* Sat. i. 2, 121). A number of the latter, in the shape of epigrams, are preserved. Of his philosophical works mentioned by *Diog.* x. 3; 24, no fewer than thirty-six books were discovered in Herculaneum, which have, for the most part, been published (Vol. Herc. iv. Introd. in Polystr. iii. a portion of which have been published). Spengel and Gros have separately edited Rhet. IV.; Sauppe, De Vitiis X.; and Petersen and Sauppe, the fragments περὶ εὐσεβείας.

[1] *Cic.* Acad. ii. 33, 106; Fin. ii. 35, 119; Ad Fam. vi. 11. According to *Virgil*, Catal. 7, 9; 10, 1, *Donat.* Vita Virg. 79, *Serv.* Ad Ecl. vi. 13, *Æn.* vi. 264, he was the teacher of Virgil. The name is variously written as Syro, Siro, Sciro, Scyro. Somewhat earlier is the grammarian Pompilius Andronicus, from Syria, who, according to *Sueton.* Illust. Gram. c. 8, lived at Rome at the same time as Gnipho, the teacher of Cæsar (*Ibid.* c. 7), neglecting his profession for the Epicurean philosophy, and afterwards at Cumæ.

[2] *Cic.* Ad Fam. xiii. 1; Ad

Att. v. 11; vii. 2; Ad Quint. Fratr. i. 2, 4, where besides him an Epicurean Plato of Sardes is mentioned, and above pp. 410, 1; 413, 1.

[3] Besides Lucretius, the most important among them are T. Albutius, called by *Cic.* Brut. 35, 131, perfectus Epicureus (*Cic.* Brut. 26, 102; Tusc. v. 37, 108: N. D. i. 33, 93; Fin. i. 3, 8 [De Orat. iii. 43, 171]; In Pison. 38, 92; Offic. ii. 14, 50; Orator. 44, 149; In Cæcil. 19, 63; Provin. Cons. 7, 15; De Orat. ii. 70, 281), and Velleius, who, as *Krische* (Forsch. 20) proves, by a gloss on Nat. De. i. 29, 82 and *Cic.* De N. D. i. 28, 79 (conf. Divin. i. 36, 79) was a native of Lanuvium, and was considered the most distinguished Epicurean of his time (*Cic.* N. D. i. 6, 15; 21, 58; conf. De Orat. iii. 21, 78). Other Epicureans were: C. Catius, a native of Gaul, named by Cicero (Ad Fam. xv. 16) as one long ago dead. By *Quintilian*, x. 1, 124, he is called levis quidem sed non injucundus tamen auctor; and the Comment. Cruqu. in *Hor.* Sat. ii. 4, 1, says that he wrote four books De Rerum Natura et De Summo Bono;—C. Cassius, the well-known leader of the conspiracy against Cæsar (*Cic.* Ad Fam. xv. 16, 19; *Plut.* Brut. 37); C. Vibius Pansa, who died as consul at Mutina, in 43 B.C. (*Cic.* Ad Fam. vii. 12 : xv. 19); Gallus (Ad Fam. vii. 26); L. Piso, the patron of

whom has obtained a higher repute than T. Lucretius
Carus.[1] His poem, carefully reproducing the Epicurean notions on natural science, is, therefore, one of
the most valuable sources for the knowledge of their
system.   Contemporary with Lucretius was the celebrated physican Asclepiades of Bithynia,[2] residing at
Rome, but to judge by the views on nature attributed to him, no genuine Epicurean, although connected with the Epicurean School.[3]

Philodemus (*Cic.* in Pis. 28, see
above, p. 413, 2 ; l. c. 9, 20 ; 16,
37 ; 18, 42 ; 25, 59 ; Post Red.
6, 14) ; Statilius (*Plut.* Brut.
12) ; a second Statilius appears
to be meant (Cat. Min. 65) ;
L. Manlius Torquatus, to whom
Cic. Fin. i. 5, 13, delegates the
representation of the Epicurean teaching.   Moreover,
T. Pomponius Atticus, the well-
known friend of Cicero, approached nearest to the Epicurean School, calling its
adherents nostri familiares
(*Cic.* Fin. v. 1, 3) and condis-
cipuli (Leg. i. 7, 21), being a
pupil of Zeno and Phædrus and
a friend of Patro's ; but his relations to philosophy were too
free to entitle him properly to
be ranked in any one School
(*Cic.* Fam. xiii. 1).   The same
observation applies also to his
friend, L. Saufeius (*Nepos,*
Att. 12 ; *Cic.* Ad Att. iv. 6).
Still less can C. Sergius Orata
(*Cic.* Fin. ii. 22, 70 ; Off. iii. 16,
67 ; De Orat. i. 39, 178), L.
Thorius Balbus (Fin. l. c.), and
Postumius (*Ibid.*) be called
Epicureans.   Nor can anything
be stated with certainty respecting L. Papirius Pœtus (*Cic.*
Ad Fam. vii. 1/ to 26), not even

from the chief passage Ep. 25,
or respecting C. Trebatius from
Cic. Ad Fam. vii. 12.   C. Memmius (from the way in which
he is spoken of *Cic.* Ad. Fam.
xiii. 1) cannot be regarded as a
member of the Epicurean
School, although *Lucret.* De
Rer. Nat. i. 24 ; v. 9, expressed
the hope of winning him.

[1] Born, according to Hieron.
(in *Eus.* Chron.), 95 B.C., he
died in his 44th year, or 51
B.C.   In Vita Virgilii, 659
ought therefore to be substituted for 699 A.U.C. It is clear,
from *Nepos,* Att. 12, that he
was dead before the assassina-
tion of Cæsar.   Teuffel (in
Pauly's Realencycl. iv. 1195)
justly disputes the statement of
Hieronymus, that he committed suicide in a fit of madness.

[2] According to *Sext.* Math.
vii. 201, a cotemporary of Antiochus of Ascalon, whose language towards him is there
quoted, and reckoned by *Galen.*
Isag. c. 4, vol. xiv. 683 among
the leaders of the logical
School of Physicians. His medical treatises are often referred
to by Galen. Plutarch in his
Placita often names him.

[3] Known for three things—

In the following century, too, several supporters of the practical philosophy of the Epicureans are known to us,[1] but no one apparently approaching Zeno or

his theory of atoms, his theory of the acquisition of knowledge, and his resolution of the soul into matter.

All bodies, he held, consist of atoms, differing, however, from the atoms of Democritus in that they owe their origin to the meeting and breaking up of greater masses, and are not in quality alike and unchangeable (ἀπαθεῖς). *Sext.* Pyrrh. iii. 32; Math. ix. 363; x. 318; viii. 220; iii. 5; *Galen.* l. c. 9, p. 698; *Dionys.*; Alex. (in *Eus.* Pr. Ev. xiv. 23, 4); *Cœl. Aurelian.* De Pass. Acut. i. 14. See *Fabric.* on Pyrrh. iii. 32. The latter is probably in error in describing the primary atoms of Asclepiades as without quality, differing only in size, form, number and arrangement. Although in this respect he resembled Heraclides, with whom he is generally classed, and applied, like him, the name ὄγκοι to atoms, still it is probable that his knowledge of Heraclides was traditionally derived from the Epicureans.

He also asserted, with Epicurus (Antiochus, in *Sext.* Math. vii. 201): τὰς μὲν αἰσθήσεις ὄντως καὶ ἀληθῶς ἀντιλήψεις εἶναι, λόγῳ δὲ μηδὲν ὅλως ἡμᾶς καταλαμβάνειν. If he at the same time maintained that our senses cannot distinguish the component parts of things, even Epicurus together with Democritus admitted this in respect of atoms.

He differs, however, entirely from Epicurus in denying the existence of a soul apart from body, and in referring every kind of notion, including the soul itself, to the action of the senses (*Sext.* Math. vii. 380; *Plut.* Plac. iv. 2, 6; *Cœl. Aurelian.* l. c. in *Fabric.* on the passage of Sext.; *Tertullian,* De An. 15). All that is otherwise stated of Asclepiades, apart from his medical views, for instance, that with Heraclitus he believed in a perpetual flux of things, is not at variance with Epicurean principles.

[1] *Quint.* Inst. vi. 3, 78, names L. Varus as an Epicurean, a friend of Augustus, perhaps the individual who, according to *Donat.* V. Virg. 79, *Serv.* on Ecl. vi. 13, attended the lectures of Syro, in company with Virgil. Horace, notwithstanding Ep. i. 4, 15, was no Epicurean, but only a man who gathered everywhere what he could make use of (Sat. i. 5, 101). In Caligula's time, a senator Pompedius was an Epicurean (*Joseph.* Antiquit. ix. 1, 5); under Nero, Aufidius Bassus, a friend of Seneca (*Sen.* Ep. 30, 1 and 3 and 5; 14), the elder Celsus (*Orig.* c. Cels. i. 8), and Diodorus, who committed suicide (*Sen.* Vi. Be. 19, 1); under Vespasian or his sons, Pollius (*Stat.* Silv. ii. 2, 113). In the first half of the second century, *Cleomedes,* Met. p. 87, complained of the honours paid to Epicurus. In the second

Phædrus in scientific importance. Rehabilitated under the Antonines by the establishment of a public chair in Athens, the Epicurean School outlived most other systems, continuing to exist as late as the fourth century after Christ.[1]

half of the same century lived Antonius, mentioned by *Galen.* De Prop. An. Affect. v. 1, and Zenobius, who, according to *Simpl.* Phys. 113, b, was an opponent of Alexander of Aphrodisias. In the first half of the third century lived Diogenes Laërtius, who, if not a perfect Epicurean himself, was at least a friend of the Epicureans. Amongst other Epicureans, the names of Athenæus (whose epigram on Epicurus is quoted by *Diog.* x. 12), Autodorus (*Diog.* v. 92), and Hermodorus (*Lucian*, Icaromen. 16) may be mentioned; but *Diog.* x. 11,

does not justify us setting down Diocles of Magnesia as an Epicurean.

[1] *Diog.* x. 9, in the first half of the third century, writes : ἥ τε διδαχὴ πασῶν σχεδὸν ἐκλιπουσῶν τῶν ἄλλων ἐσαεὶ διαμένουσα καὶ νηρίθμους ἀρχὰς ἀπολύουσα ἄλλην ἐξ ἄλλης τῶν γνωρίμων. The testimony of *Lactantius*, Inst. iii. 17, to the wide spread of Epicureanism, is not so trustworthy, although it treats it as still existing. It may be that he is only following older writers as Cicero does. See above p. 412, 1.

CHAPTER XVI.

CHARACTER AND DIVISIONS OF THE EPICUREAN
TEACHING : THE TEST-SCIENCE OF TRUTH.

CHAP.
XVI.
───────
A. *Cha-
racter of
Epicurean
system.*
(1) *Its
power of
self-pre-
servation.*

THE scientific value and capacity for development of
Epicureanism is out of all proportion to its extensive diffusion and the length of time during which
it continued to flourish. No other system troubled
itself so little about the foundation on which it
rested ; none confined itself so exclusively to the utterances of its founder. Such was the dogmatism
with which Epicurus propounded his precepts, such
the conviction he entertained of their excellence,
that his pupils were required to commit summaries
of them to memory ;[1] and the superstitious devotion
for the founder was with his approval [2] carried to

───────

[1] *Cic.* Fin. ii. 7, 20 : Quis
enim vestrum non edidicit Epicuri κυρίας δόξας ? *Diog.* 12
(according to Diocles). Epicurus often exhorted his scholars
(*Ibid.* 83 ; 85 ; 35) to commit to
memory what they had heard.
His last exhortation to his
friends was (*Diog.* 16): τῶν
δογμάτων μεμνῆσθαι.

[2] He speaks of himself and
Metrodorus in *Cic.* Fin. ii. 3, 7,
as wise men. *Plut.* N. P. Suav.
Viv. 18, 5, quotes, as coming

from him : ὡς Κολώτης μὲν αὐτὸν
φυσιολογοῦντα προσκυνήσειεν γο-
νάτων ἁψάμενος· Νεοκλῆς δὲ ὁ
ἀδελφὸς εὐθὺς ἐκ παίδων ἀποφαί-
νοιτο μηδένα σοφώτερον Ἐπικούρου
γεγονέναι μηδ᾽ εἶναι· ἡ δὲ μήτηρ
ἀτόμους ἔσχεν ἐν αὐτῇ τοαύτας,
οἷαι συνελθοῦσαι σοφὸν ἂν ἐγέν-
νησαν. Conf. *Id.* Frat. Am. 16,
p. 487 ; Adv. Col. 17, 5 ; *Cleomed.*
Meteor. p. 89. Not only was
Epicurus' birthday observed by
the Epicurean School during
his lifetime, but the 20th of

such a length, that not the slightest deviation from his tenets was on a single point permitted. Whereas, even in Cicero's time, the writings of Epicurus and Metrodorus found hardly a reader beyond the School,[1] it is asserted that as late as the first and second centuries after Christ the Epicureans clung tenaciously to their master's teaching.[2] Probably it was easier for an Epicurean than for any other thinker to act thus, he, like his master,[3] being indifferent to the

every month was celebrated as a festival, in honour of him and Metrodorus. In his testament, Epicurus especially ordered this twofold observance for the future. *Diog.* 18; *Cic.* Fin. ii. 31, 101; *Plut.* N. P. Suav. Viv. 4, 8; *Plin.* H. N. xxxv. 5. *Athen.* vii. 298, d: 'Επικούρειός τις εἰκαδιστής. Epicurus' picture is constantly referred to (*Cic.* Fin. v. 1, 3; *Plin.* l. c.). The extravagant importance attached to Epicurus in his School is proved by the high eulogies in *Lucret.* i. 62; iii. 1 and 1040; v. 1; vi. 1. Metrodorus, in *Plut.* Adv. Col. 17, 4, praises τὰ 'Επικούρου ὡς ἀληθῶς θεόφαντα ὄργια.

[1] *Cic.* Tusc. ii. 3, 8.

[2] *Sen.* Ep. 33, 4, compares the scientific independence of the Stoics with the Epicurean's dependence on the founder: Non sumus sub rege: sibi quisque se vindicat. Apud istos quicquid dicit Hermarchus, quicquid Metrodorus, ad unum refertur. Omnia quæ quisquam in illo contubernio locutus est, unius ductu et auspiciis dicta sunt. On the other hand, Numenius (in *Eus.* Pr. Ev. xiv.

5, 3), little as he can agree with their tenets, commends the Epicureans for faithfully adhering to their master's teaching, a point in which only the Pythagoreans are their equals. Of the Epicureans, it may be said: μηδ' αὐτοῖς εἰπεῖν πω ἐναντίον οὔτε ἀλλήλοις οὔτε 'Επικούρῳ μηδὲν [μηδένα] εἰς μηδὲν, ὅτου καὶ μνησθῆναι ἄξιον, ἀλλ' ἔστιν αὐτοῖς παρανόμημα, μᾶλλον δὲ ἀσέβημα, καὶ κατέγνωσται τὸ καινοτομηθέν. Thus the Epicurean School resembles a state animated by one spirit, in which there are no divisions of party.

[3] It has been already observed, p. 405, 1; 406, 1, that Epicurus ignored his obligations to his teachers Pamphilus and Nausicydes, and only confessed his debt to Democritus. All other philosophers provoked, not only his contempt, but likewise his abuse. *Diog.* 8, probably on the authority of Timocrates, communicates his remarks on Plato, Aristotle, and others. *Cic.* N. D. i. 33, 93: Cum Epicurus Aristotelem vexarit contumeliosissime, Phædoni Socratico turpissime

CHAP.
XVI.

labours of other philosophers, or unable to appreciate their merits.[1] For us this conduct of theirs has one advantage ; we can be far more certain that the Epicureans reflect the teaching of their founder than we can that this is the case with the Stoics. But this philosophical sterility, this mechanical handing down of unchangeable principles, places the intellectual value of Epicureanism on the lowest level. The servile dependance of the Epicurean School on its founder can neither excuse its mental idleness nor recommend a system so powerless to give an independent training to its supporters.

(2) *Aim of philosophy according to the Epicureans.*

The want of intellectual taste here displayed appears also in the view taken by Epicurus of the aim and business of philosophy. If among the Stoics the subordination of theory to practice was frequently felt, among the Epicureans this subordination was carried to such an extent as to lead to a depreciation of all science. The aim of philosophy was, with them, to promote human happiness. Indeed, philosophy is nothing else but an activity helping us to happiness by means of speech and thought.[2] Nor is happiness, according to Epicurus,

maledixerit. *Plut.* N. P. Suav. V. 2, 2 : Compared with Epicurus and Metrodorus, Colotes is polite ; τὰ γὰρ ἐν ἀνθρώποις αἴσχιστα ῥήματα, βωμολοχίας, ληκυθισμοὺς, κ.τ.λ. συναγαγόντες Ἀριστοτέλους καὶ Σωκράτους καὶ Πυθαγόρου καὶ Πρωταγόρου καὶ Θεοφράστου καὶ Ἡρακλείδου καὶ Ἱππάρχου, καὶ τίνος γὰρ οὐχὶ τῶν ἐπιφανῶν, κατεσκέδασαν.
[1] *Cic.* N. D. ii. 29, 73 : Nam

vobis, Vellei, minus notum est, quem ad modum quidque dicatur ; vestra enim solum legitis, vestra amatis, ceteros causa incognita condemnatis. *Ibid.* i. 34, 93 : Zeno not only despised cotemporary philosophers, but he even called Socrates a scurra Atticus, *Macrob.* Somn. i. 2 (Colotes ridiculing Plato's Republic).
[2] *Sext.* Math. xi. 169 : Ἐπί·

directly promoted by knowledge, but only indirectly in as far as knowledge ministers to practical needs, or clears away hindrances to their attainment. All science which does not serve this end is superfluous and worthless.[1] Hence Epicurus despised learning and culture, the researches of grammarians, and the lore of historians, and declared it a piece of good fortune for simplicity of feeling to be uncontaminated by learned rubbish.[2] Nor was his opinion different respecting mathematical science, of which he was wholly ignorant.[3] The calculations of mathematicians, he maintained, are based on false principles;[4]

κουρος ἔλεγε τὴν φιλοσοφίαν ἐνέργειαν εἶναι λόγοις καὶ διαλογισμοῖς τὸν εὐδαίμονα βίον περιποιοῦσαν. Conf. Epic. in *Diog.* 122 : The demand to study philosophy in youth, as well as in age, is supported on the ground, that it is never too early nor too late to be happy.

[1] It was mentioned, p. 408, 3, that Epicurus' own education was defective. Not content therewith, he upholds this defectiveness on principle. Nullam eruditionem, says the Epicurean in *Cic.* Fin. i. 21, 71, esse duxit, nisi quæ beatæ vitæ disciplinam adjuvaret. In poets, nulla solida utilitas omnisque puerilis est delectatio. Music, geometry, arithmetic, astronomy et a falsis initiis profecta vera esse non possunt, et si essent vera nihil afferrent, quo jucundius, i. e. quo melius viveremus.

[2] *Cic.* Fin. ii. 4, 12 : Vestri quidem vel optime disputant, nihil opus esse eum, philosophus qui futurus sit, scire literas.

They fetch their philosophers, like Cincinnatus, from the plough. In this spirit, Epicurus (*Diog.* 6 ; *Plut.* N. P. Suav. V. 12, 1) wrote to Pythocles : παιδείαν δὲ πᾶσαν (the παιδεία ἐγκύκλιος, the learned culture), μακάριε, φεῦγε τὸ ἀκάτιον ἀράμενος ; and to Apelles (*Plut.* l. c. ; *Athen.* xiii. 588, a) : μακαρίζω σε, ὦ οὗτος, ὅτι καθαρὸς πάσης αἰτίας (*Plut.* explains it : τῶν μαθημάτων ἀποσχόμενος) ἐπὶ φιλοσοφίαν ὥρμησας. Metrodorus asserted (*Plut.* l. c.) that it need not be a source of trouble to anyone, if he had never read a line of Homer, and did not know whether Hector were a Trojan or a Greek. The art of reading and writing, γραμματικὴ in the limited sense, was the only art recognised by Epicurus. *Sext.* Math. i. 49.

[3] *Sext.* Math. i. 1 ; *Cic.* Fin. i. 6, 20.

[4] *Cic.* Fin. i. 21 (see p. 421, 1), which probably only means, that mathematical ideas

at any rate, they contribute nothing to human happiness, and it is therefore useless and foolish to trouble oneself about them.[1] The theory of music and poetry he likewise found exceedingly irksome, although he took pleasure in music itself and the theatre;[2] and rhetoric, as an artificial guide to eloquence, seemed to him as worthless as the show-speeches which are the only result of the study thereof. The power of public speaking is a matter of practice and of momentary feeling, and hence the skilful speaker is far from being a good statesman.[3] Nor did the greater part of logical enquiries fare any better in his judgment. Himself no logician, he set little store by logic. Definitions are of no use; the theory of division and proof may be dispensed with; the philosopher does best to confine himself to words, and to leave all the logical ballast alone.[4] Of all the questions which engrossed the

cannot be applied to phenomena. Hence Acad. ii. 33, 106 (conf. Fin. i. 6, 20): Polyænus . . . Epicuro adsentiens totam geometriam falsam esse credidit. Conf. Procl. in *Eucl.* p. 85.

[1] See p. 421, 1 ; *Sext.* Math. i. 1 : Epicurus rejects mathematics ὡς τῶν μαθημάτων μηδὲν συνεργούντων πρὸς σοφίας τελείωσιν. According to *Diog.* 93, Epicurus calls astronomy τὰς ἀνδραποδώδεις τῶν ἀστρολόγων τεχνιτείας. Conf. *Diog.* 79.

[2] *Plut.* l. c. 13, 1. Philodemus, in his treatise περὶ μουσικῆς, had discussed at length the value of music, as we gather from the fragments

of the 4th Book, Vol. Herc. i. ; in particular, rejecting the notion that it has a moral effect, see col. i. 24, 28. He was even opposed to music at table (Col. 38, as Epicurus was in *Plut.* l. c.). The statement of *Diog.* 121, that only the wise man can give a right opinion on poetry and music, is not at variance with these passages.

[3] *Philodemus*, De Rhet. Vol. Herc. iv col. 3 ; 12. The same polemic is continued in the further fragments of this treatise, *Ibid.* V. Col. 6.

[4] *Cic.* Fin. i. 7, 22 : In logic iste vester plane, ut mihi quidem videtur, inermis ac nudus est. Tollit definitiones : nihil de

attention of Stoic logicians, one only, the theory of
knowledge, was studied by Epicurus, and that in a
very superficial way.[1]

Far greater, comparatively, was the importance
he attached to the study of nature,[2] but even natural science was deemed valuable, not so much for its
own sake as because of its practical use. The knowledge of natural causes is the only means of liberating the soul from the shackles of superstition; this
is the only use of natural science. If it were not
for the thought of God and the fear of death, there
would be no need of studying nature.[3] The investigation of our instincts is also of use, because it helps
us to control them, and to keep them within their
natural bounds.[4] Thus the onesided practical view

dividendo ac partiendo docet.
Non quomodo efficiatur conclu-
daturque ratio, tradit, non qua
via captiosa solvantur, ambigua distinguantur, ostendit.
Ibid. 19, 63: In dialectica
autem vestra nullam existima-
vit [Epic.] esse nec ad melius
vivendum nec ad commodius
disserendum viam. *Acad.* ii.
30, 97: Ab Epicuro, qui totam
dialecticam et contemnit et
inridet. *Diog.* 31: τὴν διαλεκτικὴν ὡς παρέλκουσαν ἀποδοκιμά-
ζουσιν· ἀρκεῖν γὰρ τοὺς φυσικοὺς
χωρεῖν κατὰ τοὺς τῶν πραγμάτων
φθόγγους.

[1] See p. 424.
[2] *Cic.* Fin. i. 19, 63: In
physicis plurimum posuit
[Epic.]. *Ibid.* 6, 17: In physicis, quibus maxime gloriatur,
primum totus est alienus.
[3] Epic. in *Diog.* x. 82 and

85: μὴ ἄλλο τι τέλος ἐκ τῆς περὶ
μετεώρων γνώσεως . . . νομίζειν
δεῖ εἶναι ἥπερ ἀταραξίαν καὶ πίστιν
βέβαιον καθάπερ καὶ ἐπὶ τῶν λοιπῶν. *Ibid.* 112: εἰ μηθὲν ἡμᾶς
αἱ περὶ τῶν μετεώρων ὑποψίαι ἠνώχ-
λουν καὶ αἱ περὶ θανάτου . . . οὐκ
ἂν προσεδεόμεθα φυσιολογίας; but
this becomes necessary, since
without knowledge of nature,
we cannot be perfectly free
from fear. The same in *Plut.*
N. P. Suav. Viv. 8, 7; Conf.
Diog. 79 and 143; *Cic.* Fin. iv.
5, 11; *Lucret.* i. 62; iii. 14; vi.
9.
[4] In *Cic.* Fin. i. 19, 63, the
Epicurean speaks of a fivefold,
or, excluding Canonic, of a
fourfold use of natural science:
fortitudo contra mortis ti-
morem; constantia contra me-
tum religionis; sedatio animi
omnium rerum occultarum ig-

of philosophy which we have already encountered in Stoicism was carried by the Epicureans to an extreme length.

Nor is it otherwise than in harmony herewith that logic did not receive a fuller or more perfect treatment in the further development of their system. Even the study of nature, going as it did far more into particulars than logic, was guided entirely by practical considerations, all scientific interest in nature being ignored Following the usual method, however, the Epicureans divided philosophy into three parts [1]—logic, natural science, and moral science. Limiting, however, the first of these parts to one branch of logic, the part which deals with the characteristics of truth, and which they therefore called neither logic, nor dialectic, but Canonic, they really reduced this part to a mere introductory appendage to the two other parts,[2] and studied Canonic as a part of natural science.[3] Moreover, natural science

noratione sublata; moderatio natura cupiditatum generibusque earum explicatis.

[1] *Diog.* 29: διαιρεῖται τοίνυν [ἡ φιλοσοφία] εἰς τρία, τό τε κανονικὸν καὶ φυσικὸν καὶ ἠθικόν. Canonic was also called περὶ κριτηρίου καὶ ἀρχῆς καὶ στοιχειωτικόν; natural science, περὶ γενέσεως καὶ φθορᾶς καὶ περὶ φύσεως; ethics, περὶ αἱρετῶν καὶ φευκτῶν καὶ περὶ βίων καὶ τέλους.

[2] *Diog.* 30: τὸ μὲν οὖν κανονικὸν ἐφόδους ἐπὶ τὴν πραγματείαν ἔχει.

[3] *Diog.* l. c.: εἰώθασι μέντοι τὸ κανονικὸν ὁμοῦ τῷ φυσικῷ συντάττειν. *Cic.* Fin. i. 19. See

p. 423, 4. Hence *Sext.* Math. vii. 14: Some reckon Epicurus amongst those who only divide philosophy into natural and moral science; whilst, according to others, he adhered to a threefold division, at the same time rejecting the Stoic logic. *Sen.* Ep. 89, 11: Epicurei duas partes philosophiæ putaverunt esse, naturalem atque moralem: rationalem removerunt, deinde cum ipsis rebus cogerentur, ambigua secernere, falsa sub specie veri latentia coarguere, ipsi quodque looum, quem de judicio et regula appellant, alio nomine

was so entirely subordinated to moral science, that
we might almost feel tempted to follow some modern
writers [1] in their view of the Epicurean system, giving
to moral science the precedence of the two other
parts, or at least of natural science.[2] The School,
however, followed the usual order, and not without
reason ;[3] for although the whole tendency of the
Epicurean Canonic and natural science can only, like
the Stoic, be explained by a reference to their moral
science, yet their moral science presupposes the test-
science of truth and natural science. We shall, therefore, do well to treat of Canonic in the first place,
and subsequently to prove how this branch of study
depends on Ethics.

Canonic or the test-science of truth, as has been
observed, is occupied with investigating the standard of truth, and with enquiring into the mode of
acquiring knowledge. The whole of formal logic,
the doctrine of the formation of conceptions and
conclusions, is omitted by Epicurus.[4] Even the theory
of the acquisition of knowledge assumes with him a
very simple form. If the Stoics were fain, notwithstanding their ideal ethics and their pantheistic
speculations, ultimately to take their stand on materialism, could Epicurus avoid doing the same?
In seeking a speculative basis for a view of life
which refers everything to the feeling of pleasure

B. *Canonic
or the test-
science of
truth.*

(1) *Sen-
sation and
percep-
tion.*

rationalem induxerunt: sed eum
accessionem esse naturalis partis existimant.
    [1] *Ritter*, iii. 463 ; *Schleier-
macher*, Gesch. d. Phil. p. 123.

    [2] *Steinhart* in the treatise
often referred to.
    [3] *Diog.* 29 ; *Sext.* Math. vii. 22.
    [4] *Cic.* Fin. i. 7, 22. See p.
422, 4.

or pain, he appealed far more unreservedly than
they had done to sensation. Now, since the senses
can alone inform us what is pleasant or unpleasant,
and what is desirable or the contrary, our judgment
as to truth or falsehood must ultimately depend on
the senses. Viewed speculatively, sensation is the
standard of truth; viewed practically, the feeling of
pleasure or pain.[1] If the senses may not be trusted,
still less may knowledge derived from reason be
trusted, reason itself being primarily and entirely
derived from the senses. There remains, therefore,
no distinctive mark of truth, and no possibility of
certain conviction. We are at the mercy of unlimited doubt. If, however, this doubt is contradictory of itself—for how can men declare they *know*,
that they can *know* nothing?—it is also contradictory
of human nature, since it would do away not only
with all knowledge but with every possibility of action, in short, with all the conditions on which human
life depends.[2] To avoid doubt we must allow that
sensation as such is always, and under all circumstances, to be trusted; nor ought the delusions of the
senses to shake our belief; the causes of these decep-

[1] *Cic.* Fin. i. 7, 22; *Sext.*
Math. vii. 203. If, according
to *Diog.* 31, and *Cic.* Acad. ii.
46, 142, Epicurus named three
criteria—πρόληψις, αἴσθησις, and
πάθη—instead of the above two,
it is only an inaccuracy of expression, πρόληψις, as we have
seen, being derived from sensation.

[2] Epicurus, in *Diog.* x. 146;

Lucr. iv. 467–519; *Cic.* Fin. i.
19, 64. Colotes (in *Plut.* Adv.
Col. 24, 3) replies to the Cyrenaic scepticism by saying:
μὴ δύνασθαι ζῆν μηδὲ χρῆσθαι τοῖς
πράγμασιν. In this case, as in
the case of the Stoics, the dogmatism in favour of the senses
is based on a practical postulate, the need of a firm basis of
conviction for human life.

tions not lying in sensation as such, but in our judgment about sensation. What the senses supply is only that an object produces this or that effect upon us, and that this or that picture has impressed our soul. The facts thus supplied are always true, only it does not follow that the object exactly corresponds with the impression we receive of it, nor that it produces on others the same impression that it produces on us. On the contrary, many different pictures may emanate from one and the same object, and these pictures may be changed on their way to the ear or eye. Pictures, too, may strike our senses with which no real objects correspond. To confound the picture with the thing, the impression made with the object making the impression, is certainly an error, but this error must not be laid to the charge of the senses, but to that of opinion.[1] Indeed, how is it possible, asks Epicurus,[2] to refute the testimony of the senses? Can reason refute it? But reason is itself dependent on the senses, and cannot bear testimony against that on which its own claims to belief depend. Or can one sense convict another of error? But different sensations do not refer to the same object, and similar sensations have equal value. Nothing remains, therefore, but to attach implicit belief to every impression of the senses. Every such

---

[1] Epic. in *Diog.* x. 50 and 147; *Sext.* Math. vii. 203–210; viii. 9; 63; 185; *Plut.* Adv. Col. 4, 3; 5, 2; 25, 2; Plac. iv. 9, 2; *Lucr.* iv. 377–519; *Cic.* Acad. ii. 25, 79; 32, 101; Fin.

i. 7, 22; N. D. i. 25, 70; *Tertull.* De An. 17. Further particulars below respecting sense-perception.

[2] *Diog.* x. 31; *Lucr.* iv. 480.

CHAP.
XVI.

(2) No-
tions.

impression is directly certain, and is accordingly
termed by Epicurus clear evidence (ἐνάργεια).[1] Nay,
more, its truth is so paramount that the impressions
of madmen, and appearances in dreams, are true
because they are caused by something real,[2] and error
only becomes possible when we go beyond sensation.
This going beyond sensation becomes, however,
a necessity. By a repetition of the same perception
a notion (πρόληψις) arises. A notion, therefore, is
nothing else but the general picture retained in the
mind of what has been perceived.[3] On these notions
retained by memory depends all speaking and thinking. They are what commonly go under the name
of things; and speech is only a means of recalling
definite perceptions[4] to the memory. Notions are

[1] Sext. Math. vii. 203 and
216. In Diog. x. 52, instead of
ἐνεργείας, we should read with
Cobet ἐναργείας. Besides this
peculiar expression, Epicurus
uses sometimes αἴσθησις, sometimes φαντασία (Sext. l. c.), for
sensation. An impression on
the senses, he calls φανταστικὴ
ἐπιβολή. Diog. 50.

[2] Diog. 32.

[3] Diog. 33 : τὴν δὲ πρόληψιν
λέγουσιν οἱονεὶ κατάληψιν ἢ δόξαν
ὀρθὴν ἢ ἔννοιαν ἢ καθολικὴν νόησιν
ἐναποκειμένην, τουτέστι μνήμην
τοῦ πολλάκις ἔξωθεν φανέντος. By
the help of this passage, Cicero's
description, N. D. i. 16, 43, must
be corrected.

[4] Diog. l. c.: ἅμα γὰρ τῷ
ῥηθῆναι ἄνθρωπος εὐθὺς κατὰ πρόληψιν καὶ ὁ τύπος αὐτοῦ νοεῖται
προηγουμένων τῶν αἰσθήσεων.
παντὶ οὖν ὀνόματι τὸ πρώτως ὑπο-
τεταγμένον ἐναργές ἐστι· καὶ οὐκ

ἂν ἐζητήσαμεν τὸ ζητούμενον, εἰ
μὴ πρότερον ἐγνώκειμεν αὐτὸ . . .
οὐδ' ἂν ὠνομάσαμέν τι μὴ πρότερον
αὐτοῦ κατὰ πρόληψιν τὸν τύπον
μαθόντες. Hence the exhortation in Epicurus' letter to
Herodotus (in Diog. x. 37):
πρῶτον μὲν οὖν τὰ ὑποτεταγμένα
τοῖς φθόγγοις δεῖ εἰληφέναι ὅπως
ἂν τὰ δοξαζόμενα ἢ ζητούμενα ἢ
ἀπορούμενα ἔχωμεν εἰς ὃ ἀνάγοντες
ἐπικρίνειν, κ.τ.λ. Every impression must be referred to definite
perceptions; apart from perceptions, no reality belongs to
our impressions ; or, as it is expressed Sext. Pyrrh. ii. 107,
Math. viii. 13, 258 : The Epicureans deny the existence of
a λεκτὸν, and that between a
thing and its name there exists
a third intermediate something
—a conception. See also Sext.
vii. 267.

presupposed in all scientific knowledge.[1] Together with sensations they form the measure of the truth of our convictions;[2] and it holds true of them as it did of sensations—that they are true in themselves and need no proof.[3] Taken by themselves, notions, like perceptions, are reflections in the soul of things on which the transforming action of the mind, changing external impressions into conceptions, has not as yet been brought to bear.

For this very reason notions are not sufficient. From appearances we must advance to their secret causes; from the known to the unknown.[4] But far too little value was attached by Epicurus to the logical forms of thought, or he would have investigated more accurately the nature of this process of advancing.[5] Thoughts, in his view, result from sensations spontaneously, and although a certain amount of reflection is necessary for the process, yet it requires no scientific guidance.[6] The thoughts arrived

(3) *Opinion.*

---

[1] *Diog.* 33. *Sext.* Math. i. 57 (xi. 21): οὔτε ζητεῖν οὔτε ἀπορεῖν ἔστι κατὰ τὸν σόφον 'Επίκουρον ἄνευ προλήψεως. *Ibid.* viii. 337, p. 521; *Plut.* De An. 6: The difficulty, that all learning presupposes knowledge, the Stoics met by φυσικαὶ ἔννοιαι, the Epicureans by προλήψεις which accordingly are the natural test of truth.

[2] See p. 426, 1. *Diog.* l. c.: ἐναργεῖς οὖν εἰσιν αἱ προλήψεις καὶ τὸ δοξαστὸν ἀπὸ προτέρου τινὸς ἐναργοῦς ἤρτηται, ἐφ' ὃ ἀναφέροντες λέγομεν.

[3] See previous note and Epic. in *Diog.* 38: ἀνάγκη γὰρ

τὸ πρῶτον ἐννόημα καθ' ἕκαστον φθόγγον βλέπεσθαι καὶ μηθὲν ἀποδείξεως προσδεῖσθαι, εἴπερ ἕξομεν τὸ ζητούμενον ἢ ἀπορούμενον καὶ δοξαζόμενον ἐφ' ὃ ἀνάξομεν.

[4] *Diog.* 33 (Conf. 38, 104): περὶ τῶν ἀδήλων ἀπὸ τῶν φαινομένων χρὴ σημειοῦσθαι.

[5] See p. 422, 4. *Steinhart*, p. 466, goes too far, in saying that Epicurus defied all law and rule in thought.

[6] *Diog.* 32: καὶ γὰρ καὶ ἐπίνοιαι πᾶσαι ἀπὸ τῶν αἰσθήσεων γεγόνασι, κατά τε περίπτωσιν (probably: the coincidence of several sensations to be distinguished from their σύνθεσις or free com-

at in this way do not stand as a higher genus above perceptions, but they are only opinions (ὑπόληψις, δόξα) without a note of truth in themselves, and depending for their truth upon sensation. That opinion may be considered a true one which is based on the testimony of the senses, or is at least not contrary to the senses, and that a false opinion in which the opposite is the case.[1] Sometimes we suppose that upon certain present impressions other impressions will follow; for instance, that a tower which appears round at a distance will appear round close at hand. In that case, if the real perception corresponds with our supposition, our opinion is true, otherwise it is false.[2] At other times we suppose that certain appearances are due to secret causes; for instance, that empty space is the cause of motion. If all appearances tally with their explanations, we may consider

bination) καὶ ἀναλογίαν καὶ ὁμοιότητα καὶ σύνθεσιν, συμβαλλομένου τι καὶ τοῦ λογισμοῦ. Conf. p. 422, 4 ; 429, 1, and the corresponding doctrine of the Stoics, p. 80, with the teaching of Epicurus, on the genesis of thoughts from sensations.

[1] *Diog.* 33 : καὶ τὸ δοξαστὸν ἀπὸ προτέρου τινὸς ἐναργοῦς ἤρτηται . . . τὴν δὲ δόξαν καὶ ὑπόληψιν λέγουσιν. ἀληθῆ τέ φασι καὶ ψευδῆ· ἂν μὲν γὰρ ἐπιμαρτυρῆται ἢ μὴ ἀντιμαρτυρῆται ἀληθῆ εἶναι· ἐὰν δὲ μὴ ἐπιμαρτυρῆται ἢ ἀντιμαρτυρῆται ψευδῆ τυγχάνειν. *Sext.* Math. vii. 211 : τῶν δοξῶν κατὰ τὸν Ἐπίκουρον αἱ μὲν ἀληθεῖς εἰσιν αἱ δὲ ψευδεῖς· ἀληθεῖς μὲν αἵ τε ἀντιμαρτυρούμεναι καὶ οὐκ ἀντιμαρτυρούμεναι πρὸς τῆς ἐναρ-

γείας, ψευδεῖς δὲ αἵ τε ἀντιμαρτυρούμεναι καὶ οὐκ ἐπιμαρτυρούμεναι πρὸς τῆς ἐναργείας. *Ritter*, iii. 486, observes that these statements are contradictory. According to Sextus, an opinion is only then true when it can be proved *and* not refuted; according to Diogenes, when it can be proved *or* not refuted. The latter is, however, clearly meant by Sextus, and is affirmed by Epicurus in *Diog.* 50 and 51.

[2] Epicur. in *Diog.* 50 ; *Ibid.* 33 ; *Sext.* vii. 212. The object of a future sensation is called by *Diog.* 38, τὸ προσμένον. *Diog.* x. 34, himself gives a perverted explanation of this term, which probably misled Steinhart, p. 466.

our suppositions correct ; if not, our suppositions are incorrect.[1] In the first case the test of the truth of an opinion is that it is supported by experience; in the latter that it is not refuted by experience.[2] Have we not here all the leading features of a theory of knowledge based purely on sensation ? The Epicurean's interest in these questions was, however, far too slight to construct with them a developed theory of materialism.

Little pains seem to have been taken by Epicurus to overcome the difficulties by which his view was beset. If all sensations as such are true, the saying of Protagoras necessarily follows that for each individual that is true which seems to him to be true, that contrary impressions about one and the same object are true, and that deceptions of the senses, so many instances of which are supplied by experience, are really impossible. To avoid these conclusions, Epicurus maintained that for each different impression there is a different object-picture. What immediately affects our senses is not the object itself, but a picture of the object, and these pictures may be innumerable, a different one being the cause of each separate sensation. Moreover, although the pictures emanating from the same object are in general nearly alike, it is possible that they may differ from one-

[1] *Sext.* l. c. 213.
[2] The two tests of truth, proof and absence of refutation, do not, therefore, as Sextus expressly says, refer to the same cases. Our suppositions in respect of external appearances must be proved, in order to be true ; our impressions of the secret causes of these appearances must not be refuted. The former test applies to opinions regarding τὸ προσμένον; the latter, to opinions regarding τὸ ἄδηλον. *Diog.* 38.

another owing to a variety of causes. If, therefore, the same object appears different to different individuals, the cause of these different sensations is not one and the same, but a different one, and different pictures must have affected their senses. If our own sensations deceive us, the blame does not belong to our senses, as though they had depicted to us unreal objects, but to our judgment for drawing unwarranted inferences from pictures [1] as to their causes.

This line of argument, however, only removes the difficulty one step further. Sensation is said always to reproduce faithfully the picture which affects the organs of sense, but the pictures do not always reproduce the object with equal faithfulness. How then can a faithful picture be known from one which is not faithful? To this question the Epicurean system can furnish no real answer. To say that the wise man knows how to distinguish a faithful from an unfaithful picture [2] is to despair of an absolute standard at all, and to make the decision of truth or error depend upon the individual's judgment. Such a statement reduces all our impressions of the properties of things to a relative level. If sensation does not show us things themselves, but only those impressions of them which happen to affect us, it does not supply us with a knowledge of things as they are, but as they happen to be related to us. It

---

[1] Compare the passages in *Sext.* vii. 206, quoted p. 427, 1.
[2] *Cic.* Acad. ii. 14, 45 : Nam qui voluit subvenire erroribus Epicurus iis, qui videntur conturbare veri cognitionem, dixitque sapientis esse opinionem a perspicuitate sejungere, nihil profecit, ipsius enim opinionis errorem nullo modo sustulit.

was, therefore, a legitimate inference from this theory
of knowledge for Epicurus to deny that colour belongs to bodies in themselves, since some only see
colour in the dark, whilst others do not.[1] Like his
predecessor, Democritus, he must have been brought
to this view by his theory of atoms. Few of the
properties belong to atoms which we perceive in
things, and hence all other properties must be explained as not belonging to the essence, but only belonging to the appearance of things.[2] The taste for
speculation was, however, too weak, and the need of
a direct truth of the senses too strong in Epicurus
for him to be able to turn his thoughts in this direction for long. Whilst allowing to certain properties
of things only a relative value, he had no wish to
doubt the reality of objects, nor to disparage the
object-pictures which furnish us with sensations.[3]

---

[1] *Plut.* Adv. Col. 7, 2 (*Stob.*
Ecl. i. 366; *Lucr.* ii. 795): ὁ
Ἐπίκουρος οὐκ εἶναι λέγων τὰ
χρώματα συμφυῆ τοῖς σώμασιν,
ἀλλὰ γεννᾶσθαι κατὰ ποιάς τινας
τάξεις καὶ θέσεις πρὸς τὴν ὄψιν.
For says Epicurus, οὐκ οἶδα ὅπως
δεῖ τὰ ἐν σκότει ταῦτα ὄντα φῆσαι
χρώματα ἔχειν. Often some see
colour where others do not; οὐ
μᾶλλον οὖν ἔχειν ἢ μὴ ἔχειν
χρῶμα ῥηθήσεται τῶν σωμάτων ἕκαστον. [2] *Simpl.* Categ 109, β (Schol.
in Arist. 92, a, 10): Since Democritus and Epicurus depute
all qualities to atoms except
those of form and mode of combination, ἐπιγίνεσθαι λέγουσι τὰς
ἄλλας ποιότητας, τάς τε ἁπλᾶς,
οἷον θερμότητας καὶ λειότητας, καὶ

τὰς κατὰ χρώματα καὶ τοὺς χυμούς.
Lucret. l. c.
[3] Compare the passages already quoted, on the truth of
the impressions of the senses,
and the words of Epicurus, in
Diog. 68 : ἀλλὰ μὴν καὶ τὰ σχήματα καὶ τὰ χρώματα καὶ τὰ μεγέθη
καὶ τὰ βάρεα καὶ ὅσα ἄλλα κατη-
γορεῖται κατὰ τοῦ σώματος ὡς ἂν
εἰς αὐτὸ βεβηκότα καὶ πᾶσιν ἐνόν-
τα ἢ τοῖς ὁρατοῖς καὶ κατὰ τὴν
αἴσθησιν αὐτὴν γνωστοῖς, οὐθ᾽ ὡς
καθ᾽ ἑαυτάς εἰσι φύσεις δοξαστέον
(οὐ γὰρ δυνατὸν ἐπινοῆσαι τοῦτο),
οὔθ᾽ ὅλως ὡς οὐκ εἰσίν, οὔθ᾽ ὡς
ἕτερά τινα προσυπάρχοντα τούτῳ
ἀσώματα οὔθ᾽ ὡς μορία τούτου,
ἀλλ᾽ ὡς τὸ ὅλον σῶμα καθόλου μὲν
ἐκ τούτων πάντων τὴν ἑαυτοῦ
φύσιν ἔχον ἀΐδιον, κ.τ.λ.

CHAPTER XVII.

THE EPICUREAN VIEWS ON NATURE.

CHAP.
XVII.

A. *General
views on
nature.*

(1) *Object,
value, and
method of
the study
of nature.*

IF EPICURUS and his followers underrated logic, to
natural science they attached a considerable value.
This value was, however, exclusively derived from a
sense of the practical advantages which a knowledge
of nature confers in opposing superstition. Without
such an object the study of nature would have
seemed wholly superfluous.[1] Such being their attitude of mind, the Epicureans were, as might have
been expected, indifferent about giving a complete
and accurate explanation of phenomena. Their one
aim was to put forward such a view of nature as
would do away with the necessity for supernatural
intervention, without at the same time pretending to
offer a sufficient solution of the problems raised by
science.[2] Whilst, therefore, devoting considerable
attention to natural science,[3] Epicurus does not seem

---

[1] Epic. in *Diog.* 143 : οὐκ ἦν
τὸν φοβούμενον περὶ τῶν κυριωτάτων λύειν μὴ κατειδότα τίς ἡ τοῦ
σύμπαντος φύσις ἀλλ' ὑποπτευό-
μενόν τι τῶν κατὰ τοὺς μύθους.
ὥστε οὐκ ἦν ἄνευ φυσιολογίας
ἀκεραίας τὰς ἡδονὰς ἀπολαμβάνειν.
For further particulars, p. 422.

[2] οὐ γὰρ δὴ ἰδιολογίας καὶ
κενῆς δόξης ὁ βίος ἡμῶν ἔχει
χρείαν, ἀλλὰ τοῦ ἀθορύβως ἡμᾶς
ζῆν. Epic. in *Diog.* 87.

[3] *Diog.* 27, mentions 37 books
of his περὶ φύσεως, besides
smaller works.

to have considered certainty to be of importance, or
even to be possible, in dealing with details of scientific study. Of the general causes of things we can
and ought to entertain a firm conviction, since the
possibility of overcoming religious prejudices and
the fears occasioned by them depends on these convictions. No such result, however, follows from the
investigation of details, which, on the contrary, only
tends to confirm prejudices in those who are not
already emancipated from them. In dealing with
details it is, therefore, enough for Epicurus to show
that various natural causes for phenomena may be
imagined, and to offer various suggestions which
dispense with the intervention of the Gods and the
myths of a belief in Providence.[1] To say that any
one of these expedients is the only possible one, is
in most cases to exceed the bounds of experience

[1] Epic. in *Diog.* 78: καὶ μὴν
καὶ τὴν ὑπὲρ τῶν κυριωτάτων αἰτίαν ἐξακριβῶσαι φυσιολογίας ἔργον εἶναι δεῖ νομίζειν καὶ τὸ
μακάριον ἐν τῇ περὶ τῶν μετεώρων
γνώσει ἐνταῦθα πεπτωκέναι· καὶ
ἐν τῷ, τίνες φύσεις αἱ θεωρούμεναι
κατὰ τὰ μετέωρα ταυτί, καὶ ὅσα
συγγενῆ πρὸς τὴν εἰς ταῦτα ἀκρί-
βειαν· ἔτι δὲ καὶ τὸ πλεοναχῶς ἐν
τοῖς τοιούτοις εἶναι [evidently μὴ
εἶναι must be read], καὶ τὸ εὐδεχο-
μένως καὶ ἄλλως πως ἔχειν, ἀλλ᾽
ἁπλῶς μὴ εἶναι ἐν ἀφθάρτῳ καὶ
μακαρίᾳ φύσει τῶν διάκρισιν ὑπο-
βαλλόντων ἢ τάραχον μηθέν· καὶ
τοῦτο καταλαβεῖν τῇ διανοίᾳ ἔστιν
ἁπλῶς οὕτως εἶναι. τὸ δ᾽ ἐν τῇ
ἱστορίᾳ πεπτωκὸς τῆς δύσεως καὶ
ἀνατολῆς καὶ τροπῆς καὶ ἐκλείψεως
καὶ ὅσα συγγενῆ τούτοις μηθὲν ἔτι
πρὸς τὸ μακάριον τῆς γνώσεως συν-
τείνειν (how very different from
Aristotle. See *Zeller,* Philosophie der Griechen, ii. b, 113, 3;
114, 3; 359, 2), ἀλλ᾽ ὁμοίως τοὺς
φόβους ἔχειν τοὺς ταῦτα κατιδόν-
τας τίνες δὲ αἱ φύσεις ἀγνοοῦντας
καὶ τίνες αἱ κυριώταται αἰτίαι, καὶ εἰ
(as if) μὴ προσῄδεσαν ταῦτα, τάχα
δὲ καὶ πλείους, ὅταν τὸ θάμβος ἐκ
τῆς τούτων προκατανοήσεως μὴ
δύνηται τὴν λύσιν λαμβάνειν κατὰ
τὴν περὶ τῶν κυριωτάτων οἰκονομίαν. (Conf. *Lucr.* vi. 50; v. 82.)
διὸ δὴ καὶ πλείους αἰτίας εὑρίσκομεν
τροπῶν, κ.τ.λ. καὶ οὐ δεῖ νομίζειν
τὴν ὑπὲρ τούτων χρείαν ἀκρίβειαν
μὴ ἀπειληφέναι ὅση πρὸς τὸ ἀτάρα-
χον καὶ μακάριον ἡμῶν συντείνει,
κ.τ.λ. *Ibid.* 104: καὶ κατ᾽ ἄλλους δὲ τρόπους πλείονας ἐνδέχε-
ται κεραυνοὺς ἀποτελεῖσθαι. μόνον
ὁ μῦθος ἀπέστω.

and human knowledge, and to go back to the capricious explanations of mythology.[1] Possibly the
world may move, and possibly it may be at rest. Possibly it may be round, or else it may be triangular, or
have any other shape. Possibly the sun and the stars
may be extinguished at setting, and be lighted afresh
at their rising. It is, however, equally possible that
they may only disappear under the earth and reappear again, or that their rising and setting may
be due to yet other causes. Possibly the waxing
and waning of the moon may be caused by the
moon's revolving; or it may be due to an atmospheric change, or to an actual increase and decrease
in the moon's size, or to some other cause. Possibly
the moon may shine with borrowed light, or it may
shine with its own, experience supplying us with
instances of bodies which give their own light, and
of those which have their light borrowed.[2] From
these and such-like statements it appears that
questions of natural science in themselves have no

---

[1] *Ibid.* 87: πάντα μὲν οὖν
γίνεται ἀσείστως κατὰ πάντων,
κατὰ πλεοναχὸν τρόπον ἐκκαθαιρο-
μένων συμφώνως τοῖς φαινομένοις,
ὅταν τις τὸ πιθανολογούμενον ὑπὲρ
αὐτῶν δεόντως καταλίπῃ. ὅταν δέ
τις τὸ μὲν ἀπολίπῃ, τὸ δὲ ἐκβάλῃ
ὁμοίως σύμφωνον ὂν τῷ φαινομένῳ
δῆλον ὅτι καὶ ἐκ παντὸς ἐκπίπτει
φυσιολογήματος ἐπὶ δὲ τὸν μῦθον
καταῤῥεῖ. *Ibid.* 98: οἱ δὲ τὸ ἐν
λαμβάνοντες (those who only
allow one explanation for every
phenomenon) τοῖς τε φανομένοις
μάχονται καὶ τοῦ τί δυνατὸν ἀνθρώπῳ θεωρῆσαι διαπεπτώκασιν. In
investigating nature, they pro-

ceed on suppositions chosen at
random (ἀξιώματα κενὰ καὶ νομο-
θεσίαι, Epic. l. c. 86). Conf. 94;
104; 113. *Lucret.* vi. 703.

[2] Epic. in *Diog.* 88; 92–95.
Many other similar instances
might be quoted. In support of
the view that the sun was extinguished at setting, Epicurus,
according to *Cleomed.* Meteora,
p. 89, is said to have appealed
to the story (respecting which
Posidonius in *Strabo,* iii. 1, 5,
p. 138) that, as it sets, the his-
sing of the ocean may be heard
on the sea-shore.

value for Epicurus. Whilst granting that only one natural explanation of phenomena is generally possible, yet in any particular case he is perfectly indifferent which explanation is adopted.

Great stress is, however, laid by him on the general explanation. In contrast with the religious view which regards the world as a system of means leading to ends, the leading business of the natural science of the Epicureans is to refer all phenomena to natural causes. To an Epicurean nothing appears more absurd than to suppose that the arrangements of nature have for their object the well-being of mankind, or that they have any object at all. The tongue is not given us for the purpose of speaking, nor the ears for the purpose of hearing. As a matter of fact it would, indeed, be more correct to say, that we speak because we have a tongue, and hear because we have ears. Natural powers have acted purely according to the law of necessity, and among their various products, there could not fail to be some presenting the appearance of purpose in their arrangement. In the case of man there have resulted many such resources and powers. But this result is by no means intentional; it is simply an accidental consequence of natural causes. In explaining nature all thought of Gods must be put out of sight, whose happiness is inconceivable, on the supposition that they care for mankind and his welfare.[1]

CHAP. XVII.

(2) *Mechanical explanation of nature.*

---

[1] The principle is thus expanded by *Lucret.* i. 1021 :—
Nam certe neque consilio primordia rerum
Ordine se suo quæque sagaci mente locarunt,
Nec quos quæque darent motus pepigere profecto ·

CHAP.
XVII.

Confining, as Epicurus did, his interest in nature completely to this general view of things, in carrying it into details he was all the more inclined to rely upon some older system. No one, however, appeared better to correspond with his tone of mind than that of Democritus, which, moreover, commended itself to him not only by absolutely banishing the idea of final cause, but in particular by referring everything to matter, and by its theory of atoms. As Epicurus placed in each individual thing taken by itself the ultimate end of action, so Democritus had theoretically made all that is real to consist in what is absolutely individual or in atoms. His natural science, therefore, seemed to present the most na-

Sed quia multa modis multis mutata per omne
Ex infinito vexantur percita plagis,
Omne genus motus et cœtus experiundo,
Tandem deveniunt in tales disposituras,
Qualibus hæc rebus consistit summa creata.

v. 156 :
Dicere porro hominum causa voluisse [*scil.* Deos] parare
Præclaram mundi naturam, &c. Desipere est. Quid enim immortalibus atque beatis
Gratia nostra queat largirier emolumenti,
Ut nostra quidquam causa gerere adgrediantur?
Quidve novi potuit tanto post ante quietos
Inlicere, ut cuperent vitam mutare priorem? . . .
Exemplum porro gignundis rebus et ipsa

Notities hominum, Dis unde est insita primum ; . . .
Si non ipsa dedit specimen natura creandi?

Conf. iv. 820; v. 78 ; 195; 419. In these views, he is only following Epicurus. Heavenly phenomena, says the latter, in *Diog.* 76, μήτε λειτουργοῦντός τινος νομίζειν δεῖ γίνεσθαι καὶ διατάττοντος ἢ διατάξαντος καὶ ἅμα τὴν πᾶσαν μακαριότητα ἔχοντος μετ᾿ ἀφθαρσίας· οὐ γὰρ συμφωνοῦσι πραγματεῖαι καὶ φροντίδες καὶ ὀργαὶ καὶ χάριτες τῇ μακαριότητι, ἀλλ᾿ ἀσθενείᾳ καὶ φόβῳ καὶ προσδεήσει τῶν πλησίον ταῦτα γίνεται. *Ibid.* 97 : ἡ θεία φύσις πρὸς ταῦτα μηδαμῇ προσαγέσθω, ἀλλ᾿ ἀλειτούργητος διατηρείσθω καὶ ἐν τῇ πάσῃ μακαριότητι. *Ibid.* 113. With these passages, *Cic.* N. D. i. 20, 52, and *Plut.* Plac. i. 7, 7 (likewise ii. 3, 2 ; *Stob.* i. 442), are quite in agreement.

tural basis for the Epicurean Ethics. If, therefore,   Chap.
the Stoics had already followed Heraclitus in their   XVII.
views of nature, Epicurus followed Democritus still
more closely, and hence, with the exception of one
single point, the additions made by Epicurus to the
theory of this philosopher are philosophically unimportant.

With Democritus Epicurus agreed in holding   (3) *Atoms
that there is no other form of reality except that of   and empty
space.*
bodily reality. Every substance, he says in the
words of the Stoics, must affect others, and be
affected by them ; and whatever affects others or is
itself affected, is corporeal. Corporeal substance is,
therefore, the only kind of substance.[1] The various
qualities of things, essential ones as well as accidental ones, are not therefore incorporeal existences,
but simply chance modes of body, the former
being called by Epicurus συμβεβηκότα, the latter,
συμπτώματα.[2] But a second something is necessary

---

[1] *Lucr.* i. 440 :—

Præterea per se quodcumque
erit aut faciet quid
Aut aliis fungi [πάσχειν] debe-
bit agentibus ipsum,
Aut erit, ut possint in eo res
esse gerique.
At facere et fungi sine corpore
nulla potest res,
Nec præbere locum porro nisi
inane vacansque.
Ergo præter inane et corpora
tertia per se
Nulla potest rerum in numero
natura relinqui.

Epic. in *Diog.* 67 : καθ᾽ ἑαυτὸ δὲ
οὐκ ἔστι νοῆσαι τὸ ἀσώματον πλὴν

ἐπὶ τοῦ κενοῦ. τὸ δὲ κεκὸν οὔτε
ποιῆσαι οὔτε παθεῖν δύναται, ἀλλὰ
κίνησιν μόνον δι᾽ ἑαυτοῦ τοῖς σώμασι παρέχεται. ὥσθ᾽ οἱ λέγοντες
ἀσώματον εἶναι τὴν ψυχὴν ματαιά-
ζουσιν. οὐθὲν γὰρ ἂν ἐδύνατο ποιεῖν οὔτε πάσχειν εἰ ἦν τοιαύτη.
[2] *Diog.* 68; 40. *Lucr.* i.
449, who expresses συμβεβηκότα
by conjuncta, and συμπτώματα
by eventa. Among the latter,
Lucretius, 459, reckons *time*,
because in itself it is nothing,
and only comes to our knowledge through motion and rest.
Likewise Epicurus, in *Diog.* 72
(conf. *Stob.* i. 252), shows that
time is composed of days and

CHAP.
XVII.

besides corporeal substance in order to explain phenomena, viz. empty space. That empty space exists
is proved by the differences of weight in bodies.
For what else could be the cause of this difference?[1]
It is proved still more conclusively by motion, motion being impossible without empty space.[2] Mind
as a moving cause, however, seems to Epicurus
altogether superfluous. Everything that exists consists of bodies and empty space, and there is no
third thing.[3]

Democritus had resolved the two conceptions of
body and empty space into the conceptions of being
and not being. True to his position, Epicurus dispensed with this speculative basis ; he holds to the
ordinary notions of empty space, and of a material
filling space,[4] and simply proves these notions by

nights, and their portions, of
states of feeling or unconscious-
ness, of motion or rest, and
hence that it is only a product
(σύμπτωμα) of these phenomena;
and these being again συμπτώματα, time is defined by the
Epicurean Demetrius (*Sext.*
Math. x. 219 ; Pyrrh. iii. 137) :
σύμπτωμα συμπτωτάτων παρεπό-
μενον ἡμέραις τε καὶ νυξὶ καὶ ὥραις
καὶ πάθεσι καὶ ἀπαθείαις καὶ κινήσεσι καὶ μοναῖς. The distinction
between abstract and sensuous
or undivided time (*Steinhart,*
l. c. 466) does not appear to
exist in Diogenes. His χρόνοι
διὰ λόγου θεωρητοὶ (*Diog.* 47)
are imperceptibly small divisions of time, tempora multa,
ratio quæ comperit esse, which,
according to *Lucret.* iv. 792, are
contained in every given time.

[1] *Lucret.* i. 358.
[2] *Lucret.* l. c. and i. 329 ;
Diog. 40 and 67 ; *Sext.* Math.
vii. 213 ; viii. 329. Most of the
remarks in *Lucret.* i. 346 and
532 point to the same fundamental idea : Without vacant
interstices, nourishment cannot
be diffused over the whole
bodies of plants or animals,
nor can noise, cold, fire and
water penetrate through solid
bodies, or any body be broken
up into parts. The same in
Themist. 40, b ; *Simpl.* De Cœlo,
Schol. in Arist. 484, a, 26.
[3] *Lucr.* i. 440 ; *Diog.* 39 ;
Plut. Adv. Col. 11, 5.
[4] Body is defined by Epicurus (*Sext.* Math. i. 21 ; x.
240 ; 257 ; xi. 226) as τὸ τριχῆ
διαστατὸν μετὰ ἀντιτυπίας, or as
σύνοδος κατὰ ἀθροισμὸν μεγέθους

the qualities of phenomena. For this very reason
Democritus' division of body into innumerable primary particles or atoms appeared to him most
necessary. All bodies known to us by sensation are
composed of parts.[1] If the process of division were
infinitely continued, all things would ultimately be
resolved into the non-existent—so Epicurus and
Democritus argue;—and conversely all things must
have been formed out of the non-existent, in defiance
of the first principle of natural science that nothing
can come from nothing, and that nothing can be
resolved into nothing.[2] Hence, we must conclude

καὶ σχήματος καὶ ἀντιτυπίας καὶ
βάρους. Emptiness is (according to *Sext.* x. 2) φύσις ἀναφὴς
or ἔρημος παντὸς σώματος. When
occupied by a body, it is called
·· ὅπος; when bodies pass through
it, it is χώρα; so that all three
expressions, as *Stob.* Ecl. i. 388,
rightly observes, are only different names for the same
thing. To the same effect is
the statement in *Plut.* Plac. i.
20.
  [1] Hence, in *Diog.* 69, ἄθροισμα and συμπεφορήμενον are used
of bodies; in *Diog.* 71, all
bodies are called συμπτώματα;
and according to Epicurus
(*Sext.* Math. x. 42), all changes
in bodies are due to local dis-
placement of the atoms. *Plut.*
Amator. 24, 3, p. 769, observes
that Epicurus deals with ἀφὴ
and συμπλοκή, but never with
ἑνότης.
  [2] Epic. in *Diog.* 40: τῶν σωμάτων τὰ μέν ἐστι συγκρίσεις τὰ δ'
ἐξ ὧν αἱ συγκρίσεις πεποίηνται·
ταῦτα δέ ἐστιν ἄτομα καὶ ἀμετά-

βλητα εἴπερ μὴ μέλλει πάντα εἰς
τὸ μὴ ὂν φθαρήσεσθαι, ἀλλ' ἰσχύ-
οντα ὑπομένειν ἐν ταῖς διαλύσεσι
τῶν συγκρίσεων . . . ὥστε τὰς
ἀρχὰς ἀτόμους ἀναγκαῖον εἶναι σωμάτων φύσεις. *Ibid.* 56; *Lucr.*
i. 147; ii. 551; 751; 790. Further arguments for the belief
in atoms in *Lucret.* i. 498:
Since a body and the space in
which it is are entirely different, both must originally
have existed without any intermingling. If things exist composed of the full and the empty,
the full by itself must exist,
and likewise the empty. Bodies
in which there is no empty
space cannot be divided. They
may be eternal, and must be so,
unless things have been produced out of nothing. Without empty space, soft bodies
could not exist, nor hard bodies
without something full. If
there were no indivisible parts,
everything must have been
long since destroyed. The regularity of phenomena presup-

CHAP.
XVII.

that the primary component parts of things can neither have come into existence nor cease to exist, nor yet be changed in their nature.[1] These primary bodies contain no empty space in themselves, and hence can neither be divided nor destroyed, nor be changed in any way.[2] They are so small that they do not impress the senses, and it is a matter of fact that we do not see them. Nevertheless they must not be regarded as mathematical atoms, the name atoms being only assigned to them because their bodily structure will not admit of division.[3] Moreover, they have neither colour, warmth, smell, nor any other property; properties only belonging to distinct materials;[4] and for this reason they must not be sought in the four elements, all of which, as experience shows, come into being and pass away.[5] They only possess the universal qualities of all corporeal things, viz. shape, size, and weight.[6]

poses unchangeable primary elements. All that is composite must ultimately consist of simple indivisible parts. If there were no indivisible parts, every body would consist of innumerable parts as many in the smaller as in the greater body (conf. Epic. in *Diog.* 56). If nature did not reduce things to their smallest parts, it could not make new things. These arguments, very unequal in value, were borrowed by Lucretius from Epicurus. Plut. in *Eus.* Pr. Ev. i. 8, 9, quotes, as an Epicurean principle, that unchangeable Being must be at the bottom of everything.

[1] Epicurus and Lucretius, l. c. *Lucr.* i. 529; *Sext.* Math.

ix. 219; x. 318; *Stob.* Ecl. i. 306; *Plut.* Pl. Phil. i. 3, 29.

[2] Epic. in *Diog.* 41; *Lucret.* i. 528; *Simpl.* De Cœlo, Schol. in Arist. 484, a, 23.

[3] *Diog.* 44 and 55; *Lucret.* i. 266, where it is proved, by many analogies, that there may be invisible bodies; *Stob.* l. c.; *Plut* l. c.; *Simpl.* Phys. 216, a.

[4] *Diog.* 44; 54; *Lucr.* ii. 736 and 841; *Plut.* l. c. See page 433, 2.

[5] *Lucret.* v. 235.

[6] *Diog.*; *Plut.* Plac. i. 3, 29. The statement there made, that Democritus only allowed to atoms size and shape, and that Epicurus added weight, is not a correct one.

Not only must atoms, like all other bodies, have shape, but there must exist among them indefinitely many varieties of shape, or it would be impossible to account for the innumerable differences of things. There cannot, however, be really an infinite number of such shapes, as Democritus maintained, in any limited body, as is intelligible of itself, nor yet in the whole universe,[1] since an unlimited number would make the arrangement of the world impossible, in the world everything being circumscribed by certain extreme limits.[2] Again, atoms must be different in point of size ; for all materials cannot be divided into particles of equal size. Yet even to this difference there must be some bounds. An atom must neither be so large as to become an object of sense, nor can it, after what has been said, be infinitely small.[3] From difference in point of size the difference of atoms in point of weight follows.[4] In point of number atoms must be unlimited, and in the same way empty space must be unbounded also. For since everything bounded must be bounded by something, it is impossible to imagine any bounds of the universe beyond which nothing exists, and hence there can be no bounds at all. The absence

---

[1] *Diog.* 42 ; *Lucr.* ii. 333 and 478; *Plut.* Plac. i. 3, 30 (where, however, it would be against the sense to substitute ἤ for μὴ as *Steinhart* l. c. p. 473 note 94 does); Alex. Aphr. in *Phi op.* Gen. et Corr. 3, b ; *Cic.* N. D. i. 24, 66. It does not, however, appear that *Lucret.* ii. 333, made the variety of

figures as great as the number of atoms. (*Ritter*, iv. 101.)

[2] *Lucret.* i. 500.

[3] *Diog.* x. 55 ; *Lucr.* ii. 381.

[4] See the passages quoted, p. 442, 6, and 445, 5. The text of *Stobæus*, Ecl. i. 346, must be corrected by the aid of these passages. *Plut.* Plac. i. 12, 5.

of bounds must apply to the mass of atoms quite as much as to empty space. If an indefinite number of atoms would not find room in a limited space, conversely a limited number of atoms would be lost in empty space, and never able to form a world.[1] In all these views Epicurus closely follows Democritus, no doubt, agreeing with him also in explaining the qualities of things by the composition of their atoms.[2]

B. *The world.*
(1) *The swerving aside of atoms.*

In deducing the origin of things from their primary causes, Epicurus, however, deviates widely from his predecessor. Atoms—so it was taught by both—have by virtue of their weight been eternally engaged in a downward motion.[3] That all bodies

[1] Epic. in *Diog.* 41: ἀλλὰ μὴν καὶ τὸ πᾶν ἄπειρόν ἐστι· τὸ γὰρ πεπερασμένον ἄκρον ἔχει· τὸ δ' ἄκρον παρ' ἕτερόν τι θεωρεῖται. ὥστε οὐκ ἔχον ἄκρον πέρας οὐκ ἔχει, πέρας δ' οὐκ ἔχον ἄπειρον ἂν εἴη καὶ οὐ πεπερασμένον. The same argument is used by *Lucret.* i. 951; 1008–1020. He continues 984, 1021: If space were limited, all bodies would collect towards its lower part by reason of their weight, and their motion would cease. Unless the quantity of matter were unlimited, the amount lost by bodies in their mutual contact could not be supplied. Conf. also *Plut.* Adv. Col. 13, 3; in *Eus.* Pr. Ev. i. 8, 9; Plac. i. 3, 28; Alex. in *Simpl.* Phys. 107, b, who mentions the argument of Epicurus quoted above as the chief argument of the Epicureans.

[2] We have but little information; but it has been already shown, p. 433, 2, and

follows too as a matter of course, that he referred all the properties of bodies to the shape and arrangement of the atoms. Whenever he found in the same body different qualities combined, he assumed that it was composed of different kinds of atoms. For instance, he asserted of wine: οὐκ εἶναι θερμὸν αὐτοτελῶς τὸν οἶνον, ἀλλ' ἔχειν τινὰς ἀτόμους ἐν αὐτῷ θερμασίας ἀποτελεστικὰς, ἑτέρας δ' αὖ ψυχρότητος. According to the difference of constitution, it has on some a cooling, on others a heating effect. *Plut.* Qu. Conviv. iii. 5, 1, 4; Adv. Col. 6. This agrees with the remarks made on Democritus in vol. i. 597.

[3] *Diog.* 43; 47; *Cic.* N. D. i. 20, 54. What idea Epicurus formed to himself of motion we are not told. We learn, however, from *Themist.* Phys. 52, b, that he replied to Aristotle's proof of motion, that no

should move downwards in empty space seemed to Epicurus a matter of course; for whatever is heavy must fall unless it is supported.[1] He was therefore opposed to the Aristotelian view that heaviness shows itself in the form of attraction towards a centre, and consequently to his further supposition that downward mode of motion only belongs to certain bodies, circular motion being for others more natural.[2] The objection that in endless space there is no above or below he could only meet by appealing to experience,[3] some things always appearing above our heads, others beneath our feet.[4] But whilst Democritus held that atoms in their downward motion meet together, thus giving rise to a rotatory motion, no such view commended itself to Epicurus. Nay rather all atoms will fall equally fast, since empty space offers no resistance, and falling perpendicularly it is impossible to see how they can meet.[5] To render a meeting possible he supposed the

constant quantities can be composed of indivisible particles (Phys. vi. 1), by saying : Whatever moves in a given line moves in the whole line, but not in the individual indivisible portions of which the line consists. With reference to the same question, the Epicureans, according to *Simpl.* Phys. 219, b, asserted that everything moves equally quickly through indivisible spaces.

[1] *Cic.* Fin. i. 6, 18; *Lucret.* i. 1074.

[2] *Lucr.* ii. 1052 (the text being faulty); *Simpl.* De Cœlo, Schol. in Arist. 510, b, 30; 486,

a, 7. The latter writer inaccurately groups Epicurus together with others (Democritus and Strato). The same point, according to *Simpl.* Phys. 113, b, divided Alexander of Aphrodisias and the Epicurean Zenobius, at the close of the second century after Christ.

[3] As Aristotle had already done.

[4] *Diog.* 60; conf. *Plut.* Def. Orac. 28, p. 425.

[5] Epic. in *Diog.* 43; 61; *Lucr.* ii. 225; *Plut.* C. Not. 43, 1, p. 1082. This objection was borrowed from Aristotle by Epicurus.

smallest possible swerving aside from the perpendicular line in falling. This assumption seemed to him indispensable, since it would be otherwise impossible to assert the freedom of the human will. For how can the will be free if everything falls according to the strict law of gravity? And for the same reason this swerving aside was not supposed to proceed from any natural necessity, but simply from the power of self-motion in the atoms.[1] In consequence of their meeting one part of the atoms rebounds—so Democritus also taught; the lighter ones are forced upwards, and from the upward and downward motions combined a rotatory motion arises.[2] When this motion takes place a clustering of atoms is the consequence, which by their own motion separate themselves from the remaining mass, and form a world of themselves.[3] Atoms being eternal and unchangeable, the process of forming worlds must go on without beginning or end;[4] and inasmuch as they are also infinite in number, and empty space is infinite also, there must be an innumerable number of worlds.[5] In the

[1] *Lucr.* ii. 216; 251; *Cic.* Fin. i. 6, 18; N. D. i. 25, 69; De Fato, 10, 22; *Plut.* An. Proct. 6, 9, p. 1015; Solert. Anim. 7, 2, p. 964; Plac. i. 12, 5; 23, 4; *Stobæus*, Ecl. i. 346, 394.

[2] *Diog.* 44; conf. 62; 90; *Plut.* Plac. i. 12, 5; Fac. Lun. 4, 5, p. 921; *Stob.* i. 346; *Lucret.* v. 432.

[3] *Diog.* 73; *Lucr.* i. 1021. See above p. 437, 1; *Plut.* Def. Or. 19, p. 420.

[4] *Cic.* Fin. i. 6, 17. See p. 444, 3.

[5] *Diog.* 45; 73; *Lucret.* ii. 1048; *Plut.* Plac. ii. 1, 3. It need hardly be remarked that by worlds world-bodies are hardly meant. In *Diog.* 88, Epicurus defines the world as a part of the heaven, surrounding the earth and stars, having a definite shape, and, towards other parts of the heaven, bounded.

character of these worlds the greatest possible variety may be supposed, since it is most unlikely
that the innumerable combinations of atoms all
brought about at random will fall out alike.
Equally impossible is it to assert that all these
worlds are absolutely dissimilar. In general, Epicurus assumed that they are extremely different both
in point of size and arrangement, and that here and
there one may be similar to our own.[1] Moreover,
since eternity affords time for all imaginable combinations of atoms, nothing can ever be brought
about now which has not already existed.[2] In one
respect all worlds are alike; they come into existence,
are liable to decay, and, like all other individual
elements, are exposed to a gradual increase and
decrease.[3] So we might have assumed from other
positions in his system. Between the individual
worlds both Democritus and Epicurus insert intermediate world-spaces, in which by the clustering
of atoms from time to time new worlds come into
being.[4]

The origin of our world is thus described. At a
certain period of time—Lucretius[5] believes at no
very distant period—a cluster of atoms of varying

[1] *Diog.* 45; 74; 88; *Plut.*
Plac. ii. 2, 2 ; 7, 3 ; *Stob.* i. 490;
Cic. N. D. ii. 18, 48 ; Acad. ii.
40, 125.

[2] Plut. in *Eus.* Pr. Ev. i. 8,
9 : Epicurus says, ὅτι οὐδὲν ξένον
ἀποτελεῖται ἐν τῷ παντὶ παρὰ τὸν
ἤδη γεγενημένον χρόνον ἄπειρον.

[3] *Diog.* 73 ; 89 ; *Lucret.* ii.
1105 ; v. 91 and 235, where the
transitory character of the

world is elaborately proved;
Cic. Fin. i. 6, 21. *Stob.* i. 418;
Epicurus makes the world decay in the greatest variety of
ways. *Plut.* Plac. ii. 4, 2.

[4] *Diog.* x. 89.

[5] v. 324, arguing that historical memory would otherwise go much further back, and
arts and sciences be of much
greater antiquity.

shape and size was formed in this definite portion of
space. These atoms meeting, there first arose from
the pressure and rebound of the quickly-falling
particles motions of every variety in every direction.
Soon the greater atoms pressing downwards, by dint
of weight forced upwards the smaller and lighter
atoms, the fiery ones topmost and with the greatest
impetus to form the ether, and afterwards those
which form the air.[1] The upper pressure ceasing,
these masses under the pressure of particles still
joining it from below, spread forth sidewards, and
thus the belts of fire and air were formed. Next
uprose those atoms out of which the sun and stars
are formed into the heights, and at the same time
the earth settled down, its inner part being partially
exhausted in those places where the sea now is. By
the influence of the warmth of the ether, and the
sun-heat, the earth-mass was bound together more
closely, the sea was pressed out of it, and the surface
assumed an uneven character.[2] The world is shut

[1] On this point see *Lucret.*
ii. 1112. The principle that
similar elements naturally con-
gregate is there explained in
this way.

[2] *Lucr.* v. 416–508; *Plut.*
Plac. i. 4. The latter view has
been referred, in vol. i. 604, to
the Atomists. It would now
appear that it must be deduced
from Epicureanism, and its
agreement with the views attributed to Leucippus in other
places explained by the well-
known connection between Epicurus and Democritus. The

views of Epicurus on the formation of the world do not
entirely agree with those of
Democritus. It was probably
with an eye to Democritus
(compare the extracts in vol. i.
608 from *Orig.* Philosoph. p.
17) that Epicurus, in *Diog.* 90,
denied that the world could be
increased from without, or that
sun and moon could in this way
be possibly absorbed in our
world. *Lucret.* ii. 1105, however, supposes an increase of
the world from without to be
possible.

off from other worlds and from empty space by those bodies which form its external boundary.[1]

Asking, in the next place, what idea must be formed of the arrangement of the world, we are met by the two principles which Epicurus is never weary of inculcating; one, that we must deduce nothing from an intentional arrangement by deity, but refer everything simply and solely to mechanical causes; the other, that in explaining phenomena the widest possible scope must be given to hypotheses of every kind, and that nothing is more absurd than to abridge the extensive range of possible explanations by exclusively deciding in favour of any one.[2] Thereby the investigation of nature loses for him its value as such, nor is it of any great interest to us to follow his speculations on nature into detail. On one point he enters a protest, viz., that the framework of heaven must not be considered the work of God,[3] nor must life and reason be attributed to the stars.[4] Otherwise, on nearly all the questions which engaged the attention of astronomers at that time, he observes the greatest indifference, treating the views of his predecessors, good and bad alike, with an easy superficiality which can only be explained by supposing him altogether careless[5] as to their truth. The state

CHAP.
XVII.

(3) *Arrangement of the universe.*

---

[1] On these moenia mundi, which, according to Lucretius, coincide with the ether or firebelt, see Epic. in *Diog.* 88; *Id.* περὶ φύσεως, xi. (Vol. Herc. ii.) col. 2; *Plut.* Plac. ii. 7, 3; *Lucr.* i. 73; ii. 1144; v. 454.

[2] On this point see page 434.

[3] See p. 437, 1.

[4] In *Diog.* 77; 81; *Lucret.* v. 78 and 114, where the contrast is more fully brought out. By ζῷα οὐράνια, in *Plut.* Plac. v. 20, 2, we must by no means think of the stars.

[5] Examples have already been met with, p. 436. A complete review of the Epicurean

of his own astronomical knowledge can, moreover, be easily seen by recalling the notorious assertion [1] that the sun, the moon, and the stars are either not at all, or only a little larger, and may possibly be even less than they appear to be. The Epicureans also thought to support their theory that the earth, borne by the air, reposes in the middle of the world —a theory which on their hypothesis of the weight of bodies is impossible [2]—by the gradual diminution in weight of the surrounding bodies.[3] It would be impossible here to go through the treatment which they gave to atmospheric and terrestrial phenomena, particularly as the principle already indicated was most freely used, and many explanations were given as being all equally possible.[4]

astronomy is not worth our while. It may be studied in the following passages : For the substance of the stars, consult *Plut.* Plac. ii. 13, 9 ; for their rising and setting, *Diog.* 92 ; *Lucr.* v. 648 ; *Cleomed.* Met. p. 87; for their revolution and deviation, *Diog.* 92 ; 112–114 ; *Lucr.* v. 509 ; 612 ; for the appearance of the moon, *Diog.* 94, and *Lucr.* v. 574, 703 ; for eclipses of sun and moon, *Diog.* 96 ; *Lucr.* v. 749 ; for changes in the length of day, *Diog.* 98 ; *Lucr.* v. 678.

[1] *Diog.* 91 ; *Cic.* Acad. ii. 26, 82 ; Fin. i. 6, 20 ; *Sen.* Qu. Nat. i. 3, 10 ; *Cleomed.* Met. ii. 1 ; *Plut.* Plac. ii. 21, 4 ; 22, 4 ; *Lucr.* v. 564. The body of the sun was considered by Epicurus (*Plut.* Plac. ii. 20, 9 ; *Stob.* i. 530) to consist of earth-like and spongy matter, saturated

with fire. According to *Lucret.* v. 471, sun and moon stand midway between ether and earth in point of density.

[2] It is still more difficult to imagine the world as stationary, which is tacitly assumed. It would then be bounded by endless space, and soon come into collision with other masses.

[3] *Lucr.* v. 534. Conf. Epic. in *Diog.* 74, and περὶ φύσεως, xi. col. 1. In the latter passage, Epicurus appeals to the fact that the earth is equidistant from the bounds of the world.

[4] Further particulars: on clouds, *Diog.* 99 ; *Lucr.* vi. 451; *Plut.* Plac. iii. 4, 3 ; on rain, *Diog.* 100 ; *Lucret.* vi. 495 ; on thunder, *Diog.* 100 ; 103 ; *Lucret.* vi. 96 ; on lightning, *Diog.* 101 ; *Lucr.* vi. 160 ; on sirocco, *Diog.* 104 ; *Lucr.* vi. 423 ; Plac. iii. 3, 2 ; on earthquakes, *Diog.*

Out of the newly-made earth plants at first grew,[1] and afterwards animals came forth, since the latter, according to Lucretius, can by no possibility have fallen from heaven.[2] In other worlds, likewise, living beings came into existence, though not necessarily in all.[3] Among these beings were originally, as Empedocles had previously supposed,[4] all sorts of composite or deformed creatures. Those, however, alone continued to exist which were fitted by nature to find support, to propagate, and to protect themselves from danger. Romantic creatures, such as centaurs or chimæras, can never have existed here, because the beings of which they are compounded would require conditions of life [5] altogether different.

Aiming, as the Epicureans did, at explaining the origin of men and animals in a purely natural manner, they likewise tried to form an idea, equally according to nature, of the original state and historical development of the human race, ignoring in this

CHAP. XVII.

(4) *Plants and animals.*

C. *Mankind.*

(1) *Origin of the*

105; *Lucr.* vi. 535; Plac. iii. 15, 11; *Sen.* Nat. Qu. vi. 20, 5; on winds, *Diog.* 106; on hail, *Diog.* 106; Plac. iii. 4, 3; on snow, thaw, ice, frost, *Diog.* 107–109; on the rainbow, *Diog.* 109; on the halo of the moon, *Diog.* 110; on comets, *Diog.* 111; on shooting-stars, *Diog.* 114. Explanations are given by Lucretius of volcanoes (vi. 639), of the overflow of the Nile (vi. 712), of Lake Avernus (vi. 738–839), of the magnet (vi. 906–1087), of the reputed chilling of the springs in summer (vi. 840).
  [1] *Lucret.* ii. 1157; v. 780.

Otherwise, we learn that the Epicureans attributed to plants a soul, just as little as the Stoics. *Plut.* Plac. v. 26, 3.
  [2] *Lucr.* ii. 1155; v. 787, giving further particulars as to the origin and maintenance of living beings, and the subsequent abatement of the productive powers of earth.
  [3] Epic. in *Diog.* 74.
  [4] Anaximander, Parmenides, Anaxagoras, Diogenes, of Apollonia, and Democritus, all taught the procreation of living beings from earth.
  [5] *Lucr.* v. 834–921.

attempt all legendary notions. On this point, notwithstanding their leaning towards materialism, they
on the whole advocated perfectly sound views. The
men of early times, so thought Lucretius, were
stronger and more powerful than the men of to-day.
Rude and ignorant as beasts, they lived in the woods
in a perpetual state of warfare with wild animals,
without justice or society.[1] The first and most important step in a social direction was the discovery
of fire, the learning to build huts, and to clothe
themselves in skins, when marriage and domestic
life began,[2] when speech, originally not a matter of
convention, but, like the noises of animals, the natural expression of thoughts and feelings, was developed.[3] The older the human race grew, the more
they learned of the arts and skill which minister to
the preservation and enjoyment of life. These arts
were first learnt by experience, under the pressure of
nature, or the compulsion of want. What had thus
been discovered was completed by reflection, the
more gifted preceding the rest as teachers.[4] In ex-

---

[1] v. 922–1008. Conf. *Plato,*
Polit. 274, B; *Arist.* Polit. ii.
8, 1269, a, 4; *Horace,* Serm. i.
3, 99, appears to have had an
eye to Lucretius.

[2] *Lucr.* v. 1009–1025.

[3] Epicurus, in *Diog.* 75, thus
sums up his views on the origin
of language: τὰ ὀνόματα ἐξ
ἀρχῆς μὴ θέσει γενέσθαι, ἀλλ'
αὐτὰς τὰς φύσεις τῶν ἀνθρώπων
καθ' ἕκαστα ἔθνη ἴδια πασχούσας
πάθη καὶ ἴδια λαμβανούσας φαντάσματα ἰδίως τὸν ἀέρα ἐκπέμπειν
. . ὕστερον δὲ κοινῶς καθ' ἕκαστα

τὰ ἔθνη τὰ ἴδια τεθῆναι πρὸς τὸ
τὰς δηλώσεις ἧττον ἀμφιβόλους
γενέσθαι ἀλλήλοις καὶ συντομω-
τέρως δηλουμένας. He who in-
vents any new thing puts, at
the same time, new words into
circulation. *Lucret.* v. 1026–
1088, explains more fully that
language is of natural origin.
On the voice, *Ibid.* iv. 522;
Plut. Plac. iv. 19, 2.

[4] Epic. in *Diog.* 75: ἀλλὰ μὴν
ὑποληπτέον καὶ τὴν τῶν ἀνθρώπων
φύσιν πολλὰ καὶ παντοῖα ὑπὸ τῶν
αὐτὴν περιεστώτων πραγμάτων δι

actly the same way civil society was developed. Individuals built strongholds, and made themselves rulers.
In time the power of kings aroused envy, and they
were massacred. To crush the anarchy which then
arose, magistrates were chosen, and order established
by penal laws.[1] It will subsequently be seen that
Epicurus explained religion in the same way by natural growth.

The apotheosis of nature, which has been apparent in Epicurus's whole view of history, becomes
specially prominent in his treatment of psychology.
This treatment could, after all that has been said, be
only purely materialistic. (The soul, like every other
real being, is a body.) In support of this view the

CHAP.
XVII.

(2) *The
soul.*

δαχθῆναί τε καὶ ἀναγκασθῆναι· τὸν
δὲ λογισμὸν τὰ ὑπὸ ταύτης παρεγ-
γυηθέντα καὶ ὕστερον ἐπακριβοῦν
καὶ προσεξευρίσκειν, ἐν μέν τισι
θᾶττον ἐν δέ τισι βραδύτερον.

Lucr. v. 1450 :—all arts
Usus et impigræ simul experien-
tia mentis
Paulatim docuit.

Ibid. 1103 :—
Inque dies magis hi victum vi-
tamque priorem
Commutare novis monstrabant
rebu' benigni
Ingenio qui præstabant et corde
vigebant.

In harmony with these premises, Lucretius then tries to
explain various inventions. The
first fire was obtained by lightning, or the friction of branches
in a storm. The sun taught
cooking (v. 1089). Forests on
fire, melting brass, first taught

men how to work in metal (v.
1239–1294). Horses and ele-
phants were used for help in
war, after attempts had been
previously made with oxen and
wild beasts (v. 1295). Men
first dressed themselves in
skins; afterwards they wore
twisted, and then woven materials (v. 1009; 1348; 1416).
The first ideas of planting and
agriculture were from the natural spread of plants (v. 1359).
The first music was in imitation
of birds; the first musical instrument was the pipe, through
which the wind was heard
to whistle; from this natural
music, artificial music only gradually grew (v. 1377). The
measure and arrangement of
time was taught by the stars
(v. 1434); and, comparatively
late, came the arts of poetry
and writing (v. 1438).
[1] *Lucr.* v. 1106.

Epicureans appealed to the mutual relations of the body and the soul, agreeing on this point with the Stoics.[1] The body of the soul, however, consists of the finest, lightest, and most easily-moved atoms, as is manifest from the speed of thought, from the instantaneous dissolution of the soul after death, and, moreover, from the fact that the soulless body is as heavy as the body in which there is a soul.[2] Hence Epicurus, again agreeing with the Stoics, describes the soul as a material resembling fire and air,[3] or, more accurately, as composed of four elements, fire, air, vapour, and a fourth nameless element. It consists of the finest atoms, and is the cause of feeling,[4] and according as one or other of these elements preponderates, the character of man is of one or the other kind.[5] Like the Stoics, Epicurus believed that the soul-element is received by generation from the parents' souls,[6] and that it is spread over the whole body,[7] growing as the body grows.[8] At the same time he makes a distinction somewhat similar to that made by the Stoics in their doctrine of the

---

[1] *Lucr.* iii. 161; *Diog.* 67. See p. 439, 1.

[2] *Lucr.* iii. 177; *Diog.* 63.

[3] *Diog.* 63 : ἡ ψυχὴ σῶμά ἐστι λεπτομερὲς παρ' ὅλον τὸ ἄθροισμα (the body), παρεσπαρμένον· προσεμφερέστατον δὲ πνεύματι θερμοῦ τινα κρᾶσιν ἔχοντι. 66 : ἐξ ἀτόμων αὐτὴν συγκεῖσθαι λειοτάτων καὶ στρογγυλοτάτων πολλῷ τινι διαφερουσῶν τῶν τοῦ πυρός.

[4] *Lucr.* iii. 231; 269; *Plut.* Plac. iv. 3, 5 (*Stob.* i. 798), conf. *Alex. Aphr.* De An. 127, b.

[5] *Lucr.* iii. 288.

[6] According to *Plut.* Plac. v. 3, 5, he considered the seed an ἀπόσπασμα ψυχῆς καὶ σώματος; and, since he believed in a feminine σπέρμα, he must have regarded the soul of the child as formed by the intermingling of the soul-atoms of both parents. *Ibid.* v. 16, 1.

[7] *Diog.* 63; *Lucret.* iii. 216; 276; 323; 370.

[8] *Metrodor.* περὶ αἰσθητῶν (Vol. Herc. vi.), col. 7.

sovereign part of the soul (ἡγεμονικόν).[1] Only the
irrational part of the soul is diffused as a principle
of life over the whole body; the rational part has its
seat in the breast.[2] To the rational part belongs
mental activity, sensation, and perception, the motion
of the will and the mind, and in this latter sense life
itself; both parts together make up one being, yet
they may exist in different conditions. The mind
may be cheerful whilst the body and the irrational
soul feel pain, or the reverse may be the case. It is
even possible that portions of the irrational soul may
be lost by the mutilation of the body, without detriment to the rational soul, or consequently to life.[3]
When, however, the connection between soul and
body is fully severed, then the soul can no longer
exist. Deprived of the surrounding shelter of the
body, its atoms are dispersed in a moment, owing to
their lightness; and the body in consequence, being
unable to exist without the soul, goes over into corruption.[4] If this view appears to hold out the most

---

[1] *Lucr.* iii. 98, contradicts
the assertion that the soul is
the harmony of the body; Epicurus having already replied
(in *Philop.* De An. E. 1) to one
of the objections urged against
it by Plato.

[2] *Diog.* 66; *Lucr.* iii. 94;
136; 396; 613; *Plut.* Plac. iv.
4, 3. Lucretius calls the rational part animus or mens, and
the irrational part anima. The
statement, Pl. Phil. iv. 23, 2,
that Epicurus made feeling reside in the organs of sense, because the ἡγεμονικὸν was feel-
ingless, can hardly be correct.

[3] *Diog.* and *Lucr.* In sleep,
a portion of the soul is supposed
to leave the body (*Lucr.* iv.
913, conf. *Tertull.* De An. 43),
whilst another part is forcibly
confined within the body. Probably this is all that is meant
by *Diog.* 66.

[4] Epic. in *Diog.* 64. *Lucr.*
iii. 417–827, gives an elaborate
proof of the mortality of the
soul. Other passages, *Plut.*
N. P. Suav. Vivi. 27, 1 and 3;
30, 5; *Sext.* Math. ix. 72, hardly
need to be referred to. Observe the contrast between Epicureanism and Stoicism. In

gloomy prospect for the future, Epicurus considers
that it cannot really be so. With life every feeling
of evil ceases,[1] and the time when we shall no longer
exist affects us just as little as the time before we
existed.[2] Nay, more, he entertains the opinion that
his teaching alone can reconcile us to death by re-
moving all fear of the nether world and its terrors.[3]

Allowing that many of these statements are natural consequences of the principles of Epicurus, the
distinction between a rational and an irrational soul
must, nevertheless, at first sight seem strange in a
system so thoroughly materialistic as was that of the
Epicureans. And yet this distinction is not stranger
than the corresponding parts of the Stoic teaching. If
the Stoic views may be referred to the distinction
which they drew in morals between the senses and the
reason, not less are the Epicurean ethics marked by
the same contrast between the general and the sensuous side of the mind. Hence Epicurus shares the
Stoic belief in an etherial origin of the human race ;[4]

Stoicism, the soul keeps the
body together; in Epicureanism, the body the soul. In
Stoicism, the soul survives the
body; in Epicureanism, this is
impossible. In Stoicism, the
mind is a power over the world,
and hence over the body; in
Epicureanism, it is on a level
with the body, and dependent
on it.

[1] Epic. in *Diog.* 124–127, for
instance : τὸ φρικωδέστατον οὖν
τῶν κακῶν ὁ θάνατος οὐδὲν πρὸς
ἡμᾶς· ἐπειδήπερ ὅταν μὲν ἡμεῖς
ὦμεν ὁ θάνατος οὐ πάρεστιν·
ὅταν.δὲ ὁ θάνατος παρῇ τόθ' ἡμεῖς

οὐκ ἐσμέν. *Id.* in *Sext.* Pyrrh.
iii. 229 (*Alex. Aphr.* Anal. Pri.
117, Top. 9. *Gell.* N. A. ii. 8,
1 ; *Stob.* Serm. 118, 30) : ὁ θάνατος οὐδὲν πρὸς ἡμᾶς· τὸ γὰρ δια-
λυθὲν ἀναισθητεῖ, τὸ δὲ ἀναισθη-
τοῦν οὐδὲν πρὸς ἡμᾶς. *Lucr.* iii.
828–975.

[2] *Lucr.* iii. 830.

[3] *Diog.* 81 ; 142 ; *Lucr.* iii.
37.

[4] *Lucr.* ii. 991 :—
Denique cœlesti sumus omnes
　　semine oriundi, &c.
999 :—
Cedit item retro de terra quod
　　fuit ante

and although this belief as at first expressed only
implies that man, like other living beings, is
composed of etherial elements, yet there is connected
with it the distinction already discused in the case
of the Stoics between the higher and the lower
parts of man, which ultimately comes to be simply
another mode of expressing the difference between
mind and matter.

Among the phenomena of the soul's life sen- (3) *Sensa-*
sation is made to harmonise with the general prin- *tion.*
ciples of the Epicurean view of nature by the aid
of Democritus' doctrine of atom-pictures (εἴδωλα).
From the surface of bodies—this is the pith of that
doctrine—the finest possible particles are constantly
being thrown off, which by virtue of their fineness,
traverse the furthest spaces in an infinitely short
time, hurrying through the void.[1] Many of these
exhalations are arrested by some obstacle soon after
their coming forth, or are otherwise thrown into
confusion. In the case of others the atoms for a
long time retain the same position and connection
which they had in bodies themselves, thus presenting
a picture of things, and only lacking corporeal
solidity. As these pictures are conveyed to the soul
by the various organs of sense, our impressions of
things arise.[2] Even these impressions, which have

In terras: et quod missum est
  ex ætheris oris
Id rursum cœli rellatum templa receptant.
  [1] Democritus, from whom
Epicurus has borrowed the rest

of this theory, makes them
mould the air.
  [2] Epic. in *Diog.* 46-50 ; 52 ;
and in the fragments of the
second book περὶ φύσεως ; *Lucr.*
iv. 26-266 ; 722; vi. 921. *Cic.* Ad

458   *THE EPICUREANS.*

CHAP.
XVII.

no corresponding real object, must be referred to
such pictures present in the soul.[1] For often pictures last longer than things themselves;[2] and often
by a casual combination of atoms pictures are formed
in the air resembling no one single thing. Sometimes, too, pictures of various kinds are combined on
their way to the senses; thus, for instance, the
notion of a Centaur is caused by the union of the
picture of a man with that of a horse, not only in
our imagination, but already previously in the atom-
picture.[3] If, therefore, sensation distorts or imperfectly represents real objects, it must be explained
as being due to some change or mutilation in the
atom-pictures before they reach our senses.[4]

In thus explaining mental impressions, the Epicureans do not allow themselves to be disturbed by
the fact that we can recall at pleasure the ideas of
all possible things. The cause of this power was
rather supposed to be the circumstance that we are
always surrounded by an innumerable number of
atom-pictures, none of which we perceive unless our
attention is directed to them. Likewise the seeming

Famil. xv. 16; *Plut.* Qu. Conviv. viii. 10, 2, 2; Plac. iv. 3, 1;
19, 2; *Sext.* Math. vii. 206;
Gell. N. A. v. 16; *Macrob.* Sat.
vii. 14; the remarks of *Lucr.*
iv. 267; 568; *Plut.* Plac. iv. 14,
2, on reflected images and the
echo belong likewise to the
doctrine of idola.

[1] For instance, the impressions in the minds of dreamers
and madmen. *Diog.* 32; *Lucr.*
iv. 730.

[2] *Plut.* Def. Orac. 19, p. 420:
εἰ δὲ χρὴ γελᾶν ἐν φιλοσοφίᾳ τὰ
εἴδωλα γελαστέον τὰ κωφὰ καὶ
τυφλὰ καὶ ἄψυχα, ἃ ποιμαίνουσιν
[sc. οἱ Ἐπικούρειοι] ἀπλέτους ἐτῶν
περιόδους ἐμφαινόμενα καὶ περινοσ-
τοῦντα πάντῃ τὰ μὲν ἔτι ζώντων
τὰ δὲ πάλαι κατακαέντων ἢ κα-
τασαπέντων ἀποῤῥυέντα.

[3] *Lucr.* l. c.

[4] *Sext.* l. c.; *Lucr.* iv.
351.

motion of forms which we behold in dreams is
explained by the hasty succession of similar atom-
pictures, appearing to us as changes of one and the
same picture.[1] But besides receiving pictures supplied from without, spontaneous motion with regard
to these pictures takes place on our part, a motion
connected in the first instance with the soul's
motion when it receives the outward impression,
but not to be regarded as a simple continuation
thereof. This independent motion gives rise to
opinion, and hence opinion is not so necessary or so
universally true as feeling. It may agree with feeling, or it may not agree with it. It may be true or
it may be false.[2] The conditions of its being true
or false have been previously investigated.[3]

Impressions also give rise to will and action, the
soul being set in motion by impressions, and this
motion extending from the soul to the body.[4] Into
the nature of will, however, Epicurus does not
appear to have instituted a more careful psychological investigation. It was enough for him to
assert the freedom of the will. This freedom he
considers absolutely indispensable, if anything we

CHAP.
XVII.

(4) *Will.*

---

[1] *Lucr.* iv. 766–819; and on
the incessant streaming forth
of images, v. 141; *Diog.* 48.

[2] Epic. in *Diog.* x. 51: τὸ δὲ
διημαρτημένον οὐκ ἂν ὑπῆρχεν, εἰ
μὴ ἐλαμβάνομεν καὶ ἄλλην τινὰ
κίνησιν ἐν ἡμῖν αὐτοῖς συνημμένην
μὲν, διάληψιν [al. διάλειψιν] δ'
ἔχουσαν κατὰ δὲ ταύτην τὴν
συνημμένην τῇ φανταστικῇ ἐπι-
βολῇ [impression on the senses],
διάληψιν δ' ἔχουσαν ἐὰν μὲν μὴ

ἐπιμαρτυρηθῇ ἢ ἀντιμαρτυρηθῇ τὸ
ψεῦδος γίνεται, ἐὰν δὲ ἐπιμαρτυρηθῇ ἢ μὴ ἀντιμαρτυρηθῇ τὸ
ἀληθές.

[3] As to terminology, Epicurus, according to *Plut.* Plac.
iv. 8, 2, *Diog.* 32, called the
faculty of sensation αἴσθησις,
and sensation itself, ἐπαίσθημα.

[4] *Lucr.* iv. 874; conf. *Galen.*
De Hipp. et Plat. v. 2, vol. v.
367, κ.

do is to be considered our own, if we are not
prepared to despair of moral responsibility altogether,
and to resign ourselves to a comfortless and inexorable necessity.[1] To make freedom possible, Epicurus
had introduced accident into the motion of atoms as
we have seen, and for the same reason he denies the
truth of disjunctive propositions which apply to the
future.[2] In the latter respect, he, no doubt, only
attacked the material truth of two clauses, without
impugning the formal accuracy of the disjunction,[3]
i.e., he did not deny that of two contradictory cases
either one or the other must happen, nor did he
deny the truth of saying: To-morrow Epicurus will
either be alive or not alive. But he disputed the
truth of each clause taken by itself. He denied the
truth of the sentence, Epicurus will be alive; and
equally that of the contradictory, Epicurus will not
be alive; on the ground that the one or the other
statement only *becomes* true by the actual realisation
of an event at present uncertain.[4] For this he

[1] *Diog.* 133 : τὸ δὲ παρ' ἡμᾶς
ἀδέσποτον· ᾧ καὶ τὸ μεμπτὸν καὶ
τὸ ἐναντίον παρακολουθεῖν πέφυκεν.
ἐπεὶ κρεῖττον ἦν τῷ περὶ θεῶν μύθῳ
κατακολουθεῖν ἢ τῇ τῶν φυσικῶν
εἱμαρμένῃ δουλεύειν.

[2] *Cic.* N. D. i. 25, 70 : [Epi-
curus] pertimuit, ne si conces-
sum esset hujusmodi aliquid :
aut vivet cras aut non vivet
Epicurus, alterutrum fieret ne-
cessarium ; totum hoc ; aut
etiam aut non negavit esse ne-
cessarium. Acad. ii. 30, 97 ;
De Fat. 10, 21.

[3] *Steinhart*, p. 466.

[4] *Cic.* De Fato, 16, 37, at

least says, referring to the above
question : Nisi forte voluimus
Epicureorum opinionem sequi,
qui tales propositiones nec veras
nec falsas esse dicunt, aut cum
id pudet illud tamen dicunt,
quod est impudentius, veras
esse ex contrariis disjunctiones,
sed quæ in his enuntiata essent
eorum neutrum esse verum.
Cicero indeed adds : O admira-
bilem licentiam et miserabilem
inscientiam dicendi ! but he
has no reason for this exclama-
tion; for the proposition :
Either A or B must follow is
not identical with the proposi-

deserves little blame. Our real charge against him
is that he did not more thoroughly investigate the
nature of the will and the conception of freedom,
and that he treats the subject of the soul as scantily
and superficially as he had treated the subject of
nature.

tion : It may be stated either of   allow the former and deny the
A or of B that it will follow.   latter. In so doing he is really
Epicurus could, therefore, justly   following Aristotle.

CHAPTER XVIII.

VIEWS OF EPICURUS ON RELIGION.

CHAP.
XVIII.

A. *Criticism of the gods and the popular faith.*

SATISFIED with the results of his own enquiries into nature, Epicurus hoped by his view of the causes of things not only to displace the superstitions of a polytheistic worship, but also to uproot the prejudice in favour of Providence. Indeed, these two objects were placed by him on exactly the same footing. So absurd did he consider the popular notions respecting the Gods, that far from blaming those who attacked them,[1] he believed it impious to acquiesce in them. Religion being, according to Lucretius, the cause of the greatest evils,[2] he who displaces it to make way for rational views of nature deserves praise as having overcome the most dangerous

---

[1] *Diog.* x. 123: οἵους δ' αὐ-τοὺς [τοὺς θεοὺς] οἱ πολλοὶ νομί-ζουσιν οὐκ εἰσίν· οὐ γὰρ φυλάτ-τουσιν αὐτοὺς οἵους νομίζουσιν. ἀσεβὴς δὲ οὐχ ὁ τοὺς τῶν πολλῶν θεοὺς ἀναιρῶν ἀλλ' ὁ τὰς τῶν πολ-λῶν δόξας θεοῖς προσάπτων. Conf. *Cic.* N. D. i. 16, 42.

[2] iii. 14; vi. 49; and, specially, the celebrated passage i. 62:—

Humana ante oculos fœde cum vita jaceret

In terris oppressa gravi sub rel-ligione,
Quæ caput a cœli regionibus ostendebat
Horribili super aspectu morta-libus instans, &c.

as far as to 101 :—

Tantum relligio potuit suadere malorum.

Conf. Epic. in *Diog.* 81, and above, p. 423, 3 ; 437, 1.

enemy of mankind. All the language of Epicurus in disparagement of the art of poetry applies in a still higher degree to the religious errors fostered by poetry.[1] Nor is it better with belief in Providence than with the popular faith. This belief is also included in the category of romance ;[2] and the doctrine of fatalism, which was the Stoic form for the same belief, was denounced as even worse than the popular faith.[3] For how, asks the Epicurean, could divine Providence have created a world in which evil abounds, in which virtue often fares ill, whilst vice is triumphant ? How could a world have been made for the sake of man, when man can only inhabit a very small portion of it ? How could nature be intended to promote man's well-being when it so often imperils his life and labour, and sends him into the world more helpless than any animal ? How can we form a conception of beings ruling over an infinite universe, and everywhere present to administer everything in every place?[4] What could have induced these beings to create a world, and how and whence could they have known how to create it, had not nature supplied them with an example?[5] In fine, how

---

[1] *Heraclit.* Alleg. Hom. c. 4: ['Επίκουρος] ἅπασαν ὁμοῦ ποιητικὴν ὥσπερ ὀλέθριον μύθων δέλεαρ ἀφοσιούμενος. *Ibid.* c. 75.

[2] *Plut.* Def. Orac. 19, p. 420: 'Επικουρείων δὲ χλευασμοὺς καὶ γέλωτας οὔτι φοβητέον οἶς τολμῶσι χρῆσθαι καὶ κατὰ τῆς προνοίας μῦθον αὐτὴν ἀποκαλοῦντες. N. P. Suav. Viv. 21, 2: διαβάλλοντες τὴν πρόνοιαν ὥσπερ παισὶν Ἐμπουσαν ἡ Ποινὴν ἀλιτηριώδη καὶ τραγικὴν ἐπιγεγραμμένην. In

Cic. N. D. i. 8, 18, the Epicurean calls πρόνοια anus fatidica, to which it was often reduced, no doubt, by the Stoics.

[3] See p. 460, 1.

[4] *Lucr.* . v. 196 ; ii. 1090 ; *Plut.* Plac. i. 7, 10. Conf. the disputation of the Stoic and Epicurean in *Lucian*, Jup. Trag. c. 35, and especially c. 46.

[5] *Lucr.* v. 165 ; conf. p. 437, 1 ; *Plut.* Plac. i. 7, 8.

CHAP.
XVIII.

B. *The
gods ac-
cording to
Epicurus.*
(1) *Rea-
sons for
his belief.*

could God be the happy Being He must be if the whole burden of caring for all things and all events lay upon Him, or He were swayed to and fro together with the body of the world?[1]   Or how could we feel any other feeling but that of fear in the presence of such a God who troubles himself about everything?[2]

With the denial of the popular Gods, the denial of demons,[3] of course, goes hand in hand, and, together with Providence, the need of prayer[4] and of prophecy is at the same time negatived.[5]   All these notions, according to Epicurus, are the result of ignorance and fear.   Pictures seen in dreams have been confounded with real existences; regularity of motion in the heavenly bodies has been mistaken by the ignorant for the work of God; events which accidentally happened in combination with others have been regarded as portents; terrific natural phenomena, storms and earthquakes, have engendered in men's minds the fear of higher powers.[6]   Fear is therefore the basis of religion;[7] and, on the other hand, freedom from fear is the primary object aimed at by philosophy.

For all that, Epicurus was unwilling to renounce

[1] *Diog.* 76; 97; 113; see p. 437, 1; *Cic.* N. D. i. 20, 52; *Plut.* Plac. i. 7, 7.
[2] *Cic.* l. c. 54.
[3] *Plut.* Def. Or. 19; Plac. i. 83.
[4] Conf. the captious argument of Hermarchus, in *Procl.* in Tim. 66, E: If prayer is necessary for everything, it is necessary for prayer, and so on, ad infin.
[5] *Diog.* 135; *Lucr.* v. 379; *Plut.* Plac. v. 1, 2; *Cic.* N. D. i. 20, 55; Divin. ii. 17, 40; *Tertull.* De An. 46.
[6] *Lucr.* v. 1159–1238; conf. iv. 33; vi. 49; *Sext.* Math. ix. 25; vi. 19; *Diog.* 98; 115.
[7] This view is especially prominent in Lucretius. See p. 462, 2. Conf. *Plut.* N. P. Suav. Viv. 21, 10; *Cic.* N. D. i. 20, 54.

belief in the Gods,[1] nor is it credible that this un-
willingness was simply a yielding to popular opinion.[2]
The language used by the Epicureans certainly gives
the impression of sincerity; and the time was past
when avowed atheism was attended with danger.
Atheism would have been as readily condoned in the
time of Epicurus as the deism which denied most
unreservedly the popular faith. It is, however, possible to trace the causes which led Epicurus to
believe that there are Gods. There was first the
general diffusion of a belief in Gods which appeared
to him to establish the truth of this belief, and hence
he declared the existence of Gods to be something
directly certain, and grounded on a primary notion
($\pi\rho\delta\lambda\eta\psi\iota s$).[3] Moreover, with his materialistic theory
of knowledge he no doubt supposed that the primary
notion which convinces us of the existence of Gods
arises from the actual contemplation of divine beings,
and from the perception of those atom-pictures from
which Democritus had already deduced the belief in
Gods.[4] And in addition to these theoretical reasons,

[1] He drew up separate trea-
tises περὶ θεῶν and περὶ ὁσιότητος.
Diog. 27 ; *Cic.* N. D. i. 41, 115 ;
Plut. N. P. Suav. Viv. 21, 11.

[2] Posidonius, in *Cic.* N. D.
i. 44, 123 ; Conf. 30, 85 ; iii.
1, 3 ; *Plut.*, l. c.

[3] Epic. in *Diog.* 123 : θεοὶ μὲν
γάρ εἰσι · ἐναργὴς μὲν γάρ ἐστιν
αὐτῶν ἡ γνῶσις. The Epicurean
in *Cic.* N. D. i. 16, 43 : Solus
enim [Epicurus] vidit, primum
esse Deos quod in omnium animis eorum notionem impressis-
set ipsa natura. Quæ est enim

gens aut quod genus hominum
quod non habeat sine doctrina
anticipationem quandam Deorum ? quam appellat πρόληψιν
Epicurus, &c. These statements
must, however, be received with
some caution, since Cicero appears to give up his own views
as to innate ideas. Inasmuch
however as he expressly refers
to Epicurus' treatise περὶ κανό-
νος, we may assume that belief
in Gods with Epicurus rests on
a general πρόληψις.

[4] In support of this view,

CHAP. XVIII.

Epicurus had also another, half æsthetical, half religious—the wish to see his ideal of happiness realised in the person of the Gods,[1] and it is this ideal which determines the character of all his notions respecting the Gods. His Gods are therefore, throughout, human beings. Religious belief only knows beings such as these, or, as Epicurus expresses it, only such beings come before us in those pictures of the Gods which present themselves to our minds, sometimes in sleep, sometimes when we are awake. Reflection, too, convinces us that the human form is the most beautiful, that to it alone reason belongs, and that it is the most appropriate form for perfectly happy beings.[2] Epicurus even went so far as to attribute to the Gods difference of sex.[3] At the same time everything must be eliminated which is not appropriate to a divine being.

see *Cic.* N. D. i. 18, 46. It is there said of the form of the Gods: A natura habemus omnes omnium gentium speciem nullam aliam nisi humanam Deorum. Quæ enim alia forma occurrit umquam aut vigilanti cuiquam aut dormienti? φυσικὴ πρόληψις is here referred to sensations derived from εἴδωλα. *Ibid.* 19, 49; and *Lucr.* vi. 76: De corpore quæ sancto simulacra feruntur In mentis hominum divinæ nuntia formæ.

[1] *Diog.* 121. *Cic.* N. D. i. 17, 45: Si nihil aliud quæreremus, nisi ut Deos pie coleremus et ut superstitione liberaremur, satis erat dictum: nam et præstans Deorum natura hominum pietate coleretur, cum et æter-

na esset et beatissima . . . et metus omnis a vi atque ira Deorum pulsus esset. *Ibid.* 20, 56: We do not fear the Gods, et pie sancteque colimus naturam excellentem atque præstantem. *Ibid.* 41, 115. *Sen.* Benef. iv. 19, 3: Epicurus denied all connection of God with the world, but, at the same time, would have him honoured as a father, propter majestatem ejus eximiam singularemque naturam.

[2] *Cic.* N. D. i. 18, 46; Divin. ii. 17, 40; *Sext.* Pyrrh. iii. 218; *Plut.* Pl. Phil. i. 7, 18 (*Stob.* i. 66); *Phædr.* (Philodem.) Fragm. col. 7; *Metrodorus*, περὶ αἰσθη-τῶν (Vol. Herc. vi.), col. 10; col. 16, 21.

[3] *Cic.* N. D i. 34, 95.

The two essential characteristics of the Gods, according to Epicurus, are immortality and perfect happiness.[1] Both of these characteristics would be impaired were we to attribute to the bodies of the Gods the same dense corporeity which belongs to our own. We must, therefore, only assign to them a body analogous to our body, etherial, and consisting of the finest atoms.[2] Such bodies would be of little use in a world like ours. In fact, they could not live in any world without being exposed to the temporal ruin which will in time overwhelm it, and, meantime, to a state of fear, which would mar their bliss. Epicurus, therefore, assigns to them the space between the worlds as their habitation, where, as Lucretius remarks, troubled by no storms, they live under a sky ever serene.[3]

Nor can these Gods be supposed to care for the world and the affairs of men, else their happiness would be marred by the most distressing occupations; but perfectly free from care and trouble, and absolutely regardless of the world, in eternal contemplation of their unchanging perfection, they enjoy the most unalloyed happiness.[4] The view which the

---

[1] Epic. in *Diog.* 123 : πρῶτον μὲν τὸν θεὸν ζῷον ἄφθαρτον καὶ μακάριον νομίζων . . . μηδὲν μήτε τῆς ἀφθαρσίας ἀλλότριον μήτε τῆς μακαριότητος ἀνοίκειον αὐτῷ πρόσαπτε, κ.τ.λ. *Ibid.* 139. *Cic.* N. D. i. 17, 45 ; 19, 51 ; *Lucr.* ii, 646; v. 165.

[2] *Cic.* N. D. ii. 23, 59 ; i. 18, 49 ; 25, 71 ; 26, 74 ; Divin. ii. 17, 40 ; *Lucr.* v. 148 ; *Metrodor.* περὶ αἰσθητῶν, col. 7 ; *Plut.* l. c.

Epicurus has, as Cicero remarks, monogrammos Deos; his Gods have only quasi corpus and quasi sanguinem. They are perlucidi and perflabiles, or, according to Lucr., tenues, so that they cannot be touched, and are indestructible.

[3] *Cic.* Divin. ii. 17, 40; *Lucr.* ii. 646 ; iii. 18 ; v. 146 ; *Sen.* Benef. iv. 19, 2.

[4] Epic. in *Diog.* 77 ; 97:

CHAP.
XVIII.

School formed to itself of this happiness we learn from Philodemus.[1] The Gods are exempt from sleep, sleep being a partial death, and not needed by beings who live without any exertion. And yet he believes that they require nourishment, though this must, of course, be of a kind suited to their nature. They also need dwellings,[2] since every being requires some place wherein to dwell. Were powers of speech to be refused to them, they would be deprived of the highest means of enjoyment—the power of conversing with their equals. Philodemus thinks it probable they use the Greek or some other closely-allied language.[3] In short, he imagines the Gods to be a society of Epicurean philosophers, who have everything that they can desire—everlasting life, no care, and perpetual opportunities of sweet converse. Only such Gods,—the Epicureans thought,[4]—need not be feared. Only such Gods are free and pure, and wor-

139; *Cic.* N. D. i. 19, 51 (amongst other things: nos autem beatam vitam in animi securitate et in omnium vacatione munerum ponimus, both of which features must therefore be attributed to the Gods); *Legg.* i. 7, 21; *Lucr.* ii. 646; iii. 1092; iv. 83; vi. 57; *Sen.* Benef. iv. 4, 1; 19, 2. Conf. p. 436; 464, 1; 466, 1.

[1] In the fragments of his treatise περὶ τῆς τῶν θεῶν εὐστοχουμένης διαγωγῆς, κατὰ Ζήνωνα, col. 12.

[2] The κλίσια discussed by Hermarchus and Pythocles, col. 13, 20, had reference to these, and not to ordinary feasts.

[3] Col. 14: The reason being

assigned that λέγονται μὴ πολὺ διαφερούσαις κατὰ τὰς ἀρθρώσεις χρῆσθαι φωναῖς, καὶ μόνον οἴδαμεν γεγονότας θεοὺς Ἑλληνίδι γλώττῃ χρωμένους. The first statement seems to refer to the words of the divine language quoted by Homer; the second statement, to stories of appearances of the Gods. For the whole tone of the system militates against our thinking of men who have afterwards become Gods. The sceptical question, Whether the Gods possess speech? raised by Carneades in *Sext.* Math. ix. 178, appears to refer to this μυθολογία Ἐπικούρου.

[4] *Cic.* N. D. i. 20, 54; *Sen.* Benef. iv. 19, 1.

shipped because of this very perfection.[1] Moreover, these Gods are innumerable. If the number of mortal beings is infinite, the law of counterpoise requires that the number of immortal beings must not be less.[2] If we have only the idea of a limited number of Gods, it is because, owing to their being so much alike,[3] we confound in our minds the innume-

---

[1] *Philodem.* De Mus. iv. (V. Herc. i.) col. 4, says that the Gods do not need this worship, but it is natural for us to show it : μάλιστα μὲν ὁσίαις προλήψεσιν, ἔπειτα δὲ καὶ τοῖς κατὰ τὸ πάτριον παραδεδομένοις ἑκάστῳ τῶν κατὰ μέρος.

[2] *Cic.* l. c. i. 19, 50, the sentence, et si quae interimant, belonging, however, to Cicero only. For Epicurus cannot have described his ease-taking Gods as sustainers of the universe.

[3] *Cic.* N. D. i. 19, 49 : (Epicurus) docet eam esse vim et naturam Deorum ut primum non sensu sed mente cernatur : nec soliditate quadam nec ad numerum ut ea, quae ille propter firmitatem στερέμνια appellat, sed imaginibus similitudine et transitione perceptis: cum infinita simillimarum imaginum species ex innumerabilibus individuis exstat et ad Deos (probably instead of Deos, which gives no sense, we should read nos. See the commentators in the editions of Moser and Kreuzer) affluat, cum maximis voluptatibus in eas imagines mentem intentam infixamque nostram intelligentiam capere quae sit et beata natura et aeterna. The meaning of

these words appears to be, that ideas of the Gods are not formed in the same way as the ideas of other solid bodies, by a number of similar pictures from the same object striking our senses (nec soliditate nec ad numerum, *Diog.* x. 95), but by single pictures emanating from innumerable divine individuals, all so much alike, that they leave behind them the impressions of perfect happiness and immortality. The passage of *Diog.* x. 139, ought probably to be corrected by that in Cicero. It runs : ἐν ἄλλοις δέ φησι, τοὺς θεοὺς λόγῳ θεωρητοὺς εἶναι· οὒς μὲν κατ' ἀριθμὸν ὑφεστῶτας, οὒς δὲ κατὰ ὁμοειδίαν ἐκ τῆς συνεχοῦς ἐπιρρύσεως τῶν ὁμοίων εἰδώλων ἐπὶ τὸ αὐτὸ ἀποτετελεσμένους ἀνθρωποειδῶς. The similarity of most of the expressions leaves no doubt that Diogenes followed the same authority as Cicero (probably the same as *Plut.* Plac. i. 7, 18 followed), but in the words οὒς μὲν κ.τ.λ., it asserts the very opposite of this and the Epicurean teaching. There must, therefore, be some error here, either due to Diogenes or a copyist. This error does not apparently belong to the words κατ' ἀριθμὸν, which Cicero renders ad numerum, so that

rable pictures of the Gods which are conveyed to our souls.

Priding themselves in contrast to the Stoics on their agreement by means of this theology with the anthropomorphic views of the popular belief, and even outdoing polytheism in the assumption of innumerable Gods,[1] the Epicureans were willing to join in the customary services of religion,[2] without being nearly so anxious as the Stoics to prove themselves in harmony with the popular creed. Whilst the Stoics in their anxiety to do this had plunged head over heels into allegory, no such tendency is observed on the part of the Epicureans. Only the poet of the School gives a few allegorical interpretations of mythical ideas, and does it with more taste and skill than is usual with the Stoics.[3]

Steinhart's suggestion, p. 477 καθ' ἁρμὸν or καθ' ἁρμοὺς is clearly wrong. It is more probably to be found in the words οὓς μὲν —οὓς δέ. We might suggest for οὓς μὲν. οὐ μέντοι.

[1] In *Phædrus* (*Philodem.* περὶ εὐσεβείας), Fragm. col. 7 (10) it is said in answer to the Stoics: ἐπιδεικνύσθωσαν τοῖς πολλοῖς ἕνα μόνον [θεὸν] ἅπαντα λέγοντες οὐδὲ πάντας ὅσους ἢ κοινὴ φήμη παρέδωκεν, ἡμῶν οὐ μόνον ὅσους φασὶν οἱ Πανέλληνες ἀλλὰ καὶ πλείονας εἶναι λεγόντων· ἔπειθ' ὅτι τοιούτους οὐδὲ μεμήκασιν ἀπολείπειν, οἵους σέβονται πάντες καὶ ἡμεῖς ὁμολογοῦμεν. ἀνθρωποειδεῖς γὰρ ἐκεῖνοι οὐ νομίζουσιν ἀλλὰ ἀέρα καὶ πνεύματα καὶ αἰθέρα, ὥστ' ἔγωγε καὶ τεθαρρηκότως εἴπαιμι τούτους Διαγόρου μᾶλλον πλημμελεῖν. It is then shown how little the natural substances of the Stoics resemble Gods (col. 9): τὰ θεῖα τοιαῦτα καταλείπουσιν ἃ καὶ γεννητὰ καὶ φθαρτὰ φαίνεται, τοῖς δὲ πᾶσιν ἡμεῖς ἀκολούθως ἀϊδίους κἀφθάρτους εἶναι δογματίζομεν. Here we have a phenomenon witnessed in modern times, Deists and Pantheists mutually accusing one another of atheism, the former missing personality, the latter missing activity in the deity of their opponents.

[2] See p. 469, 1.

[3] *Lucr.* ii. 598, explains the Mother of the Gods as meaning the earth. ii. 655, he allows the expressions, Neptune, Ceres, Bacchus, for the sea, corn, and wine. iii. 976, he interprets the pains of the nether-world as the qualms now brought on by superstition and folly.

On other points the Epicureans, not excluding Lucretius, observe towards the popular faith a negative attitude, that of opposing it by explanations; and by this attitude, without doubt, they rendered one of the most important services to humanity.

CHAPTER XIX.

THE MORAL SCIENCE OF THE EPICUREANS.   GENERAL
PRINCIPLES.

CHAP.
XIX.

A. *Plea-
sure.*
(1) *Plea-
sure the
highest
good.*

NATURAL science is intended to overcome the prejudices which stand in the way of happiness; moral
science to give positive instructions as to the nature
and means of attaining to happiness. The speculative parts of the Epicurean system had already worked
out the idea that reality belongs only to individual
things, and that all general order must be referred
to the accidental harmony of individual forces. The
same idea is now met with in the sphere of morals,
individual feeling being made the standard, and individual well-being the object of all human activity.
Natural science, beginning with external phenomena,
went back to the secret principles of these phenomena, accessible only to thought. It led from an
apparently accidental movement of atoms to a universe of regular motions. Not otherwise was the
course followed by Epicurus in moral science. Not
content with human feelings alone, nor with selfishly
referring everything to the individual taken by himself alone, that science, in more accurately defining the
conception of well-being, ascertained that the same

can only be found by rising superior to feelings and
purely individual aims, and by that very process of
referring consciousness to itself and its universal
being, which the Stoics declared to be the only path
to happiness. It is for us now to portray this development of the Epicurean platform in its most prominent features.

The only unconditional good, according to Epicurus, is pleasure; the only unconditional evil is
pain.[1] No proof of this proposition seemed to him
to be necessary; it rests on a conviction supplied by
nature herself, and is the ground and basis of all our
doing and not doing.[2] If proof, however, were required, he appealed to the fact that all living beings
from the first moment of their existence pursue pleasure and avoid pain,[3] and that consequently pleasure
is a natural good, and the normal condition of every
being.[4] Hence follows the proposition to which Epicurus in common with all the philosophers of plea-

[1] Epic. in *Diog.* 128: τὴν ἡδονὴν ἀρχὴν καὶ τέλος λέγομεν εἶναι
τοῦ μακαρίως ζῆν . . . πρῶτον
ἀγαθὸν τοῦτο καὶ σύμφυτον . . .
πᾶσα οὖν ἡδονὴ . . . ἀγαθόν. . . .
καθάπερ καὶ ἀλγηδὼν πᾶσα κακόν.
Ibid. 141. *Cic.* Fin. i. 9, 29;
Tusc. v. 26, 73: Cum præser-
tim omne malum dolore defi-
niat, bonum voluptate.

[2] *Diog.* 129: ταύτην γὰρ ἀγαθὸν
πρῶτον καὶ συγγενικὸν ἔγνωμεν
καὶ ἀπὸ ταύτης καταρχόμεθα πάσης
αἱρέσεως καὶ φευγῆς καὶ ἐπὶ ταύτην
καταντῶμεν ὡς κανόνι τῷ πάθει
τὸ ἀγαθὸν κρίνοντες. *Plut.* Adv.
Col. 27, 1.

[3] *Diog.* 137; *Cic.* Fin. i. 7,

23; 9, 30; ii. 10, 31; *Sext.*
Pyrrh. iii. 194; Math. xi. 96.

[4] *Stob.* Ecl. ii. 58: τοῦτο δ'
[the τέλος] οἱ κατ' Ἐπίκουρον
φιλοσοφοῦντες οὐ προσδέχονται
λέγειν ἐνεργούμενον, διὰ τὸ παθητικὸν ὑποτίθεσθαι τὸ τέλος, οὐ
πρακτικόν· ἡδονὴ γάρ· ὅθεν καὶ
τὴν ἔννοιαν ἀποδιδόασι τοῦ τέλους,
τὸ οἰκείως διατεθεῖσθαι ἐξ ἑαυτοῦ
πρὸς αὑτὸν χωρὶς τῆς ἐπ' ἄλλο τε
ἁπάσης ἐπιβολῆς. *Alex. Aphr.*
De An. 154, a: τοῖς δὲ περὶ Ἐπίκουρον ἡδονὴ τὸ πρῶτον οἰκεῖον
ἔδοξεν εἶναι ἁπλῶς· προϊόντων δὲ
διαρθροῦσθαι ταύτην τὴν ἡδονήν
φασι.

sure appealed, that pleasure must be the object of
life.

At the same time, this proposition was restricted
in the Epicurean system by several considerations.
In the first place, neither pleasure nor pain are simple
things. There are many varieties and degrees of
pleasure and pain, and the case may occur in which
pleasure has to be secured by the loss of other pleasures, or even by pain, or in which pain can only be
avoided by submitting to another pain, or at the cost
of some pleasure. In this case Epicurus would have
the various feelings of pleasure and pain carefully
estimated, and in consideration of the advantages
and disadvantages which they confer, would under
circumstances advise the good to be treated as an
evil, and the evil as a good. He would have pleasure forsworn if it would entail a greater corresponding pain, and pain submitted to if it holds out the
prospect of greater pleasure.[1] He also agrees with
Plato in holding that every positive pleasure presupposes a want, i.e. a pain which it proposes to
remove ; and hence he concludes that the real aim
and object of all pleasure consists in obtaining freedom from pain,[2] and that the good is nothing else

---

[1] *Diog.* 129; *Cic.* Fin. i. 14,
48; Tusc. v. 33, 95; *Sen.* De
Otio, 7, 3.
[2] Epic. in *Diog.* 139 (*Gell.*
N. A. ii. 9, 2): ὅρος τοῦ μεγέθους
τῶν ἡδονῶν ἡ παντὸς τοῦ ἀλγοῦν-
τος ὑπεξαίρεσις. *Id.* in *Diog.*
128: τούτων γὰρ [τῶν ἐπιθυμιῶν]
ἀπλανὴς θεωρία πᾶσαν αἵρεσιν καὶ
φυγὴν ἐπαναγαγεῖν οἶδεν ἐπὶ τὴν

τοῦ σώματος ὑγίειαν καὶ τὴν τῆς
ψυχῆς ἀταραξίαν. ἐπεὶ τοῦτο τοῦ
μακαρίως ζῆν ἐστι τέλος. τούτου
γὰρ χάριν ἅπαντα πράττομεν ὅπως
μήτε ἀλγῶμεν μήτε ταρβῶμεν· ὅταν
δὲ ἅπαξ τοῦτο περὶ ἡμᾶς γένηται
λύεται πᾶς ὁ τῆς ψυχῆς χειμὼν
οὐκ ἔχοντος τοῦ ζῴου βαδίζειν ὡς
πρὸς ἐνδέον τι . . . τότε γὰρ
ἡδονῆς χρείαν ἔχομεν, ὅταν ἐκ τοῦ

but emancipation from evil.[1] By a Cyrenaic neither
repose of soul nor freedom from pain, but a gentle
motion of the soul or positive pleasure was proposed
as the object of life; and hence happiness was not
made to depend on man's general state of mind, but
on the sum-total of his actual enjoyments. But
Epicurus, advancing beyond this position, recognised
both the positive and the negative side of pleasures,
both pleasure as repose, and pleasure as motion.[2]
Both aspects of pleasure, however, do not stand on
the same footing in his system. On the contrary,
the essential and immediate cause of happiness is
repose of mind — ἀταραξία. Positive pleasure is
only an indirect cause of ἀταραξία in that it removes the pain of unsatisfied craving.[3] This mental
repose, however, depends essentially on the character
of a man's mind, just as conversely positive pleasure
in systems so materialistic must depend on sensuous
attractions. It was consistent, therefore, on the part
of Aristippus to consider bodily gratification the
highest pleasure; and conversely Epicurus was no

μὴ παρεῖναι τὴν ἡδονὴν ἀλγῶμεν·
ὅταν δὲ μὴ ἀλγῶμεν οὐκέτι τῆς
ἡδονῆς δεόμεθα. *Ibid.* 131; 144;
conf. *Plut.* N. P. Sua. Viv. 3,
10; *Stob.* Serm. 17, 35; *Lucr.*
ii. 14; *Cic.* Fin. i. 11, 37.
    [1] Epicurus and Metrodorus,
in *Plut.* l. c. 7, 1.
    [2] *Diog.* 136, quotes the words
of Epicurus : ἡ μὲν γὰρ ἀταραξία
καὶ ἀπονία καταστηματικαί εἰσιν
ἡδοναί, ἡ δὲ χαρὰ καὶ εὐφροσύνη
κατὰ κίνησιν ἐνεργείᾳ βλέπονται.
Ritter. iii. 469, suggests instead

of ἐνεργείᾳ ἐναργείᾳ, but ἐνεργείᾳ
gives a very fair meaning: they
appear actually in motion. *Sen.*
Ep. 66, 45 : Apud Epicurum
duo bona sunt, ex quibus summum illud beatumque componi-
tur, ut corpus sine dolore sit,
animus sine perturbatione.
    [3] Hence *Sen.* Brevit. Vit. 14,
2 : Cum Epicuro quiescere.
Benef. iv. 4, 1 : Quæ maxima
Epicuro felicitas videtur, nihil
agit.

less consistent in subordinating it to gratification of mind.

In calling pleasure the highest object in life, says Epicurus, we do not mean the pleasures of profligacy, nor, indeed, sensual enjoyments at all, but the freedom of the body from pain, and of the soul from disturbance. Neither feasts nor banquets, neither the lawful nor unlawful indulgence of the passions, nor the joys of the table, make life happy, but a sober judgment, investigating the motives for action and for inaction, and dispelling those greatest enemies of our peace, prejudices. The root from which it springs, and, therefore, the highest good, is intelligence.[1] It is intelligence that leaves us free to acquire possession thereof, without being ever too early or too late.[2] Our indispensable wants are simple, little being necessary to ensure freedom from pain ; other things only afford change in enjoyment, by which the quantity is not increased, or else they rest on a mere sentiment.[3] The little we need may be easily attained.

B. Intellectual happiness.
(1) Intelligence.

[1] *Diog.* 131. Similar views are expressed by Metrodorus, in *Clement*, Strom. v. 614, B, in praise of philosophers who escape all evils by rising to the contemplation of the eternal καθαροὶ καὶ ἀσήμαντοι τούτου, ὃ νῦν σῶμα περιφέροντες ὀνομάζομεν. *Id.* in *Plut.* Adv. Col. 17, 4 : ποιήσωμέν τι καλὸν ἐπὶ καλοῖς, μόνον οὐ καταδύντες ταῖς ὁμοιοπαθείαις καὶ ἀπαλλαγέντες ἐκ τοῦ χαμαὶ βίου εἰς τὰ 'Επικούρου ὡς ἀληθῶς θεόφαντα ὄργια.

[2] Epic in *Diog.* 122 : μήτε νέος τις ὢν μελλέτω φιλοσοφεῖν μήτε γέρων ὑπάρχων κοπιάτω φιλοσο-

φῶν· οὔτε γὰρ ἄωρος οὐδείς ἐστιν οὔτε πάρωρος πρὸς τὸ κατὰ ψυχὴν ὑγιαῖνον. He who says it is too early or too late to study philosophy means πρὸς εὐδαιμονίαν ἢ μήπω παρεῖναι τὴν ὥραν ἢ μηκέτι εἶναι. *Id.* in *Sen.* Ep. 8, 7 : Philosophiæ servias oportet, ut tibi contingat vera libertas.

[3] Epic. in *Diog.* 127 : τῶν ἐπιθυμιῶν αἱ μέν εἰσι φυσικαὶ αἱ δὲ κεναί· καὶ τῶν φυσικῶν αἱ μὲν ἀναγκαῖαι αἱ δὲ φυσικαὶ μόνον. τῶν δὲ ἀναγκαίων αἱ μὲν πρὸς εὐδαιμονίαν εἰσὶν ἀναγκαῖαι, αἱ δὲ πρὸς τὴν τοῦ σώματος ἀοχλησίαν, αἱ δὲ πρὸς αὐτὸ τὸ ζῆν. *Ibid.* 149,

Nature makes ample provision for our happiness,
would we only receive her gifts thankfully, not for-
getting what she gives in thinking what we desire.[1]
He who lives according to nature is never poor; the
wise man living on bread and water has no reason to
envy Zeus;[2] chance has little hold on him; with him
judgment is everything,[3] and if that be right, he
need trouble himself but little about external mis-
haps.[4] Not even bodily pain appeared to Epicurus
so irresistible as to be able to cloud the wise man's
happiness. Although he regards as unnatural the
Stoic's insensibility to pain,[5] still he is of opinion that
the wise man may be happy on the rack, and can
smile at pains the most violent, exclaiming in the
midst of torture, How sweet![6] A touch of forced
sentiment may be discerned in the last expression,
and a trace of self-satisfied exaggeration is manifest
even in the beautiful language of the dying philosopher on the pains of disease.[7] Nevertheless, the

further particulars are given as
to the classes. *Ibid.* 144; *Lucr.*
ii. 20; *Cic.* Fin. i. 13, 45; Tusc.
v. 33, 94; *Plut.* N. P. Sua. Viv.
3, 10; *Eustrat.* Eth. N. 48, b;
Sen. Vit. Be. 13, 1.
  [1] *Sen.* Benef. iii. 4, 1: Epicuro . . . qui adsidue queritur,
quod adversus præterita simus
ingrati. Epic. in *Sen.* Ep. 15,
10: Stulta vita ingrata est et
trepida, tota in futurum fertur;
and *Lucr.* iii. 929.
  [2] *Diog.* 11; 130; 144; 146;
Stob. Floril. 17; 23; 30; 34;
Sen. Ep. 2, 5; 16, 7; 25, 4.
  [3] *Diog.* 144: βραχεία σοφῷ
τύχη παρεμπίπτει, τὰ δὲ μέγιστα

καὶ κυριώτατα ὁ λογισμὸς διῴκηκε.
The like in *Stob.* Ecl. ii. 354;
Cic. Fin. i. 19, 63; *Sen.* De
Const. 15, 4; Epicurus and
Metrodorus in *Cic.* Tusc. v. 9,
26, and *Plut.* Aud. Po. 14, p.
37.
  [4] *Diog.* 135: κρεῖττον εἶναι
νομίζων εὐλογίστως ἀτυχεῖν ἢ ἀλο-
γίστως εὐτυχεῖν.
  [5] *Plut.* N. P. Sua. Viv. 20, 4.
  [6] *Diog.* 118; *Plut.* l. c. 3, 9;
Sen. Ep. 66, 18; 67, 15; *Cic.*
Tusc. v. 26, 73.
  [7] *Diog.* 22, *Cic.* Fin. ii. 30,
96, Tusc. ii. 7, 17; *M. Aurel.*
ix. 41; *Sen.* Ep. 66, 47; 92, 25;
Plut. N. P. Sua. Viv. 18, 1, the

CHAP.
XIX.

principle involved is based in the spirit of the Epicurean philosophy, and borne out by the testimony
of the founder. The main thing, according to Epicurus, is not the state of the body, but the state of
the mind; bodily pleasure being of short duration,
and having much about it to unsettle; mental enjoyments only being pure and incorruptible. For the
same reason mental sufferings are more severe than
those of the body, since the body only suffers from
present ills, whilst the soul feels those past and
those to come.[1] In a life of limited duration the
pleasures of the flesh never attain their consum-
mation. Mind only, by consoling us for the limited
nature of our bodily existence, can produce a life
complete in itself, and not standing in need of unlimited duration.[2]

(2) Rea-
sons for
rising
superior to
the senses.

At the same time, the Epicureans, if consistent
with their principles, cannot deny that bodily pleasure is the earlier form, and likewise the ultimate
source, of all pleasure, and neither Epicurus nor his
favourite pupil Metrodorus shrunk from making this
admission; Epicurus declaring that he could form

latter perverting Epicurus'
words to a terrible extent.

[1] *Diog.* 137: ἔτι πρὸς τοὺς Κυ-
ρηναϊκοὺς διαφέρεται. οἱ μὲν γὰρ
χείρους τὰς σωματικὰς ἀλγηδόνας
λέγουσι τῶν ψυχικῶν . . . ὁ δὲ
τὰς ψυχικάς. τὴν γοῦν σάρκα διὰ
τὸ παρὸν μόνον χειμάζειν, τὴν δὲ
ψυχὴν καὶ διὰ τὸ παρελθὸν καὶ τὸ
παρὸν καὶ τὸ μέλλον. οὕτως οὖν
καὶ μείζονας ἡδονὰς εἶναι τῆς ψυχῆς. Further particulars in
Plut. l. c. 3, 10: *Cic.* Tusc. v.

33, 96. The Epicureans designated bodily pleasure by ἥδεσ-
θαι, mental by χαίρειν. *Plut.*
l. c. 5, 1.

[2] *Diog.* 145. Epicurus appears to have first used σάρξ to
express the body in contrast to
the soul, σῶμα, in his system,
including the soul. See *Diog.*
137; 140; 144; Metrodor. in
Plut. Colot. 31, 2. (*Plut.* in
N. P. Suav. v. 16, 9; Plut. has
γαστρί instead of σαρκί.)

no conception of the good apart from enjoyments [1]
of the senses; Metrodorus asserting that everything
good has reference to the belly.[2] Still the Epicureans did not feel themselves thereby driven to give
up the pre-eminence which they claimed for goods
of the soul over those of the body. Even the Stoics,
notwithstanding the grossness of their theory of
knowledge, never abated their demand for a knowledge of conceptions, nor ceased to subordinate the
senses to reason, notwithstanding their building a
theory of morals on nature. But all character has
vanished from their joys and their pains. Their only
distinctive feature can be found in the addition either
of memory, or of hope, or of fear [3] to the present feeling of pleasure or pain ; and their greater importance
is simply ascribed to the greater force or duration
belonging to these ideal feelings as compared with
the attractions which momentarily impress the senses.[4]

[1] *Diog.* x. 6, from Epicurus
περὶ τέλους : οὐ γὰρ ἔγωγε ἔχω τί
νοήσω τἀγαθὸν ἀφαιρῶν μὲν τὰς
διὰ χυλῶν ἡδονὰς, ἀφαιρῶν δὲ καὶ
τὰς δι' ἀφροδισίων καὶ τὰς δι' ἀκρο-
αμάτων καὶ τὰς διὰ μορφᾶς (-ῆς).
The like, in a more expanded
form, in *Cic.* Tusc. iii. 18, 41.

[2] *Plut.* l. c. 16, 9: ὡς καὶ
ἐχάρην καὶ ἐθρασυνάμην ὅτε ἔμαθον
παρ' Ἐπικούρου ὀρθῶς γαστρὶ (see
previous note) χαρίζεσθαι ; and :
περὶ γαστέρα γάρ, ὦ φυσιολόγε
Τιμόκρατες, τὸ ἀγαθόν. Conf.
ibid. 3, 1.

[3] See p. 478, 1, and Epic. in
Plut. N. P. Suav. V. 4, 10 : τὸ
γὰρ εὐσταθὲς σαρκὸς κατάστημα
καὶ τὸ περὶ ταύτης πιστὸν ἔλπισμα

τὴν ἀκροτάτην χαρὰν καὶ βεβαιο-
τάτην ἔχει τοῖς ἐπιλογίζεσθαι δυνα-
μένοις. *Ibid.* 5, 1 : τὸ μὲν ἡδόμενον τῆς σαρκὸς τῷ χαίροντι τῆς
ψυχῆς ὑπερείδοντες, αὖθις δ' ἐκ τοῦ
χαίροντος εἰς τὸ ἡδόμενον τῇ
ἐλπίδι τελευτῶντας.

[4] Conf., besides the extracts
on p. 478, 1 and 2, *Cic.* Fin. i.
17, 55 : Animi autem voluptas
et dolores nasci fatemur e corporis voluptatibus et doloribus;
it is only a misapprehension on
the part of several Epicureans
to deny this fact. Mental pleasures and pains may therefore
be the stronger ones for the
reasons assigned above.

CHAP.
XIX.

Only accidentally is the remembrance of philosophic discourses mentioned [1] as a counterpoise to bodily pain; properly speaking, mental pleasures and pains are not different from other pleasures in kind, but only in degree, by reason of their being stronger and more enduring. Accordingly Epicurus cannot escape the admission that we have no cause for rejecting gross and carnal enjoyments if these can liberate us from the fear of higher powers, of death, and of sufferings; [2] and so the only consolation he can offer in pain is the uncertain one that most violent pains either do not last long, or else put an end to our life; and the less violent ones ought to be endured since they do not exclude a counterbalacing pleasure. [3] Hence victory over the impression of the moment must be secured, not so much by a mental force stemming the tide of feeling, as by a proper estimate of the conditions and actions of the senses.

(3) *Virtue.*

In no other way can the necessity of virtue be established in the Epicurean system. Agreeing with the strictest moral philosophers, so far as to hold that virtue can be as little separated from happiness as happiness from virtue, [4] having even the testimony of opponents as to the purity and strictness

---

[1] In his last letter (*Diog.* 22), after describing his painful illness, Epicurus continues: ἀντιπαρετάττετο δὲ πᾶσι τούτοις τὸ κατὰ ψυχὴν χαῖρον ἐπὶ τῇ τῶν γεγονότων ἡμῖν διαλογισμῶν μνήμῃ.

[2] *Diog.* 142; *Cic.* Fin. ii. 7, 21.

[3] *Diog.* 140; 133; *Cic.* Fin.

i. 15, 49; *Plut.* Aud. Po. 14, p. 36; *M. Aurel.* vii. 33, 64.

[4] *Diog.* 140: οὐκ ἔστιν ἡδέως ζῆν ἄνευ τοῦ φρονίμως καὶ καλῶς καὶ δικαίως οὐδὲ φρονίμως καὶ δικαίως ἄνευ τοῦ ἡδέως. The same p. 132, 138. *Cic.* Tusc. v. 9, 26; Fin. i. 16, 50; 19, 62; *Sen.* Ep. 85, 18.

of his moral teaching, which in its results differed
in no wise from that of the Stoics;[1] Epicurus, nevertheless, holds a position strongly contrasted with that
of the Stoics as to the grounds on which his moral
theory is based. To demand virtue for its own sake
seemed to him a mere phantom of the imagination.
Those only who make pleasure their aim have a real
object in life.[2] Only a conditional value belongs to
virtue[3] as a means to happiness; or, as it is otherwise expressed,[4] Not virtue taken by itself renders a
man happy, but the pleasure arising from the exercise of virtue. This pleasure the Epicurean system
does not seek in the consciousness of duty fulfilled,

[1] *Sen.* Vit. Be. 13, 1 (conf.
12, 4): In ea quidem ipse sententia sum (invitis nec nostris
popularibus — the Stoics — dicam), sancta Epicurum et recta præcipere, et si propius ac-
cesseris tristia: voluptas enim
illa ad parvum et exile revoca-
tur, et quam nos virtuti legem
dicimus eam ille dicit voluptati
. . . itaque non dico, quod
plerique nostrorum, sectam
Epicuri flagitiorum ministram
esse, sed illud dico: male audit,
infamis est, et immerito. Ep.
33, 2: Apud me vero Epicurus
est et fortis, licet manuleatus
sit. Seneca not infrequently
quotes sayings of Epicurus, and
calls (Ep. 6, 6) Metrodorus,
Hermarchus and Polyænus,
magnos viros. Conf. *Cic.* Fin.
ii. 25, 81.
[2] Epic. in *Plut.* Adv. Col.
17, 3: ἐγὼ δ' ἐφ' ἡδονὰς συνεχεῖς
παρακαλῶ, καὶ οὐκ ἐπ' ἀρετὰς, κενὰς
καὶ ματαίας καὶ ταραχώδεις ἐχούσας
πῶν κάρπων τὰς ἐλπίδας.

[3] *Diog.* 138: διὰ δὲ τὴν ἡδονὴν
καὶ τὰς ἀρετὰς δεῖν αἱρεῖσθαι οὐ δι'
αὐτάς· ὥσπερ τὴν ἰατρικὴν διὰ τὴν
ὑγίειαν, καθά φησι καὶ Διογένης.
Cic. Fin. i. 13, 42 (conf. ad Att.
vii. 2): Istæ enim vestræ exi-
miæ pulcræque virtutes nisi
voluptatem efficerent, quis eas
aut laudabiles aut expetendas
arbitraretur? ut enim medi-
corum scientiam non ipsius
artis sed bonæ valetudinis causa
probamus, &c. . . . ; sic sapientia, quæ ars vivendi putanda
est, non expeteretur si nihil efficeret; nunc expetitur quod est
tanquam artifex conquirendæ
et comparandæ voluptatis.
Alex. Aphr. De An. 156, b: [ἡ
ἀρετὴ] περὶ τὴν ἐκλογήν ἐστι τῶν
ἡδέων κατ' Ἐπίκουρον.
[4] *Sen.* Ep. 85, 18: Epicurus
quoque judicat, cum virtutem
habeat beatum esse, sed ipsam
virtutem non satis esse ad beatam vitam, quia beatum efficiat
voluptas quæ ex virtute est, non
ipsa virtus.

or of virtuous action, but in the freedom from disquiet, fear, and dangers, which follows as a consequence from virtue. Wisdom and intelligence contribute to happiness by liberating us from the fear of the Gods and death, by making us independent of immoderate passions and vain desires, by teaching us to bear pain as something subordinate and passing, and by pointing the way to a more cheerful and natural life.[1] Self-control aids in that it points out the attitude to be assumed towards pleasure and pain, so as to receive the maximum of enjoyment and the minimum of suffering;[2] valour, in that it enables us to overcome fear and pain;[3] justice, in that it makes life possible without that fear of Gods and men, which ever haunts the transgressor.[4] To the Epicurean virtue is never an end in itself, but only a means to an end lying beyond it—a happy life—but withal a means so certain and necessary, that virtue can neither be conceived without happiness, nor happiness without virtue. Little as it may seem to be required, still even he would ever insist that an action to be right must be done not according to the letter, but according to the spirit of the law, not simply from regard to others, or by compulsion, but from delight in what is good.[5]

---

[1] *Diog.* 132; *Cic.* Fin. i. 13, 43; 19, 62.

[2] *Cic.* Fin. i. 13, 47.

[3] *Cic.* l. c. 13, 49. *Diog.* 120: τὴν δὲ ἀνδρείαν φύσει μὴ γίνεσθαι, λογισμῷ δὲ τοῦ συμφέροντος.

[4] *Cic.* Fin. i. 16, 50; *Diog.* 144; *Plut.* N. P. Sua. Viv. 6, 1; *Sen.* Ep. 97, 13 and 15. *Lucr.*

v. 1152: The criminal can never rest, and often in delirium or sleep betrays himself. Epicurus, however, refused to answer the question, Whether the wise man would do what is forbidden, if he could be certain of not being discovered? *Plut.* col. 34, 1.

[5] *Philodemus*, De Rhet. Vol.

The same claims were therefore advanced by Epicurus on behalf of his wise man as the Stoics had urged on behalf of theirs. Not only was a control over pain attributed to him, in nothing inferior to the Stoic insensibility of feeling, but he endeavoured himself to describe his life as most perfect and satisfactory in itself. Albeit not free from emotions, and being in particular susceptible to the higher feelings of the soul, such as compassion, he yet finds his philosophic activity in no wise thereby impaired.[1] Without despising enjoyment, he is altogether master of his desires, and knows how to restrain them by intelligence, so that they never exercise a harmful influence on life. He alone has an unwavering certainty of conviction ;[2] he alone knows how to do the right thing in the right way ; he alone, as Metrodorus observes,[3] knows how to be thankful. Nay, more, he is so far exalted above ordinary men, that Epicurus promises his pupils that, by carefully observing his teaching, they will dwell as Gods among men ;[4] so little can destiny influence him, that he calls him happy under all circumstances.[5] Happiness may, indeed, depend on certain external condi-

---

Herc. v. a, col. 25: The laws ought to be kept τῷ μὴ τὰ διωρισμένα μόνον, ἀλλὰ καὶ τὰ τὴν ὁμοείδειαν αὐτοῖς ἔχοντα διαφυλάττειν, κἀκεῖνα μὴ μόνον συνειδότων, ἀλλὰ κἂν λανθάνωμεν ἀπαξἁπαντας, καὶ μεθ᾽ ἡδονῆς, οὐ δι᾽ ἀνάγκην, καὶ βεβαίως, ἀλλ᾽ οὐ σαλευομένως.
[1] *Diog.* 117 ; 118 ; 119.
[2] *Plut.* Adv. Col. 19, 2.
[3] *Diog.* 118 ; *Sen.* Ep. 81, 11.

The Stoic assertion of the equality of virtues and vices was, however, denied by the Epicureans. *Diog.* 120.
[4] *Diog.* 135 ; conf. *Plut.* N. P. Sua. Vi. 7, 3 ; *Lucr.* iii. 323.
[5] *Cic.* Fin. i. 19, 61 ; v. 27, 80: Semper beatum esse sapientem. Tusc. v. 9, 26 ; *Stob.* Serm. 17, 30. See p. 477.

tions; it may even be allowed that the disposition
to happiness is not found in every nature, nor in
every person;[1] but still, when it is found, its sta-
bility is sure, nor can time affect its duration. For
wisdom—so Epicurus and the Stoics alike believed—
is indestructible,[2] and the wise man's happiness can
never be increased by time. A life, therefore, bounded
by time can be quite as complete as one not so
bounded.[3]

Different as the principles, and different as the
tone of the systems of the Stoics and of Epicurus
may be, one and the same endeavour may yet be
observed in both. It is the tendency which cha-
racterises all the post-Aristotelian philosophy—the
wish to place man in a position of absolute independence by emancipating him from connection with
the external world, and by awakening in him the
consciousness of the infinite freedom of thought.[4]

---

[1] *Diog.* 117.

[2] *Diog.* 117: τὸν ἅπαξ γενόμενον σοφὸν μηκέτι τὴν ἐναντίαν
λαμβάνειν διάθεσιν μήδ᾽ ἐπαλλάτ-
τειν ἑκόντα. The latter words
appear to admit the possibility
of an involuntary loss of wisdom, perhaps through madness.

[3] *Diog.* 126; 145; *Cic.* Fin.
i. 19, 63.

[4] See also page 476, 2.

CHAPTER XX.

THE EPICUREAN ETHICS CONTINUED: SPECIAL POINTS.

THE general principles already laid down determine
likewise the character of particular points in the
moral science of the Epicureans. Epicurus, it is
true, never developed his moral views to a systematic
theory of moral actions and states, however much
his pupils, particularly in later times, busied themselves with morality and special points in a system of
morals.[1] Moreover, his fragmentary statements and
precepts are very imperfectly recorded. Still, all that
is known corresponds with the notion which we must
form in accordance with those general views. All
the practical rules given by Epicurus aim at con-
ducting man to happiness by controlling passions
and desires. The wise man is easily satisfied. He
sees that little is necessary for supplying the wants

CHAP.
XX.

A. *The in-
dividual.*

---

[1] We gather this from the
fragments of Philodemus' treatise περὶ κακιῶ΄ καὶ τῶν ἀντικειμένων ἀγαθῶν καὶ τῶν ἐν οἷς
εἰσὶ καὶ περὶ ἅ. The 10th book
of this treatise gives a portrait
of the ὑπερήφανος, and kindred
faults, after the manner of
Theophrastus; the 9th, a mild
criticism of Xenophon's and
Aristotle's οἰκονομικός. It is objected to the latter that the
master of the house is there
made (col. ii. 30) to rise earlier
than his servants, and to go to
bed later than they do, such
conduct being ταλαίπωρον καὶ
ἀνοίκειον φιλοσόφου.

of nature, and for emancipating from pain; that
imaginary wealth knows no limit, whereas the riches
required by nature may be easily acquired;[1] that
the most simple nourishment affords as much enjoyment as the most luxurious, and is at the same time
far more conducive to health;[2] that therefore the restriction of wants rather than the increase of possessions makes really rich;[3] and that he who is not
satisfied with little will never be satisfied at all.[4] He
therefore can with Epicurus live upon bread and
water,[5] and at the same time think himself as happy

[1] *Diog.* 144; 146; 130; *Stob.*
Floril. 17, 23; *Sen.* Ep. 16, 7;
Lucr. ii. 20; iii. 59; v. 1115;
Philod. De Vit. ix. col. 12: φιλο-
σόφῳ δ' ἐστὶ πλούτου μικρόν· ὃ
παρεδώκαμεν ἀκολούθως [for thus
and not by εὐκαίρως must the
defective —ως be represented]
τοῖς καθηγεμόσιν ἐν τοῖς περὶ
πλούτου λόγοις. Conf. p. 476,
3; 477.
[2] *Diog.* 130.
[3] *Stob.* Floril. 17, 24 and 37;
Sen. Ep. 21, 7; 14, 17; 2, 5:
Honesta, inquit, res est læta
paupertas. Ep. 17, 11: Multis
parasse divitias non finis mise-
riarum fuit, sed mutatio.
[4] *Stob.* Flor. 17, 30. Conf.
Sen. Ep. 9, 20: Si cui sua non
videntur amplissima, licet totius mundi dominus sit tamen
miser est.
[5] *Diog.* 11; *Stob.* Floril. 17,
34; *Cic.* Tusc. v. 31, 89; *Sen.*
Ep. 25, 4. Epicurus lived very
abstemiously. The charge of
luxury brought against him
was fully disposed of by *Gassendi*, De Vit. et Mor. Epic. 153.
Timocrates, on the strength of

one of his letters, asserts that
he spent a mina every day on
his table. If this statement be
not a pure invention, it must
refer to the whole circle of his
friends. It could otherwise
only have happened at such a
time as the siege of Athens by
Demetrius Poliorcetes, when a
modius of wheat cost 300
drachmæ, and when Epicurus
counted out to his friends the
beans on which they lived.
Plut. Demetr. 33. The further
statement of Timocrates—
(*Diog.* 6) αὐτὸν δὶς τῆς ἡμέρας
ἐμεῖν ἀπὸ τρυφῆς)—is certainly
an unfounded calumny. The
moderation of Epicurus is admitted by *Sen.* Vit. B. 12, 4; 13,
1; and Epicurus flatters himself, in *Sen.* Ep. 18, 9: Non
toto asse pasci, Metrodorum,
qui nondum tantum profecerit,
toto; and, in *Diog.* 11, because
he was satisfied with bread and
water. *Ibid.* he writes: πέμψον
μοι τυροῦ Κυθνίου, ἵν' ὅταν βού-
λωμαι πολυτελεύσασθαι, δύνωμαι.
Still less have we any reason
to connect the diseases of which

as Zeus.[1] He eschews passions which disturb peace
of mind and the repose of life ; considering it foolish
to throw away the present in order to obtain an uncertain future, or to sacrifice life itself for the means
of a life, seeing he can only once enjoy it.[2] He
therefore neither gives way to passionate love, nor to
forbidden acts of profligacy.[3] Fame he does not

Epicurus and some of his
scholars died (as *Plut.* N. P.
Suav. V. 5, 3 does, herein following Timocrates in *Diog.* 7)
with their presumed luxurious-
ness.

[1] *Stob.* Floril. 17, 30. See
p. 477, 2.

[2] Epicurus and Metrodorus,
in *Stob.* Floril. 16, 28 ; 20. Conf.
Plut. Tran. An. 16, p. 474 : ὁ
τῆς αὔριον ἥκιστα δεόμενος, ὥς
φησιν Ἐπίκουρος, ἥδιστα πρόσεισι
πρὸς τὴν αὔριον.

[3] Serious charges on this
subject, against which Gassendi
in *Diog.* 6, defends him, are
preferred against Epicurus by
Timocrates, in *Diog.* 6 ; but
neither the testimony of Timocrates, nor the fact that a
woman of loose morality (see
above p. 406) was in his society,
can be considered conclusive.
Chrysippus in *Stob.* Floril. 63,
31, calls Epicurus ἀναίσθητος.
Epicurus is, however, far below
our standard of morality. Thus,
in the quotation on p. 479, 1,
he reckons ἡδοναὶ δι' ἀφροδισίων
among the necessary ingredients of the good. By *Eustrat.*
in Eth. N. 48, such pleasures
are included among φυσικαὶ (see
p. 476, 3), not among ἡδοναὶ
ἀναγκαῖαι. They are treated in
the same light by *Lucr.* v. 1050;
and *Plut.* Qu. Conviv. iii. 6, 1,

1, not only discusses the most
suitable time for the enjoyment of love, but quotes as the
words of Epicurus : εἰ γέρων ὁ
σοφὸς ὢν καὶ μὴ δυνάμενος πλη-
σιάζειν ἔτι ταῖς τῶν καλῶν ἀφαῖς
χαίρει καὶ ψηλαφήσεσιν (N. P.
Suav. V. 12, 3). These enjoyments, according to Epicurus,
are only then allowed when
they do not entail any bad consequences (*Diog.* 118), or produce passionate states of feeling. Hence he not only forbids
unlawful commerce (*Diog.* 118),
but declares οὐκ ἐρασθήσεσθαι
τὸν σοφόν. *Diog.* 118 ; *Stob.*
Floril. 63, 31. Eros is defined
(*Alex. Aphr.* Top. 75) = σύντονος
ὄρεξις ἀφροδισίων. Conf. *Plut.*
Amat. 19, 16, p. 765. It is consequently a passionate and disturbing state, which the wise
man must avoid. The Stoics,
on the contrary, allowed Eros
to their wise man. The same
view is taken of Eros by Lucretius, who cannot find words
strong enough to express the
restlessness and confusion en-
tailed by love, the state of dependence in which it places
man, and the loss to his fortune
and good name. His advice is
to allay passion as quickly as
possible by means of Venus
volgivaga, and to gratify it in
a calm way.

covet; and for the opinions of men he cares only so
far as to wish not to be despised, since being despised
would expose him to danger.[1] Injuries he can bear
with calmness.[2] He cares not what may happen to
him after death;[3] nor envies any for possessions
which he does not himself value.[4]

It has been already seen how Epicurus thought
to rise above pains, and to emancipate himself from
the fear of the Gods and death.[5] And it has been
further noticed that he thinks to secure by means of
his principles the same independence and happiness
which the Stoics aspired to by means of theirs. But
whilst the Stoics thought to attain this independence by crushing the senses, Epicurus was content
to restrain and regulate them. Desires he would not
have uprooted, but he would have them brought into
proper proportion to the collective end and condition
of life, into the equilibrium necessary for perfect repose of mind. Hence, notwithstanding his own simplicity, Epicurus is far from disapproving, under all
circumstances, of a fuller enjoyment of life. The
wise man will not live as a Cynic or a beggar.[6] Care
for business he will not neglect; only he will not

---

[1] *Diog.* 120 ; 140 ; *Cic.* Tusc.
ii. 12, 28 ; *Lucr.* iii. 59; 993.
[2] *Sen.* De Const. 16, 1.
[3] *Diog.* 118 : οὐδὲ ταφῆς φρον-
τιεῖν.
[4] *Lucr.* iii. 74.
[5] See p. 479, 455. A further
argument may, however, be
here quoted. In *Plut.* N. P.
Suav. Viv. 16, 3, he says : ὅτι
νόσῳ νοσῶν ἀσκίτῃ τινὰς ἑστιάσεις

φίλων συνῆγε, καὶ οὐκ ἐφθόνει τῆς
προσαγωγῆς τοῦ ὑγροῦ τῷ ὑδρωπι,
καὶ τῶν ἐσχάτων Νεοκλέους λόγων
μεμνημένος ἐτήκετο τῇ μετὰ δακ-
ρύων ἡδονῇ. It is true that a
certain mawkishness and self-
conceit may be detected in this
language.
[6] *Diog.* 119; *Philodem.* De
Vit. ix. col. 12 ; 27, 40.

give himself too much trouble therewith, and will prefer the business of education to any and every other.[1] Nor will he despise the attractions of art, although he can be content when obliged to dispense with them.[2] In short, his self-sufficiency will not consist in *using* little, but in *needing* little; and it is this freedom from wants which will add flavour to his more luxurious enjoyments.[3] Nor is his attitude towards death a different one. Not fearing death, rather seeking it when he has no other mode of escaping unendurable suffering, still, the cases in which he will resort to suicide will be rare, since he has learnt to be happy under all bodily pains. The Stoic's recommendation of suicide finds no favour with the Epicurean.[4]

[1] *Diog.* 120 ; κτήσεως προνοήσεσθαι καὶ τοῦ μέλλοντος. 121 : χρηματίσεσθαί τε ἀπὸ μόνης σοφίας ἀπορήσαντα. The limitation implied in the text would, however, seem to require μόνης. *Philodem.* in the same sense l. c. 23, 23, says that Epicurus received presents from his scholars. Conf. *Plut.* adv. col. 18, 3, also col. 15, 31.

[2] *Diog.* 121 : εἰκόνας τε ἀναθήσειν εἰ ἔχοι· ἀδιαφόρως ἕξειν ἂν μὴ σχοίη (*Cobet*, not intelligibly : ἀδιαφόρως ἂν σχοίης).

[3] Epic. in *Diog.* 130 : καὶ τὴν αὐτάρκειαν δὲ ἀγαθὸν μέγα νομίζομεν οὐχ ἵνα πάντως τοῖς ὀλίγοις χρώμεθα, ἀλλ᾽ ὅπως ἐὰν μὴ ἔχωμεν τὰ πολλὰ τοῖς ὀλίγοις χρώμεθα πεπεισμένοι γνησίως ὅτι ἥδιστα πολυτελείας ἀπολαύουσιν οἱ ἥκιστα αὐτῆς δεόμενοι.

[4] The Epicurean in *Cic.* Fin.
. 15, 49: Si tolerabiles sint

[dolores] feramus, sin minus, æquo animo e vita, cum ea non placeat, tanquam e theatro exeamus. Epic. in *Sen.* Ep. 12, 10 : Malum est in necessitate vivere, sed in necessitate vivere necessitas nulla est. On the other hand, Ep. 24, 22 : Objurgat Epicurus non minus eos qui mortem concupiscunt, quam eos, qui timent, et ait : ridiculum est currere ad mortem tædio vitæ, cum genere vitæ ut currendum esset ad mortem effeceris. *Diog.* 119, the older editions read : καὶ πηρωθεὶς τὰς ὄψεις μεθέξειν αὐτὸν τοῦ βίου. *Cobet* : μετάξε.ν αὐτὸν τοῦ βίου. Instead of πηρωθεὶς πηρωθέντα is read, or as we might prefer instead of μετάξειν μετάξει. Suicide was only allowed by Epicurus in extreme cases. In Seneca's time, when an Epicurean, Diodorus, committed

CHAP.
XX.

B. *Civil
society
and the
family.*
(1) *Civil
society.*

Fully as the wise man can suffice for himself, still Epicurus would not separate him from connection with others. Not, indeed, that he believed with the Stoics in the natural relationship of all rational beings.[1] Yet even he could form no idea of human life except in connection with human society. He does not, however, assign the same value to all forms of social life. Civil society and the state have for him the least attraction. Civil society is only an external association for the purpose of protection. Justice reposes originally on nothing but a contract entered into for purposes of mutual security.[2] Laws are only made for the sake of the wise, not to prevent their committing, but to prevent their suffering injustice.[3] Law and justice are not, therefore, binding for their own sake, but for the general good; nor is injustice to be condemned for its own sake, but only because the offender can never be free from fear of discovery and punishment.[4] There is not, therefore, any such thing as universal, unchangeable justice. The claims of justice only extend to a limited number of beings and nations—those, in fact, which were able and willing to enter into the social compact. And the particular applications of justice which constitute positive right differ in dif-

suicide, his fellow-scholars were unwilling to allow that suicide was permitted by the precepts of Epicurus (*Sen.* Vit. B. 19, 1).

[1] *Epict.* Diss. ii. 20, 6 : 'Επίκουρος ὅταν ἀναιρεῖν θέλῃ τὴν φυσικὴν κοινωνίαν ἀνθρώποις πρὸς ἀλλήλους, κ.τ.λ.

[2] *Diog.* 150 ; 154. From this point of view, *Lucr.* v. 1106, gives a long description of the rise of a state.

[3] *Stob.* Floril. 43, 139.

[4] *Diog.* 150 ; *Lucr.* v. 1149 ; *Sen.* Ep. 97, 13, and 15 ; *Plut.* Ad. Col. 34. See p. 482, 4.

ferent cases, and change with circumstances. What
is felt to be conducive to mutual security must pass
for justice; and whenever a law is seen to be inex-
pedient, it is no longer binding.[1] The wise man will
therefore only enter into political life in case and in
as far as this is necessary for his own safety. The
sovereign power is a good, inasmuch as it protects
from harm. He who pursues it, without thereby attaining this object, acts most foolishly.[2] Private
individuals living as a rule much more calmly and
safely than statesmen, it was therefore natural that the
Epicureans should be averse to public affairs; public
life, after all, is a hindrance to what is the real end-
in-chief—wisdom and happiness.[3] Their watchword
is therefore Λάθε βιώσας.[4] To them the golden
mean seemed by far the most desirable lot in life.[5]
They only advise citizens to take part in affairs of
state when special circumstances render it necessary,[6]
or when an individual has such a restless nature that

[1] *Diog.* 150–153.
[2] *Diog.* 140.
[3] *Plut.* Adv. Col. 31; 33, 4;
N. P. Sua. Viv. 16, 9; *Epictet.*
Diss. i. 23, 6; *Lucr.* v. 1125;
Cic. pro Sext. 10, 23. *Philodem.*
περὶ ῥητορικῆς (Vol. Herc. iv.)
col. 14: οὐδὲ χρησίμην ἡγούμεθα
τὴν πολιτικὴν δύναμιν, οὔτ᾽ αὐτοῖς
τοῖς κεκτημένοις, οὔτε ταῖς πόλεσιν,
αὐτὴν καθ᾽ αὑτήν· ἀλλὰ πολλάκις
αἰτίαν καὶ συμφορῶν ἀνηκέστων,
when combined with upright-
ness, it benefits the community,
and is sometimes useful; at
other times, harmful to statesmen themselves.

[4] *Plut.* De Latenter Viven-
do, c. 4. In this respect, T.
Pomponius Atticus is the true
type of an Epicurean, on
whose conduct during the civil
war and withdrawal from public
life, see *Nepos*, Att. 6.
[5] Metrodorus, in *Stob.* Floril.
45, 26: ἐν πόλει μήτε ὡς λέων
ἀναστρέφου μήτε ὡς κώνωψ· τὸ
μὲν γὰρ ἐκπατεῖται τὸ δὲ καιροφυ-
λακεῖται.
[6] Seneca well expresses the
difference on this point between Epicureans and Stoics in
the passage quoted, p. 320, 3.

he cannot be content with the quiet of private life.[1]
Otherwise they are far too deeply convinced of the
impossibility of pleasing the masses to wish even to
make the attempt.[2] For the same reason they appear
to have been partisans of monarchy. The stern and
unflinching moral teaching of the Stoics had found
its political expression in the unbending republican
spirit, so often encountered at Rome. Naturally the
soft and timid spirit of the Epicureans took shelter
under a monarchical constitution. Of their political
principles so much at least is known that they did
not consider it degrading for a wise man to pay court
to princes, and under all circumstances they recommended unconditional obedience to the powers
that be.[3]

Family life is said to have been deprecated by Epicurus equally with civil life.[4] Stated thus baldly, this
is an exaggeration. So much, however, appears to
be established, that Epicurus believed it to be generally better for the wise man to forego marriage and
the rearing of children, since he would thereby save
himself many disturbances.[5] It is also quite credible

[1] *Plut.* Tranq. An. c. 2, p.
465.

[2] Epic. in *Sen.* Ep. 29, 10 :
Nunquam volui populo placere ;
nam quæ ego scio non probat
populus, quæ probat populus
ego nescio. Similar expressions
from Stoics have been previously quoted.

[3] *Diog.* 121 : καὶ μόναρχον ἐν
καιρῷ θεραπεύσειν [τὸν σοφόν].
Lucr. v. 1125 :—

Ut satius multo jam sit parere
quietum,

Quam regere imperio res velle
et regna tenere.

[4] *Epict.* Diss. i. 23, 3 (against
Epicurus) : διατὶ ἀποσυμβουλεύεις
τῷ σοφῷ τεκνοτροφεῖν ; τί φοβῇ
μὴ διὰ ταῦτα εἰς λύπας ἐμπέσῃ ;
ii. 20, 20 : Ἐπίκουρος τὰ μὲν ἀν-
δρὸς πάντ' ἀπεκόψατο καὶ τὰ οἰκο-
δεσπότου καὶ φίλου—the last
words proving how cautiously
these statements must be understood.

[5] *Diog.* 119. The passage
is, however involved in much

that he declared the love of children towards parents to be no inborn feeling.[1] This view is, after all, only a legitimate consequence of his materialism ; but it did not oblige him to give up parental love altogether. Nay, it is asserted of him that he was anything but a stranger to family affections.[2]

The highest form of social life was considered by Epicurus to be friendship—a view which is distinctive in a system regarding the individual as the atom of society. Such a system naturally attributes more value to a connection with others freely entered upon and based on individual character and personal inclination, than to one in which a man finds himself placed without any choice, as a member of a society founded on nature or history. The basis, however, on which the Epicurean friendship rests is very superficial, regard being had mainly to its advantages, and in some degree to the natural effects of common enjoyments ;[3] but it is also treated

---

obscurity, owing to a difference of reading. The earlier text was: καὶ μὴν καὶ γαμήσειν καὶ τεκνοποιήσειν τὸν σοφὸν, ὡς Ἐπίκουρος ἐν ταῖς διαπορίαις καὶ ἐν ταῖς περὶ φύσεως. κατὰ περίστασιν δέ ποτε βίου οὐ γαμήσεω. *Cobet* reads instead : καὶ μηδὲ γαμήσειν μηδὲ τεκνοποιήσειν τὸν σοφόν . . . κατὰ περίστασιν δέ ποτε βίου γαμήσειν. What the MS. authority for this reading is, we are not told. In sense it agrees with *Hieron.* Adv. Jovin. i. 191, quoting from *Seneca*, De Matrimonio : Epicurus . . . raro dicit sapienti ineunda conjugia quia multa incommoda admixta sunt

nuptiis. Like riches, honours, health, ita et uxores sitas in bonorum malorumque confinio. grave aut esse viro sapienti venire in dubium, utrum bonam an malam ducturus sit.

[1] *Plut.* Adv. Col. 27, 6 ; De Am. Prol. 2, p. 495 ; *Epictet.* Diss. i. 23, 3.

[2] *Diog.* 10 : ἥ τε πρὸς τοὺς γονέας εὐχαριστία καὶ ἡ πρὸς τοὺς ἀδελφοὺς εὐποιία. Diogenes himself appeals to Epicurus' testament, *ibid.* 18.

[3] *Diog.* 120 ; καὶ τὴν φιλίαν διὰ τὰς χρείας [γίνεσθαι] . . . συνίστασθαι δὲ αὐτὴν κατὰ κοινωνίαν ἐν ταῖς ἡδοναῖς. Epic. *Ibid.*

in such a way, that its scientific imperfection has no influence on its moral importance. Only one portion of the School, and that not the most consistent, maintained that friendship is pursued in the first instance for the sake of its own use and pleasure, but that it subsequently becomes an unselfish love.[1] Moreover, the assumption that among the wise there exists a tacit agreement requiring them to love one another as much as they love themselves, is clearly only a lame shift.[2] Still, the Epicureans were of opinion that a grounding of friendship on motives of utility was not inconsistent with holding it in the highest esteem.

Friendly connection with others affords in short so pleasant a feeling of security, that it entails the most enjoyable consequences; and since this connection can only then exist when friends love one another as themselves, it follows that self-love and the love of a friend must be equally strong.[3]

Even this inference sounds forced, nor does it

---

148 (also in *Cic.* Fin. i. 20, 68): καὶ τὴν ἐν αὑτοῖς τοῖς ὡρισμένοις ἀσφάλειαν φιλίας μάλιστα κτήσει δεῖ νομίζειν συντελουμένην. (*Cobet*, however, reads: φιλίας μάλιστα κατιδεῖν εἶναι συντελυμένην, in which case φιλίᾳ should be substituted for φιλίας or else κτήσει for κατιδεῖν.) *Sen.* Ep. 9, 8: The wise man needs a friend, non ad hoc quod Epicurus dicebat in hac ipsa epistola (a letter in which Stilpo's cynical self-contentment is blamed), ut habeat, qui sibi ægro adsideat, succurrat in vincula conjecto vel inopi; sed ut habeat aliquem, cui ipsi ægro adsideat,

quem ipse circumventum hostili custodia liberet. *Cic.* Fin. i. 20, 66 : Cum solitudo et vita sine amicis insidiarum et metus plena sit, ratio ipsa monet amicitias comparare, quibus partis confirmatur animus et a spe pariendarum voluptatum sejungi non potest, etc. On the same grounds, *Philodem.* De Vit. ix. (V. Herc. iii.) col. 24, argues that it is much better to cultivate friendship than to withdraw from it.

[1] *Cic.* Fin. i. 20, 69.
[2] *Ibid.* 70.
[3] *Cic.* Fin. i. 20, 67.

fully state the grounds on which Epicurus's view of
the value of friendship reposes. That view, in fact,
was anterior to all the necessary props of the system.
What Epicurus requires is primarily enjoyment. The
first conditions of such enjoyment, however, are inward repose of mind, and the removal of fear of disturbances. But as to trusting his own powers for
satisfying these conditions, Epicurus was far too
effeminate and dependent on externals. He needed
the support of others, not only to obtain their help
in necessity and trouble, and to console himself with
this view for the uncertainty of the future, but still
more, to make sure of himself and his principles
by having the approval of others, thus obtaining an
inward satisfaction which he could not otherwise have
had. Thus, the approval of friends is to him the
pledge of the truth of his convictions. In sympathy
with them his mind first attains to a strength by
means of which it is able to rise above the changing
circumstances of life. General ideas are for him too
abstract, too unreal. A philosopher who considers
individual beings as alone real, and perceptions as
absolutely true, cannot feel quite happy and sure of
his ground, unless he finds others go with him.[1]
The enjoyment which he seeks is the enjoyment
of his own cultivated personality; and wherever
this standard prevails, particular value is attached

[1] The same need finds expression in the advice given by
Epicurus (*Sen.* Ep. 11, 8; 25,
5): Let every one choose some
distinguished man as his pattern, that so he may live, as it
were, perpetually under his
eye. Man requires a stranger
to give him moral support.

CHAP.
XX.

to the personal relations of society, and to friend-ship.[1]

Hence Epicurus expresses himself on the value and necessity of friendship in a manner far exceed-ing the grounds on which he based it. Friendship is unconditionally the highest of earthly goods.[2] It is far more important in whose company we eat and drink, than what we eat and drink.[3] In case of emer-gency the wise man will not shrink from suffering the greatest pains, even death, for his friend.[4]

It is well known that the conduct of Epicurus and his followers was in harmony with these pro-fessions. The Epicurean friendship is hardly less celebrated than the Pythagorean.[5] There may be an offensive mawkishness and a tendency to weak mutual admiration apparent in the relations of Epicurus to his friends,[6] but of the sincerity of his feelings there

---

[1] As illustrations in modern times, the réunions of the French freethinkers, or the societies of Rousseau, Mendels-sohn, Jacobi, may be mentioned. It deserves notice that in these societies, as amongst the Epi-cureans, an important part was played by women. This is quite natural, when philosophy is confined to cultivated inter-course and conversation.

[2] *Diog.* 148 : ὧν ἡ σοφία παρα-σκευάζεται εἰς τὴν τοῦ ὅλου βίου μακαριότητα πολὺ μέγιστόν ἐστιν ἡ τῆς φιλίας κτῆσις. *Cic.* Fin. ii. 25, 80 : Epicurus exalts friendship to heaven. In *Diog.* 120, Cobet reads instead of the usual φίλον τε οὐδένα κτήσεσθαι [τὸν σοφὸν], which is altogether

untrustworthy, φίλων τε οὐδὲν κτήσεσθαι.

[3] *Sen.* Ep. 19, 10, with the addition : Nam sine amico vis-ceratio leonis ac lupi vita est.

[4] *Plut.* Adv. Col. 8, 7 ; *Diog.* 121. We have no reason to suppose, with *Ritter*, iii. 474, that this was not the expres-sion of a real sentiment. That it is inconsistent we can well say.

[5] The Epicureans in *Cic.* Fin. i. 20, 65 : At vero Epi-curus una in domo et ea quidem angusta quam magnos quanta-que amoris conspiratione con-sentientes tenuit amicorum greges, quod fit etiam nunc ab Epicureis. *Ibid.* ii. 25, 80.

[6] Instances have already

can be no doubt. One single expression, that referring to the property of friends,¹ is enough to prove what a high view Epicurus held of friendship; and there is evidence to show that he aimed at a higher improvement of his associates.²

In other respects Epicurus bore the reputation of being a kind, benevolent, and genial companion.³ His teaching, likewise, bears the same impress. It meets the inexorable sternness of the Stoics by insisting on compassion and forgiveness,⁴ and supersedes its own egotism by the maxim that it is more

occurred, p. 418, 2, of the extravagant honours required by Epicurus; nor did he fail to eulogise his friends, as the fragments of his letters to Leontion, Themista, and Pythocles (*Diog.* 5) prove. When Metrodorus had tried to obtain the release of a captive friend, Epicurus applauds him (*Plut.* N. P. Sua. Vit. 15, 5, Adv. Col. 33, 2): ὡς εὖ τε καὶ νεανικῶς ἐξ ἄστεως ἅλαδε κατέβη Μίθρῳ τῷ Σύρῳ βοηθήσων. *Ibid.* 15, 8, he expresses his thanks for a present: δαΐως τε καὶ μεγαλοπρεπῶς ἐπεμελήθητε ἡμῶν τὰ περὶ τὴν τοῦ σίτου κομιδὴν, καὶ οὐρανομήκη σημεῖα ἐνδέδειχθε τῆς πρὸς ἐμὲ εὐνοίας He wrote of Pythocles before he was 18 : οὐκ εἶναι φύσιν ἐν ὅλῃ τῇ Ἑλλάδι ἀμείνω, καὶ τερατικῶς αὐτὸν εὖ ἀπαγγέλλειν, καὶ πάσχειν αὖ τὸ τῶν γυναικῶν, εὐχόμενος ἀνεμέσητα εἶναι πάντα καὶ ἀνεπίφθονα τῆς ὑπερβολῆς τοῦ νεανισκοῦ (*Plut.* Adv. Col. 29, 2); and he also said (*Philodem.* περὶ παῤῥησίας, Fr. 6, V. Herc. v. 2, 11): ὡς διὰ Πυθοκλέα τύχην

θεώσει παρὰ τὸ τεθεμισμένον. Compare the remarks on p. 488, 3.

¹ *Diog.* 11 : τόν τε Ἐπίκουρον μὴ ἀξιοῦν εἰς τὸ κοινὸν κατατίθεσθαι τὰς οὐσίας καθάπερ τὸν Πυθαγόραν κοινὰ τὰ τῶν φίλων λέγοντα. ἀπιστούντων γὰρ εἶναι τὸ τοιοῦτον· εἰ δ᾽ ἀπίστων οὐδὲ φίλων.

² *Philodem.* περὶ παῤῥησίας (V. Herc. v. 2), Fr. 15 ; 72 ; 73, mentions Epicurus and Metrodorus as patterns of genial frankness towards friends. Probably the words in *Sen.* Ep. 28, 9—initium salutis est notitia peccati--are taken from a moral exhortation addressed to a friend.

³ Not only does Diogenes (9) praise his unsurpassed benevolence, his kindness to his slaves, and his general geniality, but Cicero calls him (Tusc. ii. 19, 44) vir optimus, and (Fin. ii. 25, 80) bonum virum et comem et humanum.

⁴ *Diog.* 118: οὔτε κολάσειν οἰκέτας ἐλεήσειν μέντοι, καὶ συγ-

blessed to give than to receive.[1] The number of
such maxims on record is, no doubt, limited ; nevertheless, the whole tone of the Epicurean School is
a pledge of the humane and generous character of
its moral teaching.[2] To this trait the Epicurean
School owes its greatest importance in history. By
its theory of utility it undoubtedly did much harm,
partly indicating, partly helping on the moral decline of the classic nations. Still, by drawing man
away from the outer world within himself, by teaching him to look for happiness in the beautiful type
of a cultivated mind content with itself, it contributed quite as much, after a gentler fashion, as Stoicism by its sterner tone, to the development and
the extension of a more independent and more universal morality.

γνώμην τινὶ ἔξειν τῶν σπουδαίων.
121: ἐπιχαρίσεσθαί τινι ἐπὶ τῷ
διορθώματι.
    [1] *Plut.* N. P. Sua. Vi. 15, 4
(similarly C. Princ. Philos. 3,
2, p. 778) : αὐτοὶ δὲ δήπου λέγουσιν ὡς τὸ εὖ ποιεῖν ἥδιόν ἐστι τοῦ
πάσχειν.   Conf. *Alex. Aphr.*
Top. 123. A similar maxim is
attributed by *Ælian.* V. H. xiii.
13, to Ptolemy Lagi.   Conf.
Acts xx. 35.
    [2] *Cic.* Fin. ii. 25, 81: Et

ipse bonus vir fuit et multi
Epicurei fuerunt et hodie sunt,
et in amicitiis fideles et in omni
vita constantes et graves nec
voluptate sed officio consilia
moderantes. Atticus is a well-
known example of genuine
human kindness and ready self-
sacrifice, and Horace may be
also quoted as an illustration
of the same character. See
Steinhart's remarks, *l. c.* p. 470.

CHAPTER XXI.

THE EPICUREAN SYSTEM AS A WHOLE : ITS POSITION
IN HISTORY.

It has often been urged against the Epicurean philosophy, that it is deficient both in coherence and consistency. Nor is this objection without foundation. If we come to the study of this philosophy with the demand for a complete scientific groundwork, or a strictly logical development, there will certainly result therefrom a feeling of dissatisfaction. It is not difficult to show in what contradictions Epicurus was involved ; in professing to trust the senses wholly and entirely, and yet going beyond the senses to the hidden causes of things; in despising logical forms and laws, and at the same time building up his whole system on deductions ; in holding that all sensations are true, but yet maintaining that a portion of the realities which they represent as belonging to things is only relative. Nor were other inconsistencies wanting; his acknowledging at one time only natural causes and laws, and ignoring any such thing as free will and imagination, and yet at another time, by the doctrine of the swerving aside of atoms and of the human will, elevating unexplained caprice to the

CHAP.
XXI.

A. *Inner connection of the Epicurean teaching.*

rank of law; his referring all pleasures and pains to bodily sensations, and yet calling mental states the higher and more important states; nay, more, his deducing from a basis of selfishness rules and precepts of humanity, justice, love, faithfulness, and devotion. It ought not, however, to be forgotten that the Stoics, to whom the claim of clear and consistent thought cannot be denied, were involved in similar difficulties. The Stoics, like the Epicureans, built up a rational system on a basis of the senses. They, too, constructed an ideal theory of morals on a material groundwork of metaphysics. They, too, declared that universal law is the only active power, whilst they maintained that reality belongs only to the world of matter. They, too, deduced a strict theory of virtue from the principle of self-preservation; not to mention the inconsistent attitude which they assumed towards the popular religion. To deny to the Stoics a unity and connectedness of system, because of these scientific defects and inconsistencies, would be felt to be doing them an injustice. And can Epicureanism be fairly condemned, when its faults are essentially of the same kind (though a little more obvious) as those of the Stoics, without a single extenuating plea being admitted on its behalf?

The strongest plea to be advanced in its favour is that the development of the Epicurean system does not pretend to rest upon an intellectual platform. Epicurus sought in philosophy a path to happiness, a school of practical wisdom. For him knowledge has only a secondary value, as contributing to this end, and indeed, both the tone and the results of his intellectual activity were determined by a reference to this end. In the case of the Stoics, however, it has been already seen that the comparative subordination of Logic and Natural Science to Moral Science, the going back to the older view of nature, the vindication of the truth of the senses and of the reality of matter, grew out of their peculiarly one-sided view of the scope of philosophy. In the case of Epicurus the same results appear, and all the more markedly, since Epicurus did not, like the Stoics, look for happiness in subordination to a universal law, but in individual gratification or pleasure. For him the recognition of a universal law had not the same value as for the Stoics; and consequently Epicurus did not feel the same need of a scientific method as they had done. He could therefore more exclusively content himself with the impressions of the senses, regarding them as the only unfailing source of knowledge. No necessity compelled him to advance from pure materialism to a view of matter in which it is described as possessing a soul and made to be the bearer of reason. In fact, the more exclusively everything was referred by him to mechanical causes, the more easily could he regard the individual with his pursuit of happiness as independent of all superhuman forces, and left entirely to himself and his natural powers. No system in ancient times has so consistently carried out the mechanical view of nature as that of the Atomists. None, therefore, afforded such a strong metaphysical support to the Epicurean views of the absolute worth of the individual. It was, therefore, as natural for Epicurus to build on the teaching of Democritus as for the Stoics to build on that of Heraclitus. But Epicurus, influenced probably more by practical than by scientific considerations, allowed himself, by his theory of the swerving aside of atoms, to destroy the consistency of the theory of Democritus.[1]

It is hardly necessary to notice here how the distinctive features of the Epicurean morals were developed out of their theory of happiness, in marked contrast to the Stoic teaching. The happiness of Epicurus, however, does not depend upon sensual gratification as such, but upon repose of mind and cheerfulness of disposition. Hence his theory of morals, notwithstanding its foundation in pleasure, bears a nobler character, which is seen in its language as to the wise man's relations to the pains and desires of the body, to poverty and riches, to life and death, no less than in the mild humanity and the warm and hearty appreciation of friendship by the Epicurean School. Certainly the rationalising spirit of that School was opposed to any religious belief which supposed an intervention of God in the course of the world, or the world's influence on man for weal or woe; but its appeal to the senses without criticism raised no objection to admitting divine beings, from whom no such intervention need be feared. Nay, more, this belief seemed the most natural ground for explaining the popular belief in Gods. It

[1] See p. 445.

satisfied an inborn and apparently keenly-felt want by supplying an appropriate object of devotion, and a standard by which to test the accuracy of moral ideas. Hence, notwithstanding scientific defects and contradictions, the whole system of Epicurus bears a definite stamp. All the essential parts of that system are subservient to one and the same end. The consistent working out of a scientific view of nature is looked for in vain ; but there is no lack of consistency arising from an undeniable reference of the individual to a definite and practical standard.

Looking to the wider historical relations of the Epicurean system, the first point which calls for remark is the relation of that system to Stoicism. The contrast between the two Schools is obvious ; attention having been already drawn to it on all the more important points. It is likewise well known that a constant rivalry existed between the two Schools during their whole careers, that the Stoics looked down on the Epicureans, and circulated many calumnies with respect to their morals. For these statements proofs may be found in the preceding pages. Nevertheless, the two Schools are related in so many respects, that they can only be regarded as parallel links connected in one chain, their differences being varieties where the same main tendency exists. Both agree in the general character of their philosophy. In both practical considerations prevail over speculation. Both treat natural science and logic as sciences subsidiary to ethics—natural science especially in view of its bearing on religion.

B. *His-
torical
position
of Epicu-
reanism.*
(1) *Rela-
tion to
Stoicism.*

(*a*) *Points
of agree-
ment.*

Both, however, attach more importance to natural science than to logic. If the Epicurean neglect of scientific rule forms a contrast to the care which the Stoics devoted thereto, both parts are at least agreed in one thing—in displaying greater independence in investigating the question as to a test of truth. By both this standard was placed in the senses; and to all appearances both were led to take this view by the same cause; appeals to the senses being a consequence of their purely practical way of looking at things. Moreover, both employed against scepticism the same practical postulate—the argument that knowledge must be possible, or no certainty of action would be possible. They even agree in not being content with the phenomena supplied by the senses as such, although Epicurus as little approved of the Stoic theory of irresistible impressions as he did of their logical analysis of the forms of thought. With such appeals to the senses how could there be any other result but materialism both in the Stoic and Epicurean systems? But it is strange that the materialism in both Schools should be based on the same definition of reality, corresponding with their practical way of looking at things.[1]

(b) Points of difference.

In the expansion and more detailed setting forth of materialistic views the systems diverge, more widely, perhaps, than the philosophers themselves, whose leading they professed to follow. These differences appear particularly on the subject of nature, the Stoics regarding nature as a system of design,

[1] Conf. p. 126, 2, with 439, 1.

the Epicureans explaining it as a mechanical product. Whilst the Stoics adhered to fatalism, and saw God everywhere, the Epicureans held the theory of atoms, and the theory of necessity. Whilst the Stoics were speculatively orthodox, the Epicureans were irreligious freethinkers. Both meet again in that branch of natural science which is most important in respect of morals—the part dealing with man. Both hold that the soul is a fiery atmospheric substance. Even the proof for this view, derived from the mutual influence of body and soul, is common to both. Both distinguish between the higher and the lower parts of the soul, and thus even the Epicureans in their psychology allow a belief in the superiority of reason to the senses, and in the divine origin of the soul.

The arena of the warmest dispute between the two Schools is, however, ethics. Yet, even on this ground, they are more nearly related than appears at first sight. No greater contrast appears to be possible than that between the Epicurean theory of pleasure and the Stoic theory of virtue; and true it is that the two theories are diametrically opposite. Nevertheless, not only are both aiming at one and the same end—the happiness of mankind—but the conditions of happiness are also laid down by both in the same spirit. According to Zeno virtue, according to Epicurus pleasure, is the highest and only good; but the former making virtue consist essentially in withdrawal from the senses or insensibility; the latter seeking pleasure in repose of mind or imperturbability, are both expressing the same belief.

CHAP.
XXI.

Man can only find unconditional and enduring satisfaction, when by means of knowledge he attains to a condition of mind at rest with itself, and also to an independence of external attractions and misfortunes. The same unlimited appeal to personal truth is the common groundwork of both systems. Both have expanded this idea under the same form—that of the ideal wise man—for the most part with the same features. The wise man of Epicurus is, as we have seen, superior to pain and want; he enjoys an excellence which cannot be lost; and he lives among men a very God in intelligence and happiness. Thus, when worked out into details, the difference in the estimate of pleasure and virtue by the Stoics and Epicureans seems to vanish. Neither the Stoic can separate happiness from virtue, nor the Epicurean separate virtue from happiness.

But, whilst recommending a living for society, both systems take no real interest in social life. The recognition of a natural society amongst mankind, of certain positive relations to state and family, above all, a clear enunciation of a citizenship of the world, characterise the Stoics. The pursuit of friendship, and the gentle humanity of their ethics, characterise the Epicureans. Together with these peculiarities one common feature cannot be ignored. Both have renounced the political character of the old propriety of conduct, and diverting their attention from public life, seek to find a basis for universal morality in the simple relation of man to man.

The united weight of all these points of resemblance is sufficient to warrant the assertion that, notwithstanding their differences, the Stoics and Epicureans stand on the same footing, and that the sharpness of the contrast between them is owing to their laying hold of opposite sides of one and the same principle. Abstract personality, and self-consciousness developed into a generic idea, is for both the highest aim. Compared with it not only the state of the senses, but the scientific knowledge of things, and the realisation of moral ideas in a commonwealth, are of minor importance. In this self-consciousness happiness consists. To implant it in man is the object of philosophy, and knowledge is only of value when and in as far as it ministers to this end. The point of difference between the two Schools is only their view of the conditions under which that certainty of consciousness is attained. The Stoics hope to attain it by the entire subordination of the individual to universal law. The Epicureans, on the other hand, are of opinion that man can only then be content in himself when he is restrained by nothing external to himself. The first condition of happiness consists in liberating individual life from all dependence on others, and all disturbing causes. The former, therefore, make virtue, the latter make personal well-being or pleasure, the highest good. By the Epicureans, however, pleasure is usually conceived of as of a purely negative character, as being freedom from pain, and is referred to the whole of human life. Hence it is always made to depend on the moderation of desires, on indifference to outward ills, and the state of the senses, on intelligence and actions conformable with intelligence, in short, on virtue and wisdom. Hence, too, the Epicureans arrive by a roundabout course at the same result as the Stoics— the conviction that happiness can only be the lot of those who are altogether independent of external things, and in the enjoyment of perfect inward harmony.

(2) *Relation to Aristippus.*

Towards the older philosophy Epicureanism bears nearly the same relation as Stoicism. True it is that Epicurus and his School would not recognise their obligation to either one or other of his predecessors.[1]

[1] It has been already stated, p. 405, 1, 4, that Epicurus admitted his debt to Democritus, but not without some reserve, otherwise claiming to be entirely self-taught. With this exception, he professed to have learned nothing from the ancient teachers, and expressed himself with such conceit and scorn, as to spare neither them nor their writings. *Diog.* 8, besides mentioning his abuse of Nausiphanes (sup. 342, 1), refers also to his calling the Platonists Διονυσοκόλακας, Plato himself in irony the *golden* Plato, Heraclitus κυκητής, Democritus Ληρόκριτος, Antidorus Σαινίδωρος, the Cynics ἐχθροὺς τῆς Ἑλλάδος, the Dialecticians πολυφθονέρους, Pyrrho ἀμαθής and ἀπαίδευτος, and charging Aristotle and Protagoras with vices in their youth. Diogenes refuses to allow that any of these statements are true, Epicurus' friendliness being well known. But the devotion of Epicurus to his friends and admirers does not exclude hatred and injustice towards his predecessors, see p. 418, 2, of whom a fair estimate was rendered impossible by the superficial nature of his knowledge and the one-sidedness of his point of view. *Sext.* Math i. 2, attests τὴν πρὸς τοὺς περὶ Πλάτωνα καὶ Ἀριστοτέλη καὶ τοὺς ὁμοίους δυσμένειαν; *Plut.* Adv. Col. 26, 1, mentions a false objection to Arcesilaus; and *Cic.* N. D. i. 33, 93, says: Cum Epicurus Aristotelem vexarit contumeliosissime, Phædoni Socratico turpissime maledixerit, etc. The rude jokes mentioned by Diogenes are in harmony with a man whom *Cic.* N. D. ii. 17, 46, calls homo non aptissimus ad jocandum minimeque resipiens patriam. On these jokes he apparently prided himself as well as on a certain bombastic elegance. See p. 496, 6. In this Epicurus was followed by his pupils. *Cic.* N. D. i. 34, 93, says of Zeno:

But far from disproving the influence of previous systems on his own, this conduct only shows the personal vanity of Epicurus. Epicureanism, like Stoicism, starts with the object of bringing down science from metaphysical speculation to the simpler form of a practical science of life. Both systems of philosophy, therefore, turn away from Plato and Aristotle, whose labours they notably neglect, to Socrates and those Socratic Schools which, without more extensive meddling with science, are content with ethics. Circumstances, however, led Epicurus to follow Aristippus as Zeno had followed Antisthenes. Not only in morals did Epicurus derive his principle of pleasure from the Cyrenaics; he likewise derived from them his theory of knowledge, that the sense-impressions are the only source of ideas, and that every feeling is true in itself. Nor can he altogether deny the assertion that feelings only furnish direct information respecting our personal states, and hence respecting the relative properties of things. With the Cyrenaics, too, he taught that true pleasure can only be secured by philosophic intelligence, and that this intelligence aims, before all things, at liberating the mind from passion, fear, and superstition. At the same time, he is by no means prepared to follow the Cyrenaics unreservedly. His theory of morals differs, as has already been seen, from the Cyrenaic

---

Non oos solum, qui tunc erant, Apollodorum, Silum, ceteros figebat maledictis, sed Socratem ipsum . . . scurram Atticum fuisse dicebat (according to

Cic. Brut. 85, 292, Epicurus had already expressed a disparaging opinion of the Socratic irony), Chrysippum nunquam nisi Chrysippam vocabat.

theory in this important particular, that not sensual and individual pleasure, but mental repose and the whole state of the mind is regarded as the ultimate end, and the highest good in life. It was thus impossible for him to be content, as the Cyrenaics were, with feelings only, with individual and personal impressions. He could not help pursuing a conviction reposing on a real knowledge of things, since only on such a conviction can an equable and certain tone of mind depend.

(3) Relation to Democritus.

Epicurus, therefore, not only differed from Aristippus with regard to feelings, in referring all feelings to impressions from without, of which he considered them true representations, but he felt himself called upon to meet the Cyrenaic contempt for theories of nature, just as the Stoics had met the Cynic contempt for science. To the physics of Democritus he looked for a scientific basis for his ethics, just as they had looked to the system of Heraclitus. But the closer he clung to Democritus, owing to the weakness of his own interest in nature, the more it becomes apparent that his whole study of nature was subservient to a moral purpose, and hence of a purely relative value. Accordingly, he had not the least hesitation in setting consistency at defiance, by assuming the swerving aside of atoms and the freedom of the will. It is not only altogether improbable that Epicurus was only a second edition of Democritus—for history knows of no such repetitions—but as a matter of fact it is false. A more accurate observation proves that even when the two philosophers

agree in individual statements, the meaning which
they attach to these assertions and the whole spirit
of their systems is widely divergent. Democritus
aims at explaining natural phenomena by natural
causes. He wishes, in short, for a *science* of nature
purely for its own sake. Epicurus wishes for a *view*
of nature able to avert disturbing influences from
man's inner life. Natural science stands with him
entirely in the service of ethics. If in point of substance his system is borrowed from another system,
yet its whole position and treatment supposes an entirely new view of things. The Socratic introspection, and the Sophistic resolution of natural philosophy into personal rationalising, are its historical
antecedents ; and it owes its existence to the general
aversion of thought for pure theory, which constitutes the common peculiarity of all the post-Aristotelian philosophy.

Excepting the systems named, Epicureanism is
connected with no other previous system, so far as is
known. Even its attack upon those systems appears to have consisted of general dogmatic and
superficial statements. Still it must not be forgotten
that Epicureanism presupposes the line of thought
originated by Socrates, not only as found in the col-
lateral Cyrenaic branch, but as found in the main line
of regular development by Plato and Aristotle. The
view of Plato and Aristotle, distinguishing the immaterial essence from the sensible appearance of
things, and attributing reality only to the former,
is undoubtedly attacked by Epicurus as by Zeno, on

CHAP.
XXI.

(4) *Rela-
tion to
Aristotle
and Plato.*

metaphysicsl grounds, by his materialism. Practically, however, he approaches very much nearer to
this view in all those points in which his teaching
deviates from the Cyrenaic, and resembles that of
the Stoics.

It has been observed on a former occasion that
the indifference to the immediate conditions of the
senses, the withdrawal of the mind within itself, the
contentment with itself of the thinking subject,
which Epicurus required no less than the Stoics and
cotemporary Sceptics, is nothing but a consequence
of the idealism of Plato and Aristotle. Even the
materialism of the post-Aristotelian systems, it is
said, was by no means a going back to the old pre-
Socratic philosophy of nature, but only a one-sided
practical apprehension of that idealism. These systems only deny a soul in nature or a soul in man,
because they look exclusively to consciousness and
to personal activity for independence of the senses.
The correctness of this observation may be easily
proved from the Epicurean teaching, notwithstanding the severity and harshness of its materialism.
Why was it that Epicurus relentlessly banished
from nature all immaterial causes and all idea of
purpose? And why did he confine himself exclusively to a mechanical explanation of nature?
Was it not because he felt afraid that the admission
of any other than material causes would imperil the
certainty of consciousness; because he feared to lose
the firm groundwork of reality by admitting invisible forces, and to expose human life to influences

beyond calculation if he were to allow of anything immaterial? Yet how slightly, in his view of life, does he adhere to present facts, since his wise man is made to enjoy perfect happiness by himself alone, independent of everything external. The same ideal is reproduced in the Epicurean Gods. In their isolated contemplation of themselves, what else do they resemble but the God of Aristotle, who, aloof from all intermeddling with the world, meditates on himself alone? No doubt the independent existence of the thinking mind is held only by Aristotle in a pure and dignified manner. By Epicurus it is pourtrayed in a sensuous, and, therefore, a contradictory form. But the connection of the views of both cannot be ignored. A similar relation exists generally between the Epicurean philosophy and that of Plato and Aristotle.[1] Little as the former can be compared with the latter in breadth and depth, it must not, therefore, be regarded as an intellectual monstrosity. Epicureanism is a tenable though one-sided expression of a certain stage in the development of the intellect of Greece.

---

[1] Compare in this connection the quotations from Metrodorus on p. 476, 1.

PART IV.

THE SCEPTICS—PYRRHO AND THE OLDER
ACADEMY.

CHAPTER XXII.

PYRRHO.

Chap.
XXII.
_____

A. *His-*
torical
position of
Scepti-
cism.
(1) *Its re-*
lation to
cotem-
porary
dogmatic
systems.

STOICISM and Epicureanism are alike in one respect:
they commence the pursuit of happiness with definite
dogmatic statements. The Sceptic Schools, however,
attempt to reach the same end by denying every
dogmatic position. Varied as the paths may be,
the result is in all cases the same; happiness is made
to consist in the exaltation of the mind above all
external objects, in the withdrawal of man within
his own thinking self. Moving in the same sphere
as the cotemporary dogmatic systems, the post-Aristotelian Scepticism takes a practical view of the
business of philosophy, and estimates the value of
theoretical enquiries by their influence on the state
and happiness of man. It moreover agrees with
cotemporary systems in its ethical view of life; the
object at which it aims is the same as that at which
those systems aim—repose of mind, and imperturba-

bility. It differs, however, from them, none the less; for the Epicureans and Stoics make mental repose to depend on a knowledge of the world and its laws, whereas the Sceptics are of opinion that it can only be obtained by despairing of all knowledge. Hence, with the former, morality depends on a positive conviction as to the highest Good; with the latter, morality consists in indifference to all that appears as Good to men. Important as this difference may be, it must not therefore be forgotten that Scepticism generally revolves in the same sphere as Stoicism and Epicureanism, and that in renouncing all claim to knowledge, and all interest in the external world, it is only pushing to extremes that withdrawal of man into himself which we have seen to be the common feature of these Schools. Not only, therefore, do these three lines of thought belong to one and the same epoch, but such is their internal connection, that they may be regarded as three branches of a common stock.

More than one point of departure was offered to Scepticism by the earlier philosophy. The Megarian criticism and the Cynic teaching had taken up a position subversive of all connection of ideas, and of all knowledge. Pyrrho, too, had received from the School of Democritus an impulse to doubt.[1] In

(2) Causes producing it.

---

[1] Democritus had denied all truth to sensuous impressions. The same sceptical tone was more strongly apparent in Metrodorus (Aristocl. in *Eus.* Pr. Ev. xiv. 19, 5; *Sext.* Math. vii. 88; *Epiphan.* Exp. Fid. 1088, A), although, notwithstanding his usual agreement with the physical views of Democritus (*Plut.* in *Eus.* l. c. i. 8, 11; *id.* Fac. Lun. 15, 3, p. 928; *Sen.* Nat. Qu. vi. 19), he cannot be considered a full

particular, the development of the Platonic and Aristotelian speculations by those who were not able to
follow them, had made men distrustful of all speculation, until they at last doubted the possibility of
all knowledge. Not seldom do Sceptical theories
follow times of great philosophical originality. Still
stronger in the sequel was the impulse given by the
Stoic and Epicurean systems. Related as these systems are to Scepticism by their practical tone, it was
natural that they should afford fuel to Scepticism. At
the same time the unsatisfactory groundwork upon
which they were built, and the contrast between their
moral and physical teaching, promoted destructive
criticism. If, according to the Stoics and Epicureans, the individual and the universal elements in

Sceptic. Scepticism appears to have passed from him to Pyrrho, Anaxarchus being the middleman (see p. 518, 2, 3), and herewith may be combined the Sceptical imperturbability. This doctrine of imperturbability being held by Epicurus, the pupil of Nausiphanes, it might be supposed that before Pyrrho's time a doctrine not unlike that of Pyrrho had been developed in the School of Democritus, from whom it was borrowed by Epicurus. The connection is, however, uncertain. We have seen that the doubts of Democritus only extended to sense-impressions, not to intellectual knowledge. The case of Metrodorus was similar. His sceptical expressions refer only to the ordinary conditions of human knowledge, that of ideas derived from the senses; greater dependence is, however, placed on thought. We must therefore take the statement ὅτι πάντα ἐστὶν ὃ ἄν τις νοῆσαι subject to this limitation. Anaxarchus is said (*Sext.* Math. vii. 87) to have compared the world to a stage-scene, which involves no greater scepticism than the similar expressions used by Plato as to the phenomenal world. However much, therefore, these individuals may have contributed to Pyrrhonism, a simple transference of Scepticism from Democritus to Pyrrho is not to be thought of. And as regards imperturbability, Epicurus may have borrowed the expression from Pyrrho, whom, according to *Diog.* ix. 64 and 69, he both knew and esteemed.

the personal soul, the isolation of the individual as CHAP.
an independent atom, and his being merged in a pan- XXII.
theistic universe, stand over against one another
without being reconciled; among the Sceptics this
contrast has given place to neutrality. Neither the
Stoic nor the Epicurean theory can claim acceptation;
neither the unconditional value of pleasure, nor yet
the unconditional value of virtue; neither the truth
of the senses nor the truth of rational knowledge;
neither the Atomist's view of nature, nor the Pantheistic view as it found expression in Heraclitus,
can be vindicated. The only thing which remains
certain amid universal uncertainty is abstract personality content with itself, a personality forming at
once the starting-point and the goal of the two contending systems.

The important back-influence of Stoicism and
Epicureanism upon Scepticism may be best gathered
from the fact that Scepticism only attained a wide
extension and a more comprehensive basis in the
New Academy after the appearance of those systems.
Before that time its leading features had been indeed
laid down by Pyrrho, but they had never been developed into a permanent School of Scepticism, nor
given rise to an expanded theory of doubt.

Pyrrho was a native of Elis,[1] and may therefore (3) *Pyrrho*
have early made the acquaintance of the Elean and *and his followers.*

[1] Aristocl. in *Eus.* Pr. Ev.
xiv. 18, 1; *Diog.* ix. 61. We
are indebted almost exclusively
to Diogenes for our information respecting Pyrrho. Besides
Antigonus the Carystian, Apollodorus, Alexander Polyhistor,
Diocles, &c., are the chief authorities drawn upon by Diogenes.

CHAP.
XXII.

Megarian criticism—that criticism, in fact, which
was the precursor of subsequent Scepticism. It can,
however, hardly be true that Bryso was his instructor.[1]
To Anaxarchus, a follower of Democritus, he attached
himself, accompanying that philosopher with Alexander's army as far as India.[2] Still he is less indebted
to Anaxarchus for the sceptical than for the ethical
parts of his teaching.[3]   At a later period he resided

---

[1] Attention has been drawn
to the chronological difficulties
in ' Socrates and the Socratic
Schools,' p. 255, note 1 (2nd
edition).   Either Pyrrho is
falsely called a pupil of Bryso,
or Bryso is falsely called the
son of Stilpo.   The former
seems more probable, *Diog.*
ix. 61, having derived his statement from Alexander's διαδοχαί,
and it is quite the style of the
compilers of διαδοχαί to assign
a Megarian teacher to a Sceptic
whose connection with that
School was sufficiently obvious.

[2] *Diog.* ix. 61 ; Aristocl. l. c.
18, 20; 17, 8.   We gather from
them that Pyrrho was originally a painter. *Suidas* Πύρρων
only copies the present text of
Diogenes with a few mistakes.

[3] Besides the passage quoted
from Sextus, p. 515, 1, which is
little known, we have no proof
of the sceptical tone in Anaxarchus which *Sextus*, Math. vii.
48, ascribes to him, and since
the latter quotes no proofs, it
may be assumed that he had
none. Anaxarchus appears to
have been unjustly included
among the Sceptics, like so
many others who were called
Sceptics by later writers on the
strength of a single word or

expression. According to other
accounts, he belonged to the
School of Democritus. *Plut.*
Tranq. An. 4, p. 466. In *Valer.*
Max. viii. 14, ext. 2, he pro-
pounds to Alexander the doctrine of an infinite number of
worlds ; and *Clemens*, Strom. i.
287, B, quotes a fragment, in
which, agreeing with Democritus, he observes that πολυ-
μαθία is only useful where it is
properly made use of. Like
Epicurus, Anaxarchus followed
Democritus, calling happiness
the highest object of our desire;
and this assertion probably
gained for him the epithet ὁ
εὐδαιμονικὸς (*Clemens*, l. c.;
Athen. vi. 250; xii. 548, b; *Æl.*
V. H. ix. 37).   In other respects, he differed from Democritus. For first he is charged
by Clearch. in *Athen.* xii. 548,
b, with a luxurious indulgence
far removed from the earnest
and pure spirit of Democritus;
and according to *Plut.* Alex.
52, he had, when in Asia, renounced the independence of a
philosopher for a life of pleasure; and Timon, in *Plut.* Virt.
Mor. 6, p. 446, says he was led
away by φύσις ἡδονοπλὴξ contrary to his better knowledge.
Again, he is said to have com-

in his native city,[1] honoured by his fellow-citizens,[2] but in poor circumstances,[3] which he bore with his characteristic repose of mind.[4] He died, it would appear, at an advanced age,[5] between 275 and 270 B.C., leaving no writings behind.[6] Even the ancients, therefore, only knew his teaching by that of his pupils, among whom Timon of Phlius was the most

mended in Pyrrho (*Diog.* ix. 63) an indifference which went a good deal beyond the imperturbability of Democritus ; and Timon commends him for his κύνικον μένος. He meets external pain with the haughty pride expressed in his much-admired dictum under the blows of Nitocreon's club—*Diog.* ix. 59 ; *Plut.* Virt. Mor. c. 10, p. 449 ; *Clemens*, Strom. iv. 496, D; *Valer. Max.* iii. 3, ext. 4 ; *Plin.* Hist. Nat. vii. 87; *Tertull.* Apol. 50; *Dio Chrysos.* Or. 37, p. 126, R. But he treats men with the same contempt ; and whilst meeting the Macedonian conqueror with an air of independence, he spoils the whole by adroit flattery. Conf. *Plut.* Alex. 52 ; Ad Prine. Iner. 4, p. 781; Qu. Conv. ix. 1, 2, 5 ; *Æl.* V. H. ix. 37 ; *Athen.* vi. 250. His indifference was, at any rate, very much lacking in nobility. Respecting Anaxarchus, see *Lusac.* Lect. Att. 181.

[1] *Diog.* ix. 64 ; 109.
[2] According to *Diog.* 64, they made him head-priest, and, on his account, allowed to philosophers immunity from taxation. According to Diocles (*Diog.* 65), the Athenians presented him with citizenship for his services in putting a Thracian prince Cotys to death.

[3] *Diog.* 66 ; 62.
[4] Examples in *Diog.* 67. It sounds, however, highly improbable ; and doubts were expressed by Ænesidemus whether his indifference ever went to the extent described by Antigonus, *Ibid.* 62, of not getting out of the way of carriages and precipices, so that he had to be preserved from danger by his friends. He must, moreover, have enjoyed a special good fortune to attain the age of 90, notwithstanding such senseless conduct.
[5] All the dates here are very uncertain. Neither the date of his death nor of his birth is given, and the notice in Suidas that he lived after the 111 Olympiad (336–332 B.C.) is of no avail. If, however, as *Diog.* 62, says, he attained the age of 90, and if he joined Anaxarchus at Alexander's first invasion of Asia, being then between 24 and 30, the statements above given are true.
[6] *Diog.* Pro. 16 ; 102 ; Aristocl. in *Eus.* Pr. Ev. xiv. 18, 1 ; better authorities than *Sext.* Math. i. 282, or *Plut.* Alex. Fort. i. 10, p. 331. Neither does Sextus say that the supposed poem on Alexander was extant. The whole statement is evidently untrustworthy.

important.[1] Besides Timon several other of his pupils are known by name.[2] His School, however, was short-lived.[3] Soon after Timon it seems to have

[1] Timon (see *Wachsmuth,* De Timone Phliasio, Leipzig, 1859) was a native of Phlius (*Diog.* ix. 109). A public dancer at first (*Diog.* 109; Aristocl. in *Eus.* Pr. Ev. xiv. 18, 12), when tired of this mode of life he repaired to Megara, to hear Stilpo (*Diog.* 109). Stilpo being alive in the third century, and Timon's birth having happened approximately between 325–315 B.C., the connection is not so impossible as Wachsmuth, p. 5, and Preller, Hist. Phil. Gr. et Rom. 398, suppose, though in the uncertainty of chronological data it cannot be positively stated. Subsequently Timon became acquainted with Pyrrho, and removed with his wife to Elis, leaving his staunch admirers (*Diog.* 109, 69; *Aristocl.* l. c. 11, 14, 21). He then appeared as a teacher in Chalcis, and, having amassed a fortune, concluded his life in Athens (*Diog.* 110; 115). It appears from *Diog.* 112 and 115, that he survived Arcesilaus (who died 241 B.C.), having nearly attained the age of 90. His death may therefore be approximately fixed in 230, his birth in 320 B.C. For his life and character, see *Diog.* 110; 112–115; *Athen.* x. 438, a; *Æl.* V. H. ii. 41. Of his numerous writings, the best known is a witty and pungent satire on previous and cotemporary philosophers. Respecting this satire (*Diog.* 110) consult *Wachsmuth,* p. 9 and 3. The

latter, p. 51, has collected the fragments.

[2] *Diog.* 67–69, mentions, besides Timon, a certain Eurylochus as his pupil, who, however, was not very successful in the way of keeping his temper; also Philo, an Athenian, Hecataeus of Abdera, the well-known historian (on whom see *Müller,* Fragm. Hist. Gr. ii. 384); and Nausiphanes, the teacher of Epicurus. The last assertion is only tenable on the supposition that Nausiphanes appeared as a teacher only a few years after Pyrrho, for Pyrrho cannot have returned to Elis before 322 B.C., and Epicurus must have left the School of Nausiphanes before 310 B.C. See p. 406, 3. According to *Diog.* 64, Epicurus must have become acquainted with Pyrrho whilst a pupil of Nausiphanes. Nausiphanes is said not to have agreed with Pyrrho, but only to have admired his character (*Diog.* l. c.), so that he cannot properly be called his pupil. Numenius, mentioned by *Diog.* 102 (Conf. 68), among Pyrrho's συνήθεις, is suspicious, Ænesidemus being named at the same time, and it may be questioned whether he as well as Ænesidemus does not belong to a later period of Scepticism.

[3] According to *Diog.* 115, Menodotus (a Sceptic belonging to the latter half of the second century after Christ) asserted that Timon left no successor, the School being in

become extinct.[1] Those who were disposed to be sceptical now joined the New Academy, towards whose founder even Timon made no secret of his grudge.[2]

The little which is known of Pyrrho's teaching may be summed up in the three following statements: We can know nothing as to the nature of things: Hence the right attitude towards them is to withhold judgment: The necessary result of suspending judgment is imperturbability. He who will live happily—for happiness is the starting-point with the Sceptics—must, according to Timon, take these things into consideration: What is the nature of things? What ought our attitude to things to be? What is the gain resulting from these relations?[3] To the first of these three questions Pyrrho can only reply by saying that things are altogether inaccessible to knowledge, and that whatever property may be attributed to a thing, with equal justice the oppo-

abeyance from Timon to Ptolemæus, i.e., until the second half of the first century B.C. Sotion and Hippobotus, however, asserted that his pupils were Dioscurides, Nicolochus, Euphranor, and Praÿlus. His son too, the physician Xanthus, likewise followed his father. (*Diog.* 109.) That, however, Timon was himself a physician, as *Wachsmuth*, p. 5, supposes, does not follow with certainty from the words: ἰατρικὸν ἐδίδαξε, since these only mean he had been instructed in medicine. On the other hand, according to *Suid.* Πύρρων, the second Pyrrho, called Timon's pupil, was a changeling. If Aratus of Soli

was a pupil of his (*Suid.*῎Αρατος; conf. *Diog.* ix. 113), he was certainly not an adherent of his views. See p. 43, 2.

[1] In *Diog.* 116, Eubulus is called a pupil of Euphranor, also on the authority of Sotion and Hippobotus. If Ptolemæus is named as the next one after him, no philosopher of Pyrrho's ἀγωγὴ can have been known for 150 years.

[2] *Diog.* 114.

[3] Aristocl. in *Eus.* Pr. Ev. xiv. 18, 2 : ὁ δέ γε μαθητὴς αὐτοῦ Τίμων φησὶ δεῖν τὸν μέλλοντα εὐδαιμονήσειν εἰς τρία ταῦτα βλέπειν· πρῶτον μὲν ὁποῖα πέφυκε τὰ πράγματα· δεύτερον δὲ, τίνα χρὴ τρόπον ἡμᾶς πρὸς αὐτὰ διακεῖσθαι·

site may be predicated.[1] In support of this statement
Pyrrho appears to have argued that neither the senses
nor reason furnish certain knowledge.[2] The senses
do not show things as they are, but only as they appear to be.[3] Rational knowledge, even where it
seems to be most certain, in the sphere of morals,
does not depend upon real knowledge, but only upon
tradition and habit.[4] Against every statement the
opposite may be advanced with equal justice.[5] If,
however, neither the senses nor reason alone can furnish trustworthy testimony, no more can the two
combined, and thus the third way is barred, by which
we might possibly have advanced to knowledge.[6] How
many more of the arguments quoted by the later
Sceptics belong to Pyrrho it is impossible to say.
The short duration and diffusion of Pyrrho's School
renders it probable that with him Scepticism was not

τελευταῖον δὲ τί περιέσται τοῖς
οὕτως ἔχουσιν.

[1] Aristocl. 1. c.: τὰ μὲν οὖν
πράγματά φησιν αὐτὸν (Pyrrho)
ἀποφαίνειν ἐπίσης ἀδιάφορα καὶ
ἀστάθμητα καὶ ἀνεπίκριτα, διὰ
τοῦτο [τὸ] μήτε τὰς αἰσθήσεις
ἡμῶν μήτε τὰς δόξας ἀληθεύειν
ἢ ψεύδεσθαι. *Diog.* ix. 61: οὐ
γὰρ μᾶλλον τόδε ἢ τόδε εἶναι
ἕκαστον. *Gell.* xi. 5, 4: Pyrrho is
said to have stated οὐ μᾶλλον οὕτως ἔχει τόδε ἢ ἐκείνως ἢ οὐθετέρως.

[2] See the above-quoted passage of Aristocles and *Diog.* ix.
114.

[3] Timon, in *Diog.* ix. 105:
τὸ μέλι ὅτι ἐστὶ γλυκὺ οὐ τίθημι·
τὸ δ' ὅτι φαίνεται ὁμολογῶ.

[4] *Diog.* ix. 61: οὐδὲν γὰρ ἔφα-
σκεν οὔτε καλὸν οὔτε αἰσχρὸν οὔτε

δίκαιον οὔτε ἄδικον, καὶ ὁμοίως ἐπὶ
πάντων, μηδὲν εἶναι τῇ ἀληθείᾳ,
νόμῳ δὲ καὶ ἔθει πάντα τοὺς ἀνθρώπους πράττειν, οὐ γὰρ μᾶλλον
τόδε ἢ τόδε εἶναι ἕκαστον. *Sext.*
Math. xi. 140: οὔτε ἀγαθόν τί
ἐστι φύσει οὔτε κακόν, ἀλλὰ πρὸς
ἀνθρώπων ταῦτα νόῳ κέκριται κατὰ
τὸν Τίμωνα.

[5] In this sense the words of
Ænesidemus, in *Diog.* ix. 106,
must be understood: οὐδέν φησιν
ὁρίζειν τὸν Πύρρωνα· δογματικῶς
διὰ τὴν ἀντιλογίαν. See note 1.

[6] *Diog.* ix. 114, on Timon:
συνεχές τε ἐπιλέγειν εἰώθει πρὸς
τοὺς τὰς αἰσθήσεις μετ' ἐπιμαρτυ-
ροῦντος τοῦ νοῦ ἐγκρίνοντας· συν-
ῆλθεν Ἀτταγᾶς τε καὶ Νουμήνιος.
The meaning of this proverb
has been already explained.

far advanced. The same result appears to follow from its further development in the Academy. The ten τρόποι, or aspects under which sceptical objections were grouped, cannot with certainty be attributed to any one before Ænesidemus.[1] Portions of the arguments used at a later day may be borrowed from Pyrrho and his pupils,[2] but it is impossible to discriminate these portions with certainty.

Thus, if knowledge of things proves to be a failure, there only remains as possible an attitude of pure Scepticism ; and therein is contained the answer to the second question. We know nothing whatever of the real nature of things, and hence can neither believe nor assert anything as to their nature. We cannot say of anything that it *is* or *is not* ; but we must abstain from every opinion, allowing that of all which appears to us to be true, the opposite may with equal justice be true.[3] Accordingly, all our state-

(2) *With-holding of judgment.*

---

[1] *Diog.* ix. 79 refers these τρόποι to Pyrrho, but inasmuch as he was there describing Sceptic views, the author of which to his mind was Pyrrho, nothing follows from his statement. *Sext.* Pyrrh. i. 36 generally attributes them to the ancient Sceptics, by whom, according to Math. vii. 345, he understood Ænesidemus and his followers. Aristocles, l. c. 18, 11, refers them to Ænesidemus, and they may easily have been referred to Pyrrho by mistake, since Ænesidemus himself (*Diog.* ix. 106) and subsequent writers (Favorin. in *Gell.* xi. 5, 5 ; *Philostr.* Vit. Soph. i. 491) call every kind of

sceptical statement λόγοι or τρόποι Πυρρώνειοι. That they cannot belong to Pyrrho in the form in which they are presented by Sextus and Diogenes is clear, since they obviously refer to later views.

[2] *Sext.* Math. vi. 66 ; x. 197 quotes an argument of Timon against the reality of time, and further states (Math. iv. 2) that Timon, in his conflict with the philosophers of nature, maintained that no assertion should be made without proof : in other words, he denied dogmatism, every proof supposing something established, i.e. another proof, and so on for ever.

[3] Aristocl. l. c. 18, 3 : διὰ

CHAP.
XXII.

ments (as the Cyrenaics taught) only express individual opinions, and not absolute realities. We cannot deny that things *appear* to be of this or the
other kind ; but we can never say that they are so.[1]
Even the assertion that things are of this or the
other kind, is not an assertion, but a confession by
the individual of his state of mind.[2] Hence, too, the
universal maxim of being undecided cannot be taken
as an established principle, but only as a confession,
and, therefore, as only problematical.[3] It must, however, remain a matter of doubt how far the captious
turns of expression by which the Sceptics thought
to parry the attacks of their opponents, come from
Pyrrho's School. The greater part, it is clear, came
into use in the struggle with the Dogmatists, the
lively play of which is not older than the develop-

τοῦτο οὖν μηδὲ πιστεύειν αὐταῖς
δεῖν, ἀλλ' ἀδοξάστους καὶ ἀκλινεῖς
καὶ ἀκραδάντους εἶναι περὶ ἑνὸς
ἑκάστου λέγοντας ὅτι οὐ μᾶλλον
ἔστιν ἢ οὐκ ἔστιν, ἢ καὶ ἔστι καὶ
οὐκ ἔστιν, ἢ οὔτε ἔστιν οὔτ' οὐκ
ἔστιν. *Diog.* ix. 61. *Ibid.* 76 :
οὐ μᾶλλον means, according to
Timon, τὸ μηδὲν ὁρίζειν ἀλλὰ
ἀπροσθετεῖν.
    [1] Ænesidèm. in *Diog.* ix.
106 : οὐδὲν ὁρίζειν τὸν Πύρρωνα
δογματικῶς διὰ τὴν ἀντιλογίαν,
τοῖς δὲ φαινομένοις ἀκολουθεῖν.
Timon, *Ibid.* 105. See p. 522, 3.
    [2] *Diog.* ix. 103 : περὶ μὲν ὧν
ὡς ἄνθρωποι πάσχομεν ὁμολογοῦμεν
. . . περὶ δὲ ὧν οἱ δογματικοὶ δια-
βεβαιοῦνται τῷ λόγῳ φάμενοι κα-
τειλῆφθαι ἐπέχομεν περὶ τούτων ὡς
ἀδήλων· μόνα δὲ τὰ πάθη γινώσκομεν. τὸ μὲν γὰρ ὅτι ὁρῶμεν ὁμολογοῦμεν καὶ τὸ ὅτι τόδε νοοῦμεν

γινώσκομεν, πῶς δ' ὁρῶμεν ἢ πῶς
νοοῦμεν ἀγνοοῦμεν· καὶ ὅτι τόδε
λευκὸν φαίνεται διηγηματικῶς λέγομεν οὐ διαβεβαιούμενοι εἰ καὶ
ὄντως ἐστί . . . καὶ γὰρ τὸ φαινόμενον τιθέμεθα οὐχ ὡς καὶ τοιοῦτον
ὄν· καὶ ὅτι πῦρ καίει αἰσθανόμεθα·
εἰ δὲ φύσιν ἔχει καυστικήν, ἐπέχομεν.
    [3] *Diog.* l. c.: περὶ δὲ τῆς Οὐδὲν
ὁρίζω φωνῆς καὶ τῶν ὁμοίων λέγομεν ὡς οὐ δογμάτων· οὐ γάρ εἰσιν
ὅμοια τῷ λέγειν ὅτι σφαιροειδής
ἐστιν ὁ κόσμος· ἀλλὰ γὰρ τὸ μὲν
ἄδηλον, αἱ δὲ ἐξομολογήσεις εἰσίν.
ἐν ᾧ οὖν λέγομεν μηδὲν ὁρίζειν
οὐδ' αὐτὸ τοῦτο ὁριζόμεθα. *Diog.*
states even this view in its
later form, probably following
Sext. Pyrrh. i. 197, but agreeing
in substance with the quotations from Timon and Pyrrho.

ment of the Stoic theory of knowledge by Chrysippus, and the criticism of Carneades to which it gave rise. In this despairing of anything like certain conviction consists *ἀφασία, ἀκαταληψία* or *ἐποχὴ,* the withholding of judgment or state of indecision which Pyrrho and Timon regard as the only true attitude in speculation,[1] and from which the whole School derived its distinctive name.[2]

From this state of indecision, Timon, in reply to the third question, argues that mental imperturbability or *ἀταραξία* proceeds, which can alone conduct to true happiness.[3] Men are disturbed by views and prejudices which mislead them into efforts of passion. Only the Sceptic who has suspended all judgment is in a condition to regard things with absolute calmness, unruffled by passion or desire.[4] He

(3) Mental imperturbability.

---

[1] *Diog.* ix. 61 and 107; Aristocl. l. c. The expressions ἀφασία, ἀκαταληψία, ἐποχὴ, invariably mean the same thing. Later writers use instead of them, ἀρρεψία, ἀγνωσία τῆς ἀληθείας, κ.τ.λ. If, according to Aristocles and Diog. 107, Timon first mentioned ἀφασία on occasion of the first of his questions, this statement is obviously inaccurate.

[2] Πυρρώνειοι, σκεπτικοὶ, ἀπορητικοὶ, ἐφεκτικοὶ, ζητητικοί. Conf. *Diog.* 69.

[3] Aristocl. l. c. 2: τοῖς μέντοι διακειμένοις οὕτω περιέσεσθαι Τίμων φησὶ πρῶτον μὲν ἀφασίαν ἔπειτα δ᾽ ἀταραξίαν. *Diog.* 107: τέλος δὲ οἱ σκεπτικοί φασι τὴν ἐποχὴν, ᾗ σκιᾶς τρόπον ἐπακολουθεῖ ἡ ἀταραξία, ὥς φασιν οἵ τε περὶ τὸν Τίμωνα καὶ Αἰνεσίδημον.

Apathy is substituted for ataraxy in *Diog.* 108; *Cic.* Acad. ii. 42, 130.

[4] Timon, in Aristocl. l. c. 18, 14, speaking of Pyrrho:—

ἀλλ᾽ οἷον τὸν ἄτυφον ἐγὼ ἴδον ἠδ᾽ ἀδάμαστον
πᾶσιν, ὅσοις δάμνανται ὁμῶς ἄφατοί τε φατοί τε (conf. *Wachsmuth,* p. 62)
λαῶν ἔθνεα κοῦφα, βαρυνόμεν᾽ ἔνθα καὶ ἔνθα
ἐκ παθέων δόξης τε καὶ εἰκαίης νομοθήκης.

Id. in *Sext.* Math. xi. 1: The Sceptic lives—

ῥῆστα μεθ᾽ ἡσυχίης
αἰεὶ ἀφροντίστως καὶ ἀκινήτως κατὰ ταὐτὰ
μὴ προσέχων δειλοῖς ἡδυλόγου σοφίης.

Id. in *Diog.* 65.

knows that it is a fond delusion to suppose that one
external condition is preferable to another.[1] In reality
only the tone of mind or virtue possesses value.[2] Thus,
by withdrawing within himself, man reaches happiness, which is the goal of all philosophy.[3] Absolute
inactivity being, however, impossible, the Sceptic
will act on probabilities, and hence follow custom;[4]
but at the same time he will be conscious that this
conduct does not rest on a basis of firm conviction.[5]
To this province only of uncertain opinion all positive judgments respecting good and evil belong.
Only in this conditional form will Timon allow of
goodness and divine goodness as standards of conduct.[6] The real object of this Scepticism is, therefore, a purely negative one—indifference. It cannot
even be proved[7] that Pyrrho's School so far acom-

[1] *Cic.* Fin. ii. 13, 43 : Quæ
(externals) quod Aristoni et
Pyrrhoni omnino visa sunt pro
nihilo, ut inter optime valere
et gravissime ægrotare nihil
prorsus dicerent interesse. iii.
3, 11 : Cum Pyrrhone et Aristone qui omnia exæquent.
Acad. ii. 42, 130 : Pyrrho autem
ea ne sentire quidem sapientem,
quæ ἀπάθεια nominatur. *Epictet.*
Fragm. 93 (in *Stob.* Serm. 121,
28): Πύῤῥων ἔλεγεν μηδὲν διαφέρειν ζῆν ἢ τεθνάναι.

[2] *Cic.* Fin. iv. 16, 43 : Pyrrho
... qui virtute constituta nihil
omnino quod appetendum sit
relinquat. The same *Ibid.* ii.
13, 43 ; iii. 4, 12.

[3] See p. 521, 3 ; 525, 3.

[4] *Diog.* 105 : ὁ Τίμων ἐν τῷ
Πύθωνί φησι μὴ ἐκβεβηκέναι [τὸν
Πύῤῥωνα] τὴν συνήθειαν. καὶ ἐν
τοῖς ἰνδαλμοῖς οὕτω λέγει· ἀλλὰ

τὸ φαινόμενον παντὶ σθένει οὗπερ
ἂν ἔλθῃ. (Conf. *Sext.* Math.
vii. 30.) *Ibid.* 106, of Pyrrho :
τοῖς δὲ φαινομένοις ἀκολουθεῖν.
See p. 519, 4.

[5] See p. 524, 1, 2.

[6] *Sext.* Math. xi. 20: κατὰ δὲ
τὸ φαινόμενον τούτων ἕκαστον ἔχομεν ἔθος ἀγαθὸν ἢ κακὸν ἢ ἀδιάφορον προσαγορεύειν· καθάπερ καὶ
ὁ Τίμων ἐν τοῖς ἰνδαλμοῖς ἔοικε
δηλοῦν ὅταν φῇ

ἦ γὰρ ἐγὼν ἐρέω ὥς μοι καταφαί-
νεται εἶναι
μῦθον ἀληθείης ὀρθὸν ἔχων κανό-
να·
ὡς ἡ τοῦ θείου τε φύσις καὶ τἀγα-
θοῦ αἰεὶ,
ἐξ ὧν ἰσότατος γίγνεται ἀνδρὶ
βίος.

[7] According to an anecdote
preserved by Antigonus of Carystus (Aristocl. 1. c. 18, 19;

modated itself to life, as to make moderation rather
than indifference the regulating principle for unavoidable actions and desires. In this direction the
School seems to have done but little.

CHAP.
XXII.

Diog. ix. 66), Pyrrho apologised for being agitated by saying: It is difficult to lay aside humanity altogether. This language only proves what his aim was, and that he had found no mediating principle between the apathy required by his system and practical needs. Neither do the remarks of *Ritter*, iii. 451, prove that the doctrine of moderation belongs to Pyrrho and his school.

CHAPTER XXIII.

THE NEW ACADEMY.

CHAP.
XXIII.

A. *Arcesi-laus.*
(1) *Denial of knowledge.*

PLATO's School was the first to put Scepticism on a firmer footing, and to cultivate it as a system. It has been already remarked that after the time of Xenocrates this School gradually deserted speculative enquiries, limiting itself to Ethics. To this new tendency it consistently adhered, when shortly after the beginning of the third century before Christ it took a fresh lease of life. Instead, however, of simply ignoring theoretical knowledge, as it had hitherto done, it assumed towards knowledge an attitude of opposition, hoping to arrive at security and happiness in life by being persuaded of the impossibility of knowledge. How far this result was due to the example set by Pyrrho it is impossible to establish authoritatively. But it is not in itself probable that the learned originator of this line of thought in the Academy should have ignored the views of a philosopher whose work had been carried on at Elis in his own lifetime, and whose most distinguished pupil, a personal acquaintance of his own, was then working at Athens as a prolific writer.[1] The whole tone

[1] Conf. *Diog.* ix. 114. Tennemann's view (Gesch. d. Phil. iv. 190), that Arcesilaus arrived at his conclusions indepen-

and character, moreover, of the Scepticism of the
New Academy betrays everywhere the presence of
Stoic influences. By the confidence of its assertions it provokes contradiction and doubt, without
its being necessary to seek an explanation by improbable conjectures as to the personal relations of Arcesilaus and Zeno.[1]

This connection of the New Academy with Stoicism can be proved in the case of its first founder,[2]
Arcesilaus.[3] The doubts of this philospher are directed

dently of Pyrrho, does not appear to be tenable.
[1] Numen. in *Eus.* Pr. Ev.
xiv. 5, 10; 6, 5, says that Zeno
and Arcesilaus were fellow-
pupils under Polemo, and that
their rivalry whilst at school
was the origin of the later
quarrels between the Stoa and
the Academy. The same may
have been stated by Antiochus,
since *Cic.* Acad. i. 9, 35, ii. 24,
76, appeals to him to prove
their acquaintance at school.
Still the assertion is valueless.
There can be no doubt that
both Zeno and Arcesilaus were
pupils of Polemo, but it is
hardly possible that they can
have been under him at the
same time; nor if they were,
would the intellectual differences of the two schools be referred simply to their personal
relations.
[2] *Cic.* De Orat. ii. 18, 68;
Diog. iv. 28; *Eus.* Pr. Ev. xiv.
4, 16; *Sext.* Pyrrh. i. 220. *Clemens*, Strom. i. 301, C, calls
Arcesilaus the founder of the
New (second or middle) Academy.

[3] Arcesilaus (see *Geffers*,
De Arcesila. Gött. 1842, Gymn.
Progr.) was born at Pitane, in
Æolia (*Strabo*, xiii. 1, 67, p. 614;
Diog. iv. 28). His birth year is
not stated; but as Lacydes
(*Diog.* iv. 61) was his successor
in 240 B.C., and he was then 75
years of age (*Diog.* 44), it must
have been about 315 B.C. Having enjoyed the instruction of
the mathematician Autolycus
in his native town, he repaired
to Athens, where he was first a
pupil of Theophrastus, but was
gained for the Academy by
Crantor (*Diog.* 29; Numen. in
Eus. xiv. 6, 2). With Crantor
he lived on the most intimate
terms; but as Polemo was the
president of the Academy, he is
usually called a pupil of Polemo
(*Cic.* De Orat. iii. 18, 67; Fin.
v. 31, 94; *Strabo*). On the
death of Polemo, he was probably a pupil of Crates; but it
is not asserted by *Diog.* 33, or
Numen. in *Eus.* l. c. xiv. 5, 10,
that he was a pupil of either
Pyrrho, Menedemus, or Diodorus. If Eusebius seems to
imply it, it would seem to be a

not only to knowledge derived from the senses, but
to rational knowledge as well.[1] The principal object
of his attack was, however, the Stoic theory of irresistible impressions;[2] and in overthrowing that theory
Arcesilaus, it would seem, believed he had exploded
every possibility of rational knowledge; for the Stoic
appeal to the senses he regarded as the only possible
form of a theory of knowledge, and the theories of

misunderstanding of the statement that he made use of their
teaching. Fortified with extraordinary acuteness, penetrating wit, and ready speech
(*Diog.* 30; 34; 37; *Cic.* Acad.
ii. 6, 18; Numen. in *Eus.* xiv. 6,
2; *Plut.* De Sanit. 7, p. 126;
Qu. Conv. vii. 5, 3, 7; ii. 1, 10, 4;
Stob. Floril. ed. Mein. iv. 193,
28), learned, particularly in
mathematics (*Diog.* 32), and
well acquainted with native
poets (*Diog.* 30, who mentions
his own attempts at poetry,
quoting some of his epigrams),
he appears to have early distinguished himself. From *Plut.*
Adv. Col. 26, p. 1121, it appears
that in Epicurus' lifetime, consequently before 270 B.C., he
had propounded his sceptical
views with great success. Apollodorus, however, appears to
have placed his career too early
(*Diog.* 45), in making his ἀκμὴ
between 300 and 296 B.C. On
the death of Crates, the conduct of the School devolved
upon Arcesilaus (*Diog.* 32),
through whom it attained no
small note (*Strabo*, i. 2, 2, p.
15; *Diog.* 37; Numen. in *Eus.*
xiv. 6, 14). From public matters he held aloof, and lived in

retirement (*Diog.* 39), esteemed
even by opponents for his pure,
gentle, and genial character
(*Diog.* 37; quoting many individual traits, 44; vii. 171; ix.
115; *Cic.* Fin. v. 31, 94; *Plut.*
De Adulat. 22, p. 63; Coh. Ira,
13, p. 461. *Ælian*, V. H. xiv.
96). On his relations to Cleanthes, conf. *Diog.* vii. 171; *Plut.*
De Adulat. 11, p. 55. He left no
writings (*Diog.* 32; *Plut.* Alex.
Virt. 4, p. 328).

[1] *Cic.* De Orat. iii. 18, 67:
Arcesilas primum ... ex variis
Platonis libris sermonibusque
Socraticis hoc maxime arripuit,
nihil esse certi quod aut sensibus aut animo percipi possit:
quem ferunt ... aspernatum
esse omne animi sensusque judicium, primumque instituisse
... non quid ipse sentiret os-
tendere, sed contra id, quod
quisque se sentire dixisset, dis-
putare. This is, in fact, the
calumniandi licentia with which
Augustin., herein doubtless following Cicero, c. Acad. iii. 17,
39, charges him, contra omnia
velle dicere quasi ostentationis
causa.

[2] Conf. Numen. in *Eus.* Pr.
Ev. xiv. 6, 12, and above, p. 86, 4.

Plato and Aristotle he ignored altogether. Indeed,
no peculiar arguments against knowledge are referred
to him. The old sceptical arguments of Plato and
Socrates, of Anaxagoras, Empedocles, Democritus,
Heraclitus, and Parmenides, are repeated,[1] all of
which apply only to the knowledge of the senses, and
not to rational knowledge. Nevertheless, Arcesilaus
aimed at overthrowing the latter along with the former.[2] For the opinion that he only used doubt as a
preparation to or means for concealing genuine Platonism,[3] is opposed to all credible authorities. It appears, however, all the more clearly, that to him it
seemed unnecessary to refute the theory of a knowledge existing independently of the senses.

The Stoic arguments in favour of irresistible impressions Arcesilaus met by asserting that an intermediate something between knowledge and opinion,
a kind of conviction common to the wise and the
unwise, such as the Stoic κατάληψις, is inconceivable ;
the wise man's conviction being always knowledge,
and that of the fool always opinion.[4] Going then
farther into the idea of φαντασία καταληπτική, he endeavoured to show that it contained an internal contradiction ; for to conceive (κατάληψις) is to approve

---

[1] *Plut.* Adv. Col. 26,2; *Cic.*
Acad. i. 12, 44. Ritter's view
of the latter passage that Arcesilaus dwelt on the diversities
of philosophic teaching in the
view of refuting it (iii. 478)
appears to be so entirely without foundation, that he rather
appealed to its unanimity to
confront doubt.

[2] *Cic.* De Orat. iii. 18. See
p. 530, 1.
[3] *Sext.* Pyrrh. i. 234; *Diocles* of Cnidus, in Numen. in
Eus. Pr. Ev. xiv. 6, 5; *Augustin,*
c. Acad. iii. 17, 38. Geffers regards Arcesilaus as a true follower of the older Academy.
[4] *Sext.* Math. vii. 153.

(συγκατάθεσις), and approval never applies to sensation, but only to thoughts and general ideas.[1] Lastly,
if the Stoics regarded force of conviction as the distinctive mark of a true or irresistible conception, and
as belonging to it in distinction from every other, the
Sceptic rejoined that such conceptions do not exist,
and that no true conception is of such a nature, but
that a false one may be equally irresistible.[2] If no
certainty of perception is possible, no knowledge is
possible.[3] And since the wise man—for on this
point Arcesilaus agrees with the Stoics—must only
consider knowledge, and not opinion, nothing remains for him but to abstain from all and every
statement, and to despair of any certain conviction.[4]

---

[1] *Sext.* Math. l. c. 154.

[2] *Cic.* Acad. ii. 24, 27. Zeno
asserted : An irresistible or
conceptional perception is such
an impression of a real object
as cannot possibly come from
an unreal one. Arcesilaus endeavoured to prove nullum tale
visum esse a vero, ut non ejusdem modi etiam a falso posset
esse. The same view in *Sext.*
l. c. To these may be added
discussions on deceptions of the
senses and contradictions in
the statements of the senses
in *Sext.* vii. 408, and otherwise
attributed to the Academicians.
Conf. *Cic.* N. D. i. 25, 70 : Ur-
gebat Arcesilas Zenonem, cum
ipse falsa omnia diceret, quæ
sensibus viderentur, Zenon autem nonnulla visa esse falsa,
non omnia. To these attacks
on Zeno *Plut.* De An. (Fr. vii.)
1, probably refers : ὅτι οὐ τὸ
ἐπιστητὸν αἴτιον τῆς ἐπιστήμης ὡς

'Αρκεσίλαος. οὕτω γὰρ καὶ ἀνε-
πιστημοσύνη τῆς ἐπιστήμης αἴτια
φανεῖται. All that is here attributed to Arcelaus is the assertion that ἐπιστητὸν is the cause
of ἐπιστήμη, and that it is so
when it produces a φαντασία
καταληπτική. The connection
in which these statements were
made by Arcesilaus was probably this : If there is such a
thing as knowledge, there must
be objects which produce it.
These objects, however, do not
exist, there being no object
which does not admit a false
opinion equally well with a true
one.

[3] *Sext.* 155 : μὴ οὔσης δὲ καταληπτικῆς φαντασίας οὐδὲ κατάληψις γενήσεται· ἦν γὰρ καταλη-
πτικῇ φαντασίᾳ συγκατάθεσις. μὴ
οὔσης δὲ καταλήψεως πάντα ἔσται
ἀκατάληπτα.

[4] *Sext.* l. c.; *Cic.* Acad. i.
12, 45 ; ii. 20, 66 ; *Plut.* Adv.

It is therefore impossible to know anything, nor can CHAP.
XXIII. we even know for certain that we do not know anything.[1] It was quite in accordance with this theory for Arcesilaus to lay down no definite view in his lectures, but only to refute the views of others.[2] Even his disparaging remarks on dialectic,[3] supposing them to be genuine,[4] are not at variance with this conduct. He might consider the arguments of the Stoics and the sophisms of the Megarians as useless, whilst, at the same time, he was convinced that no real knowledge could be attained by any other means. He might even have inferred from their sterility, that thought leads to truth quite as little as the senses. There is no real difference between the result at which he arrived and that of Pyrrho.[5]

Col. 24, 2; *Eus.* Pr. Ev. xiv. 4, 16; 6, 4. By *Sext.* Pyrrh. i. 233, it is thus expressed: Arcesilaus regards ἐποχή as being a good in every case, συγκατάθεσις as an evil.

[1] *Cic.* Acad. i. 12, 45.

[2] *Cic.* Fin. ii. 1, 2; v. 4, 11; De Orat. iii. 18, 67; *Diog.* iv. 28; Conf. *Plut.* C. Not. 37, 7.

[3] *Stob.* Floril. 82, 4: Ἀρκεσίλαος ὁ φιλόσοφος ἔφη τοὺς διαλεκτικοὺς ἐοικέναι τοῖς ψηφοπαίκταις (jugglers), οἵτινες χαριέντως παραλογίζονται; and, *Ibid.* 10 (under the heading: Ἀρκεσιλάου ἐκ τῶν Σερήνου ἀπομνημονευμάτων): διαλεκτικὴν δὲ φεῦγε, συγκυκᾷ τἄνω κάτω.

[4] The authority is a very uncertain one, particularly as Arcesilaus left nothing in writing, and they would seem to belong more fittingly to the Chian Aristo (see p. 59) than to Arcesilaus. Still, if Chrysippus condemned the dialectic of the Sceptics (according to p. 66, 1), Arcesilaus may very well have condemned that of the Stoics and Megarians. Does not even *Cic.* Acad. ii. 28, 91, probably following Carneades (see p. 541, 4), object to dialectic, because it furnishes no knowledge?

[5] This fact is not only recognised by Numen. in *Eus.* Pr. Ev. xiv. 6, 4, but by *Sext.* Pyrrh. i. 232. Nor does the difference apply to Arcesilaus (see p. 533, 1) which the later Sceptics made between themselves and the Academicians, viz. that they asserted the principle of doubt tentatively,

CHAP.
XXIII.

(2) *Probability.*

If opponents asserted that by denying knowledge all possibility of action is denied,[1] Arcesilaus declined to accede to this statement. No firm conviction is, as he maintained, necessary for a decision of the will; for an action to come about, a perception influences the will immediately, leaving the question as to its truth entirely out of sight.[2] In order to act sensibly we need no knowledge. For this purpose probability is quite enough ; anyone can follow probability, even though he is conscious of the uncertainty of all knowledge. Thus probability is the highest standard for practical life.[3] We are but scantily informed how

whereas the Academicians had asserted it absolutely. Even Sextus asserts it with some diffidence (πλὴν εἰ μὴ λέγοι τις ὅτι κ.τ.λ.). On account of this connection with Pyrrho, the Stoic Aristo called Arcesilaus (following Il. vi. 181) : πρόσθε Πλάτων, ὄπιθεν Πύῤῥων, μέσσος Διόδωρος. *Sext.* l. c.; Numen. in *Eus.* Pr. Ev. xiv. 5, 11 ; *Diog.* iv. 33.

[1] It has been already seen that this was the key to the position which the Stoics and Epicureans took up against the Sceptics.

[2] *Plut.* Adv. Col. 26, 3, protecting Arcesilaus against the attacks of Kolotes, says: The opponents of Scepticism cannot show that ἐποχὴ leads to inactivity, for πάντα πειρῶσι καὶ στρέφουσιν αὐτοῖς οὐχ ὑπήκουσεν ἡ ὁρμὴ γενέσθαι συγκατάθεσις οὐδὲ τῆς ῥοπῆς ἀρχὴν ἐδέξατο τὴν αἴσθησιν, ἀλλ' ἐξ ἑαυτῆς ἀγωγὸς ἐπὶ τὰς πράξεις ἐφάνη μὴ δεομένη τοῦ προστίθεσθαι. Perception arises

and influences the will without συγκατάθεσις. Since this statement was controverted by Chrysippus (*Plut.* Sto. Rep. 47, 12. See above 87, 1), there can be no doubt that it was propounded by Arcesilaus.

[3] *Sext.* Math. vii. 158 : ἀλλ' ἐπεὶ μετὰ ταῦτα ἔδει καὶ περὶ τῆς τοῦ βίου διεξαγωγῆς ζητεῖν ἥ τις οὐ χωρὶς κριτηρίου πέφυκεν ἀποδίδοσθαι, ἀφ' οὗ καὶ ἡ εὐδαιμονία, τουτέστι τὸ τοῦ βίου τέλος, ἤρτημένην ἔχει τὴν πίστιν, φησὶν ὁ Ἀρκεσίλαος, ὅτι ὁ περὶ πάντων ἐπέχων κανονιεῖ τὰς αἱρέσεις καὶ φυγὰς καὶ κοινῶς τὰς πράξεις τῷ εὐλόγῳ, κατὰ τοῦτό τε προερχόμενος τὸ κριτήριον κατορθώσει· τὴν μὲν γὰρ εὐδαιμονίαν περιγίνεσθαι διὰ τῆς φρονήσεως, τὴν δὲ φρόνησιν κινεῖσθαι ἐν τοῖς κατορθώμασι, τὸ δὲ κατόρθωμα εἶναι (according to the Stoic definition) ὅπερ πραχθὲν εὔλογον ἔχει τὴν ἀπολογιαν. ὁ προσέχων οὖν τῷ εὐλόγῳ κατορθώσει καὶ εὐδαιμονήσει. It is a mistake to suppose, with Numen. in *Eus.* Pr. Ev. xiv. 6,

Arcesilaus applied this principle to the sphere of morals, but a few of his utterances are on record,[1] all
bearing witness to the beautiful spirit of moderation
in the moral theory of the Academy, which was
otherwise exemplified in his own life.[2]

Comparing with the theory of Arcesilaus, that
which was propounded by Carneades a century later,
the same leading features are found to be underlying; but all points have been more carefully worked
out, and placed on a wider footing. Of the immediate followers of Arcesilaus[3] it can only be stated

4, that Arcesilaus denied probabilities.

[1] In *Plut.* Tran. An. 9, g, E,
p. 470, he gives the advice
rather to devote attention to
oneself and one's own life than
to works of art and other external things. In *Stob.* Floril.
95, 17, he says: Poverty is bur-
densome, but educates for virtue. *Ibid.* 43, 91: Where there
are most laws, there are most
transgressions of law. *Plut.*
Cons. ad Apoll. 15, p. 110, has
a saying of his as to the folly
of the fear of death. *Id.* De
Sanit. 7, p. 126, Qu. Conv. vii.
5, 3, 7, records a somewhat
severe judgment on adulterers
and prodigals. Quite unique
is the statement in *Tertull.* Ad
Nation. ii. 2: Arcesilaus held
that there were three kinds of
Gods (in other words he divided
the popular Gods into three
classes): the Olympian, the
stars, and the Titans. It implies
that he criticised the belief in
the Gods. It also appears by
the language used in *Plut.* C.
Not. 37, 7, respecting the Stoic

theory of a κρᾶσις δι' ὅλου, that
his criticism of dogmatism extended to natural science.

[2] Conf. p. 529, 3 g, E.

[3] *Geffers*, De Arcesilæ Suc-
cessoribus (including Carneades): Gött. 1845. Arcesilaus
was succeeded by *Lacydes* of
Cyrene, who died 240 B.C., after
presiding over the School for
26 years, having entrusted it in
his lifetime (probably only
shortly before his death) to the
care of the Phocæans Telecles
and Euandros (*Diog.* iv. 59–€̄.).
The statements made in *Diog.*
l. c., Numen. in *Eus.* Pr. Ev.
xiv. 7, *Plut.* De Adul. 22, p. 63,
Ælian, V. H. ii. 41, *Athen*, x.
438, a, xiii. 606, c, *Plin.* H. N.
x. 22, 51, referring particularly
to individual peculiarities
which he appears to have had,
must be received with caution,
and particularly the smack
which *Diog.* 59 passingly mentions and Numenius depicts
with intolerable garrulity. *Diog.*
calls him ἀνὴρ σεμνότατος καὶ
οὐκ ὀλίγους ἐσχηκὼς ζηλωτάς·
φιλόπονός τε ἐκ νέου καὶ πένης·

that they clung to their teacher. It may be presumed that they did little in the way of expansion,
since the ancients are silent as to their labours, only
Carneades [1] being mentioned as the continuer of the

μὲν, εὔχαρις δ' ἄλλως καὶ εὐόμιλος.
To his admirers belongs Attalus I. of Pergamum. A visit to
his court was however declined
in skilful language (*Diog.* 60,
which *Geffers*, p. 5 clearly mis-
understands). In doctrine, he
deviated little from Arcesilaus,
and, having been the first to
commit to writing the teaching
of the New Academy (*Suid.*
Λακ· ἔγραψε φιλόσοφα καὶ περὶ
φύσεως—the latter is somewhat
extraordinary for a Sceptic)
was by some mistake called its
founder (*Diog.* 59). According
to *Diog.* vii. 183, see p. 46, 1, he
appears to have taught in the
Academy during Arcesilaus'
lifetime. Panaretus (*Athen.* xii.
552, d; *Æl.* V. H. x. 6), Demo-
phanes, and Ecdemus or Ecde-
lus (*Plutarch.* Philopon. 1 Arab.
5, 7) are also called pupils of
Arcesilaus. The most distinguished pupil of Lacydes, according to *Eus.* xiv. 7, 12, was
Aristippus of Cyrene, also mentioned by *Diog.* ii. 83. Another,
Paulus, is also mentioned by
Timotheus, in *Clemens*, Strom.
496, D. His successors were
Telecles and Euandros, who
jointly presided over the School.
Euander, however, according to
Cic. Acad. ii. 6, 16, *Diog.* 60,
Eus. l. c., having survived his
colleague, was followed by He-
gesinus (*Diog.* 60; *Cic.* l. c.) or
Hegesilaus (as he is called by
Clemens, Strom. p. 301, c), the
immediate predecessor of Car-

neades. Respecting these individuals nothing is known beyond the names.

[1] Carneades, the son of Epi-
comus or Philocomus, was born
at Cyrene (*Diog.* iv. 62; *Strabo*,
xvii. 3, 22, p. 838; *Cic.* Tusc.
iv. 3, 5), and died, according
to Apollodorus (*Diog.* 65), 129
B.C., in his 85th year. *Lucian*,
Macrob. 20 assigns to him the
same age. With less probability *Cic.* Acad. ii. 6, 16, *Valer.
Max.* viii. 7, 5, extend his age
to 90, making his birth year
213 B.C. Later admirers find
a remarkable fact in his birthday happening, like Plato's, on
the Carnean festival (*Plut.* Qu.
Conv. viii. 1, 2, 1). Little is
known of his life. He was a
disciple and follower of Hegesi-
nus, but at the same time received instruction in dialectic
(*Cic.* Acad. ii. 30, 98) from the
Stoic Diogenes, and studied
with indefatigable zeal (*Diog.*
62) philosophic literature, and
in particular the writings of
Chrysippus (*Diog.* 62; *Plut.*
Sto. Rep. 10, 44; *Eus.* Pr. Ev.
xiv. 7, 13). In 156 B.C. he took
part in the well-known association of philosophers, and produced the greatest impression
on his Roman hearers by the
force of his language and the
boldness with which he attacked
the current principles of morals.
Shortly before his death, probably also at an earlier period,
he became blind (*Diog.* 66).

Academic Scepticism. The importance attaching to
Carneades is therefore all the greater, and he is in
consequence called the founder of the third or New
Academy.[1] Nor is this done without reason, witness
the admiration which his talents called forth among
cotemporaries and posterity,[2] and the flourishing con-

He left no writings, the preservation of his doctrines being
the work of his pupils, in particular of Clitomachus (*Diog.*
66, 67; *Cic.* Acad. ii. 31, 98;
32, 102). Respecting his character, we may gather from a
few expressions that, whilst
vigorous in disputation (*Diog.*
63; *Gell.* N. A. vi. 14, 10), he
was not wanting in a repose of
mind harmonising with his
principles (*Diog.* 66). That he
was a just man, notwithstanding his speech against justice,
we can well believe (*Quintil.*
xii. 1, 35).

The quotation in *Diog.* 64
(ἡ συστήσασα φύσις καὶ διαλύσει)
does not indicate fear of death,
but simple resignation to the
course of nature. Still less so
does his language on Antipater's
suicide (and also what is quoted
in *Stob.* Floril. 119, 19) indicate
a faint-hearted attempt at imitation afterwards abandoned,
but only a not very witty ridiculing of an action which appeared to Carneades eminently
mad.

[1] *Sext.* Pyrrh. i. 220; *Eus.*
Pr. Ev. xiv. 7, 12; *Lucian. Macrob.* 20.

[2] His School held him in
such esteem, that it not only
considered him, together with
Plato, because of his birthday
(unless the idea grew out of

his name), to be a special favourite of Apollo, but that tradition said an eclipse of the
moon (*Suid.* Καρν. adds an
eclipse of the sun) comme-
morated his death; συμπάθειαν,
ὡς ἂν εἴποι τις, αἰνιττομένου τοῦ
μεθ' ἥλιον καλλίστου τῶν ἄστρων
(*Diog.* 64). *Strabo*, xvii. 3, 22,
p. 838, says of him: οὗτος δὲ
τῶν ἐξ Ἀκαδημίας ἄριστος φιλοσόφων ὁμολογεῖται; and there was
only one opinion among the
ancients regarding the force of
his logic, and the power and
attraction of his eloquence,
aided as these were by unusually powerful organs (see
the anecdotes in *Plut.* Garrul.
21, p. 513; *Diog.* 63). Conf.
Diog. 62; *Cic.* Fin. iii. 12, 41;
De Orat. ii. 38, 161; iii. 18, 68;
Gell. N. A. vi. 14, 10; Numen.
in *Eusebius*, Pr. Ev. xiv. 8, 2
and 5; *Lactant.* Inst. v. 14;
Plut. Cato Maj. 22. The latter,
speaking of his success at Rome,
says: μάλιστα δ' ἡ Καρνεάδου χάρις,
ἧς δύναμίς τε πλείστη καὶ δόξα τῆς
δυνάμεως οὐκ ἀποδέουσα . . . ὡς
πνεῦμα τὴν πόλιν ἠχῆς ἐνέπλησε.
καὶ λόγος κατεῖχεν. ὡς ἀνὴρ Ἕλλην
εἰς ἔκπληξιν ὑπερφυής, πάντα κη-
λῶν καὶ χειρούμενος, ἔρωτα δεινὸν
ἐμβέβληκε τοῖς νέοις, ὑφ' οὗ τῶν
ἄλλων ἡδονῶν καὶ διατριβῶν ἐκ-
πεσόντες ἐνθουσιῶσι περὶ φιλοσοφίαν.

CHAP.
XXIII.

(1) *Negative side of his teaching.*

(a) *Denial of possibility of formal knowledge.*

dition in which he left his School.[1] Himself a pupil
of Chrysippus, and resembling him in tone of mind,[2]
Carneades expanded not only the negative side of
the Sceptical theory in all directions with an acuteness entitling him to the first place among the ancient
Sceptics, but he was also the first to investigate the
positive side of Scepticism, the doctrine of probability, and to determine the degrees and conditions
of probability. By his labours in both ways he carried the philosophy of Scepticism to its greatest
scientific perfection.

As regards the negative side of these investigations, or the refutation of dogmatism, the attacks of
Carneades were directed partly against the formal
possibility of knowledge, and partly against the chief
actual results of the knowledge of his day, and in
both respects he had mainly to do with the Stoics,[3]
little as he confined himself to them.

To prove the impossibility of knowledge in general, he appeals sometimes to experience. There is
no kind of conviction which does not sometimes deceive us; consequently there is none which guaran-
tees its own truth.[4] Going then further into the

---

[1] *Cic.* Acad. ii. 6, 16.
[2] See p. 536, note.
[3] *Sext.* Math. vii. 159: ταῦτα
καὶ ὁ ᾿Αρκεσίλαος. ὁ δὲ Καρνεάδης
οὐ μόνον τοῖς Στωϊκοῖς ἀλλὰ καὶ
πᾶσι τοῖς πρὸ αὐτοῦ ἀντιδιετάσσετο
περὶ τοῦ κριτηρίου. In Math. ix.
1, Sextus charges the School of
Carneades with unnecessary
diffuseness in discussing the
fundamental principles of every

system. The Stoics were, however, the chief object of his attack. *Cic.* Tusc. v. 29, 82;
N. D. ii. 65, 162; *Plut.* Garrul.
23, p. 514; *Augustin.* c. Acad.
iii. 17, 39.
[4] *Sext.* l. c.: καὶ δὴ πρῶτος
μὲν αὐτῷ καὶ κοινὸς πρὸς πάντας
ἐστὶ λόγος καθ᾿ ὃν παρίσταται ὅτι
οὐδέν ἐστιν ἁπλῶς ἀληθείας κριτήριον, οὐ λόγος οὐκ αἴσθησις οὐ φαν-

nature of our notions, he argues, that since notions consist in the change produced on the soul by impressions from without, they must, to be true, not only furnish information as to themselves, but also as to the objects producing them. Now, this is by no means always the case, many notions avowedly giving a false impression of things. Hence the note of truth cannot reside in an impression as such, but only in a true impression.[1] It is, however, impossible to distinguish with certainty a true impression from one that is false. For independently of dreams, visions, and the fancies of madmen, in short, of all the unfounded chimeras which force themselves on our notice under the guise of truth,[2] it is still undeniable that many false notions resemble true ones most unmistakably. The transition, too, from truth to falsehood is so gradual, the interval between the two is occupied by intermediate links so innumerable, and gradations so slight, that they imperceptibly go one into the other, and it becomes impossible to draw a boundary line between the two opposite spheres.[3] Not content with proving this

---

τασία οὐκ ἄλλο τι τῶν ὄντων·
πάντα γὰρ ταῦτα συλλήβδην δια-
ψεύδεται ἡμᾶς.

[1] *Sext.* l. c. 160–163.

[2] Conf. *Sext.* vii. 403; *Cic.* Acad. ii. 15, 47; 28, 89—Carneades being undoubtedly meant, although not mentioned by name. For the further sceptical arguments in Cicero tally with those which Sextus attributes to Carneades, and those here quoted are refuted by An-

tiochus, whose immediate adversary was Carneades.

[3] According to *Cic.* Acad. ii. 13, 40; 26, 83, the Academic system of proof rests on the four following propositions: (1) that there are false notions; (2) that these cannot be known, i.e. be recognised as true; (3) that of two indistinguishable notions, it is impossible to know the one and not the other; (4) that there is no true notion by

assertion in regard to the impression of the senses,
Carneades went on to prove it with regard to general
notions based on experience and intellectual conceptions.[1] He showed that it is impossible for us to
distinguish objects so much alike as one egg is from
another; that at a certain distance the painted surface
seems raised, and a square tower seems round; that
an oar in the water seems broken, and the neck-
plumage of a pigeon assumes different colours in
the sun; that objects on the shore seem to be moving
as we sail by, and so forth;[2] in all of which cases
the same strength of conviction belongs to the false as
to the true impressions.[3] He showed further that this
applies equally to purely intellectual ideas; that
many logical difficulties cannot be solved;[4] that no

the side of which a false one
cannot be placed not distin-
guishable from it. The second
and third of these propositions
not being denied at all, and the
first one only being denied by
Epicurus in regard to impressions on the senses, all importance attaches to the fourth
proposition, to which *Sextus,*
vii. 164 and 402, and Numen.
in *Eus.* Pr. Ev. xiv. 8, 4, look
as the pith of the proof.

[1] *Cic.* Acad. ii. 15, 42 : Divi-
dunt enim in partes et eas
quidem magnas : primum in
sensus, deinde in ea, quæ du-
cuntur a sensibus et ab omni
consuetudine, quam obscurari
volunt (the συνήθεια against
which Chrysippus already directed severe attacks. See p.
46, 2 ; 91, 2) tum perveniunt
ad eam partem, ut ne ratione
quidem et conjectura ulla res

percipi possit. Hæc autem
universa etiam concidunt minu-
tius.

[2] *Sext.* vii. 409 ; *Cic.* Acad.
ii. 26, 84 ; 7, 19 ; 25, 79 : Numen. in *Eus.* Pr. Ev. xiv. 8, 5.
Therewith is probably connected the statement in *Galen,*
De Opt. Doct. c. 2, vol. i. 45, κ,
to the effect that Carneades
persistently denied the axiom
that things that are equal to a
third are equal to one another.
His assertion probably comes
to this that it may be possible
to distinguish two things as
unequal, which cannot be distinguished from a third, that
therefore two things may appear equal to a third without
being or appearing equal to
one another.

[3] *Sext.* 402 and 408.

[4] The fallacy called ψευδόμενος is carefully investigated

absolute distinction can be drawn between much and little, in short, between all differences in quantity; and that it is the most natural course in all such cases to follow Chrysippus, and to avoid the dangerous inferences which may be drawn by withholding judgment.[1] Arguing from these facts, Carneades concluded at first in regard to impressions of the senses, that there is no such thing as φαντασία καταληπτικὴ in the Stoic sense of the term, in other words, that no perception contains in itself characteristics, by virtue of which its truth may be inferred with certainty.[2] This fact being granted, the possibility is in his opinion precluded of there residing in the understanding a standard for the distinction of truth from falsehood. The understanding—and this belief was shared by his opponents—must derive its material from the senses.[3] Logic tests the formal accuracy of combinations of thought, but gives no insight into their import.[4] Direct proofs of the uncertainty of intellectual convictions are not therefore needed. The same result may also be attained in a more personal way, by raising the question, how individuals obtain their

in *Cic.* Acad. ii. 30, 95 (by Carneades as he says, 98), as an instance in point.

[1] *Sext.* 416; *Cic.* l. c. 29, 92. Since Chrysippus tried to meet the chain-argument, it may be supposed that this fallacy had been used by Arcesilaus against the Stoics.

[2] *Sext.* vii. 164; *Augustin.* c. Acad. ii. 5, 11.

[3] *Sext.* 165.

[4] *Cic.* Acad. ii. 28, 91, who here appears to be following Philo, and, subsequently, Carneades as well. Carneades also gives utterance to a similar view of dialectic in *Stob.* Floril. 93, 13 (conf. *Plut.* C. Not. 2, 4), comparing it to a polypus consuming its own tentacles. It is able, he conceives, to expose fallacies, but not to discover truth.

CHAP.
XXIII.

knowledge. He can only be said to know a thing who has formed an opinion respecting it. In the mean time, until he has decided in favour of some definite opinion, he has still no knowledge. And what dependence can be placed on the judgment of one who has no knowledge?[1]

(b) *Attack on the scientific knowledge of the time.*

(a) *The physical views of the Stoics attacked.*

In these formal enquiries into the possibility of knowledge, Carneades had chiefly to deal with the Stoics, with whom he holds a common ground in his appeal to the senses. The Stoics were also his chief opponents in his polemic against the material results of the dogmatic philosophy. Natural science having throughout the period of the post-Aristotelian philosophy been subordinated to ethics, ethics likewise engaged more attention at the hands of Carneades than science.[2] In as far as he studied Natural science, he appears to have been entirely opposed to the Stoic treatment of the subject, and to this circumstance we owe it, that better information is forthcoming regarding his scientific, or rather his theological investigations, than regarding his moral views. The Stoic theories of God and of final causes[3] afforded ample scope for the exercise of his ingenuity, and from the ground he occupied it cannot have been difficult for him to expose the weak points of that

---

[1] *Cic.* Acad. ii. 36, 117. Carneades is not mentioned by name, but there can be no doubt that the reference is to some Academician, and it is probable that it was the work of Carneades.

[2] *Diog.* iv. 62.

[3] *Cic.* N. D. i. 2, 5, after a brief description of the Stoical views of Gods: Contra quos Carneades ita multa disseruit, ut excitaret homines non socordes ad veri investigandi cupiditatem.

theory. The Stoics had appealed in support of the belief in God to the *consensus gentium.* How close at hand was the answer,[1] that the universality of this belief was neither proved to exist, nor as a matter of fact did it, but that in no case could the opinion of an ignorant multitude decide anything. The Stoics thought to find a proof of divine providence in the manner in which portents and prophecies come true. To expose the delusion, no very expanded criticism of divination was necessary.[2] Going beyond this, Carneades proceded to call in question the cardinal point of the Stoic system—the belief in God, the doctrine of the soul and reason of the universe, and of the presence of design in its arrangements. How, he asks, is the presence of design manifested? Whence all the things which cause destruction and danger to men if it be true that God has made the world for the sake of man?[3] If reason is praised as the highest gift of God, is it not manifest that the majority of men only use it to make themselves worse than brutes? In bestowing such a gift God must have been taking but little

[1] *Cic.* N. D. i. 23, 62; iii. 4, 11. Here, too, Carneades is not mentioned by name, but the reference to him is clear by Cicero's remarking that he is quoting the Academic view.

[2] Conf. *Cic.* N. D. iii. 5, 11.

[3] The Academician in *Cic.* Acad. ii. 38, 120. That these arguments were used by Carneades is clear from Plut. in *Porphyr.* De Abst. iii. 20, where the latter vindicates against the Stoics the existence of vermin, of poisonous plants, of beasts of prey. In answer to Chrysippus' assertion, that the final cause of a pig is to be killed, Carneades argues: A pig, therefore, by being killed, must attain the object for which it was destined; it is always beneficial for a thing to attain its object —therefore it must be beneficial to a pig to be killed and eaten.

CHAP.
XXIII.

care of this majority.[1] Even if we attribute to man direct blame for the misuse of reason, still, why has God bestowed on him a reason which can be so much abused?[2] Moreover, the Stoics themselves say that a wise man can nowhere be found? They admit, too, that folly is the greatest misfortune. How, then, can they speak of the care bestowed by God on men, when on their own confession, the whole of mankind is sunk in the deepest misery?[3] But allowing that the Gods could not bestow virtue and wisdom upon all, they could, at least, have taken care that it should go well with the good. Instead of this, the experience of a hundred cases shows that the upright man comes to a miserable end; that crime succeeds; and that the criminal can enjoy the fruits of his misdeeds undisturbed. Where, then, is the agency of Providence?[4] The facts being entirely different to what the Stoics suppose, what becomes of their inferences? Allowing the presence of design in the world, and granting that the world is as beautiful and good as possible, why is it inconceivable that nature should have formed the world according to natural laws without the intervention of God? Admitting, too, the connection of parts in the universe, why should not this connection be the result simply of natural forces, without a soul of the universe or a deity?[5] Who can pretend to be so intimately ac-

[1] *Cic.* N. D. iii. 25, 65–70. It is here presumed that the leading thoughts in Cicero's description belong to the School of Carneades.

[2] *Ibid.* 31, 76.
[3] *Ibid.* 32, 79.
[4] *Cic.* N. D. iii. 32, 80.
[5] *Cic.* Acad. ii. 38, 120; N. D. iii. 11, 28.

quainted with the powers of nature, as to be able to prove the impossibility of this assumption? Zeno argued that rational things are better than things irrational, that the world is the best possible, and must therefore be rational. Man, says Socrates, can only derive his soul from the world; therefore the world must have a soul. But what, replies the Academician,[1] is there to show that reason is best for the world, if it be the best for us? or that there must be a soul even in nature for nature to produce a soul? What man is not able to produce, that, argues Chrysippus, must have been produced by a higher being—by deity. But to this inference the same objection was raised by the Academicians as to the former one, viz., that it confounds two different points of view. There may, indeed, be a Being higher than man. But why must there needs be a rational man-like Being? Why a God? Why not nature herself?[2] Nor did the argument seem to an Academician more conclusive, that as every house is destined to be inhabited, so, too, the world must be intended for the habitation of God. To this there was the obvious reply:[3] If the world were a house, it might be so; but the very point at issue is whether it is a house constructed for a definite purpose, or whether it is simply an undesigned result of natural forces.

Not content with attacking the conclusiveness of the arguments upon which the Stoics built their belief in a God, the scepticism of the Academy

(β) Theological views of the Stoics attacked.

[1] *Cic.* N. D. iii. 8, 21; 10, 26; 11, 27.
[2] *Ibid.* 10, 25.
[3] L. c.

sought to demonstrate that the idea of God itself
was an untenable one. The line of argument which
Carneades struck out for this purpose is essentially
the same as that used in modern times to deny the
personality of God. The ordinary view of God regards Him as an infinite, but, at the same time, as
a separate Being, possessing the qualities and living
the life of an individual. To this view Carneades
objected, on the ground that the first assertion
contradicts the second; and argues that it is impossible to apply the characteristics of personal existence to God without limiting His infinite nature.
Whatever view we may take of God, we must regard
Him as a living Being; and every living being is
composite, having parts and passions, and is hence
destructible.[1] Moreover, every living being has a
sense-nature. Far, therefore, from refusing such a
nature to God, Carneades attributed to Him, in the
interest of omniscience, far more organs of sense
than the five we possess. Now, everything capable
of impressions through the senses is also liable to
change; sensation, according to the definition of
Chrysippus, being nothing more than a change of
soul; and every such being must be capable of pleasure and pain, without which sensation is inconceivable. Whatever is capable of change is liable to
destruction; whatever is susceptible to pain is also
liable to deterioration, pain being caused by deterioration, and is also liable to destruction.[2] As the

---

[1] *Cic.* N. D. iii. 12, 29; 14,
34.

[2] *Cic.* N. D. iii. 13, 32. More
fully *Sext.* Math. ix. 139-147.

capacity for sensation, so too the desire for what is in harmony with nature, and the dislike of what is opposed to nature, belong to the conditions of life. Whatever has the power of destroying any being is opposed to the nature of that being, everything that lives being exposed to annihilation.[1] Advancing from the conception of a living being to that of a rational being, all virtues would have to be attributed to God as well as bliss. But how, asks Carneades, can any virtue be ascribed to God? Every virtue supposes an imperfection, in overcoming which it consists. He only is continent who might possibly be incontinent, and persevering who might be indulgent. To be brave, a man must be exposed to danger; to be magnanimous, he must be exposed to misfortunes. A being not feeling attraction for pleasure, nor aversion for pain and difficulties, dangers and misfortunes, would not be capable of virtue. Just as little could we predicate prudence of a being not susceptible of pleasure and pain; prudence consisting in knowing what is good, bad, and morally indifferent. But how can there be any such knowledge where there is no susceptibility to pleasure or pain? Or how can a being be conceived of capable of feeling pleasure, but incapable of feeling pain, since pleasure can only be known by contrast with pain, and the possibility of increasing life always supposes the possibility of lessening it. Nor is it otherwise

Here too Carneades is expressly mentioned. But without being mentioned the agreement with Cicero would show that we were dealing with his views.

[1] *Cic.; Ibid.* Further proofs of the transient nature of all earthly beings are there given.

with intelligence (εὐβουλία). He only is intelligent who always discovers what will subserve his purpose. If, however, he must discover it, it cannot have been previously known to him. Hence intelligence can only belong to a being who is ignorant about much. Such a being can never feel sure that sooner or later something will not cause his ruin. He will therefore be exposed to fear. A being susceptible of pleasure and exposed to pain, a being who has to contend with dangers and difficulties, and who feels pain and fear, must inevitably, so thought Carneades, be finite and destructible. If, therefore, we cannot conceive of God except in this form, we cannot conceive of Him at all, our conception being self-destructive.[1]

There is yet another reason, according to Carneades, why God cannot have any virtue; because virtue is above its possessor, and there can be nothing above God.[2] Moreover, what is the position of God in regard to speech? It was easy to show the absurdity of attributing speech to Him,[3] but to call Him speechless (ἄφωνος) seemed also to be opposed to the general belief.[4] Quite independently, how-

---

[1] *Sext.* Math. ix. 152–175, quotes the same argument for σωφροσύνη, and so does *Cic.* N. D. iii. 15, 38, both without mentioning Carneades by name, but since both writers introduce these proofs in the same position of a longer argument, in which Carneades is expressly mentioned both before and after, there can be no doubt that to him they refer.

[2] *Sext.* ix. 176. The argument has a look of sophistry about it. It alludes to the important question which engaged so much attention in the middle ages, viz. How in Deity the universal side is related to the individual, whether goodness and reason are for God a law independent of His will or not.

[3] As Epicurus did. See p. 468, 3.

[4] *Sext.* 178.

ever, of details, the inconceivableness of God appears, so soon as the question is raised, whether the deity is limited or unlimited, material or immaterial. God cannot be unlimited; for what is unlimited is necessarily immoveable—because it has no place—and soulless—since by virtue of its boundlessness it cannot form a whole permeated by a soul; but God we ordinarily think of both as moving and as endowed with a soul. Nor can God be limited; for all that is limited is incomplete. Moreover, God cannot be immaterial, for Carneades, like the Stoics, held that what is immaterial possesses neither soul, feeling, nor activity. Neither can he be material, all composite bodies being liable to change and destruction, and simple bodies, fire, water, and the like, possessing neither life nor reason.[1] If, then, all the forms under which we think of God are impossible, His existence cannot be asserted.

Easier work lay before the Sceptics in criticising polytheistic views of religion and their defence by the Stoics. Among the arguments employed by Carneades to overthrow them, certain chain-arguments are prominently mentioned, by means of which he endeavoured to show that the popular belief has no distinctive marks for the spheres of God and man.

(γ) Polytheistic views attacked.

---

[1] *Sext.* l. c. 148-151; 180. That Sextus here refers to Carneades is clear from his agreement with *Cic.* N. D. 12, 29-31; 14, 34. Cicero introduces his remarks with the words: Illa autem, quæ Carneades afferebat, quemadmodum dissolvitis? Sextus himself seems to refer not only individual arguments, but the whole series of them, to Carneades, when he continues, 182: ἠρώτηνται δὲ καὶ ὑπὸ τοῦ Καρνεάδου καὶ σωριτικῶς τινες, κ.τ.λ.

If Zeus is a God, he argues, his brother Poseidon
must likewise be one, and if he is one, the rivers and
streams must also be Gods. If Helios is a God, the
appearance of Helios above the earth, or day, must
be a God; and, consequently, month, year, morning,
midday, evening, must all be Gods.[1] Polytheism is
here refuted by establishing an essential similarity
between what is accepted as God and what is avowedly not a God. It may readily be supposed that
this was not the only proof of the acuteness of Carneades' reasoning.[2]

Divination, to which the Stoics attached especial
importance,[3] was stoutly assailed. Carneades proved
that no peculiar range of subjects belonged thereto,
but that in all cases admitting professional judgment
experts pass a better judgment than diviners.[4] To
know accidental events beforehand is impossible;
it is useless to know those that are necessary and
unavoidable, nay, more, it would even be harmful.[5]
No casual connection can be conceived of between
a prophecy and the ensuing realisation.[6] If the
Stoics met him by pointing to fulfilled prophecies,
he replied that the coincidence was accidental,[7] at

[1] *Sext.* 182–190. More fully
in *Cic.* N. D. iii. 17, 43. Sextus also observes, 190: καὶ ἄλλους
δὴ τοιούτους σωρείτας ἐρωτῶσιν
οἱ περὶ τὸν Καρνεάδην εἰς τὸ μὴ
εἶναι θεούς.

[2] To him, or probably to his
School, belongs the learned argument in *Cic.* N. D. iii. 21, 53,
to 23, 60, proving the want of
unity in traditional myths by
the multiplicity of Gods of the

same name. The whole drift
of this argument shows that it
was borrowed from some Greek
treatise.

[3] See *Cic.* Divin. i. 4, 7 ; 7,
12.

[4] *Ibid.* ii. 3, 9.

[5] *Ibid.* v. 13 ; but Carneades is not here mentioned by
name.

[6] *Ibid.* i. 13, 23 ; 49, 109.

[7] *Cic.* l.c. and Divin. ii. 21,48.

the same time declaring many such stories to be
without doubt false.[1]

Connected probably with these attacks on divination was the defence by Carneades of the freedom of
the will. The Stoic fatalism he refuted by an appeal
to the fact that our decision is free; and since the
Stoics appealed in support of their view to the law
of causality, he likewise attacked this law.[2] In so
doing his intention was not to assert anything positive respecting the nature of the human will, but
only to attack the Stoic proposition, and if for his
own part he adhered to the old Academic doctrine
of a free will, he still regarded that doctrine as only
probable.

Less information exists as to the arguments by
which Carneades sought to assail the current principles of morality. Nevertheless, enough is known
to indicate the course taken by his Scepticism within
this sphere. In the second of the celebrated speeches
which he delivered at Rome in the year 156 B.C.,[3] he
denied that there is such a thing as natural right:
all laws are only positive civil institutions devised by
men for the sake of safety and advantage, and for
the protection of the weak; and hence he is regarded
as foolish who prefers justice to interest, which after

---

[1] *Cic.* l. c. ii. 11, 27.
[2] *Cic.* De Fato, 11, 23; 14,
31. The freedom of the will,
he there says, may be asserted
even granting that every motion is referred to a cause, for
it is not necessary that this law
should hold good of the will.

He will therefore confine it to
bodily motion, and not allow it
unconditional validity.
[3] *Lact.* Instit. v. 14, following *Cic.* De Rep. iii. 4; *Plut.*
Cato Maj. c. 22; *Quintil.* Instit. xii. 1, 35.

all is the only unconditional end. In support of
these statements he appealed to the fact that laws
change with circumstances, and are different in different countries. He pointed to the example of all
great nations, such as the Romans, all of whom
attained to greatness by unrighteous means. He
impressed into his service the many casuistical
questions raised by the Stoics, expressing the
opinion that in all these cases it is better to commit
the injury which brings advantage — for instance, to
murder another to save one's own life — rather than
to postpone advantage to right, and hence inferred
that intelligence is a state of irreconcileable opposition to justice.[1]

This free criticism of dogmatic views could not
fail to bring Carneades to the same result as his
predecessors. Knowledge is absolutely impossible.
A man of sense will look at everything from all
sides and invariably withhold judgment, thus guarding himself against error.[2] And to this conviction

---

[1] *Lactant.* l. c. 16; *Cic.* De
Rep. iii. 8–12; 14; 17; Fin. ii.
18, 59. On the above casuistical cases see De Off. iii. 13;
23, 89, and above, p. 299, 2.
Probably Carneades was the
cause of the study of casuistry
among the later Stoics.

[2] *Cic.* Acad. ii. 34, 108; conf.
31, 98. In *Id.* Att. xiii. 21, he
compares this ἐποχή to the
drawing up of a charioteer, or
to the guard of a pugilist. No
doubt it is with reference to
ἐποχή that *Alex. Aphr.* De An.
154 a, says: The Academicians
consider ἀπτωσία the πρῶτον οἰ-

κεῖον, πρὸς ταύτην γάρ φασιν ἡμᾶς
οἰκείως ἔχειν πρώτην, ὥστε μηδὲν
προσπταίειν. ἀπτωσία or ἀπροπτωσία is, according to the Stoic
definition (*Diog.* vii. 46) = ἐπιστήμη τοῦ πότε δεῖ συγκατατίθεσθαι καὶ μή. It consists, therefore, in not giving a hasty
assent to any proposition. According to the Sceptics, this is
only possible, and you are only
then safe from error, when you
give assent to none whatever.
ἀπροσπτωσία becomes then identical with ἐποχή or ἄγνοια, which
Max. Tyr. Diss. 35, 7, speaks
of as the ultimate end of Car-

he clings so persistently that he altogether refuses to listen to the objection that the wise man must be at least *convinced* of the impossibility of any firm conviction.[1] The earlier Sceptics, far from attributing an equal value to all notions on this account, had not dispensed with reasons for actions and thoughts. This point was now taken up by Carneades, who in attempting to establish the conditions and degrees of probability, hoped to obtain a clue as to the kind of convinction which was still permitted in his system. However much we may despair of knowledge, some stimulus and groundwork for action is needed. Certain suppositions must therefore be assumed, from which the pursuit of happiness must start.[2] To these so much weight must be attached that they are allowed to decide our conduct, but we must be on our guard against considering them to be true, or to be something really known and conceived. Nor must we forget that

neades. Hence Carneades, as Arcesilaus had done before him, spoke for and against every subject, without expressing a decided opinion. *Cic.* N. D. i. 5, 11; Acad. ii. 18, 60; Divin. ii. 72, 150; Rep. iii. 5, 8; Tusc. v. 4, 11; *Eus.* Pr. Ev. xiv. 7, 12.

[1] *Cic.* Acad. ii. 9, 28.

[2] *Sext.* Math. vii. 166 : ἀπατούμενος δὲ καὶ αὐτὸς [ὁ Καρνεάδης] τι κριτήριον ηρός τε τὴν τοῦ βίου διεξαγωγὴν καὶ πρὸς τὴν τῆς εὐδαιμονίας περίκτησιν δυνάμιν ἀπαναγκάζεται καὶ καθ' αὐτὸν περὶ τούτου διατάττεσθαι, κ.τ.λ. *Cic.* Acad. ii. 31, 99 (of Clitomachus): Etenim contra naturam

esset, si probabile nihil esset, et sequitur omnis vitæ . . . eversio. *Ibid.* 101; 32, 104 : Nam cum placeat, eum qui de omnibus rebus contineat se de assentiendo, moveri tamen et agere aliquid, reliquit ejusmodi visa, quibus ad actionem excitemur, etc. Hence the assurance (*Ibid.* 103 ; *Stob.* Floril. ed. Mein. iv. 234) that the Academicians do not wish to go into the question of perception. They accept it as a phenomenon of consciousness, and a basis of action, but they deny that it strictly furnishes knowledge. The senses are ὑγιεῖς, but not ἀκριβεῖς.

CHAP.
XXIII.

even the nature of our true ideas is such as that of false ones may be, and that the truth of ideas can never be known with certainty. Hence we shall withhold all assent, not allowing any ideas to be true, but only to have the appearance of truth (ἀληθῆ φαίνεσθαι) or probability (ἔμφασις, πιθανότης).[1] In every notion two things need to be considered, the relation to the object represented which makes it either true or false, and the relation to the subject who has the notion, which makes it *seem* either true or false. The former relation is, for the reasons already quoted, quite beyond the compass of our judgment; the latter, the relation of a notion to ourselves, falls within the sphere of consciousness.[2] So long as a notion seemingly true is cloudy and indistinct, like an object contemplated from a distance, it makes no great impression on us. When, on the contrary, the appearance of truth is strong, it produces in us a belief[3] strong enough to determine us to action, although it does not come up to the impregnable certainty of knowledge.[4]

[1] *Sext.* and *Cic.* l. c.
[2] *Sext.* l. c. 167–170.
[3] *Ibid.* 171–173; or, as it is expressed by Cicero, Acad. ii. 24, 78 : It is possible nihil percipere et tamen opinari. It is of no importance that Philo and Metrodorus said Carneades had proved this statement, whereas Clitomachus had stated, hoc magis ab eo disputatum quam probatum. Acad. ii. 48, 148; 21, 67, attributes the statement to Carneades, without any qualification, adding only : Ad-

sensurum (aliquando, as the latter passage adds) non percepto, i.e. opinaturum sapientem.

[4] Conf. *Augustin.* c. Acad. ii. 11, 26 (undoubtedly in point of matter and probably in terms following Cicero) : Id probabile vel verisimile Academici vocant, quod nos ad agendum sine adsensione potest invitare. Sine adsensione autem dico, ut id quod agimus non opinemur verum esse aut non id scire arbitremur, agamus tamen. To

Belief, however, like probability, is of several degrees. The lowest degree of probability arises when a notion produces by itself an impression of truth, without being taken in connection with other notions. The next higher degree is when that impression is confirmed by the agreement of all notions which are related to it. The third and highest degree is when an investigation of all these notions results in producing the same corroboration for all. In the first case a notion is called probable (πιθανή); in the second probable and undisputed (πιθανὴ καὶ ἀπερίσπαστος); in the third probable, undisputed, and tested (πιθανὴ καὶ ἀπερίσπαστος καὶ περιωδευμένη).[1] Within each one of these three classes different gradations of probability are again possible.[2] The distinguishing marks, which must be considered in the investigation of probability, appear to have been investigated by Carneades in the spirit of the Aristotelian logic.[3] In proportion to the greater or less practical importance of a question, or to the accuracy of investigation which the circumstances allow, we must adhere to one or the other degree of probability.[4] Although no one of them is of such a nature as to exclude the possibility of error, this circumstance need not deprive us of certainty in

the same effect, *Euseb.* Pr. Ev. xiv. 7, 12 : Carneades declared it impossible to withhold judgment on all points, and asserted πάντα μὲν εἶναι ἀκατάληπτα, οὐ πάντα δὲ ἄδηλα. Conf. *Cic.* Acad. ii. 17, 54, where the objection is raised to the New Academicians : Ne hoc quidem cernunt, omnia se reddere incerta, quod nolunt ; ea dico incerta, quae ἄδηλα Græci.

[1] *Sext.* 1. c. 173; 175–182; Pyrrh. i. 227; conf. *Cic.* Acad. ii. 11, 33 ; 31, 99 ; 32, 104.

[2] *Sext.* l. c. 173 ; 181.

[3] *Ibid.* 176 ; 183.

[4] *Ibid.* 184.

respect to actions, provided we have once convinced
ourselves that the absolute certainty of our practical
premisses is not possible.[1] Just as little shall we
hesitate to affirm or deny anything in that conditional way which is alone possible after what has
been stated. Assent will be given to no notion in
the sense of its being absolutely true, but to many
notions in the sense that we consider them highly
probable.[2]

*(b) Moral
and re-
ligious
view of
life.*

Among questions about which the greatest possible
certainty is felt to be desirable, Carneades, true to
his whole position, gave a prominent place to principles of morals ;[3] life and action being the principal
things with which the theory of probability has to
do.[4] We hear, therefore, that he thoroughly discussed the fundamental questions of Ethics, the
question as to the highest Good.[5] On this subject he

[1] *Sext.* 1. c. 174; *Cic.* Acad.
ii. 31, 99.
[2] *Cic.* 1. c. 32, 103; 48, 148.
This explanation does away
with the charge of inconsistency
which is brought against Carneades in *Cic.* Acad. ii. 18, 59;
21, 67; 24, 78 (see p. 554, 3), on
the ground that he allowed, in
contradistinction to Arcesilaus,
that the wise man will sometimes follow opinion, and will
give his assent to certain statements. Numen. in *Eus.* Pr. Ev.
xiv. 8, 7, even asserts that he
expressed his own convictions
to his friends in private; but
this assertion is no more true
of him than of Arcesilaus (see
p. 531, 3), as may be seen from
the passage on p. 557, 2,

[3] *Sext.* Pyrrh. i. 226: ἀγαθὸν
γάρ τί φασιν εἶναι οἱ Ἀκαδημαϊκοὶ
καὶ κακὸν, οὐχ ὥσπερ ἡμεῖς, ἀλλὰ
μετὰ τοῦ πεπεῖσθαι ὅτι πιθανόν
ἐστι μᾶλλον ὃ λέγουσιν εἶναι ἀγαθὸν ὑπάρχειν ἢ τὸ ἐναντίον; καὶ
ἐπὶ τοῦ κακοῦ ὁμοίως.
[4] See p. 553, 2; 554, 4.
[5] Here the question arises :
Whence does the Sceptic derive
his conviction as to probabilities in morals? and as perception is not available for the
purpose, Geffers concludes (De
Arc. Successor. 20) that Carneades assumed a peculiar source
of conviction in the mind. For
such an assumption, however,
our authorities give no proof.
It cannot be gathered from the
hypothetical language respect-

distinguished six, or relatively four, different views. If the primary object of desire can in general only consist of those things which correspond with our nature, and which consequently call our emotions into exercise, the object of desire must be either pleasure, or absence of pain, or conformity with nature. In each of these three cases two opposite results are possible : either the highest Good may consist in the attainment of a purpose, or else in the activity which aims at its attainment. The latter is the view of the Stoics only, and arises from regarding natural activity or virtue as the highest Good. Hence the six possible views are practically reduced to four, which taken by themselves alone, or else in combination, include all existing views respecting the highest Good.[1] But so ambiguously did Carneades express himself as to his particular preference of any one view, that even Clitomachus declared he was ignorant as to his real opinions.[2] It was only tentatively and for the purpose of refuting the Stoics, that he propounded the statement that the highest Good consists in the enjoyment of such things as afford satisfaction to the primary impulses

ing the freedom of the will in *Cic.* De Fato, ii. 23. See p. 551, 2. Nor is it, indeed, necessary that Carneades, who never pretended to hold any psychological theory, should have had any opinion on the subject. Supposing he did have it, he might have appealed to experience quite as readily or more so than the Stoics, and have been content with the fact that certain things are far more agreeable or disagreeable, and either promote or disturb happiness.

[1] *Cic.* Fin. v. 6, 16, to 8, 23 ; Conf. Tusc. v. 29, 84; *Ritter,* iii. 686, has hardly expressed with accuracy Carneades' division, which he would otherwise hardly have accused of being inaccurate and superficial.

[2] *Cic.* Acad. ii. 45, 139.

of nature.[1] Nevertheless, the matter has often been placed in such a light as though Carneades had propounded this statement on his own account; and the statement itself has been quoted to prove that he considered the satisfaction of natural impulses apart from virtue as an end in itself.[2] It is also asserted that he approximated to the view of Callipho, which does not appear to have been essentially different from that of the older Academy.[3] The same leaning to the older Academy and its doctrine of moderation appears in other recorded parts of the Ethics of Carneades. The pain caused by misfortune he wished to lessen by thinking beforehand of its possibility;[4] and after the destruction of Carthage he deliberately asserted before Clitomachus that the wise man would never allow himself to be disturbed, not even by the downfall of his country.[5]

[1] *Cic.* Acad. ii. 42, 131: Introducebat etiam Carneades, non quo probaret, sed ut opponeret Stoicis, summum bonum esse frui iis rebus, quas primas natura conciliavisset (οἰκειοῦν). Similarly Fin. v. 7, 20; Tusc. v. 30, 84. This view differs from that of the Stoics, because it makes the highest Good consist not in natural activity as such, but in the enjoyment of natural goods.

[2] *Cic.* Fin. ii. 11, 35: Ita tres sunt fines expertes honestatis, unus Aristippi vel Epicuri (pleasure), alter Hieronymi (freedom from pain), Carneadis tertius (the satisfaction of natural instincts). Conf. *Ibid.* v. 7, 20; 8, 22.

[3] *Cic.* Acad. ii. 45, 139: Ut Calliphontem sequar, cujus quidem sententiam Carneades ita studiose defensitabat, ut eam probare etiam videretur. Callipho is reckoned among those who consider honestas cum aliqua accessione—or, as it is said, Fin. v. 8, 21; 25, 73; Tusc. v. 30, 85, voluptas cum honestate—the highest Good.

[4] *Plut.* Tranq. An. 16, p. 475.

[5] *Cic.* Tusc. iii. 22, 54. Let it be observed that this view of Carneades is specially placed under the head of conviction on probabilities. It is said, he attacked the proposition, videri fore in aegritudine sapientem patria capta. The other state-

one time identifying the satisfaction of natural instincts with virtue, and at another time making them
distinct from virtue, which is attributed to Carneades,
is an inconsistency for which probably Cicero is
alone responsible. The real meaning of Carneades can
only be that virtue consists in an activity directed
towards the possession of what is according to nature,
and hence that it cannot be separated from this [1] as
the highest Good. For the same reason, virtue, in
his opinion, supplies all that is requisite for happiness.[2] Hence, when it is stated that notwithstanding
his scepticism on moral subjects, Carneades was a
thoroughly upright man,[3] we have not only no reason
to doubt this statement as to his personal character,
but we can even discern that it was a practical and
legitimate consequence of his philosophy. It may
appear to us inconsistent to build on a foundation of
absolute doubt the certainty of practical conduct ;
nevertheless, it is an inconsistency deeply rooted in
all the scepticism of post-Aristotelian times. That
scepticism Carneades brought to completeness, and
in logically developing his theory, even its scientific
defects came to light.

For the same reason we may also give credit to

[1] He explicitly says, Fin. v. 7, 18, that as each one defines the highest good, so he deter-mines the honestum (the καλὸν, virtue). The view of the Stoics, he says, places the honestum and bonum in an activity aim-ing at what is according to nature ; adding that, according to the view which places it in the possession of what is ac- cording to nature, the prima secundum naturam are also prima in animis quasi virtutum igniculi et semina.

[2] See p. 560, 3, and *Plut.* Tranq. An. 19, p. 477, where, however, the greater part seems to belong to Plutarch.

[3] *Quintil.* Instit. xii. 1, 35. See above 536, 1, end.

the statement that Carneades, like the later Sceptics, notwithstanding his sharp criticisms on the popular and philosophic theology of his age, never intended to deny the existence of divine agencies.[1] On this point he acted like a true Sceptic. He expressed doubts as to whether anything could be known about God, but for practical purposes he accepted the belief in God as an opinion more or less probable and useful.

Taking all things into account, the philosophic importance of Carneades and the School of which he was the head cannot be estimated at so low a value as would be the case were the New Academy merely credited with entertaining shallow doubts, and Carneades' theory of probabilities deduced from rhetorical rather than from philosophical considerations.[2] For the last assertion there is no ground whatever; Carneades distinctly avowed that a conviction resting on probabilities seemed indispensable for practical needs and actions. On this point, too, he is wholly in accord with all the forms of Scepticism, not only with the New Academy, but also with Pyrrho and the later Sceptics. He differs from them only in the degree of accuracy with which he investigates the varieties and conditions of probability; but a

[1] *Cic.* N. D. iii. 17, 44 : Hæc Carneades aiebat, non ut Deos tolleret. Quid enim philosopho minus conveniens?—sed ut Stoicos nihil de Diis explicare vinceret. In this sense the Academician in Cicero (i. 22, 62) frequently asserts, that he would not destroy belief in God, but that he finds the arguments unsatisfactory. Likewise *Sextus*, Pyrrh. iii. 2 : τῷ μὲν βίῳ κατακολουθοῦντες ἀδοξάστως φαμὲν εἶναι θεοὺς καὶ σέβομεν θεοὺς καὶ προνοεῖν αὐτοὺς φαμέν.

[2] *Ritter*, iii. 730, 694.

question of degree can least of all be urged against
a philosopher. Nor should doubts be called shallow
which the ancients even in subsequent times could
only very inadequately dissipate, and which throw
light on several of the deepest problems of life by
the critical investigations they occasioned. No doubt,
in the despair of attaining to knowledge at all, and
in the attempt to reduce everything to opinion more
or less certain, indications may be seen of the exhaustion of the intellectual spirit, and of the extinction of philosophic originality. Nevertheless it must
never be forgotten that the Scepticism of the New
Academy was not only in harmony with the course
naturally taken by Greek philosophy as a whole, but
that it was pursued with an acuteness and a scientific
vigour leaving no doubt that it was a really important link in the chain of philosophic development.

In Carneades this Scepticism attained its highest
growth. The successor of Carneades, Clitomachus,[1]

[1] Clitomachus was a native
of Carthage, hence called by
Max. Tyr. Diss. 10, 3, ὁ Λίβυς,
and originally bore the name
of Hasdrubal. At home he
devoted himself to study, and
wrote several treatises in his
mother tongue (τῇ ἰδίᾳ φωνῇ ἐν
τῇ πατρίδι ἐφιλοσόφει). When
40 years of age (according to
Steph. Byz. De urbe Καρχηδὼν :
28), he came to Athens, was
initiated by Carneades into
Greek philosophy, and devoted
himself to it with such zeal and
success (*Cic.* Acad. ii. 6, 17 ;
31, 98 ; *Athen.* ix. 402, c) that
he became esteemed as a philosopher and productive as a
writer (*Diog.* iv. 67). Treatises
of his are mentioned by *Cic.*
Acad. ii. 31, 98 ; 32, 102 ; *Diog.*
ii. 92. He died (according to
Stob. Floril. vii. 55) by suicide,
not before 110 B.C. (as *Zumpt*
remarks, Ueber d. philosoph.
Schulen in Ath. Abh. d. Berl.
Akad., Jahrg. 1842. Hist. Philol.
Kl. p. 67), since, according to
Cic. De Orat. i. 11, 45, L. Cras-
sus, during his quæstorship,
met him at Athens, which falls
at the earliest in this year. He
must then have been very old.

is known as the literary exponent of the views taught
by Carneades.[1] At the same time we hear of his
being accurately acquainted with the teaching of the
Peripatetics and Stoics ; and although it was no
doubt his first aim to refute the dogmatism of these
Schools, it would appear that Clitomachus entered
into the connection of their doctrines more fully
than is usually the case with opponents.[2] As to his
fellow-pupil, Charmidas (or Charmadas),[3] one wholly
unimportant utterance is our only guide for determining his views.[4] For ascertaining the philosophy
of the other pupils of Carneades,[5] nothing but the

[1] *Diog.* iv. 67 ; *Cic.* Acad.
ii. 32, 102.

[2] As the peculiar observation in *Diog.* iv. proves : ἀνὴρ
ἐν ταῖς τρισὶν αἱρέσεσι διαπρέψας,
ἔν τε τῇ ᾿Ακαδημαϊκῇ καὶ περιπα-
τητικῇ καὶ στωϊκῇ.

[3] According to *Cic.* Acad. ii.
6, 17 ; De Orat. i. 11, 45 ; Orator, 16, 51, Charmadas was a
pupil of Carneades, whom he
followed not only in teaching
but in method. He must have
survived Clitomachus, since he
taught at the same time with
Philo. See p. 566, 1. Philo,
however, according to Clitomachus, undertook the presidency of the School (*Eus.* Pr.
Ev. xiv. 8, 9). According to
Cic. De Orat. ii. 88, 360, Tusc.
i. 24, 59, he was remarkable
for a good memory.

[4] *Cic.* De Orat. i. 18, 84 :
Charmadas asserted, eos qui
rhetores nominabantur et qui
dicendi præcepta traderent nihil plane tenere, neque posse
quenquam facultatem assequi

dicendi, nisi qui philosopho-
rum inventa didicissent. *Sext.*
Math. ii. 20, also mentions the
hostile attitude of Clitomachus
and Charmadas towards rhe-
toricians, at whom both he and
the School to which he belongs
tilt. His fellow-disciple Agnon
drew up a treatise, according
to *Quintil.* ii. 17, 15, entitled
' Charges against the rhetori-
cians.'   Ritter's inferences,
that Charmadas recommended
philosophy as the only way to
eloquence, and thus openly
avowed the end of the philosophical doctrine of probability,
iii. 695, make far too much of
a chance expression, which
really says nothing but what
the Stoics, and before them
Plato, had said.

[5] In addition to Clitomachus and Charmadas, *Cic.* Acad.
ii. 6, 16, mentions Hagnon and
Melanthius of Rhodes, the former of whom is also mentioned
by Quintilian. (See *Athen.*
xiii. 602, d.) Cicero adds that

scantiest fragments have been preserved. The statement of Polybius that the Academic School degenerated into empty subtleties, and thereby became an
object of contempt,[1] may deserve no great amount
of belief ; but it does seem probable that the School
made no important advance on the path marked out

Metrodorus of Stratonice passed
for a friend of Carneades ; he
had joined him from among the
Epicureans (*Diog.* x. 9). This
Metrodorus must neither be
confounded with Metrodorus of
Skepsis, the pupil of Charmadas (see p. 566, 1), nor with
the Metrodorus distinguished
as a painter, 168 B.C., whom
Æmilius Paulus brought to
Rome (*Plin.* H. N. xxxv. 11,
135). The former must have
been younger, the latter older,
than Metrodorus of Stratonice.
A pupil of Melanthius (*Diog.*
ii. 64), and also of Carneades
in his later years (*Plut.* An.
Sen. S. Ger. Resp. 13, 1, p. 791),
was Æschines of Naples, according to *Cic.* De Orat. i. 11,
45, a distinguished teacher in
the Academic School, likewise
towards the close of the second
century. Another pupil, Men-
tor, was by Carneades forbidden
the School, because he was
caught with his concubine
(*Diog.* iv. 63 ; Numen. in *Eus.*
Pr. Ev. xiv. 8, 7).

¹ Exc. Vatic. xii. 26 : καὶ γὰρ
ἐκείνων [τῶν ἐν ᾽Ακαδημίᾳ] τινὲς
βουλόμενοι περί τε τῶν προφανῶς
καταληπτῶν εἶναι δοκούντων καὶ
περὶ τῶν ἀκαταλήπτων εἰς ἀπορίαν
ἄγειν τοὺς προσμαχομένους τοιαύταις χρῶνται παραδοξολογίαις καὶ
τοιαύτας εὐποροῦσι πιθανότητας,

ὥστε διαπορεῖν, ἀδύνατόν [l. εἰ δυ-
νατόν] ἐστι, τοὺς ἐν ᾽Αθήναις ὄντας
ὀσφραίνεσθαι τῶν ἐψομένων ὠῶν ἐν
᾽Εφέσῳ, καὶ διστάζειν, μή πω καθ᾽
ὃν καιρὸν ἐν ᾽Ακαδημίᾳ διαλέγονται
περὶ τούτων οὐχ ὑπὲρ ἄλλων ἄρ᾽ ἐν
οἴκῳ κατακείμενοι τούτους διατί-
θενται τοὺς λόγους· ἐξ ὧν δι᾽ ὑπερ-
βολὴν τῆς παραδοξολογίας εἰς δια-
βολὴν ἤχασιτὴν ὅλην αἵρεσιν, ὥστε
καὶ τὰ καλῶς ἀπορούμενα παρὰ τοῖς
ἀνθρώποις εἰς ἀπιστίαν ἤχθαι, καὶ
χωρὶς τῆς ἰδίας ἀστοχίας καὶ τοῖς
νέοις τοιοῦτον ἐντετόκασι ζῆλον,
ὥστε τῶν μὲν ἠθικῶν καὶ πραγμα-
τικῶν λόγων μηδὲ τὴν τυχοῦσαν
ἐπίνοιαν ποιεῖσθαι, δι᾽ ὧν ὄνησις
τοῖς φιλοσοφοῦσι, περὶ δὲ τὰς ἀνω-
φελεῖς καὶ παραδόξους εὑρεσιλογίας
κενοδοξοῦντες κατατρίβουσι τοὺς
βίους. In the time of Carneades, whose cotemporary Polybius was, and to whom the remark of the enthusiasm of
youth for Sceptical teaching
refers, such depreciatory language could not have been used
of the Academy. The historical value, therefore, of the
whole passage is suspicious. It
bears, besides, so entirely the
mark of exaggeration, that it
is no more useful as giving a
view of the Academy than are
the caricatures of opponents
for conveying any idea of modern German philosophy.

CHAP.
XXIII. by himself and Arcesilaus. It did not even continue true to that path for very long. Not a generation after the death of its most celebrated teacher, and even among his own pupils,[1] that eclecticism began to appear, the general and simultaneous spread of which ushered in a new period in the history of the post-Aristotelian philosophy.

[1] Among these pupils the tendency to lay stress on the doctrine of probabilities in relation to Scepticism was already strong. Proof may be found not only in the accounts already given us of Clitomachus and Æschines, but also in the circumstance that many of the older writers made the fourth Academy date from Philo and Charmidas, the fifth from Antiochus (*Sext.* Pyrrh. i. 220; *Eus.* Pr. Ev. xiv. 4, 16). At a still earlier date, Metrodorus is said to have departed from the platform of Carneades. *Augustin.* c. Acad. iii. 18, 41, after speaking of Antiochus and his renunciation of Scepticism, says: Quamquam et Metrodorus id antea facere tentaverat, qui primus dicitur esse confessus, non decreto placuisse Academicis, nihil posse comprehendi, sed necessario contra Stoicos hujus modi eos arma sumsisse. Probably Augustin borrowed this passage from a lost treatise of Cicero, and hence it may be relied upon. The Metrodorus referred to is probably Metrodorus of Stra-tonice (see p. 564, 5), mentioned by *Cic.* Acad. ii. 6, 16. Metrodorus of Skepsis might also be suggested (*Strabo,* xiii. 155, p. 609; xvi. 4, 16, p. 775; *Plut.* Lucull. 22; *Diog.* v. 84; *Cic.* De Orat. ii. 88, 360; 90, 365; iii. 20, 75; Tusc. i. 24, 59; *Plin.* Hist. Nat. vii. 24, 89; *Quintil.* x. 6, 1; xi. 2, 22; *Müller,* Hist. Gr. iii. 203), who first learned rhetoric at Chalcedon, afterwards entered the service of Mithridates, and was put to death by his orders, B.C. 70, at an advanced age. *Cic.* De Orat. iii. 20, 75, calls him an Academician; and he is mentioned, *Ibid.* i. 11, 45, as a pupil of Charmadas. The language quoted by Augustin may have come from the treatise περὶ συνηθείας (*Strabo,* p. 775). He is otherwise only known as a rhetorician and politician. The same remark applies to the language in *Cic.* Acad. ii. 24, 78 (see p. 554, 3). We do not know who is the Metrodorus referred to. It may, however, be inferred that it is the same Metrodorus who is mentioned by Augustin.

INDEX.

400; instructor of Sphærus the Stoic, 44; views of, 62; holds later theory to some extent, 76; view of perceptions, 78; view of life according to nature, 228; sad view of life, 272; view of the seat of efficient force, 147; view of the destruction of the world, 165; view of separate existence, 218; holds that all pleasure is contrary to nature, 237; determines the relations of the virtues, 262; Herillus a fellow-student of, 281; teaches indefectible virtue, 295; agrees with Aristo, 298; moral character of, 309; submission to destiny, 333; death of, 336; view of Stoicism, 342; seeks for moral ideas, 355; explanation of myths, 361; distinguishes two kinds of fire, 397; a counterpart of Xenocrates, 400; allegorical interpretation of mythology, 361, 362, 364, 368; preparation for later teaching, 370; teaching of, 44, 45, 46, 54, 62; logical treatises of, 63; view of the common source of virtue, 257; moral view of life, 272; the successors of, 273; specially honours the sun, 146, 165, 362; views on the soul, 217; view of divination, 370.

Cleomenes, Spartan reformer, 44.
Clitomachus, 557, 558, 560, 563.
Colotes, an Epicurean, 409.
Composite judgment of Stoics, 113; inference, 119.
Conceptions formed from perceptions, 79; truth of, 135; relation to perceptions, 83; primary, a standard of truth, 90; highest, of Stoics, 98; Socratic theory of, 9.
Condensation, a cause of being, 140.
Connection, inner, of Stoic system, 381.

Consensus gentium, appealed to by Stoics, 543.
Constantine, 32.
Conversion, Stoic theory of, 275.
Conviction or assent, 88.
Cornutus, a Stoic, 53, 368.
Cosmopolitanism of Stoics, 35, 326.
Course of the world, 332.
Crates the Cynic, 37; teacher of Zeno, 40.
Criticism of popular faith by Stoics, 344.
Cronos, 367.
Cyclopes, 369.
Cynic, appeal to nature, 91; Epicurean view of life, 488; life, 306; Zeno at one time, 322; strength of will, 389; contempt for theory, 390, 510; view of wise man, 488; ideas, 40; teaching, 515; a precursor of Scepticism, 515; nominalism, 84; School, precursor of Stoicism, 17; onesidedness of, 306; philosophy, 28; followed by Aristo, 281, 297; virtue, 282; ethics, 386.
Cynicism, 43, 91, 92, 238; of the Stoics, 305; instances of, 307; a consequence of Stoic principles, 308, 385, 387, 389, 390; attraction of, for Zeno, 401.
Cynics, 223, 239, 273, 277, 288, 308; meagre teaching of, 37, 255; appeal to nature, 92; connections of Stoics with, 291, 317, 323, 389, 390; followed by Aristo, 297; precursors of Stoics, 327.
Cyprus, Citium in, 36.
Cyrenaic, 48; School, 44, 511; a precursor of Epicurean, 17, 511; view of pleasure as the object of life, 475, 510.
Cyrenaics, theory of pleasure followed by Epicurus, 509; content with feelings, 510; view of language, 524.

INDEX. 573

END

End-in-chief, of Stoics, 187.
Ἐνδεικτικὸν σημεῖον, 115.
Ἐνδιάθετος λόγος, 72, n. 2.
Ἔννοιαι κοιναὶ of Stoics, 81.
Epaminondas, 11.
Ephesus, birthplace of Heraclitus, 393.
Epictetus, 299 ; a freedman, 325; native of Phrygia, 36 ; a Stoic, 53, 92 ; of later times, 316 ; dissuades from matrimony, 324 ; religious language of, 328 ; view of demons, 351.
Epicurean, 415, 419, 431, 437, 463, 489 ; view of Stoicism, 311; philosophy, 499 ; divisions of, 424 ; antecedents of, 16; system, character of, 418, 425, 432, 472, 474, 480, 481, 504, 516 ; outlived others, 417 ; developed, 500 ; historical relations of, 503 ; self-contentment, 17 ; imperturbability, 21 ; School, 29, 44, 415, 420 ; tone of, 498 ; appreciates friendship, 502 ; doctrines, 411; theory, 517 ; inner connection of, 499 ; ethics, 439, 456 ; friendship, 493, 495, 506 ; Gods, nature of, 467 ; canonic, 415 ; views on nature, 434, 457 ; view of virtue, 481, 482 ; moral science, 485 ; theory of pleasure, 505, 481.
Epicureanism, 26, 400, 403 ; scientific value of, 418 ; intellectual value, 420 ; grows out of Cyrenaic teaching, 17 ; power of self-preservation, 418 ; established in Rome, 411 ; historical position of, 503 ; relation to Stoicism, 400, 403, 503, 508, 514, 515 ; relation to Aristippus, 508 ; relation to Democritus, 510 ; to Aristotle and Plato, 511 ; to older philosophy, 508 ; aims at a practical science of life, 509 ; vindicated, 500, 513
Epicureans, 412, 414, 420, 458 ; of the Roman period, 411 ;

EPI

regard individual side in man, 25 ; distinguished from Stoics, 183, 372 ; points of agreement with, 507, 508, 515, 516 ; charged with impropriety by opponents, 407 ; view of divination, 372 ; aim of philosophy, 420 ; divide philosophy into three parts, 424 ; indifferent to explaining phenomena, 434 ; refer them to natural causes, 437 ; consider the earth the centre of the universe, 450 ; on the relations of body and soul, 454, 479, 505 ; negative attitude of, towards popular faith, 471 ; averse to public affairs, 491 ; build a rational system on a base of the senses, 500 ; hold theory of atoms, 505 ; irreligious freethinkers, 505 ; practical philosophy of, 416 ; onesidedness of, 424 ; explain man's origin naturally, 451 ; materialism of, 456 ; sincerity of, 465 ; view of the Gods, 468 ; on bodily pleasures, 478, 506 ; moral science of, 485 ; friends of monarchy, 492 ; view of friendship, 494.
Epicurus, school of, subordinate theory to practice, 19 ; view of the world as unlimited, 203, 409 ; of empty space, 445, 44 ; life of, 404 ; writings unread in Cicero's time, 419 ; despised learning, 421, 501 ; theory of knowledge, 423; on certainty of the senses, 427 ; on standard of truth, 431 ; a voluminous writer, 47 ; views on colour, 433 ; undervalues logic, 434, 425; undervalues natural science, 436, 438, 511 ; and mind, 440, 513; relations to Democritus, 439, 444, 502, 510 ; does not investigate psychologically, 459 ; does not give up belief in Gods, 465, 466 ; position of, contrasted with the Stoics, 481, 456, 484,

Panætius, a later Stoic and scholar of Antipater, 51 ; not a severe Stoic, 286 ; teacher of Posidonius, 298 ; treatise of, 302 ; followed by Cicero, 315 ; treatise on divination, 371 ; denies omens, 374.

Pantheism of Stoics, 126, 156, 517 ; dissented from by Boëthus, 159.

Παράθεσις, 106, n. 2 ; defined, 137, n. 1.

Parmenides, sceptical arguments of, 531.

Patro, an Epicurean, 414.

Peloponnesian war, 10.

Peloponnesus, 13.

Penelope, suitors of, 60.

Perceptions derived by Stoics from impressions, 77 ; the basis of conceptions, 79, 83 ; a standard, 76 ; irresistible, the standard of truth, 87 ; sole source of truth, 135 ; Epicurean view of, 425.

Perfect duties, 287.

Pericles, age of, 9.

Peripatetic School, 29, 301 ; approached by Herillus the Stoic, 43 ; on the human soul, 397 ; materialism, 133 ; view of emotions, 253 ; goes back to earlier view, 301 ; philosophy, 133 ; debt of Stoics to, 402 ; notion, 244 ; doctrine, 397 ; views, 398, 281 ; view of goods, 559.

Peripatetics, opposed to the Stoics, 62, 66 ; the Sorites of the, 120 ; logic of, 124 ; ground occupied by, 133 ; view of emotions, 253 ; teaching of, 49, 398, 564 ; theory of goods, 559 ; attacked by Stoics, 233 ; not the cause of Zeno's materialism, 134.

Persæus, a Stoic and pupil of Zeno, 43 ; fellow pupil of Aristo, 298.

Persian war, 9 ; Greek dependence on empire, 12.

φαντασίαι, 77 ; καταληπτικαί, 89, 531, 541.

Phædrus, an Epicurean, 413, 414, 417.

Philo, a pupil of Diodorus, 38.

Philodemus, an Epicurean, 413, 468 ; view of the Gods, 468.

Philosophy, Stoic divisions of, 66 ; Epicurean divisions of, 424.

Phlius, birthplace of Timon, 519.

Phrygian, Epictetus, 36.

Φύσις, 228, 350, 209.

Πιθανή, 555.

Πιθανότης, 555.

Planets, Stoic view of, 208 ; Epicurean view of, 451.

Plato, 55, 126, 305, 323, 509, 511, 513, 531 ; perfection of Greek philosophy in, 1 ; the study of, 126 ; example, 187 ; many-sidedness of, 402 ; merits and defects of, 1 ; idealism of, 2, 9, 130 ; flaws in teaching of, 3 ; dialectical exclusiveness of, 4 ; antagonistic currents in, 45 ; general conceptions of, 18 ; denies virtue in great men, 274 ; view of demons, 351 ; theory of final causes, 396 ; system of, connected with Greek character, 7 ; doctrine of the four elements, 197 ; view of the stars, 205 ; of the seat of life, 214 ; view of the soul, 215 ; on the regulation of emotions, 252 ; permits a lie, 305 ; prejudice against foreigners, 326 ; view of pleasure, 474 ; places knowledge above action, 256 ; advocates community of wives, 310 ; distinguishes supreme and popular gods, 348 ; known to Epicurus, 405 ; sceptical arguments of, 531 ; pure speculation of, 57 ; metaphysical notions of, 133 ; example of, 187, 258 ; time of, 178 ; teaching of, 252, 399, 405 ; formal and final causes of, 141 ; relation of

Sciro, an Epicurean, 413.
Scylla, Stoic explanation of, 369.
Secondary goods, 280.
Seleucia, birthplace of Diogenes, 49.
Seneca, 219, 239, 285, 299, 306, 316, 319, 325, 326, 335, 337, 339, 351; a Stoic, 53; in harmony with the Stoics, 154; opinion on wickedness, 273; defends external possessions, 285; views on customs, 306; age of, 274; a later Stoic, 316; his views on friendship, 318, 319; on the wise man's independence, 335; on suicide, 337, 339; denies the use of prayer, 344; view of demons, 351.
Sensation, Epicurean view of, 425, 457.
Senses, Epicurean superiority to, 478.
Septimus Severus, Emperors after, 32.
Sextus Empiricus, a Stoic authority, 53.
Sidon, birthplace of Zeno the Epicurean, 412.
Simple judgment, 110, 111.
Sirens explained, 369.
Social relations, Stoic view of, 311.
Society, origin and use of, 311; Epicurean views on, 490.
Socrates, 274, 292, 305, 306, 501, 509, 511; definition of the good, 229; of virtue, 59, 255; sceptical arguments of, 531; view of natural science, 60; line of thought presupposed by Epicureanism, 511; philosophic ideas of, 2; practical philosophy of, 17; differs from past Aristotelian philosophy, 18; view of means and ends, 185; time of, 225; defines the good as the useful, 229; an example of wisdom, 274, 292, 306; per-

mitted a lie, 305; sceptical arguments of, 531; on the derivation of the soul, 545; relations of Stoics to, 387, 391, 396.
Socratic, old, teaching, 401; dictum, 245, 247; introspection, 511; views, 388; theory of conceptions, 9; teaching, 255; philosophy, 392; School, 509.
Soli, birthplace of Chrysippus, 45; of Aratus, 43.
Something, the highest conception, 98.
Sophists, practical philosophy of, 18; fallacies fostered by, 122.
Sorites, the, of the Peripatetics developed by the Stoics, 120.
Soul, of the parts, 213; nature of, 210; the individual, 216; God as, 148; Stoic views of, 210; Epicurean views of, 453; materialistic view of, 210.
Space, 196.
Sparta, rivalry of, with Athens, 11, 13.
Spartan reformer, Cleomenes, 44.
Spartans, 14.
Σπερματικοὶ λόγοι. *See* λόγοι.
Sphærus, a Stoic and pupil of Zeno, 44; from the Bosporus, 44; logical researches of, 64; treatise on divination, 371.
Spinoza, 219.
Standard of truth. *See* Knowledge. Stoic, 86; need of, 86; irresistible impressions, 87; primary conceptions, 90; Epicurean, 431. *See* Canonic.
Stars, Stoic view of, 204.
Stilpo, combined Cynic and Megarian teaching, 37; School of, 385; connected with Zeno, 392.
Στοὰ ποικιλή, 38, 327.
Stobæus has preserved extracts from writings of Teles, 48; and definitions of virtues, 261.
Stoic, 49, 132, 251, 313, 324, 346, 374, 517, 531; apathy, 121; doc-

trine fully expanded by Chrysippus, 47, 48; appeal to the senses, 530; assertion, 185; bias, 304; citizenship of the world, 327; notions of Providence, 177, 388; conception, 397; theory of the good, 290, 559; wise man, 335; enquiries, 170; *Ethics*, 249, 278, 383; two currents of thought in, 382; main features of, 383; explanation of myths, 367, 368; fatalism, 175, 551; influence of, 529; insensibility to pain, 477; κατάληψις, 531; virtue, 398, 334, 58, 505; apathy, 316; pantheism, 176; morality, 229, 333, 390, 342; necessity, 176; philosophers, 298, 322; citizenship of the world, 328, 506; materialism, 384, 385; system, 91, 394, 68, 91, 125, 138, 152, 173, 223, 249, 277, 301, 351, 354, 381, 394, 504, 516, 543; *Philosophy*, 334; authorities for, 53; divisions of, 66; practical character of, 134; scope of, 381; as a whole, 400; political antecedents of, 16; doctrine expanded, 47; problem proposed to, 56; enquiries into duties, 302; practical character, 56; necessity for knowledge, 58; position towards logic and natural science, 59; relative importance of parts, 68; onesidedness of, 402; place in history, 400; theory of intermingling, 137; of irresistible impressions, 530; *Logic* of, 70, 121; field of, 70; words and thoughts, 73; formality of, 75, 92, 119; estimate of, 123; categories, 97; theory of illation, 121; *Knowledge*, theory of, 75, 525; prominent points in, 77; prophecy, 379; platform, 335, 353; point of view, 48, 90; polytheism, 549; preference for argument,

65; principles, logical result of, 311; principles, 153, 219, 225, 256, 293; propositions, 310, 551; views on nature; 194; *School*, 29, 62, 64, 69, 168, 274, 286, 297, 299, 300, 307, 336, 351, 388; founded by Zeno, 36; Chrysippus president of, 45; a School of reasoners, 66; φαντασία, 541; severity, 286; skill, 363; speculation, 173; *System*, inner connection of, 381; teaching, 55, 59, 67, 69, 84, 133, 221, 257, 316, 456; theology, 545; treatment of science, 542.

Stoicism, 26, 69, 326, 339, 357, 380; growing out of Cynicism, 17, 91, 392, 402; relation of, to previous system, 387; related to Cynics, 387; to Socrates, 387; to Aristotle, 396; to Megarians, 392; to Heraclitus, 392; to Plato, 399; later, founded by Chrysippus, 45; historical ingredients of, 400; form fixed, 48; Eratosthenes won for, 48; as traditionally known, 56; features of, 239; a religious system, 342; essentially practical, 380, 385; insists on self-sufficiency of virtue, 389; preserved original character of Socratic philosophy, 391; stern tone of, 498; and the theory of pleasure, 560; entered the Roman world under Panætius, 51; declared man independent of his fellows, 311; makes a dogma of fatalism, 332; connection with religion, 341; with popular faith, 343: ethical side of, 382; scientific side of, 383; elements combined in, 386; relation of Epicurean system to, 503, 508, 509, 514, 517.

Stoics [*see Table of Contents*], 276, 314, 393, 398, 512; of the Roman period, 36, 326, 492; School of the, 19 ; feel the need of philosophic speculation, 20 ; history of, 35 *sq.* ; take their name from Stoa ποικιλή, 38 ; highest conception of, 99 ; look at accuracy of expression, 118 ; seek a standard of truth, 20 ; demand a knowledge of conceptions, 479 ; logic of, 96, 97, 123, 223 ; sorites, 120 ; did little for natural science, 20 ; opposed to Sceptics, 21 ; teach original unity of human family, 21, 490 ; apologetical writings of, 25 ; regard universâl element, 25 ; belief from idea, 36 ; develope the doctrine of the syllogism, 65 ; problem proposed to, 56 ; view of virtue, 59, 128, 272, 300 ; unity of virtue, 266 ; differ generally from Aristo, 62 ; their views expanded by Chrysippus, 64 ; make three divisions of philosophy, 66 ; development of teaching, 69 ; their view of thoughts and words, 74 ; had no distinct theory of knowledge before Chrysippus, 76 ; attach importance to the senses, 77 ; make perceptions the source of notions, 82, 91 ; λεκτὸν of, 92 ; consider material objects alone real, 84, 94 ; admit the existence of immaterial attributes, 106 ; enumerate sentences, 110 ; discuss modality of judgments, 115 ; attached great value to the theory of illation, 116 ; strive to find firm ground, 123 ; their view of knowledge, 129 ; ground occupied by, 134, 135 ; deny the freedom of the will, 179, 217 ; distinguished from Epicureans, 183, 470 ; agreement with, 454, 481, 484, 500, 507, 508, 516 ; follow Aristotle, 194 ; do not explain irregular impulses, 248 ; classify errors,

261 ; divide mankind into two classes, 269 ; the wise man of, 270, 271, 291, 295, 304, 317, 383 ; influenced by Academy, 399 ; agrees with Arcesilaus, 532 ; opponent of Carneades, 542, 564 ; driven into admissions, 287 ; compelled to recognise differences of degree, 293 ; connection with Cynics, 305, 307, 308, 327, 388, 402, 510 ; insist on justice and mercy, 315 ; pay great attention to domestic life, 321 ; view of suicide, 336, 338 ; of lying, 305 ; ethical principles of, 385 ; aim at independence, 488 ; inexorable sternness of, 497 ; subordinate logic and natural science to moral science, 507 ; adhere to fatalism, 505 ; appeal to consensus gentium, 543 ; theological views of, attacked by Sceptics, 545 ; view of the soul, 211, 214, 215, 222 ; supposed connection with Heraclitus, 135, 394 ; materalism of, 139, 210, 385, 425 ; hold one primary force, 143, 146 ; view of Deity, 148, 152, 154 ; view of popular Gods, 358, 362, 366, 368, 369, 549 ; identify God and the world, 156, 348, 349 ; theology of, 341 ; pantheism of, 159 ; view of nature, 194, 223, 351, 373 ; view of the resolution of the world, 165, 203 ; view of the seat of generative power, 173 ; view of divination, 175, 370, 377, 550 ; prophecy, 373, 374, 375, 378 ; view of relation of man to destiny, 182, 301 ; view of the unity of the world, 183, 231 ; of the perfections of the world, 187 ; of physical evil, 188 ; view of moral evil, 189, 191 ; inconsistencies of, 193 ; view of time and space, 197 ; hold two active elements, 179,

DATE DUE

GAYLORD